Race, Class, and Gender
in the United States

An Integrated Study

Race, Class, and Gender in the United States

An Integrated Study

FIFTH EDITION

Paula S. Rothenberg

William Paterson University of New Jersey

WORTH PUBLISHERS

Race, Class, and Gender in the United States, Fifth Edition
Copyright © 2001 by Worth Publishers
Copyright © 1998 by St. Martin's Press
All rights reserved

Manufactured in the United States of America

ISBN: 1-57259-950-2

Printing: 1 2 3 4 5   04 03 02 01

Executive Editor: Alan McClare
Production Editor: Margaret Comaskey
Art Director: Barbara Reingold
Design: Paul Lacy
Cover Design: Wiktor Sadowski
Production Manager: Barbara Anne Seixas
Composition: TSI Graphics Inc.
Printing and Binding: R. R. Donnelley & Sons Company

Library of Congress Cataloging-in-Publication Data

Race, class, and gender in the United States: an integrated study / [edited by] Paula S. Rothenberg—5th ed.
      p. cm.
   Includes bibliographical references and index.
   ISBN 1-57259-950-2
   1. Racism. 2. Sexism. 3. Social classes—United States. 4. Sex discrimination against women—United States. 5. United States—Race relations. I. Rothenberg, Paula S., 1943–

HT1521.R335 2000
305.8′00973—dc21

00–035427

Worth Publishers
41 Madison Avenue
New York, NY 10010
www.worthpublishers.com

Contents

PART IV: THE ECONOMICS OF RACE, CLASS, AND GENDER IN THE UNITED STATES   253

PART V: MANY VOICES, MANY LIVES: SOME CONSEQUENCES OF RACIAL, GENDER, AND CLASS INEQUALITY   321

PART VI: HOW IT HAPPENED: RACE AND GENDER ISSUES IN U.S. LAW   427

PART VII: MAINTAINING RACE, CLASS, AND GENDER HIERARCHIES: SOCIAL CONTROL 507

PART VIII: MAKING A DIFFERENCE 583

Preface

As in the past, this new edition undertakes the study of issues of race, gender, and sexuality within the context of class. The opening section of the book introduces these issues by simultaneously examining the ways in which each has been socially constructed and by examining the social construction of difference or hierarchy itself, which underlies all of them. Part II takes an in-depth look at racism, sexism, heterosexism, and class privilege and introduces the concepts of patriarchy and white privilege. Designed to focus on both the similarities and the differences between and among these forms of oppression and to emphasize the ways in which they intersect, the structure of this book continually explores the interlocking nature of these systems as they work in combination to impact on virtually every aspect of life in U.S. society today.

One of the greatest impediments to teaching this material to college-age students is the belief held by many that discrimination based on race, gender, sexual orientation, or class is a thing of the past. A surprising number are convinced that unfair treatment, if it ever existed, has largely been eliminated, while another group believes that if unfair treatment exists, it is white people or white men who are currently disadvantaged. This has prompted the introduction of a new section to this edition, one which takes a look at "Discrimination in Everyday Life." Using newspaper accounts of individual and institutional discrimination, this section makes a compelling case for the continuing existence of unfair and unequal treatment based on people's race/ethnicity, class, gender, sexual orientation, or some combination of them. It is guaranteed to produce some lively classroom discussion.

New selections consider the ways in which changing U.S. demographics and recent immigration history have complicated both racial and ethnic categories as well as the relationships between and among groups within those categories. And several readings compare and contrast the successes and failures of various racial and ethnic groups and the causes for the same. By broadening the consideration of issues of ethnicity and race, this new edition reflects some of the ways in which this discourse is changing during the first part of the new century. Additional attention is also paid to examining both white skin privilege and class privilege and making them more visible to readers who are sometimes reluctant to recognize that the flip side of discrimination is privilege.

Throughout this book, issues of gender are framed in inclusive terms to include attention to the socialization of men and boys as well as that of women and girls. Attention is paid to some of the ways in which male socialization leads to misogyny and homophobia, and a number of articles make it clear that male privilege has its price. On the other hand, several new articles present more positive accounts of the experiences of individuals and groups as they claim identities that were previously viewed by many as problematic. For example, in Part V, a new article entitled "Out of the Closet but Not Out of Middle School" now shares space with Tommy Avicolli's poignant childhood memories recounted in "He Defies You Still: The Memoirs of a Sissy," and a piece by Kate Bornstein invites us to move beyond the dualistic nature of traditional sexual categorization. Finally, Part VIII, "Making a Difference," the concluding section of the book, has been substantially revised to provide students with additional specific examples of what it might mean to work toward social change.

Organization and Structure

Individual instructors may wish to modify the order of presentation of readings to conform to their own vision of how this complex and challenging material is best presented. The articles included in the fifth edition provide considerable flexibility in this respect. The Mantsios article on class, which now appears in Part II, could easily be used early in Part IV to frame the discussion of the economics of race, class, and gender in the United States. The selection by Chandra Talpade Mohanty in Part V, "On Being South Asian in North America," might well be used in conjunction with essays in Parts I and II to illustrate the ways in which identity is constructed and contextualized. Instructors might want to assign Sonia Shah's "Asian American?" and Delina D. Pryce's "Black Latina," along with the Mohanty piece and other selections from Part V, when they teach about the social construction of race/ethnicity, gender, class, and sexuality in Part I. Articles that focus on male socialization and men's experience might be grouped together for a special section on "the social construction of masculinity." These include the Messner piece in Part I, the Johnson piece in Part II, "No Means No" and "Minority Private-School Students Claim Police Harassment" in Part III, along with the Sabo, Avicolli, Copeland, Bornstein, and other pieces in Parts III and V, as well as "White Lies" and "Pulling Train" in Part VII and the Bronski and Thompson pieces in Part VIII.

I continue to place the historical materials in Part VI, fairly late in the book, because I continue to believe that students are more likely to read and digest this material after their interest has been captured by the more contemporary readings. To my mind, this ordering helps students see that history holds answers to perplexing contemporary questions rather than simply providing "background" for them. Other instructors will undoubtedly prefer to use the historical material earlier. Countless other reorderings will emerge from the contents, depending on each instructor's own vision for the course being taught. I think this flexibility is one of the strong points of a collection that is genuinely interdisciplinary and inclusive.

In the new edition, I have tried to continue to enlarge the scope of vision and deepen the analysis that prompted this book in the first place. I have been helped by conversations with my own students at William Paterson University during the fall of 1999 and with faculty and students throughout the country who have shared their experiences in using the text with me. The fact that so many have found the book useful confirms my own belief that these topics are an essential part of a liberal education today. It is unthinkable that students graduating from college in the twenty-first century would fail to grapple with issues of diversity, difference, and inequality in the course of their studies. This book is intended to facilitate that inquiry and analysis.

Acknowledgments

Many people contributed to this book. First, I owe a profound debt to the old 12th Street study group, with whom I first studied black history and first came to understand the centrality of the issue of race. I am also indebted to the group's members, who provided me with a lasting example of what it means to commit one's life to the struggle for justice for all people.

Next, I owe an equally profound debt to my friends and colleagues in the New Jersey Project on Inclusive Scholarship, Curriculum, and Teaching and to friends, colleagues, and students at William Paterson University who have been involved in the various race and gender projects we have carried out for some years now. I have learned a great deal from all of them. I am especially grateful to J. Samuel Jordan and Leslie Agard-Jones: colleagues, teachers, and friends.

Many other people contributed to this new edition by helping me track down articles or information or by discussing various topics with me. In particular I would like to thank: Steve Shalom; Jo-Ann Pilardi; Naomi Miller; Greg Mantsios; Lahoucine Ouzgane; Janice Bogstad; Patricia E. Russo; Maragret Tacardon; Deb Figart; Rick Schultz; Arlene Hirschfelder and Dennis White of the Association of American Indian Affairs; Evelyn Canolli of the National Committee on Pay Equity; Marion Saviola of the Center for Independence of the Disabled, New York City; and Paula Ettelbrick, Legislative Counsel for the Empire State Pride Agenda. In addition, Jack Meacham's counsel and perspective were particularly helpful to me as I rethought this edition, and Jill Hamburg generously shared volumes of material as well as her perspective on teaching it.

I am also grateful to the following reviewers: Michel Coconis (Grand Valley State University), Elizabeth Cramer (Virginia Commonwealth University), Donna Langston (Minnesota State University), Pedro Noguera (University of California, Berkeley), Keith Osajima (University of Redlands), Thomas Sanchez (University of Nebraska), Betsy A. Smith (Florida International University), and Cookie White Stephan (New Mexico State University).

Additional thanks to the faculty and students, too numerous to name, at the many colleges and universities where I have lectured during the past several years. Their generous sharing of bibliographies, articles, insights, and questions has enriched this book immeasurably.

The new edition has benefited greatly from the professional contributions of many people at Worth Publishers. In particular, I would like to thank my editor, Alan McClare, who restored my faith in the role that a truly professional editor can play in the production of a book. I would also like to thank Chris Narozny, Margaret Comaskey, Barbara Seixas, Barbara Reingold, and Scott Hitchcock for their important contributions.

Finally, I want to thank my partner Greg Mantsios and our children, Alexi and Andrea, for a lifetime of conversation and shared readings, the benefits of which are reflected on every page of this edition.

About the Author

Paula S. Rothenberg is Director of the New Jersey Project on Inclusive Scholarship, Curriculum, and Teaching and a professor at the William Paterson University of New Jersey. She attended the University of Chicago and received her undergraduate degree from New York University, where she also did her graduate work. Rothenberg has lectured and consulted on multicultural and gender issues and curriculum transformation at hundreds of colleges and universities throughout the country. Her articles and essays appear in journals and anthologies across the disciplines, and many have been widely reprinted. Rothenberg is co-editor of *Creating an Inclusive College Curriculum: A Teaching Sourcebook from the New Jersey Project*, as well as co-editor of several highly successful college text anthologies, including *Feminist Frameworks*. Her most recent book is *Invisible Privilege: A Memoir about Race, Class, and Gender*.

Race, Class, and Gender in the United States

An Integrated Study

Introduction

It is impossible to make sense out of either the past or the present without using race, class, gender, and sexuality as central categories of description and analysis. Ironically, many of us are the products of an educational system that has taught us *not* to use these categories and, hence, taught us *not* to see the differences in power and privilege that surround us. As a result, things that some people identify as clear examples of sexism or racism appear to others to be simply "the way things are." Understandably, this often makes conversation difficult and frustrating. A basic premise of this book is that much of what passes for a neutral perspective across the disciplines and in cultural life already "smuggles in" elements of class, race, and gender bias and distortion. Because the so-called neutral point of view is so pervasive, it is often difficult to identify. One of the goals of this text is to help the reader learn to recognize some of the ways in which issues of race, class, and gender are embedded in ordinary discourse and daily life. Learning to identify and employ race, class, and gender as fundamental categories of description and analysis is essential if we wish to understand our own lives and the lives of others.

Beginning Our Study

Beginning our study together makes apparent some immediate differences from other academic enterprises. Whereas students and faculty in an introductory literature or chemistry class do not begin the semester with deeply felt and firmly entrenched attitudes toward the subject, almost every student in a course that deals with issues of race, class, gender, and sexuality enters the room on the first day with strong feelings, and almost every faculty member does so as well. This can have either very good or very bad consequences. Under the best conditions and if we acknowledge them head on, these feelings can provide the basis for a passionate and personal study of the topics and can make this course something out of the ordinary, one which has real long-term meanings for both students and teachers. But if we fail to find a way to channel these feelings in a positive way, they can function as obstacles that prevent the study from ever beginning in earnest. For this reason, it is important to acknowledge the existence of these feelings and devise some ground rules for classroom interactions, rules that help create an atmosphere that encourages candid and respectful dialogue.

Approaching this material presents many challenges. Racism, sexism, heterosexism, and class privilege are all systems of oppression with their own particular history and their own intrinsic logic (or illogic), and it is important to explore each of these systems in its own right; at the same time, these systems operate in conjunction with each other to form an enormously complex set of interlocking and self-perpetuating relations of domination and subordination. It is essential that we understand the ways in which these systems overlap and intersect and play off each other. For purposes of analysis, it may be necessary to talk as if it were possible to abstract race or sexuality from, say, gender and class, and subject it to exclusive scrutiny for a time, even though such distinctions are never possible in reality. When we engage in this kind of abstraction, we should never lose sight of the fact that any particular woman or man has an ethnic background, class location, age, sexual orientation, religious orientation, gender, and so forth, and all these characteristics are inseparable from the person and from each other. Always, the particular combination of these identities shapes the individual and locates him or her in society.

It is also true that in talking about racism, sexism, and heterosexism within the context of class, we may have to make generalizations about the experience of different groups of people, even as we affirm that each individual is unique. For example, in order to highlight similarities in the experiences of some individuals, this book often talks about "people of color" or "women of color," even though these terms are somewhat problematic. When I refer to "women" in this book instead of "white women" or "women of color," it is usually in order to focus on the particular experiences or the legal status of women qua women. In doing so, I use language in much the same way that one might author a guide to "the anatomy of the cat." There is no such thing as "the cat" any more than there is "a woman" or there are "people of color." Yet for the purposes of discussion and analysis, it is often necessary to make artificial distinctions in order to focus on particular aspects of experience that may not be separable in reality. Language both mirrors reality and helps to structure it. No wonder, then, that it is so difficult to use our language in ways that adequately address our topics.

Structure of the Book

This book begins with an examination of the ways in which race, class, gender, and sexuality have been socially constructed in the United States as "difference" in the form of hierarchy. Part I treats the idea of difference itself as a social construct, one that underlies and grounds racism, sexism, class privilege, and homophobia. Each of the authors included would agree that while some of these differences may appear to be "natural" or given in nature, they are in fact socially constructed, and the meanings and values associated with these differences create a hierarchy of power and privilege which, precisely because it does appear to be "natural," is used to rationalize inequality. Part II introduces the concept of "oppression" in order to examine racism, sexism, heterosexism, and class privilege as interlocking *systems* of oppression which ensure advantages for some and diminished opportunities for others. Part III provides us with concrete examples of how these systems of oppression operate in contemporary society. Through the use of newspaper articles, we get a first-hand look at the kinds of discrimination faced by members of groups subject to unequal and discriminatory treatment.

What exactly does it mean to claim that someone or some group of people is "different"? What kind of evidence might be offered to support this claim? What does it mean to construct differences? And how does society treat people who are categorized in this way? The readings in Parts I, II, and III of this book are intended to initiate a dialogue about the ways in which U.S. society constructs difference and the social, political, and personal consequences that flow from that construction. The readings encourage us to think about the meaning of racism, sexism, heterosexism, and class privilege.

Defining racism and sexism is always a volatile undertaking. Most of us have fairly strong feelings about race and gender relations and have a stake in the way those relations are portrayed and analyzed. Definitions, after all, are powerful. They can focus attention on certain aspects of reality and make others disappear. They may even end up assigning blame or responsibility for the phenomena under consideration. Parts I, II, and III are intended to initiate this process of definition. The readings allow us to discuss the ways in which we have been taught to think about race, class, and gender difference and to examine how these differences manifest themselves in daily life. The project of this entire volume is to carry this enterprise further, deepening our understanding of these phenomena, their manifestations, and their intersections.

Part IV provides statistics and analyses that demonstrate the impact of race, class, and gender difference on people's lives. Whereas previous selections depend primarily on narrative to define, describe, and illustrate discrimination and oppression, the material in Part IV presents current data, much of it drawn from U.S. government sources, that document the ways in which socially constructed differences mean real differences in opportunity, expectations, and treatment. These differences are brought to life in the articles, poems, and stories in Part V, which offer glimpses into the lives of women and men of different ethnic and class backgrounds, expressing their sexuality and cultures in a variety of ways. Although many selections are highly personal, each points beyond the individual's experience to social policy or practice or culturally conditioned attitudes.

When people first begin to recognize the enormous toll that racism, sexism, heterosexism, and class privilege take on our lives, they often are overwhelmed. How can we reconcile a belief that the United States extends liberty and justice and equal opportunity for all with the reality presented in these pages? How did it happen? At this point, we must turn to history.

Part VI highlights important aspects of the history of subordinated groups in the United States by focusing on historical documents that address race and gender issues in U.S. law since the beginning of the Republic. When these documents are read in the context of the earlier material describing race, gender, and class difference in contemporary society, history becomes a way of using the past to make sense of the present. Focusing on the legal status of women of all colors and men of color allows us to telescope hundreds of years of history to manageable size, while still providing the historical information needed to make sense of contemporary society.

Our survey of racism and sexism in the United States, past and present, has shown that these phenomena can assume different forms in different contexts. For some, the experiences that Richard Wright describes in "The Ethics of Living Jim Crow" (Part I) are still all too real today, but for others they reflect a crude, blatant racism that seems incompatible with contemporary life. How, then, are racism, sexism, homophobia, and class privilege perpetuated in contemporary society? Why do these divisions and the accompanying differences in opportunity and achievement continue? How are they reproduced? Why is it so difficult to recognize the reality that lies behind a rhetoric of equality of opportunity and justice for all? Part VII offers some suggestions.

A classic essay on sex-role conditioning draws an important distinction between discrimination (which frustrates choices already made) and the force of a largely unconscious gender-role ideology (which compromises one's ability to choose).* In Part VII our discussion of stereotypes, violence, ideology, and social control is concerned with analyzing how the way we conceive of others—and, equally important, the way we come to conceive of ourselves—helps perpetuate racism, sexism, heterosexism, and class privilege. The discussion moves beyond the specificity of stereotypes; it analyzes how modes of conceptualizing reality itself are conditioned by forces that are not always obvious. Racism, sexism, and classism are not only systems of oppression that provide advantages and privileges to some, not simply identifiable attitudes, policies, and practices that affect individual lives—racism, sexism, heterosexism, and classism operate on a basic level to structure what we come to think of as "reality." In this way, they limit our possibilities and personhood. They cause us to internalize beliefs that distort our perspective and expectations and make it more difficult to identify the origins of unequal and unjust distribution of resources. We grow up being taught that the prevailing hierarchy in society is natural and inevitable, perhaps even desirable, and so we fail to identify the unequal distribution itself as a problem.

Finally, Part VIII offers suggestions for moving beyond racism, classism, and sexism. The selections are intended to stimulate discussion about the kinds of changes we might wish to explore in order to transform society. They offer a variety of ideas about the causes of and cures for the pervasive social and economic inequality and injustice that are documented in this volume and offer us examples of some concrete steps that we can take to become agents of social change. But rather than providing definitive solutions, they are meant to initiate a process of reflection and debate about these social ills and about the kinds of changes that can help address them.

---

*Sandra L. Bem and Daryl Bem, "Homogenizing the American Woman," in *Beliefs, Attitudes, and Human Affairs* by D. J. Bem (Monterey, CA: Brooks/Cole, 1970), pp. 89–99.

PART I

The Social Construction of Difference: Race, Class, Gender, and Sexuality

EVERY SOCIETY GRAPPLES WITH THE QUESTION of how to distribute its wealth, power, and opportunities. In some cases the distribution is relatively egalitarian and in others it is dramatically unequal. Those societies that tend toward a less egalitarian distribution have adopted various ways to apportion privilege; some have used age, others have used ancestry. Like many others, U.S. society places a priority on sex and race. To this end, race and gender differences have been portrayed as unbridgeable and immutable. Men and women have been portrayed as polar opposites with innately different abilities and capacities. The very personality traits that were considered positive in a man were seen as signs of dysfunction in a woman, and the qualities that were praised in women were often ridiculed in men. In fact, until very recently, introductory psychology textbooks provided a description of neurosis in a woman that was virtually identical to their description of a healthy male personality.

Race difference has been similarly portrayed. White-skinned people of European origins have viewed themselves as innately superior in intelligence and ability to people with darker skin or different physical characteristics. As both the South Carolina Slave Code of 1712 and the Dred Scott Decision in Part VI make clear, "Negroes" were believed to be members of a different and lesser race. Their enslavement, like the genocide carried out against Native Americans, was justified based on this assumed difference. In the Southwest, Anglo landowners claimed that "Orientals" and Mexicans were naturally suited to perform certain kinds of brutal, sometimes crippling, farm labor to which whites were "physically unable to adapt."[1] Women from various Asian populations have been said to be naturally suited to the tedious and precise labor required in the electronics industry (an appeal to supposedly innate race and gender differences).

Class status, too, has been correlated with supposed differences in innate ability and moral worth. Property qualifications for voting have been used not only to prevent African Americans from exercising the right to vote, but to exclude poor whites as well. From the beginnings of U.S. society, being a person of property was considered an indication of superior intelligence and character. The most dramatic expression of this belief is found in Calvinism, which taught that success in business was a sign of being in God's grace and, similarly, that being poor was a punishment inflicted by the Almighty.

In Part I we begin with a different premise. All the readings in this section argue that, far from reflecting natural and innate differences among people, the categories of gender, race, and class are themselves socially constructed. Rather than being "given" in nature, they reflect culturally constructed differences that maintain the prevailing distribution of power and privilege in a society, and they change in relation to changes in social, political, and economic life.

At first this may seem to be a strange claim. On the face of it, whether a person is male or female or a member of a particular race seems to be a straightforward question of biology. But like most differences that are alleged to be "natural" and "immutable," or unchangeable, the categories of race and gender are far more complex than they might seem. While it is true that most (though, as Judith Lorber points out in Selection 5, not all) of us are born unambiguously "male" or "female" as defined by our chromosomes or genitalia, the meaning of being a man or a woman differs from culture to culture and within each society. It is this difference in connotation or meaning that theorists point to when they claim that gender is socially constructed.

Social scientist distinguish between "sex," which is, in fact, a biologically based category, and "gender," which refers to the particular set of socially constructed meanings that are associated with each sex. These are seen to vary over time and place so that what is understood as "naturally" masculine or feminine behavior in one society may be the exact opposite of what is considered "natural" for women or men in another culture. Furthermore, while it is true that most societies have sex-role stereotypes that identify certain jobs or activities as appropriate for women and others for men, and claim that these divisions reflect "natural" differences in ability and/or interest, there is little consistency in what kinds of tasks have been so categorized. Whereas in many cultures strenuous physical activity is considered to be more appropriate to men than women, in one society where women are responsible for such labor the heaviest loads are described as being "so heavy only a woman can lift it." In some societies it is women who are responsible for agricultural labor, and in others it is men. Even within cultures that claim that women are unsuited for heavy manual labor, some women (usually women of color and poor, white working women) have always been expected and required to perform back-breaking physical work—on plantations, in factories, on farms, in commercial laundries, and in their homes. The actual lives of real women and real men throughout history stand in sharp contrast to the images of masculinity and femininity that have been constructed by society and then rationalized as reflecting innate differences between the sexes.

In addition to pointing out the enormous differences in how societies have defined what is "naturally" feminine or masculine, and using these disparities to challenge the notion of an innate masculine or feminine nature, some theorists, such as Ruth Hubbard and Judith Lorber, use the phrase "the social construction of gender" to make an even more profoundly challenging claim. They argue that the notion of difference itself is constructed and suggest that the claim that women and men are naturally and profoundly different reflects a political and social decision rather than a distinction given in nature. Anthropologist Gayle Rubin explains it this way:

> Gender is a socially imposed division of the sexes. . . Men and women are, of course, different. But they are not as different as day and night, earth and sky, yin and yang, life and death. In fact from the standpoint of nature, men and women are closer to each other than either is to anything else—for instance mountains, kangaroos, or coconut palms. The idea that men and women are more different from one another than either is from anything else must come from somewhere other than nature.[2]

In fact, we might go on to argue, along with Rubin, that "far from being an expression of natural differences, exclusive gender identity is the suppression of natural similarities."[3] Boys and girls, women and men are under enormous pressure from the earliest ages to conform to sex-role stereotypes that divide basic human attributes between the two sexes. Mike Messner illustrates this point dramatically in Selection 6 by analyzing the way girls and boys throw a baseball. In Selection 7, Sandra Lipsitz Bem goes on to argue that differences between women and men are never merely differences but are constructed hierarchically so that women are always portrayed as different in the sense of being deviant and deficient. Central to this construction of difference is the social construction of sexuality, a process Ruth Hubbard and Jonathan Ned Katz analyze in Selections 8 and 9. In a society where parents thought of their job as raising "human beings" instead of boys and girls, we would likely find all people sharing a wide range of human attributes, and the belief that men and women naturally occupy two mutually exclusive categories would not structure social, political, and economic life.

The idea of race has been socially constructed in similar ways. The claim that race is a social construction takes issue with the once popular belief that people were born into different races with innate, biologically based differences in intellect, temperament, and character. The idea of ethnicity, in contrast to race, focuses on the shared social/cultural experiences and heritages of various groups and divides or categorizes them according to these shared experiences and traits. The important difference here is that those who talk of race and racial identity believe that they are dividing people according to biological or genetic similarities and differences, whereas those who talk of ethnicity simply point to commonalities that are understood as social, not biological, in origin.

Contemporary historian Ronald Takaki suggests that in the United States "race . . . has been a social construction that has historically set apart racial minorities from European immigrant groups."[4] Michael Omi and Howard Winant, authors of Selection 1, would agree. They maintain that race is more a political categorization than a biological or scientific category. They point to the relatively arbitrary way in which the category has been constructed and suggest that changes in the meaning and use of racial distinctions can be correlated with economic and political changes in U.S. society. Dark-skinned men and women from Spain were once classified as "white" along with fair-skinned immigrants from England and Ireland, whereas early Greek immigrants were often classified as "Orientals" and subjected to the same discrimination that Chinese and Japanese immigrants experienced under the laws of California and other western states. In South Africa, Japanese immigrants were categorized as "white," not "black" or "colored," presumably because the South African economy depended on trade with Japan. In contemporary U.S. society, dark-skinned Latin people are often categorized as "black" by individuals who continue to equate something called "race" with skin color. In Selection 3, Karen Brodkin provides a detailed account of the specific ways in which the status and classifications of one group, Jewish immigrants to the United States, changed over time as a result of and in relation to economic, political, and social changes in our society.

The claim that race is a social construction is not meant to deny the obvious differences in skin color and physical characteristics that people manifest. It simply sees these differences on a continuum of diversity rather than as reflecting innate genetic differences among peoples. Scientists have long argued that all human beings are descended from a common stock. Some years ago the United Nations published a pictorial essay called *The Family of Man.* It included numerous photographs of people from all over the world and challenged readers to survey the enormous diversity among the people depicted and point out where one race ended and another began. Of course, it was impossible to do so. The photographs did not reflect sharply distinguished races but simply diversity on one and the same continuum.

The opening line of the autobiographical account by Richard Wright (Selection 2) provides another opportunity to think about the ways in which race is socially constructed. Wright begins his account by announcing, "My first lesson in how to live as a Negro came when I was quite small." Although it is true that Wright was born with dark skin, an unambiguous physical characteristic, it was for others to define the meaning of being black. As Wright's selection makes clear, in the South during the early 1900s it was primarily whites who defined what it meant to be a "Negro." They did so by making clear what behavior would be acceptable and what behavior would provoke violence, perhaps even death. In Part VII of this book, William Chafe draws an analogy between the way in which (white) women and black men have been socialized in this country under the threat of violence to conform to rigid race and gender roles. The irony is that when this socialization is successful, its results are used to support the claim that sex and race stereotypes are valid and reflect innate differences.

Writing about racism, Algerian-born French philosopher Albert Memmi once explained that racism consists of stressing a difference between individuals or populations. The difference can be real or imagined and in itself doesn't entail racism (or, by analogy, sexism). It is not difference itself that leads to subordination, but the interpretation of difference. it is the assigning of a value to a particular difference in a way that discredits an individual or group to the advantage of another that transforms mere difference into deficiency.[5] In this country, both race and gender difference have been carefully constructed as hierarchy. This means that in the United States, not only are women described as different from men, but that difference is understood to leave them deficient. The same is true of race. Not only are people of color described as different from white people, but that difference, too, is understood as deviance from an acceptable norm—even as pathology—and in both cases difference is used to rationalize racism and sexism.

The social construction of class is analogous but not identical to that of race and gender. Differences between rich and poor, which result from particular ways of structuring the economy, are socially constructed as innate differences among people. They are then used to rationalize or justify the unequal distribution of wealth and power that results from economic decisions made to perpetuate privilege. In addition, straightforward numerical differences in earnings are rarely the basis for conferring class status. For example, school teachers and college professors are usually considered to have a higher status than plumbers and electricians even though the latter groups' earnings are often significantly higher. Where people are presumed to fit into the class hierarchy has less to do with clear-cut numerical categories than it does with the socially constructed superiority of those who perform mental labor (i.e., work with their heads) over those who perform manual labor (i.e., work with their hands). In addition, the status of various occupations and the class position they imply often changes, depending on whether the occupation is predominantly female or male and according to its racial composition as well.

Equally significant, differences in wealth and family income have been overladen with value judgments and stereotypes to the extent that identifying someone as a member of the middle class, working class, or underclass carries implicit implications about his or her moral character and ability. As Herbert Gans suggests in Selection 10, various ways of classifying and portraying poor people in this country have been used to imply that their poverty reflected a personal failure rather than a social problem for which society as a whole might be held responsible. In the nineteenth century, proponents of Calvinism and social Darwinism maintained that being poor in itself indicated that an individual was morally flawed and thus deserved his or her poverty—again relieving society of any responsibility for social ills.

Finally, class difference can be said to be socially constructed in a way that parallels the construction of race and gender as difference. In this respect, U.S. society is organized in such a way as to make hierarchy or class itself appear natural and inevitable. We grade and rank children from their earliest ages and claim to be sorting them according to something called "natural ability." The tracking that permeates our system of education both reflects and creates the expectation that there are A people, B people, C people, and so forth. Well before high school, children come to define themselves and others in just this way and accept this kind of classification as natural. Consequently, quite apart from accepting the particular mythology or ideology of class difference prevailing at any given moment (i.e., "the poor are lazy and worthless" versus "the poor are meek and humble and will inherit the earth"), we come to think it natural and inevitable that there should be class differences in the first place. In the final essay in Part I, Jean Baker Miller asks and answers the question "What do people do to people who are different from them and why?"

NOTES

1. Ronald Takaki, *A Different Mirror: Multicultural American History* (Boston: Little, Brown, 1993), p. 321.

2. Gayle Rubin, "The Traffic in Women," in *Toward an Anthropology of Women*, Rayna R. Reiter, ed. (New York: Monthly Review Press, 1975), p. 179.

3. Ibid., p. 180.

4. Takaki, *Different Mirror*.

5. Albert Memmi, *Dominated Man* (Boston: Beacon Press, 1968).

Racial Formations

Michael Omi and Howard Winant

In 1982–83, Susie Guillory Phipps unsuccessfully sued the Louisiana Bureau of Vital Records to change her racial classification from black to white. The descendant of an eighteenth-century white planter and a black slave, Phipps was designated "black" in her birth certificate in accordance with a 1970 state law which declared anyone with at least one-thirty-second "Negro blood" to be black. The legal battle raised intriguing questions about the concept of race, its meaning in contemporary society, and its use (and abuse) in public policy. Assistant Attorney General Ron Davis defended the law by pointing out that some type of racial classification was necessary to comply with federal record-keeping requirements and to facilitate programs for the prevention of genetic diseases. Phipps's attorney, Brian Begue, argued that the assignment of racial categories on birth certificates was unconstitutional and that the one-thirty-second designation was inaccurate. He called on a retired Tulane University professor who cited research indicating that most whites have one-twentieth "Negro" ancestry. In the end, Phipps lost. The court upheld a state law which quantified racial identity, and in so doing affirmed the legality of assigning individuals to specific racial groupings.[1]

The Phipps case illustrates the continuing dilemma of defining race and establishing its meaning in institutional life. Today, to assert that variations in human physiognomy are racially based is to enter a constant and intense debate. *Scientific* interpretations of race have not been alone in sparking heated controversy; *religious* perspectives have done so as well.[2] Most centrally, of course, race has been a matter of *political* contention. This has been particularly true in the United States, where the concept of race has varied enormously over time without ever leaving the center stage of US history.

What Is Race?

Race consciousness, and its articulation in theories of race, is largely a modern phenomenon. When European explorers in the New World "discovered" people who looked different than themselves, these "natives" challenged then existing

From Michael Omi and Howard Winant, *Racial Formations in the United States: From the 1960s to the 1980s* (London: Routledge, 1986). Reprinted by permission of the authors.

conceptions of the origins of the human species, and raised disturbing questions as to whether *all* could be considered in the same "family of man."[3] Religious debates flared over the attempt to reconcile the Bible with the existence of "racially distinct" people. Arguments took place over creation itself, as theories of polygenesis questioned whether God had made only one species of humanity ("monogenesis"). Europeans wondered if the natives of the New World were indeed human beings with redeemable souls. At stake were not only the prospects for conversion, but the types of treatment to be accorded them. The expropriation of property, the denial of political rights, the introduction of slavery and other forms of coercive labor, as well as outright extermination, all presupposed a worldview which distinguished Europeans—children of God, human beings, etc.—from "others." Such a worldview was needed to explain why some should be "free" and others enslaved, why some had rights to land and property while others did not. Race, and the interpretation of racial differences, was a central factor in that worldview.

In the colonial epoch science was no less a field of controversy than religion in attempts to comprehend the concept of race and its meaning. Spurred on by the classificatory scheme of living organisms devised by Linnaeus in *Systema Naturae*, many scholars in the eighteenth and nineteenth centuries dedicated themselves to the identification and ranking of variations in humankind. Race was thought of as a *biological* concept, yet its precise definition was the subject of debates which, as we have noted, continue to rage today. Despite efforts ranging from Dr. Samuel Morton's studies of cranial capacity[4] to contemporary attempts to base racial classification on shared gene pools,[5] the concept of race has defied biological definition. . . .

Attempts to discern the *scientific meaning* of race continue to the present day. Although most physical anthropologists and biologists have abandoned the quest for a scientific basis to determine racial categories, controversies have recently flared in the area of genetics and educational psychology. For instance, an essay by Arthur Jensen which argued that hereditary factors shape intelligence not only revived the "nature or nurture" controversy, but raised highly volatile questions about racial equality itself.[6] Clearly the attempt to establish a *biological* basis of race has not been swept into the dustbin of history, but is being resurrected in various scientific arenas. All such attempts seek to remove the concept of race from fundamental social, political, or economic determination. They suggest instead that the truth of race lies in the terrain of innate characteristics, of which skin color and other physical attributes provide only the most obvious, and in some respects most superficial, indicators.

Race as a Social Concept

The social sciences have come to reject biologistic notions of race in favor of an approach which regards race as a *social* concept. Beginning in the eighteenth century, this trend has been slow and uneven, but its direction clear. In the nineteenth century Max Weber discounted biological explanations for racial conflict and instead highlighted the social and political factors which engendered such conflict.[7] The work of pioneering cultural anthropologist Franz Boas was crucial in refuting the scientific racism of the early twentieth century by rejecting the connection between race and culture, and the assumption of a continuum of "higher" and "lower" cultural groups. Within the contemporary social science literature, race is assumed to be a variable which is shaped by broader societal forces.

Race is indeed a pre-eminently *sociohistorical* concept. Racial categories and the meaning of race are given concrete expression by the specific social relations and historical context in which they are embedded. Racial meanings have varied tremendously over time and between different societies.

In the United States, the black/white color line has historically been rigidly defined and enforced. White is seen as a "pure" category. Any racial intermixture makes one "nonwhite." In the movie *Raintree County*, Elizabeth Taylor describes the worst of fates to befall whites as "havin' a little Negra blood in ya' — just one little teeny drop and a person's all Negra."[8] This thinking flows from what Marvin Harris has characterized as the principle of *hypo-descent*:

> By what ingenious computation is the genetic tracery of a million years of evolution unraveled and each man [sic] assigned his proper social box? In the United States, the mechanism employed is the rule of hypo-descent. This descent rule requires Americans to believe that anyone who is known to have had a Negro ancestor is a Negro. We admit nothing in between. . . . "Hypo-descent" means affiliation with the subordinate rather than the superordinate group in order to avoid the ambiguity of intermediate identity. . . . The rule of hypo-descent is, therefore, an invention, which we in the United States have made in order to keep biological facts from intruding into our collective racist fantasies.[9]

The Susie Guillory Phipps case merely represents the contemporary expression of this racial logic.

By contrast, a striking feature of race relations in the lowland areas of Latin America since the abolition of slavery has been the relative absence of sharply defined racial groupings. No such rigid descent rule characterizes racial identity in many Latin American societies. Brazil, for example, has historically had less rigid conceptions of race, and thus a variety of "intermediate" racial categories exist. Indeed, as Harris notes, "One of the most striking consequences of the Brazilian system of racial identification is that parents and children and even brothers and sisters are frequently accepted as representatives of quite opposite racial types."[10] Such a possibility is incomprehensible within the logic of racial categories in the US.

To suggest another example: the notion of "passing" takes on new meaning if we compare various American cultures' means of assigning racial identity. In the United States, individuals who are actually "black" by the logic of hypo-descent have attempted to skirt the discriminatory barriers imposed by law and custom by attempting to "pass" for white.[11] Ironically, these same individuals would not be able to pass for "black" in many Latin American societies.

Consideration of the term "black" illustrates the diversity of racial meanings which can be found among different societies and historically within a given society. In contemporary British politics the term "black" is used to refer to all non-whites. Interestingly this designation has not arisen through the racist discourse of groups such as the National Front. Rather, in political and cultural movements, Asian as well as Afro-Caribbean youth are adopting the term as an expression of self-identity.[12] The wide-ranging meanings of "black" illustrate the manner in which racial categories are shaped politically.[13]

The meaning of race is defined and contested throughout society, in both collective action and personal practice. In the process, racial categories themselves are formed, transformed, destroyed and re-formed. We use the term *racial formation* to refer to the process by which social, economic and political forces determine the content and importance of racial categories, and by which they are in turn shaped by racial meanings. Crucial to this formulation is the treatment of race as a *central axis* of social relations which cannot be subsumed under or reduced to some broader category or conception.

Racial Ideology and Racial Identity

The seemingly obvious, "natural" and "common sense" qualities which the existing racial order exhibits themselves testify to the effectiveness of the racial formation process in constructing racial meanings and racial identities.

One of the first things we notice about people when we meet them (along with their sex) is their race. We utilize race to provide clues about *who* a person is. This fact is made painfully obvious when we encounter someone whom we cannot conveniently racially categorize—someone who is, for example, racially "mixed" or of an ethnic/racial group with which we are not familiar. Such an encounter becomes a source of discomfort and momentarily a crisis of racial meaning. Without a racial identity, one is in danger of having no identity.

Our compass for navigating race relations depends on preconceived notions of what each specific racial group looks like. Comments such as, "Funny, you don't look black," betray an underlying image of what black should be. We also become disoriented when people do not act "black," "Latino," or indeed "white." The content of such stereotypes reveals a series of unsubstantiated beliefs about who these groups are and what "they" are like.[14]

In US society, then, a kind of "racial etiquette" exists, a set of interpretative codes and racial meanings which operate in the interactions of daily life. Rules shaped by our perception of race in a comprehensively racial society determine the "presentation of self,"[15] distinctions of status, and appropriate modes of conduct. "Etiquette" is not mere universal adherence to the dominant group's rules, but a more dynamic combination of these rules with the values and beliefs of subordinated groupings. This racial "subjection" is quintessentially ideological.

Everybody learns some combination, some version, of the rules of racial classification, and of their own racial identity, often without obvious teaching or conscious inculcation. Race becomes "common sense"—a way of comprehending, explaining and acting in the world.

Racial beliefs operate as an "amateur biology," a way of explaining the variations in "human nature."[16] Differences in skin color and other obvious physical characteristics supposedly provide visible clues to differences lurking underneath. Temperament, sexuality, intelligence, athletic ability, aesthetic preferences and so on are presumed to be fixed and discernible from the palpable mark of race. Such diverse questions as our confidence and trust in others (for example, clerks or salespeople, media figures, neighbors), our sexual preferences and romantic images, our tastes in music, films, dance, or sports, and our very ways of talking, walking, eating and dreaming are ineluctably shaped by notions of race. Skin color "differences" are thought to explain perceived differences in intellectual, physical and artistic temperaments, and to justify distinct treatment of racially identified individuals and groups.

The continuing persistence of racial ideology suggests that these racial myths and stereotypes cannot be exposed as such in the popular imagination. They are, we think, too essential, too integral, to the maintenance of the US social order. Of course, particular meanings, stereotypes and myths can change, but the presence of a *system* of racial meanings and stereotypes, of racial ideology, seems to be a permanent feature of US culture.

Film and television, for example, have been notorious in disseminating images of racial minorities which establish for audiences what people from these groups look like, how they behave, and "who they are."[17] The power of the media lies not only in their ability to reflect the dominant racial ideology, but in their capacity to shape that ideology in the first place. D. W. Griffith's epic *Birth of a Nation,* a sympathetic treatment of the rise of the Ku Klux Klan during Reconstruction, helped to generate, consolidate and "nationalize" images of blacks which had been more disparate (more regionally specific, for example) prior to the film's appearance.[18] In US television, the necessity to define characters in the briefest and most condensed manner has led to the perpetuation of racial caricatures, as racial stereotypes serve as shorthand for scriptwriters, directors and actors, in commercials, etc. Television's tendency to address the "lowest common denominator" in order to render programs "familiar" to an enormous and diverse audience leads it regularly to assign and reassign racial characteristics to particular groups, both minority and majority.

These and innumerable other examples show that we tend to view race as something fixed and immutable—something rooted in "nature." Thus we mask the historical construction of racial categories, the shifting meaning of race, and the crucial role of politics and ideology in shaping race relations. Races do not emerge full-blown. They are the results of diverse historical practices and are continually subject to challenge over their definition and meaning.

Racialization: The Historical Development of Race

In the United States, the racial category of "black" evolved with the consolidation of racial slavery. By the end of the seventeenth century, Africans whose specific identity was Ibo, Yoruba, Fulani, etc. were rendered "black" by an ideology of exploitation based on racial logic—the establishment and maintenance of a "color line." This of course did not occur overnight. A period of indentured servitude which was not rooted in racial logic preceded the consolidation of racial slavery. With slavery, however, a racially based understanding of society was set in motion which resulted in the shaping of a specific *racial* identity not only for the slaves but for the European settlers as well. Winthrop Jordan has observed: "From the initially common term *Christian*, at mid-century there was a marked shift toward the terms *English* and *free*. After about 1680, taking the colonies as a whole, a new term of self-identification appeared—*white*."[19]

We employ the term *racialization* to signify the extension of racial meaning to a previously racially unclassified relationship, social practice or group. Racialization is an ideological process, an historically specific one. Racial ideology is constructed from pre-existing conceptual (or, if one prefers, "discursive") elements and emerges from the struggles of competing political projects and ideas seeking to articulate similar elements differently. An account of racialization processes that avoids the pitfalls of US ethnic history[20] remains to be written.

Particularly during the nineteenth century, the category of "white" was subject to challenges brought about by the influx of diverse groups who were not of the same Anglo-Saxon stock as the founding immigrants. In the nineteenth century, political and ideological struggles emerged over the classification of Southern Europeans, the Irish and Jews, among other "non-white" categories.[21] Nativism was only effectively curbed by the institutionalization of a racial order that drew the color line *around*, rather than *within*, Europe.

By stopping short of racializing immigrants from Europe after the Civil War, and by subsequently allowing their assimilation, the American racial order was reconsolidated in the wake of the tremendous challenge placed before it by the abolition of racial slavery.[22] With the end of Reconstruction in 1877, an effective program for limiting the emergent class struggles of the later nineteenth century was forged: the definition of the working class *in racial terms*—as "white." This was not accomplished by any legislative decree or capitalist maneuvering to divide the working class, but rather by white workers themselves. Many of them were recent immigrants, who organized on racial lines as much as on traditionally defined class lines.[23] The Irish on the West Coast, for example, engaged in vicious anti-Chinese race-baiting and committed many pogrom-type assaults on Chinese in the course of consolidating the trade union movement in California.

Thus the very political organization of the working class was in important ways a racial project. The legacy of racial conflicts and arrangements shaped the definition of interests and in turn led to the consolidation of institutional patterns (e.g., segregated unions, dual labor markets, exclusionary legislation) which perpetuated the color line *within* the working class. Selig Perlman, whose study of the development of the labor movement is fairly sympathetic to this process, notes that:

> The political issue after 1877 was racial, not financial, and the weapon was not merely the ballot, but also "direct action"—violence. The anti-Chinese agitation in California, culminating as it did in the Exclusion Law passed by Congress in 1882, was doubtless the most important single factor in the history of American labor, for without it the entire country might have been overrun by Mongolian [*sic*] labor and *the labor movement might have become a conflict of races instead of one of classes.*[24]

More recent economic transformations in the US have also altered interpretations of racial identities and meanings. The automation of southern agriculture and the augmented labor demand of the postwar boom transformed blacks from a largely rural, impoverished labor force to a largely urban, working-class group by 1970.[25] When boom became bust and liberal welfare statism moved rightwards, the majority of blacks came to be seen, increasingly, as part of the "underclass," as state "dependents." Thus the particularly deleterious effects on blacks of global and national economic shifts (generally rising unemployment rates, changes in the employment structure away from reliance on labor intensive work, etc.) were explained once again in the late 1970s and 1980s (as they had been in the 1940s and mid-1960s) as the result of defective black cultural norms, of familial disorganization, etc.[26] In this way new racial attributions, new racial myths, are affixed to "blacks."[27] Similar changes in racial identity are presently affecting Asians and Latinos, as such economic forces as increasing Third World impoverishment and indebtedness fuel immigration and high interest rates, Japanese competition spurs resentments, and US jobs seem to fly away to Korea and Singapore.[28] . . .

Once we understand that race overflows the boundaries of skin color, super-exploitation, social stratification, discrimination and prejudice, cultural domination and cultural resistance, state policy (or of any other particular social relationship we list), once we recognize the racial dimension present to some degree in *every* identity, institution and social practice in the United States—once we have done this, it becomes possible to speak of *racial formation.* This recognition is hard-won; there is a continuous temptation to think of race as an *essence,* as something fixed, concrete and objective, as (for example) one of the categories just enumerated. And there is also an opposite temptation: to see it as a mere illusion, which an ideal social order would eliminate.

In our view it is crucial to break with these habits of thought. The effort must be made to understand race as *an unstable and "decentered" complex of social meanings constantly being transformed by political struggle.* . . .

NOTES

1. *San Francisco Chronicle*, 14 September 1982, 19 May 1983. Ironically, the 1970 Louisiana law was enacted to supersede an old Jim Crow statute which relied on the idea of "common report" in determining an infant's race. Following Phipps's unsuccessful attempt to change her classification and have the law declared unconstitutional, a legislative effort arose which culminated in the repeal of the law. See *San Francisco Chronicle*, 23 June 1983.

2. The Mormon church, for example, has been heavily criticized for its doctrine of black inferiority.

3. Thomas F. Gossett notes:

> Race theory . . . had up until fairly modern times no firm hold on European thought. On the other hand, race theory and race prejudice were by no means unknown at the time when the English colonists came to North America. Undoubtedly, the age of exploration led many to speculate on race differences at a period when neither Europeans nor Englishmen were prepared to make allowances for vast cultural diversities. Even though race theories had not then secured wide acceptance or even sophisticated formulation, the first contacts of the Spanish with the Indians in the Americas can now be recognized as the beginning of a struggle between conceptions of the nature of primitive peoples which has not yet been wholly settled. (Thomas F. Gossett, *Race: The History of an Idea in America* [New York: Schocken Books, 1965], p. 16).

Winthrop Jordan provides a detailed account of early European colonialists' attitudes about color and race in *White Over Black: American Attitudes Toward the Negro, 1550–1812* (New York: Norton, 1977 [1968]), pp. 3–43.

4. Pro-slavery physician Samuel George Morton (1799–1851) compiled a collection of 800 crania from all parts of the world which formed the sample for his studies of race. Assuming that the larger the size of the cranium translated into greater intelligence, Morton established a relationship between race and skull capacity. Gossett reports that:

> In 1849, one of his studies included the following results: The English skulls in his collection proved to be the largest, with an average cranial capacity of 96 cubic inches. The Americans and Germans were rather poor seconds, both with cranial capacities of 90 cubic inches. At the bottom of the list were the Negroes with 83 cubic inches, the Chinese with 82, and the Indians with 79. (Ibid., p. 74).

On Morton's methods, see Stephen J. Gould, "The Finagle Factor," *Human Nature* (July 1978).

5. Definitions of race founded upon a common pool of genes have not held up when confronted by scientific research which suggests that the differences *within* a given human population are greater than those *between* populations. See L. L. Cavalli-Sforza, "The Genetics of Human Populations," *Scientific American* (September 1974), pp. 81–9.

6. Arthur Jensen, "How Much Can We Boost IQ and Scholastic Achievement?" *Harvard Educational Review*, vol. 39 (1969), pp. 1–123.

7. Ernst Moritz Manasse, "Max Weber on Race," *Social Research*, vol. 14 (1947), pp. 191–221.

8. Quoted in Edward D. C. Campbell, Jr., *The Celluloid South: Hollywood and the Southern Myth* (Knoxville: University of Tennessee Press, 1981), pp. 168–70.

9. Marvin Harris, *Patterns of Race in the Americas* (New York: Norton, 1964), p. 56.

10. Ibid., p. 57.

11. After James Meredith had been admitted as the first black student at the University of Mississippi, Harry S. Murphy announced that he, and not Meredith, was the first black student to attend "Ole Miss." Murphy described himself as black but was able to pass for white and spent nine months at the institution without attracting any notice (ibid., p. 56).

12. A. Sivanandan, "From Resistance to Rebellion: Asian and Afro-Caribbean Struggles in Britain," *Race and Class*, vol. 23, nos. 2–3 (Autumn–Winter 1981).

13. Consider the contradictions in racial status which abound in the country with the most rigidly defined racial categories—South Africa. There a race classification agency is employed to adjudicate claims for upgrading of official racial identity. This is particularly necessary for the "coloured" category. The apartheid system considers Chinese as "Asians" while the Japanese are accorded the status of "honorary whites." This logic nearly detaches race from any grounding in skin color and other physical attributes and nakedly exposes race as a juridical category subject to economic, social and political influences. (We are indebted to Steve Talbot for clarification of some of these points.)

14. Gordon W. Allport, *The Nature of Prejudice* (Garden City, New York: Doubleday, 1958), pp. 184–200.

15. We wish to use this phrase loosely, without committing ourselves to a particular position on such social psychological approaches as symbolic interactionism, which are outside the scope of this study. An interesting study on this subject is S. M. Lyman and W. A. Douglass, "Ethnicity: Strategies of Individual and Collective Impression Management," *Social Research*, vol. 40, no. 2 (1973).

16. Michael Billig, "Patterns of Racism: Interviews with National Front Members," *Race and Class*, vol. 20, no. 2 (Autumn 1978), pp. 161–79.

17. "Miss San Antonio USA Lisa Fernandez and other Hispanics auditioning for a role in a television soap opera did not fit the Hollywood image of real Mexicans and had to darken their faces before filming." Model Aurora Garza said that their faces were bronzed with powder because they looked too white. "'I'm a real Mexican [Garza said] and very dark anyway. I'm even darker right now because I have a tan. But they kept wanting me to make my face darker and darker'" (*San Francisco Chronicle*, 21 September 1984). A similar dilemma faces Asian American actors who feel that Asian character lead roles inevitably go to white actors who make themselves up to be Asian. Scores of Charlie Chan films, for example, have been made with white leads (the last one was the 1981 *Charlie Chan and the Curse of the Dragon Queen*). Roland Winters, who played in six Chan features, was asked by playwright Frank Chin to explain the logic of casting a white man in the role of Charlie Chan: "'The only thing I can think of is, if you want to cast a homosexual in a show, and you get a homosexual, it'll be awful. It won't be funny . . . and maybe there's something there . . .'" (Frank Chin, "Confessions of the Chinatown Cowboy," *Bulletin of Concerned Asian Scholars*, vol. 4, no. 3 [Fall 1972]).

18. Melanie Martindale-Sikes, "Nationalizing 'Nigger' Imagery Through 'Birth of a Nation'," paper prepared for the 73rd Annual Meeting of the American Sociological Association, 4–8 September 1978, in San Francisco.

19. Winthrop D. Jordan, op. cit., p. 95; emphasis added.

20. Historical focus has been placed either on particular racially defined groups or on immigration and the "incorporation" of ethnic groups. In the former case the characteristic

ethnicity theory pitfalls and apologetics such as functionalism and cultural pluralism may be avoided, but only by sacrificing much of the focus on race. In the latter case, race is considered a manifestation of ethnicity.

21. The degree of antipathy for these groups should not be minimized. A northern commentator observed in the 1850s: "An Irish Catholic seldom attempts to rise to a higher condition than that in which he is placed, while the Negro often makes the attempt with success." Quoted in Gossett, op. cit., p. 288.

22. This analysis, as will perhaps be obvious, is essentially DuBoisian. Its main source will be found in the monumental (and still largely unappreciated) *Black Reconstruction in the United States, 1860–1880* (New York: Atheneum, 1977 [1935]).

23. Alexander Saxton argues that:

North Americans of European background have experienced three great racial confrontations: with the Indian, with the African, and with the Oriental. Central to each transaction has been a totally one-sided preponderance of power, exerted for the exploitation of nonwhites by the dominant white society. In each case (but especially in the two that began with systems of enforced labor), white workingmen have played a crucial, yet ambivalent, role. They have been both exploited and exploiters. On the one hand, thrown into competition with nonwhites as enslaved or "cheap" labor, they suffered economically; on the other hand, being white, they benefited by that very exploitation which was compelling the nonwhites to work for low wages or for nothing. Ideologically they were drawn in opposite directions. *Racial identification cut at right angles to class consciousness.* (Alexander Saxton, *The Indispensable Enemy: Labor and the Anti-Chinese Movement in California* (Berkeley and Los Angeles: University of California Press, 1971), p. 1; emphasis added.)

24. Selig Perlman, *The History of Trade Unionism in the United States* (New York: Augustus Kelley, 1950), p. 52; emphasis added.

25. Whether southern blacks were "peasants" or rural workers is unimportant in this context. Sometime during the 1960s blacks attained a higher degree of urbanization than whites. Before World War II most blacks had been rural dwellers and nearly 80 percent lived in the South.

26. See George Gilder, *Wealth and Poverty* (New York: Basic Books, 1981); Charles Murray, *Losing Ground* (New York: Basic Books, 1984).

27. A brilliant study of the racialization process in Britain, focused on the rise of "mugging" as a popular fear in the 1970s, is Stuart Hall *et al.*, *Policing the Crisis* (London: Macmillan, 1978).

28. The case of Vincent Chin, a Chinese American man beaten to death in 1982 by a laid-off Detroit auto worker and his stepson who mistook him for Japanese and blamed him for the loss of their jobs, has been widely publicized in Asian American communities. On immigration conflicts and pressures, see Michael Omi, "New Wave Dread: Immigration and Intra–Third World Conflict," *Socialist Review*, no. 60 (November–December 1981).

2

The Ethics of Living Jim Crow:
An Autobiographical Sketch

Richard Wright

I

My first lesson in how to live as a Negro came when I was quite small. We were living in Arkansas. Our house stood behind the railroad tracks. Its skimpy yard was paved with black cinders. Nothing green ever grew in that yard. The only touch of green we could see was far away, beyond the tracks, over where the white folks lived. But cinders were good enough for me and I never missed the green growing things. And anyhow cinders were fine weapons. You could always have a nice hot war with huge black cinders. All you had to do was crouch behind the brick pillars of a house with your hands full of gritty ammunition. And the first woolly black head you saw pop out from behind another row of pillars was your target. You tried your very best to knock it off. It was great fun.

I never fully realized the appalling disadvantages of a cinder environment till one day the gang to which I belonged found itself engaged in a war with the white boys who lived beyond the tracks. As usual we laid down our cinder barrage, thinking that this would wipe the white boys out. But they replied with a steady bombardment of broken bottles. We doubled our cinder barrage, but they hid behind trees, hedges, and the sloping embankments of their lawns. Having no such fortifications, we retreated to the brick pillars of our homes. During the retreat a broken milk bottle caught me behind the ear, opening a deep gash which bled profusely. The sight of blood pouring over my face completely demoralized our ranks. My fellow-combatants left me standing paralyzed in the center of the yard, and scurried for their homes. A kind neighbor saw me and rushed me to a doctor, who took three stitches in my neck.

I sat brooding on my front steps, nursing my wound and waiting for my mother to come from work. I felt that a grave injustice had been done me. It was all right to throw cinders. The greatest harm a cinder could do was leave a bruise. But broken bottles were dangerous; they left you cut, bleeding, and helpless.

When night fell, my mother came from the white folks' kitchen. I raced down the street to meet her. I could just feel in my bones that she would understand. I knew she would tell me exactly what to do next time. I grabbed her hand and babbled out the whole story. She examined my wound, then slapped me.

"How come yuh didn't hide?" she asked me. "How come yuh awways fightin'?"

I was outraged, and bawled. Between sobs I told her that I didn't have any trees or hedges to hide behind. There wasn't a thing I could have used as a trench. And you couldn't throw very far when you were hiding behind the brick pillars of a house. She grabbed a barrel stave, dragged me home, stripped me naked, and beat me till I had a fever of one hundred and two. She would smack my rump with the stave, and, while the skin was still smarting, impart to me gems of Jim Crow wisdom. I was never to throw cinders any more. I was never to fight any more wars. I was never, never, under any conditions, to fight *white* folks again. And they were absolutely right in clouting me with the broken milk bottle. Didn't I know she was working hard every day in the hot kitchens of the white folks to make money to take care of me? When was I ever going to learn to be a good boy? She couldn't be bothered with my fights. She finished by telling me that I ought to be thankful to God as long as I lived that they didn't kill me.

All that night I was delirious and could not sleep. Each time I closed my eyes I saw monstrous white faces suspended from the ceiling, leering at me.

From that time on, the charm of my cinder yard was gone. The green trees, the trimmed hedges, the cropped lawns grew very meaningful, became a symbol. Even today when I think of white folks, the hard, sharp outlines of white houses surrounded by trees, lawns, and hedges are present somewhere in the background of my mind. Through the years they grew into an overreaching symbol of fear.

It was a long time before I came in close contact with white folks again. We moved from Arkansas to Mississippi. Here we had the good fortune not to live behind the railroad tracks, or close to white neighborhoods. We lived in the very heart of the local Black Belt. There were black churches and black preachers; there were black schools and black teachers; black groceries and black clerks. In fact, everything was so solidly black that for a long time I did not even think of white folks, save in remote and vague terms. But this could not last forever. As one grows older one eats more. One's clothing costs more. When I finished grammar school I had to go to work. My mother could no longer feed and clothe me on her cooking job.

There is but one place where a black boy who knows no trade can get a job, and that's where the houses and faces are white, where the trees, lawns, and hedges are green. My first job was with an optical company in Jackson, Mississippi. The morning I applied I stood straight and neat before the boss, answering all his questions with sharp yessirs and nosirs. I was very careful to pronounce my *sirs* distinctly, in order that he might know that I was polite, that I knew where I was, and that I knew he was a *white* man. I wanted that job badly.

He looked me over as though he were examining a prize poodle. He questioned me closely about my schooling, being particularly insistent about how much mathematics I had had. He seemed very pleased when I told him I had had two years of algebra.

"Boy, how would you like to try to learn something around here?" he asked me.

"I'd like it fine, sir," I said, happy. I had visions of "working my way up." Even Negroes have those visions.

"All right," he said. "Come on."

I followed him to the small factory.

"Pease," he said to a white man of about thirty-five, "this is Richard. He's going to work for us."

Pease looked at me and nodded.

I was then taken to a white boy of about seventeen.

"Morrie, this is Richard, who's going to work for us."

"Whut yuh sayin' there, boy!" Morrie boomed at me.

"Fine!" I answered.

The boss instructed these two to help me, teach me, give me jobs to do, and let me learn what I could in my spare time.

My wages were five dollars a week.

I worked hard, trying to please. For the first month I got along O.K. Both Pease and Morrie seemed to like me. But one thing was missing. And I kept thinking about it. I was not learning anything and nobody was volunteering to help me. Thinking they had forgotten that I was to learn something about the mechanics of grinding lenses, I asked Morrie one day to tell me about the work. He grew red.

"Whut yuh tryin' t' do, nigger, get smart?" he asked.

"Naw; I ain' tryin' t' git smart," I said.

"Well, don't, if yuh know whut's good for yuh!"

I was puzzled. Maybe he just doesn't want to help me, I thought. I went to Pease.

"Say, are yuh crazy, you black bastard?" Pease asked me, his gray eyes growing hard.

I spoke out, reminding him that the boss had said I was to be given a chance to learn something.

"Nigger, you think you're white, don't you?"

"Naw, sir!"

"Well, you're acting mighty like it!"

"But, Mr. Pease, the boss said . . ."

Pease shook his fist in my face.

"This is a *white* man's work around here, and you better watch yourself!"

From then on they changed toward me. They said good-morning no more. When I was just a bit slow in performing some duty, I was called a lazy black son-of-a-bitch.

Once I thought of reporting all this to the boss. But the mere idea of what would happen to me if Pease and Morrie should learn that I had "snitched" stopped me. And after all the boss was a white man, too. What was the use?

The climax came at noon one summer day. Pease called me to his workbench. To get to him I had to go between two narrow benches and stand with my back against a wall.

"Yes, sir," I said.

"Richard, I want to ask you something," Pease began pleasantly, not looking up from his work.

"Yes, sir," I said again.

Morrie came over, blocking the narrow passage between the benches. He folded his arms, staring at me solemnly.

I looked from one to the other, sensing that something was coming.

"Yes, sir," I said for the third time.

Pease looked up and spoke very slowly.

"Richard, Mr. Morrie here tells me you called me *Pease*."

I stiffened. A void seemed to open up in me. I knew this was the show-down.

He meant that I had failed to call him Mr. Pease. I looked at Morrie. He was gripping a steel bar in his hands. I opened my mouth to speak, to protest, to assure Pease that I had never called him simply *Pease*, and that I had never had any intentions of doing so, when Morrie grabbed me by the collar, ramming my head against the wall.

"Now, be careful, nigger!" snarled Morrie, baring his teeth. "*I* heard yuh call 'im *Pease*! 'N' if yuh say yuh didn't, yuh're callin' me a *lie*, see?" He waved the steel bar threateningly.

If I had said: No, sir, Mr. Pease, I never called you *Pease*, I would have been automatically calling Morrie a liar. And if I had said: Yes, sir, Mr. Pease, I called you *Pease*, I would have been pleading guilty to having uttered the worst insult that a Negro can utter to a southern white man. I stood hesitating, trying to frame a neutral reply.

"Richard, I asked you a question!" said Pease. Anger was creeping into his voice.

"I don't remember calling you *Pease*, Mr. Pease," I said cautiously. "And if I did, I sure didn't mean . . ."

"You black son-of-a-bitch! You called me *Pease*, then!" he spat, slapping me till I bent sideways over a bench. Morrie was on top of me, demanding:

"Didn't yuh call 'im *Pease*? If yuh say yuh didn't, I'll rip yo' gut string loose with this bar, yuh black granny dodger! Yuh can't call a white man a lie 'n' git erway with it, you black son-of-a-bitch!"

I wilted. I begged them not to bother me. I knew what they wanted. They wanted me to leave.

"I'll leave," I promised. "I'll leave right *now*."

They gave me a minute to get out of the factory. I was warned not to show up again, or tell the boss.

I went.

When I told the folks at home what had happened, they called me a fool. They told me that I must never again attempt to exceed my boundaries. When you are working for white folks, they said, you got to "stay in your place" if you want to keep working.

II

My Jim Crow education continued on my next job, which was portering in a clothing store. One morning, while polishing brass out front, the boss and his twenty-year-old son got out of their car and half dragged and half kicked a Negro woman into the store. A policeman standing at the corner looked on, twirling his night-stick. I watched out of the corner of my eye, never slackening the strokes of my chamois upon the brass. After a few minutes, I heard shrill screams coming from the rear of the store. Later the woman stumbled out, bleeding, crying, and holding her stomach. When she reached the end of the block, the policeman grabbed her and accused her of being drunk. Silently, I watched him throw her into a patrol wagon.

When I went to the rear of the store, the boss and his son were washing their hands at the sink. They were chuckling. The floor was bloody and strewn with wisps of hair and clothing. No doubt I must have appeared pretty shocked, for the boss slapped me reassuringly on the back.

"Boy, that's what we do to niggers when they don't want to pay their bills," he said, laughing.

His son looked at me and grinned.

"Here, hava cigarette," he said.

Not knowing what to do, I took it. He lit his and held the match for me. This was a gesture of kindness, indicating that even if they had beaten the poor old woman, they would not beat me if I knew enough to keep my mouth shut.

"Yes, sir," I said, and asked no questions.

After they had gone, I sat on the edge of a packing box and stared at the bloody floor till the cigarette went out.

That day at noon, while eating in a hamburger joint, I told my fellow Negro porters what had happened. No one seemed surprised. One fellow, after swallowing a huge bite, turned to me and asked:

"Huh! Is tha' all they did t' her?"

"Yeah. Wasn't tha' enough?" I asked.

"Shucks! Man, she's a lucky bitch!" he said, burying his lips deep into a juicy hamburger. "Hell, it's a wonder they didn't lay her when they got through."

III

I was learning fast, but not quite fast enough. One day, while I was delivering packages in the suburbs, my bicycle tire was punctured. I walked along the hot, dusty road, sweating and leading my bicycle by the handle-bars.

A car slowed at my side.

"What's the matter, boy?" a white man called.

I told him my bicycle was broken and I was walking back to town.

"That's too bad," he said, "Hop on the running board."

He stopped the car. I clutched hard at my bicycle with one hand and clung to the side of the car with the other.

"All set?"

"Yes, sir," I answered. The car started.

It was full of young white men. They were drinking. I watched the flask pass from mouth to mouth.

"Wanna drink, boy?" one asked.

I laughed as the wind whipped my face. Instinctively obeying the freshly planted precepts of my mother, I said:

"Oh, no!"

The words were hardly out of my mouth before I felt something hard and cold smash me between the eyes. It was an empty whisky bottle. I saw stars, and fell backwards from the speeding car into the dust of the road, my feet becoming entangled in the steel spokes of my bicycle. The white men piled out and stood over me.

"Nigger, ain' yuh learned no better sense'n tha' yet?" asked the man who hit me. "Ain't yuh learned t' say *sir* t' a white man yet?"

Dazed, I pulled to my feet. My elbows and legs were bleeding. Fists doubled, the white man advanced, kicking my bicycle out of the way.

"Aw, leave the bastard alone. He's got enough," said one.

They stood looking at me. I rubbed my shins, trying to stop the flow of blood. No doubt they felt a sort of contemptuous pity, for one asked:

"Yuh wanna ride t' town now, nigger? Yuh reckon yuh know enough t' ride now?"

"I wanna walk," I said, simply.

Maybe it sounded funny. They laughed.

"Well, walk, yuh black son-of-a-bitch!"

When they left they comforted me with:

"Nigger, yuh sho better be damn glad it wuz us yuh talked t' tha' way. Yuh're a lucky bastard, 'cause if yuh'd said tha' t' somebody else, yuh might've been a dead nigger now."

IV

Negroes who have lived South know the dread of being caught alone upon the streets in white neighborhoods after the sun has set. In such a simple situation as this the plight of the Negro in America is graphically symbolized. While white strangers may be in these neighborhoods trying to get home, they can pass unmolested. But the color of a Negro's skin makes him easily recognizable, makes him suspect, converts him into a defenseless target.

Late one Saturday night I made some deliveries in a white neighborhood. I was pedaling my bicycle back to the store as fast as I could, when a police car, swerving toward me, jammed me into the curbing.

"Get down and put up your hands!" the policemen ordered.

I did. They climbed out of the car, guns drawn, faces set, and advanced slowly.

"Keep still!" they ordered.

I reached my hands higher. They searched my pockets and packages. They seemed dissatisfied when they could find nothing incriminating. Finally, one of them said:

"Boy, tell your boss not to send you out in white neighborhoods after sundown."

As usual, I said:

"Yes, sir."

V

My next job was a hall-boy in a hotel. Here my Jim Crow education broadened and deepened. When the bell-boys were busy, I was often called to assist them. As many of the rooms in the hotel were occupied by prostitutes, I was constantly called to carry them liquor and cigarettes. These women were nude most of the time. They did not bother about clothing, even for bell-boys. When you went into their rooms, you were supposed to take their nakedness for granted, as though it startled you no more than a blue vase or a red rug. Your presence awoke in them no sense of shame, for you were not regarded as human. If they were alone, you could steal sidelong glimpses at them. But if they were receiving men, not a flicker of your eyelids could show. I remember one incident vividly. A new woman, a huge, snowy-skinned blonde, took a room on my floor. I was sent to wait upon her. She was in bed with a thick-set man; both were nude and uncovered. She said she wanted some liquor and slid out of bed and waddled across the floor to get her money from a dresser drawer. I watched her.

"Nigger, what in hell you looking at?" the white man asked me, raising himself upon his elbows.

"Nothing," I answered, looking miles deep into the blank wall of the room.

"Keep your eyes where they belong, if you want to be healthy!" he said.

"Yes, sir."

VI

One of the bell-boys I knew in this hotel was keeping steady company with one of the Negro maids. Out of a clear sky the police descended upon his home and arrested him, accusing him of bastardy. The poor boy swore he had had no intimate relations with the girl. Nevertheless, they forced him to marry her. When the child arrived, it was found to be much lighter in complexion than either of the two supposedly legal parents. The white men around the hotel made a great joke of it. They spread the rumor that some white cow must have scared the poor girl while she was carrying the baby. If you were in their presence when this explanation was offered, you were supposed to laugh.

VII

One of the bell-boys was caught in bed with a white prostitute. He was castrated and run out of town. Immediately after this all the bell-boys and hall-boys were called together and warned. We were given to understand that the boy who had been castrated was a "mighty, mighty lucky bastard." We were impressed with the fact that next time the management of the hotel would not be responsible for the lives of "trouble-makin' niggers." We were silent.

VIII

One night, just as I was about to go home, I met one of the Negro maids. She lived in my direction, and we fell in to walk part of the way home together. As we passed the white night-watchman, he slapped the maid on her buttock. I turned around, amazed. The watchman looked at me with a long, hard, fixed-under stare. Suddenly he pulled his gun and asked:

"Nigger, don't yuh like it?"

I hesitated.

"I asked yuh don't yuh like it?" he asked again, stepping forward.

"Yes, sir," I mumbled.

"Talk like it, then!"

"Oh, yes sir!" I said with as much heartiness as I could muster.

Outside, I walked ahead of the girl, ashamed to face her. She caught up with me and said:

"Don't be a fool! Yuh couldn't help it!"

This watchman boasted of having killed two Negroes in self-defense.

Yet, in spite of all this, the life of the hotel ran with an amazing smoothness. It would have been impossible for a stranger to detect anything. The maids, the hall-boys, and the bell-boys were all smiles. They had to be.

IX

I had learned my Jim Crow lessons so thoroughly that I kept the hotel job till I left Jackson for Memphis. It so happened that while in Memphis I applied for a job at a branch of the optical company. I was hired. And for some reason, as long as I worked there, they never brought my past against me.

Here my Jim Crow education assumed quite a different form. It was no longer brutally cruel, but subtly cruel. Here I learned to lie, to steal, to dissemble. I learned to play that dual role which every Negro must play if he wants to eat and live.

For example, it was almost impossible to get a book to read. It was assumed that after a Negro had imbibed what scanty schooling the state furnished he had no further need for books. I was always borrowing books from men on the job. One day I mustered enough courage to ask one of the men to let me get books from the library in his name. Surprisingly, he consented. I cannot help but think that he consented because he was a Roman Catholic and felt a vague sympathy for Negroes, being himself an object of hatred. Armed with a library card, I obtained books in the following manner: I would write a note to the librarian, saying: "Please let this nigger boy have the following books." I would then sign it with the white man's name.

When I went to the library, I would stand at the desk, hat in hand, looking as unbookish as possible. When I received the books desired I would take them home. If the books listed in the note happened to be out, I would sneak into the lobby and forge a new one. I never took any chances guessing with the white librarian about what the fictitious white man would want to read. No doubt if any of the white patrons had suspected that some of the volumes they enjoyed had been in the home of a Negro, they would not have tolerated it for an instant.

The factory force of the optical company in Memphis was much larger than that in Jackson, and more urbanized. At least they liked to talk, and would engage the Negro help in conversation whenever possible. By this means I found that many subjects were taboo from the white man's point of view. Among the topics they did not like to discuss with Negroes were the following: American white women; the Ku Klux Klan; France, and how Negro soldiers fared while there; French women; Jack Johnson; the entire northern part of the United States; the Civil War; Abraham Lincoln; U. S. Grant; General Sherman; Catholics; the Pope; Jews; the Republican Party; slavery; social equality; Communism; Socialism; the 13th and 14th Amendments to the Constitution; or any topic calling for positive knowledge or manly self-assertion on the part of the Negro. The most accepted topics were sex and religion.

There were many times when I had to exercise a great deal of ingenuity to keep out of trouble. It is a southern custom that all men must take off their hats when they enter an elevator. And especially did this apply to us blacks with rigid force. One day I stepped into an elevator with my arms full of packages. I was forced to ride with my hat on. Two white men stared at me coldly. Then one of them very kindly lifted my hat and placed it upon my armful of packages. Now the most accepted response for a Negro to make under such circumstances is to look at the white man out of the corner of his eye and grin. To have said: "Thank you!" would have made the white man *think* that you *thought* you were receiving from him a personal service. For such an act I have seen Negroes take a blow in the mouth. Finding the first alternative distasteful, and the second dangerous, I hit upon an acceptable course of action which fell safely between these two poles. I immediately—no sooner than my hat was lifted—pretended that my packages were about to spill, and appeared deeply distressed with keeping them in my arms. In this fashion I evaded having to acknowledge his service, and, in spite of adverse circumstances, salvaged a slender shred of personal pride.

How do Negroes feel about the way they have to live? How do they discuss it when alone amongst themselves? I think this question can be answered in a single sentence. A friend of mine who ran an elevator once told me:

"Lawd, man! Ef it wuzn't fer them polices 'n' them ol' lynch-mobs, there wouldn't be nothin' but uproar down here!"

3

How Jews Became White

Karen Brodkin

The American nation was founded and developed by the Nordic race, but if a few more million members of the Alpine, Mediterranean and Semitic races are poured among us, the result must inevitably be a hybrid race of people as worthless and futile as the good-for-nothing mongrels of Central America and Southeastern Europe.
(KENNETH ROBERTS, QTD. IN CARLSON AND COLBURN 1972:312)

It is clear that Kenneth Roberts did not think of my ancestors as white like him. The late nineteenth and early decades of the twentieth centuries saw a stready stream of warnings by scientists, policymakers, and the popular press that "mongrelization" of the Nordic or Anglo-Saxon race—the real Americans—by inferior European races (as well as inferior non-European ones) was destroying the fabric of the nation. I continue to be surprised to read that America did not always regard its immigrant European workers as white, that they thought people from different nations were biologically different. My parents, who are first-generation U.S.-born eastern European Jews, are not surprised. They expect anti-Semitism to be a part of the fabric of daily life, much as I expect racism to be part of it. They came of age in a Jewish world in the 1920s and 1930s at the peak of anti-semitism in the United States (Gerber 1986). They are proud of their upward mobility and think of themselves as pulling themselves up by their own bootstraps. I grew up during the 1950s in the Euroethnic New York suburb of Valley Stream where Jews were simply one kind of white folks and where ethnicity meant little more to my generation than food and family heritage. Part of my familized ethnic heritage was the belief that Jews were smart and that our success was the result of our own efforts and abilities, reinforced by a culture that valued sticking together, hard work, education,

From Steven Gregory and Roger Sanjek, eds., *Race* (New Brunswick, NJ: Rutgers University Press, 1994), pp. 78–102. Reprinted by permission of the author.

and deferred gratification. Today, this belief in a Jewish version of Horatio Alger has become an entry point for racism by some mainstream Jewish organizations against African Americans especially, and for their opposition to affirmative action for people of color (Gordon 1964; Sowell 1981; Steinberg 1989: chap. 3).

It is certainly true that the United States has a history of anti-Semitism and of beliefs that Jews were members of an inferior race. But Jews were hardly alone. American anti-Semitism was part of a broader pattern of late-nineteenth-century racism against all southern and eastern European immigrants, as well as against Asian immigrants. These views justified all sorts of discriminatory treatment including closing the doors to immigration from Europe and Asia in the 1920s.[1] This picture changed radically after World War II. Suddenly the same folks who promoted nativism and xenophobia were eager to believe that the Euro-origin people whom they had deported, reviled as members of inferior races, and prevented from immigrating only a few years earlier were now model middle-class white suburban citizens.

It was not an educational epiphany that made those in power change their hearts, their minds, and our race. Instead, it was the biggest and best affirmative action program in the history of our nation, and it was for Euromales. There are similarities and differences in the ways each of the European immigrant groups became "whitened." I want to tell the story in a way that links anti-Semitism to other varieties of anti-European racism, because this foregrounds what Jews shared with other Euroimmigrants and shows changing notions of whiteness to be part of America's larger system of institutional racism.

Euroraces

The U.S. "discovery" that Europe had inferior and superior races came in response to the great waves of immigration from southern and eastern Europe in the late nineteenth century. Before that time, European immigrants—including Jews— had been largely assimilated into the white population. The twenty-three million European immigrants who came to work in U.S. cities after 1880 were too many and too concentrated to disperse and blend. Instead, they piled up in the country's most dilapidated urban areas, where they built new kinds of working-class ethnic communities. Since immigrants and their children made up more than 70 percent of the population of most of the country's largest cities, urban America came to take on a distinctly immigrant flavor. The golden age of industrialization in the United States was also the golden age of class struggle between the captains of the new industrial empires and the masses of manual workers whose labor made them rich. As the majority of mining and manufacturing workers, immigrants were visibly major players in these struggles (Higham 1955:226; Steinberg 1989:36).[2]

The Red Scare of 1919 clearly linked anti-immigrant to anti-working-class sentiment—to the extent that the Seattle general strike of native-born workers was blamed on foreign agitators. The Red Scare was fueled by economic depression, a massive postwar strike wave, the Russian revolution, and a new wave of postwar immigration. . . .

Not surprisingly, the belief in European races took root most deeply among the wealthy U.S.-born Protestant elite, who feared a hostile and seemingly unassimilable working class. By the end of the nineteenth century, Senator Henry Cabot Lodge pressed Congress to cut off immigration to the United States; Teddy Roosevelt raised the alarm of "race suicide" and took Anglo-Saxon women to task for allowing "native" stock to be outbred by inferior immigrants. In the twentieth century, these fears gained a great deal of social legitimacy thanks to the efforts of an influential network of aristocrats and scientists who developed theories of eugenics—breeding for a "better" humanity—and scientific racism. Key to these efforts was Madison Grant's influential *Passing of the Great Race*, in which he shared his discovery that there were three or four major European races ranging from the superior Nordics of northwestern Europe to the inferior southern and eastern races of Alpines, Mediterraneans, and, worst of all, Jews, who seemed to be everywhere in his native New York City. Grant's nightmare was race mixing among Europeans. For him, "the cross between any of the three European races and a Jew is a Jew" (qtd. in Higham 1955:156). He didn't have good things to say about Alpine or Mediterranean "races" either. For Grant, race and class were interwoven: the upper class was racially pure Nordic, and the lower classes came from the lower races.

Far from being on the fringe, Grant's views resonated with those of the nonimmigrant middle class. A *New York Times* reporter wrote of his visit to the Lower East Side:

> This neighborhood, peopled almost entirely by the people who claim to have been driven from Poland and Russia, is the eyesore of New York and perhaps the filthiest place on the western continent. It is impossible for a Christian to live there because he will be driven out, either by blows or the dirt and stench. Cleanliness is an unknown quantity to these people. They cannot be lifted up to a higher plane because they do not want to be. If the cholera should ever get among these people, they would scatter its germs as a sower does grain. (qtd. in Schoener 1967:58)[3]

Such views were well within the mainstream of the early-twentieth-century scientific community. Grant and eugenicist Charles B. Davenport organized the Galton Society in 1918 in order to foster research and to otherwise promote eugenics and immigration restriction.[4] . . .

By the 1920s, scientific racism sanctified the notion that real Americans were white and real whites came from northwest Europe. Racism animated laws excluding and expelling Chinese in 1882, and then closing the door to immigration by virtually all Asians and most Europeans in 1924 (Saxton 1971, 1990). Northwestern European ancestry as a requisite for whiteness was set in legal concrete when the Supreme Court denied Bhagat Singh Thind the right to become a naturalized citizen under a 1790 federal law that allowed whites the right to become naturalized citizens. Thind argued that East Indians were the real Aryans and Caucasians, and therefore white. The Court countered that the United States only wanted blond Aryans and Caucasians, "that the blond Scandinavian and the brown Hindu have a common ancestor in the dim reaches of antiquity, but the average man knows perfectly well that there are unmistakable and profound differences between them today" (Takaki 1989:298–299). A narrowly defined white, Christian race was also built into the 1705 Virginia "Act concerning servants and slaves." This statute stated "that no negroes, mulattos and Indians or other infidels or jews, Moors, Mahometans or other infidels shall, at any time, purchase any christian servant, nor any other except of their own complexion" (Martyn 1979:111).[5]

The 1930 census added its voice, distinguishing not only immigrant from "native" whites, but also native whites of native white parentage, and native whites of immigrant (or mixed) parentage. In distinguishing immigrant (southern and eastern Europeans) from "native" (northwestern Europeans), the census reflected the racial distinctions of the eugenicist-inspired intelligence tests.[6]

Racism and anti-immigrant sentiment in general and anti-Semitism in particular flourished in higher education. Jews were the first of the Euroimmigrant groups to enter colleges in significant numbers, so it wasn't surprising that they faced the brunt of discrimination there.[7] The Protestant elite complained that Jews were unwashed, uncouth, unrefined, loud, and pushy. Harvard University President A. Lawrence Lowell, who was also a vice president of the Immigration Restriction League, was openly opposed to Jews at Harvard. The Seven Sisters schools had a reputation for "flagrant discrimination." . . .

Anti-Semitic patterns set by these elite schools influenced standards of other schools, made anti-Semitism acceptable, and "made the aura of exclusivity a desirable commodity for the college-seeking clientele" (Synott 1986:250; and see Karabel 1984; Silberman 1985; Steinberg 1989: chaps. 5, 9). Fears that colleges "might soon be overrun by Jews" were publicly expressed at a 1918 meeting of the Association of New England Deans. In 1919 Columbia University took steps to decrease the number of entering Jews by a set of practices that soon came to be widely adopted. . . .

Columbia's quota against Jews was well known in my parents' community. My father is very proud of having beaten it and of being admitted to Columbia Dental School on the basis of his sculpting skill. In addition to demonstrating academic qualifications, he was asked to carve a soap ball, which he did so well and fast that his Protestant interviewer was willing to accept him. Although he became a teacher instead because the dental school tuition was too high, he took me to the dentist every week of my childhood and prolonged the agony by discussing the finer points of tooth filling and dental care. My father also almost failed the speech test required for his teaching license because he didn't speak "standard"—that is, nonimmigrant, nonaccented—English. For my parents and most of their friends,

English was a second language learned when they went to school, since their home language was Yiddish. They saw the speech test as designed to keep all ethnics, not just Jews, out of teaching. . . .

My parents' conclusion is that Jewish success, like their own, was the result of hard work and of placing a high value on education. They went to Brooklyn College during the Depression. My mother worked days and started school at night, and my father went during the day. Both their families encouraged them. More accurately, their families expected this effort from them. Everyone they knew was in the same boat, and their world was made up of Jews who advanced as they did. The picture of New York—where most Jews lived—seems to back them up. In 1920, Jews made up 80 percent of the students at New York's City College, 90 percent of Hunter College, and before World War I, 40 percent of private Columbia University. By 1934, Jews made up almost 24 percent of all law students nationally, and 56 percent of those in New York City. Still, more Jews became public school teachers, like my parents and their friends, than doctors or lawyers (Steinberg 1989:137, 227). Steinberg has debunked the myth that Jews advanced because of the cultural value placed on education. This is not to say that Jews did not advance. They did. "Jewish success in America was a matter of historical timing. . . . [T]here was a fortuitous match between the experience and skills of Jewish immigrants, on the one hand, and the manpower needs and opportunity structures, on the other" (1989:103). Jews were the only ones among the southern and eastern European immigrants who came from urban, commercial, craft, and manufacturing backgrounds, not least of which was garment manufacturing. They entered the United States in New York, center of the nation's booming garment industry, soon came to dominate its skilled (male) and "unskilled" (female) jobs, and found it an industry amenable to low-capital entrepreneurship. As a result, Jews were the first of the new European immigrants to create a middle class of small businesspersons early in the twentieth century. Jewish educational advances followed this business success and depended upon it, rather than creating it (see also Bodnar 1985 for a similar argument about mobility).

In the early twentieth century, Jewish college students entered a contested terrain in which the elite social mission was under challenge by a newer professional training mission. Pressure for change had begun to transform the curriculum and reorient college from a gentleman's bastion to a training ground for the middle-class professionals needed by an industrial economy. "The curriculum was overhauled to prepare students for careers in business, engineering, scientific farming, and the arts, and a variety of new professions such as accounting and pharmacy that were making their appearance in American colleges for the first time" (Steinberg 1989:229). Occupational training was precisely what drew Jews to college. In a setting where disparagement of intellectual pursuits and the gentleman's C were badges of distinction, it was not hard for Jews to excel.

How we interpret Jewish social mobility in this milieu depends on whom we compare Jews to. Compared with other immigrants, Jews were upwardly mobile.

But compared with that of nonimmigrant whites, their mobility was very limited and circumscribed. Anti-immigrant racist and anti-Semitic barriers kept the Jewish middle class confined to a small number of occupations. Jews were excluded from mainstream corporate management and corporately employed professions, except in the garment and movie industries, which they built. Jews were almost totally excluded from university faculties (and the few that made it had powerful patrons). Jews were concentrated in small businesses, and in professions where they served a largely Jewish clientele (Davis 1990:146 n. 25; Silberman 1985:88–117; Sklare 1971:63–67). . . .

My parents' generation believed that Jews overcame anti-Semitic barriers because Jews are special. My belief is that the Jews who were upwardly mobile were special among Jews (and were also well placed to write the story). My generation might well counter our parents' story of pulling themselves up by their own bootstraps with, "But think what you might have been without the racism and with some affirmative action!" And that is precisely what the postwar boom, the decline of systematic, public anti-immigrant racism and anti-Semitism, and governmental affirmative action extended to white males.

Euroethnics into Whites

By the time I was an adolescent, Jews were just as white as the next white person. Until I was eight, I was a Jew in a world of Jews. Everyone on Avenue Z in Sheepshead Bay was Jewish. I spent my days playing and going to school on three blocks of Avenue Z, and visiting my grandparents in the nearby Jewish neighborhoods of Brighton Beach and Coney Island. There were plenty of Italians in my neighborhood, but they lived around the corner. They were a kind of Jew, but on the margins of my social horizons. Portuguese were even more distant, at the end of the bus ride, at Sheepshead Bay. . . . We left that world in 1949 when we moved to Valley Stream, Long Island, which was Protestant, Republican, and even had farms until Irish, Italian, and Jewish exurbanites like us gave it a more suburban and Democratic flavor. Neither religion nor ethnicity separated us at school or in the neighborhood. Except temporarily. In elementary school years, I remember a fair number of dirt-bomb (a good suburban weapon) wars on the block. Periodically one of the Catholic boys would accuse me or my brother of killing his God, to which we would reply, "Did not" and start lobbing dirt-bombs. Sometimes he would get his friends from Catholic school, and I would get mine from public school kids on the block, some of whom were Catholic. Hostilities lasted no more than a couple of hours and punctuated an otherwise friendly relationship. They ended by junior high years, when other things became more important. Jews, Catholics, and Protestants, Italians, Irish, Poles, and "English" (I don't remember hearing WASP as a kid) were mixed up on the block and in school. We thought of ourselves as middle class and very enlightened because our ethnic backgrounds seemed so irrelevant to high school culture. We didn't see race (we thought), and racism was not part of our peer consciousness, nor were the immigrant or working-class histories of our families.

Like most chicken and egg problems, it's hard to know which came first. Did Jews and other Euroethnics become white because they became middle class? That is, did money whiten? Or did being incorporated in an expanded version of white-ness open up the economic doors to a middle-class status? Clearly, both tendencies were at work. Some of the changes set in motion during the war against fascism led to a more inclusive version of whiteness. Anti-Semitism and anti-European racism lost respectability. The 1940 census no longer distinguished native whites of native parentage from those, like my parents, of immigrant parentage, so that Euro-immigrants and their children were more securely white by submersion in an expanded notion of whiteness. (This census also changed the race of Mexicans to white [U.S. Bureau of the Census, 1940:4].) Theories of nurture and culture re-placed theories of nature and biology. Instead of dirty and dangerous races who would destroy U.S. democracy, immigrants became ethnic groups whose children had successfully assimilated into the mainstream and risen to the middle class. In this new myth, Euroethnic suburbs like mine became the measure of U.S. democ-racy's victory over racism. Jewish mobility became a new Horatio Alger story. In time and with hard work, every ethnic group would get a piece of the pie, and the United States would be a nation with equal opportunity for all its people to become part of a prosperous middle-class majority. And it seemed that Euroethnic immi-grants and their children were delighted to join middle America.[8]

This is not to say that anti-Semitism disappeared after World War II, only that it fell from fashion and was driven underground. . . .

Although changing views on who was white made it easier for Euroethnics to become middle class, it was also the case that economic prosperity played a very powerful role in the whitening process. Economic mobility of Jews and other Euroethnics rested ultimately on U.S. postwar economic prosperity with its enor-mously expanded need for professional, technical, and managerial labor, and on government assistance in providing it. The United States emerged from the war with the strongest economy in the world. . . . The postwar period was a historic moment for real class mobility and for the affluence we have erroneously come to believe was the U.S. norm. It was a time when the old white and the newly white masses became middle class.

The GI Bill of Rights, as the 1944 Serviceman's Readjustment Act was known, was arguably the most massive affirmative action program in U.S. history. It was created to develop needed labor-force skills, and to provide those who had them with a life-style that reflected their value to the economy. The GI benefits ulti-mately extended to sixteen million GIs (veterans of the Korean War as well) in-cluded priority in jobs—that is, preferential hiring, but no one objected to it then; financial support during the job search; small loans for starting up businesses; and, most important, low-interest home loans and educational benefits, which included tuition and living expenses (Brown 1946; Hurd 1946; Mosch 1975; *Postwar Jobs for Veterans* 1945; Willenz 1983). This legislation was rightly regarded as one of the most revolutionary postwar programs. I call it affirmative action because it was aimed at and disproportionately helped male, Euro-origin GIs. . . .

Education and Occupation

It is important to remember that prior to the war, a college degree was still very much a "mark of the upper class" (Willenz 1983:165). Colleges were largely finishing schools for Protestant elites. Before the postwar boom, schools could not begin to accommodate the American masses. Even in New York City before the 1930s, neither the public schools nor City College had room for more than a tiny fraction of potential immigrant students.

Not so after the war. The almost eight million GIs who took advantage of their educational benefits under the GI Bill caused "the greatest wave of college building in American history" (Nash et al. 1986:885). White male GIs were able to take advantage of their educational benefits for college and technical training, so they were particularly well positioned to seize the opportunities provided by the new demands for professional, managerial, and technical labor. "It has been well documented that the GI educational benefits transformed American higher education and raised the educational level of that generation and generations to come. With many provisions for assistance in upgrading their educational attainments veterans pulled ahead of nonveterans in earning capacity. In the long run it was the nonveterans who had fewer opportunities" (Willenz 1983:165).[9] . . .

Even more significantly, the postwar boom transformed the U.S. class structure—or at least its status structure—so that the middle class expanded to encompass most of the population. Before the war, most Jews, like most other Americans, were working class. Already upwardly mobile before the war relative to other immigrants, Jews floated high on this rising economic tide, and most of them entered the middle class. Still, even the high tide missed some Jews. As late as 1973, some 15 percent of New York's Jews were poor or near-poor, and in the 1960s, almost 25 percent of employed Jewish men remained manual workers (Steinberg 1989:89–90).

Educational and occupational GI benefits really constituted affirmative action programs for white males because they were decidedly not extended to African Americans or to women of any race. White male privilege was shaped against the backdrop of wartime racism and postwar sexism. During and after the war, there was an upsurge in white racist violence against black servicemen in public schools, and in the KKK, which spread to California and New York (Dalfiume 1969:133–134). The number of lynchings rose during the war, and in 1943 there were antiblack race riots in several large northern cities. Although there was a wartime labor shortage, black people were discriminated against in access to well-paid defense industry jobs and in housing. In 1946 there were white riots against African Americans across the South, and in Chicago and Philadelphia as well. Gains made as a result of the wartime Civil Rights movement, especially employment in defense-related industries, were lost with peacetime conversion as black workers were the first fired, often in violation of seniority (Wynn 1976:114, 116). White women were also laid off, ostensibly to make jobs for demobilized servicemen, and in the long run women lost most of the gains they had made in wartime (Kessler-Harris 1982). We now know that women did not leave the labor force in any significant numbers but instead were forced to find inferior jobs, largely nonunion, parttime, and clerical.

Theoretically available to all veterans, in practice women and black veterans did not get anywhere near their share of GI benefits. Because women's units were not treated as part of the military, women in them were not considered veterans and were ineligible for Veterans' Administration (VA) benefits (Willenz 1983:168). The barriers that almost completely shut African-American GIs out of their benefits were more complex. In Wynn's portrait (1976:115), black GIs anticipated starting new lives, just like their white counterparts. Over 43 percent hoped to return to school and most expected to relocate, to find better jobs in new lines of work. The exodus from the South toward the North and far West was particularly large. So it wasn't a question of any lack of ambition on the part of African-American GIs.

Rather, the military, the Veterans' Administration, the U.S. Employment Service, and the Federal Housing Administration (FHA) effectively denied African-American GIs access to their benefits and to the new educational, occupational, and residential opportunities. Black GIs who served in the thoroughly segregated armed forces during World War II served under white officers, usually southerners (Binkin and Eitelberg 1982: Dalfiume 1969; Foner 1974; Johnson 1967; Nalty and MacGregor 1981). African-American soldiers were disproportionately given dishonorable discharges, which denied them veterans' rights under the GI Bill. Thus between August and November 1946, 21 percent of white soldiers and 39 percent of black soldiers were dishonorably discharged. Those who did get an honorable discharge then faced the Veterans' Administration and the U.S. Employment Service. The latter, which was responsible for job placements, employed very few African Americans, especially in the South. This meant that black veterans did not receive much employment information, and that the offers they did receive were for low-paid and menial jobs. "In one survey of 50 cities, the movement of blacks into peacetime employment was found to be lagging far behind that of white veterans: in Arkansas 95 percent of the placements made by the USES for Afro-Americans were in service or unskilled jobs" (Nalty and MacGregor 1981:218, and see 60–61). African Americans were also less likely than whites, regardless of GI status, to gain new jobs commensurate with their wartime jobs, and they suffered more heavily. For example, in San Francisco by 1948, black Americans "had dropped back halfway to their pre-war employment status" (Wynn 1976:114, 116).[10]

Black GIs faced discrimination in the educational system as well. Despite the end of restrictions on Jews and other Euroethnics, African Americans were not welcome in white colleges. Black colleges were overcrowded, and the combination of segregation and prejudice made for few alternatives. About twenty thousand black veterans attended college by 1947, most in black colleges, but almost as many, fifteen thousand, could not gain entry. Predictably, the disproportionately few African Americans who did gain access to their educational benefits were able, like their white counterparts, to become doctors and engineers, and to enter the black middle class (Walker 1970).

Suburbanization

In 1949, ensconced at Valley Stream, I watched potato farms turn into Levittown and into Idlewild (later Kennedy) Airport. This was a major spectator sport in our first years on suburban Long Island. A typical weekend would bring various aunts, uncles, and cousins out from the city. After a huge meal we would pile in the car—itself a novelty—to look at the bulldozed acres and comment on the match-box construction. During the week, my mother and I would look at the houses going up within walking distance.

Bill Levitt built a basic 900–1,000-square-foot, somewhat expandable house for a lower-middle-class and working-class market on Long Island, and later in Pennsylvania and New Jersey (Gans 1967). Levittown started out as two thousand units of rental housing at sixty dollars a month, designed to meet the low-income housing needs of returning war vets, many of whom, like my Aunt Evie and Uncle Julie, were living in quonset huts. By May 1947, Levitt and Sons had acquired enough land in Hempstead Township on Long Island to build four thousand houses, and by the next February, he'd built six thousand units and named the development after himself. After 1948, federal financing for the construction of rental housing tightened, and Levitt switched to building houses for sale. By 1951 Levittown was a development of some fifteen thousand families. . . .

At the beginning of World War II, about 33 percent of all U.S. families owned their houses. That percentage doubled in twenty years. Most Levittowners looked just like my family. They came from New York City or Long Island; about 17 percent were military, from nearby Mitchell Field; Levittown was their first house; and almost everyone was married. The 1947 inhabitants were over 75 percent white collar, but by 1950 more blue-collar families moved in, so that by 1951, "barely half" of the new residents were white collar, and by 1960 their occupational profile was somewhat more working class than for Nassau County as a whole. By this time too, almost one-third of Levittown's people were either foreign-born or, like my parents, first-generation U.S. born (Dobriner 1963:91, 100).

The FHA was key to buyers and builders alike. Thanks to it, suburbia was open to more than GIs. People like us would never have been in the market for houses without FHA and VA low-down-payment, low-interest, long-term loans to young buyers.[11] . . .

The FHA believed in racial segregation. Throughout its history, it publicly and actively promoted restrictive covenants. Before the war, these forbade sale to Jews and Catholics as well as to African Americans. The deed to my house in Detroit had such a covenant, which theoretically prevented it from being sold to Jews or African Americans. Even after the Supreme Court ended legal enforcement of restrictive covenants in 1948, the FHA continued to encourage builders to write them against African Americans. FHA underwriting manuals openly insisted on racially homogeneous neighborhoods, and their loans were made only in white neighborhoods. I bought my Detroit house in 1972 from Jews who were leaving a largely African-American neighborhood. By that time, after the 1968 Fair Housing Act, restrictive covenants were a dead letter (although blockbusting by realtors was rapidly replacing it).

With the federal government behind them, virtually all developers refused to sell to African Americans. Palo Alto and Levittown, like most suburbs as late as 1960, were virtually all white. Out of 15,741 houses and 65,276 people, averaging 4.2 people per house, only 220 Levittowners, or 52 households, were "nonwhite." In 1958 Levitt announced publicly at a press conference to open his New Jersey development that he would not sell to black buyers. This caused a furor, since the state of New Jersey (but not the U.S. government) prohibited discrimination in federally subsidized housing. Levitt was sued and fought it, although he was ultimately persuaded by township ministers to integrate. . . .

The result of these policies was that African Americans were totally shut out of the suburban boom. An article in *Harper's* described the housing available to black GIs. "On his way to the base each morning, Sergeant Smith passes an attractive air-conditioned, FHA-financed housing project. It was built for service families. Its rents are little more than the Smiths pay for their shack. And there are half-a-dozen vacancies, but none for Negroes" (qtd. in Foner 1974:195).

Where my family felt the seductive pull of suburbia, Marshall Berman's experienced the brutal push of urban renewal. In the Bronx in the 1950s, Robert Moses's Cross-Bronx Expressway erased "a dozen solid, settled, densely populated neighborhoods like our own; . . . something like 60,000 working- and lower-middle-class people, mostly Jews, but with many Italians, Irish and Blacks thrown in, would be thrown out of their homes. . . . For ten years, through the late 1950s and early 1960s, the center of the Bronx was pounded and blasted and smashed" (1982:292).

Urban renewal made postwar cities into bad places to live. At a physical level, urban renewal reshaped them, and federal programs brought private developers and public officials together to create downtown central business districts where there had formerly been a mix of manufacturing, commerce, and working-class neighborhoods. Manufacturing was scattered to the peripheries of the city, which were ringed and bisected by a national system of highways. Some working-class neighborhoods were bulldozed, but others remained (Greer 1965; Hartman 1975;

Squires 1989). In Los Angeles, as in New York's Bronx, the postwar period saw massive freeway construction right through the heart of old working-class neighborhoods. In East Los Angeles and Santa Monica, Chicano and African-American communities were divided in half or blasted to smithereens by the highways bringing Angelenos to the new white suburbs, or to make way for civic monuments like Dodger Stadium (Pardo 1990; Social and Public Arts Resource Center 1990:80, 1983:12–13).

Urban renewal was the other side of the process by which Jewish and other working-class Euroimmigrants became middle class. It was the push to suburbia's seductive pull. The fortunate white survivors of urban renewal headed disproportionately for suburbia, where they could partake of prosperity and the good life. . . .

If the federal stick of urban renewal joined the FHA carrot of cheap mortgages to send masses of Euros to the suburbs, the FHA had a different kind of one-two punch for African Americans. Segregation kept them out of the suburbs, and redlining made sure they could not buy or repair their homes in the neighborhoods where they were allowed to live. The FHA practiced systematic redlining. This was a system developed by its predecessor, the Home Owners Loan Corporation (HOLC), which in the 1930s developed an elaborate neighborhood rating system that placed the highest (green) value on all-white, middle-class neighborhoods, and the lowest (red) on racially nonwhite or mixed and working-class neighborhoods. High ratings meant high property values. The idea was that low property values in redlined neighborhoods made them bad investments. The FHA was, after all, created by and for banks and the housing industry. Redlining warned banks not to lend there, and the FHA would not insure mortgages in such neighborhoods. Redlining created a self-fulfilling prophecy. "With the assistance of local realtors and banks, it assigned one of the four ratings to every block in every city. The resulting information was then translated into the appropriate color [green, blue, yellow, and red] and duly recorded on secret 'Residential Security Maps' in local HOLC offices. The maps themselves were placed in elaborate 'City Survey Files,' which consisted of reports, questionnaires, and workpapers relating to current and future values of real estate" (Jackson 1985:197).[12]

FHA's and VA's refusal to guarantee loans in redlined neighborhoods made it virtually impossible for African Americans to borrow money for home improvement or purchase. Because these maps and surveys were quite secret, it took the 1960s Civil Rights movement to make these practices and their devastating consequences public. As a result, those who fought urban renewal or who sought to make a home in the urban ruins found themselves locked out of the middle class. They also faced an ideological assault that labeled their neighborhoods slums and called those who lived in them slum dwellers (Gans 1962).

The record is very clear that instead of seizing the opportunity to end institutionalized racism, the federal government did its best to shut and double seal the postwar window of opportunity in African Americans' faces. It consistently refused to combat segregation in the social institutions that were key for upward mobility: education, housing, and employment. Moreover, federal programs that were themselves designed to assist demobilized GIs and young families systematically discriminated against African Americans. Such programs reinforced white/nonwhite racial distinctions even as intrawhite racialization was falling out of fashion. This other side of the coin, that white men of northwestern or southeastern European ancestry were treated equally in theory and in practice with regard to the benefits they received, was part of the larger postwar whitening of Jews and other eastern and southern Europeans.

The myth that Jews pulled themselves up by their own bootstraps ignores the fact that it took federal programs to create the conditions whereby the abilities of Jews and other European immigrants could be recognized and rewarded rather than denigrated and denied. The GI Bill and FHA and VA mortgages were forms of affirmative action that allowed male Jews and other Euro-American men to become suburban homeowners and to get the training that allowed them—but not women vets or war workers—to become professionals, technicians, salesmen, and managers in a growing economy. Jews' and other white ethnics' upward mobility was the result of programs that allowed us to float on a rising economic tide. To African Americans, the government offered the cement boots of segregation, redlining, urban renewal, and discrimination.

Those racially skewed gains have been passed across the generations, so that racial inequality seems to maintain itself "naturally," even after legal segregation ended. Today, in a shrinking economy where downward mobility is the norm, the children and grandchildren of the postwar beneficiaries of the economic boom have some precious advantages. For example, having parents who own their own homes or who have decent retirement benefits can make a real difference in young people's ability to take on huge college loans or to come up with a down payment for a house. Even this simple inheritance helps perpetuate the gap between whites and nonwhites. Sure Jews needed ability, but ability was not enough to make it. The same applies even more in today's long recession.

NOTES

This is a revised and expanded version of a paper published in *Jewish Currents* in June 1992 and delivered at the 1992 meetings of the American Anthropological Association in the session *Blacks and Jews, 1992: Reaching across the Cultural Boundaries* organized by Angela Gilliam. I would like to thank Emily Abel, Katya Gibel Azoulay, Edna Bonacich, Angela Gilliam, Isabelle Gunning, Valerie Matsumoto, Regina Morantz-Sanchez, Roger Sanjek, Rabbi Chaim Seidler-Feller, Janet Silverstein, and Eloise Klein Healy's writing group for uncovering wonderful sources and for critical readings along the way.

1. Indeed, Boasian and Du Boisian anthropology developed in active political opposition to this nativism; on Du Bois, see Harrison and Nonini 1992.

2. On immigrants as part of the industrial work force, see Steinberg 1989:36.

3. I thank Roger Sanjek for providing me with this source.

4. It was intended, as Davenport wrote to the president of the American Museum of Natural History, Henry Fairfield Osborne, as "an anthropological society . . . with a central governing body, self-elected and self-perpetuating, and very limited in members, and also confined to native Americans who are anthropologically, socially and politically sound, no Bolsheviki need apply" (Barkan 1991:67–68).

5. I thank Valerie Matsumoto for telling me about the Thind case and Katya Gibel Azoulay for providing this information to me on the Virginia statute.

6. "The distinction between white and colored" has been "the only racial classification which has been carried through all the 15 censuses." "Colored" consisted of "Negroes" and "other races": Mexican, Indian, Chinese, Japanese, Filipino, Hindu, Korean, Hawaiian, Malay, Siamese, and Samoan. (U.S. Bureau of the Census, 1930:25, 26).

7. For why Jews entered colleges earlier than other immigrants, and for a challenge to views that attribute it to Jewish culture, see Steinberg 1989.

8. Indeed, Jewish social scientists were prominent in creating this ideology of the United States as a meritocracy. Most prominent of course was Nathan Glazer, but among them also were Charles Silberman and Marshall Sklare.

9. The belief was widespread that "the GI Bill . . . helped millions of families move into the middle class" (Nash et al. 1986:885). A study that compares mobility among veterans and nonveterans provides a kind of confirmation. In an unnamed small city in Illinois, Havighurst and his colleagues (1951) found no significant difference between veterans and nonveterans, but this was because apparently very few veterans used any of their GI benefits.

10. African Americans and Japanese Americans were the main target of wartime racism (see Murray 1992). By contrast, there were virtually no anti–German American or anti–Italian American policies in World War II (see Takaki 1989:357–406).

11. See Eichler 1982:5 for homeowning percentages; Jackson (1985:205) found an increase in families living in owner-occupied buildings, rising from 44 percent in 1934 to 63 percent in 1972; see Monkkonen 1988 on scarcity of mortgages; and Gelfand 1975, esp. chap. 6, on federal programs.

12. These ideas from the real estate industry were "codified and legitimated in 1930s work by University of Chicago sociologist Robert Park and real estate professor Homer Hoyt" (Jackson 1985:198–199).

REFERENCES

Binkin, Martin, and Mark J. Eitelberg. 1982. *Blacks and the Military*. Washington, D.C.: Brookings.

Bodnar, John. 1985. *The Transplanted: A History of Immigrants in Urban America*. Bloomington: Indiana University Press.

Brody, David. 1980. *Workers in Industrial America: Essays of the Twentieth Century Struggle*. New York: Oxford University Press.

Brown, Francis J. 1946. *Educational Opportunities for Veterans*. Washington, D.C.: Public Affairs Press, American Council on Public Affairs.

Carlson, Lewis H., and George A. Colburn. 1972. *In Their Place: White America Defines Her Minorities, 1850–1950*. New York: Wiley.

Dalfiume, Richard M. 1969. *Desegregation of the U.S. Armed Forces: Fighting on Two Fronts, 1939–1953*. Columbia: University of Missouri Press.

Davis, Mike. 1990. *City of Quartz*. London: Verso.

Dobriner, William M. 1963. *Class in Suburbia*. Englewood Cliffs, N.J.: Prentice-Hall.

Eichler, Ned. 1982. *The Merchant Builders*. Cambridge, Mass.: MIT Press.

Fields, Barbara Jeanne. 1990. Slavery, Race, and Ideology in the United States of America. *New Left Review* 181:95–118.

Foner, Jack. 1974. *Blacks and the Military in American History: A New Perspective*. New York: Praeger.

Gans, Herbert. 1962. *The Urban Villagers*. New York: Free Press.

———. 1967. *The Levittowners*. New York: Pantheon.

Gordon, Milton. 1964. *Assimilation in American Life*. New York: Oxford University Press.

Hartman, Chester. 1975. *Housing and Social Policy*. Englewood Cliffs, N.J.: Prentice-Hall.

Higham, John. 1955. *Strangers in the Land*. New Brunswick, N.J.: Rutgers University Press.

Hurd, Charles. 1946. *The Veterans' Program: A Complete Guide to Its Benefits, Rights, and Options*. New York: McGraw-Hill.

Jackson, Kenneth T. 1985. *Crabgrass Frontier: The Suburbanization of the United States*. New York: Oxford University Press.

Johnson, Jesse J. 1967. *Ebony Brass: An Autobiography of Negro Frustration amid Aspiration*. New York: Frederick.

Karabel, Jerome. 1984. Status-Group Struggle, Organizational Interests, and the Limits of Institutional Autonomy. *Theory and Society* 13:1–40.

Kessler-Harris, Alice. 1982. *Out to Work: A History of Wage-Earning Women in the United States*. New York: Oxford University Press.

Martyn, Byron Curti. 1979. Racism in the U.S.: A History of Anti-Miscegenation Legislation and Litigation. Ph.D. diss., University of Southern California.

Mosch, Theodore R. 1975. *The GI Bill: A Breakthrough in Educational and Social Policy in the United States*. Hicksville, N.Y.: Exposition.

Nalty, Bernard C., and Morris J. MacGregor, eds. 1981. *Blacks in the Military: Essential Documents*. Wilmington, Del.: Scholarly Resources.

Nash, Gary B., Julie Roy Jeffrey, John R. Howe, Allen F. Davis, Peter J. Frederick, and Allen M. Winkler. 1986. *The American People: Creating a Nation and a Society*. New York: Harper and Row.

Pardo, Mary. 1990. Mexican-American Women Grassroots Community Activists: "Mothers of East Los Angeles." *Frontiers* 11:1–7.

Postwar Jobs for Veterans. 1945. Annals of the American Academy of Political and Social Science 238 (March).

Saxton, Alexander. 1971. *The Indispensible Enemy*. Berkeley and Los Angeles: University of California Press.

———. 1990. *The Rise and Fall of the White Republic*. London: Verso.

Silberman, Charles. 1985. *A Certain People: American Jews and Their Lives Today*. New York: Summit.

Sklare, Marshall. 1971. *America's Jews*. New York: Random House.

Sowell, Thomas. 1981. *Ethnic America: A History*. New York: Basic.

Steinberg, Stephen. 1989. *The Ethnic Myth: Race, Ethnicity, and Class in America*. 2d ed. Boston: Beacon.

Synott, Marcia Graham. 1986. Anti-Semitism and American Universities: Did Quotas Follow the Jews? In *Anti-Semitism in American History*, ed. David A. Gerber. Urbana: University of Illinois Press, 233–274.

Takaki, Ronald. 1989. *Strangers from a Different Shore*. Boston: Little, Brown.

Tobin, Gary A., ed. 1987. *Divided Neighborhoods: Changing Patterns of Racial Segregation*. Beverly Hills: Sage.

U.S. Bureau of the Census. 1930. *Fifteenth Census of the United* States. Vol. 2. Washington, D.C.: U.S. Government Printing Office.

———. 1940. *Sixteenth Census of the United States*. Vol. 2. Washington, D.C.: U.S. Government Printing Office.

Walker, Olive. 1970. The Windsor Hills School Story. *Integrated Education: Race and Schools* 8(3): 4–9.

Willenz, June A. 1983. *Women Veterans: America's Forgotten Heroines*. New York: Continuum.

Wynn, Neil A. 1976. *The Afro-American and the Second World War*. London: Elek.

4

Rethinking Women's Biology

Ruth Hubbard

Women's biology is a social construct and a political concept, not a scientific one, and I mean that in at least three ways. The first can be summed up in Simone de Beauvoir's (1953) dictum "One isn't born a woman, one becomes a woman." This does not mean that the environment shapes us, but that the concept, woman (or man), is a socially constructed one that little girls (or boys) try to fit as we grow up. Some of us are better at it than others, but we all try, and our efforts have biological as well as social consequences (a false dichotomy because our biological and social attributes are related dialectically). How active we are, what clothes we wear, what games we play, what we eat and how much, what kinds of schools we go to, what work we do, all affect our biology as well as our social being in ways we cannot sort out. So, one isn't born a woman (or man), one becomes one.

The concept of women's biology is socially constructed, and political, in a second way because it is not simply women's description of our experience of our biology. Women's biology has been described by physicians and scientists who, for historical reasons, have been mostly economically privileged, university-educated men with strong personal and political interests in describing women in ways that make it appear "natural" for us to fulfill roles that are important for their well-being, personally and as a group. Self-serving descriptions of women's biology date back at least to Aristotle. But if we dismiss the early descriptions as ideological, so are the descriptions scientists have offered that characterize women as weak, over-emotional, and at the mercy of our raging hormones, and that construct our entire being around the functions of our reproductive organs. No one has suggested that men are just walking testicles, but again and again women have been looked on as though they were walking ovaries and wombs.

In the nineteenth century, when women tried to get access to higher educa-tion, scientists initially claimed we could not be educated because our brains are too small. When that claim became untenable, they granted that we could be edu-cated the same as men but questioned whether we should be, whether it was good for us. They based their concerns on the claim that girls need to devote much en-ergy to establishing the proper functioning of their ovaries and womb and that if they divert this energy to their brains by studying, their reproductive organs will shrivel, they will become sterile, and the race will die out.

This logic was steeped in race and class prejudice. The notion that women's reproductive organs need careful nurturing was used to justify excluding upper-class girls and young women from higher education but not to spare the working-class, poor, or black women who were laboring in the factories and homes of the upper class. If anything, these women were said to breed too much. In fact, their ability to have many children despite the fact that they worked so hard was taken as evidence that they were less highly evolved than upper-class women; for them breeding was "natural," as for animals.

Finally, and perhaps most importantly, our concept of ourselves is socially con-structed and political because our society's interpretation of what is and is not nor-mal and natural affects what we do. It therefore affects our biological structure and functioning because, as I have said before, what we do and how our bodies and minds function are connected dialectically. Thus norms are self-fulfilling prophe-cies that do not merely describe how we are but prescribe how we should be.

5

The Social Construction of Gender

Judith Lorber

Until the eighteenth century, Western philosophers and scientists thought that there was one sex and that women's internal genitalia were the inverse of men's external genitalia: the womb and vagina were the penis and scrotum turned inside out (Laqueur 1990). Current Western thinking sees women and men as so different physically as to sometimes seem two species. The bodies, which have been mapped inside and out for hundreds of years, have not changed. What has changed are the justifications for gender inequality. When the social position of all human beings was believed to be set by natural law or was considered God-given, biology was irrelevant; women and men of different classes all had their assigned places. When scientists began to question the divine basis of social order and replaced faith with empirical knowledge, what they saw was that women were very different from men in that they had wombs and menstruated. Such anatomical differences destined them for an entirely different social life from men.

In actuality, the basic bodily material *is* the same for females and males, and except for procreative hormones and organs, female and male human beings have similar bodies (Naftolin and Butz 1981). Furthermore, as has been known since the middle of the nineteenth century, male and female genitalia develop from the same fetal tissue, and so infants can be born with ambiguous genitalia (Money and Ehrhardt 1972). When they are, biology is used quite arbitrarily in sex assignment. Suzanne Kessler (1990) interviewed six medical specialists in pediatric intersexuality and found that whether an infant with XY chromosomes and anomalous genitalia was categorized as a boy or a girl depended on the size of the penis—if a penis was very small, the child was categorized as a girl, and sex-change surgery was used to make an artificial vagina. In the late nineteenth century, the presence or absence of ovaries was the determining criterion of gender assignment for hermaphrodites because a woman who could not procreate was not a complete woman (Kessler 1990, 20).

Yet in Western societies, we see two discrete sexes and two distinguishable genders because our society is built on two classes of people, "women" and "men." Once the gender category is given, the attributes of the person are also gendered: Whatever a "woman" is has to be "female"; whatever a "man" is has to be "male." Analyzing the social processes that construct the categories we call "female and male," "women and men," and "homosexual and heterosexual" uncovers the ideology and power differentials congealed in these categories (Foucault 1978). This article will use a familiar area of social life—sports—to show how myriad physiological differences are transformed into similar-appearing, gendered social bodies. My perspective goes beyond accepted feminist views that gender is a cultural overlay that modifies physiological sex differences. That perspective assumes either that there are two fairly similar sexes distorted by social practices into two genders with purposefully different characteristics or that there are two sexes whose essential differences are rendered unequal by social practices. I am arguing that bodies differ in many ways physiologically, but they are completely transformed by social practices to fit into the salient categories of a society, the most pervasive of which are "female" and "male" and "women" and "men."

Neither sex nor gender are pure categories. Combinations of incongruous genes, genitalia, and hormonal input are ignored in sex categorization, just as combinations of incongruous physiology, identity, sexuality, appearance, and behavior are ignored in the social construction of gender statuses. Menstruation, lactation, and gestation do not demarcate women from men. Only some women are pregnant and then only some of the time; some women do not have a uterus or ovaries. Some women have stopped menstruating temporarily, others have reached menopause, and some have had hysterectomies. Some women breastfeed some of the time, but some men lactate (Jaggar 1983, 165fn). Menstruation, lactation, and gestation are individual experiences of womanhood (Levesque-Lopman 1988), but not determinants of the social category "woman," or even "female." Similarly, "men are not always sperm-producers, and in fact, not all sperm producers are men. A male-to-female transsexual, prior to surgery, can be socially a woman, though still potentially (or actually) capable of spermatogenesis" (Kessler and McKenna [1978] 1985, 2).

When gender assignment is contested in sports, where the categories of competitors are rigidly divided into women and men, chromosomes are now used to determine in which category the athlete is to compete. However, an anomaly common enough to be found in several women at every major international sports competition are XY chromosomes that have not produced male anatomy or physiology because of a genetic defect. Because these women are women in every way significant for sports competition, the prestigious International Amateur Athletic Federation has urged that sex be determined by simple genital inspection (Kolata 1992). Transsexuals would pass this test, but it took a lawsuit for Renée Richards, a male-to-female transsexual, to be able to play tournament tennis as a woman, despite his male sex chromosomes (Richards 1983). Oddly, neither basis for gender categorization—chromosomes nor genitalia—has anything to do with sports prowess (Birrell and Cole 1990).

In the Olympics, in cases of chromosomal ambiguity, women must undergo "a battery of gynecological and physical exams to see if she is 'female enough' to compete. Men are not tested" (Carlson 1991, 26). The purpose is not to categorize women and men accurately, but to make sure men don't enter women's competitions, where, it is felt, they will have the advantage of size and strength. This practice sounds fair only because it is assumed that all men are similar in size and strength and different from all women. Yet in Olympics boxing and wrestling matches, men are matched within weight classes. Some women might similarly successfully compete with some men in many sports. Women did not run in marathons until about twenty years ago. In twenty years of marathon competition, women have reduced their finish times by more than one-and-one-half hours; they are expected to run as fast as men in that race by 1998 and might catch up with men's running times in races of other lengths within the next fifty years because they are increasing their fastest speeds more rapidly than are men (Fausto-Sterling 1985, 213–18).

The reliance on only two sex and gender categories in the biological and social sciences is as epistemologically spurious as the reliance on chromosomal or genital tests to group athletes. Most research designs do not investigate whether physical skills or physical abilities are really more or less common in women and men (Epstein 1988). They start out with two social categories ("women," "men"), assume they are biologically different ("female," "male"), look for similarities within them and differences between them, and attribute what they have found for the social categories to sex differences (Gelman, Collman, and Maccoby 1986). These designs rarely question the categorization of their subjects into two and only two groups, even though they often find more significant within-group differences than between-group differences (Hyde 1990). The social construction perspective on sex and gender suggests that instead of starting with the two presumed dichotomies in each category—female, male; woman, man—it might be more useful in gender studies to group patterns of behavior and only then look for identifying markers of the people likely to enact such behaviors.

What Sports Illustrate

Competitive sports have become, for boys and men, as players and as spectators, a way of constructing a masculine identity, a legitimated outlet for violence and aggression, and an avenue for upward mobility (Dunning 1986; Kemper 1990, 167–206; Messner 1992). For men in Western societies, physical competence is an important marker of masculinity (Fine 1987; Glassner 1992; Majors 1990). In professional and collegiate sports, physiological differences are invoked to justify women's secondary status, despite the clear evidence that gender status overrides physiological capabilities. Assumptions about women's physiology have influenced rules of competition; subsequent sports performances then validate how women and men are treated in sports competitions.

Gymnastic equipment is geared to slim, wiry, prepubescent girls and not to mature women; conversely, men's gymnastic equipment is tailored for muscular, mature men, not slim, wiry prepubescent boys. Boys could compete with girls, but are not allowed to; women gymnasts are left out entirely. Girl gymnasts are just that—little girls who will be disqualified as soon as they grow up (Vecsey 1990). Men gymnasts have men's status. In women's basketball, the size of the ball and rules for handling the ball change the style of play to "a slower, less intense, and less exciting modification of the 'regular' or men's game" (Watson 1987, 441). In the 1992 Winter Olympics, men figure skaters were required to complete three triple jumps in their required program; women figure skaters were forbidden to do more than *one*. These rules penalized artistic men skaters and athletic women skaters (Janofsky 1992). For the most part, Western sports are built on physically trained men's bodies:

> Speed, size, and strength seem to be the essence of sports. Women *are* naturally inferior at "sports" so conceived.
>
> But if women had been the historically dominant sex, our concept of sport would no doubt have evolved differently. Competitions emphasizing flexibility, balance, strength, timing, and small size might dominate Sunday afternoon television and offer salaries in six figures. (English 1982, 266, emphasis in original)

Organized sports are big businesses and, thus, who has access and at what level is a distributive or equity issue. The overall status of women and men athletes is an economic, political, and ideological issue that has less to do with individual physiological capabilities than with their cultural and social meaning and who defines and profits from them (Messner and Sabo 1990; Slatton and Birrell 1984). Twenty years after the passage of Title IX of the U.S. Civil Rights Act, which forbade gender inequality in any school receiving federal funds, the *goal* for collegiate sports in the next five years is 60 percent men, 40 percent women in sports participation, scholarships, and funding (Moran 1992).

How access and distribution of rewards (prestigious and financial) are justified is an ideological, even moral, issue (Birrell 1988, 473–76; Hargreaves 1982). One way is that men athletes are glorified and women athletes ignored in the mass media. Messner and his colleagues found that in 1989, in TV sports news in the United States, men's sports got 92 percent of the coverage and women's sports 5 percent, with the rest mixed or gender-neutral (Messner, Duncan, and Jensen 1993). In 1990, in four of the top-selling newspapers in the United States, stories on men's sports outnumbered those on women's sports 23 to 1. Messner and his colleagues also found an implicit hierarchy in naming, with women athletes most likely to be called by first names, followed by Black men athletes, and only white men athletes routinely referred to by their last names. Similarly, women's collegiate sports teams are named or marked in ways that symbolically feminize and trivialize them—the men's team is called Tigers, the women's Kittens (Eitzen and Baca Zinn 1989).

Assumptions about men's and women's bodies and their capacities are crafted in ways that make unequal access and distribution of rewards acceptable (Hudson 1978; Messner 1988). Media images of modern men athletes glorify their strength and power, even their violence (Hargreaves 1986). Media images of modern women athletes tend to focus on feminine beauty and grace (so they are not really athletes) or on their thin, small, wiry androgynous bodies (so they are not really women). In coverage of the Olympics,

> loving and detailed attention is paid to pixie-like gymnasts; special and extended coverage is given to graceful and dazzling figure skaters; the camera painstakingly records the fluid movements of swimmers and divers. And then, in a blinding flash of fragmented images, viewers see a few minutes of volleyball, basketball, speed skating, track and field, and alpine skiing, as television gives its nod to the mere existence of these events. (Boutilier and SanGiovanni 1983, 190)

Extraordinary feats by women athletes who were presented as mature adults might force sports organizers and audiences to rethink their stereotypes of women's capabilities, the way elves, mermaids, and ice queens do not. Sports, therefore, construct men's bodies to be powerful; women's bodies to be sexual. As Connell says,

> The meanings in the bodily sense of masculinity concern, above all else, the superiority of men to women, and the exaltation of hegemonic masculinity over other groups of men which is essential for the domination of women. (1987, 85)

In the late 1970s, as women entered more and more athletic competitions, supposedly good scientific studies showed that women who exercised intensely would cease menstruating because they would not have enough body fat to sustain ovulation (Brozan 1978). When one set of researchers did a yearlong study that compared 66 women—21 who were training for a marathon, 22 who ran more than an hour a week, and 23 who did less than an hour of aerobic exercise a week—they discovered that only 20 percent of the women in any of these groups had "normal" menstrual cycles every month (Prior et al. 1990). The dangers of intensive training for women's fertility therefore were exaggerated as women began to compete successfully in arenas formerly closed to them.

Given the association of sports with masculinity in the United States, women athletes have to manage a contradictory status. One study of women college basketball players found that although they "did athlete" on the court—"pushing, shoving, fouling, hard running, fast breaks, defense, obscenities and sweat" (Watson 1987, 441), they "did woman" off the court, using the locker room as their staging area:

> While it typically took fifteen minutes to prepare for the game, it took approximately fifteen minutes after the game to shower and remove the sweat of an athlete,

and it took another thirty minutes to dress, apply make-up and style hair. It did not seem to matter whether the players were going out into the public or getting on a van for a long ride home. Average dressing time and rituals did not change. (Watson 1987, 443)

Another way women manage these status dilemmas is to redefine the activity or its result as feminine or womanly (Mangan and Park 1987). Thus women body-builders claim that "flex appeal is sex appeal" (Duff and Hong 1984, 378).

Such a redefinition of women's physicality affirms the ideological subtext of sports that physical strength is men's prerogative and justifies men's physical and sexual domination of women (Hargreaves 1986; Messner 1992, 164–72; Olson 1990; Theberge 1987; Willis 1982). When women demonstrate physical strength, they are labeled unfeminine:

> It's threatening to one's takeability, one's rapeability, one's femininity, to be strong and physically self-possessed. To be able to resist rape, not to communicate rapeability with one's body, to hold one's body for uses and meanings other than that can transform what *being a woman means.* (MacKinnon 1987, 122, emphasis in original)

Resistance to that transformation, ironically, was evident in the policies of American women physical education professionals throughout most of the twentieth century. They minimized exertion, maximized a feminine appearance and manner, and left organized sports competition to men (Birrell 1988, 461–62; Mangan and Park 1987).

* * *

Social Bodies and the Bathroom Problem

People of the same racial ethnic group and social class are roughly the same size and shape—but there are many varieties of bodies. People have different genitalia, different secondary sex characteristics, different contributions to procreation, different orgasmic experiences, different patterns of illness and aging. Each of us experiences our bodies differently, and these experiences change as we grow, age, sicken, and die. The bodies of pregnant and nonpregnant women, short and tall people, those with intact and functioning limbs and those whose bodies are physically challenged are all different. But the salient categories of a society group these attributes in ways that ride roughshod over individual experiences and more meaningful clusters of people.

I am not saying that physical differences between male and female bodies don't exist, but that these differences are socially meaningless until social practices transform them into social facts. West Point Military Academy's curriculum is designed to produce leaders, and physical competence is used as a significant measure of leadership ability (Yoder 1989). When women were accepted as West Point cadets, it became clear that the tests of physical competence, such as rapidly scaling an eight-foot wall, had been constructed for male physiques—pulling oneself up and over using upper-body strength. Rather than devise tests of physical competence for women, West Point provided boosters that mostly women used—but that lost them test points—in the case of the wall, a platform. Finally, the women themselves figured out how to use their bodies successfully. Janice Yoder describes this situation:

> I was observing this obstacle one day, when a woman approached the wall in the old prescribed way, got her fingertips grip, and did an unusual thing: she walked her dangling legs up the wall until she was in a position where both her hands and feet were atop the wall. She then simply pulled up her sagging bottom and went over. She solved the problem by capitalizing on one of women's physical assets: lower-body strength. (1989, 530)

In short, if West Point is going to measure leadership capability by physical strength, women's pelvises will do just as well as men's shoulders.

The social transformation of female and male physiology into a condition of inequality is well illustrated by the bathroom problem. Most buildings that have gender-segregated bathrooms have an equal number for women and for men. Where there are crowds, there are always long lines in front of women's bathrooms but rarely in front of men's bathrooms. The cultural, physiological, and demographic combinations of clothing, frequency of urination, menstruation, and child care add up to generally greater bathroom use by women than men. Thus, although an equal number of bathrooms seems fair, equity would mean more women's bathrooms or allowing women to use men's bathrooms for a certain amount of time (Molotch 1988).

The bathroom problem is the outcome of the way gendered bodies are differentially evaluated in Western cultures: Men's social bodies are the measure of what is "human." Gray's *Anatomy*, in use for 100 years, well into the twentieth century, presented the human body as male. The female body was shown only where it differed from the male (Laqueur 1990, 166–67). Denise Riley says that if we envisage women's bodies, men's bodies, and human bodies "as a triangle of identifications, then it is rarely an equilateral triangle in which both sexes are pitched at matching distances from the apex of the human" (1988, 197). Catharine MacKinnon also contends that in Western society, universal "humanness" is male because

> virtually every quality that distinguishes men from women is already affirmatively compensated in this society. Men's physiology defines most sports, their needs define auto and health insurance coverage, their socially defined biographies define workplace expectations and successful career patterns, their perspectives and concerns define quality in scholarship, their experiences and obsessions define merit, their objectification of life defines art, their military service defines citizenship, their presence defines family, their inability to get along with each other—their wars and rulerships—define history, their image defines god, and their genitals define sex. For each of their differences from women, what amounts to an affirmative

action plan is in effect, otherwise known as the structure and values of American society. (1987, 36)

The Paradox of Human Nature

Gendered people do not emerge from physiology or hormones but from the exigencies of the social order, mostly, from the need for a reliable division of the work of food production and the social (not physical) reproduction of new members. The moral imperatives of religion and cultural representations reinforce the boundary lines among genders and ensure that what is demanded, what is permitted, and what is tabooed for the people in each gender is well known and followed by most. Political power, control of scarce resources, and, if necessary, violence uphold the gendered social order in the face of resistance and rebellion. Most people, however, voluntarily go along with their society's prescriptions for those of their gender status because the norms and expectations get built into their sense of worth and identity as a certain kind of human being and because they believe their society's way is the natural way. These beliefs emerge from the imagery that pervades the way we think, the way we see and hear and speak, the way we fantasize, and the way we feel. There is no core or bedrock human nature below these endlessly looping processes of the social production of sex and gender, self and other, identity and psyche, each of which is a "complex cultural construction" (Butler 1990, 36). The paradox of "human nature" is that it is *always* a manifestation of cultural meanings, social relationships, and power politics—"not biology, but culture, becomes destiny" (Butler 1990, 8).

Feminist inquiry has long questioned the conventional categories of social science, but much of the current work in feminist sociology has not gone beyond adding the universal category "women" to the universal category "men." Our current debates over the global assumptions of only two categories and the insistence that they must be nuanced to include race and class are steps in the direction I would like to see feminist research go, but race and class are *also* global categories (Collins 1990; Spelman 1988). Deconstructing sex, sexuality, and gender reveals many possible categories embedded in the social experiences and social practices of what Dorothy Smith calls the "everyday/everynight world" (1990, 31–57). These emergent categories group some people together for comparison with other people without prior assumptions about who is like whom. Categories can be broken up and people regrouped differently into new categories for comparison. This process of discovering categories from similarities and differences in people's behavior or responses can be more meaningful for feminist research than discovering similarities and differences between "females" and "males" or "women" and "men" because the social construction of the conventional sex and gender categories already assumes differences between them and similarities among them. When we rely only on the conventional categories of sex and gender, we end up finding what we looked for—we see what we believe, whether it is that "females" and "males" are essentially different or that "women" and "men" are essentially the same.

REFERENCES

Birrell, Susan J. 1988. Discourses on the gender/sport relationship: From women in sport to gender relations. In *Exercise and sport science reviews.* Vol. 16, edited by Kent Pandolf. New York: Macmillan.

Birrell, Susan J., and Sheryl L. Cole. 1990. Double fault: Renée Richards and the construction and naturalization of difference. *Sociology of Sport Journal* 7:1–21.

Boutilier, Mary A., and Lucinda SanGiovanni. 1983. *The sporting woman.* Champaign, IL: Human Kinetics.

Brozan, Nadine. 1978. Training linked to disruption of female reproductive cycle. *New York Times,* 17 April.

Butler, Judith. 1990. *Gender trouble: Feminism and the subversion of identity.* New York and London: Routledge & Kegan Paul.

Carlson, Alison. 1991. When is a woman not a woman? *Women's Sport and Fitness* March:24–29.

Collins, Patricia Hill. 1990. *Black feminist thought: Knowledge, consciousness, and the politics of empowerment.* Boston: Unwin Hyman.

Connell, R. W. 1987. *Gender and power.* Stanford, CA: Stanford University Press.

Duff, Robert W., and Lawrence K. Hong. 1984. Self-images of women bodybuilders. *Sociology of Sport Journal* 2:374–80.

Dunning, Eric. 1986. Sport as a male preserve: Notes on the social sources of masculine identity and its transformations. *Theory, Culture and Society* 3:79–90.

Eitzen, D. Stanley, and Maxine Baca Zinn. 1989. The deathleticization of women: The naming and gender marking of collegiate sport teams. *Sociology of Sport Journal* 6:362–70.

English, Jane. 1982. Sex equality in sports. In *Femininity, masculinity, and androgyny,* edited by Mary Vetterling-Braggin. Boston: Littlefield, Adams.

Epstein, Cynthia Fuchs. 1988. *Deceptive distinctions: Sex, gender and the social order.* New Haven, CT: Yale University Press.

Fausto-Sterling, Anne. 1985. *Myths of gender: Biological theories about women and men.* New York: Basic Books.

Fine, Gary Alan. 1987. *With the boys: Little League baseball and preadolescent culture.* Chicago: University of Chicago Press.

Foucault, Michel. 1978. *The history of sexuality: An introduction.* Translated by Robert Hurley. New York: Pantheon.

Gelman, Susan A., Pamela Collman, and Eleanor E. Maccoby. 1986. Inferring properties from categories versus inferring categories from properties: The case of gender. *Child Development* 57:396–404.

Glassner, Barry. 1992. Men and muscles. In *Men's lives,* edited by Michael S. Kimmel and Michael A. Messner. New York: Macmillan.

Hargreaves, Jennifer A., ed. 1982. *Sport, culture, and ideology.* London: Routledge & Kegan Paul.

_____. 1986. Where's the virtue? Where's the grace? A discussion of the social production of gender relations in and through sport. *Theory, Culture, and Society* 3:109–21.

Hudson, Jackie. 1978. Physical parameters used for female exclusion from law enforcement and athletics. In *Women and sport: From myth to reality*, edited by Carole A. Oglesby. Philadelphia: Lea and Febiger.

Hyde, Janet Shibley. 1990. Meta-analysis and the psychology of gender differences. *Signs: Journal of Women in Culture and Society* 16:55–73.

Jaggar, Alison M. 1983. *Feminist politics and human nature*. Totowa, NJ: Rowman & Allanheld.

Janofsky, Michael. 1992. Yamaguchi has the delicate and golden touch. *New York Times*, 22 February.

Kemper, Theodore D. 1990. *Social structure and testosterone: Explorations of the socio-biosocial chain*. New Brunswick, NJ: Rutgers University Press.

Kessler, Suzanne J. 1990. The medical construction of gender: Case management of intersexed infants. *Signs: Journal of Women in Culture and Society* 16:3–26.

Kessler, Suzanne J., and Wendy McKenna. [1978] 1985. *Gender: An ethnomethodological approach*. Chicago: University of Chicago Press.

Kolata, Gina. 1992. Track federation urges end to gene test for femaleness. *New York Times*, 12 February.

Laqueur, Thomas. 1990. *Making sex: Body and gender from the Greeks to Freud*. Cambridge, MA: Harvard University Press.

Levesque-Lopman, Louise. 1988. *Claiming reality: Phenomenology and women's experience*. Totowa, NJ: Rowman & Littlefield.

MacKinnon, Catharine. 1987. *Feminism unmodified*. Cambridge, MA: Harvard University Press.

Majors, Richard. 1990. Cool pose: Black masculinity in sports. *In Sport, men, and the gender order: Critical feminist perspectives*, edited by Michael A. Messner and Donald F. Sabo. Champaign, IL: Human Kinetics.

Mangan, J. A., and Roberta J. Park. 1987. *From fair sex to feminism: Sport and the socialization of women in the industrial and post-industrial eras*. London: Frank Cass.

Messner, Michael A. 1988. Sports and male domination: The female athlete as contested ideological terrain. *Sociology of Sport Journal* 5:197–211.

_____. 1992. *Power at play: Sports and the problem of masculinity*. Boston: Beacon Press.

Messner, Michael A., Margaret Carlisle Duncan, and Kerry Jensen. 1993. Separating the men from the girls: The gendered language of televised sports. *Gender & Society* 7:121–37.

Messner, Michael A., and Donald F. Sabo, eds. 1990. *Sport, men, and the gender order: Critical feminist perspectives*. Champaign, IL: Human Kinetics.

Molotch, Harvey. 1988. The restroom and equal opportunity. *Sociological Forum* 3:128–32.

Money, John, and Anke A. Ehrhardt. 1972. *Man & woman, boy & girl*. Baltimore, MD: Johns Hopkins University Press.

Moran, Malcolm. 1992. Title IX: A 20-year search for equity. *New York Times* Sports Section, 21, 22, 23 June.

Naftolin, F., and E. Butz, eds. 1981. Sexual dimorphism. *Science* 211:1263–1324.

Olson, Wendy. 1990. Beyond Title IX: Toward an agenda for women and sports in the 1990s. *Yale Journal of Law and Feminism* 3:105–51.

Prior, Jerilynn C., Yvette M. Yigna, Martin T. Shechter, and Arthur E. Burgess. 1990. Spinal bone loss and ovulatory disturbances. *New England Journal of Medicine* 323:1221–27.

Richards, Renée, with Jack Ames. 1983. *Second serve*. New York: Stein and Day.

Riley, Denise. 1988. *Am I that name? Feminism and the category of women in history*. Minneapolis: University of Minnesota Press.

Slatton, Bonnie, and Susan Birrell. 1984. The politics of women's sport. *Arena Review* 8.

Smith, Dorothy E. 1990. *The conceptual practices of power: A feminist sociology of knowledge*. Toronto: University of Toronto Press.

Spelman, Elizabeth. 1988. *Inessential woman: Problems of exclusion in feminist thought*. Boston: Beacon Press.

Theberge, Nancy. 1987. Sport and women's empowerment. *Women's Studies International Forum* 10:387–93.

Vecsey, George. 1990. Cathy Rigby, unlike Peter, did grow up. *New York Times* Sports Section, 19 December.

Watson, Tracey. 1987. Women athletes and athletic women: The dilemmas and contradictions of managing incongruent identities. *Sociological Inquiry* 57:431–46.

Willis, Paul. 1982. Women in sport in ideology. In *Sport, culture, and ideology*, edited by Jennifer A. Hargreaves. London: Routledge & Kegan Paul.

Yoder, Janice D. 1989. Women at West Point: Lessons for token women in male-dominated occupations. In *Women: A feminist perspective*, edited by Jo Freeman, 4th ed. Palo Alto, CA: Mayfield.

6

Ah, Ya Throw Like a Girl!

Mike Messner

Although the sociology department at U.C. Berkeley is situated on the fourth floor of a very ugly post-war building, the place does have one thing going for it: the fourth floor balcony overlooks the women's softball field. There I have spent not a few fine afternoons in the past few years basking in the sunshine and watching some of the most talented softball players in the nation.

When I am joined on the balcony (usually only briefly) by my hard-working friends and colleagues who kid me about "taking the day off in the sun," I retort that I am actually doing *research* at this very moment. After all, I *am* doing my dissertation on "sports and male identity" (great thing about sociology: everything is data).

From Michael A. Messner and Donald F. Sabo, eds., *Sex, Violence and Power in Sports: Rethinking Masculinity* (Freedom, CA: The Crossing Press, 1992). Reprinted by permission of the author.

One spring day I was enjoying a beautifully played pitchers' duel between Cal's women and another top-ranked team. It was late in the game, with the score tied 1–1 when I was joined in my personal left field pavillion by a friendly and gentle man who is nearing the end of a very successful career as a sociologist at U.C.B. Suddenly, with a runner on first via a rare base-on-balls from the Cal pitcher, the batter drove the ball on a line into left-center field. The left fielder managed to run the ball down, turn, and fire a strike to the shortstop just at the edge of the infield, who in turn spun and threw perfectly, laser-like, to the plate, nailing the lead runner. What precision teamwork and execution! And the game was still tied!

My fellow fan smiled, as did I, and shook his head. "You know, it amazes me to see a woman throw like that. I always thought that there was something about the female arm that made it impossible to throw like a man."

I'm 8 years old and I'm playing Little League Baseball for the first time and my dad's the coach! It's my first tryout/practice and it's an exciting, confusing, scary affair, with what seems like hundreds of boys, all with identical green caps and leather mitts facing each other in two long lines, throwing balls back and forth as fathers furiously race around coaching, criticizing, encouraging, demonstrating, and scrawling mysterious things on clipboards.

Later at home, my father informs me that there are two boys on the team who throw like girls, and that I, unfortunately, am one of them! By the next practice, he tells me, we will have corrected that problem. That evening, with glove and cap securely in place, I anxiously face my father on the front lawn. And we play catch. For quite a while. I am concentrating, working hard to throw correctly ("like a *man*"), pulling my arm back as far as I can and snapping the ball overhand, just past my ear. When I do this, it feels very strange—I really have very little control over the flight of the ball, and it hurts my shoulder a bit—but I am rewarded with the knowledge that *this is how men throw the ball.* If I learn this, I won't embarrass either myself or my father. When at times I inadvertently revert to what feels like a more natural and more easily controllable throwing style (more of a shot-put style, with hand and ball starting just behind the ear, and elbow leading the way), I immediately am rewarded with a return throw that sails far over my head and lands two or three houses down. "Run! *Run* after that ball! You won't have to chase it anymore when you quit throwing like a girl!"

Simple behavior-modification, actually. And it worked—I learned very rapidly how to throw properly. But it wasn't really the having to run after the ball that taught me: it was the threat to my very fragile sense of maleness. The *fear*—oh, the fear of being thought a sissy—a *girl!*

I was momentarily taken aback that a renowned sociologist would have such a "biological" explanation for gender differences between women and men. I explained to him that, indeed, "throwing like a girl" is actually a more anatomically natural motion for the human arm. "Throwing like a man" is a learned action which can, repeated over time, actually seriously damage the arm.

A few years ago, a sportswriter did an informal survey of major league pitchers, asking of those who had played Little League as youngsters just how many of them had been pitchers in their youth. The astounding answer: *zero*. Stories of Little Leaguers burning their arms out for life are common. The destruction of young shoulders and elbows has led to some Little Leagues outlawing curve balls. Others have even instituted systems in which adults do all the pitching for 8-and 9-year-olds.

"Throwing like a man" is an unnatural act, an act that (like most aspects of "masculinity") must be learned. Indeed, I learned it at a very young age, as did most of my male peers. And while I was on the front lawn with Dad, my older sister Linda was God-knows-where, but certainly not playing ball. Only this past summer did she join a softball team and learn how to throw a ball. She's a natural athlete who had to wait until the age of 31 to get some simple coaching.

Things change far too slowly for most of us, but it is a fact that things are changing. People are changing. As we men begin to question the traditional meaning of "maleness" and reject those aspects of the traditional male role which have been oppressive to others and destructive to ourselves, we discover new ways to be men. After a 15-year break, I, for one, have taken up pitching a baseball to a friend who used to be a catcher. I throw exclusively submarine-style (almost underhand) which does not hurt my shoulder like overhand throwing always has. And we do it just for the simple joy of throwing and catching the ball.

As women become more and more visible and competent at tasks (including sports) that are traditionally "male territory," our conceptions of masculinity and femininity are being challenged. While watching women play softball, my professor friend learned something about the social basis for traditional differences between men and women. My sister not only plays softball, but coaches her 9-year-old daughter Jennifer's team, where she is determined to teach the girls how to throw a ball accurately and safely, among other things. And with this kind of role model and a changing social context, Jennifer is a girl who plays with a sense of enjoyment and confidence that was never allowed her mother. She loves to play. And she even loves to be the "bat-girl" for her father's city-league softball team. The first time she went to clear a bat away from home plate, she was confronted by a boy about her age who said to her derisively, "There's no such *thing* as a bat-*girl!*"

"Watch me," she replied.

7

In a Male-Centered World, Female Differences Are Transformed into Female Disadvantages

Sandra Lipsitz Bem

Two journalists called me recently, one from *The New York Times* to talk about sex differences in the brain, the other from ABC News to talk about the connection between hormones and sexual harassment. Both asked me essentially the same questions, ones that I, a feminist psychologist, am often asked: What differences between men and women do I think *really* exist? And are these differences inconsistent with feminist demands for gender equality?

The idea that there might be fundamental biological differences that limit the chances for gender equality has played a central role in both cultural and scientific debates in the United States for 150 years. The debates began in the nineteenth century with highly respected scientists using unsubstantiated arguments about biological differences between the sexes to oppose feminists' demands for both women's suffrage and women's higher education. The debate continues today with, for example, sociobiologists hypothesizing that gender inequality is built into our genes. Other scientists, including psychologists, conduct study after empirical study of male/female differences in human beings and in animals. These studies would be of much less interest to journalists and the general public alike, I suspect, if the issue of biological differences were not so often coupled with the issue of equality.

With the emergence of "identity politics" during roughly the last 15 years, this long-standing debate has expanded in a new direction. Members of marginalized groups, both inside academe and out, have begun to base their claims for equality not, as they tended to do in the past, on their similarities to dominant social groups, but on the ways in which they are different, whether biologically or historically. More specifically, they have begun to argue that their differences from the

Originally published in *The Chronicle of Higher Education*, August 17, 1994, section 2, pp. B1–B2. Reprinted by permission of the author.

dominant groups require the society to adopt new and different social policies and practices.

To give but a few examples, members of various minority groups whose native language is not English have demanded that official government communications be available in their native tongues. Working women have demanded not just equal pay for equal work but equal pay for work of comparable value. Lesbians and gay men have demanded the extension of spousal rights and benefits to same-sex domestic partners. As a result, diversity, multiculturalism, political correctness, and "dead white European male" perspectives—all of which have to do with sensitivity to cultural differences—have become the red-hot academic and political buzz-words of the 1990s.

In recent years, this new "sensitivity to difference" model of equality has won me over. At the same time, however, I also believe that two critical points relating to difference and inequality have not been adequately clarified in either academic debate or the news media.

The first point is that the search for fundamental biological differences between men and women is misguided. We already know the truly potent differences between the sexes—women can become pregnant and can breast-feed their infants, while men, on average, are bigger and stronger. Even if we were to discover differences with more power than these have to shape our lives or to limit our chances for equality, the fact remains that biological differences are given real meaning by the ways in which a culture interprets and uses them.

Put somewhat differently, social change—what I like to call cultural invention—can so radically transform the context in which human beings live their lives that people can often be liberated from what in earlier times were thought to be intrinsic biological limitations. This, of course, is why human beings can fly today even though they have no wings.

The problem for women thus is not simply that they are different from men, whether biologically or in some other way. The problem for women—and what limits their chances for equality—is that they are different from men in a social world that disguises what are really just male standards or norms as gender-neutral principles. In other words, the difficulties women face stem from the fact that they are different from men in an "androcentric" or male-centered world, one in which almost all policies and practices are so completely organized around male experience that they fit men better than they do women—and hence automatically transform any and all male/female differences into female disadvantages.

This privileging of male experience frequently involves the male body. Consider, for example, that the Centers for Disease Control included in their early diagnostic criteria for HIV infection only those medical conditions that showed up in men, thereby denying women access both to the appropriate diagnosis for their medical conditions and to emerging experimental treatments.

Consider as well that the U.S. Supreme Court ruled in the 1970s that pregnancy could be excluded from an employer's disability-insurance package, even if it covered every medical condition that could conceivably occur in a man—including those, like diseases of the prostate, that are unique to men. Why? Because, the Court argued, pregnancy is "unique to women" and thus deviates from what, in an androcentric society, are seen as "normal," thus gender-neutral, medical conditions.

This analysis of inequality as the hidden—or at least the disguised—institutional privileging of the dominant group's perspective and experience underlies the demand by so many marginalized groups in the 1990s that America's policies and practices finally be made more sensitive to difference. This analysis is also what has enabled many scholars like myself to realize that the "universalized" analysis of difference—done without considering the social and cultural contexts—that has characterized research on gender for the last 150 years is fundamentally misguided.

If we want to understand gender inequality, it is much more important to shift from an analysis of difference *per se* to an analysis of the ways in which the social structure privileges some people's differences at the expense of others'.

This shift from difference *per se* to the politics of difference has not yet taken place—or not yet gone far enough—in the world of social science. But it is exactly what has taken place—and exactly what has been needed—in the world of politics. Many marginalized groups have taken whatever category of difference has been used against them historically and transformed its meaning: They have begun to use their differences as the basis of both collective identity and political resistance.

I wholly support this move—whether by lesbians and gay men for open acceptance in the military or by American Indians for another rendition of the Christopher Columbus story. I believe that it is only by demanding that our social institutions be sensitive to the difference of some people's perspectives and experience from those of the dominant group that we can insure that our institutions (rich, white, heterosexual, and male-centered) will ever stop transforming such differences into disadvantages.

There is a danger in this political strategy that we must guard against, however. It is that we, the members of marginalized groups, will ourselves begin to "over-solidify" the very categories of difference to which we are demanding sensitivity. I already see this phenomenon—making our differences seem more intrinsically real than they actually are—in at least two contemporary contexts.

First, many gay males have promoted the existence of a "gay gene," even though many cultures exist in which sexual attraction and behavior are structured so differently from our culture's that the distinction between heterosexual and homosexual people doesn't even arise.

Second, some feminists who came to prominence in the 1980s and who emphasize female differences have celebrated an alleged female predisposition to be concerned about human relationships rather than about the struggles for dominance that allegedly concern males.

It is important not to overemphasize these categories of difference because they are not, in fact, eternal or universal or natural categories. They are, rather, categories that historically have been largely shaped by those in power, to serve as both the foundation and the rationale for their privilege. Giving advantages to some people and not to others requires as a first step that people be divided into rigid (and frequently dichotomous) categories.

Furthermore, it also requires that the categories be made to seem like the natural fault lines of the social world, as if they divided nature at its joints rather than just divided culture at the convenience of the privileged. Dividing people in this way so polarizes differences related to sex and race—which do have a kernel of biological reality at their base—that the full spectrum of natural human diversity is denied.

I call this process of dichotomizing people into two sexes and of making sex matter in virtually every domain of social life "gender polarization." It not only dictates mutually exclusive scripts for males and females—scripts that constrain everything from modes of dress and social roles to ways of expressing emotion and experiencing sexual desire. It also defines any person or behavior that deviates from these scripts as problematic—unnatural, immoral, biologically anomalous, or psychologically pathological.

Taken together, these two processes construct what appears to be a *natural* link—or match—between the sex of one's body and the character of one's psyche and sexuality. This illusion not only makes everything other than exclusive heterosexuality appear to be unnatural; it also motivates both women and men to create identities, personalities, and sexualities that mirror the different and unequal roles assigned to them in an androcentric and gender-polarized social world. It can easily lead the individual to become an unwitting collaborator in reproducing gender inequality, for example by predisposing women to construct identities around deference and men to construct identities around dominance.

Although they might not use exactly the same language that I use, almost all feminists would probably agree that feminism's primary project must be to challenge the marginalization of women by exposing and eradicating androcentrism. However, not all feminists necessarily believe, as I do, that feminism's second major project should be to challenge the allegedly natural links long assumed to exist among sex, psyche, and sexuality. I'm thinking here, in particular, of the long-standing cultural belief that men are naturally masculine, women are naturally feminine, and everyone is naturally heterosexual.

Challenging these assumptions is essential to feminism, because they provide the foundation for gender inequality. Furthermore, if we do not challenge them, I believe we break faith with our foremothers in the women's-suffrage movement, who challenged conventional definitions of real women and men by daring even to speak in public.

8

The Social Construction of Sexuality

Ruth Hubbard

There is no "natural" human sexuality. This is not to say that our sexual feelings are "unnatural" but that whatever feelings and activities our society interprets as sexual are channeled from birth into socially acceptable forms of expression.

Western thinking about sexuality is based on the Christian equation of sexuality with sin, which must be redeemed through making babies. To fulfill the Christian mandate, sexuality must be intended for procreation, and thus all forms of sexual expression and enjoyment other than heterosexuality are invalidated. Actually, for most Christians nowadays just plain heterosexuality will do, irrespective of whether it is intended to generate offspring.

These ideas about sexuality set up a major contradiction in what we tell children about sex and procreation. We teach them that sex and sexuality are about becoming mommies and daddies and warn them not to explore sex by themselves or with playmates of either sex until they are old enough to have babies. Then, when they reach adolescence and the entire culture pressures them into heterosexual activity, whether they themselves feel ready for it or not, the more "enlightened" among us tell them how to be sexually (meaning heterosexually) active without having babies. Surprise: It doesn't work very well. Teenagers do not act "responsibly"—teenage pregnancies and abortions are on the rise and teenage fathers do not acknowledge and support their partners and babies. Somewhere we forget that we have been telling lies. Sexuality and procreation are not linked in societies like ours. On the contrary, we expect youngsters to be heterosexually active from their teens on but to put off having children until they are economically independent and married, and even then to have only two or, at most, three children.

Other contradictions: This society, on the whole, accepts Freud's assumption that children are sexual beings from birth and that society channels their polymorphously perverse childhood sexuality into the accepted forms. Yet we expect our children to be asexual. We raise girls and boys together more than is done in many societies while insisting that they must not explore their own or each other's sexual parts or feelings.

What if we acknowledged the separation of sexuality from procreation and encouraged our children to express themselves sexually if they were so inclined? What if we, further, encouraged them to explore their own bodies as well as those of friends of the same and the other sex when they felt like it? They might then be able to feel at home with their sexuality, have some sense of their own and other people's sexual needs, and know how to talk about sexuality and procreation with their friends and sexual partners before their ability to procreate becomes an issue for them. In this age of AIDS and other serious sexually transmitted infections, such a course of action seems like essential preventive hygiene. Without the embarrassment of unexplored and unacknowledged sexual needs, contraceptive needs would be much easier to confront when they arise. So, of course, would same-sex love relationships.

Such a more open and accepting approach to sexuality would make life easier for children and adolescents of either sex, but it would be especially advantageous for girls. When a boy discovers his penis as an organ of pleasure, it is the same organ he is taught about as his organ of procreation. A girl exploring her pleasurable sensations finds her clitoris, but when she is taught about making babies, she hears about the functions of the vagina in sex and birthing. Usually, the clitoris goes unmentioned, and she doesn't even learn its name until much later. Therefore for boys there is an obvious link between procreation and their own pleasurable, erotic explorations; for most girls, there isn't.

Individual Sexual Scripts

Each of us writes our own sexual script out of the range of our experiences. None of this script is inborn or biologically given. We construct it out of our diverse life situations, limited by what we are taught or what we can imagine to be permissible and correct. There is no unique female sexual experience, no male sexual experience, no unique heterosexual, lesbian, or gay male experience. We take the experiences of different people and sort and lump them according to socially significant categories. When I hear generalizations about *the* sexual experience of some particular group, exceptions immediately come to mind. Except that I refuse to call them exceptions: They are part of the range of our sexual experiences. Of course, the similar circumstances in which members of a particular group find themselves will give rise to group similarities. But we tend to exaggerate them when we go looking for similarities within groups or differences between them.

This exaggeration is easy to see when we look at the dichotomy between "the heterosexual" and "the homosexual." The concept of "the homosexual," along with many other human typologies, originated toward the end of the nineteenth century. Certain kinds of behavior stopped being attributed to particular persons and came to define them. A person who had sexual relations with someone of the same sex became a certain kind of person, a "homosexual"; a person who had sexual relations with people of the other sex, a different kind, a "heterosexual."

This way of categorizing people obscured the hitherto accepted fact that many people do not have sexual relations exclusively with persons of one or the other sex. (None of us has sex with a kind of person; we have sex with a person.) This categorization created the stereotypes that were popularized by the sex reformers, such as Havelock Ellis and Edward Carpenter, who biologized the "difference." "The homosexual" became a person who is different by nature and therefore should not be made responsible for his or her so-called deviance. This definition served the purpose of the reformers (although the laws have been slow to change), but it turned same-sex love into a medical problem to be treated by doctors rather than punished by judges—an improvement, perhaps, but not acceptance or liberation. . . .

Toward a Nondeterministic Model of Sexuality

. . . Some gay men and lesbians feel that they were born "different" and have always been homosexual. They recall feeling strongly attracted to members of their own sex when they were children and adolescents. But many women who live with men and think of themselves as heterosexual also had strong affective and erotic ties to girls and women while they were growing up. If they were now in loving relationships with women, they might look back on their earlier loves as proof that they were always lesbians. But if they are now involved with men, they may be tempted to devalue their former feelings as "puppy love" or "crushes."

Even within the preferred sex, most of us feel a greater affinity for certain "types" than for others. Not any man or woman will do. No one has seriously suggested that something in our innate makeup makes us light up in the presence of only certain women or men. We would think it absurd to look to hormone levels or any other simplistic biological cause for our preference for a specific "type" within a sex. In fact, scientists rarely bother to ask what in our psychosocial experience shapes these kinds of tastes and preferences. We assume it must have something to do with our relationship to our parents or with other experiences, but we do not probe deeply unless people prefer the "wrong" sex. Then, suddenly, scientists begin to look for specific causes.

Because of our recent history and political experiences, feminists tend to reject simplistic, causal models of how our sexuality develops. Many women who have thought of themselves as heterosexual for much of their life and who have been married and have had children have fallen in love with a woman (or women) when they have had the opportunity to rethink, refeel, and restructure their lives.

The society in which we live channels, guides, and limits our imagination in sexual as well as other matters. Why some of us give ourselves permission to love people of our own sex whereas others cannot even imagine doing so is an interesting question. But I do not think it will be answered by measuring our hormone levels or by trying to unearth our earliest affectional ties. As women begin to speak freely about our sexual experiences, we are getting a varied range of information with which we can reexamine, reevaluate, and change ourselves. Lately, increasing numbers of women have begun to acknowledge their "bisexuality"—the fact that they can love women and men in succession or simultaneously. People fall in love with individuals, not with a sex. Gender need not be a significant factor in our choice, although for some of us it may be.

9

The Invention of Heterosexuality

Jonathan Ned Katz

Heterosexuality is old as procreation, ancient as the lust of Eve and Adam. That first lady and gentleman, we assume, perceived themselves, behaved, and felt just like today's heterosexuals. We suppose that heterosexuality is unchanging, universal, essential: ahistorical.

Contrary to that common sense conjecture, the concept of heterosexuality is only one particular historical way of perceiving, categorizing, and imagining the social relations of the sexes. Not ancient at all, the idea of heterosexuality is a modern invention, dating to the late nineteenth century. The heterosexual belief, with its metaphysical claim to eternity, has a particular, pivotal place in the social universe of the late nineteenth and twentieth centuries that it did not inhabit earlier. This essay traces the historical process by which the heterosexual idea was created as ahistorical and taken-for-granted. . . .

By not studying the heterosexual idea in history, analysts of sex, gay and straight, have continued to privilege the "normal" and "natural" at the expense of the "abnormal" and "unnatural." Such privileging of the norm accedes to its domination, protecting it from questions. By making the normal the object of a thoroughgoing historical study we simultaneously pursue a pure truth and a sex-radical

I'm grateful to Lisa Duggan, Judith Levine, Sharon Thompson, Carole S. Vance, and Jeffrey Weeks for comments on a recent version of this manuscript, and to Manfred Herzer and his editor, John DeCecco, for sharing, prepublication, Herzer's most recent research on Kertbeny. I'm also indebted to John Gagnon, Philip Greven, and Catharine R. Stimpson for bravely supporting my (unsuccessful) attempts to fund research for a full-length study of heterosexual history.

From *Socialist Review* 20 (January–March 1990): 7–34 Reprinted by permission of the author.

and subversive goal: we upset basic preconceptions. We discover that the hetero-sexual, the normal, and the natural have a history of changing definitions. Studying the history of the term challenges its power.

Contrary to our usual assumption, past Americans and other peoples named, perceived, and socially organized the bodies, lusts, and intercourse of the sexes in ways radically different from the way we do. If we care to understand this vast past sexual diversity, we need to stop promiscuously projecting our own hetero and homo arrangement. Though lip-service is often paid to the distorting, ethnocentric effect of such conceptual imperialism, the category heterosexuality continues to be applied uncritically as a universal analytical tool. Recognizing the time-bound and culturally-specific character of the heterosexual category can help us begin to work toward a thoroughly historical view of sex. . . .

Before Heterosexuality: Early Victorian True Love, 1820–1860

In the early nineteenth-century United States, from about 1820 to 1860, the heterosexual did not exist. Middle-class white Americans idealized a True Womanhood, True Manhood, and True Love, all characterized by "purity"—the freedom from sensuality.[1] Presented mainly in literary and religious texts, this True Love was a fine romance with no lascivious kisses. This ideal contrasts strikingly with late nineteenth- and twentieth-century American incitements to a hetero sex.*

Early Victorian True Love was only realized within the mode of proper procre-ation, marriage, the legal organization for producing a new set of correctly gen-dered women and men. Proper womanhood, manhood, and progeny—not a normal male-female eros—was the main product of this mode of engendering and of human reproduction.

The actors in this sexual economy were identified as manly men and womanly women and as procreators, not specifically as erotic beings or heterosexuals. Eros did not constitute the core of a heterosexual identity that inhered, democratically, in both men and women. True Women were defined by their distance from lust. True Men, though thought to live closer to carnality, and in less control of it, as-pired to the same freedom from concupiscence.

Legitimate natural desire was for procreation and a proper manhood or wom-anhood; no heteroerotic desire was thought to be directed exclusively and natu-rally toward the other sex; lust in men was roving. The human body was thought of

---

*Some historians have recently told us to revise our idea of sexless Victorians: their experience and even their ideology, it is said, were more erotic than we previously thought. Despite the revisionists, I argue that "purity" was indeed the dominant, early Victorian, white middle-class standard. For the de-bate on Victorian sexuality see John D'Emilio and Estelle Freedman, *Intimate Matters: A History of Sexuality in America* (New York: Harper & Row, 1988), p. xii.

as a means towards procreation and production; penis and vagina were instruments of reproduction, not of pleasure. Human energy, thought of as a closed and severely limited system, was to be used in producing children and in work, not wasted in libidinous pleasures.

The location of all this engendering and procreative labor was the sacred sanctum of early Victorian True Love, the home of the True Woman and True Man — a temple of purity threatened from within by the monster masturbator, an archetypal early Victorian cult figure of illicit lust. The home of True Love was a castle far removed from the erotic exotic ghetto inhabited most notoriously then by the prostitute, another archetypal Victorian erotic monster. . . .

Late Victorian Sex-Love: 1860–1892

"Heterosexuality" and "homosexuality" did not appear out of the blue in the 1890s. These two eroticisms were in the making from the 1860s on. In late Victorian America and in Germany, from about 1860 to 1892, our modern idea of an eroticized universe began to develop, and the experience of a heterolust began to be widely documented and named. . . .

In the late nineteenth-century United States, several social factors converged to cause the eroticizing of consciousness, behavior, emotion, and identity that became typical of the twentieth-century Western middle class. The transformation of the family from producer to consumer unit resulted in a change in family members' relation to their own bodies; from being an instrument primarily of work, the human body was integrated into a new economy, and began more commonly to be perceived as a means of consumption and pleasure. Historical work has recently begun on how the biological human body is differently integrated into changing modes of production, procreation, engendering, and pleasure so as to alter radically the identity, activity, and experience of that body.[2]

The growth of a consumer economy also fostered a new pleasure ethic. This imperative challenged the early Victorian work ethic, finally helping to usher in a major transformation of values. While the early Victorian work ethic had touted the value of economic production, that era's procreation ethic had extolled the virtues of human reproduction. In contrast, the late Victorian economic ethic hawked the pleasures of consuming, while its sex ethic praised an erotic pleasure principle for men and even for women.

In the late nineteenth century, the erotic became the raw material for a new consumer culture. Newspapers, books, plays, and films touching on sex, "normal" and "abnormal," became available for a price. Restaurants, bars, and baths opened, catering to sexual consumers with cash. Late Victorian entrepreneurs of desire incited the proliferation of a new eroticism, a commoditized culture of pleasure.

In these same years, the rise in power and prestige of medical doctors allowed these upwardly mobile professionals to prescribe a healthy new sexuality. Medical men, in the name of science, defined a new ideal of male-female relationships that included, in women as well as men, an essential, necessary, normal eroticism. Doctors, who had earlier named and judged the sex-enjoying woman a "nymphomaniac," now began to label women's *lack* of sexual pleasure a mental disturbance, speaking critically, for example, of female "frigidity" and "anesthesia."*

By the 1880s, the rise of doctors as a professional group fostered the rise of a new medical model of Normal Love, replete with sexuality. The new Normal Woman and Man were endowed with a healthy libido. The new theory of Normal Love was the modern medical alternative to the old Cult of True Love. The doctors prescribed a new sexual ethic as if it were a morally neutral, medical description of health. The creation of the new Normal Sexual had its counterpart in the invention of the late Victorian Sexual Pervert. The attention paid the sexual abnormal created a need to name the sexual normal, the better to distinguish the average him and her from the deviant it.

Heterosexuality: The First Years, 1892–1900

In the periodization of heterosexual American history suggested here, the years 1892 to 1900 represent "The First Years" of the heterosexual epoch, eight key years in which the idea of the heterosexual and homosexual were initially and tentatively formulated by U.S. doctors. The earliest-known American use of the word "heterosexual" occurs in a medical journal article by Dr. James G. Kiernan of Chicago, read before the city's medical society on March 7, 1892, and published that May—portentous dates in sexual history.[3] But Dr. Kiernan's heterosexuals were definitely not exemplars of normality. Heterosexuals, said Kiernan, were defined by a mental condition, "psychical hermaphroditism." Its symptoms were "inclinations to both sexes." These heterodox sexuals also betrayed inclinations "to abnormal methods of gratification," that is, techniques to insure pleasure without procreation. Dr. Kiernan's heterogeneous sexuals did demonstrate "traces of the normal sexual appetite" (a touch of procreative desire). Kiernan's normal sexuals were implicitly defined by a monolithic other-sex inclination and procreative aim. Significantly, they still lacked a name.

Dr. Kiernan's article of 1892 also included one of the earliest-known uses of the word "homosexual" in American English. Kiernan defined "Pure homosexuals" as persons whose "general mental state is that of the opposite sex." Kiernan thus defined homosexuals by their deviance from a gender norm. His heterosexuals displayed a double deviance from both gender and procreative norms.

---

*This reference to females reminds us that the invention of heterosexuality had vastly different impacts on the histories of women and men. It also differed in its impact on lesbians and heterosexual women, homosexual and heterosexual men, the middle class and working class, and on different religious, racial, national, and geographic groups.

Though Kiernan used the new words heterosexual and homosexual, an old procreative standard and a new gender norm coexisted uneasily in his thought. His word heterosexual defined a mixed person and compound urge, abnormal because they wantonly included procreative and non-procreative objectives, as well as same-sex and different-sex attractions.

That same year, 1892, Dr. Krafft-Ebing's influential *Psychopathia Sexualis* was first translated and published in the United States.[4] But Kiernan and Krafft-Ebing by no means agreed on the definition of the heterosexual. In Krafft-Ebing's book, "hetero-sexual" was used unambiguously in the modern sense to refer to an erotic feeling for a different sex. "Homo-sexual" referred unambiguously to an erotic feeling for a "same sex." In Krafft-Ebing's volume, unlike Kiernan's article, heterosexual and homosexual were clearly distinguished from a third category, a "psycho-sexual hermaphroditism," defined by impulses toward both sexes.

Krafft-Ebing hypothesized an inborn "sexual instinct" for relations with the "opposite sex," the inherent "purpose" of which was to foster procreation. Krafft-Ebing's erotic drive was still a reproductive instinct. But the doctor's clear focus on a different-sex versus same-sex sexuality constituted a historic, epochal move from an absolute procreative standard of normality toward a new norm. His definition of heterosexuality as other-sex attraction provided the basis for a revolutionary, modern break with a centuries-old procreative standard.

It is difficult to overstress the importance of that new way of categorizing. The German's mode of labeling was radical in referring to the biological sex, masculinity or femininity, and the pleasure of actors (along with the procreant purpose of acts). Krafft-Ebing's heterosexual offered the modern world a new norm that came to dominate our idea of the sexual universe, helping to change it from a mode of human reproduction and engendering to a mode of pleasure. The heterosexual category provided the basis for a move from a production-oriented, procreative imperative to a consumerist pleasure principle—an institutionalized pursuit of happiness. . . .

Only gradually did doctors agree that heterosexual referred to a normal, "other-sex" eros. This new standard-model heterosex provided the pivotal term for the modern regularization of eros that paralleled similar attempts to standardize masculinity and femininity, intelligence, and manufacturing.[5] The idea of heterosexuality as the master sex from which all others deviated was (like the idea of the master race) deeply authoritarian. The doctors' normalization of a sex that was hetero proclaimed a new heterosexual separatism—an erotic apartheid that forcefully segregated the sex normals from the sex perverts. The new, strict boundaries made the emerging erotic world less polymorphous—safer for sex normals. However, the idea of such creatures as heterosexuals and homosexuals emerged from the narrow world of medicine to become a commonly accepted notion only in the early twentieth century. In 1901, in the comprehensive *Oxford English Dictionary*, "heterosexual" and "homosexual" had not yet made it.

The Distribution of the Heterosexual Mystique: 1900–1930

In the early years of this heterosexual century the tentative hetero hypothesis was stabilized, fixed, and widely distributed as the ruling sexual orthodoxy: The Heterosexual Mystique. Starting among pleasure-affirming urban working-class youths, southern blacks, and Greenwich-Village bohemians as defensive subculture, heterosex soon triumphed as dominant culture.[6]

In its earliest version, the twentieth-century heterosexual imperative usually continued to associate heterosexuality with a supposed human "need," "drive," or "instinct" for propagation, a procreant urge linked inexorably with carnal lust as it had not been earlier. In the early twentieth century, the falling birth rate, rising divorce rate, and "war of the sexes" of the middle class were matters of increasing public concern. Giving vent to heteroerotic emotions was thus praised as enhancing baby-making capacity, marital intimacy, and family stability. (Only many years later, in the mid-1960s, would heteroeroticism be distinguished completely, in practice and theory, from procreativity and male-female pleasure sex justified in its own name.)

The first part of the new sex norm—hetero—referred to a basic gender divergence. The "oppositeness" of the sexes was alleged to be the basis for a universal, normal, erotic attraction between males and females. The stress on the sexes' "oppositeness," which harked back to the early nineteenth century, by no means simply registered biological differences of females and males. The early twentieth-century focus on physiological and gender dimorphism reflected the deep anxieties of men about the shifting work, social roles, and power of men over women, and about the ideals of womanhood and manhood. That gender anxiety is documented, for example, in 1897, in *The New York Times'* publication of the Reverend Charles Parkhurst's diatribe against female "andromaniacs," the preacher's derogatory, scientific-sounding name for women who tried to "minimize distinctions by which manhood and womanhood are differentiated."[7] The stress on gender difference was a conservative response to the changing social-sexual division of activity and feeling which gave rise to the independent "New Woman" of the 1880s and eroticized "Flapper" of the 1920s.

The second part of the new hetero norm referred positively to sexuality. That novel upbeat focus on the hedonistic possibilities of male-female conjunctions also reflected a social transformation—a revaluing of pleasure and procreation, consumption and work in commercial, capitalist society. The democratic attribution of a normal lust to human females (as well as males) served to authorize women's enjoyment of their own bodies and began to undermine the early Victorian idea of the pure True Woman—a sex-affirmative action still part of women's struggle. The twentieth-century Erotic Woman also undercut nineteenth-century feminist assertion of women's moral superiority, cast suspicions of lust on women's passionate romantic friendships with women, and asserted the presence of a menacing female monster, "the lesbian."[8] . . .

In the perspective of heterosexual history, this early twentieth-century struggle for the more explicit depiction of an "opposite-sex" eros appears in a curious new light. Ironically, we find sex-conservatives, the social purity advocates of censorship and repression, fighting against the depiction not just of sexual perversity but also of the new normal heterosexuality. That a more open depiction of normal sex had to be defended against forces of propriety confirms the claim that heterosexuality's predecessor, Victorian True Love, had included no legitimate eros. . . .

The Heterosexual Steps Out: 1930–1945

In 1930, in *The New York Times*, heterosexuality first became a love that dared to speak its name. On April 30th of that year, the word "heterosexual" is first known to have appeared in *The New York Times Book Review*. There, a critic described the subject of André Gide's *The Immoralist* proceeding "from a heterosexual liaison to a homosexual one." The ability to slip between sexual categories was referred to casually as a rather unremarkable aspect of human possibility. This is also the first known reference by *The Times* to the new hetero/homo duo.[9]

The following month the second reference to the hetero/homo dyad appeared in *The New York Times Book Review*, in a comment on Floyd Dell's *Love in the Machine Age*. This work revealed a prominent antipuritan of the 1930s using the dire threat of homosexuality as his rationale for greater heterosexual freedom. *The Times* quoted Dell's warning that current abnormal social conditions kept the young dependent on their parents, causing "infantilism, prostitution and homosexuality." Also quoted was Dell's attack on the "inculcation of purity" that "breeds distrust of the opposite sex." Young people, Dell said, should be "permitted to develop normally to heterosexual adulthood." "But," *The Times* reviewer emphasized, "such a state already exists, here and now." And so it did. Heterosexuality, a new gender-sex category, had been distributed from the narrow, rarified realm of a few doctors to become a nationally, even internationally, cited aspect of middle-class life.[10] . . .

Heterosexual Hegemony: 1945–1965

The "cult of domesticity" following World War II—the reassociation of women with the home, motherhood, and child-care; men with fatherhood and wage work outside the home—was a period in which the predominance of the hetero norm went almost unchallenged, an era of heterosexual hegemony. This was an age in which conservative mental-health professionals reasserted the old link between heterosexuality and procreation. In contrast, sex-liberals of the day strove, ultimately with success, to expand the heterosexual ideal to include within the boundaries of normality a wider-than-ever range of nonprocreative, premarital, and extramarital behaviors. But sex-liberal reform actually helped to extend and secure the dominance of the heterosexual idea, as we shall see when we get to Kinsey.

The postwar sex-conservative tendency was illustrated in 1947, in Ferdinand Lundberg and Dr. Marnia Farnham's book, *Modern Woman: The Lost Sex.* Improper masculinity and femininity was exemplified, the authors decreed, by "engagement in heterosexual relations . . . with the complete intent to see to it that they do not eventuate in reproduction."[11] Their procreatively defined heterosex was one expression of a postwar ideology of fecundity that, internalized and enacted dutifully by a large part of the population, gave rise to the postwar baby boom.

The idea of the feminine female and masculine male as prolific breeders was also reflected in the stress, specific to the late 1940s, on the homosexual as sad symbol of "sterility"—that particular loaded term appears incessantly in comments on homosex dating to the fecund forties.

In 1948, in *The New York Times Book Review*, sex liberalism was in ascendancy. Dr. Howard A. Rusk declared that Alfred Kinsey's just published report on *Sexual Behavior in the Human Male* had found "wide variations in sex concepts and behavior." This raised the question: "What is 'normal' and 'abnormal'?" In particular, the report had found that "homosexual experience is much more common than previously thought," and "there is often a mixture of both homo and hetero experience."[12]

Kinsey's counting of orgasms indeed stressed the wide range of behaviors and feelings that fell within the boundaries of a quantitative, statistically accounted heterosexuality. Kinsey's liberal reform of the hetero/homo dualism widened the narrow, old hetero category to accord better with the varieties of social experience. He thereby contradicted the older idea of a monolithic, qualitatively defined, natural procreative act, experience, and person.[13]

Though Kinsey explicitly questioned "whether the terms 'normal' and 'abnormal' belong in a scientific vocabulary," his counting of climaxes was generally understood to define normal sex as majority sex. This quantified norm constituted a final, society-wide break with the old qualitatively defined reproductive standard. Though conceived of as purely scientific, the statistical definition of the normal as the-sex-most-people-are-having substituted a new, quantitative moral standard for the old, qualitative sex ethic—another triumph for the spirit of capitalism.

Kinsey also explicitly contested the idea of an absolute, either/or antithesis between hetero and homo persons. He denied that human beings "represent two discrete populations, heterosexual and homosexual." The world, he ordered, "is not to be divided into sheep and goats." The hetero/homo division was not nature's doing: "Only the human mind invents categories and tries to force facts into separated pigeon-holes. The living world is a continuum."[14]

With a wave of the taxonomist's hand, Kinsey dismissed the social and historical division of people into heteros and homos. His denial of heterosexual and homosexual personhood rejected the social reality and profound subjective force of a historically constructed tradition which, since 1892 in the United States, had cut the sexual population in two and helped to establish the social reality of a hetero-sexual and homosexual identity.

On the one hand, the social construction of homosexual persons has led to the development of a powerful gay liberation identity politics based on an ethnic group model. This has freed generations of women and men from a deep, painful, socially induced sense of shame, and helped to bring about a society-wide liberal-ization of attitudes and responses to homosexuals.[15] On the other hand, contesting the notion of homosexual and heterosexual persons was one early, partial resis-tance to the limits of the hetero/homo construction. Gore Vidal, rebel son of Kinsey, has for years been joyfully proclaiming:

> there is no such thing as a homosexual or a heterosexual person. There are only homo- or heterosexual acts. Most people are a mixture of impulses if not practices, and what anyone does with a willing partner is of no social or cosmic significance.
>
> So why all the fuss? In order for a ruling class to rule, there must be arbitrary prohibitions. Of all prohibitions, sexual taboo is the most useful because sex in-volves everyone. . . . we have allowed our governors to divide the population into two teams. One team is good, godly, straight; the other is evil, sick, vicious.[16]

* * *

Heterosexuality Questioned: 1965–1982

By the late 1960s, anti-establishment counterculturalists, fledgling feminists, and homosexual-rights activists had begun to produce an unprecedented critique of sexual repression in general, of women's sexual repression in particular, of mar-riage and the family—and of some forms of heterosexuality. This critique even found its way into *The New York Times.*

In March 1968, in the theater section of that paper, freelancer Rosalyn Regelson cited a scene from a satirical review brought to New York by a San Francisco troupe:

> a heterosexual man wanders inadvertently into a homosexual bar. Before he realizes his mistake, he becomes involved with an aggressive queen who orders a drink for him. Being a broadminded liberal and trying to play it cool until he can back out of the situation gracefully, he asks, "How do you like being a ah homosexual?" To which the queen drawls drily, "How do you like being ah whatever it is you are?"

Regelson continued:

> The Two Cultures in confrontation. The middle-class liberal, challenged today on many fronts, finds his last remaining fixed value, his heterosexuality, called into question. The theater . . . recalls the strategies he uses in dealing with this ultimate threat to his world view.[17]

* * *

Heterosexual History: Out of the Shadows

Our brief survey of the heterosexual idea suggests a new hypothesis. Rather than naming a conjunction old as Eve and Adam, heterosexual designates a word and concept, a norm and role, an individual and group identity, a behavior and feeling, and a peculiar sexual-political institution particular to the late nineteenth and twentieth centuries.

Because much stress has been placed here on heterosexuality as word and concept, it seems important to affirm that heterosexuality (and homosexuality) came into existence before it was named and thought about. The formulation of the heterosexual idea did not create a heterosexual experience or behavior; to suggest otherwise would be to ascribe determining power to labels and concepts. But the titling and envisioning of heterosexuality did play an important role in consolidating the construction of the heterosexual's social existence. Before the wide use of the word "heterosexual," I suggest, women and men did not mutually lust with the same profound, sure sense of normalcy that followed the distribution of "heterosexual" as universal sanctifier.

According to this proposal, women and men make their own sexual histories. But they do not produce their sex lives just as they please. They make their sexualities within a particular mode of organization given by the past and altered by their changing desire, their present power and activity, and their vision of a better world. That hypothesis suggests a number of good reasons for the immediate inauguration of research on a historically specific heterosexuality.

The study of the history of the heterosexual experience will forward a great intellectual struggle still in its early stages. This is the fight to pull heterosexuality, homosexuality, and all the sexualities out of the realm of nature and biology [and] into the realm of the social and historical. Feminists have explained to us that anatomy does not determine our gender destinies (our masculinities and femininities). But we've only recently begun to consider that *biology does not settle our erotic fates*. The common notion that biology determines the object of sexual desire, or that physiology and society together cause sexual orientation, are determinisms that deny the break existing between our bodies and situations and our desiring. Just as the biology of our hearing organs will never tell us why we take pleasure in Bach or delight in Dixieland, our female or male anatomies, hormones, and genes will never tell us why we yearn for women, men, both, other, or none. That is because desiring is a self-generated project of individuals within particular historical cultures. Heterosexual history can help us see the place of values and judgments in the construction of our own and others' pleasures, and to see how our erotic tastes—our aesthetics of the flesh—are socially institutionalized through the struggle of individuals and classes.

The study of heterosexuality in time will also help us to recognize the *vast historical diversity of sexual emotions and behaviors*—a variety that challenges the monolithic heterosexual hypothesis. John D'Emilio and Estelle Freedman's

Intimate Matters: A History of Sexuality in America refers in passing to numerous substantial changes in sexual activity and feeling: for example, the widespread use of contraceptives in the nineteenth century, the twentieth-century incitement of the female orgasm, and the recent sexual conduct changes by gay men in response to the AIDS epidemic. It's now a commonplace of family history that people in particular classes feel and behave in substantially different ways under different historical conditions.[18] Only when we stop assuming an invariable essence of heterosexuality will we begin the research to reveal the full variety of sexual emotions and behaviors.

The historical study of the heterosexual experience can help us *understand the erotic relationships of women and men in terms of their changing modes of social organization.* Such modal analysis actually characterizes a sex history well underway.[19] This suggests that the eros-gender-procreation system (the social ordering of lust, femininity and masculinity, and baby-making) has been linked closely to a society's particular organization of power and production. To understand the subtle history of heterosexuality we need to look carefully at correlations between (1) society's organization of eros and pleasure; (2) its mode of engendering persons as feminine or masculine (its making of women and men); (3) its ordering of human reproduction; and (4) its dominant political economy. This General Theory of Sexual Relativity proposes that substantial historical changes in the social organization of eros, gender, and procreation have basically altered the activity and experience of human beings within those modes.[20]

A historical view locates heterosexuality and homosexuality in time, helping us distance ourselves from them. This distancing can help us formulate new questions that clarify our long-range sexual-political goals: What has been and is the social function of sexual categorizing? Whose interests have been served by the division of the world into heterosexual and homosexual? Do we dare not draw a line between those two erotic species? Is some sexual naming socially necessary? Would human freedom be enhanced if the sex-biology of our partners in lust was of no particular concern, and had no name? In what kind of society could we all more freely explore our desire and our flesh?

As we move [into the year 2000], a new sense of the historical making of the heterosexual and homosexual suggests that these are ways of feeling, acting, and being with each other that we can together unmake and radically remake according to our present desire, power, and our vision of a future political-economy of pleasure.

REFERENCES

1. Barbara Welter, "The Cult of True Womanhood: 1820–1860," *American Quarterly*, vol. 18 (Summer 1966); Welter's analysis is extended here to include True Men and True Love.

2. See, for example, Catherine Gallagher and Thomas Laqueur, eds., "The Making of the Modern Body: Sexuality and Society in the Nineteenth Century," *Representations*, no. 14 (Spring 1986) (republished, Berkeley: University of California Press, 1987).

3. Dr. James G. Kiernan, "Responsibility in Sexual Perversion," *Chicago Medical Recorder*, vol. 3 (May 1892), pp. 185–210.

4. R. von Krafft-Ebing, *Psychopathia Sexualis, with Especial Reference to Contrary Sexual Instinct: A Medico-Legal Study*, trans. Charles Gilbert Chaddock (Philadelphia: F. A. Davis, 1892), from the 7th and revised German ed. Preface, November 1892.

5. For the standardization of gender see Lewis Terman and C. C. Miles, *Sex and Personality, Studies in Femininity and Masculinity* (New York: McGraw Hill, 1936). For the standardization of intelligence see Lewis Terman, *Stanford-Binet Intelligence Scale* (Boston: Houghton Mifflin, 1916). For the standardization of work, see "scientific management" and "Taylorism" in Harry Braverman, *Labor and Monopoly Capital: The Degradation of Work in the Twentieth Century* (New York: Monthly Review Press, 1974).

6. See D'Emilio and Freedman, *Intimate Matters*, pp. 194–201, 231, 241, 295–96; Ellen Kay Trimberger, "Feminism, Men, and Modern Love: Greenwich Village, 1900–1925," in *Powers of Desire: The Politics of Sexuality*, ed. Ann Snitow, Christine Stansell, Sharon Thompson (New York: Monthly Review Press, 1983), pp. 131–52; Kathy Peiss, "'Charity Girls' and City Pleasures: Historical Notes on Working Class Sexuality, 1880–1920," in *Powers of Desire*, pp. 74–87; and Mary P. Ryan, "The Sexy Saleslady: Psychology, Heterosexuality, and Consumption in the Twentieth Century," in her *Womanhood in America*, 2nd ed. (New York: Franklin Watts, 1979), pp. 151–82.

7. [Rev. Charles Parkhurst], "Woman. Calls Them Andromaniacs. Dr. Parkhurst So Characterizes Certain Women Who Passionately Ape Everything That Is Mannish. Woman Divinely Preferred. Her Supremacy Lies in Her Womanliness, and She Should Make the Most of It—Her Sphere of Best Usefulness the Home," *The New York Times*, May 23, 1897, p. 16:1.

8. See Lisa Duggan, "The Social Enforcement of Heterosexuality and Lesbian Resistance in the 1920s," in *Class, Race, and Sex: The Dynamics of Control*, ed. Amy Swerdlow and Hanah Lessinger (Boston: G. K. Hall, 1983), pp. 75–92; Rayna Rapp and Ellen Ross, "The Twenties Backlash: Compulsory Heterosexuality, the Consumer Family, and the Waning of Feminism," in *Class, Race, and Sex*; Christina Simmons, "Companionate Marriage and the Lesbian Threat," *Frontiers*, vol. 4, no. 3 (Fall 1979), pp. 54–59; and Lillian Faderman, *Surpassing the Love of Men* (New York: William Morrow, 1981).

9. Louis Kronenberger, review of André Gide, *The Immoralist*, *New York Times Book Review*, April 20, 1930, p. 9.

10. Henry James Forman, review of Floyd Dell, *Love in the Machine Age* (New York: Farrar & Rinehart), *New York Times Book Review*, September 14, 1930, p. 9.

11. Ferdinand Lundberg and Dr. Marnia F. Farnham, *Modern Woman: The Lost Sex* (New York: Harper, 1947).

12. Dr. Howard A. Rusk, *New York Times Book Review*, January 4, 1948, p. 3.

13. Alfred Kinsey, Wardell B. Pomeroy, Clyde E. Martin, *Sexual Behavior in the Human Male* (Philadelphia: W. B. Saunders, 1948), pp. 199–200.

14. Kinsey, *Sexual Behavior*, pp. 637, 639.

15. See Steven Epstein, "Gay Politics, Ethnic Identity: The Limits of Social Constructionism," *Socialist Review* 93/93 (1987), pp. 9–54.

16. Gore Vidal, "Someone to Laugh at the Squares With" [Tennessee Williams], *New York Review of Books*, June 13, 1985; reprinted in his *At Home: Essays, 1982–1988* (New York: Random House, 1988), p. 48.

17. Rosalyn Regelson, "Up the Camp Staircase," *The New York Times*, March 3, 1968, Section II, p. 1:5.

18. D'Emilio and Freedman, *Intimate Matters*, pp. 57–63, 268, 356.

19. Ryan, *Womanhood*; John D'Emilio, "Capitalism and Gay Identity," in *Powers of Desire*, pp. 100–13; Jeffrey Weeks, *Coming Out: Homosexual Politics in Britain from the Nineteenth Century to the Present* (London: Quartet Books, 1977); D'Emilio and Freedman, *Intimate Matters*; Katz, "Early Colonial Exploration, Agriculture, and Commerce: The Age of Sodomitical Sin, 1607–1740," *Gay/Lesbian Almanac*, pp. 23–65.

20. This tripartite system is intended as a revision of Gayle Rubin's pioneering work on the social-historical orgainization of eros and gender. See "The Traffic in Women: Notes on the Political-Economy of Sex," in *Toward an Anthropology of Women*, ed. Rayna R. Reiter (New York: Monthly Review Press, 1975), pp. 157–210, and "Thinking Sex: Notes for a Radical Theory of the Politics of Sexuality," in *Pleasure and Danger: Exploring Female Sexuality*, ed. Carole S. Vance (Boston: Routledge & Kegan Paul, 1984), pp. 267–329.

10

Deconstructing the Underclass

Herbert Gans

A Matter of Definition?

Buzzwords for the undeserving poor are hardly new, for in the past the poor have been termed paupers, rabble, white trash, and the dangerous classes. Today, however, Americans do not use such harsh terms in their public discourse, whatever people may say to each other in private. Where possible, euphemisms are employed, and if they are from the academy, so much the better. A string of these became popular in the 1960s; the most famous is Oscar Lewis's anthropological concept *culture of poverty*, a term that became his generation's equivalent of underclass.

When Gunnar Myrdal invented or reinvented the term underclass in his 1962 book *Challenge to Affluence*, he used the word as a purely economic concept, to describe the chronically unemployed, underemployed, and underemployables being created by what we now call the post-industrial economy. He was thinking of people being driven to the margins, or entirely out, of the modern economy, here and elsewhere; but his intellectual and policy concern was with reforming that economy, not with changing or punishing the people who were its victims.

Some other academics, this author included, used the term with Myrdal's definition in the 1960s and 1970s. However, gradually the users shifted from Myrdal's concern with unemployment to poverty, so that by the late 1970s social scientists had begun to identify the underclass with acute or persistent poverty rather than joblessness. Around the same time a very different definition of the underclass also emerged that has become the most widely used, and is also the most dangerous.

That definition has two novel elements. The first is racial, for users of this definition see the underclass as being almost entirely black and Hispanic. Second, it

From *Journal of the American Planning Association* 271 (Summer 1990). Reprinted by permission of the *Journal of the American Planning Association*.

adds a number of behavioral patterns to an economic definition—and almost always these patterns involve behavior thought to be undeserving by the definers.

Different definers concentrate on somewhat different behavior patterns, but most include antisocial or otherwise harmful behavior, such as crime. Many definers also focus on various patterns that are *deviant* or aberrant from what they consider middle class norms, but that in fact are not automatically or always harmful, such as common law marriage. Some definers even measure membership in the underclass by deviant answers to public opinion poll questions. . . .

In the past five years the term's diverse definitions have remained basically unchanged, although the defining attempt itself has occasioned a very lively, often angry, debate among scholars. Many researchers have accepted much or all of the now-dominant behavioral definition; some have argued for a purely economic one, like Myrdal's; and some—this author included—have felt that the term has taken on so many connotations of undeservingness and blameworthiness that it has become hopelessly polluted in meaning, ideological overtone and implications, and should be dropped—with the issues involved studied via other concepts. Basically the debate has involved positions usually associated with the Right and the Left, partisans of the former arguing that the underclass is the product of the unwillingness of the black poor to adhere to the American work ethic, among other cultural deficiencies, and the latter claiming that the underclass is a consequence of the development of the post-industrial economy, which no longer needs the unskilled poor.

The debate has swirled in part around William J. Wilson, the University of Chicago sociologist and author of *The Truly Disadvantaged* (1987), who is arguably the most prominent analyst of the underclass in the 1980s. He focuses entirely on the black underclass and insists that this underclass exists mainly because of large-scale and harmful changes in the labor market, and its resulting spatial concentration as well as the isolation of such areas from the more affluent parts of the black community. One of his early definitions also included a reference to aberrant behavior patterns, although his most recent one, offered in November 1989, centers around the notion of "weak attachment to the labor force," an idea that seems nearly to coincide with Myrdal's, especially since Wilson attributes that weakness to faults in the economy rather than in the jobless.

Wilson's work has inspired a lot of new research, not only about the underclass but about poverty in general, and has made poverty research funding, public and private, available again after a long drought. Meanwhile, various scholars have tried to resolve or reorient the political debate, but without much luck, for eventually the issue always boils down to whether the fault for being poor and the responsibility for change should be assigned more to poor people or more to the economy and the state. At the same time, journalistic use of the so-called behavioral definition of the underclass has increased—and so much so that there is a danger of researchers and policy analysts being carried along by the popularity of this definition of the term in the public discourse. . . .

The Power of Buzzwords and Labels

The behavioral definition of the underclass, which in essence proposes that some very poor people are somehow to be selected for separation from the rest of society and henceforth treated as especially undeserving, harbors many dangers—for their civil liberties and ours, for example, for democracy, and for the integration of society. But the rest of this essay will concentrate on what seem to me to be the major dangers for planners. The *first* danger of the term is its unusual power as a buzzword. It is a handy euphemism; while it seems inoffensively technical on the surface, it hides within it all the moral opprobrium Americans have long felt toward those poor people who have been judged to be undeserving. Even when it is being used by journalists, scholars, and others as a technical term, it carries with it this judgmental baggage. . . .

A *second* and related danger of the term is its use as a racial codeword that subtly hides anti-black and anti-Hispanic feelings. A codeword of this kind fits in with the tolerant public discourse of our time, but it also submerges and may further repress racial—and class—antagonisms that continue to exist, yet are sometimes not expressed until socio-political boiling points are reached. Racial and class codewords—and codewords of any kind—get in the way of planners, however, because the citizenry may read codewords even though planners are writing analytical concepts.

A *third* danger of the term is its flexible character. Given the freedom of definition available in a democracy, anyone can decide, or try to persuade others, that yet additional people should be included in the underclass. For example, it is conceivable that in a city, region, or country with a high unemployment rate, powerless competitors for jobs, such as illegal immigrants or even legal but recently arrived workers, might be added to the list of undeserving people. . . .

The *fourth* danger of the term, a particularly serious one, is that it is a synthesizing notion—or what William Kornblum has more aptly called a lumping one— that covers a number of different people. Like other synthesizing notions that have moved far beyond the researchers' journals, it has also become a stereotype. Stereotypes are lay generalizations that are necessary in a very diversified society, and are useful when they are more or less accurate. When they are not, however, or when they are also judgmental terms, they turn into *labels*, to be used by some people to judge, and usually to stigmatize, other people, often those with less power or prestige. . . .

Insofar as poor people keep up with the labels the rest of society sticks on them, they are aware of the latest one. We do not all know the "street-level" consequences of stigmatizing labels, but they cannot be good. One of the likely, and most dangerous, consequences of labels is that they can become self-fulfilling prophecies. People publicly described as members of the underclass may begin to feel that they *are* members of such a class and are therefore unworthy in a new way. At the least, they now have to fight against yet another threat to their self-respect, not to mention another reason for feeling that society would just as soon have them disappear.

More important perhaps, people included in the underclass are quickly treated accordingly in their relations with the private and public agencies in which, like the rest of us, they are embedded—from workplaces, welfare agencies, and schools to the police and the courts. We know from social research that teachers with negative images of their pupils do not expect them to succeed and thus make sure, often unconsciously, that they do not; likewise, boys from single parent families who are picked up by the police are often thought to be wild and therefore guilty because they are assumed to lack male parental control. We know also that areas associated with the underclass do not get the same level of services as more affluent areas. After all, these populations are not likely to protest. . . .

Social Policy Implications

The remaining dangers are more directly relevant for planners, other policy researchers, and policy makers. The most general one, and the *fifth* on my list, is the term's interference with antipoverty policy and other kinds of planning. This results in part from the fact that underclass is a quite distinctive synthesizing term that lumps together a variety of highly diverse people who need different kinds of help. Categorizing them all with one term, and a buzzword at that, can be disastrous, especially if the political climate should demand that planners formulate a single "underclass policy." Whether one thinks of the poorest of the poor as having problems or as making problems for others, or both, they cannot be planned for with a single policy. For example, educational policies to prevent young people from dropping out of school, especially the few good ones in poor areas, have nothing to do with housing policies for dealing with various kinds of homelessness and the lack of affordable dwellings. Such policies are in turn different from programs to reduce street crime, and from methods of discouraging the very poor from escaping into the addictions of drugs, alcohol, mental illness, or pentecostal religion—which has its own harmful side effects. To be sure, policies relevant to one problem may have positive overlaps for another, but no single policy works for all the problems of the different poverty-stricken populations. Experts who claim one policy can do it all, like education, are simply wrong.

This conclusion applies even to jobs and income grant policies. Although it is certain that all of the problems blamed on the people assigned to the underclass would be helped considerably by policies to reduce sharply persistent joblessness and poverty, *and generally before other programs are implemented*, these policies also have limits. While all poor people need economic help, such help will not alone solve other problems some of them have or make for others. Although the middle class does not mug, neither do *the* poor; only a small number of poor male youngsters and young adults do so. Other causal factors are also involved, and effective antipoverty planning has to be based on some understanding of these factors and how to overcome them. Lumping concepts like the underclass can only hurt this effort.

A related or *sixth* danger stems from the persuasive capacity of concepts or buzzwords. These terms may become so *reified* through their use that people think they represent actual groups or aggregates, and may also begin to believe that being in what is, after all, an imaginary group is a *cause* of the characteristics included in its definition. Sometimes journalists and even scholars—especially those of conservative bent—appear to think that becoming very poor and acting in antisocial or deviant ways is an *effect* of being in the underclass. When the underclass becomes a causal term, however, especially on a widespread basis, planners, as well as politicians and citizens, are in trouble; sooner or later, someone will argue that the only policy solution is to lock up everyone described as an underclass member.

Similar planning problems develop if and when the reification of a term leads to its being assigned *moral* causality. Using notions that blame victims may help the blamers to feel better by blowing off the steam of righteous indignation, but it does not eliminate the problems very poor people have or make. Indeed, those who argue that all people are entirely responsible for what they do sidestep the morally and otherwise crucial issue of determining how much responsibility should be assigned to people who lack resources, who are therefore under unusual stress, and who lack effective choices in many areas of life in which even moderate income people can choose relatively freely. . . .

The *seventh* danger of the term, and one also particularly salient for planners, stems from the way the underclass has been analyzed. As already noted, some researchers have tried to identify underclass neighborhoods. Planners must be especially sensitive to the dangers of the underclass neighborhood notion, because, once statistically defined "neighborhoods," or even sets of adjacent census tracts, are marked with the underclass label, the politicians who make the basic land use decisions in the community may propose a variety of harmful policies, such as moving all of a city's homeless into such areas, or declaring them ripe for urban renewal because of the undeservingness of the population. Recall that this is how much of the federal urban renewal of the 1950s and 1960s was justified. In addition, neighborhood policies generally rest on the assumption that people inside the boundaries of such areas are more homogeneous than they in fact are, and that they remain inside boundaries that are more often nothing but lines on a map. Since very poor people tend to suffer more from public policies than they benefit, and since they have fewer defenses than more affluent people against harmful policies, "neighborhood policies" may hurt more often than they will help.

A related danger—and my *eighth*—stems from William J. Wilson's "concentration and isolation" hypotheses. Wilson argues that the economic difficulties of the very poorest blacks are compounded by the fact that as the better-off blacks move out, the poorest are more and more concentrated, having only other very poor people, and the few institutions that minister to them, as neighbors. This concentration causes social isolation, among other things, Wilson suggests, because the very poor are now isolated from access to the people, job networks, role models, institutions, and other connections that might help them escape poverty.

Wilson's hypotheses, summarized all too briefly here, are now being accepted as dogma by many outside the research community. Fortunately, they are also being tested in a number of places, but until they are shown to be valid, planners should probably go slowly with designing action programs—especially programs to reduce concentration. In the minimal-vacancy housing markets in which virtually all poor people live, such a policy might mean having to find a new, and surely more costly, dwelling unit, or having to double up with relatives, or in some cases being driven into shelters or into the streets. Even if working- and middle-class areas were willing to accept relocatees from deconcentrated areas, a response that seems unlikely, the relocatees could not afford to live in such areas—although many would flourish if they had the money to do so. Meanwhile, the dysfunctions of dispersal may be as bad as those of overconcentration, not because the latter has any virtues, but because, until an effective jobs-and-income-grants program has gone into operation, requiring very poor people to move away from the neighborly support structures they *do* have may deprive them of their only resources.

While it may be risky to attempt deconcentration at this stage, it is worth trying to reduce isolation. One form of isolation, the so-called urban-suburban mismatch between jobless workers residing in cities and available suburban jobs, is already being attacked again, which is all to the good. Perhaps something has been learned from the failures of the 1960s to reduce the mismatch. We must bear in mind, however, that in some or perhaps many cases the physical mismatch is only a cover for class and racial discrimination, and the widespread unwillingness of white suburban employers—and white workers—to have black coworkers. . . .

The *ninth* danger is inherent in the concept of an underclass. While it assumes that the people assigned to the underclass are poor, the term itself sidesteps issues of poverty. It also permits analysts to ignore the dramatic recent increases in certain kinds of poverty, or persisting poverty, and hence the need for resuming effective antipoverty programs. For example, terms like underclass make it easier for conservative researchers to look at the homeless mainly as mentally ill or the victims of rent control, and frees them of any need to discuss the disappearance of jobs, SROs [single-room occupancies], and other low income housing.

Indeed, to the extent that the underclass notion is turned into a synonym for the undeserving poor, the political conditions for reinstituting effective antipoverty policy are removed. If the underclass is undeserving, then the government's responsibility is limited to beefing up the courts and other punitive agencies and institutions that try to isolate the underclass and protect the rest of society from it. Conversely, the moral imperative to help the poor through the provision of jobs and income grants is reduced. Describing the poor as undeserving has long been an effective if immoral short-term approach to tax reduction. . . .

NOTES

I am grateful to Michael Katz for his helpful comments on an earlier draft of this essay.

Kornblum, William. 1984. Lumping the Poor: What *Is* the Underclass. *Dissent.* September: 295–302.

Lewis, Oscar. 1969. The Culture of Poverty. In *On Understanding Poverty,* edited by Daniel P. Moynihan. New York: Basic.

Myrdal, Gunnar. 1962. *The Challenge to Affluence.* New York: Pantheon.

Wilson, William J. 1987. *The Truly Disadvantaged: The Inner City, the Underclass, and Public Policy.* Chicago: University of Chicago Press.

11

Domination and Subordination

Jean Baker Miller

What do people do to people who are different from them and why? On the individual level, the child grows only via engagement with people very different from her/himself. Thus, the most significant difference is between the adult and the child. At the level of humanity in general, we have seen massive problems around a great variety of differences. But the most basic difference is the one between women and men.

On both levels it is appropriate to pose two questions. When does the engagement of difference stimulate the development and the enhancement of both parties to the engagement? And, conversely, when does such a confrontation with difference have negative effects: When does it lead to great difficulty, deterioration, and distortion and to some of the worst forms of degradation, terror, and violence—both for individuals and for groups—that human beings can experience? It is clear that "mankind" in general, especially in our Western tradition but in some others as well, does not have a very glorious record in this regard.

It is not always clear that in most instances of difference there is also a factor of inequality—inequality of many kinds of resources, but fundamentally of status and

From Jean Baker Miller, *Toward a New Psychology of Women.* © 1976, 1986 by Jean Baker Miller. Reprinted by permission of Beacon Press, Boston.

power. One useful way to examine the often confusing results of these confrontations with difference is to ask: What happens in situations of inequality? What forces are set in motion? While we will be using the terms "dominant" and "subordinate" in the discussion, it is useful to remember that flesh and blood women and men are involved. Speaking in abstractions sometimes permits us to accept what we might not admit to on a personal level.

Temporary Inequality

Two types of inequality are pertinent for present purposes. The first might be called temporary inequality. Here, the lesser party is *socially* defined as unequal. Major examples are the relationships between parents and children, teachers and students, and, possibly, therapists and clients. There are certain assumptions in these relationships which are often not made explicit, nor, in fact, are they carried through. But they are the social structuring of the relationship.

The "superior" party presumably has more of some ability or valuable quality, which she/he is supposed to impart to the "lesser" person. While these abilities vary with the particular relationship, they include emotional maturity, experience in the world, physical skills, a body of knowledge, or the techniques for acquiring certain kinds of knowledge. The superior person is supposed to engage with the lesser in such a way as to bring the lesser member up to full parity; that is, the child is to be helped to become the adult. Such is the overall task of this relationship. The lesser, the child, is to be given to, by the person who presumably has more to give. Although the lesser party often also gives much to the superior, these relationships are *based in service* to the lesser party. That is their *raison d'être*.

It is clear, then, that the paramount goal is to end the relationship; that is, to end the relationship of inequality. The period of disparity is meant to be temporary. People may continue their association as friends, colleagues, or even competitors, but not as "superior" and "lesser." At least this is the goal.

The reality is that we have trouble enough with this sort of relationship. Parents or professional institutions often tip toward serving the needs of the donor instead of those of the lesser party (for example, schools can come to serve teachers or administrators, rather than students). Or the lesser person learns how to be a good "lesser" rather than how to make the journey from lesser to full stature. Overall, we have not found very good ways to carry out the central task: to foster the movement from unequal to equal. In childrearing and education we do not have an adequate theory and practice. Nor do we have concepts that work well in such other unequal so-called "helping" relationships as healing, penology, and rehabilitation. Officially, we say we want to do these things, but we often fail.

We have a great deal of trouble deciding on how many rights "to allow" to the lesser party. We agonize about how much power the lesser party shall have. How much can the lesser person express or act on her or his perceptions when these definitely differ from those of the superior? Above all, there is great difficulty in maintaining the conception of the lesser person *as a person of as much intrinsic worth as the superior.*

A crucial point is that power is a major factor in all of these relationships. But power alone will not suffice. Power exists and it has to be taken into account, not denied. The superiors hold all the real power, but power will not accomplish *the task.* It will not bring the unequal party up to equality.

Our troubles with these relationships may stem from the fact that they exist within the context of a second type of inequality that tends to overwhelm the ways we learn to operate in the first kind. The second type molds the very ways we perceive and conceptualize what we are doing in the first, most basic kind of relationships.

The second type of inequality teaches us how to enforce inequality, but not how to make the journey from unequal to equal. Most importantly, its consequences are kept amazingly obscure—in fact they are usually denied. . . . However, the underlying notion is that this second type has determined, and still determines, the only ways we can think and feel in the first type.

Permanent Inequality

In these relationships, some people or groups of people are defined as unequal by means of what sociologists call ascription; that is, your birth defines you. Criteria may be race, sex, class, nationality, religion, or other characteristics ascribed at birth. Here, the terms of the relationships are very different from those of temporary inequality. There is, for example, no notion that superiors are present primarily to help inferiors, to impart to them their advantages and "desirable" characteristics. There is no assumption that the goal of the unequal relationship is to end the inequality; in fact, quite the reverse. A series of other governing tendencies are in force, and occur with great regularity. . . . While some of these elements may appear obvious, in fact there is a great deal of disagreement and confusion about psychological characteristics brought about by conditions as obvious as these.

Dominants

Once a group is defined as inferior, the superiors tend to label it as defective or substandard in various ways. These labels accrete rapidly. Thus, blacks are described as less intelligent than whites, women are supposed to be ruled by emotion, and so on. In addition, the actions and words of the dominant group tend to be destructive of the subordinates. All historical evidence confirms this tendency. And, although they are much less obvious, there are destructive effects on the dominants as well. The latter are of a different order and are much more difficult to recognize.

Dominant groups usually define one or more acceptable roles for the subordinate. Acceptable roles typically involve providing services that no dominant group wants to perform for itself (for example, cleaning up the dominant's waste products). Functions that a dominant group prefers to perform, on the other hand, are carefully guarded and closed to subordinates. Out of the total range of human possibilities, the activities most highly valued in any particular culture will tend to be enclosed within the domain of the dominant group; less valued functions are relegated to the subordinates.

Subordinates are usually said to be unable to perform the preferred roles. Their incapacities are ascribed to innate defects or deficiencies of mind or body, therefore immutable and impossible of change or development. It becomes difficult for dominants even to imagine that subordinates are capable of performing the preferred activities. More importantly, subordinates themselves can come to find it difficult to believe in their own ability. The myth of their inability to fulfill wider or more valued roles is challenged only when a drastic event disrupts the usual arrangements. Such disruptions usually arise from outside the relationship itself. For instance, in the emergency situation of World War II, "incompetent" women suddenly "manned" the factories with great skill.

It follows that subordinates are described in terms of, and encouraged to develop, personal psychological characteristics that are pleasing to the dominant group. These characteristics form a certain familiar cluster: submissiveness, passivity, docility, dependency, lack of initiative, inability to act, to decide, to think, and the like. In general, this cluster includes qualities more characteristic of children than adults—immaturity, weakness, and helplessness. If subordinates adopt these characteristics they are considered well-adjusted.

However, when subordinates show the potential for, or even more dangerously have developed other characteristics—let us say intelligence, initiative, assertiveness—there is usually no room available within the dominant framework for acknowledgement of these characteristics. Such people will be defined as at least unusual, if not definitely abnormal. There will be no opportunities for the direct application of their abilities within the social arrangements. (How many women have pretended to be dumb!)

Dominant groups usually impede the development of subordinates and block their freedom of expression and action. They also tend to militate against stirrings of greater rationality or greater humanity in their own members. It was not too long ago that "nigger lover" was a common appellation, and even now men who "allow their women" more than the usual scope are subject to ridicule in many circles.

A dominant group, inevitably, has the greatest influence in determining a culture's overall outlook—its philosophy, morality, social theory, and even its science. The dominant group, thus, legitimizes the unequal relationship and incorporates it into society's guiding concepts. The social outlook, then, obscures the true nature of this relationship—that is, the very existence of inequality. The culture explains the events that take place in terms of other premises, premises that are inevitably false, such as racial or sexual inferiority. While in recent years we have learned about many such falsities on the larger social level, a full analysis of the psychological implications still remains to be developed. In the case of women, for example, despite overwhelming evidence to the contrary, the notion persists that women are meant to be passive, submissive, docile, secondary. From this premise, the outcome of therapy and encounters with psychology and other "sciences" are often determined.

Inevitably, the dominant group is the model for "normal human relationships." It then becomes "normal" to treat others destructively and to derogate them, to obscure the truth of what you are doing, by creating false explanations, and to oppose actions toward equality. In short, if one's identification is with the dominant group, it is "normal" to continue in this pattern. Even though most of us do not like to think of ourselves as either believing in, or engaging in, such dominations, it is, in fact, difficult for a member of a dominant group to do otherwise. But to keep on doing these things, one need only behave "normally."

It follows from this that dominant groups generally do not like to be told about or even quietly reminded of the existence of inequality. "Normally" they can avoid awareness because their explanation of the relationship becomes so well integrated *in other terms*; they can even believe that both they and the subordinate group share the same interests and, to some extent, a common experience. If pressed a bit, the familiar rationalizations are offered: the home is "women's natural place," and we know "what's best for them anyhow."

Dominants prefer to avoid conflict—open conflict that might call into question the whole situation. This is particularly and tragically so, when many members of the dominant group are not having an easy time of it themselves. Members of a dominant group, or at least some segments of it, such as white working-class men (who are themselves also subordinates), often feel unsure of their own narrow toehold on the material and psychological bounties they believe they desperately need. What dominant groups usually cannot act on, or even see, is that the situation of inequality in fact deprives them, particularly on the psychological level.

Clearly, inequality has created a state of conflict. Yet dominant groups will tend to suppress conflict. They will see any questioning of the "normal" situation as threatening; activities by subordinates in this direction will be perceived with alarm. Dominants are usually convinced that the way things are is right and good, not only for them but especially for the subordinates. All morality confirms this view, and all social structure sustains it.

It is perhaps unnecessary to add that the dominant group usually holds all of the open power and authority and determines the ways in which power may be acceptably used.

Subordinates

What of the subordinates' part in this? Since dominants determine what is normal for a culture, it is much more difficult to understand subordinates. Initial expressions of dissatisfaction and early actions by subordinates always come as a surprise;

they are usually rejected as atypical. After all, dominants *knew* that all women needed and wanted was a man around whom to organize their lives. Members of the dominant group do not understand why "they"—the first to speak out—are so upset and angry.

The characteristics that typify the subordinates are even more complex. A subordinate group has to concentrate on basic survival. Accordingly, direct, honest reaction to destructive treatment is avoided. Open, self-initiated action in its own self-interest must also be avoided. Such actions can, and still do, literally result in death for some subordinate groups. In our own society, a woman's direct action can result in a combination of economic hardship, social ostracism, and psychological isolation—and even the diagnosis of a personality disorder. Any one of these consequences is bad enough. . . .

It is not surprising then that a subordinate group resorts to disguised and indirect ways of acting and reacting. While these actions are designed to accommodate and please the dominant group, they often, in fact, contain hidden defiance and "put ons." Folk tales, black jokes, and women stories are often based on how the wily peasant or sharecropper outwitted the rich landowner, boss, or husband. The essence of the story rests on the fact that the overlord does not even know that he has been made a fool of.

One important result of this indirect mode of operation is that members of the dominant group are denied an essential part of life—the opportunity to acquire self-understanding through knowing their impact on others. They are thus deprived of "consensual validation," feedback, and a chance to correct their actions and expressions. Put simply, subordinates won't tell. For the same reasons, the dominant group is deprived also of valid knowledge about the subordinates. (It is particularly ironic that the societal "experts" in knowledge about subordinates are usually members of the dominant group.)

Subordinates, then, know much more about the dominants than vice versa. They have to. They become highly attuned to the dominants, able to predict their reactions of pleasure and displeasure. Here, I think, is where the long story of "feminine intuition" and "feminine wiles" begins. It seems clear that these "mysterious" gifts are in fact skills, developed through long practice, in reading many small signals, both verbal and nonverbal.

Another important result is that subordinates often know more about the dominants than they know about themselves. If a large part of your fate depends on accommodating to and pleasing the dominants, you concentrate on them. Indeed, there is little purpose in knowing yourself. Why should you when your knowledge of the dominants determines your life? This tendency is reinforced by many other restrictions. One can know oneself only through action and interaction. To the extent that their range of action or interaction is limited, subordinates will lack a realistic evaluation of their capacities and problems. Unfortunately, this difficulty in gaining self-knowledge is even further compounded.

Tragic confusion arises because subordinates absorb a large part of the untruths created by the dominants; there are a great many blacks who feel inferior to whites, and women who still believe they are less important than men. This internalization of dominant beliefs is more likely to occur if there are few alternative concepts at hand. On the other hand, it is also true that members of the subordinate group have certain experiences and perceptions that accurately reflect the truth about themselves and the injustice of their position. Their own more truthful concepts are bound to come into opposition with the mythology they have absorbed from the dominant group. An inner tension between the two sets of concepts and their derivations is almost inevitable.

From a historical perspective, despite the obstacles, subordinate groups have tended to move toward greater freedom of expression and action, although this progress varies greatly from one circumstance to another. There were always some slaves who revolted; there were some women who sought greater development or self-determination. Most records of these actions are not preserved by the dominant culture, making it difficult for the subordinate group to find a supporting tradition and history.

Within each subordinate group, there are tendencies for some members to imitate the dominants. This imitation can take various forms. Some may try to treat their fellow subordinates as destructively as the dominants treat them. A few may develop enough of the qualities valued by the dominants to be partially accepted into their fellowship. Usually they are not wholly accepted, and even then only if they are willing to forsake their own identification with fellow subordinates. "Uncle Toms" and certain professional women have often been in this position. (There are always a few women who have won the praise presumably embodied in the phrase "she thinks like a man.")

To the extent that subordinates move toward freer expression and action, they will expose the inequality and throw into question the basis for its existence. And they will make the inherent conflict an open conflict. They will then have to bear the burden and take the risks that go with being defined as "troublemakers." Since this role flies in the face of their conditioning, subordinates, especially women, do not come to it with ease.

What is immediately apparent from studying the characteristics of the two groups is that mutually enhancing interaction is not probable between unequals. Indeed, conflict is inevitable. The important questions, then, become: Who defines the conflict? Who sets the terms? When is conflict overt or covert? On what issues is the conflict fought? Can anyone win? Is conflict "bad," by definition? If not, what makes for productive or destructive conflict?

Suggestions for Further Reading

Alba, Richard D. *Ethnic Identity: The Transformation of White American Identity.* New Haven: Yale University Press, 1990.

Berkhofer, Robert F., Jr. *The White Man's Indian: Images of the American Indian from Columbus to the Present.* New York: Vintage, 1978.

Connell, R. W. *Masculinities.* Berkeley, CA: University of California Press, 1995.

De Beauvoir, Simone. *The Second Sex.* New York: Alfred A. Knopf, 1952.

Doty, William G. *The Myths of Masculinity.* New York: Crossroad Publishing, 1993.

Epstein, Cynthia Fuchs. *Deceptive Distinctions: Sex, Gender, and the Social Order.* New Haven: Yale University Press; New York: Russell Sage Foundation, 1988.

Frankenberg, Ruth. *White Women, Race Matters.* Minneapolis: University of Minnesota Press, 1993.

Funderburg, Lise. *Black, White, Other Biracial Americans Talk about Race and Identity.* New York: William Morrow, 1994.

Gould, Stephen. *The Mismeasure of Man.* New York: W. W. Norton, 1984.

Gregory, Steven, and Roger Sanjek, eds. *Race.* New Brunswick, NJ: Rutgers University Press, 1994.

Haizlip, Shirlee Taylor. *The Sweeter the Juice.* New York: Simon & Schuster, 1994.

Hubbard, Ruth. *The Politics of Women's Biology.* New Brunswick, NJ: Rutgers University Press, 1990.

Katz, Jonathan Ned. *The Invention of Heterosexuality.* New York: Dutton, 1995.

Lipman-Blumen, Jean. *Gender Roles and Power.* Englewood Cliffs, NJ: Prentice-Hall, 1984.

Lopez, Ian F. Haney. *White by Law: The Legal Construction of Race.* New York: New York University Press, 1996.

Lowe, M., and R. Hubbard, eds. *Women's Nature: Rationalizations of Inequality.* New York: Pergamon Press, 1983.

Memmi, Albert. *Dominated Man.* Boston: Beacon Press, 1969.

Montague, M. F. Ashley. *Man's Most Dangerous Myth.* New York: Harper & Row, 1952.

Omi, Michael, and Howard Winant. *Racial Formations in the United States.* New York: Routledge and Kegan Paul, 1986.

Sanday, Peggy R. *Female Power and Male Dominance: On the Origins of Sexual Inequality.* New York: Cambridge University Press, 1981.

Smith, Dorothy. *The Everyday World as Problematic: A Feminist Sociology.* Boston: Northeastern Press, 1987.

Williams, Gregory Howard. *Life on the Color Line.* New York: Dutton, 1995.

Understanding Racism, Sexism, Heterosexism, and Class Privilege

IN PART II, WE SPEND SOME TIME ANALYZING SYSTEMS of oppression and examining the relations of dominance and subordination they incorporate almost seamlessly into daily life. Racism, sexism, heterosexism, and class privilege are systems of advantage that provide those with the "right" race, sex, sexual orientation, and class (or some combination of these) with opportunities and rewards that are unavailable to other individuals and groups in society. Sometimes they work in isolation from each other but most often they operate in combination to create a system of advantage and disadvantage that enhances the life chances of some while limiting the life chances of others.

The construction of difference as deviance or deficiency underlies the systems of oppression that determine how power, privilege, wealth, and opportunity are distributed. We are surrounded by differences every day, but our society chooses to place a value on only some of them. By valuing the characteristics and lifestyles of certain individuals or groups and devaluing those of others, society constructs some of its members as "other." These "others" are understood to be less deserving, less intelligent, even less human. Once this happens, it is possible to distribute wealth, opportunity, and justice unequally without appearing to be unfair. The social construction of race, class, gender, and sexuality as difference—where being white, male, European, heterosexual, and prosperous is the norm and everyone else is considered less able and less worthy—lies at the heart of racism, sexism, heterosexism, and classism.

Some people are uncomfortable with words like "racism," "sexism," and "oppression," which seem to them highly charged and unnecessarily accusatory. They prefer to talk about discrimination and prejudice. However, those who wish to emphasize the complex, pervasive, and self-perpetuating nature of the system of beliefs, policies, practices, and attitudes that enforces the relations of subordination and domination in our society find the term "discrimination" too narrow and too limited to do so effectively. Words like "racism," "sexism," and "oppression" are more appropriate because they capture the comprehensive nature of the systems being studied. In Selection 6, Marilyn Frye does a good job of explaining the meaning of "oppression" in the course of using that concept to convey the pervasive nature of sexism. Frye uses the metaphor of a birdcage to illustrate how a system of oppression, in this case sexism, imprisons its victims through a set of interlocking impediments to motion. Taken alone, none of the barriers seems very powerful or threatening; taken together they are unyielding. They constitute a cage which appears light and airy, masking the fact that its occupants are trapped as completely as if they were in a sealed vault.

Racism and sexism are systems of advantage based on race and sex. In the United States racism perpetuates an interlocking system of institutions, attitudes, privileges, and rewards that work to the benefit of white people just as sexism works to the advantage of men. In Selection 1 Beverley Daniels Tatum elaborates on this definition of racism (originally offered by David Wellman in his book *Portraits of White Racism*), and discusses the resistance some of those of us who are white feel toward acknowledging both the existence of racism and the advantages it bestows on us. As Tatum observes, many prefer to define racism in terms of racial prejudice because by adopting this definition it is possible to say that people of color as well as white people can be racist. For many people in this society, being able to say so seems to satisfy a deep emotional need. Confronted with behavior or speech that is hateful, they wish to use the strongest words they can to condemn and deplore it. Once racism is defined as a system of advantages based on race, it is no longer possible to attribute racism to people of color because clearly they do not systematically benefit from racism, only white people do. This, of course, does not deny that people of all colors are capable of hateful and hurtful behavior, nor does it prevent us from taking them to task for their prejudice. But it does mean that we will reserve the term "racism" to refer specifically to the comprehensive system of advantages that work to the benefit of white people in the United States. For more on this important and provocative distinction, you will want to turn directly to the essay by Tatum.

In the following selection, Rita Chaudhry Sethi reminds us how easy it is, in certain parts of the United States, to think of racial conflict in black and white terms. Sethi rejects this simplistic racial paradigm because it leaves no room for the racism that Asian Americans experience. According to Sethi, white America constructs Asian Americans as a model minority, and Asian Americans themselves, and for their own reasons, tend to minimize anti-Asian discrimination as well. As a result, the racism that Asian Americans experience in the United States is often rendered invisible or trivialized. Sethi's project is to uncover the hidden racism directed against Asians and by doing so to broaden the use of the term. Although she does not argue the point directly, unlike Tatum, Sethi seems willing to use the term "racism" to describe certain behavior and attitudes that occur within and among communities of color.

In Selection 4, Manning Marable further deepens our understanding of racism. While Tatum tends to focus on broad interpersonal issues and Sethi is concerned with cultural conflict, Marable's focus is on the conditions under which people of color live in contemporary U.S. society and the forms of social control used to keep the prevailing hierarchy in place. In the course of his discussion, he draws parallels between racism and sexism as systems of domination and looks at the nature of what he calls the "new racism" we are now encountering.

The term "sexism" refers to the oppression of women by men in a society that is largely patriarchal. As defined by Alan Johnson in Selection 5, a patriarchal society is male-dominated, male-identified, and male-centered. In such a society, every institution and aspect of culture contrives to rationalize and perpetuate the dominance of men and the subordination of women. Marilyn Frye's article asks us to look closely at examples of some seemingly innocent but oppressive social rituals that perpetuate these relations of domination. She takes as her paradigm or model the "male door-opening ritual" and argues that its meaning and implications go far beyond the conscious intentions of the man who opens the door. The point is that sexism and racism can be perpetuated by people who are just trying to be nice. As you think about her example, remember that Frye is analyzing the implications of a social practice, not looking at any individual's motives for carrying out that ritual.

The use of the term "heterosexism" parallels that of the other two and, according to Suzanne Pharr in Selection 7, creates the assumption that the world is and must be heterosexual at the same time that it rationalizes the existing distribution of power and privilege that flows from this assumption. In her essay Pharr argues that economics, violence, and homophobia, or fear of lesbians and gays, are the most effective weapons of sexism and makes it clear that homophobia and heterosexism are oppressive of all women, not just those of us who are not exclusively heterosexual. For more current statistics on economic inequality (which continue to support Pharr's claims), take a look at the material in Part IV of this book.

Finally, class privilege refers to the system of advantages that continues to ensure that wealth, power, opportunity, and privilege go hand in hand. In Selection 10, Greg Mantsios explores some of the myths about class that mislead people about their real-life chances and documents the impact of class position on daily life. While many in the United States are oblivious to the full force of class privilege, the statistics in this article suggest that the class position of one's family, not hard work, intelligence, or determination, is probably the single most significant determinant of future success. This gap between people's beliefs about what it takes to succeed and the tremendous role that class privilege plays in determining who is successful provides a dramatic illustration of the effectiveness of systems of oppression in terms of both perpetuating the current systems of advantage and rendering their continuing operation invisible to so many.

These are strong and disturbing claims, and they are likely to provoke equally strong reactions from many people reading this introduction. Some will feel angry, others will feel depressed and discouraged, some will feel uncomfortable, others will be skeptical, and some will simply feel confused. This is understandable. If what you have just read is true, then things in the United States are neither as fair nor as equitable as most of us would like them to be. If some people, as these definitions suggest, have more than their share, then others have less than they deserve, and each of us must wonder where we will stand in the final computation. Further, many readers who are white and working class or middle class will be hard pressed to imagine what kind of privilege they exercise. They look at their own lives and the lives of their parents and friends and see people who have worked very hard for everything they have achieved. The idea that they are privileged may seem very foreign to them. The same will be true for other readers as well. Heterosexism, class privilege, male privilege? "What have these abstract and politically charged terms got to do with me?" they ask. "I work hard, try to get ahead, wish others well, and feel more like a victim myself than a victimizer." This understandable response underscores how effectively the systems of oppression we are discussing function in contemporary society to rationalize the hierarchy they create, often making its operation invisible both to those who benefit from it and to those who are shortchanged by it. In addition, it points to the complicated and ambiguous nature of privilege, which means that a single individual can be privileged in some respects at the very same time he or she is disadvantaged in other respects. Let us examine these two points in more detail.

Many people who are privileged fail to realize that this is the case because the systems of oppression we are studying so effectively make the current distribution of privilege and power appear almost "natural." In addition, some of us, including those of us who are disadvantaged, grow up believing things about ourselves and others that make our life choices and opportunities, or lack of same, seem inevitable or deserved. (Take a look, if you haven't already done so, at Sandra Bem's article in Part I.) In many cases, people with privileges have enjoyed them for so long that they have simply come to take them for granted. Instead of recognizing them as special benefits that come with, for example, white skin, they just assume that these privileges are things to which they have a right. (For more on this topic see Peggy McIntosh's essay, Selection 9, which does an excellent job of examining how white privilege works.)

In other cases, privilege may be difficult to identify and acknowledge because the individual is privileged in some respects but not in others. For example, those who are privileged by virtue of their sex or sexual orientation may be disadvantaged in other respects, say by virtue of their race/ethnicity or their class position or both. The disadvantages they experience in some areas may seem so unfair and so egregious that they prevent them from recognizing the privileges they nonetheless enjoy. For example, a poor, white, single mother who receives public assistance and who feels very much at the mercy of an unfair and inhumane system might still be able to call upon her white skin privilege or her heterosexual privilege in certain situations and yet be oblivious to that privilege because she feels so disadvantaged in other respects. A working-class or lower-middle-class white male who has trouble stretching his paycheck to cover all his expenses may be so preoccupied with his financial situation that he doesn't recognize the male privilege and white skin privilege from which he nonetheless benefits—privileges which may not feel at all like privileges to him because he takes them for granted and regards them as "natural" and "normal." And finally, since most people are basically decent and fair, those of us who are privileged are often simply reluctant to acknowledge that we have unfair advantages over others because that would require that we reevaluate our sense of who we are and what we have accomplished in our lives. The complicated nature of relations of privilege, dominance, and subordination are examined by Aida Hurtado in Selection 8. Hurtado, whose fundamental claim is that each oppressed group in the United States has its own unique relationship to white men and the particular nature of that relationship is what shapes each form of subordination, devotes much of her essay to analyzing the ways in which the subordination of women of color and white women differ in contemporary society.

As should by now be clear, each of the thinkers whose work is included in Part II shares the belief that the various systems of oppression operate in relation to each other, forming an interlocking system of advantages and disadvantages that rationalize and preserve the prevailing distribution of power and privilege in society. As you read these articles, try to keep an open mind about this claim. If these thinkers are correct, they have something important to tell us about this society and the forces that will be in place as each of us goes about creating our own future. Reading some of this material may make some people temporarily uncomfortable, but failing to grapple with it may leave us all the more vulnerable to the forces that play a compelling role in determining the life chances of the individuals and groups that make up our society.

1

Defining Racism: *"Can We Talk?"*

Beverley Daniels Tatum

Early in my teaching career, a White student I knew asked me what I would be teaching the following semester. I mentioned that I would be teaching a course on racism. She replied, with some surprise in her voice, "Oh, is there still racism?" I assured her that indeed there was and suggested that she sign up for my course. Fifteen years later, after exhaustive media coverage of events such as the Rodney King beating, the Charles Stuart and Susan Smith cases, the O. J. Simpson trial, the appeal to racial prejudices in electoral politics, and the bitter debates about affirmative action and welfare reform, it seems hard to imagine that anyone would still be unaware of the reality of racism in our society. But in fact, in almost every audience I address, there is someone who will suggest that racism is a thing of the past. There is always someone who hasn't noticed the stereotypical images of people of color in the media, who hasn't observed the housing discrimination in their community, who hasn't read the newspaper articles about documented racial bias in lending practices among well-known banks, who isn't aware of the racial tracking pattern at the local school, who hasn't seen the reports of rising incidents of racially motivated hate crimes in America—in short, someone who hasn't been paying attention to issues of race. But if you are paying attention, the legacy of racism is not hard to see, and we are all affected by it.

The impact of racism begins early. Even in our preschool years, we are exposed to misinformation about people different from ourselves. Many of us grew up in neighborhoods where we had limited opportunities to interact with people different from our own families. When I ask my college students, "How many of you grew up in neighborhoods where most of the people were from the same racial group as your own?" almost every hand goes up. There is still a great deal of social segregation in our communities. Consequently, most of the early information we receive about "others"—people racially, religiously, or socioeconomically different from ourselves—does not come as the result of firsthand experience. The secondhand information we do receive has often been distorted, shaped by cultural stereotypes, and left incomplete.

From Beverley Daniels Tatum, *"Why Are All the Black Kids Sitting Together in the Cafeteria?" and Other Conversations about Race* (New York: Basic Books, 1997), pp. 3–13.

Some examples will highlight this process. Several years ago one of my students conducted a research project investigating preschoolers' conceptions of Native Americans.[1] Using children at a local day care center as her participants, she asked these three- and four-year-olds to draw a picture of a Native American. Most children were stumped by her request. They didn't know what a Native American was. But when she rephrased the question and asked them to draw a picture of an Indian, they readily complied. Almost every picture included one central feature: feathers. In fact, many of them also included a weapon—a knife or tomahawk—and depicted the person in violent or aggressive terms. Though this group of children, almost all of whom were White, did not live near a large Native American population and probably had had little if any personal interaction with American Indians, they all had internalized an image of what Indians were like. How did they know? Cartoon images, in particular the Disney movie *Peter Pan*, were cited by the children as their number-one source of information. At the age of three, these children already had a set of stereotypes in place. Though I would not describe three-year-olds as prejudiced, the stereotypes to which they have been exposed become the foundation for the adult prejudices so many of us have.

Sometimes the assumptions we make about others come not from what we have been told or what we have seen on television or in books, but rather from what we have *not* been told. The distortion of historical information about people of color leads young people (and older people, too) to make assumptions that may go unchallenged for a long time. Consider this conversation between two White students following a discussion about the cultural transmission of racism:

"Yeah, I just found out that Cleopatra was actually a Black woman."

"What?"

The first student went on to explain her newly learned information. The second student exclaimed in disbelief, "That can't be true. Cleopatra was beautiful!"

What had this young woman learned about who in our society is considered beautiful and who is not? Had she conjured up images of Elizabeth Taylor when she thought of Cleopatra? The new information her classmate had shared and her own deeply ingrained assumptions about who is beautiful and who is not were too incongruous to allow her to assimilate the information at that moment.

Omitted information can have similar effects. For example, another young woman, preparing to be a high school English teacher, expressed her dismay that she had never learned about any Black authors in any of her English courses. How was she to teach about them to her future students when she hadn't learned about them herself? A White male student in the class responded to this discussion with frustration in his response journal, writing "It's not my fault that Blacks don't write books." Had one of his elementary, high school, or college teachers ever told him that there were no Black writers? Probably not. Yet because he had never been exposed to Black authors, he had drawn his own conclusion that there were none.

Stereotypes, omissions, and distortions all contribute to the development of prejudice. *Prejudice* is a preconceived judgment or opinion, usually based on limited information. I assume that we all have prejudices, not because we want them, but simply because we are so continually exposed to misinformation about others. Though I have often heard students or workshop participants describe someone as not having "a prejudiced bone in his body," I usually suggest that they look again. Prejudice is one of the inescapable consequences of living in a racist society. Cultural racism—the cultural images and messages that affirm the assumed superiority of Whites and the assumed inferiority of people of color—is like smog in the air. Sometimes it is so thick it is visible, other times it is less apparent, but always, day in and day out, we are breathing it in. None of us would introduce ourselves as "smog-breathers" (and most of us don't want to be described as prejudiced), but if we live in a smoggy place, how can we avoid breathing the air? If we live in an environment in which we are bombarded with stereotypical images in the media, are frequently exposed to the ethnic jokes of friends and family members, and are rarely informed of the accomplishments of oppressed groups, we will develop the negative categorizations of those groups that form the basis of prejudice.

People of color as well as Whites develop these categorizations. Even a member of the stereotyped group may internalize the stereotypical categories about his or her own group to some degree. In fact, this process happens so frequently that it has a name, *internalized oppression*. Some of the consequences of believing the distorted messages about one's own group will be discussed in subsequent chapters.

Certainly some people are more prejudiced than others, actively embracing and perpetuating negative and hateful images of those who are different from themselves. When we claim to be free of prejudice, perhaps what we are really saying is that we are not hatemongers. But none of us is completely innocent. Prejudice is an integral part of our socialization, and it is not our fault. Just as the preschoolers my student interviewed are not to blame for the negative messages they internalized, we are not at fault for the stereotypes, distortions, and omissions that shaped our thinking as we grew up.

To say that it is not our fault does not relieve us of responsibility, however. We may not have polluted the air, but we need to take responsibility, along with others, for cleaning it up. Each of us needs to look at our own behavior. Am I perpetuating and reinforcing the negative messages so pervasive in our culture, or am I seeking to challenge them? If I have not been exposed to positive images of marginalized groups, am I seeking them out, expanding my own knowledge base for myself and my children? Am I acknowledging and examining my own prejudices, my own rigid categorizations of others, thereby minimizing the adverse impact they might have on my interactions with those I have categorized? Unless we engage in these and other conscious acts of reflection and reeducation, we easily repeat the process with our children. We teach what we were taught. The unexamined prejudices of the parents are passed on to the children. It is not our fault, but it is our responsibility to interrupt this cycle.

Racism: A System of Advantage Based on Race

Many people use the terms *prejudice* and *racism* interchangeably. I do not, and I think it is important to make a distinction. In his book *Portraits of White Racism*, David Wellman argues convincingly that limiting our understanding of racism to prejudice does not offer a sufficient explanation for the persistence of racism. He defines racism as a "system of advantage based on race."[2] In illustrating this definition, he provides example after example of how Whites defend their racial advantage—access to better schools, housing, jobs—even when they do not embrace overtly prejudicial thinking. Racism cannot be fully explained as an expression of prejudice alone.

This definition of racism is useful because it allows us to see that racism, like other forms of oppression, is not only a personal ideology based on racial prejudice, but a *system* involving cultural messages and institutional policies and practices as well as the beliefs and actions of individuals. In the context of the United States, this system clearly operates to the advantage of Whites and to the disadvantage of people of color. Another related definition of racism, commonly used by antiracist educators and consultants, is "prejudice plus power." Racial prejudice when combined with social power—access to social, cultural, and economic resources and decision-making—leads to the institutionalization of racist policies and practices. While I think this definition also captures the idea that racism is more than individual beliefs and attitudes, I prefer Wellman's definition because the idea of systematic advantage and disadvantage is critical to an understanding of how racism operates in American society.

In addition, I find that many of my White students and workshop participants do not feel powerful. Defining racism as prejudice plus power has little personal relevance. For some, their response to this definition is the following: "I'm not really prejudiced, and I have no power, so racism has nothing to do with me." However, most White people, if they are really being honest with themselves, can see that there are advantages to being White in the United States. Despite the current rhetoric about affirmative action and "reverse racism," every social indicator, from salary to life expectancy, reveals the advantages of being White.[3]

The systematic advantages of being White are often referred to as White privilege. In a now well-known article, "White Privilege: Unpacking the Invisible Knapsack," Peggy McIntosh, a White feminist scholar, identified a long list of societal privileges that she received simply because she was White.[4] She did not ask for them, and it is important to note that she hadn't always noticed that she was receiving them. They included major and minor advantages. Of course she enjoyed greater access to jobs and housing. But she also was able to shop in department stores without being followed by suspicious salespeople and could always find appropriate hair care products and makeup in any drugstore. She could send her child to school confident that the teacher would not discriminate against him on the basis of race. She could also be late for meetings, and talk with her mouth full, fairly confident that these behaviors would not be attributed to the fact that she was

White. She could express an opinion in a meeting or in print and not have it labeled the "White" viewpoint. In other words, she was more often than not viewed as an individual, rather than as a member of a racial group.

This article rings true for most White readers, many of whom may have never considered the benefits of being White. It's one thing to have enough awareness of racism to describe the ways that people of color are disadvantaged by it. But this new understanding of racism is more elusive. In very concrete terms, it means that if a person of color is the victim of housing discrimination, the apartment that would otherwise have been rented to that person of color is still available for a White person. The White tenant is, knowingly or unknowingly, the beneficiary of racism, a system of advantage based on race. The unsuspecting tenant is not to blame for the prior discrimination, but she benefits from it anyway.

For many Whites, this new awareness of the benefits of a racist system elicits considerable pain, often accompanied by feelings of anger and guilt. These uncomfortable emotions can hinder further discussion. We all like to think that we deserve the good things we have received, and that others, too, get what they deserve. Social psychologists call this tendency a "belief in a just world."[5] Racism directly contradicts such notions of justice.

Understanding racism as a system of advantage based on race is antithetical to traditional notions of an American meritocracy. For those who have internalized this myth, this definition generates considerable discomfort. It is more comfortable simply to think of racism as a particular form of prejudice. Notions of power or privilege do not have to be addressed when our understanding of racism is constructed in that way.

The discomfort generated when a systemic definition of racism is introduced is usually quite visible in the workshops I lead. Someone in the group is usually quick to point out that this is not the definition you will find in most dictionaries. I reply, "Who wrote the dictionary?" I am not being facetious with this response. Whose interests are served by a "prejudice only" definition of racism? It is important to understand that the system of advantage is perpetuated when we do not acknowledge its existence.

Racism: For Whites Only?

Frequently someone will say, "You keep talking about White people. People of color can be racist, too." I once asked a White teacher what it would mean to her if a student or parent of color accused her of being racist. She said she would feel as though she had been punched in the stomach or called a "low-life scum." She is not alone in this feeling. The word *racist* holds a lot of emotional power. For many White people, to be called racist is the ultimate insult. The idea that this term might only be applied to Whites becomes highly problematic for after all, can't people of color be "low-life scum" too?

Of course, people of any racial group can hold hateful attitudes and behave in racially discriminatory and bigoted ways. We can all cite examples of horrible hate crimes which have been perpetrated by people of color as well as Whites. Hateful behavior is hateful behavior no matter who does it. But when I am asked, "Can people of color be racist?" I reply, "The answer depends on your definition of racism." If one defines racism as racial prejudice, the answer is yes. People of color can and do have racial prejudices. However, if one defines racism as a system of advantage based on race, the answer is no. People of color are not racist because they do not systematically benefit from racism. And equally important, there is no systematic cultural and institutional support or sanction for the racial bigotry of people of color. In my view, reserving the term *racist* only for behaviors committed by Whites in the context of a White-dominated society is a way of acknowledging the ever-present power differential afforded Whites by the culture and institutions that make up the system of advantage and continue to reinforce notions of White superiority. (Using the same logic, I reserve the word *sexist* for men. Though women can and do have gender-based prejudices, only men systematically benefit from sexism.)

Despite my best efforts to explain my thinking on this point, there are some who will be troubled, perhaps even incensed, by my response. To call the racially motivated acts of a person of color acts of racial bigotry and to describe similar acts committed by Whites as racist will make no sense to some people, including some people of color. To those, I will respectfully say, "We can agree to disagree." At moments like these, it is not agreement that is essential, but clarity. Even if you don't like the definition of racism I am using, hopefully you are now clear about what it is. If I also understand how you are using the term, our conversation can continue — despite our disagreement.

Another provocative question I'm often asked is "Are you saying all Whites are racist?" When asked this question, I again remember that White teacher's response, and I am conscious that perhaps the question I am really being asked is, "Are you saying all Whites are bad people?" The answer to that question is of course not. However, all White people, intentionally or unintentionally, do benefit from racism. A more relevant question is what are White people as individuals doing to interrupt racism? For many White people, the image of a racist is a hood-wearing Klan member or a name-calling Archie Bunker figure. These images represent what might be called *active racism*, blatant, intentional acts of racial bigotry and discrimination. *Passive racism* is more subtle and can be seen in the collusion of laughing when a racist joke is told, of letting exclusionary hiring practices go unchallenged, of accepting as appropriate the omissions of people of color from the curriculum, and of avoiding difficult race-related issues. Because racism is so ingrained in the fabric of American institutions, it is easily self-perpetuating.[6] All that is required to maintain it is business as usual.

I sometimes visualize the ongoing cycle of racism as a moving walkway at the airport. Active racist behavior is equivalent to walking fast on the conveyor belt. The person engaged in active racist behavior has identified with the ideology of

White supremacy and is moving with it. Passive racist behavior is equivalent to standing still on the walkway. No overt effort is being made, but the conveyor belt moves the bystanders along to the same destination as those who are actively walking. Some of the bystanders may feel the motion of the conveyor belt, see the active racists ahead of them, and choose to turn around, unwilling to go to the same destination as the White supremacists. But unless they are walking actively in the opposite direction at a speed faster than the conveyor belt—unless they are actively antiracist—they will find themselves carried along with the others.

So, not all Whites are actively racist. Many are passively racist. Some, though not enough, are actively antiracist. The relevant question is not whether all Whites are racist, but how we can move more White people from a position of active or passive racism to one of active antiracism. The task of interrupting racism is obviously not the task of Whites alone. But the fact of White privilege means that Whites have greater access to the societal institutions in need of transformation. To whom much is given, much is required.

It is important to acknowledge that while all Whites benefit from racism, they do not all benefit equally. Other factors, such as socioeconomic status, gender, age, religious affiliation, sexual orientation, mental and physical ability, also play a role in our access to social influence and power. A White woman on welfare is not privileged to the same extent as a wealthy White heterosexual man. In her case, the systematic disadvantages of sexism and classism intersect with her White privilege, but the privilege is still there. This point was brought home to me in a 1994 study conducted by a Mount Holyoke graduate student, Phyllis Wentworth.[7] Wentworth interviewed a group of female college students, who were both older than their peers and were the first members of their families to attend college, about the pathways that led them to college. All of the women interviewed were White, from working-class backgrounds, from families where women were expected to graduate from high school and get married or get a job. Several had experienced abusive relationships and other personal difficulties prior to coming to college. Yet their experiences were punctuated by "good luck" stories of apartments obtained without a deposit, good jobs offered without experience or extensive reference checks, and encouragement provided by willing mentors. While the women acknowledged their good fortune, none of them discussed their Whiteness. They had not considered the possibility that being White had worked in their favor and helped give them the benefit of the doubt at critical junctures. This study clearly showed that even under difficult circumstances, White privilege was still operating.

It is also true that not all people of color are equally targeted by racism. We all have multiple identities that shape our experience. I can describe myself as a light-skinned, well-educated, heterosexual, able-bodied, Christian African American woman raised in a middle-class suburb. As an African American woman, I am systematically disadvantaged by race and by gender, but I systematically receive benefits in the other categories, which then mediate my experience of racism and sexism. When one is targeted by multiple isms—racism, sexism, classism, heterosexism, ableism, anti-Semitism, ageism—in whatever combination, the effect is intensified. The particular combination of racism and classism in many communities of color is life-threatening. Nonetheless, when I, the middle-class Black mother of two sons, read another story about a Black man's unlucky encounter with a White police officer's deadly force, I am reminded that racism by itself can kill.

* * *

NOTES

1. C. O'Toole, "The effect of the media and multicultural education on children's perceptions of Native Americans" (senior thesis, Department of Psychology and Education, Mount Holyoke College, South Hadley, MA, May 1990).

2. For an extended discussion of this point, see David Wellman, *Portraits of White racism* (Cambridge: Cambridge University Press, 1977), ch. 1.

3. For specific statistical information, see R. Farley, "The common destiny of Blacks and Whites: Observations about the social and economic status of the races," pp. 197–233 in H. Hill and J. E. Jones, Jr. (Eds.), *Race in America: The struggle for equality* (Madison: University of Wisconsin Press, 1993).

4. P. McIntosh, "White privilege: Unpacking the invisible knapsack," *Peace and Freedom* (July/August 1989): 10–12.

5. For further discussion of the concept of "belief in a just world," see M. J. Lerner, "Social psychology of justice and interpersonal attraction," in T. Huston (Ed.), *Foundations of interpersonal attraction* (New York: Academic Press, 1974).

6. For a brief historical overview of the institutionalization of racism and sexism in our legal system, see "Part V: How it happened: Race and gender issues in U.S. law," in P. S. Rothenberg (Ed.), *Race, class, and gender in the United States: An integrated study*, 3d ed. (New York: St. Martin's Press, 1995).

7. P. A. Wentworth, "The identity development of non-traditionally aged first-generation women college students: An exploratory study" (master's thesis, Department of Psychology and Education, Mount Holyoke College, South Hadley, MA, 1994).

2

Smells Like Racism

Rita Chaudhry Sethi

When I started my first job after college, Steve Riley, an African American activist, asked me: "So, how do you feel being black?" I confessed, "I am not black." "In America," Steve responded, "if you're not white, you're black."

U.S. discourse on racism is generally framed in these simplistic terms: the stark polarity of black/white conflict. As it is propagated, it embraces none of the true complexities of racist behavior. Media sensationalism, political expedience, intellectual laziness, and legal constraints conspire to narrow the scope of cognizable racism. What remains is a pared-down image of racism, one that delimits the definition of its forms, its perpetrators, and, especially, its victims. Divergent experiences are only included in the hierarchy of racial crimes when they sufficiently resemble the caricature. Race-based offenses that do not conform to this model are permitted to exist and fester without remedy by legal recourse, collective retribution, or even moral indignation.

Asians' experiences exist in the penumbra of actionable racial affronts. Our cultural, linguistic, religious, national, and color differences do not, as one might imagine, form the basis for a modified paradigm of racism; rather, they exist on the periphery of offensiveness. The racial insults we suffer are usually trivialized; our reactions are dismissed as hypersensitivity or regarded as a source of amusement. The response to a scene where a Korean-owned store is being destroyed with a bat in the 1993 film *Falling Down* (a xenophobic and racist diatribe on urban life)[1] reflects how mainstream America/American culture responds to the phenomenon of anti-Asian violence:

> There was, in the theater where I saw the film, a good deal of appreciative laughter and a smattering of applause during this scene, which of course flunks the most obvious test of comparative racism: imagine a black or an Orthodox Jew, say, in that Korean's place and you imagine the theater's screen being ripped from the walls. Asians, like Arabs, remain safe targets for the movies' casual racism.[2]

The perpetuation of the caricature of racism is attributable to several complex and symbiotic causes. First, Asians often do not ascribe racist motivation to

From Karin Aguilar-San Juan, ed., *The State of Asian America.* Copyright © 1994 by South End Press, 116 Saint Botolph Street, Boston, MA 02115. Reprinted by permission of the publisher.

the discrimination they suffer, or they have felt that they could suffer the injustice of racial intolerance, in return for being later compensated by the fruits of economic success. Second, many Asians do not identify with other people of color. Sucheta Mazumdar posits that South Asians exclude themselves from efforts at political mobilization because of their rigid self-perception as Aryan, not as people of color.[3]

The final and most determinative factor, however, is the perspective that excludes the experiences of Asians (and other people of color) from the rubric of racism. Whites would deny us our right to speak out against majority prejudice, partially because it tarnishes their image of Asians as "model" minorities; other people of color would deny us the same because of monopolistic sentiments that they alone endure real racism.

For example, a poll conducted by *The Wall Street Journal* and NBC News revealed that "most American voters thought that Asian Americans did not suffer discrimination" but in fact received too many "special advantages."[4] Similarly, when crimes against Asians were on the rise in housing projects in San Francisco, the Housing Authority was loathe to label the crimes as racially motivated, despite the clear racial bias involved.[5] The deputy director of the Oakland Housing Authority's response to the issue was: "There may be some issues of race in it, but it's largely an issue of people who don't speak English feeling very isolated and not having a support structure to deal with what's happening to them."[6]

Other minorities reject Asian claims of racial victimization by pointing to economic privilege or perceived whiteness.[7] Such rejections even occur among different Asian groups. Chinese Americans in San Francisco attempted to classify Indians as white for the purposes of the California Minority Business Enterprise Statute: "If you are a white, male buyer in the City, all else being equal, would you buy from another Caucasian [i.e., Indian] or from a person of the Mongolian race?"[8]

The perspective of some people of color that there is a monopoly on oppression is debilitating to an effort at cross-ethnic coalition building. Our experiences are truly distinct, and our battles will in turn be unique; but if we are to achieve a community, we must begin to educate ourselves about our common denominator as well as our different histories and struggles. Ranking and diminishing relative subjugation and discrimination will only subvert our goal of unity. Naheed Islam expresses this sentiment in part of a poem addressed to African American women:

> Ah Sister! What have they done to us! Separated, segregated, unable to love one another, to cross the color line. I am not trying to cash in on your chains. I have my own. The rape, plunder, pain of dislocation is not yours alone. We have different histories, different voices, different ways of expressing our anger, but they used the same bullets to reach us all.[9]

The combination of white America refusing to acknowledge anti-Asian discrimination, and minority America minimizing anti-Asian discrimination, foists a formidable burden upon Asians: to combat our own internalized racial alienation, and to fight extrinsic racial classifications by both whites and other minority groups. It also renders overly simplistic those suggestions that if South Asians simply became "sufficiently politicized" they could overcome fragmentation in the struggle by people of color.[10]

As activists, a narrow-minded construct of racism impairs our political initiatives to use racism as a banner that unites all people of color in a common struggle.[11] The mainstream use of the word "racism" does not embrace Asian experiences, and we are not able to include ourselves in a definition that minimizes our encounters with racism. Participation in an antiracism campaign, therefore, is necessarily limited to those involved in a battle against racism that fits within the confines of the black/white paradigm, and conversely relegates anti-Asian racism to a lesser realm in terms of both exposure and horribleness.

We need to be more sophisticated in our analysis of racism, and less equivocal in our condemnation. In doing so, we will expand the base of opposition against anti-Asian racism, and forge an alliance against all its myriad forms. The first step in this process is for Asians to apply a racial analysis to our lives. This involves developing a greater understanding of how racism has operated socially and institutionally in this country against ourselves and other people of color, as well as acknowledging our own complicity; and secondly, accepting ourselves as people of color, with a shared history of being targeted as visibly Other. Only then can we act in solidarity with other efforts at ending racism.

Anti-Asian Racism: Fashioning a More Inclusive Paradigm

Racism takes on manifold creative and insidious expressions. Intra-racism, racism among different racial communities, and internalized racism all complicate an easy understanding of the phenomenon. My project here is to uncover shrouded racism perpetrated against Asians, particularly South Asians, in an attempt to broaden the use of the term.

Accent

It is only since 1992 that the Courts have begun to realize the legitimacy of discrimination based upon accent.[12] Immigrants, primarily those not of European descent,[13] suffer heightened racism because of their accents, including job discrimination and perpetual taunting and caricaturization. This is a severe and pervasive form of racism that is often not acknowledged as racist, or even offensive. Even among Asians there is a high degree of denial about the accent discrimination that is attributable to race. In a letter to the *New York Times*, an Asian man blithely encouraged immigrants to maintain their accents, without acknowledging the potential discrimination that we face, though he personally was "linguistically gifted" with an "American accent."

The man wrote, "Fellow immigrants, don't worry about the way you speak until Peter Jennings eliminates his Canadian accent."[14]

Accent discrimination is linked directly to American jingoism, and its accompanying virulently anti-immigrant undertones. In the aforementioned movie *Falling Down*, the protagonist has the following exchange with a Korean grocer:

Mr. Lee: Drink eighty-five cent. You pay or go.

Foster: This "fie," I don't understand a "fie." There's a "v" in the word. It's "fie-vah." You don't got "v's" in China?

Mr. Lee: Not Chinese. I'm Korean.

Foster: Whatever. You come to my country, you take my money, you don't even have the grace to learn my language?[15]

A person's accent is yet another symbol of otherness, but it is one that even U.S.-born minorities do not regard as a target for race-based discrimination. Language is implicitly linked with race, and must be treated as such.

Subversive Stereotyping

The myths that are built based on the commonality of race are meant to depersonalize and simplify people. To many, the Indian persona is that of a greedy, unethical, cheap immigrant. This stereotype is reflected in popular culture, where its appearance gives it credibility, thereby reinforcing the image. In the television comedy *The Simpsons*, a purportedly politically sensitive program, one of the characters is a South Asian owner of a convenience store. In one episode, in an effort to make a sale, he says, "I'll sell you expired baby food for a nickel off." Similarly, in the program *Star Trek: Deep Space Nine*, an alien race called the Firengi (Hindi for foreigner) are proprietors and sleazy entrepreneurs who take advantage of any opportunity for wealth, regardless of the moral cost.[16]

These constructs are reified in everyday life as people respond to Indians as if they have certain inherent qualities. Indian physicians, for example, are perceived as shoddy practitioners, who are greedy and disinterested in the health of their patients. In successful medical malpractice suits, Indian doctors are routinely required to pay higher penalties.[17] Similarly, in the now-famous "East Side Butcher" case, where an Indian doctor was convicted of performing illegal abortions, there was no racial analysis despite the fact that no one had been prosecuted for that crime in New York State since the early 1980s despite the fact that hundreds of illegal abortions are performed annually.[18] Another Indian doctor, less than two weeks later, was found guilty of violations in her mammography practice and fined the largest amount in New York State history in such a case. One can not help but wonder if these convictions were, at least in part, motivated by the stereotype of the Indian immigrant.[19]

The Onus

A white, liberal woman once asked my friend Ritu if she wasn't being overly sensitive for taking offense when people put their feet near her face (a high insult in Indian culture), when she could not fairly expect people to understand her culture. The onus is always on us, as outsiders, to explain and justify our culture while also being expected to know and understand majority culture.[20] Constant cultural slights about cows, bindis, and Gandhi are deemed appropriate by the majority while we are expected to subjugate expression of our culture to an understanding and acceptance of American culture. As another example, the swastika is an extremely common, ancient Hindu symbol. However, Hindus cannot wear or display the swastika in America because of Hitler's appropriation of it, and the expectation that we suppress our cultural symbols in an attempt to understand the affront to Jewish Americans. The assumption that it is our normative responsibility to make our culture secondary is racist because it suggests that one culture should be more free to express itself than another.

Religious Fanaticism

Eastern religions are commonly perceived as fraudulent, cultish, and fanatical; they are rarely perceived as equally legitimate as the spiritual doctrines of the Judeo-Christian tradition. The story of immaculate conception is accepted as plausible, while the multiarmed, multiheaded God is an impossible fantasy. Hinduism is portrayed as Hare Krishnas chanting with shaved heads and orange robes; and Islam is characterized as a rigid, violent, military religion. These hyperbolic characterizations are responsible for the fear of religion that causes local communities to refuse to permit places of worship in their neighborhoods.[21]

Western appropriation of Hindu terms reflects the perception of religion as charlatanical; the words have been reshaped through their use in the English language with an edge of irreverence or disbelief.

	Hindi Meaning	**English Use**
1. Guru	Religious teacher	Purported head; self-designated leader
2. Nirvana	Freedom from endless cycle of rebirth	Psychedelic ecstasy; drug-induced high
3. Pundit	Religious scholar	One with claimed knowledge
4. Mantra	A meditative tool; repetition of word or phrase	Mindless chant

Similarly, during times of political crisis (the 1991 Persian Gulf War; the February 1993 World Trade Center bombing), Islam has been the object of derision as a dangerous and destructive religion. After the suspects from the World Trade Center bombing were identified as Muslims, the media, the FBI, and mainstream America responded with gross anti-Muslim rhetoric. A professor in Virginia pointed out the ignorant conflation of the entire Muslim population into one extremist monolith:

> Not all Islamic revivalists are Islamic fundamentalists, and not all Islamic fundamentalists are political activists, and not all Islamic political activists are radical and prone to violence.[22]

Muslims have linked these characterizations of their religion to racial demonization.[23] The *New York Post* carried a headline entitled "The Face of Hate" with the face of a dark-skinned, bearded man of South Asian or Middle Eastern descent (the accused bomber). Similarly, the *New York Times* described the work of courtroom artists: "the defendant's beakish nose, hollow cheeks, cropped beard and the sideways tilt of his head."[24] In an Op-Ed piece in the *New York Times,* one Muslim responded to this description: "Such racial stereotyping serves nothing except to feed an existing hate and fear."[25]

Indicia of Culturalness

Indicia that identify us as Other are generally used as vehicles for discrimination; with East Asians, eye-shape provides the target for racial harassment. South Asians' unique attributes are warped for use as racist artillery: attire (we are towel heads and wear loin cloths and sheets); costume (we are dot-heads); and odor (we are unclean and smelly). Nila Gupta has written about the power of smell, and its identification of South Asians as targets for racist behavior:[26]

> it is spring
> she walks a strong walk
> but they are waiting
> for her in the air
> they can't smell curry and oil poori and dahl for breakfast
> scents they are trained to hate
> confusion
> like hunting dogs after prey
> enraged
> thrown off the scent
> by a river
> enraged
> was she trying to pass?

Gupta's poem recounts a moment of racial discrimination as it is manifested in the degradation of cultural characteristics. When we explore racism, and its effect upon different ethnic and cultural groups, we must also examine the unique ways that specific groups experience racism, and the more neutral proxies and buzzwords used to signify race.

Class Conflicts/Economic Envy

Racism and economic tension are inextricable because race discrimination against Asians has often been manifested as class competition, and vice versa. Since the early 1800s, when Asians became a source of cheap labor for the railroads, we have been an economic threat. As Asians have more recently been portrayed as the prosperous minority, the favored child of America, there has inevitably been sibling rivalry. When auto workers beat up Vincent Chin, was it Japanese competition in the auto industry or unbridled racism that motivated the murderers? When African Americans targeted Korean-owned stores in the riots in Los Angeles after the Rodney King verdict, was it the economic hardship of the inner city and perceived Asian advantages or was it simply racism? The answer is that race and class are inseparable because of the inherent difficulty in identifying the primary or motivating factor; any racial analysis must consider economic scapegoating as an avenue for racial harassment and racial victimization as an excuse for expressing economic tensions.

Conceptual and Perspective Differences

When an immigrant perspective clashes with a white American perspective, the conflict should be considered a racial one. Values such as individuality, privacy, confrontation, competition, and challenging the status quo are considered positive and healthy; however, these components of the liberal state are not necessarily virtues elsewhere. When Hawaiian children do not respond to competitive models of teaching, but thrive in group activities; and when Punjabi children defer to authority, rather than challenge their teachers out of intellectual "curiosity," they are harmed by their inability to function in an essentially and uniquely "American" world. Identifying the differences in perspective and lifestyle between Asian immigrants and Americans will help in recognizing arenas in which we will be at a cultural/racial disadvantage.[27]

A Case Study in Anti-Asian Racism: The Dotbusters of Jersey City

In early fall of 1986, Asian Indians in New Jersey were the targets of racial terrorism. Houses and businesses were vandalized, and graffitied with racial slurs, women had their saris pulled, Indians on the street were harassed and assaulted, and a 28-year-old man was beaten into a coma. The *Jersey Journal* received and printed a letter from a group calling themselves the Dotbusters threatening all Asian Indians in Jersey City, and promising to drive them out of Jersey City. Teenagers in Dickinson High School were found with Dotbuster IDs. In spite of the obvious danger to the community, the police were unresponsive and denied that any Indians should truly be concerned.

The most heinous incident was the murder of Navroze Mody, a 30-year-old Citicorp executive. Navroze was bludgeoned to death with bricks by a group of young Latinos. Long after he had lost consciousness, he was repeatedly propped up and beaten further. His white companion was not touched. Four of the eleven attackers were indicted for manslaughter; two of the indicted were also accused of assaulting two Indian students two weeks before killing Navroze.

Despite the context in which the murder occurred, the incident was not generally perceived as racist in motive by the mainstream, the press, or the Indian community. The ways that Indians were targeted made it convenient to try to find other names for their encounters with racism. Their experiences were unrecognizable as the caricature of racism, and there was a collective refusal to be expansive and open-minded in interpreting what was happening.

The tone for the general characterization of the crime as not racially motivated was set by Hudson County prosecutor Paul DePascale, assigned to Mody's case. Although he conceded that: "There was no apparent motive for the assault other than the fact that the victim was an Asian American,"[28] he refused to pursue criminal charges for racial bias.[29]

The press, a reflection of mainstream sentiment, was reluctant to label the crime as racial in nature. Even *The Village Voice*, a liberal newspaper, carried a story asking above the headline: "Was his [Navroze Mody's] murder racially motivated?"[30] One newspaper accepted the racial motive by qualifying it as a "new" racism/"new" bigotry. The defendants' supporters saw no racial animus against Indians in the crime, inquiring instead: "Do you think there would be justice if it was the other way around? If the Indian were alive and the Puerto Rican dead?"[31]

Indians-at-large were mystified about the source of the anti-Asian wave of violence and found it difficult to accept as pure racism. People looked for other potential justifications and alternative labels.[32] One community leader remarked, "We pay our taxes," and characterized the Indian community as "faultless immigrants" in an effort to distinguish Asian Indians from African Americans and Latinos.[33] A second-generation Indian lawyer characterized such attacks as "national origin" discrimination, rather than racism.[34] Such denial prevented Asian Indians from making the obvious connection to other groups victimized because of their race.

The uncommonness of the anti-Indian discrimination obfuscated the real racism that rested at its core. Economic envy was the most obvious nonracial analysis proffered for escalating crimes against Asians. One Jersey City resident commented: "I've been in this country all my life and they come here and plop down $200,000 for a house."[35] Part of the infamous Dotbuster letter contained similar comments to journalist Ronald Leir: "You say that Indians are good businessmen. Well I suppose if I had 15 people living in my apartment I'd be able to save money too."[36]

Another major source of attack was traditional Indian attire. According to one community leader: "The number two factor for racism is that we look different."[37] Similarly, the hate group, the Dotbusters, takes its name from the cosmetic dot, or bindi, worn by many Indian women on their foreheads.

Finally, Indian languages and residential clustering create a sense of exclusive cohesiveness that threatens Jersey City's non-Asian communities. Anything that represented the insular-seeming culture was the object of harrassment and hatred. Indian religion and cuisine were mocked, and Indians were repeatedly characterized as smelly (due to the lingering scents of cooking spice).

Despite the heinousness of the crime, the Mody case, and anti-Indian violence, did not receive sufficient public attention or outrage. During the same time that the case was being tried, the Howard Beach case[38] was in the headlines of all major newspapers. Of the four Howard Beach attackers, three received manslaughter convictions; of the eleven attackers in the Mody case, three were convicted of aggravated assault, and one of simple assault. Perhaps it was because Asian Indians did not know how to employ the political system that the verdicts returned did not fit the crimes committed. Perhaps it was because the attackers were also minorities. But the main reason why justice was not served was because the racism that Indians were enduring did not fit the neat, American paradigm for racial violence.

In 1993, we can no longer see the world in black and white, where "those who don't fit the color scheme become shadows."[39] Lessons from our battles with bigotry should convince us that our understanding of it and the machinery we have built to fight it are hopelessly obsolete. Denying the richness of our community of people of color ultimately undermines the objective of unity, and hampers our political work combating racism. During the late '80s, the left fought to find a common ground for people of color to coalesce; however, it is now the time to refine our collective mission to truly encompass the range of diversity among us. Any movement forged upon the principles of equality and tolerance can only be legitimate if it represents its margins.

NOTES

1. While the film generated much debate about the possible ironic intent of its stereotyping, the reactions of moviegoers showed that the irony was lost on most audiences.

2. Godfrey Cheshire, complete citation for article not available.

3. Mazumdar, Sucheta, "Race and Racism: South Asians in the United States," *Frontiers of Asian American Studies.*

4. Polner, Murray, "Asian-Americans Say They Are Treated Like Foreigners," *The New York Times,* March 7, 1993, Section B, p. 1.

5. Racial slurs were rampant (including "Go home, Chinaman" and accent harassment) and tension between the Asian and African American community was worsening.

The fact that the perpetrators were African American might have contributed to the general reluctance to characterize these crimes as racially motivated. Again, this reflects an inability, or an unwillingness, to intellectually digest racism between non-white races, as it falls outside of the narrow black/white paradigm.

6. Chin, Steven A., "Asians Terrorized in Housing Projects," *San Francisco Examiner*, January 17, 1993, p. B1.

7. Witness this morsel of divisiveness: In Miami, where large Latino and African American populations coexist, a Cuban woman was sworn in as State Attorney General. Many in the African American community were dismayed by this decision, and responded by stripping Cubans of their "rank" as a minority. One black lawyer commented: "Cubans are really 'white people whose native language is Spanish'" and others agreed that Cuban Americans should be "disqualified because they have higher income levels than other minorities." Certainly there is complexity in this conflict; however, the net result is that people who could be in alliance based on race are divided. Rohter, Larry, "Black-Cuban Rift Extends to Florida Law School," *The New York Times*, March 19, 1993, p. B16L.

8. Transcript of San Francisco Board of Supervisors Special Session of Economic and Social Policy Committee, April 30, 1991.

9. Islam, Naheed, "Untitled," from *Smell This*, an official publication of The Center for Racial Education, Berkeley, CA, 1991.

10. Mazumdar, *supra* at p. 36.

11. Here, and throughout this chapter, I am operating within the constructs of our existing political reality. I am not addressing the normative question of whether people of color should be in coalition against racism, but given that it has been our primary organizing principle, how can we be more effective and inclusive?

12. Interestingly, the case was brought by the EEOC while under the tenure of Joy Cherian, a naturalized Indian. The Commission's 1980 guidelines covering this type of discrimination were written by an Indian, and the case was brought by an Indian plaintiff. Is that what it takes to obtain recognition of the racism that we experience?

13. The Executive Assistant for the Commissioner noted: "If an employer has an applicant who speaks with a French accent . . . or with an English accent, they say, 'How cute.' But if he speaks with a Hispanic accent they say, 'What's wrong with this guy?'"

14. Letter to the editor from Yan Hong Krompacky, "Immigrants, Don't Be in Such a Hurry to Shed Your Accents," *The New York Times*, March 4, 1993.

15. Foster then proceeds to demolish Mr. Lee's grocery store with a bat, in much the same way that Japanese cars were hatefully demolished just before Vincent Chin's death.

16. That such stereotypes exist in two programs that are perceived as being among the more progressive on television is itself indicative of the continuing denial that anti-Asian racism exists.

17. According to several medical malpractice attorneys.

18. This was exacerbated further by the fact that Dr. Hayat's sentence was so severe that even the District Attorney's Office had expected less and was "pleasantly surprised." Perez-Pena, Richard, "Prison Term for Doctor Convicted in Abortions," *The New York Times*, June 15, 1993, p. B1.

19. These stereotypes find expression everywhere. I was haggling for a pair of earrings in Times Square, and the vendor asked me if I was Indian. When I replied that I was, he responded, "Oh, I should have guessed. Indians don't want to take anything out of their pockets."

20. In an effort to better integrate into American culture, and mend relations with ethnic groups in New York City, Korean grocers are taking seminars to learn to smile more frequently, supposedly rare in their culture. *The New York Times*, March 22, 1993.

21. "It's the Hindus! Circle the Zoning Laws." Viewpoint by Bob Weiner, *Newsday*, April 26, 1993, p. 40.

22. Steinfeld, Peter, "Many Varieties of Fundamentalism," *The New York Times*, no date. An even better response was: [the World Trade bomber suspect's] "variety of fundamentalism was not any more representative of Islam than the people in Waco are representative of [mainstream] Christianity." *Id.*

23. Op Ed Letter to Editor, "Don't Let Trade Center Blast Ignite Witch Hunt," March 23, 1993.

24. "Surprises in a Crowded Courtroom," Moustafa Bayami, March 5, 1993.

25. *Ibid.*

26. Gupta, Nila, "So She Could Walk," from *The Best of Fireweed*; Women's Press, Canada (1986).

27. Many Asians find themselves in low-ranking jobs in the corporate world because their skills have little application in the old boy cultural network. This is due in part to different concepts of authority and competition, as much as it is pure racial bigotry. My point is that the two should be viewed together to truly understand the full flourish of racism.

28. Vicente, Raul Jr., "Cops Arrest Two as Dotbusters," *Gold Coast*, March 24–March 31, 1988, p. 4.

29. His failure to label this as a racially motivated crime may in fact be racially motivated. In March of 1988 there was opposition by the Inter Departmental Minority Police Action Council in Jersey City to his appointment as the city's acting police director because of alleged discrimination against a black woman officer. "Minority Cops Blast Director," *Gold Coast*, March 31, 1988, p. 7.

30. "Racial Terror on The Gold Coast," *The Village Voice*, January 26, 1988.

31. *Jersey Journal*, March 1, 1988.

32. The collective denial precluded group solutions. Around the same time in Elmhurst 25 African American and Indian families were "preyed" upon in Queens. However, Indians were uninterested in forging an alliance with the African American community to fight ongoing racial harassment. Pais, Arthur, "Long Island Families Were Apathetic and Tearful When Harassed," *India Abroad*, July 31, 1987, p. 1.

33. Walt, Vivienne, "A New Racism Gets Violent in New Jersey," *Newsday*, April 6, 1988, p. 5.

34. Spoken at the Strategy Session for the case of Dr. Kaushal Sharan, March 28, 1993, by a representative of the *Indian American Magazine*.

35. Walt, Vivienne, "A New Racism Gets Violent in New Jersey," *Newsday*, April 6, 1988, p. 5.

36. Letter to *Jersey Journal* on August 5, 1987.

37. Walt, Vivienne, "A New Racism Gets Violent in New Jersey," *Newsday*, April 6, 1988, p. 5.

38. A 1986 attack by white youths in Queens where a group of African Americans were stranded; one person died when he was chased onto a highway by the mob.

39. Zia, Helen, "Another American Racism," *The New York Times*, letter to the editor.

3

Racial Relations Becoming More Complex across Country

Jonathan Tilove

HOUSTON   As a trouble-shooter with the U.S. Justice Department, Efrain Martinez negotiates racial peace in and around America's fourth-largest city.

There are, of course, the classic black-and-white or brown-and-white conflicts. But often now, it is blacks and browns who are butting heads over jobs and power. And increasingly, Martinez finds himself mediating disputes involving peoples who barely existed here 20 years ago.

The Houston area, for example, has one of the nation's largest Vietnamese communities, and over the years Martinez, in his sotto voce style, has defused violent confrontations between Vietnamese fishermen and the Ku Klux Klan, between Vietnamese merchants and black customers and between Vietnamese and Latino residents of the same condominium.

In the past year, he even brokered a truce between Vietnamese and Chinese members of the board of a new Tao temple, prompting one member of the board to gush, "You a hero. You stop a war."

Nationally, and especially in those cities like Houston that are magnets for immigrants, race and ethnic relations are becoming more complexly contentious. In part it is simple math: Greater diversity yields more diverse points of conflict. But a wealth of survey research indicates that inter-minority hostilities and negative attitudes often are more pronounced than those that exist between whites and minorities, though the more polite white attitudes may be as much a function of more affluent distance as meaningful commitment.

Still, Asians in Los Angeles are far more likely than whites to view most blacks and Hispanics as unintelligent, while most Hispanics and Asians—but only a minority of whites—think blacks prefer welfare to self-sufficiency. In New York City, Hispanics and Asians are more likely than whites to think blacks provoke hostility.

In return, blacks more than whites in both New York and Los Angeles consider Asians difficult to get along with. In Houston, blacks rate their relationship with Asians as worse than their relationship with whites.

From *The Star-Ledger*, December 26, 1996. Reprinted by permission of Newhouse News Services, Washington, DC.

"If we posit the original Rodney King question—'Can we all get along?'—the answer is a resounding no," says James Johnson Jr., a professor of business, sociology and geography at the University of North Carolina at Chapel Hill, and the former director of the Center for the Study of Urban Poverty at UCLA.

"I think we're really headed toward more intolerance," says Johnson, who is black.

Diversity's Effect

Not everyone is so sure.

University of Houston sociologist Nestor Rodriguez says it remains to be seen whether Houston's transformation from a city that was more than half Anglo (which is what they call whites here) in 1980, to one that will be 29 percent Anglo, 25 percent black, 39 percent Hispanic and 7 percent Asian by the year 2000, will prove its doing or undoing.

"I have a sense of Houston becoming better," says Rodriguez. He takes hope from the fact that his survey this year of Houston's black and Hispanic communities discovered black ambivalence—rather than one-sided anger—about immigration and people speaking Spanish at work.

Houston, with the largest black population and largest Hispanic immigrant population of any city in the South, has enjoyed relative racial calm. People variously credit its size and sprawl, its deep-seated conservatism and the almost small-town relationships of the leaders of its various racial and ethnic communities. They also credit the deft capacity of the oligarchy that has always run America's freest enterprise city to accommodate as necessary to keep a lid on.

"Our city fathers have always been tremendously successful at smelling a rat, calling it a rat, and driving the rat away," says Barbara Lange, a black woman who serves on the board of the Houston Inter-Ethnic Forum, formed to foster city-wide dialogue on these issues.

Rodriguez thinks Johnson's pessimism is premature, a consequence of looking at race relations through the fractured prism of Los Angeles.

But Johnson says that is not a prism but a window on the future.

"Los Angeles is the cutting edge and leading end of this wave of things to come," he warns.

That whites should now express the most benign racial attitudes of any group may be the final irony for a nation whose racial order was built on bedrock notions of white supremacy, a legacy that still heavily conditions the way new immigrants encounter and evaluate blacks. But there is a logical explanation.

Tolerance of the Affluent

A 1994 National Conference [of Christians and Jews] survey conducted nationally by Louis Harris confirmed that minorities were more likely to stereotype one another than whites were. But, it noted a complementary pattern: "The affluent are more tolerant."

It may be a function of education and sophistication. But it may also be that affluent whites living in comfortable suburbs or gated communities, with children ensconced in good public or private schools, can afford greater tolerance.

One in five whites exited Houston's city limits in the 1980s. Only about one in 10 students in the Houston Independent School District are white. In his annual survey of ethnic relations in Houston, Rice University sociologist Stephen Klineberg discovered that whites are increasingly likely to support principles of ethnic tolerance, and yet oppose government programs designed to support greater social and economic equality.

"Anglos don't support educating minorities of any color," says Rosemary Covalt, a Hispanic activist deeply involved in school politics. Instead, she says, "Anglos play blacks against Hispanics and Hispanics against blacks."

Yet Covalt acknowledges that most of her scrapes are with blacks over control of the schools, and those fights can be quite ugly, though she finds them more satisfying than contending with Anglo reserve.

"Anglos don't vent. They can't, they won't, they don't," says Covalt, though she was pleased to hear cries of white anger emanating from the affluent suburb of Kingwood when it was recently annexed by the city of Houston. "I've never seen so many angry Anglos in my life," says a delighted Covalt.

Dynamics of Friction

Efrain Martinez sketches out Houston's new racial dynamics on a paper napkin. At the top he writes "Heaven," and underlines it. Just below the line he writes, "whites," and at the very bottom of the napkin, he writes, "Hispanics."

"And here," he says, placing his pen point mid-napkin, "are blacks." He explains that many Hispanics see blacks standing between them and their share of public jobs and political power.

The friction with Hispanics is understandable, says Michael Harris, a popular black radio talk host on KCOH in Houston, who often uses his show to foster interethnic dialogue. "They are fighting for the same things we are fighting for. White people have the whole pie."

In the private sector, blacks see immigrants taking jobs that once might have been theirs. The fundamental problem, says Klineberg, is that immigrants are arriving in a city "increasingly unable to produce enough well-paid jobs for the workers who are already here."

The story of South Central Los Angeles, says James Johnson, is immigrants settling in a black community from which the good, industrial jobs have vanished. The employers that remain prefer cheaper, more pliant Hispanic immigrant labor for jobs at the bottom of the economy. And ethnic networks keep those jobs "in the family."

Even a term like "Hispanic immigrant labor," though, obscures more than it illuminates.

At the day labor site in the heavily immigrant neighborhood of Gulfton, more than 200 men gather daily in search of landscaping or construction jobs. Most all the laborers are Hispanic but, says Gonzalo Fernandez, a neighborhood organizer who helps at the site, there are distinct differences among them.

He explains: "The Guatemalans more easily agree to low wages. They come from the most conflicted area of Guatemala, they suffered a lot and they don't want to put up more of a fight than they already put up with in their home country. The Hondurans get the most frustrated because they don't want to work for less than $6 or $7."

As opposed to the black–Hispanic competition, the Asian–black (and sometimes Asian–Latino) relationship in Houston or New York or Los Angeles is often defined by the merchant–customer interaction, which Queens College sociologist Pyong Gap Min says is made to order for negative stereotyping.

Min, the author of a new book, *Caught in the Middle: Korean Merchants in America's Multiethnic Cities*, says those Korean merchants, most arriving from middle-class backgrounds in a thoroughly homogenous country, suddenly find themselves working in poor, black communities with high levels of violence, family breakup and other problems.

Min's New York City survey found that most Korean merchants believed that black people were generally less intelligent, less honest and more criminally oriented than white people.

That same survey found that nearly two-thirds of native-born blacks in New York thought the Korean businesses drained resources from their community, and that about one in five blacks thought Koreans to be a "rude and nasty people."

In Houston, as well, says Rodney Penn, head of Houston's Black United Front, relations at the corner store are defining. "That's the face of the Asian community," he says.

Helping Asian Merchants

Glenda Joe, a chain-smoking Asian-American activist (she is of Irish and Chinese descent) with a blond streak and a Texas twang, wrote a handbook detailing how Asian merchants can get along better with black customers.

"They may not come from a culture where the customer is always right," explains Joe, who grew up working at her father's store in the black community. He knew all about extending credit and developing friendships.

But Victoria Hyonchu Kwon, who has written a book about Koreans in Houston, says it is a very hard-working, insular, self-sufficient community and, as a rule they are just not that interested in getting to know poor black people, or any other non-Koreans for that matter.

Most searing on the psyche of the immigrant community, of course, are the many occasions on which Asian businesses in the black community have been robbed in Houston and other cities, with sometimes fatal consequences.

"Everybody knows someone who has been killed," says Joe.

Dr. Tinh Van Tran, the president of the Vietnamese Community of Houston and Vicinity, who has worked closely with Efrain Martinez resolving many disputes involving his people, recalls a recent occasion when he slowed down to pick up some hitchhikers who were black.

As he slowed, though, Tran recalls, "my mind remembered that my adopted sister got robbed, got beaten." The assailant was black. "I put my foot on the accelerator," he says, acknowledging the unfairness.

Joe Feagin, a leading scholar on race and racism, says immigrants arrive with a melange of home-grown and imported prejudices.

"Latin Americans have a great deal of racism and discrimination against darker-skinned people, Indians and those of African descent, even though their whole ideology is that they don't," he says.

But, he says, you don't have to have lived a day in the United States to have already been deeply influenced by the racial images promulgated in its media.

For example, Feagin says, a Taiwanese graduate student of his at the University of Florida interviewed people in rural Taiwan and found, "They had negative attitudes toward African-Americans even though they hadn't met one. They pick it up from American media."

And, on their arrival in America, Feagin says existing racist tendencies "are immediately reinforced."

"That is the trend," says the Rev. Alcides Alvarenga, the young Salvadoran pastor of a mission church in Gulfton. "We tend to adopt [white American] attitudes and prejudices."

But, he adds, "we do not condone that."

In the end, this attention to skin color and racial identity can be especially vexing for those who don't fit any of the conventional categories.

Romulo and Eva Sandoval are Garifunas from Honduras, the descendants of the survivors of a ship-wrecked slave ship on its way from Africa to the New World.

In Honduras, they say, their racial and ethnic identity was not particularly problematic. But in Houston, they find themselves caught in the middle of the racial crossfire.

White Americans mostly see them as black. That means that at their mostly white church some people assume that they must have become associated with the church through an affiliated drug abuse program. A woman asks Eva, a very well-educated and well-spoken English teacher, whether she works at K-Mart or Wal-Mart. The well-meaning pastor takes pains to inform parishioners that the Sandovals are from good Honduran families.

At the same time, Romulo says, American-born blacks view them as "not really black." And Eva recalls how two Mexican-American women who were her best friends in college heartbreakingly left her out of their wedding parties.

Eva's older sister came to Texas when she was two. "Ask her race and she says, 'black.'" Eva arrived when she was seven. "I'm just Hispanic."

"I find myself being very lonely," says Eva. "I think I have the best of both worlds but when I try to find someone like me I can't find anybody. Have you read that story. 'The Man Without a Country'? Sometimes I feel like that."

4

Racism and Sexism

Manning Marable

What is racism? How does the system of racial discrimination that people of color experience today differ from the type of discrimination that existed in the period of Jim Crow, or legal racial segregation? How is the rich spectrum of cultural groups affected by practices of discrimination within America's "democratic society" today? What parallels can be drawn between sexism, racism, and other types of intolerance, such as anti-Semitism, anti-Arabism, homophobia, and handicapism? What kinds of national and international strategies are needed for a multicultural democracy in the whole of American society and throughout the Western world? And finally, what do we need to do to not just see beyond our differences, but to realize our commonalities and deepen each other's efforts to seize our full freedom and transform the nature of society?

Let's begin with point one: Racism is the system of ignorance, exploitation, and power used to oppress African Americans, Latinos, Asians, Pacific Americans, Native Americans, and other people on the basis of ethnicity, culture, mannerisms, and color. Point two: When we try to articulate an agenda of multicultural democracy, we run immediately into the stumbling block of stereotypes—the device at the heart of every form of racism today. Stereotypes are at work when people are not viewed as individuals with unique cultural and social backgrounds, with different religious traditions and ethnic identities, but as two-dimensional characters bred from the preconceived attitudes, half-truths, ignorance, and fear of closed minds. When seen through a stereotype, a person isn't viewed as a bona fide human being, but as an object onto which myths and half-truths are projected.

This article appeared as "Racism and Multicultural Democracy" in Chester Hartman, ed., *Double Exposure: Poverty and Race in America* (Armonk, NY: M. E. Sharpe, 1997), pp. 151–160.

There are many ways that we see stereotypes degrade people, but perhaps most insidious is the manner in which stereotypes deny people their own history. In a racist society like our own, people of color are not viewed as having their own history or culture. Everything must conform to the so-called standards of white bourgeois society. Nothing generated by people of color is accepted as historically original, dynamic, or creative. This even applies to the way in which people of color are miseducated about their own history. Indeed, the most insidious element of stereotypes is how people who are oppressed themselves begin to lose touch with their own traditions of history, community, love, celebration, struggle, and change.

In the 1980s we saw a proliferation of racist violence, most disturbingly on college campuses. Why the upsurge of racism? Why was it occurring in the 1980s, and why does this disease continue to spread into the 1990s? How is it complicit with other systemic crises we now face within the political, economic, and social structures of our society?

First, we need to be clear about how we recognize racism. Racism is never accidental within a social structure or institution. It is the systematic exploitation of people of color in the process of production and labor, the attempt to subordinate our cultural, social, educational, and political life. The key concepts here are subordinate and systemic. The dynamics of racism attempt to inflict a subordinate position for people of color.

Racism in the 1990s means lower pay for equal work. It means a process that sustains inequality within the income structure of this country. Institutional racism in America's economic system today means that the rhetoric of equal opportunity in the marketplace remains, in effect, a hoax for most people of color. Between 1973 and 1993, the real average earnings for young Hispanic males age eighteen to twenty-nine declined by 27 percent. For African American males in this age group, the decline was a devastating 48 percent.

Pushing Drugs

What else intensifies racism and inequality in the 1990s? Drugs. We are witnessing the complete disintegration of America's inner cities, the home of millions of Latinos and Blacks. We see the daily destructive impact of gang violence inside our neighborhoods and communities, which is directly attributable to the fact that for twenty years the federal government has done little to address the crisis of drugs inside the ghetto and the inner city. For people of color, crack addiction has become part of the new urban slavery, a method of disrupting lives and regulating masses of young people who would otherwise be demanding jobs, adequate health care, better schools, and control of their own communities. Is it accidental that this insidious cancer has been unleashed within the very poorest urban neighborhoods, and that the police concentrate on petty street dealers rather than on those who actually control and profit from the drug traffic? How is it possible that thousands and thousands of pounds of illegal drugs can be transported throughout the country, in airplanes, trucks, and automobiles, to hundreds of central distribution centers with thousands of employees, given the ultra-high-tech surveillance and intelligence capacity of law enforcement officers? How, unless crack presents a systemic form of social control?

The struggle we have now is not simply against the system. It's against the kind of insidious violence and oppressive behavior that people of color carry out against each other. What I'm talking about is the convergence between the utility of a certain type of commodity—addictive narcotics—and economic and social problems that are confronting the system. That is, the redundancy, the unemployment of millions of people of color, young women and men, living in our urban centers. The criminal justice system represents one type of social control. Crack and addictive narcotics represent another. If you're doing organizing within the Black community, it becomes impossible to get people and families to come out to your community center when there are crack houses all around the building. It becomes impossible to continue political organizing when people are afraid for their own lives. This is the new manifestation of racism in which we see a form of social control existing in our communities, the destruction of social institutions, and the erosion of people's ability to fight against the forms of domination that continuously try to oppress them.

Women's Freedom

How do we locate the connections between racism and sexism? There are many direct parallels, both in theory and in practice, between these two systems of domination. A good working definition of sexism is the subordination of women's social, cultural, political, and educational rights as human beings and the unequal distribution of power and resources between women and men based on gender. Sexism is a subsocial dynamic, like racism, in that the dynamic is used to subordinate one part of the population to another.

How does sexism function in the economic system? Women experience it through the lack of pay equity—the absence of equal pay for comparable work performed by women and men on the job. Sexism exists in the stratification of the vocational hierarchy by gender, which keeps women disproportionately at the bottom. The upper levels of the corporations are dominated by white wealthy males, as is the ownership of productive forces and property. Women consequently have less income mobility and frequently are defined as "homemakers," a vocation for which there is absolutely no financial compensation, despite sixty to eighty hours of work per week.

Sexism within cultural and social institutions means the domination of males in decision-making positions. Males control the majority of newspapers, the film industry, radio, and television. Sexist stereotypes of both males and females are thus perpetuated through the dominant cultural institutions, advertising and broadcast media.

In political institutions, sexism translates into an unequal voice and influence within the government. The overwhelming majority of seats in the Congress, state legislatures, courts, and city councils are controlled by white men. The United States has one of the lowest percentages of women represented within its national legislature among Western democratic societies.

And finally, like racism, the wire that knots sexist mechanisms together, that perpetuates women's inequality within the fabric of the social institution, is violence. Rape, spouse abuse, and sexual harassment on the job are all essential to the perpetuation of a sexist society. For the sexist, violence is the necessary and logical part of an unequal, exploitative relationship. Rape and sexual harassment are therefore not accidental to the structure of gender relations within a sexist order. This is why progressives must first target the issue of violence against women, in the struggle for human equality and a nonsexist environment. This is why we must fight for women's right to control their own bodies.

Sexism and racism combine with class exploitation to produce a three-edged mode of oppression for women of color. Economically, African American, Latina, and Native American women are far below white women in terms of income, job security, and job mobility. The median income of a Black woman who is also a single parent with children is below twelve thousand dollars annually. One-third of all Black people live below the federal government's poverty line. And more than three-quarters of that number are Black women and their children.

Black and Latina women own virtually no sizable property; they head no major corporations; they only rarely are the heads of colleges and universities; they possess no massive real estate holdings; they are not on the Supreme Court; few are in the federal court system; they are barely represented in Congress; and they represent tiny minorities in state legislatures or in the leadership of both major parties. Only a fractional percentage of the attorneys and those involved in the criminal justice system are African American women. It is women of color, not white women, who are overwhelmingly harassed by police, arrested without cause, and who are the chief victims of all types of crimes.

Sexism and racism are not perpetuated biologically like a disease or drug addiction; both behaviors are learned within a social framework and have absolutely no ground in hereditary biology. They are perpetuated by stereotypes, myths, and irrational fears that are rooted in a false sense of superiority. Both sexism and racism involve acts of systemic coercion—job discrimination, legal domination, and political underrepresentation. And both sexism and racism may culminate in acts of physical violence.

Education

What are some other characteristics of the new racism we are now encountering? What we see in general is a duplicitous pattern that argues that African Americans and other people of color are moving forward, whereas their actual material conditions are being pushed back. Look at America's education system. The number of doctoral degrees being granted to Blacks, for example, is falling. The Reagan administration initiated budget cuts in education, replacing government grants with loans, and deliberately escalated unemployment for low-income people, making it difficult to afford tuition at professional schools. Between 1981 and 1995, the actual percentage of young African American adults between the ages eighteen and twenty-six enrolled in colleges and universities declined by more than 20 percent. A similar crisis is occurring in our public school systems. In many cities, the dropout rate for nonwhite high school students exceeds 40 percent. Across the United States, more than fifteen hundred teenagers of color drop out of school every day. And many of those who stay in school do not receive adequate training to prepare them for the realities of today's high-tech labor market.

Despite the curricular reforms of the 1970s and 1980s, American education retains a character of elitism and cultural exclusivity. The overwhelming majority of faculty at American colleges are white males: less than 5 percent of all college faculty today are African Americans. The basic pattern of elitism and racism in colleges conforms to the dynamics of Third World colonialism. At nearly all white academic institutions, the power relationship between whites as a group and people of color is unequal. Authority is invested in the hands of a core of largely white male administrators, bureaucrats, and influential senior faculty. The board of trustees or regents is dominated by white, conservative, affluent males. Despite the presence of academic courses on minorities, the vast majority of white students take few or no classes that explore the heritage or cultures of non-Western peoples or domestic minorities. Most courses in the humanities and social sciences focus narrowly on topics or issues from the Western capitalist experience and minimize the centrality and importance of non-Western perspectives. Finally, the university or college divorces itself from the pressing concerns, problems, and debates that relate to Blacks, Hispanics, or even white working-class people. Given this structure and guiding philosophy, it shouldn't surprise us that many talented nonwhite students fail to achieve in such a hostile environment.

The Color of Our Prisons

The racial oppression that defines U.S. society today is most dramatically apparent in the criminal justice system and the prisons. Today, about half the inmates in prisons and jails, more than 750,000 people, are African Americans. One-quarter of all African American males in their twenties today are in prison, on probation or parole, or awaiting trial. According to a 1991 survey, about one-third of all prisoners were unemployed at the time of their arrest, while two-thirds of all prisoners have less than a high-school-level education and few marketable skills. The prisons of our country have become vast warehouses for the poor and unemployed, for low-wage workers and the poorly educated, and, most especially, for Latino and African American males.

Toward a Multicultural Democracy

So what do we need in this country? How do we begin to redefine the nature of democracy? Not as a thing, but as a process. Democracy is a dynamic concept. African Americans twenty-five years ago did not have the right to eat in many restaurants, we couldn't sit down in the front seats of buses or planes, we couldn't vote in the South, we weren't allowed to use public toilets or drink from water fountains marked "For Whites Only." All of that changed through struggle, commitment, and an understanding that democracy is not something you do once every four years when you vote. It's something that you live every single day.

* * *

5

Patriarchy

Allan Johnson

What is patriarchy? A society is patriarchal to the degree that it is *male-dominated, male-identified,* and *male-centered.* It also involves as one of its key aspects the oppression of women. Patriarchy is male-dominated in that positions of authority—political, economic, legal, religious, educational, military, domestic—are generally reserved for men. Heads of state, corporate CEOs and board members, religious leaders, school principals, members of legislatures at all levels of government, senior law partners, tenured full professors, generals and admirals, and even those identified as "head of household" all tend to be male under patriarchy. When a woman finds her way into such positions, people tend to be struck by the exception to the rule, and wonder how she'll measure up against a man in the same position. It's a test we rarely apply to men ("I wonder if he'll be as good a president as a woman would be") except, perhaps, on those rare occasions when men venture into the devalued domestic and other "caring" work most women do. Even then, men's failure to measure up can be interpreted as a sign of superiority, a trained incapacity that actually protects their privileged status ("You change the diaper, I'm no good at that sort of thing").

From Allan Johnson, *The Gender Knot: Unraveling Our Patriarchal Legacy* (Philadelphia: Temple University Press, 1997), pp. 3–23.

In the simplest sense, male dominance creates power differences between men and women. It means, for example, that men can claim larger shares of income and wealth. It means they can shape culture in ways that reflect and serve men's collective interests by, for example, controlling the content of films and television shows, passing laws that allow husbands to rape their wives, or adjudicating rape and sexual harassment cases in ways that put the victim rather than the defendant on trial. Male dominance also promotes the idea that men are superior to women. In part this occurs because we don't distinguish between the superiority of *positions* in a hierarchy and the kinds of people who usually occupy them.[1] This means that if superior positions are occupied by men, it's a short leap to the idea that *men* must be superior. If presidents, generals, legislators, priests, popes, and corporate CEOs are all men (with a few token women as exceptions to prove the rule), then men as a group become identified with superiority even though most men aren't powerful in their individual lives. In this sense, *every* man's standing in relation to women is enhanced by the male monopoly over authority in patriarchal societies.

Patriarchal societies are *male-identified* in that core cultural ideas about what is considered good, desirable, preferable, or normal are associated with how we think about men and masculinity. The simplest example of this is the still widespread use of male pronouns and nouns to represent people in general. When we routinely refer to human beings as "man" or to doctors as "he," we construct a symbolic world in which men are in the foreground and women in the background, marginalized as outsiders and exceptions to the rule.[2] (This practice can back people into some embarrassingly ridiculous corners, as in the anthropology text that described man as a "species that breast-feeds his young.") But male identification amounts to much more than this, for it also takes men and men's lives as the standard for defining what is normal. The idea of a career, for example, with its 60-hour weeks, is defined in ways that assume the career-holder has something like a wife at home to perform the vital support work of taking care of children, doing laundry, and making sure there's a safe, clean, comfortable haven for rest and recuperation from the stress of the competitive male-dominated world. Since women generally don't have wives, they find it harder to identify with and prosper within this male-identified model.

Another aspect of male identification is the cultural description of masculinity and the ideal man in terms that closely resemble the core values of society as a whole. These include qualities such as control, strength, efficiency, competitiveness, toughness, coolness under pressure, logic, forcefulness, decisiveness, rationality, autonomy, self-sufficiency, and control over any emotion that interferes with other core values (such as invulnerability).[3] These male-identified qualities are associated with the work valued most in most patriarchal societies—such as business, politics, war, athletics, law, and medicine—because this work has been organized in ways that require such qualities for success. In contrast, qualities such as inefficiency, cooperation, mutuality, equality, sharing, compassion, caring, vulnerability, a readiness to negotiate and compromise, emotional expressiveness, and intuitive and other nonlinear ways of thinking are all devalued *and* culturally associated with femininity and femaleness.

Of course, femaleness isn't devalued entirely. Women are often prized for their beauty as objects of male sexual desire, for example, but as such they are often possessed and controlled in ways that ultimately devalue them. There is also a powerful cultural romanticizing of women in general and mothers in particular, but it is a tightly focused sentimentality (as on Mother's Day or Secretaries' Day) that has little effect on how women are regarded and treated on a day-to-day basis. And, like all sentimentality, it doesn't have much weight when it comes to actually doing something to support women's lives by, for example, providing effective and affordable child day-care facilities for working mothers, or family leave policies that allow working women to attend to the caring functions for which we supposedly value them so highly.

Because patriarchy is male-identified, when most women look out on the world they see themselves reflected as women in a few narrow areas of life such as "caring" occupations (teaching, nursing, child care) and personal relationships. To see herself as a leader, for example, a woman must first get around the fact that leadership itself has been gendered through its identification with maleness and masculinity as part of patriarchal culture. While a man might have to learn to see himself as a manager, a woman has to be able to see herself as a *woman* manager who can succeed in spite of the fact that she isn't a man. As a result, any woman who dares strive for standing in the world beyond the sphere of caring relationships must choose between two very different cultural images of who she is and ought to be. For her to assume real public power—as in politics, corporations, or her church—she must resolve a contradiction between her culturally based identity as a woman, on the one hand, and the male-identified *position* that she occupies on the other. For this reason, the more powerful a woman is under patriarchy, the more "unsexed" she becomes in the eyes of others as her female cultural identity recedes beneath the mantle of male-identified power and the masculine images associated with it. With men the effect is just the opposite: the more powerful they are, the more aware we are of their maleness. Power looks sexy on men but not on women.

But for all the pitfalls and limitations, some women do make it to positions of power. What about Margaret Thatcher, Queen Elizabeth I, Catherine the Great, Indira Gandhi, and Golda Meir? Doesn't their power contradict the idea that patriarchy is male-dominated? The answer is that patriarchy can accommodate a limited number of powerful women so long as the society retains its essential patriarchal character, especially in being male-identified.[4] Although some individual women have wielded great power, it has always been in societies organized on a patriarchal model. Each woman was surrounded by powerful men—generals, cabinet ministers, bishops, and wealthy aristocrats or businessmen—whose collective interests she supported and without whom she could not have ruled as she did.

And not one of these women could have achieved and held her position without embracing core patriarchal values. Indeed, part of what makes these women stand out as so exceptional is their ability to embody values culturally defined as masculine: they've been tougher, more decisive, more aggressive, more calculating, and more emotionally controlled than most men around them.[5] These women's power, however, has nothing to do with whether women in general are subordinated under patriarchy. It also doesn't mean that putting more women in positions of authority will by itself do much for women unless we also change the patriarchal character of the systems in which they operate. . . .

Since patriarchy identifies power with men, the vast majority of men who aren't powerful but are instead dominated by other men can still feel some connection with the *idea* of male dominance and with men who *are* powerful. It is far easier, for example, for an unemployed working-class man to identify with male leaders and their displays of patriarchal masculine toughness than it is for women of any class. When upper-class U.S. President George Bush "got tough" with Saddam Hussein, for example, men of all classes could identify with his acting out of basic patriarchal values. In this way, male identification gives even the most lowly placed man a cultural basis for feeling some sense of superiority over the otherwise most highly placed woman (which is why a construction worker can feel within his rights as a man when he sexually harasses a well-dressed professional woman who happens to walk by).[6] . . .

In addition to being male-dominated and male-identified, patriarchy is *male-centered*, which means that the focus of attention is primarily on men and what they do. Pick up any newspaper or go to any movie theater and you'll find stories primarily about men and what they've done or haven't done or what they have to say about either. With rare exceptions, women are portrayed as along for the ride, fussing over their support work of domestic labor and maintaining love relationships, providing something for men to fight over, or being foils that reflect or amplify men's heroic struggle with the human condition. If there's a crisis, what we see is what men did to create it and how men dealt with it.

If you want a story about heroism, moral courage, spiritual transformation, endurance, or any of the struggles that give human life its deepest meaning and significance, men and masculinity are usually the terms in which you must see it. (To see what I mean, make a list of the twenty most important movies you've ever seen and count how many focus on men as the central characters whose experience forms the point of the story.) Male experience is what patriarchal culture offers to represent *human* experience and the enduring themes of life, even when these are most often about women in the actual living of them. . . .

A male center of focus is everywhere. Research makes clear, for example, what most women probably already know: that men dominate conversations by talking more, interrupting more, and controlling content.[7] When women suggest ideas in business meetings, they often go unnoticed until a man makes the same suggestion and receives credit for it (or, as a cartoon caption put it, "Excellent idea Ms. Jones. Perhaps one of the men would like to suggest it"). In classrooms at all levels of schooling, boys and men command center stage and receive the lion's share of attention.[8] Even when women gather together, they must often resist the ongoing assumption that no situation can be complete or even entirely real unless a man is there to take the center position. How else do we understand the experience of groups of women who go out for drinks and conversation and are approached by men who ask, "Are you ladies alone?"

* * *

Women and Patriarchy

At the heart of patriarchy is the oppression of women, which takes several forms. Historically, for example, women have been excluded from major institutions such as church, state, universities, and the professions. Even when they've been allowed to participate, it's generally been at subordinate, second-class levels. . . .

Because patriarchy is male-identified and male-centered, women and the work they do tends to be devalued, if not made invisible. In their industrial capitalist form, for example, patriarchal cultures do not define the unpaid domestic work that women do as real work, and if women do something, it tends to be valued less than when men do it. As women's numbers in male-dominated occupations increase, the prestige and income that go with them tend to decline, a pattern found in a variety of occupations, from telephone operator and secretary to psychotherapist.[9] Like many minorities, women are routinely repressed in their development as human beings through neglect and discrimination in schools[10] and in occupational hiring, development, promotion, and rewards. Anyone who doubts that patriarchy is an oppressive system need only spend some time with the growing literature documenting not only economic, political, and other institutionalized sexism, but pervasive violence, from pornography to the everyday realities of wife battering, sexual harassment, and sexual assault.[11]

* * *

The power of patriarchy is also reflected in its ability to absorb the pressures of superficial change as a defense against deeper challenges. Every social system has a certain amount of "give" in it that allows some change to occur, and in the process leaves deep structures untouched and even invisible. Indeed, the "give" plays a critical part in maintaining the status quo by fostering illusions of fundamental change and acting as a systemic shock absorber. It keeps us focused on symptoms while root causes go unnoticed and unremarked; and it deflects the power we need to take the risky deeper journey that leads to the heart of patriarchy and our involvement in it.

* * *

We'd Rather Not Know

We're as stuck as we are primarily because we can't or won't acknowledge the roots of patriarchy and our involvement in it. We show no enthusiasm for going deeper than a surface obsession with sex and gender. We resist even saying the word "patriarchy" in polite conversation. We act as if patriarchy weren't there, because the realization that it does exist is a door that swings only one way and we can't go back again to not knowing. We're like a family colluding in silence over dark secrets of damage and abuse, or like "good and decent Germans" during the Holocaust who "never knew" anything terrible was being done. We cling to the illusion that everything is basically all right, that bad things don't happen to good people, that good people can't participate in the production of evil, and that if we only leave things alone they'll stay pretty much as they are and, we often like to think, always have been.

Many women, of course, do dare to see and speak the truth, but they are always in danger of being attacked and discredited in order to maintain the silence. Even those who would never call themselves feminists often know there is something terribly wrong with the structures of dominance and control that are so central to life in modern societies and without which we think we cannot survive. The public response to feminism has been ferociously defensive precisely because feminism touches such a deep nerve of truth and the denial that keeps us from it. If feminism were truly ridiculous, it would be ignored. But it isn't ridiculous, and so it provokes a vigorous backlash.

We shouldn't be too hard on ourselves for hanging on to denial and illusions about patriarchy. Letting go is risky business, and patriarchy is full of smoke and mirrors that make it difficult to see what has to be let go of. It's relatively easy to accept the idea of patriarchy as male-dominated and male-identified, for example, and even as male-centered. Many people, however, have a much harder time seeing women as oppressed.[12] This is a huge issue that sparks a lot of arguments, and for that reason it will take several chapters to do it justice. Still, it's worthwhile outlining a basic response here.

The reluctance to see women as oppressed has several sources. The first is that many women enjoy race or class privilege and it's difficult for many to see them as oppressed without, as Sam Keen put it, insulting "truly oppressed" groups such as the lower classes or racial minorities.[13] How, for example, can we count upper-class women among the oppressed and lower-class men among their oppressors?

Although Keen's objection has a certain logic to it, it rests on a confusion between the position of women and men as groups and as individuals. To identify "female" as an oppressed status under patriarchy doesn't mean that every woman suffers its consequences to an equal degree, just as living in a racist society doesn't mean that every person of color suffers equally or that every white person shares equally in the benefits of race privilege. Living in patriarchy does mean, however, that every woman must come to grips with an inferior gender *position* and that whatever she achieves will be *in spite of* that position. With the exception of child care and other domestic work and a few paid occupations related to it, women in almost every field of adult endeavor must labor under the presumption that they are inferior to men, that they are interlopers from the margins of society who must justify their participation. Men may have such experiences because of their race, ethnicity, or other minority standing, but rarely if ever because they're men.

It is in this sense that patriarchies are male-dominated even though most individual men may not *feel* dominant, especially in relation to other men. This is a crucial insight that rests on the fact that when we talk about societies, words like "dominance" and "oppression" describe relations between categories of people such as whites and Hispanics, lower and upper classes, or women and men. How dominance and oppression actually play out among individuals is another issue. Sexism, for example, is an ideology, a set of ideas that promote male privilege in part by portraying women as inferior to men. But depending on other social factors such as race, class, or age, individual men will vary in their ability to take advantage of sexism and the benefits it produces. We can make a similar argument about women and the price they pay for belonging to a subordinate group. Upper-class women, for example, are insulated to some degree from the oppressive effects of being women under patriarchy, such as discrimination in the workplace. Their class privilege, however, exists *in spite of* their subordinate standing as women, which they can never completely overcome, especially in relation to husbands.[14] No woman is immune, for example, to the cultural devaluing of women's bodies as sexual objects to be exploited in public and private life, or the ongoing threat of sexual and domestic violence. To a rapist, the most powerful woman in the land is first and foremost a woman, and this more than anything else culturally marks her as a potential victim.

Along with not seeing women as oppressed, we resist seeing men as a privileged oppressor group. This is especially true of men who are aware of their own suffering, who often argue that men and women are both oppressed because of their gender and that neither oppresses the other. Undoubtedly men do suffer because of their participation in patriarchy, but it isn't because men are oppressed *as men*. For women, gender oppression is linked to a cultural devaluing of femaleness itself. Women are subordinated and treated as inferior because they are culturally defined as inferior *as women*, just as many racial and ethnic minorities are devalued simply because they aren't considered to be white. Men, however, do not suffer because maleness is devalued as an oppressed status in relation to some higher, more powerful one. Instead, to the extent that men suffer as men—and not because they're also poor or a racial or ethnic minority—it's because they belong to the dominant gender group in a system of gender oppression, which both privileges them and exacts a price in return.

A key to understanding this is that a group cannot oppress itself. A group can inflict injury on itself, and its members can suffer from their position in society. But if we say that a group can oppress or persecute *itself* we turn the concept of social oppression into a mere synonym for socially caused suffering, which it isn't.[15]

Oppression is a social phenomenon that happens between different groups in a society; it is a system of social inequality through which one group is positioned to dominate and benefit from the exploitation and subordination of another. This means not only that a group cannot oppress itself, but also that it cannot be oppressed *by society*. Oppression is a relation that exists *between groups*, not between groups and society as a whole.

To understand oppression, then, we must distinguish it from suffering that has other social roots. Even the massive suffering inflicted on men through the horrors of war is not an oppression of men *as men*, because there is no system in which a group of non-men enforces and benefits from men's suffering. The systems that control the machinery of war are themselves patriarchal, which makes it impossible for them to oppress men as men. Warfare *does* oppress racial and ethnic minorities and the poor, who are often served up as cannon fodder by privileged classes whose interests war most often serves. Some 80 percent of all U.S. troops who served in Vietnam, for example, were from working- and lower-class backgrounds.[16] But this oppression is based on race and class, not gender. . . . If war made men truly disposable *as men*, we wouldn't find monuments and cemeteries in virtually every city and town in the United States dedicated to fallen soldiers (with no mention of their race or class), or endless retrospectives on the fiftieth anniversary of every milestone in World War II.

Rather than devalue or degrade patriarchal manhood, warfare celebrates and affirms it. As I write this on the fiftieth anniversary of the Normandy invasion, I can't help but feel the power of the honor and solemn mourning accorded the casualties of war, the deep respect opponents often feel for one another, and the countless monuments dedicated to men killed while trying to kill other men whose names, in turn, are inscribed on still more monuments.[17] But these ritual remembrances do more than sanctify sacrifice and tragic loss, they also sanctify war itself and the patriarchal institutions that promote it. Military leaders whose misguided orders, blunders, and egomaniacal schemes brought death to tens of thousands, for example, earn not ridicule, disgust, and scorn but a curious historical immunity framed in images of noble tragedy and heroic masculine endeavor. In stark contrast to massive graveyards of honored dead, the memorials, the annual speeches and parades, there are no monuments to the millions of women and children caught in the slaughter and bombed, burned, starved, raped, and left homeless. An estimated nine out of ten wartime casualties are civilians, not soldiers, and these include a huge proportion of children and women,[18] but there are no great national cemeteries devoted to *them*. War, after all, is a man's thing.

Perhaps one of the deepest reasons for denying the reality of women's oppression is that we don't want to admit that a real basis for conflict exists between men and women. We don't want to admit it because, unlike other groups involved in social oppression, such as whites and blacks, females and males really need each other, if only as parents and children. This can make us reluctant to see how patriarchy puts us at odds regardless of what we want or how we feel about it. Who wants to consider the role of gender oppression in everyday married and family life? Who wants to know how dependent we are on patriarchy as a system, how deeply our thoughts, feelings, and behavior are embedded in it? Men resist seeing the oppression of their mothers, wives, sisters, and daughters because we've participated in it, benefited from it, and developed a vested interest in it.

✻   ✻   ✻

We can move toward a clearer and more critical awareness of what patriarchy is about, of what gets in the way of working to end it, and new ways for all of us— men in particular—to participate in its long evolutionary process of turning into something else. Patriarchy is our collective legacy, and there's nothing we can do about that or the condition in which we received it. But we can do a lot about what we pass on to those who follow us.

NOTES

1. See Marilyn French, *Beyond Power: On Men, Women, and Morals* (New York: Summit Books, 1985), 303.

2. There is a lot of research that shows how such uses of language affect people's perceptions. See, for example, Mykol C. Hamilton, "Using Masculine Generics: Does Generic 'He' Increase Male Bias in the User's Imagery?" *Sex Roles* 19, nos. 11/12 (1988): 785–799; Wendy Martyna, "Beyond the 'He/Man' Approach: The Case for Nonsexist Language," *Signs* 5 (1980): 482–493; Casey Miller and Kate Swift, *Words and Women*, updated ed. (New York: HarperCollins, 1991); and Joseph W. Schneider and Sally L. Hacker, "Sex Role Imagery in the Use of the Generic 'Man' in Introductory Texts: A Case in the Sociology of Sociology," *American Sociologist* 8 (1973): 12–18.

3. Note that I'm *not* describing actual men and women here, but cultural *ideas* about men and women under patriarchy. As concepts, masculinity and femininity play a complex role in patriarchal societies.

4. Just as a white-racist society can accommodate a certain number of powerful people of color so long as they do not challenge white privilege and the institutions that support it.

5. See, for example, Carole Levin's *The Heart and Stomach of a King: Elizabeth I and the Politics of Sex and Power* (Philadelphia: University of Pennsylvania Press, 1994).

6. See Carol Brooks Gardner, *Passing By: Gender and Public Harassment* (Berkeley: University of California Press, 1995).

7. For more on gender and interaction, see Robin Lakoff, *Language and Woman's Place* (New York: Harper and Row, 1975) and *Talking Power: The Politics of Language in Our Lives* (New York: Basic Books, 1990). See also Deborah Tannen, *Conversational Style: Analyzing Talk among Friends* (Norwood, N.J.: Ablex, 1984); idem, *You Just Don't Understand: Women and Men in Conversation* (New York: William Morrow, 1990).

8. See American Association of University Women, *How Schools Shortchange Girls* (Washington, D.C.: American Association of University Women, 1992); and Myra Sadker and David M. Sadker, *Failing at Fairness: How America's Schools Cheat Girls* (New York: Charles Scribner's Sons, 1994).

9. See Paula England and D. Dunn, "Evaluating Work and Comparable Worth," *Annual Review of Sociology* 14 (1988): 227–248.

10. See American Association of University Women, *How Schools Shortchange Girls*; and Sadker and Sadker, *Failing at Fairness*.

11. See Susan Brownmiller, *Against Our Will: Men, Women, and Rape* (New York: Simon and Schuster, 1975); Andrea Dworkin, *Woman Hating* (New York: E. P. Dutton, 1974); Susan Faludi, *Backlash: The Undeclared War Against American Women* (New York: Crown Publishers, 1991); Marilyn French, *The War Against Women* (New York: Summit Books, 1992); Gardner, *Passing By*; Diana E. H. Russell, *Rape in Marriage* (New York: Macmillan, 1982); idem, *Sexual Exploitation: Rape, Child Sexual Abuse, and Workplace Harassment* (Beverly Hills, Calif.: Sage Publications, 1984); Medical News and Perspectives, *Journal of the American Medical Association* 264, no. 8 (1990): 939; Laura Lederer, ed., *Take Back the Night: Women on Pornography* (New York: William Morrow, 1980); Diana E. H. Russell, ed., *Making Violence Sexy: Feminist Views on Pornography* (New York: Teachers College Press, 1993); and Catharine MacKinnon, *Only Words* (Cambridge: Harvard University Press, 1993).

12. For more on this, see Marilyn Frye, *The Politics of Reality: Essays in Feminist Theory* (Freedom, Calif.: Crossing Press, 1983).

13. Sam Keen, *Fire in the Belly: On Being a Man* (New York: Bantam, 1991), 203.

14. See, for example, Susan A. Ostrander, *Women of the Upper Class* (Philadelphia: Temple University Press, 1984).

15. See Frye, *Politics of Reality*, 1–16.

16. Christian G. Appy, *Working-Class War: American Combat Soldiers in Vietnam* (Chapel Hill: University of North Carolina Press, 1993).

17. It is useful to note that in thirteenth-century Europe peasants were not allowed to participate in battle, since the nobility's monopoly over the tools and skills of warfare was its main basis for power and domination over land and peasants. Although knights undoubtedly suffered considerably from their endless wars with one another, one could hardly argue that their obligation to fight rendered them an oppressed group. Whatever price they paid for their dominance, the concept of oppression is not the word to describe it. For a lively history of this era, see Barbara Tuchman, *A Distant Mirror* (New York: Alfred A. Knopf, 1978).

18. Save the Children. Study results reported in *The Boston Globe*, 17 November 1994, 23.

6

Oppression

Marilyn Frye

It is a fundamental claim of feminism that women are oppressed. The word "oppression" is a strong word. It repels and attracts. It is dangerous and dangerously fashionable and endangered. It is much misused, and sometimes not innocently.

The statement that women are oppressed is frequently met with the claim that men are oppressed too. We hear that oppressing is oppressive to those who oppress as well as to those they oppress. Some men cite as evidence of their oppression their much-advertised inability to cry. It is tough, we are told, to be masculine. When the stresses and frustrations of being a man are cited as evidence that oppressors are oppressed by their oppressing, the word "oppression" is being stretched to meaninglessness; it is treated as though its scope includes any and all human experience of limitation or suffering, no matter the cause, degree or consequence. Once such usage has been put over on us, then if ever we deny that any person or group is oppressed, we seem to imply that we think they never suffer and have no feelings. We are accused of insensitivity, even of bigotry. For women, such accusation is particularly intimidating, since sensitivity is one of the few virtues that has been assigned to us. If we are found insensitive, we may fear we have no redeeming traits at all and perhaps are not real women. Thus are we silenced before we begin: the name of our situation drained of meaning and our guilt mechanisms tripped.

But this is nonsense. Human beings can be miserable without being oppressed, and it is perfectly consistent to deny that a person or group is oppressed without denying that they have feelings or that they suffer.

We need to think clearly about oppression, and there is much that mitigates against this. I do not want to undertake to prove that women are oppressed (or that men are not), but I want to make clear what is being said when we say it. We need this word, this concept, and we need it to be sharp and sure.

The root of the word "oppression" is the element "press." *The press of the crowd; pressed into military service; to press a pair of pants; printing press; press the button.* Presses are used to mold things or flatten them or reduce them in bulk, sometimes to reduce them by squeezing out the gases or liquids in them.

Something pressed is something caught between or among forces and barriers which are so related to each other that jointly they restrain, restrict or prevent the thing's motion or mobility. Mold. Immobilize. Reduce.

The mundane experience of the oppressed provides another clue. One of the most characteristic and ubiquitous features of the world as experienced by oppressed people is the double bind—situations in which options are reduced to a very few and all of them expose one to penalty, censure or deprivation. For example, it is often a requirement upon oppressed people that we smile and be cheerful. If we comply, we signal our docility and our acquiescence in our situation. We need not, then, be taken note of. We acquiesce in being made invisible, in our occupying no space. We participate in our own erasure. On the other hand, anything but the sunniest countenance exposes us to being perceived as mean, bitter, angry or dangerous. This means, at the least, that we may be found "difficult" or unpleasant to work with, which is enough to cost one one's livelihood; at worst, being seen as mean, bitter, angry or dangerous has been known to result in rape, arrest, beating and murder. One can only choose to risk one's preferred form and rate of annihilation.

Another example: It is common in the United States that women, especially younger women, are in a bind where neither sexual activity nor sexual inactivity is all right. If she is heterosexually active, a woman is open to censure and punishment for being loose, unprincipled or a whore. The "punishment" comes in the form of criticism, snide and embarrassing remarks, being treated as an easy lay by men, scorn from her more restrained female friends. She may have to lie and hide her behavior from her parents. She must juggle the risks of unwanted pregnancy and dangerous contraceptives. On the other hand, if she refrains from heterosexual activity, she is fairly constantly harassed by men who try to persuade her into it and pressure her to "relax" and "let her hair down"; she is threatened with labels like "frigid," "uptight," "man-hater," "bitch" and "cocktease." The same parents who would be disapproving of her sexual activity may be worried by her inactivity because it suggests she is not or will not be popular, or is not sexually normal. She may be charged with lesbianism. If a woman is raped, then if she has been heterosexually active she is subject to the presumption that she liked it (since her activity is presumed to show that she likes sex), and if she has not been heterosexually active, she is subject to the presumption that she liked it (since she is supposedly "repressed and frustrated"). Both heterosexual activity and heterosexual nonactivity are likely to be taken as proof that you wanted to be raped, and hence, of course, weren't *really* raped at all. You can't win. You are caught in a bind, caught between systematically related pressures.

Women are caught like this, too, by networks of forces and barriers that expose one to penalty, loss or contempt whether one works outside the home or not, is on welfare or not, bears children or not, raises children or not, marries or not, stays married or not, is heterosexual, lesbian, both or neither. Economic necessity; confinement to racial and/or sexual job ghettos; sexual harassment; sex discrimination; pressures of competing expectations and judgments about *women, wives* and *moth-*

ers (in the society at large, in racial and ethnic subcultures and in one's own mind); dependence (full or partial) on husbands, parents or the state; commitment to political ideas; loyalties to racial or ethnic or other "minority" groups; the demands of self-respect and responsibilities to others. Each of these factors exists in complex tension with every other, penalizing or prohibiting all of the apparently available options. And nipping at one's heels, always, is the endless pack of little things. If one dresses one way, one is subject to the assumption that one is advertising one's sexual availability; if one dresses another way, one appears to "not care about oneself" or to be "unfeminine." If one uses "strong language," one invites categorization as a whore or slut; if one does not, one invites categorization as a "lady"—one too delicately constituted to cope with robust speech or the realities to which it presumably refers.

The experience of oppressed people is that the living of one's life is confined and shaped by forces and barriers which are not accidental or occasional and hence avoidable, but are systematically related to each other in such a way as to catch one between and among them and restrict or penalize motion in any direction. It is the experience of being caged in: all avenues, in every direction, are blocked or booby-trapped.

Cages. Consider a birdcage. If you look very closely at just one wire in the cage, you cannot see the other wires. If your conception of what is before you is determined by this myopic focus, you could look at that one wire, up and down the length of it, and be unable to see why a bird would not just fly around the wire any time it wanted to go somewhere. Furthermore, even if, one day at a time, you myopically inspected each wire, you still could not see why a bird would have trouble going past the wires to get anywhere. There is no physical property of any one wire, *nothing* that the closest scrutiny could discover, that will reveal how a bird could be inhibited or harmed by it except in the most accidental way. It is only when you step back, stop looking at the wires one by one, microscopically, and take a macroscopic view of the whole cage, that you can see why the bird does not go anywhere; and then you will see it in a moment. It will require no great subtlety of mental powers. It is perfectly *obvious* that the bird is surrounded by a network of systematically related barriers, no one of which would be the least hindrance to its flight, but which, by their relations to each other, are as confining as the solid walls of a dungeon.

It is now possible to grasp one of the reasons why oppression can be hard to see and recognize: one can study the elements of an oppressive structure with great care and some good will without seeing the structure as a whole, and hence without seeing or being able to understand that one is looking at a cage and that there are people there who are caged, whose motion and mobility are restricted, whose lives are shaped and reduced.

The arresting of vision at a microscopic level yields such common confusion as that about the male door-opening ritual. This ritual, which is remarkably widespread across classes and races, puzzles many people, some of whom do and some of whom do not find it offensive. Look at the scene of the two people approaching a door. The male steps slightly ahead and opens the door. The male holds the door open while the female glides through. Then the male goes through. The door closes after them. "Now how," one innocently asks, "can those crazy womenslibbers say that is oppressive? The guy *removed* a barrier to the lady's smooth and unruffled progress." But each repetition of this ritual has a place in a pattern, in fact in several patterns. One has to shift the level of one's perception in order to see the whole picture.

The door-opening pretends to be a helpful service, but the helpfulness is false. This can be seen by noting that it will be done whether or not it makes any practical sense. Infirm men and men burdened with packages will open doors for able-bodied women who are free of physical burdens. Men will impose themselves awkwardly and jostle everyone in order to get to the door first. The act is not determined by convenience or grace. Furthermore, these very numerous acts of unneeded or even noisome "help" occur in counterpoint to a pattern of men not being helpful in many practical ways in which women might welcome help. What *women* experience is a world in which gallant princes charming commonly make a fuss about being helpful and providing small services when help and services are of little or no use, but in which there are rarely ingenious and adroit princes at hand when substantial assistance is really wanted either in mundane affairs or in situations of threat, assault or terror. There is no help with the (his) laundry; no help typing a report at 4:00 A.M.; no help in mediating disputes among relatives or children. There is nothing but advice that women should stay indoors after dark, be chaperoned by a man, or when it comes down to it, "lie back and enjoy it."

The gallant gestures have no practical meaning. Their meaning is symbolic. The door-opening and similar services provided are services which really are needed by people who are for one reason or another incapacitated—unwell, burdened with parcels, etc. So the message is that women are incapable. The detachment of the acts from the concrete realities of what women need and do not need is a vehicle for the message that women's actual needs and interests are unimportant or irrelevant. Finally, these gestures imitate the behavior of servants toward masters and thus mock women, who are in most respects the servants and caretakers of men. The message of the false helpfulness of male gallantry is female dependence, the invisibility or insignificance of women, and contempt for women.

One cannot see the meanings of these rituals if one's focus is riveted upon the individual event in all its particularity, including the particularity of the individual man's present conscious intentions and motives and the individual woman's conscious perception of the event in the moment. It seems sometimes that people take a deliberately myopic view and fill their eyes with things seen microscopically in order not to see macroscopically. At any rate, whether it is deliberate or not, people can and do fail to see the oppression of women because they fail to see macroscopically and hence fail to see the various elements of the situation as systematically related in larger schemes.

As the cageness of the birdcage is a macroscopic phenomenon, the oppressiveness of the situations in which women live our various and different lives is a macroscopic phenomenon. Neither can be *seen* from a microscopic perspective. But when you look macroscopically you can see it—a network of forces and barriers which are systematically related and which conspire to the immobilization, reduction and molding of women and the lives we live.

7

Homophobia as a Weapon of Sexism

Suzanne Pharr

Patriarchy—an enforced belief in male dominance and control—is the ideology and sexism the system that holds it in place. The catechism goes like this: Who do gender roles serve? Men and the women who seek power from them. Who suffers from gender roles? Women most completely and men in part. How are gender roles maintained? By the weapons of sexism: economics, violence, homophobia.

Why then don't we ardently pursue ways to eliminate gender roles and therefore sexism? It is my profound belief that all people have a spark in them that yearns for freedom, and the history of the world's atrocities—from the Nazi concentration camps to white dominance in South Africa to the battering of women—is the story of attempts to snuff out that spark. When that spark doesn't move forward to full flame, it is because the weapons designed to control and destroy have wrought such intense damage over time that the spark has been all but extinguished.

Sexism, that system by which women are kept subordinate to men, is kept in place by three powerful weapons designed to cause or threaten women with pain and loss. . . .

We have to look at economics not only as the root cause of sexism but also as the underlying, driving force that keeps all the oppressions in place. In the United States, our economic system is shaped like a pyramid, with a few people at the top, primarily white males, being supported by large numbers of unpaid or low-paid workers at the bottom. When we look at this pyramid, we begin to

From Suzanne Pharr, *Homophobia: A Weapon of Sexism.* Published by Chardon Press; distributed by the Women's Project, 2224 Main St., Little Rock, AR 72206. Reprinted by permission of the Women's Project.

understand the major connection between sexism and racism because those groups at the bottom of the pyramid are women and people of color. We then begin to understand why there is such a fervent effort to keep those oppressive systems (racism and sexism and all the ways they are manifested) in place to maintain the unpaid and low-paid labor.

Susan DeMarco and Jim Hightower, writing for *Mother Jones,* report that *Forbes* magazine indicated that "the 400 richest families in America last year had an average net worth of $550 million each. These and less than a million other families—roughly 1 percent of our population—are at the prosperous tip of our society. . . . In 1976, the wealthiest 1 percent of America's families owned 19.2 percent of the nation's total wealth. (This sum of wealth counts all of America's cash, real estate, stocks, bonds, factories, art, personal property, and anything else of financial value.) By 1983, those at this 1 percent tip of our economy owned 34.3 percent of our wealth. . . . *Today, the top 1 percent of Americans possesses more net wealth than the bottom 90 percent.*" (My italics.) (May, 1988, pp. 32–33)

In order for this top-heavy system of economic inequity to maintain itself, the 90 percent on the bottom must keep supplying cheap labor. A very complex, intricate system of institutionalized oppressions is necessary to maintain the status quo so that the vast majority will not demand its fair share of wealth and resources and bring the system down. Every institution—schools, banks, churches, government, courts, media, etc.—as well as individuals must be enlisted in the campaign to maintain such a system of gross inequity.

What would happen if women gained the earning opportunities and power that men have? What would happen if these opportunities were distributed equitably, no matter what sex one was, no matter what race one was born into, and no matter where one lived? What if educational and training opportunities were equal? Would women spend most of our youth preparing for marriage? Would marriage be based on economic survival for women? What would happen to issues of power and control? Would women stay with our batterers? If a woman had economic independence in a society where women had equal opportunities, would she still be thought of as owned by her father or husband?

Economics is the great controller in both sexism and racism. If a person can't acquire food, shelter, and clothing and provide them for children, then that person can be forced to do many things in order to survive. The major tactic, worldwide, is to provide unrecompensed or inadequately recompensed labor for the benefit of those who control wealth. Hence, we see women performing unpaid labor in the home or filling low-paid jobs, and we see people of color in the lowest-paid jobs available.

The method is complex: limit educational and training opportunities for women and for people of color and then withhold adequate paying jobs with the excuse that people of color and women are incapable of filling them. Blame the economic victim and keep the victim's self-esteem low through invisibility and distortion within the media and education. Allow a few people of color and women to succeed among the profitmakers so that blaming those who don't "make it" can be intensified. Encourage those few who succeed in gaining power now to turn against those who remain behind rather than to use their resources to make change for all. Maintain the myth of scarcity—that there are not enough jobs, resources, etc., to go around—among the middle class so that they will not unite with laborers, immigrants, and the unemployed. The method keeps in place a system of control and profit by a few and a constant source of cheap labor to maintain it.

If anyone steps out of line, take her/his job away. Let homelessness and hunger do their work. The economic weapon works. And we end up saying, "I would do this or that—be openly who I am, speak out against injustice, work for civil rights, join a labor union, go to a political march, etc.—if I didn't have this job. I can't afford to lose it." We stay in an abusive situation because we see no other way to survive. . . .

Violence against women is directly related to the condition of women in a society that refuses us equal pay, equal access to resources, and equal status with males. From this condition comes men's confirmation of their sense of ownership of women, power over women, and assumed right to control women for their own means. Men physically and emotionally abuse women because they *can*, because they live in a world that gives them permission. Male violence is fed by their sense of their *right* to dominate and control, and their sense of superiority over a group of people who, because of gender, they consider inferior to them.

It is not just the violence but the threat of violence that controls our lives. Because the burden of responsibility has been placed so often on the potential victim, as women we have curtailed our freedom in order to protect ourselves from violence. Because of the threat of rapists, we stay on alert, being careful not to walk in isolated places, being careful where we park our cars, adding incredible security measures to our homes—massive locks, lights, alarms, if we can afford them—and we avoid places where we will appear vulnerable or unprotected while the abuser walks with freedom. Fear, often now so commonplace that it is unacknowledged, shapes our lives, reducing our freedom. . . .

Part of the way sexism stays in place is the societal promise of survival, false and unfulfilled as it is, that women will not suffer violence if we attach ourselves to a man to protect us. A woman without a man is told she is vulnerable to external violence and, worse, that there is something wrong with her. When the male abuser calls a woman a lesbian, he is not so much labeling her a woman who loves women as he is warning her that by resisting him, she is choosing to be outside society's protection from male institutions and therefore from wide-ranging, unspecified, ever-present violence. When she seeks assistance from woman friends or a battered women's shelter, he recognizes the power in woman bonding and fears loss of her servitude and loyalty: the potential loss of his control. The concern is not affectional/sexual identity: the concern is disloyalty and the threat is violence.

The threat of violence against women who step out of line or who are disloyal is made all the more powerful by the fact that women do not have to do anything—they may be paragons of virtue and subservience—to receive violence against our lives: the violence still comes. It comes because of the woman-hating that exists throughout society. Chance plays a larger part than virtue in keeping women safe. Hence, with violence always a threat to us, women can never feel completely secure and confident. Our sense of safety is always fragile and tenuous.

Many women say that verbal violence causes more harm than physical violence because it damages self-esteem so deeply. Women have not wanted to hear battered women say that the verbal abuse was as hurtful as the physical abuse: to acknowledge that truth would be tantamount to acknowledging that *virtually every woman is a battered woman.* It is difficult to keep strong against accusations of being a bitch, stupid, inferior, etc., etc. It is especially difficult when these individual assaults are backed up by a society that shows women in textbooks, advertising, TV programs, movies, etc. as debased, silly, inferior, and sexually objectified, and a society that gives tacit approval to pornography. When we internalize these messages, we call the result "low self-esteem," a therapeutic individualized term. It seems to me we should use the more political expression: when we internalize these messages, we experience *internalized sexism,* and we experience it in common with all women living in a sexist world. The violence against us is supported by a society in which woman-hating is deeply imbedded.

In "Eyes on the Prize," a 1987 Public Television documentary about the Civil Rights Movement, an older white woman says about her youth in the South that it was difficult to be anything different from what was around her when there was no vision for another way to be. Our society presents images of women that say it is appropriate to commit violence against us. Violence is committed against women because we are seen as inferior in status and in worth. It has been the work of the women's movement to present a vision of another way to be.

Every time a woman gains the strength to resist and leave her abuser, we are given a model of the importance of stepping out of line, of moving toward freedom. And we all gain strength when she says to violence, "Never again!" Thousands of women in the last fifteen years have resisted their abusers to come to this country's 1100 battered women's shelters. There they have sat down with other women to share their stories, to discover that their stories again and again are the same, to develop an analysis that shows that violence is a statement about power and control, and to understand how sexism creates the climate for male violence. Those brave women are now a part of a movement that gives hope for another way to live in equality and peace.

Homophobia works effectively as a weapon of sexism because it is joined with a powerful arm, heterosexism. Heterosexism creates the climate for homophobia with its assumption that the world is and must be heterosexual and its display of power and privilege as the norm. Heterosexism is the systemic display of homophobia in the institutions of society. Heterosexism and homophobia work together to enforce compulsory heterosexuality and that bastion of patriarchal power, the nuclear family. The central focus of the rightwing attack against women's liberation is that women's equality, women's self-determination, women's control of our own bodies and lives will damage what they see as the crucial societal institution, the nuclear family. The attack has been led by fundamentalist ministers across the country. The two areas they have focused on most consistently are abortion and homosexuality, and their passion has led them to bomb women's clinics and to recommend deprogramming for homosexuals and establishing camps to quarantine people with AIDS. To resist marriage and/or heterosexuality is to risk severe punishment and loss.

It is not by chance that when children approach puberty and increased sexual awareness they begin to taunt each other by calling these names: "queer," "faggot," "pervert." It is at puberty that the full force of society's pressure to conform to heterosexuality and prepare for marriage is brought to bear. Children know what we have taught them, and we have given clear messages that those who deviate from standard expectations are to be made to get back in line. The best controlling tactic at puberty is to be treated as an outsider, to be ostracized at a time when it feels most vital to be accepted. Those who are different must be made to suffer loss. It is also at puberty that misogyny begins to be more apparent, and girls are pressured to conform to societal norms that do not permit them to realize their full potential. It is at this time that their academic achievements begin to decrease as they are coerced into compulsory heterosexuality and trained for dependency upon a man, that is, for economic survival.

There was a time when the two most condemning accusations against a woman meant to ostracize and disempower her were "whore" and "lesbian." The sexual revolution and changing attitudes about heterosexual behavior may have led to some lessening of the power of the word *whore*, though it still has strength as a threat to sexual property and prostitutes are stigmatized and abused. However, the word *lesbian* is still fully charged and carries with it the full threat of loss of power and privilege, the threat of being cut asunder, abandoned, and left outside society's protection.

To be a lesbian is to be *perceived* as someone who has stepped out of line, who has moved out of sexual/economic dependence on a male, who is woman-identified. A lesbian is perceived as someone who can live without a man, and who is therefore (however illogically) against men. A lesbian is perceived as being outside the acceptable, routinized order of things. She is seen as someone who has no societal institutions to protect her and who is not privileged to the protection of individual males. Many heterosexual women see her as someone who stands in contradiction to the sacrifices they have made to conform to compulsory heterosexuality. A lesbian is perceived as a threat to the nuclear family, to male dominance and control, to the very heart of sexism.

Gay men are perceived also as a threat to male dominance and control, and the homophobia expressed against them has the same roots in sexism as does homophobia against lesbians. Visible gay men are the objects of extreme hatred and fear by heterosexual men because their breaking ranks with male heterosexual solidarity is seen as a damaging rent in the very fabric of sexism. They are seen as betrayers, as traitors who must be punished and eliminated. In the beating and killing of gay men we see clear evidence of this hatred. When we see the fierce homophobia expressed toward gay men, we can begin to understand the ways sexism also affects males through imposing rigid, dehumanizing gender roles on them. The two circumstances in which it is legitimate for men to be openly physically affectionate with one another are in competitive sports and in the crisis of war. For many men, these two experiences are the highlights of their lives, and they think of them again and again with nostalgia. War and sports offer a cover of all-male safety and dominance to keep away the notion of affectionate openness being identified with homosexuality. When gay men break ranks with male roles through bonding and affection outside the arenas of war and sports, they are perceived as not being "real men," that is, as being identified with women, the weaker sex that must be dominated and that over the centuries has been the object of male hatred and abuse. Misogyny gets transferred to gay men with a vengeance and is increased by the fear that their sexual identity and behavior will bring down the entire system of male dominance and compulsory heterosexuality.

If lesbians are established as threats to the status quo, as outcasts who must be punished, homophobia can wield its power over all women through lesbian baiting. Lesbian baiting is an attempt to control women by labeling us as lesbians because our behavior is not acceptable, that is, when we are being independent, going our own way, living whole lives, fighting for our rights, demanding equal pay, saying no to violence, being self-assertive, bonding with and loving the company of women, assuming the right to our bodies, insisting upon our own authority, making changes that include us in society's decision-making; lesbian baiting occurs when women are called lesbians because we resist male dominance and control. And it has little or nothing to do with one's sexual identity.

To be named as lesbian threatens all women, not just lesbians, with great loss. And any woman who steps out of role risks being called a lesbian. To understand how this is a threat to all women, one must understand that any woman can be called a lesbian and there is no real way she can defend herself: there is no way to credential one's sexuality. ("The Children's Hour," a Lillian Hellman play, makes this point when a student asserts two teachers are lesbians and they have no way to disprove it.) She may be married or divorced, have children, dress in the most feminine manner, have sex with men, be celibate—but there are lesbians who do all those things. *Lesbians look like all women and all women look like lesbians.* There is no guaranteed method of identification, and as we all know, sexual identity can be kept hidden. (The same is true for men. There is no way to prove their sexual identity, though many go to extremes to prove heterosexuality.) Also, women are not necessarily born lesbian. Some seem to be, but others become lesbians later in life after having lived heterosexual lives. Lesbian baiting of heterosexual women would not work if there were a definitive way to identify lesbians (or heterosexuals).

We have yet to understand clearly how sexual identity develops. And this is disturbing to some people, especially those who are determined to discover how lesbian and gay identity is formed so that they will know where to start in eliminating it. (Isn't it odd that there is so little concern about discovering the causes of heterosexuality?) There are many theories: genetic makeup, hormones, socialization, environment, etc. But there is no conclusive evidence that indicates that heterosexuality comes from one process and homosexuality from another.

We do know, however, that sexual identity can be in flux, and we know that sexual identity means more than just the gender of people one is attracted to and has sex with. To be a lesbian has as many ramifications as for a woman to be heterosexual. It is more than sex, more than just the bedroom issue many would like to make it: it is a woman-centered life with all the social interconnections that entails. Some lesbians are in long-term relationships, some in short-term ones, some date, some are celibate, some are married to men, some remain as separate as possible from men, some have children by men, some by alternative insemination, some seem "feminine" by societal standards, some "masculine," some are doctors, lawyers and ministers, some laborers, housewives and writers: what all share in common is a sexual/affectional identity that focuses on women in its attractions and social relationships.

If lesbians are simply women with a particular sexual identity who look and act like all women, then the major difference in living out a lesbian sexual identity as opposed to a heterosexual identity is that as lesbians we live in a homophobic world that threatens and imposes damaging loss on us for *being who we are*, for choosing to live whole lives. Homophobic people often assert that homosexuals have the choice of not being homosexual; that is, we don't have to act out our sexual identity. In that case, I want to hear heterosexuals talk about their willingness not to act out their sexual identity, including not just sexual activity but heterosexual social interconnections and heterosexual privilege. It is a question of wholeness. It is very difficult for one to be denied the life of a sexual being, whether expressed in sex or in physical affection, and to feel complete, whole. For our loving relationships with humans feed the life of the spirit and enable us to overcome our basic isolation and to be interconnected with humankind.

If, then, any woman can be named a lesbian and be threatened with terrible losses, what is it she fears? Are these fears real? Being vulnerable to a homophobic world can lead to these losses:

- *Employment.* The loss of job leads us right back to the economic connection to sexism. This fear of job loss exists for almost every lesbian except perhaps those who are self-employed or in a business that does not require societal approval. Consider how many businesses or organizations you know that will hire and protect people who are openly gay or lesbian.
- *Family.* Their approval, acceptance, love.
- *Children.* Many lesbians and gay men have children, but very, very few gain custody in court challenges, even if the other parent is a known abuser. Other children may be kept away from us as though gays and lesbians are abusers. There are written and unwritten laws prohibiting lesbians and gays from being foster parents or from adopting children. There is an irrational fear that children in contact with lesbians and gays will become homosexual through influence or that they will be sexually abused. Despite our knowing that 95 percent of those who sexually abuse children are heterosexual men, there are no policies keeping heterosexual men from teaching or working

with children, yet in almost every school system in America, visible gay men and lesbians are not hired through either written or unwritten law.

- *Heterosexual privilege and protection.* No institutions, other than those created by lesbians and gays—such as the Metropolitan Community Church, some counseling centers, political organizations such as the National Gay and Lesbian Task Force, the National Coalition of Black Lesbians and Gays, the Lambda Legal Defense and Education Fund, etc.—affirm homosexuality and offer protection. Affirmation and protection cannot be gained from the criminal justice system, mainline churches, educational institutions, the government.

- *Safety.* There is nowhere to turn for safety from physical and verbal attacks because the norm presently in this country is that it is acceptable to be overtly homophobic. Gay men are beaten on the streets; lesbians are kidnapped and "deprogrammed." The National Gay and Lesbian Task Force, in an extended study, has documented violence against lesbians and gay men and noted the inadequate response of the criminal justice system. One of the major differences between homophobia/heterosexism and racism and sexism is that because of the Civil Rights Movement and the women's movement racism and sexism are expressed more covertly (though with great harm); because there has not been a major, visible lesbian and gay movement, it is permissible to be overtly homophobic in any institution or public forum. Churches spew forth homophobia in the same way they did racism prior to the Civil Rights Movement. Few laws are in place to protect lesbians and gay men, and the criminal justice system is wracked with homophobia.

- *Mental health.* An overtly homophobic world in which there is full permission to treat lesbians and gay men with cruelty makes it difficult for lesbians and gay men to maintain a strong sense of well-being and self-esteem. Many lesbians and gay men are beaten, raped, killed, subjected to aversion therapy, or put in mental institutions. The impact of such hatred and negativity can lead one to depression and, in some cases, to suicide. The toll on the gay and lesbian community is devastating.

- *Community.* There is rejection by those who live in homophobic fear, those who are afraid of association with lesbians and gay men. For many in the gay and lesbian community, there is a loss of public acceptance, a loss of allies, a loss of place and belonging.

- *Credibility.* This fear is large for many people: the fear that they will no longer be respected, listened to, honored, believed. They fear they will be social outcasts.

The list goes on and on. But any one of these essential components of a full life is large enough to make one deeply fear its loss. A black woman once said to me in a workshop, "When I fought for Civil Rights, I always had my family and community to fall back on even when they didn't fully understand or accept what I was doing. I don't know if I could have borne losing them. And you people don't have either with you. It takes my breath away."

What does a woman have to do to get called a lesbian? Almost anything, sometimes nothing at all, but certainly anything that threatens the status quo, anything that steps out of role, anything that asserts the rights of women, anything that doesn't indicate submission and subordination. Assertiveness, standing up for oneself, asking for more pay, better working conditions, training for and accepting a non-traditional (you mean a man's?) job, enjoying the company of women, being financially independent, being in control of one's life, depending first and foremost upon oneself, thinking that one can do whatever needs to be done, but above all, working for the rights and equality of women.

In the backlash to the gains of the women's liberation movement, there has been an increased effort to keep definitions man-centered. Therefore, to work on behalf of women must mean to work against men. To love women must mean that one hates men. A very effective attack has been made against the word *feminist* to make it a derogatory word. In current backlash usage, *feminist* equals *man-hater* which equals *lesbian*. This formula is created in the hope that women will be frightened away from their work on behalf of women. Consequently, we now have women who believe in the rights of women and work for those rights while from fear deny that they are feminists, or refuse to use the word because it is so "abrasive."

So what does one do in an effort to keep from being called a lesbian? She steps back into line, into the role that is demanded of her, tries to behave in such a way that doesn't threaten the status of men, and if she works for women's rights, she begins modifying that work. When women's organizations begin doing significant social change work, they inevitably are lesbian-baited; that is, funders or institutions or community members tell us that they can't work with us because of our "man-hating attitudes" or the presence of lesbians. We are called too strident, told we are making enemies, not doing good. . . .

In my view, homophobia has been one of the major causes of the failure of the women's liberation movement to make deep and lasting change. (The other major block has been racism.) We were fierce when we set out but when threatened with the loss of heterosexual privilege, we began putting on brakes. Our best-known nationally distributed women's magazine was reluctant to print articles about lesbians, began putting a man on the cover several times a year, and writing articles about women who succeeded in a man's world. We worried about our image, our being all right, our being "real women" despite our work. Instead of talking about the elimination of sexual gender roles, we stepped back and talked about "sex role stereotyping" as the issue. Change around the edges for middle-class white women began to be talked about as successes. We accepted tokenism and integration, forgetting that equality for all women, for all people— and not just equality of white middle-class women with white men—was the goal that we could never put behind us.

But despite backlash and retreats, change is growing from within. The women's liberation movement is beginning to gain strength again because there are women who are talking about liberation for all women. We are examining sexism, racism, homophobia, classism, anti-Semitism, ageism, ableism, and imperialism, and we see everything as connected. This change in point of view represents the third wave of the women's liberation movement, a new direction that does not get mass media coverage and recognition. It has been initiated by women of color and lesbians who were marginalized or rendered invisible by the white heterosexual leaders of earlier efforts. The first wave was the 19th and early 20th century campaign for the vote; the second, beginning in the 1960s, focused on the Equal Rights Amendment and abortion rights. Consisting of predominantly white middle-class women, both failed in recognizing issues of equality and empowerment for all women. The third wave of the movement, multi-racial and multi-issued, seeks the transformation of the world for us all. We know that we won't get there until everyone gets there; that we must move forward in a great strong line, hand in hand, not just a few at a time.

We know that the arguments about homophobia originating from mental health and Biblical/religious attitudes can be settled when we look at the sexism that permeates religious and psychiatric history. The women of the third wave of the women's liberation movement know that *without the existence of sexism, there would be no homophobia.*

Finally, we know that as long as the word *lesbian* can strike fear in any woman's heart, then work on behalf of women can be stopped; the only successful work against sexism must include work against homophobia.

8

The Color of Privilege

Aída Hurtado

Each oppressed group in the United States is positioned in a particular and distinct relationship to white men, and each form of subordination is shaped by this relational position. Men of Color and white men maintain power over women, particularly within their respective groups. Gender alone, however, does not determine either a superordinate or subordinate position. In a highly industrialized society

From Aída Hurtado, *The Color of Privilege* (Ann Arbor: The University of Michigan Press, 1996), pp. 1–25.

run by a complex hierarchical bureaucracy and based on individualistic competition, many socially constructed markers of group membership are used to allocate power (Apfelbaum 1979). Class, ethnicity, race, and sexuality are but a few. As we develop a discourse for discussing our group memberships, as our consciousness about the mechanisms of subordination evolves, and as previously silenced groups speak, we can begin to form a picture of contemporary forms of subordination and their psychological effects (Connell 1985, 264). . . .

The Structural Position of Women in the United States

In the United States Blacks, Native Americans, and Latinos are predominantly working class, as are some Asian groups.[1] On every measure of standard of living (income, years of education, household makeup) most groups of Color are positioned structurally below the white population. This is especially the case for women in these racial and ethnic groups. The socioeconomic position of women of Color, as a group, affects their relational position to the highest income holders in the United States—white men. Women of Color's structural position has not historically been an integral part of white feminist analyses, primarily because most white feminists have overemphasized gender oppression as overriding other socioeconomic characteristics as the basis for subordination. Although in the last five years the infusion of race and class into feminist analyses has been one of the most heated and prolific debates in feminist writings, it is still very much the practice to collapse differences among women, especially when comparing them to men (specifically, when the comparison involves white men).

The recent awareness about the differences among women from different ethnic/racial groups has not erased the persistent practice in statistical reporting in the media to aggregate the socioeconomic status of all groups of women, thus hiding their substantial differences (*San Jose Mercury News* 1988; *Los Angeles Times* 1992; James 1994). The reports usually begin by stating the aggregate differences in pay for women and men, which state, for example, that women have reached 70 percent of pay parity with men (*San Jose Mercury News* 1988). A closer examination of the statistics quoted usually shows that not only do the headlines collapse differences among women; they usually also exaggerate women's gains and so reduce the differences between women and men. In fact, most of the stories that follow show that white women reach, on average, 68 percent of pay parity with white men, but Black women reach only 61 percent, and Hispanic women reached barely 55 percent.[2]

White women tend to earn more money than women of Color because, as a group, they tend to be able to stay in school longer than many women of Color (Ortíz 1995). White women are more likely to finish high school (86 percent, in contrast to 77 percent of Black women and 63 percent of Hispanic women) and receive more of the bachelor's degrees awarded to women (83.5 percent, in contrast to 7 percent of Black women, 0.4 percent of Native Americans, 3.5 percent of Hispanic women, and 3.6 percent of Asian Americans, based on the total number of bachelor's degrees awarded to women nationwide in 1991) (Carter and Wilson 1993, 47–49, 55). White women therefore earn substantially higher incomes, even though certain groups of women of Color (e.g., Black women) are more likely than white women to stay in the labor force without interruption. Recent figures show that the median annual income for women of Mexican descent is $4,556; for Puerto Rican women, $4,473; for Vietnamese women, $4,694; for Japanese women, $7,410; for Filipina women, $8,253; and for Black women, $14,036. On the other hand, the median income for white women is $15,575 (Taeuber 1991; Bennett 1995; Ortíz 1995). All women experience job segregation, but white women's current educational attainment gives them a brighter future than that of women of Color (Woo 1985).[3] In the past few years in the United States the college enrollment of all women fourteen to thirty-four years old has been nearing that of men. Close to half (49 percent) of all graduate students in 1980 were women, compared to less than a third (29 percent) in 1970 (Taeuber and Baldisera 1986, 13–15). In fact, between 1982 and 1992 the number of Ph.D. degrees received by women rose 28.8 percent while falling 7.5 percent for all men and 8.9 percent for white men specifically. Although these school figures do not include a separate category for women of Color, it is safe to conclude that, given the high school and college graduation rates quoted earlier, the doctoral degrees increasingly going to women are predominantly going to white women (Kelley 1994).[4] Moreover, the 1991 figures for first-time professional degrees verifies this assumption: of the 39 percent professional degrees granted to women that year, 3.7 percent went to Hispanics, 6.8 percent went to African Americans, 5.6 percent to Asians, 0.4 percent to Native Americans, but 82.3 percent went to white women (Carter and Wilson 1993, 57). Of most relevance to my argument that white women have an economic cushion because of their relationship to male family members are the figures that show that, on average, about 89 percent of Hispanic and African American college students come from families with annual incomes less than $40,000 (Wyche and Graves 1992) and from families that, on average, have two more family members than white families (Hurtado et al. 1993).

Increasingly, women are becoming the sole supporters of their families. The number of single-parent families has almost doubled since 1970; one in five families with children is now maintained by a woman. Women of Color are more likely than white women, however, to maintain families (44 percent of Black women, 39 percent of Puerto Rican women, 23 percent of Native American women, 20 percent of Mexican American women, and 20 percent of Cuban women, compared to 13 percent of white women) (Ortíz 1995).[5] Furthermore, women of Color are more likely to be heads of households living in poverty (52 percent of Black households and 53 percent of Hispanic households, compared to 27 percent of white households), more likely to be divorced (35 percent of Black women, compared to 14 percent of white women), and more likely to have larger families (40 percent of Black women, 60 percent of Hispanic women, but only 20 percent of white women had four or more people to support). In addition, teenage mothers are more likely to be Black women than white women (58 percent of teenage mothers are Black, compared to 13 percent white) (Taeuber and Baldisera 1986, 9–10). These figures remained virtually unchanged in 1991 (*Poverty in the United States: 1991*, Ser. P-60, no. 181 1993).

These measures reveal that women of Color stay fewer years in school, have fewer dollars to spend, and bear more economic burdens than any other group in this country. White women also suffer economically, but their economic situation is not as dire as that of women of Color. More specifically, white women's relationship to white men (the highest earners in society) as daughters, wives, or sisters gives them an "economic cushion" (Palmer 1983). . . .

White men need white women in a way that they do not need women of Color because women of Color cannot fulfill white men's need for racially pure offspring. This fact creates differences in the relational position of the groups—distance from and access to the source of privilege, white men. Thus, white women, as a group, are subordinated through seduction, women of Color, as a group, through rejection. Class position, of course, affects the probability of obtaining the rewards of seduction and the sanctions of rejection. Working-class white women are socialized to believe in the advantages of marrying somebody economically successful, but the probability of obtaining that goal is lower for them than for middle- or upper-class white women (Ostrander 1984). Class position affects women of Color as well. Although rejected by most white men as candidates to reproduce offspring, middle-class women of Color may be accepted into some white middle-class social circles in the well-documented role of token (Apfelbaum 1979, 199; Pettigrew and Martin 1987). Class privilege functions to one degree or another regardless of race, and white privilege functions to one degree or another regardless of class (Higginbotham 1985).

The Dual Construction of Womanhood

. . . The definition of *woman* is constructed differently for white women and for women of Color, though sexuality is the marking mechanism through which the subordination of each is maintained.[6] The construction of white womanhood also eroticizes potency (as male) and victimization/frailty (as female). As Catherine MacKinnon surmises:

> Women who resist or fail, including those who never did fit—for example, black and lower-class women who cannot survive if they are soft and weak and incompetent, assertively self-respecting women, women with ambitions of male dimensions—are considered less female, lesser women. Women who comply or succeed are elevated as models, tokenized by success on male terms or portrayed as consenting to their natural place and dismissed as having participated if they complain. (1982, 530)

White women are persuaded to become the partners of white men and are seduced into accepting a subservient role that meets the material needs of white men. As Audre Lorde describes it:

> White women face the pitfall of being seduced into joining the oppressor under the pretense of sharing power. This possibility does not exist in the same way for women of color. The tokenism that is sometimes extended to us is not an invitation to join power: our racial "otherness" is a visible reality that makes it quite clear. For white women there is a wider range of pretended choices and rewards for identifying with patriarchal power and its tools. (1984, 118–19)

The patriarchal invitation to power is only a pretended choice for white women because, as in all cases of tokens, their inclusion is dependent on complete and constant submission. As John Stuart Mill observed: "It was not sufficient for [white] women to be slaves. They must be willing slaves, for the maintenance of patriarchal order depends upon the consensus of women. It depends upon women playing their part . . . voluntarily suppressing the evidence that exposes the false and arbitrary nature of man-made categories and the reality which is built on those categories" (quoted in Spender 1980, 101–2).

The genesis of the construction of "woman" for Black women in the United States is in slavery.[7] During slavery Black women were required to be as masculine as men in the performance of work and were as harshly punished as men, but they were also raped (A. Y. Davis 1981, 5). Many Black women were broken and destroyed, but the majority who survived "acquired qualities considered taboo by the nineteenth-century ideology of womanhood." As Angela Davis puts it: "[Black women's] awareness of their endless capacity for hard work may have imparted to them a confidence in their ability to struggle for themselves, their families, and their people" (1981, 11).[8]

Many white men perceive women of Color primarily as workers (Castillo 1991, 27) and as objects of sexual power and aggression. Their sexual objectification of women of Color allows white men to express power and aggression sexually, without the emotional entanglements of, and the rituals that are required in, relationships with women of their own group (Rich 1979, 291–95; hooks 1981, 58; Palmer 1983, 156). In many ways the dual conception of woman based on race—"white goddess / black she-devil, chaste virgin / nigger whore, the blond blue-eyed doll / the exotic 'mulatto' object of sexual craving"—has freed many women of Color from the distraction of the rewards of seduction (Rich 1979, 291). Women of Color "do not receive the respect and treatment—mollycoddling and condescending as it sometimes is—afforded to white women" (Joseph 1981, 27).

* * *

Political Socialization and Survival Skills

Women of Color are marginalized in U.S. society from the time they are born. Marginalization is not a status conferred on them as they step outside the confines of ascribed roles; rather, as Audre Lorde poignantly describes, it is a condition of their lives that is communicated to them by the hatred of strangers. A consciousness of this hatred and the political reasons behind it begins in childhood:

> I don't like to talk about hate. I don't like to remember the cancellation and hatred, heavy as my wished-for death, seen in the eyes of so many white people from the time I could see. It was echoed in newspapers and movies and holy pictures and comic books and Amos 'n' Andy radio programs. I had no tools to dissect it, no language to name it.
> The AA subway train to Harlem. I clutch my mother's sleeve. . . . On one side of me a man reading a paper. On the other, a woman in a fur hat staring at me. Her mouth twitches as she stares and then her gaze drops down, pulling mine with it. Her leather-gloved hand plucks at the line where my new blue snowpants and her sleek fur coat meet. She jerks her coat closer to her. I look. I do not see whatever terrible thing she is seeing on the seat between us—probably a roach. But she has communicated her horror to me. It must be something very bad from the way she is looking, so I pull my snowsuit closer to me away from it, too. When I look up the woman is still staring at me, her nose holes and eyes huge. And suddenly I realize there is nothing crawling up the seat between us: it is me she doesn't want her coat to touch. . . . No word has been spoken. I'm afraid to say anything to my mother because I don't know what I've done. I look at the sides of my snowpants, secretly. Is there something on them? Something's going on here I do not understand, but I will never forget it. Her eyes. The flared nostrils. The hate. (Lorde 1984, 147–48)

Experiences such as these force women of Color to acquire survival skills as early as five years of age (A. Y. Davis 1974; Joseph 1981, 32–33, 40; Moraga and Anzaldúa 1981). Many children of Color serve as the official translators for their monolingual relatives in disputes with companies and agencies unresponsive to poor, working-class people. Early interaction with the public sphere helps many women of Color to develop a public identity and the political skills to fend off state intervention. Women of Color do not have the rewards of seduction offered to them. Relatively few get a high school diploma, even fewer finish college, and only an infinitesimal number obtain graduate degrees (Segura 1986; Cuadraz 1992). Most women of Color have to contribute to the economic survival of their families, and therefore their commitment to obtaining an education, acquiring economic independence, and practicing a profession is part of economic survival (Pesquera 1985). In addition, the low-income status of most women of Color means that they must acquire such survival skills as sustaining informal networks of support, practicing alternative forms of health care, and organizing for political and social change (Trotter and Chavira 1981; Brant 1984; Hurtado 1987–88; Castillo 1995).

By comparison, the childhoods of many white middle-class feminists were protected by classism and racism. As a consequence, many do not acquire their political consciousness of gender oppression until they become adults (Friedan 1963, 73–94). Lacking experience in challenging authorities, and white men in particular, white feminists often seem surprised at the harshness with which the power structure responds to threat, and they do not have well-developed defenses to fend off the attacks. They often turn their anger inward rather than seeing it as a valid response (Tavris 1982, 25–45). In planning political actions, some adopt white men's approaches, others reject them totally. White liberal feminists, for instance, have had a significant impact at the macro level because they have adopted the bureaucratic language and sociopolitical rules that are congenial to the power structure (Jaggar 1983, 197, 286–87). White radical feminists reject men's approaches and are successful at the micro level of interaction in developing modes of political organizing that are consensual and nonhierarchical (Trebilcot 1979).

In contrast, the political skills of feminists of Color are neither the conventional political skills of white liberal feminists nor the free-spirited approaches of white radical feminists. Instead, feminists of Color train to be urban guerrillas by doing battle every day with the apparatus of the state (Moraga and Anzaldúa 1981; Sandoval 1991). Their tactics are not recorded or published for others to study and are often misunderstood by white middle-class feminists. One basic tactic is using anger effectively (Moraga and Anzaldúa 1981; hooks 1984; Lorde 1984, 129; Anzaldúa 1987, 15–23).

> Women of color in America have grown up within a symphony of anger, at being silenced, at being unchosen, at knowing that when we survive, it is in spite of a world that takes for granted our lack of humanness, and which hates our very existence outside of its service. And I say symphony rather than cacophony because we have had to learn to orchestrate those furies so that they do not tear us apart. We have had to learn to move through them and use them for strength and force and insight within our daily lives. Those of us who did not learn this difficult lesson did not survive. And part of my anger is always libation for my fallen sisters. (Lorde 1984, 119)

The loss of children is one of the main reasons for the anger felt by many women of Color. There is a contemporary ring to Sojourner Truth's words, "I have borne thirteen children and seen them most all sold off to slavery" (Stanton, Anthony, and Gage 1889, 117). Drugs, prison, discrimination, poverty, and racism continue to deprive women of Color of their children at alarming rates in contemporary U.S. society.[9] For example, in 1990 the homicide rate for nonwhite males ages fifteen to nineteen was 92 per 100,000, in comparison to white males in that age group, for whom the rate was 13 per 100,000. The 1990 rate among nonwhite teenage males was twice that of 1985. In 1990 Blacks of all ages made up half of the nation's homicide victims, although they constitute about 12 percent of the nation's population (*San Francisco Chronicle*, 2 February 1995). These losses and their meaning for the survival of future generations often distinguish the concerns of feminists of Color from those of white women. "Some problems we share as women, some we do not. You fear your children will grow up to join the patriarchy and testify against you, we fear our children will be dragged from a car and shot down in the street and you will turn your backs upon the reasons they are dying" (Lorde 1984, 131–32).

* * *

Clearly, whether women are subordinated by white men through seduction or rejection, the results are detrimental to women's humanity. Advantages gained by women of Color because of their distance from white men amount to nothing more than the "deformed equality of equal oppression [to that of men of Color]" (A. Y. Davis 1971, 8). The privileges that white women acquire because of their closeness to white men give them only empty choices. As a seventy-three-year-old Black woman observes: "My mother used to say that the black woman is the white man's mule and the white woman is his dog. Now, she said that to say this: we do the heavy work and get beat whether we do it well or not. But the white woman is closer to the master and he pats them on the head and lets them sleep in the house, but he ain't gonna' treat neither one like he was dealing with a person" (quoted in Collins 1986, 17). Seen as obstinate mules or as obedient dogs, both groups are objectified. Neither is seen as fully human; both are eligible for race-, class-, and gender-specific modes of domination (18). In a patriarchal society all women are oppressed, and ultimately that is what unites them.

Neither a valid analysis of women's subordination nor an ethnically and racially diverse feminist movement is likely to emerge if white middle-class feminists do not integrate their own privilege from association with white men into their analysis of gender subordination (Frye 1992, 9). This requires an awareness that their subordination, based on seduction, has separated them from other women who are subordinated by rejection. This separation can be bridged, but first white women must develop a new kind of consciousness and renounce the privilege that comes from their relationship to white men.

If women of Color are to embrace a feminist movement, then they, too, must expand their consciousness of gender oppression. They, too, must understand differences in the dynamics of seduction and rejection and, in particular, that seduction is no less oppressive than rejection.

NOTES

1. Asian Americans, as a group, are stereotyped as the "model minority," a group to be emulated by less successful people of Color. Close examination of the statistics of achieved attainment indicates, however, that the structural integration of different Asian groups (e.g., Japanese, Filipino, Vietnamese, Chinese) is at best uneven and at worst deceptive. Scholars in Asian American studies have highlighted the importance of taking into account bases of

stratification such as gender, foreign-born versus U.S.-born native, language competency in English, the geographical distribution of the Asian population within metropolitan areas of high-income/high-cost-of-living locales (e.g., San Francisco, Los Angeles, Hawaii, and New York), historical wave of immigration, and number of wage-earning family members. These factors in combination paint a very different picture of Asian American advancement, especially for women. For example, most Asian Americans (especially women) are overqualified, as measured by formal education, and underpaid when compared to their white male counterparts. In fact, once regional variation is adjusted for, Filipino and Chinese Americans had a median annual income equivalent to African American men in four mainland Standard Metropolitan Statistical Areas (SMSAs)—Chicago, Los Angeles/Long Beach, New York, San Francisco/Oakland (Woo 1992, 177). For presentations of the intricacies of measuring the structural position of Asian Americans, see Susuki 1977; Woo 1985; Cabezas and Kawaguchi 1987.

2. I use the word *Hispanic* only when the source cited uses that label and does not list figures for individual Latino groups. For accuracy I use the ethnic/racial labels used in the original sources. I cite data separately for different groups of women when available.

3. Asian women as a group have an impressive educational attainment record. Yet, while education facilitates mobility among Asian American women, a large proportion of them continue to be in clerical or administrative support jobs. For example, in 1980 close to a third of native-born Filipinas who were college educated continued to be in clerical administrative support jobs. Deborah Woo indicates that for Asian American women: "Education improves mobility but it promises less than the 'American Dream.' For Asian women, it seems to serve less as an opportunity for mobility than a hedge against jobs as service workers and as machine operatives or assembly workers—the latter being an area where foreign-born Asian women are far more likely than their Anglo male or female counterparts to concentrate. The single largest category of employment here is as seamstresses or 'textile sewing machine operators' in garment factories" (1985, 331–32).

4. Again, this newspaper article follows the practice of aggregating all "women" when there is substantial variation in different groups of women's educational achievement.

5. An exception to this are Asian American women, 13 percent of whom are heads of households (Ortíz 1995).

6. Catherine MacKinnon argues that it is women's sexuality that is the marking mechanism for their domination, while gender is the outcome of their subordinated sexuality: "sexuality is the linchpin of gender inequality" (1982, 533).

7. Afrocentric scholarship is beginning to document how gender and all aspects of social life were conceptualized prior to slavery. These labors will educate all of us on the distortion that slavery imposed on the lives of its victims.

8. As the United States expanded to the west by colonizing native people and importing labor, other women of Color experienced similar treatment. Marta Cotera documents that among the martyrs and victims of social injustice were such women as Juanita of Downieville, California, who was lynched in 1851; Chipita Rodriguez, who was the only woman to be executed in Texas; and countless other Chicanas who were killed by Texas Rangers during their raids on Chicano communities (1977, 24).

9. In addition to incarceration rates, a recent newspaper article reported that, although pregnancy-related deaths continue to decline, Black women are still three times more likely to die from complications than white women. The Federal Centers for Disease Control and Prevention attribute this difference in death rates between Black and white pregnant women to the quality of care these women receive. Black women are twice as likely as white

women not to receive prenatal care; only about 60 percent of pregnant Black women receive prenatal care, in comparison to three-fourths of all pregnant women (*San Francisco Chronicle*, 13 January 1995).

BIBLIOGRAPHY

Anzaldúa, Gloria. 1987. *Borderlands—La Frontera: The New Mestiza*. San Francisco: Spinsters / Aunt Lute.

Apfelbaum, Erika. 1979. "Relations of Domination and Movements for Liberation: An Analysis of Power between Groups." In *The Social Psychology of Intergroup Relations*, ed. William G. Austin and Stephen Worchel, 188–204. Monterey, Calif.: Brooks/Cole Publishing.

Bennett, Claudette E. 1995. *The Black Population in the United States: March 1994 and 1993*. U. S. Bureau of the Census, Current Population Reports, P20–480. Washington, D.C.: U. S. Government Printing Office.

Brant, Beth, ed. 1984. *A Gathering of Spirit: Writing and Art of North American Indian Women*. Montpelier, Vt.: Sinister Wisdom Books.

Cabezas, Amado, and Gary Kawaguchi. 1987. "Empirical Evidence for Continuing Asian American Income Inequality: The Human Capital Model and Labor Market Segmentation." Paper presented at the Fourth Asian American Studies Conference of the Association of Asian American Studies, San Francisco State University, 19–21 March.

Carter, Deborah J., and Reginald Wilson. 1993. *Twelfth Annual Status Report: Minorities in Higher Education*. Washington, D. C.: American Council on Education.

Castillo, Ana. 1995. *Massacre of the Dreamers*. New York: Plume Book.

_____. 1991. "La Macha: Toward a Beautiful Whole Self." In *Chicana Lesbians: The Girls Our Mothers Warned Us About*, ed. Carla Trujillo, 24–48. Berkeley, Calif.: Third Woman Press.

Collins, Patricia Hill. 1986. "Learning from the Outsider Within: The Sociological Significance of Black Feminist Thought." *Social Problems* 33(6): 14–32.

Connell, R. W. 1985. "Theorizing Gender." *Sociology* 19(2): 260–72.

Davis, Angela Y. 1981. *Women, Race and Class*. New York: Random House.

_____. 1974. *With My Mind on Freedom: An Autobiography*. New York: Bantam Books.

_____. 1971. "Reflections on the Black Woman's Role in the Community of Slaves." *Black Scholar* 3(4): 3–15.

Friedan, Betty. 1963. *The Feminine Mystique*. New York: Penguin.

Frye, Marilyn. 1992. *Willful Virgin*. Freedom, Calif.: The Crossing Press.

"The Good News: It's No Longer 59 Cents; Bad News: Income Gap between Women and Men Continues to Loom Large." 1992. *Los Angeles Times*, 30 December, B6.

Higginbotham, Elizabeth. 1985. "Race and Class Barriers to Black Women's College Attendance." *Journal of Ethnic Studies* 13: 89–107.

"Homicide Rates Highest in South—U. S. Record Worst in Developed World." 1995. *San Francisco Chronicle*, 2 February, A3, col. 5.

hooks, bell. 1984. *Feminist Theory from Margin to Center*. Boston: South End Press.

_____. 1981. *Ain't I a Woman? Black Women and Feminism*. Boston: South End Press.

Hurtado, Aída. 1987–88. "A View from Within: Midwife Practices in South Texas." *International Quarterly of Community Health Education* 8 (4): 317–39.

Jaggar, Alison. 1983. *Feminist Politics and Human Nature.* Totowa, N. J.: Rowman and Allanheld.

James, Aley. 1994. "The Pay Gap Narrows, but . . . (the Gap between Men and Women's Salaries Has Narrowed, but Much of That Is Due to Lower Wages for Men)." *Fortune*, September, 32.

Joseph, Gloria I. 1981. "White Promotion, Black Survival." In *Common Differences: Conflicts in Black and White Feminists' Perspectives*, ed. Gloria I. Joseph and Jill Lewis, 19–42. New York: Anchor.

Kelley, Dennis. 1994. "Ph.D.s Go to More Women." *USA Today*, 17 January, 1D.

Lorde, Audre. 1984. *Sister Outsider*. Trumansburg, N. Y.: Crossing Press.

MacKinnon, Catherine A. 1982. "Feminism, Marxism, Method, and the State: An Agenda for Theory." *Signs: Journal of Women in Culture and Society* 7(31): 515–44.

Moraga, Cherríe, and Gloria Anzaldúa, eds. 1981. *This Bridge Called My Back: Writings by Radical Women of Color*. Watertown, Mass.: Persephone Press.

Ortíz, Vilma. 1995. "The Diversity of Latino Families." In *Understanding Latino Families: Scholarship, Policy, and Practice*, ed. Ruth E. Zambrana, 18–39. Thousand Oaks, Calif.: Sage Publications.

Ostrander, Susan, 1984. *Women of the Upper Class*. Philadelphia: Temple University Press.

Palmer, Phyllis Marynick. 1983. "White Women / Black Women: The Dualism of Female Identity and Experience in the United States." *Feminist Studies* 91(1): 151–70.

Pesquera, Beatríz. 1985. "Work and Family: A Comparative Analysis of Professional, Clerical, and Blue-Collar Chicana Workers." Ph.D. diss., Sociology Department, Univeristy of California, Berkeley.

Pettigrew, Thomas F., and Joanne Martin. 1987. "Shaping the Organizational Context for Black American Inclusion." *Journal of Social Issues* 43: 41–78.

Pregnancy Deaths More Common for Blacks." 1995. *San Francisco Chronicle*, 13 January, A3.

Rich, Adrienne. 1979. *On Lies, Secrets, and Silence: Selected Prose, 1966–1973*. New York: W. W. Norton.

Sandoval, Chela. 1991. "U. S. Third World Feminism: The Thoery and Method of Oppositional Consciousness in the Postmodern World." *Genders* 10 (spring): 1–24.

Segura, Denise. 1986. "Chicanas and Mexican Immigrant Women in the Labor Market: A Study of Occupational Mobility and Stratification." Ph.D. diss., Sociology Department, University of California, Berkeley.

Spender, Dale. 1980. *Man Made Langauge*. London: Routledge, Chapman and Hall.

Stanton, Elizabeth Cady, Susan B. Anthony, and Matilda Joslyn Gage, eds. 1889. *History of Woman Suffrage*, 2d ed. Rochester, N. Y.: Susan B. Anthony.

Susuki, Bob H. 1977. "Education and the Socialization of Asian Americans: A Revisionist Analysis of the 'Model Minority' Thesis." *Amerasia Journal* 4(2): 23–51.

Taeuber, Cynthia M. 1991. *Statistical Handbook on Women in America*. Phoenix, Ariz.: Oryx Press.

Taeuber, Cynthia M., and Victor Baldisera, 1986. *Women in the American Economy*. U. S. Bureau of the Census, Current Population Reports, Series P–23, no. 146. Washington, D. C.: U. S. Government Printing Office.

Tavris, Carol. 1982. *Anger: The Misunderstood Emotion*. New York: Simon and Schuster.

Trebilcot, Joyce. 1979. "Conceiving Women: Notes on the Logic of Feminism." *Sinister Wisdom* (11): 43–50.

Trotter, Robert T., III, and Juan Antonio Chavira. 1981. *Curanderismo: Mexican/American Folk Healing.* Athens: University of Georgia Press.

U. S. Bureau of the Census. 1993. *Poverty in the United States: 1991.* U. S. Department of Commerce, Series P–60, no. 181. Washington D. C.: U. S. Government Printing Office.

"Women Reached 70% of Pay Parity with Men in '87." 1988. *San Jose Mercury News,* 2 February, C1.

Woo, Deborah. 1992. "The Gap between Striving and Achieving: The Case for Asian American Women." In *Race, Class, and Gender in the United States: An Integrated Study,* ed. Paula S. Rothenberg, 174–82. New York: St. Martin's Press.

_____. 1985. "The Socioeconomic Status of Asian American Women in the Labor Force: An Alternative View." *Sociological Perspectives* 28(3): 307–38.

Wyche, Karen Fraser, and Graves, Sherryl B. 1992. "Minority Women in Academia— Access and Barriers to Professional Participation." *Psychology of Women Quarterly* 16 (4): 429–37.

9

White Privilege:
Unpacking the Invisible Knapsack

Peggy McIntosh

Through work to bring materials from Women's Studies into the rest of the curriculum, I have often noticed men's unwillingness to grant that they are overprivileged, even though they may grant that women are disadvantaged. They may say they will work to improve women's status, in the society, the university, or the curriculum, but they can't or won't support the idea of lessening men's. Denials which amount to taboos surround the subject of advantages which men gain from women's disadvantages. These denials protect male privilege from being fully acknowledged, lessened or ended.

Thinking through unacknowledged male privilege as a phenomenon, I realized that since hierarchies in our society are interlocking, there was most likely a phenomenon of white privilege which was similarly denied and protected. As a white person, I realized I had been taught about racism as something which puts others at a disadvantage, but had been taught not to see one of its corollary aspects, white privilege, which puts me at an advantage.

I think whites are carefully taught not to recognize white privilege, as males are taught not to recognize male privilege. So I have begun in an untutored way to ask what it is like to have white privilege. I have come to see white privilege as an invisible package of unearned assets which I can count on cashing in each day, but about which I was "meant" to remain oblivious. White privilege is like an invisible weightless knapsack of special provisions, maps, passports, codebooks, visas, clothes, tools and blank checks.

Describing white privilege makes one newly accountable. As we in Women's Studies work to reveal male privilege and ask men to give up some of their power, so one who writes about having white privilege must ask, "Having described it, what will I do to lessen or end it?"

After I realized the extent to which men work from a base of unacknowledged privilege, I understood that much of their oppressiveness was unconscious. Then I remembered the frequent charges from women of color that white women whom they encounter are oppressive. I began to understand why we are justly seen as oppressive, even when we don't see ourselves that way. I began to count the ways in which I enjoy unearned skin privilege and have been conditioned into oblivion about its existence.

My schooling gave me no training in seeing myself as an oppressor, as an unfairly advantaged person, or as a participant in a damaged culture. I was taught to see myself as an individual whose moral state depended on her individual moral will. My schooling followed the pattern my colleague Elizabeth Minnich has pointed out: whites are taught to think of their lives as morally neutral, normative, and average, and also ideal, so that when we work to benefit others, this is seen as work which will allow "them" to be more like "us."

I decided to try to work on myself at least by identifying some of the daily effects of white privilege in my life. I have chosen those conditions which I think in my case *attach somewhat more to skin-color privilege* than to class, religion, ethnic status, or geographical location, though of course all these other factors are intricately intertwined. As far as I can see, my African American co-workers, friends and acquaintances with whom I come into daily or frequent contact in this particular time, place, and line of work cannot count on most of these conditions.

1. I can if I wish arrange to be in the company of people of my race most of the time.
2. If I should need to move, I can be pretty sure of renting or purchasing housing in an area which I can afford and in which I would want to live.
3. I can be pretty sure that my neighbors in such a location will be neutral or pleasant to me.

4. I can go shopping alone most of the time, pretty well assured that I will not be followed or harassed.

5. I can turn on the television or open to the front page of the paper and see people of my race widely represented.

6. When I am told about our national heritage or about "civilization," I am shown that people of my color made it what it is.

7. I can be sure that my children will be given curricular materials that testify to the existence of their race.

8. If I want to, I can be pretty sure of finding a publisher for this piece on white privilege.

9. I can go into a music shop and count on finding the music of my race represented, into a supermarket and find the staple foods which fit with my cultural traditions, into a hairdresser's shop and find someone who can cut my hair.

10. Whether I use checks, credit cards, or cash, I can count on my skin color not to work against the appearance of financial reliability.

11. I can arrange to protect my children most of the time from people who might not like them.

12. I can swear, or dress in secondhand clothes, or not answer letters, without having people attribute these choices to the bad morals, the poverty, or the illiteracy of my race.

13. I can speak in public to a powerful male group without putting my race on trial.

14. I can do well in a challenging situation without being called a credit to my race.

15. I am never asked to speak for all the people of my racial group.

16. I can remain oblivious of the language and customs of persons of color who constitute the world's majority without feeling in my culture any penalty for such oblivion.

17. I can criticize our government and talk about how much I fear its policies and behavior without being seen as a cultural outsider.

18. I can be pretty sure that if I ask to talk to "the person in charge," I will be facing a person of my race.

19. If a traffic cop pulls me over or if the IRS audits my tax return, I can be sure I haven't been singled out because of my race.

20. I can easily buy posters, postcards, picture books, greeting cards, dolls, toys, and children's magazines featuring people of my race.

21. I can go home from most meetings of organizations I belong to feeling somewhat tied in, rather than isolated, out-of-place, outnumbered, unheard, held at a distance, or feared.

22. I can take a job with an affirmative action employer without having co-workers on the job suspect that I got it because of my race.

23. I can choose public accommodation without fearing that people of my race cannot get in or will be mistreated in the places I have chosen.

24. I can be sure that if I need legal or medical help, my race will not work against me.
25. If my day, week, or year is going badly, I need not ask of each negative episode or situation whether it has racial overtones.
26. I can choose blemish cover or bandages in "flesh" color and have them more or less match my skin.

I repeatedly forgot each of the realizations on this list until I wrote it down. For me white privilege has turned out to be an elusive and fugitive subject. The pressure to avoid it is great, for in facing it I must give up the myth of meritocracy. If these things are true, this is not such a free country; one's life is not what one makes it; many doors open for certain people through no virtues of their own.

In unpacking this invisible knapsack of white privilege, I have listed conditions of daily experience which I once took for granted. Nor did I think of any of these perquisites as bad for the holder. I now think that we need a more finely differentiated taxonomy of privilege, for some of these varieties are only what one would want for everyone in a just society, and others give license to be ignorant, oblivious, arrogant and destructive.

I see a pattern running through the matrix of white privilege, a pattern of assumptions which were passed on to me as a white person. There was one main piece of cultural turf; it was my own turf, and I was among those who could control the turf. *My skin color was an asset for any move I was educated to want to make.* I could think of myself as belonging in major ways, and of making social systems work for me. I could freely disparage, fear, neglect, or be oblivious to anything outside of the dominant cultural forms. Being of the main culture, I could also criticize it fairly freely.

In proportion as my racial group was being made confident, comfortable, and oblivious, other groups were likely being made inconfident, uncomfortable, and alienated. Whiteness protected me from many kinds of hostility, distress, and violence, which I was being subtly trained to visit in turn upon people of color.

For this reason, the word "privilege" now seems to me misleading. We usually think of privilege as being a favored state, whether earned or conferred by birth or luck. Yet some of the conditions I have described here work to systematically overempower certain groups. Such privilege simply *confers dominance* because of one's race or sex.

I want, then, to distinguish between earned strength and unearned power conferred systemically. Power from unearned privilege can look like strength when it is in fact permission to escape or to dominate. But not all of the privileges on my list are inevitably damaging. Some, like the expectation that neighbors will be decent to you, or that your race will not count against you in court, should be the norm in a just society. Others, like the privilege to ignore less powerful people, distort the humanity of the holders as well as the ignored groups.

We might at least start by distinguishing between positive advantages which we can work to spread, and negative types of advantages which unless rejected will always reinforce our present hierarchies. For example, the feeling that one belongs within the human circle, as Native Americans say, should not be seen as privilege for a few. Ideally it is an *unearned entitlement*. At present, since only a few have it, it is an unearned advantage for them. This paper results from a process of coming to see that some of the power which I originally saw as attendant on being a human being in the U.S. consisted in *unearned advantage* and *conferred dominance*.

I have met very few men who are truly distressed about systemic, unearned male advantage and conferred dominance. And so one question for me and others like me is whether we will be like them, or whether we will get truly distressed, even outraged, about unearned race advantage and conferred dominance and if so, what we will do to lessen them. In any case, we need to do more work in identifying how they actually affect our daily lives. Many, perhaps most, of our white students in the U.S. think that racism doesn't affect them because they are not people of color; they do not see "whiteness" as a racial identity. In addition, since race and sex are not the only advantaging systems at work, we need similarly to examine the daily experience of having age advantage, or ethnic advantage, or physical ability, or advantage related to nationality, religion, or sexual orientation.

Difficulties and dangers surrounding the task of finding parallels are many. Since racism, sexism, and heterosexism are not the same, the advantaging associated with them should not be seen as the same. In addition, it is hard to disentangle aspects of unearned advantage which rest more on social class, economic class, race, religion, sex and ethnic identity than on other factors. Still, all of the oppressions are interlocking, as the Combahee River Collective Statement of 1977 continues to remind us eloquently.

One factor seems clear about all of the interlocking oppressions. They take both active forms which we can see and embedded forms which as a member of the dominant group one is taught not to see. In my class and place, I did not see myself as a racist because I was taught to recognize racism only in individual acts of meanness by members of my group, never in invisible systems conferring unsought racial dominance on my group from birth.

Disapproving of the systems won't be enough to change them. I was taught to think that racism could end if white individuals changed their attitudes. [But] a "white" skin in the United States opens many doors for whites whether or not we approve of the way dominance has been conferred on us. Individual acts can palliate, but cannot end, these problems.

To redesign social systems we need first to acknowledge their colossal unseen dimensions. The silences and denials surrounding privilege are the key political tool here. They keep the thinking about equality or equity incomplete, protecting unearned advantage and conferred dominance by making these taboo subjects. Most talk by whites about equal opportunity seems to me now to be about equal opportunity to try to get into a position of dominance while denying that *systems* of dominance exist.

It seems to me that obliviousness about white advantage, like obliviousness about male advantage, is kept strongly inculturated in the United States so as to maintain the myth of meritocracy, the myth that democratic choice is equally available to all. Keeping most people unaware that freedom of confident action is there for just a small number of people props up those in power, and serves to keep power in the hands of the same groups that have most of it already.

Though systemic change takes many decades, there are pressing questions for me and I imagine for some others like me if we raise our daily consciousness on the perquisites of being light-skinned. What will we do with such knowledge? As we know from watching men, it is an open question whether we will choose to use unearned advantage to weaken hidden systems of advantage, and whether we will use any of our arbitrarily-awarded power to try to reconstruct power systems on a broader base.

10

Class in America:
Myths and Realities (2000)

Gregory Mantsios

People in the United States don't like to talk about class. Or so it would seem. We don't speak about class privileges, or class oppression, or the class nature of society. These terms are not part of our everyday vocabulary, and in most circles they are associated with the language of the rhetorical fringe. Unlike people in most other parts of the world, we shrink from using words that classify along economic lines or that point to class distinctions: phrases like "working class," "upper class," and "ruling class" are rarely uttered by Americans.

For the most part, avoidance of class-laden vocabulary crosses class boundaries. There are few among the poor who speak of themselves as lower class; instead, they refer to their race, ethnic group, or geographic location. Workers are more likely to identify with their employer, industry, or occupational group than with other workers, or with the working class.[1]

Neither are those at the other end of the economic spectrum likely to use the word "class." In her study of thirty-eight wealthy and socially prominent women, Susan Ostrander asked participants if they considered themselves members of the upper class. One participant responded, "I hate to use the word 'class.' We are responsible, fortunate people, old families, the people who have something."

Another said, "I hate [the term] upper class. It is so non–upper class to use it. I just call it 'all of us,' those who are wellborn."[2]

It is not that Americans, rich or poor, aren't keenly aware of class differences — those quoted above obviously are; it is that class is not in the domain of public discourse. Class is not discussed or debated in public because class identity has been stripped from popular culture. The institutions that shape mass culture and define the parameters of public debate have avoided class issues. In politics, in primary and secondary education, and in the mass media, formulating issues in terms of class is unacceptable, perhaps even un-American.

There are, however, two notable exceptions to this phenomenon. First, it is acceptable in the United States to talk about "the middle class." Interestingly enough, such references appear to be acceptable precisely because they mute class differences. References to the middle class by politicians, for example, are designed to encompass and attract the broadest possible constituency. Not only do references to the middle class gloss over differences, but these references also avoid any suggestion of conflict or exploitation.

This leads us to the second exception to the class-avoidance phenomenon. We are, on occasion, presented with glimpses of the upper class and the lower class (the language used is "the wealthy" and "the poor"). In the media, these presentations are designed to satisfy some real or imagined voyeuristic need of "the ordinary person." As curiosities, the ground-level view of street life and the inside look at the rich and the famous serve as unique models, one to avoid and one to aspire to. In either case, the two models are presented without causal relation to each other: one is not rich because the other is poor. Similarly, when social commentators or liberal politicians draw attention to the plight of the poor, they do so in a manner that obscures the class structure and denies class exploitation. Wealth and poverty are viewed as one of several natural and inevitable states of being: differences are only differences. One may even say differences are the American way, a reflection of American social diversity.

We are left with one of two possibilities: either talking about class and recognizing class distinctions are not relevant to U.S. society, or we mistakenly hold a set of beliefs that obscure the reality of class differences and their impact on people's lives.

Let us look at four common, albeit contradictory, beliefs about the United States.

Myth 1: The United States is fundamentally a classless society. Class distinctions are largely irrelevant today, and whatever differences do exist in economic standing are, for the most part, insignificant. Rich or poor, we are all equal in the eyes of the law, and such basic needs as health care and education are provided to all regardless of economic standing.

Myth 2: We are, essentially, a middle-class nation. Despite some variations in economic status, most Americans have achieved relative affluence in what is widely recognized as a consumer society.

Myth 3: We are all getting richer. The American public as a whole is steadily moving up the economic ladder, and each generation propels itself to greater economic well-being. Despite some fluctuations, the U.S. position in the global economy has brought previously unknown prosperity to most, if not all, North Americans.

Myth 4: Everyone has an equal chance to succeed. Success in the United States requires no more than hard work, sacrifice, and perseverance: "In America, anyone can become a millionaire; it's just a matter of being in the right place at the right time."

In trying to assess the legitimacy of these beliefs, we want to ask several important questions. Are there significant class differences among Americans? If these differences do exist, are they getting bigger or smaller, and do these differences have a significant impact on the way we live? Finally, does everyone in the United States really have an equal opportunity to succeed?

The Economic Spectrum

We will begin by looking at differences. An examination of available data reveals that variations in economic well-being are in fact immense. Consider the following:

- The wealthiest 20 percent of the American population holds 85 percent of the total household wealth in the country. That is, they own nearly seven-eighths of all the consumer durables (such as houses, cars, and stereos) and financial assets (such as stocks, bonds, property, and savings accounts).[3]
- Approximately 144,000 Americans, or 0.1 percent of the adult working population, earn more than $1 million **annually,** with many of these individuals earning over $10 million and some earning over $100 million annually. It would take the average American, earning $34,000 per year, more than 65 **lifetimes** to earn $100 million.[4]

Affluence and prosperity are clearly alive and well in certain segments of the United States population. However, this abundance is in contrast to the poverty and despair that is also prevalent in the United States. At the other end of the spectrum:

- A total of 13 percent of the American population—that is, one of every eight[5]— live below the government's official poverty line (calculated in 1999 at $8,500 for an individual and $17,028 for a family of four).[6] These poor include a significant number of homeless people—approximately two million Americans.
- Approximately one out of every five children in the United States under the age of eighteen lives in poverty.[7]

The contrast between rich and poor is sharp, and with nearly one-third of the American population living at one extreme or the other, it is difficult to argue that we live in a classless society. The income gap between rich and poor in the United States (measured as the percentage of total income held by the wealthiest 20 percent of the population versus the poorest 20 percent) is approximately 11 to 1, one of the highest ratios in the industrialized world. The ratio in Japan and Germany, by contrast, is 4 to 1.[8]

Reality 1: There are enormous differences in the economic status of American citizens. A sizable proportion of the U.S. population occupies opposite ends of the economic spectrum.

In the middle range of the economic spectrum:

- Sixty percent of the American population hold less than 4 percent of the nation's wealth.[9]
- While the real income of the top 1 percent of U.S. families skyrocketed by 89 percent during the economic growth period from 1977 to 1995, the income of the middle fifth of the population actually declined by 13 percent during that same period.[10] This led one prominent economist to describe economic growth as a "spectator sport for the majority of American families."[11]

The level of inequality is sometimes difficult to comprehend fully with dollar figures and percentages. To help his students visualize the distribution of income, the well-known economist Paul Samuelson asked them to picture an income pyramid made of children's blocks, with each layer of blocks representing $1,000. If we were to construct Samuelson's pyramid today, the peak of the pyramid would be much higher than the Eiffel Tower, yet almost all of us would be within six feet of the ground.[12] In other words, the distribution of income is heavily skewed; a small minority of families take the lion's share of national income, and the remaining income is distributed among the vast majority of middle-income and low-income families. Keep in mind that Samuelson's pyramid represents the distribution of income, not wealth. The distribution of wealth is skewed even further.

Reality 2: The middle class in the United States holds a very small share of the nation's wealth, and its income—in constant dollars—is declining.

Lottery millionaires and celebrity salaries notwithstanding, evidence suggests that the level of inequality in the United States is getting higher. Census data show the gap between the rich and the poor to be the widest since the government began collecting information in 1947. Furthermore, the percentage of households earning between $25,000 and $75,000 has been falling steadily since 1969, while the percentage of households earning less than $25,000 has actually increased between 1989 and 1997.[13] And economic polarization is expected to increase over the next several decades.[14]

Reality 3: The middle class is shrinking in size, and the gap between rich and poor is bigger than it has ever been.

American Life-Styles

At last count, nearly 35 million Americans across the nation lived in unrelenting poverty.[15] Yet, as political scientist Michael Harrington once commented,

"America has the best dressed poverty the world has ever known."[16] Clothing disguises much of the poverty in the United States, and this may explain, in part, its middle-class image. With increased mass marketing of "designer" clothing and with shifts in the nation's economy from blue-collar (and often better-paying) manufacturing jobs to white-collar and pink-collar jobs in the service sector, it is becoming increasingly difficult to distinguish class differences based on appearance.[17]

Beneath the surface, there is another reality. Let us look at some "typical" and not-so-typical life-styles.

American Profile No. 1

Name:	Harold S. Browning
Father:	manufacturer, industrialist
Mother:	prominent social figure in the community
Principal child-rearer:	governess
Primary education:	an exclusive private school on Manhattan's Upper East Side
	Note: a small, well-respected primary school where teachers and administrators have a reputation for nurturing student creativity and for providing the finest educational preparation
	Ambition: "to become President"
Supplemental tutoring:	tutors in French and mathematics
Summer camp:	sleep-away camp in northern Connecticut
	Note: camp provides instruction in the creative arts, athletics, and the natural sciences
Secondary education:	a prestigious preparatory school in Westchester County
	Note: classmates included the sons of ambassadors, doctors, attorneys, television personalities, and well-known business leaders
	After-school activities: private riding lessons
	Ambition: "to take over my father's business"
	High-school graduation gift: BMW
Family activities:	theater, recitals, museums, summer vacations in Europe, occasional winter trips to the Caribbean
	Note: as members of and donors to the local art museum, the Brownings and their children attend private receptions and exhibit openings at the invitation of the museum director
Higher education:	an Ivy League liberal arts college in Massachusetts
	Major: economics and political science
	After-class activities: debating club, college newspaper, swim team
	Ambition: "to become a leader in business"

First full-time job (age 23):	assistant manager of operations, Browning Tool and Die, Inc. (family enterprise)
Subsequent employment:	*3 years*—executive assistant to the president, Browning Tool and Die
	Responsibilities included: purchasing (materials and equipment), personnel, and distribution networks
	4 years—advertising manager, Lackheed Manufacturing (home appliances)
	3 years—director of marketing and sales, Comerex, Inc. (business machines)
Present employment (age 38):	executive vice president, SmithBond and Co. (digital instruments)
	Typical daily activities: review financial reports and computer printouts, dictate memoranda, lunch with clients, initiate conference calls, meet with assistants, plan business trips, meet with associates
	Transportation to and from work: chauffeured company limousine
	Annual salary: $315,000
	Ambition: "to become chief executive officer of the firm, or one like it, within the next five to ten years"
Present residence:	eighteenth-floor condominium on Manhattan's Upper West Side, eleven rooms, including five spacious bedrooms and terrace overlooking river
	Interior: professionally designed and accented with elegant furnishings, valuable antiques, and expensive artwork
	Note: building management provides doorman and elevator attendant; family employs au pair for children and maid for other domestic chores
Second residence:	farm in northwestern Connecticut, used for weekend retreats and for horse breeding (investment/hobby)
	Note: to maintain the farm and cater to their needs when they are there, the Brownings employ a part-time maid, groundskeeper, and horse breeder

Harold Browning was born into a world of nurses, maids, and governesses. His world today is one of airplanes and limousines, five-star restaurants, and luxurious living accommodations. The life and life-style of Harold Browning is in sharp contrast to that of Bob Farrell.

American Profile No. 2

Name:	Bob Farrell
Father:	machinist
Mother	retail clerk
Principal child-rearer:	mother and sitter
Primary education:	a medium-size public school in Queens, New York, characterized by large class size, outmoded physical facilities, and an educational philosophy emphasizing basic skills and student discipline

Ambition: "to become President"

Supplemental tutoring:	none
Summer camp:	YMCA day camp

Note: emphasis on team sports, arts and crafts

Secondary education:	large regional high school in Queens

Note: classmates included the sons and daughters of carpenters, postal clerks, teachers, nurses, shopkeepers, mechanics, bus drivers, police officers, salespersons

After-school activities: basketball and handball in school park

Ambition: "to make it through college"

High-school graduation gift: $500 savings bond

Family activities:	family gatherings around television set, bowling, an occasional trip to the movie theater, summer Sundays at the public beach
Higher education:	a two-year community college with a technical orientation

Major: electrical technology

After-school activities: employed as a part-time bagger in local supermarket

Ambition: "to become an electrical engineer"

First full-time job (age 19):	service-station attendant

Note: continued to take college classes in the evening

Subsequent employment:	mail clerk at large insurance firm, manager trainee, large retail chain
Present employment (age 38):	assistant sales manager, building supply firm

Typical daily activities: demonstrate products, write up product orders, handle customer complaints, check inventory

Transportation to and from work: city subway

Annual salary: $39,261

Ambition: "to open up my own business"

Additional income: $6,100 in commissions from evening and weekend work as salesman in local men's clothing store

Present residence:	the Farrells own their own home in a working-class neighborhood in Queens

Bob Farrell and Harold Browning live very differently: the life-style of one is privileged; that of the other is not so privileged. The differences are class differences, and these differences have a profound impact on the way they live. They are differences between playing a game of handball in the park and taking riding lessons at a private stable; watching a movie on television and going to the theater; and taking the subway to work and being driven in a limousine. More important, the difference in class determines where they live, who their friends are, how well they are educated, what they do for a living, and what they come to expect from life.

Yet, as dissimilar as their life-styles are, Harold Browning and Bob Farrell have some things in common. They live in the same city, they work long hours, and they are highly motivated. More important, they are both white males.

Let us look at someone else who works long and hard and is highly motivated. This person, however, is black and female.

	American Profile No. 3
Name:	Cheryl Mitchell
Father:	janitor
Mother:	waitress
Principal child-rearer:	grandmother
Primary education:	large public school in Ocean Hill-Brownsville, Brooklyn, New York
	Note: rote teaching of basic skills and emphasis on conveying the importance of good attendance, good manners, and good work habits; school patrolled by security guards
	Ambition: "to be a teacher"
Supplemental tutoring:	none
Summer camp:	none
Secondary education:	large public school in Ocean Hill-Brownsville
	Note: classmates included sons and daughters of hairdressers, groundskeepers, painters, dressmakers, dishwashers, domestics
	After-school activities: domestic chores, part-time employment as babysitter and housekeeper
	Ambition: "to be a social worker"
	High-school graduation gift: corsage
Family activities:	church-sponsored socials
Higher education:	one semester of local community college
	Note: dropped out of school for financial reasons

First full-time job (age 17):	counter clerk, local bakery
Subsequent employment:	file clerk with temporary service agency, supermarket checker
Present employment (age 38):	nurse's aide at a municipal hospital
	Typical daily activities: make up hospital beds, clean out bedpans, weigh patients and assist them to the bathroom, take temperature readings, pass out and collect food trays, feed patients who need help, bathe patients, and change dressings
	Annual salary: $14,024
	Ambition: "to get out of the ghetto"
Present residence:	three-room apartment in the South Bronx, needs painting, has poor ventilation, is in a high-crime area
	Note: Cheryl Mitchell lives with her four-year-old son and her elderly mother

When we look at the lives of Cheryl Mitchell, Bob Farrell, and Harold Browning, we see life-styles that are very different. We are not looking, however, at economic extremes. Cheryl Mitchell's income as a nurse's aide puts her above the government's official poverty line.[18] Below her on the income pyramid are 35 million poverty-stricken Americans. Far from being poor, Bob Farrell has an annual income as an assistant sales manager that puts him in the fifty-first percentile of the income distribution.[19] More than 50 percent of the U.S. population earns less money than Bob Farrell. And while Harold Browning's income puts him in a high-income bracket, he stands only a fraction of the way up Samuelson's income pyramid. Well above him are the 144,000 individuals whose annual salary exceeds $1 million. Yet Harold Browning spends more money on his horses than Cheryl Mitchell earns in a year.

Reality 4: Even ignoring the extreme poles of the economic spectrum, we find enormous class differences in the life-styles among the haves, the have-nots, and the have-littles.

Class affects more than life-style and material well-being. It has a significant impact on our physical and mental well-being as well.

Researchers have found an inverse relationship between social class and health. Lower-class standing is correlated to higher rates of infant mortality, eye and ear disease, arthritis, physical disability, diabetes, nutritional deficiency, respiratory disease, mental illness, and heart disease.[20] In all areas of health, poor people do not share the same life chances as those in the social class above them. Furthermore, lower-class standing is correlated with a lower quality of treatment for illness and disease. The results of poor health and poor treatment are borne out in the life expectancy rates within each class. Researchers have found that the higher your class standing, the higher your life expectancy. Conversely, they have also found that within each age group, the lower one's class standing, the higher the death rate; in some age groups, the figures are as much as two and three times as high.[21]

Reality 5: From cradle to grave, class standing has a significant impact on our chances for survival.

The lower one's class standing, the more difficult it is to secure appropriate housing, the more time is spent on the routine tasks of everyday life, the greater is the percentage of income that goes to pay for food and other basic necessities, and the greater is the likelihood of crime victimization.[22] Class can predict chances for both survival and success.

Class and Educational Attainment

School performance (grades and test scores) and educational attainment (level of schooling completed) also correlate strongly with economic class. Furthermore, despite some efforts to make testing fairer and schooling more accessible, current data suggest that the level of inequity is staying the same or getting worse.

In his study for the Carnegie Council on Children fifteen years ago, Richard De Lone examined the test scores of over half a million students who took the College Board exams (SATs). His findings were consistent with earlier studies that showed a relationship between class and scores on standardized tests; his conclusion: "the higher the student's social status, the higher the probability that he or she will get higher grades."[23] Fifteen years after the release of the Carnegie report, College Board surveys reveal data that are no different: test scores still correlate strongly with family income.

Average Combined Scores by Income (400 to 1600 scale)[24]

Family Income	Median Score
More than $100,000	1130
$80,000 to $100,000	1082
$70,000 to $80,000	1058
$60,000 to $70,000	1043
$50,000 to $60,000	1030
$40,000 to $50,000	1011
$30,000 to $40,000	986
$20,000 to $30,000	954
$10,000 to $20,000	907
less than $10,000	871

These figures are based on the test results of 1,302,903 SAT takers in 1999.

A little more than twenty years ago, researcher William Sewell showed a positive correlation between class and overall educational achievement. In comparing the top quartile (25%) of his sample to the bottom quartile, he found that students from upper-class families were twice as likely to obtain training beyond high school and four times as likely to attain a postgraduate degree. Sewell concluded: "Socioeconomic background . . . operates independently of academic ability at every stage in the process of educational attainment."[25]

Today, the pattern persists. There are, however, two significant changes. On the one hand, the odds of getting into college have improved for the bottom quartile of the population, although they still remain relatively low compared to the top. On the other hand, the chances of completing a college degree have deteriorated markedly for the bottom quartile. Researchers estimate the chances of completing a four-year college degree (by age 24) to be nineteen times as great for the top 25 percent of the population as it is for the bottom 25 percent. "Those from the bottom quartile of family income . . . are faring worse than they have at any time in the 23 years of published Current Population Survey data."[26]

Reality 6: Class standing has a significant impact on chances for educational attainment.

Class standing, and consequently life chances, are largely determined at birth. Although examples of individuals who have gone from rags to riches abound in the mass media, statistics on class mobility show these leaps to be extremely rare. In fact, dramatic advances in class standing are relatively few. One study showed that fewer than one in five men surpass the economic status of their fathers.[27] For those whose annual income is in six figures, economic success is due in large part to the wealth and privileges bestowed on them at birth. Over 66 percent of the consumer units with incomes of $100,000 or more have some inherited assets. Of these units, over 86 percent reported that inheritances constituted a substantial portion of their total assets.[28]

Economist Harold Wachtel likens inheritance to a series of Monopoly games in which the winner of the first game refuses to relinquish his or her cash and commercial property for the second game. "After all," argues the winner, "I accumulated my wealth and income by my own wits." With such an arrangement, it is not difficult to predict the outcome of subsequent games.[29]

Reality 7: All Americans do not have an equal opportunity to succeed. Inheritance laws ensure a greater likelihood of success for the offspring of the wealthy.

Spheres of Power and Oppression

When we look at society and try to determine what it is that keeps most people down—what holds them back from realizing their potential as healthy, creative, productive individuals—we find institutionally oppressive forces that are largely beyond their individual control. Class domination is one of these forces. People do not choose to be poor or working class; instead, they are limited and confined by the opportunities afforded or denied them by a social and economic system. The class structure in the United States is a function of its economic system—capitalism, a system that is based on private rather than public ownership and control of commercial enterprises, and on the class division between those who own and control and those who do not. Under capitalism, these enterprises are governed by the need to produce a profit for the owners, rather than to fulfill collective needs.

Racial and gender domination are other such forces that hold people down. Although there are significant differences in the way capitalism, racism, and sexism affect our lives, there are also a multitude of parallels. And although race, class, and gender act independently of each other, they are at the same time very much interrelated.

On the one hand, issues of race and gender oppression cut across class lines. Women experience the effects of sexism whether they are well-paid professionals or poorly paid clerks. As women, they face discrimination and male domination, as well as catcalls and stereotyping. Similarly, a black man faces racial oppression, is subjected to racial slurs, and is denied opportunities because of his color. Regardless of their class standing, women and members of minority races are confronted with oppressive forces precisely because of their gender, color, or both.

On the other hand, class oppression permeates other spheres of power and oppression, so that the oppression experienced by women and minorities is also differentiated along class lines. Although women and minorities find themselves in subordinate positions vis-à-vis white men, the particular issues they confront may be quite different, depending on their position in the class structure. Inequalities in the class structure distinguish social functions and individual power, and these distinctions carry over to race and gender categories.

Power is incremental, and class privileges can accrue to individual women and to individual members of a racial minority. At the same time, class-oppressed men, whether they are white or black, have privileges afforded them as men in a sexist society. Similarly, class-oppressed whites, whether they are men or women, have privileges afforded them as whites in a racist society. Spheres of power and oppression divide us deeply in our society, and the schisms between us are often difficult to bridge.

Whereas power is incremental, oppression is cumulative, and those who are poor, black, and female have all of the forces of classism, racism, and sexism bearing down on them. This cumulative oppression is what is meant by the double and triple jeopardy of women and minorities.

Furthermore, oppression in one sphere is related to the likelihood of oppression in another. If you are black and female, for example, you are much more likely to be poor or working class than you would be as a white male. Census figures show that the incidence of poverty varies greatly by race and gender.

Chances of Being Poor in America[30]

White male/ female	White female head*	Hispanic male/ female	Hispanic female head*	Black male/ female	Black female head*
1 in 10	1 in 4	1 in 4	1 in 2	1 in 4	1 in 2

*Persons in families with female householder, no husband present.

In other words, being female and being nonwhite are attributes in our society that increase the chances of poverty and of lower-class standing.

Reality 8: Racism and sexism compound the effects of classism in society.

NOTES

1. See Jay MacLead, *Ain't No Makin' It: Aspirations and Attainment in a Lower-Income Neighborhood* (Boulder, Colo.: Westview Press, 1995); Benjamin DeMott, *The Imperial Middle* (New York: Morrow, 1990); Ira Katznelson, *City Trenches: Urban Politics and Patterning of Class in the United States* (New York: Pantheon Books, 1981); Charles W. Tucker, "A Comparative Analysis of Subjective Social Class: 1945–1963," *Social Forces*, no. 46, June 1968, pp. 508–514; Robert Nisbet, "The Decline and Fall of Social Class," *Pacific Sociological Review*, vol. 2, Spring 1959, pp. 11–17; and Oscar Glantz, "Class Consciousness and Political Solidarity," *American Sociological Review*, vol. 23, August 1958, pp. 375–382.

2. Susan Ostander, "Upper-Class Women: Class Consciousness as Conduct and Meaning," in G. William Domhoff, *Power Structure Research*, Beverly Hills, CA, Sage Productions, 1980, pp. 78–79. Also see, Stephen Birmingham, *America's Secret Aristocracy*, Boston, Little Brown, 1987.

3. Jared Bernstein, Lawrence Hishel, and John Schmitt, *The State of Working America: 1998–99*, ILR Press, Cornell University Press, 1998, p. 262.

4. The number of individuals filing tax returns showing a gross adjusted income of $1 million or more in 1997 was 144, 459 (Internal Revenue Service, *Statistics of Income Bulletin, Summer 1999*, Washington, DC, 1999, p. 268). The total civilian employment in 1997 was 129,588,000 (U.S. Bureau of Labor Statistics, 1997).

5. Joseph Dalaker, U.S. Bureau of the Census, "Current Population Reports," series P60–207, *Poverty in the United States: 1998*, Washington, DC, U.S. Government Printing Office, 1999, p. v.

6. "Preliminary Estimates of Weighted Average Poverty Thresholds in 1999," Department of Commerce, Bureau of Census, 2000.

7. Ibid, p. v.

8. See The Center on Budget and Policy Priorities, Economic Policy Institute, "Pulling Apart: State-by-State Analysis of Income Trends," January 2000, fact sheet; U.S. Department of Commerce, "Current Population Reports: Consumer Income," Washington, DC, 1993; The World Bank, "World Development Report: 1992",

Washington, DC, International Bank for Reconstruction and Development, 1992; The World Bank "World Development Report 1999/2000," pp. 238–239.

9. Jared Bernstein et al., op. cit., p. 262

10. Derived from Ibid, p. 95.

11. Alan Blinder, quoted by Paul Krugman, in "Disparity and Despair," *U.S. News and World Report*, March 23, 1992. p. 54.

12. Paul Samuelson, *Economics*, 10th ed., New York, McGraw-Hill, 1976, p. 84.

13. "Money Income of Households, Families, and Persons in the United States: 1992," U.S. Department of Commerce, "Current Population Reports: Consumer Income" series P60–184, Washington, DC, 1993, p. B6. Also, Jared Bernstein et al., op. cit., p. 61.

14. Paul Blumberg, *Inequality in an Age of Decline*, New York, Oxford University Press, 1980.

15. U.S. Census Bureau, 1999, op. cit., p. v.

16. Michael Harrington, *The Other America*, New York, Macmillan, 1962, p. 12–13.

17. Stuart Ewen and Elizabeth Ewen, *Channels of Desire: Mass Images and the Shaping of American Consciousness*, New York, McGraw-Hill, 1982.

18. This is based on the 1999 poverty threshold of $13,290 for a family of three.

19. Based on a median income in 1998 of $38,885.

20. E. Pamuk, D. Makuc, K. Heck, C. Reuben, and K. Lochner, *Socioeconomic Status and Health Chartbook, Health, United States, 1998*, Hyattsville, MD, National Center for Health Statistics, 1998, pp. 145–159; Vincente Navarro "Class, Race, and Health Care in the United States," in, Bersh Berberoglu, *Critical Perspectives in Sociology*, 2nd ed., Dubuque, IA, Kendall/Hunt, 1993, pp. 148–156; Melvin Krasner, *Poverty and Health in New York City*, United Hospital Fund of New York, 1989. See also U.S. Dept. of Health and Human Services, *Health Status of Minorities and Low Income Groups*, 1985; and Dan Hughes, Kay Johnson, Sara Rosenbaum, Elizabeth Butler, and Janet Simons, *The Health of America's Children*, The Children's Defense Fund, 1988.

21. E. Pamuk et al., op. cit.; Kenneth Neubeck and Davita Glassberg, *Sociology; A Critical Approach*, New York, McGraw-Hill, 1996, pp. 436–438; Aaron Antonovsky, "Social Class, Life Expectancy, and Overall Mortality," in *The Impact of Social Class*, New York, Thomas Crowell, 1972, pp. 467–491. See also Harriet Duleep, "Measuring the Effect of Income on Adult Mortality Using Longitudinal Administrative Record Data," *Journal of Human Resources*, vol. 21, no. 2, Spring 1986.

22. E. Pamuk et al., op. cit., fig. 20; Dennis W. Roncek, "Dangerous Places: Crime and Residential Environment," *Social Forces*, vol. 60, no. 1, September 1981, pp. 74–96.

23. Richard De Lone, *Small Futures*, New York, Harcourt Brace Jovanovich, 1978, pp. 14–19.

24. Derived from The College Entrance Examination Board, "1999, A Profile of College Bound Seniors: SAT Test Takers," www.collegeboard.org/sat/cbsenior/yr1999/NAT/natbk499.html#income

25. William H. Sewell, "Inequality of Opportunity for Higher Education," *American Sociological Review*, vol. 36, no. 5, 1971, pp. 793–809.

26. The Mortenson Report on Public Policy Analysis of Opportunity for Postsecondary Education, "Postsecondary Education Opportunity," Iowa City, IA, September 1993, no. 16.

27. De Lone, op. cit., pp. 14–19.

28. Howard Tuchman, *Economics of the Rich*, New York, Random House, 1973, p. 15.

29. Howard Wachtel, *Labor and the Economy*, Orlando, FL, Academic Press, 1984, pp. 161–162.

30. Derived from Census, 1999, op. cit., p. vi.

Suggestions for Further Reading

Baird, Robert M., and Stuart E. Rosenbaum. *Bigotry, Prejudice, and Hatred.* Buffalo, NY: Prometheus Press, 1992.

Cose, Ellis. *The Rage of a Privileged Class.* New York: Collins, 1994.

DeMott, Benjamin. *The Trouble with Friendship: Why Americans Can't Think Straight about Race.* New York: Atlantic Monthly Press, 1995.

Dusky, Lorraine. *Still Unequal: The Shameful Truth about Women and Justice in America.* New York: Crown Books, 1996.

Dyer, Richard. *White.* London and New York: Routledge, 1997.

Essed, Philomena. *Everyday Racism.* Claremont, CA: Hunter House, 1990.

Faludi, Susan. *Backlash: The Undeclared War against American Women.* New York: Crown Publishers, 1991.

Harris, Leonard. *Racism.* New York: Humanities Books, 1999.

Kadi, Joanne. *Thinking Class: Sketches from a Cultural Worker.* Boston: South End Press, 1996.

Kimmel, Michael. *The Gendered Society.* Oxford University Press, 2000.

King, Larry L. *Confessions of a White Racist.* New York: Viking Press, 1971.

Kleg, Milton. *Hate, Prejudice and Racism.* Albany: State University of New York Press, 1996.

Levin, Jack, and William Levin. *The Function of Discrimination and Prejudice,* 2nd ed. New York: Harper & Row, 1982.

Lipsitz, George. *The Possessive Investment in Whiteness.* Philadelphia: Temple University Press, 1998.

Pharr, Suzanne. *Homophobia as a Weapon of Sexism.* Chardon Press, 1988.

Pincus, F. L., and H. J. Erlich. *Race and Ethnic Conflict: Contending Views on Prejudice, Discrimination and Ethnoviolence.* Boulder, CO: Westview, 1994.

Ronai, Carol R., et al. *Everyday Sexism in the Third Millenium.* New York and London: Routledge. 1997.

Shipler, David K. *A Country of Strangers: Blacks and Whites in America.* New York: Knopf, 1997.

Wellman, David T. *Portraits of White Racism.* Cambridge: Cambridge University Press, 1977.

Discrimination in Everyday Life

THE SYSTEMS OF OPPRESSION WE HAVE BEEN STUDYING—racism, sexism, heterosexism, and class privilege—express themselves in everyday life in a variety of ways. Sometimes they are reflected in the prejudiced attitudes that people carry with them into the workplace or the community; sometimes they erupt in racist, sexist, or homophobic utterances that reach us across the playground or through our car radio. Sometimes they are in evidence in the discriminatory policies and practices of government and business as they carry out their routine operations. In Part III we will have an opportunity to read newspaper stories about incidents in which individuals or groups were discriminated against because of their race/ethnicity, gender, sexual orientation, class position, or some combination of them.

Refusing to hire a qualified person because of his or her race/ethnicity, gender, or sexual orientation, or refusing to rent that person an apartment or sell him or her a home is a fairly straightforward example of discrimination. Most people would agree that such behavior is unfair or unjust. But once we move beyond these clear-cut cases, it becomes difficult to reach agreement. Is the joke told by a popular radio personality that portrays women in a derogatory way sexist and racist or is it merely a joke? Does the fact that most major U.S. corporations have few if any women in senior management positions in itself indicate discriminatory hiring policies? Is the underrepresentation of women and men of color in medical schools in the United States de facto proof of racism in the society, or does it merely reflect a shortage of qualified applicants? Who determines what it means to be qualified? How do we arrive at the criteria according to which students are admitted to colleges and professional schools, or by which senior management is hired? Is it possible that the very criteria employed already reflect a subtle but pervasive race, class, and gender bias? Can individuals and institutions be racist, sexist, and homophobic in the course of their normal, everyday operation quite apart from—even without—their conscious or explicit intent? These are just some of the questions that are raised by the newspaper articles that appear in Part III.

The first article in this Part provides an excerpt from a 1981 report issued by the United States Commission on Civil Rights. It provides a historical overview of the kinds of discrimination against women and "minorities" that is part of our shared history. In addition, it offers some categories and distinctions which will prove useful as we read about the cases in the news articles that follow. According to this report, discrimination can take many forms. It can exist at the level of individual attitudes and behavior, as when a doctor refuses to treat patients because of their sexual orientation; it can be carried out through the routine application of the rules, policies, and practices of organizations when they unfairly prevent members of certain groups from, for example, receiving a promotion or being given highly valued work assignments; and it can be carried out in the day-to-day, unexamined practices of schools, government agencies, and other institutions so that it is so pervasive within the social structure as to constitute structural discrimination. Structural discrimination refers to an interlocking cycle of discrimination by which discrimination in one area, for example, education, leads to discrimination in other areas, such as employment and housing, creating a cycle of discrimination and disadvantage from which it is difficult to emerge.

As the articles in this Part make clear, discrimination of every type is a fact of life in every area of contemporary society. Why, then, do so many people, in particular, so many college students, seem to believe that racism and sexism are largely things of the past? Perhaps because so many people mistakenly believe that whether an act is discriminatory or racist can be determined by examining the motives of the person involved rather than looking at the consequences of the act itself. In fact, racism and sexism can be unintentional as well as intentional, and good people who mean well can inadvertently do and say things that are racist and sexist or homophobic. For example, the recruiter who fails to hire a woman because he believes that women will be uncomfortable functioning within the prevailing company culture may indeed have meant well, but intentions aside, this is a clear example of discrimination because it effectively denies women access to certain jobs. If the company culture is not welcoming to women, the right thing to do is to change that culture, not deny women employment.

As the members of the U.S. Commission on Civil Rights point out, even superficially "color blind" or "gender neutral" organizational practices can result in placing women and men of color or white women at a disadvantage. Seemingly innocuous height requirements for a particular job may discriminate disproportionately against members of certain ethnic groups or women; "standard" ways of posting job openings may exclude those who are not part of the "old boys' network," and even those of us who mean no harm can reinforce heterosexism, racism, sexism, or class privilege by our unexamined and seemingly innocent choices. As the news clippings in this Part make clear, racism, sexism, heterosexism, and class privilege are part of both our past and our present, part of our history, and part of everyday life. Learning to recognize discrimination is an essential prerequisite for acting to end it.

1

The Problem: *Discrimination*

U.S. Commission on Civil Rights

Making choices is an essential part of everyday life for individuals and organizations. These choices are shaped in part by social structures that set standards and influence conduct in such areas as education, employment, housing, and government. When these choices limit the opportunities available to people because of their race, sex, or national origin, the problem of discrimination arises.

Historically, discrimination against minorities and women was not only accepted but it was also governmentally required. The doctrine of white supremacy used to support the institution of slavery was so much a part of American custom and policy that the Supreme Court in 1857 approvingly concluded that both the North and the South regarded slaves "as beings of an inferior order, and altogether unfit to associate with the white race, either in social or political relations; and so far inferior, that they had no rights which the white man was bound to respect."[1] White supremacy survived the passage of the Civil War amendments to the Constitution and continued to dominate legal and social institutions in the North as well as the South to disadvantage not only blacks,[2] but other racial and ethnic groups as well—American Indians, Alaskan Natives, Asian and Pacific Islanders and Hispanics.[3]

While minorities were suffering from white supremacy, women were suffering from male supremacy. Mr. Justice Brennan has summed up the legal disabilities imposed on women this way:

> [T]hroughout much of the 19th century the position of women in our society was, in many respects, comparable to that of blacks under the pre–Civil War slave codes. Neither slaves nor women could hold office, serve on juries, or bring suit in their own names, and married women traditionally were denied the legal capacity to hold or convey property or to serve as legal guardians of their own children.[4]

In 1873 a member of the Supreme Court proclaimed, "Man is, or should be, woman's protector and defender. The natural and proper timidity and delicacy

From *Affirmative Action in the 1980s*. U.S. Commission on Civil Rights 65 (January 1981): 9–15.

which belongs to the female sex evidently unfits it for many of the occupations of civil life."[5] Such romantic paternalism has alternated with fixed notions of male superiority to deny women in law and in practice the most fundamental of rights, including the right to vote, which was not granted until 1920;[6] the Equal Rights Amendment has yet to be ratified.[7]

White and male supremacy are no longer popularly accepted American values. The blatant racial and sexual discrimination that originated in our conveniently forgotten past, however, continues to manifest itself today in a complex interaction of attitudes and actions of individuals, organizations, and the network of social structures that make up our society.

Individual Discrimination

The most common understanding of discrimination rests at the level of prejudiced individual attitudes and behavior. Although open and intentional prejudice persists, individual discriminatory conduct is often hidden and sometimes unintentional.[8] Some of the following are examples of deliberately discriminatory actions by consciously prejudiced individuals. Some are examples of unintentionally discriminatory actions taken by persons who may not believe themselves to be prejudiced but whose decisions continue to be guided by deeply ingrained discriminatory customs.

- Personnel officers whose stereotyped beliefs about women and minorities justify hiring them for low level and low paying jobs exclusively, regardless of their potential experience or qualifications for higher level jobs.[9]
- Administrators, historically white males, who rely on "word-of-mouth" recruiting among their friends and colleagues, so that only their friends and protégés of the same race and sex learn of potential job openings.[10]
- Employers who hire women for their sexual attractiveness or potential sexual availability rather than their competence, and employers who engage in sexual harassment of their female employees.[11]
- Teachers who interpret linguistic and cultural differences as indications of low potential or lack of academic interest on the part of minority students.[12]
- Guidance counselors and teachers whose low expectations lead them to steer female and minority students away from "hard" subjects, such as mathematics and science, toward subjects that do not prepare them for higher paying jobs.[13]
- Real estate agents who show fewer homes to minority buyers and steer them to minority or mixed neighborhoods because they believe white residents would oppose the presence of black neighbors.[14]
- Families who assume that property values inevitably decrease when minorities move in and therefore move out of their neighborhoods if minorities do move in.[15]

- Parole boards that assume minority offenders to be more dangerous or more unreliable than white offenders and consequently more frequently deny parole to minorities than to whites convicted of equally serious crimes.[16]

These contemporary examples of discrimination may not be motivated by conscious prejudice. The personnel manager is likely to deny believing that minorities and women can only perform satisfactorily in low level jobs and at the same time allege that other executives and decisionmakers would not consider them for higher level positions. In some cases, the minority or female applicants may not be aware that they have been discriminated against—the personnel manager may inform them that they are deficient in experience while rejecting their applications because of prejudice; the white male administrator who recruits by word-of-mouth from his friends or white male work force excludes minorities and women who never learn of the available positions. The discriminatory results these activities cause may not even be desired. The guidance counselor may honestly believe there are no other realistic alternatives for minority and female students.

Whether conscious or not, open or hidden, desired or undesired, these acts build on and support prejudicial stereotypes, deny their victims opportunities provided to others, and perpetuate discrimination, regardless of intent.

Organizational Discrimination

Discrimination, though practiced by individuals, is often reinforced by the well-established rules, policies, and practices of organizations. These actions are often regarded simply as part of the organization's way of doing business and are carried out by individuals as just part of their day's work.

Discrimination at the organizational level takes forms that are similar to those on the individual level. For example:

- Height and weight requirements that are unnecessarily geared to the physical proportions of white males and, therefore, exclude females and some minorities from certain jobs.[17]
- Seniority rules, when applied to jobs historically held only by white males, make more recently hired minorities and females more subject to layoff—the "last hired, first fired" employee—and less eligible for advancement.[18]
- Nepotistic membership policies of some referral unions that exclude those who are not relatives of members who, because of past employment practices, are usually white.[19]
- Restrictive employment leave policies, coupled with prohibitions on part-time work or denials of fringe benefits to part-time workers, that make it difficult for the heads of single parent families, most of whom are women, to get and keep jobs and meet the needs of their families.[20]

- The use of standardized academic tests or criteria, geared to the cultural and educational norms of the middle-class or white males, that are not relevant indicators of successful job performance.[21]
- Preferences shown by many law and medical schools in the admission of children of wealthy and influential alumni, nearly all of whom are white.[22]
- Credit policies of banks and lending institutions that prevent the granting of mortgage monies and loans in minority neighborhoods, or prevent the granting of credit to married women and others who have previously been denied the opportunity to build good credit histories in their own names.[23]

Superficially "color blind" or "gender neutral," these organizational practices have an adverse effect on minorities and women. As with individual actions, these organizational actions favor white males, even when taken with no conscious intent to affect minorities and women adversely, by protecting and promoting the status quo arising from the racism and sexism of the past. If, for example, the jobs now protected by "last hired, first fired" provisions had always been integrated, seniority would not operate to disadvantage minorities and women. If educational systems from kindergarten through college had not historically favored white males, many more minorities and women would hold advanced degrees and thereby be included among those involved in deciding what academic tests should test for. If minorities had lived in the same neighborhoods as whites, there would be no minority neighborhoods to which mortgage money could be denied on the basis of their being minority neighborhoods.

In addition, these barriers to minorities and women too often do not fulfill legitimate needs of the organization, or these needs can be met through other means that adequately maintain the organization without discriminating. Instead of excluding all women on the assumption that they are too weak or should be protected from strenuous work, the organization can implement a reasonable test that measures the strength actually needed to perform the job or, where possible, develop ways of doing the work that require less physical effort. Admissions to academic and professional schools can be decided not only on the basis of grades, standardized test scores, and the prestige of the high school or college from which the applicant graduated, but also on the basis of community service, work experience, and letters of recommendation. Lending institutions can look at the individual and his or her financial ability rather than the neighborhood or marital status of the prospective borrower.

Some practices that disadvantage minorities and women are readily accepted aspects of everyday behavior. Consider the "old boy" network in business and education built on years of friendship and social contact among white males, or the exchanges of information and corporate strategies by business acquaintances in racially or sexually exclusive country clubs and locker rooms paid for by the employer.[24] These actions, all of which have a discriminatory impact on minorities and women, are not necessarily acts of conscious prejudice. Because such actions are so often considered part of the "normal" way of doing things, people have difficulty recognizing that they are discriminating and therefore resist abandoning these practices despite the clearly discriminatory results. Consequently, many decision-makers have difficulty considering, much less accepting, nondiscriminatory alternatives that may work just as well or better to advance legitimate organizational interests but without systematically disadvantaging minorities and women.

This is not to suggest that all such discriminatory organizational actions are spurious or arbitrary. Many may serve the actual needs of the organization. Physical size or strength at times may be a legitimate job requirement; sick leave and insurance policies must be reasonably restricted; educational qualifications are needed for many jobs; lending institutions cannot lend to people who cannot reasonably demonstrate an ability to repay loans. Unless carefully examined and then modified or eliminated, however, these apparently neutral rules, policies, and practices will continue to perpetuate age-old discriminatory patterns into the structure of today's society.

Whatever the motivation behind such organizational acts, a process is occurring, the common denominator of which is unequal results on a very large scale. When unequal outcomes are repeated over time and in numerous societal and geographical areas, it is a clear signal that a discriminatory process is at work.

Such discrimination is not a static, one-time phenomenon that has a clearly limited effect. Discrimination can feed on discrimination in self-perpetuating cycles.[25]

- The employer who recruits job applicants by word-of-mouth within a predominantly white male work force reduces the chances of receiving applications from minorities and females for open positions. Since they do not apply, they are not hired. Since they are not hired, they are not present when new jobs become available. Since they are not aware of new jobs, they cannot recruit other minority or female applicants. Because there are no minority or female employees to recruit others, the employer is left to recruit on his own from among his predominantly white and male work force.[26]
- The teacher who expects poor academic performance from minority and female students may not become greatly concerned when their grades are low. The acceptance of their low grades removes incentives to improve. Without incentives to improve, their grades remain low. Their low grades reduce their expectations, and the teacher has no basis for expecting more of them.[27]
- The realtor who assumes that white home owners do not want minority neighbors "steers" minorities to minority neighborhoods. Those steered to minority neighborhoods tend to live in minority neighborhoods. White neighborhoods then remain white, and realtors tend to assume that whites do not want minority neighbors.[28]
- Elected officials appoint voting registrars who impose linguistic, geographic, and other barriers to minority voter registration. Lack of minority registration leads to low voting rates. Lower minority voting rates lead to the election of fewer minorities. Fewer elected minorities leads to the appointment of voting registrars who maintain the same barriers.[29]

Structural Discrimination

Such self-sustaining discriminatory processes occur not only within the fields of employment, education, housing, and government but also between these structural areas. There is a classic cycle of structural discrimination that reproduces itself. Discrimination in education denies the credentials to get good jobs. Discrimination in employment denies the economic resources to buy good housing. Discrimination in housing confines minorities to school districts providing inferior education, closing the cycle in a classic form.[30]

With regard to white women, the cycle is not as tightly closed. To the extent they are raised in families headed by white males, and are married to or live with white males, white women will enjoy the advantages in housing and other areas that such relationships to white men can confer. White women lacking the sponsorship of white men, however, will be unable to avoid gender-based discrimination in housing, education, and employment. White women can thus be the victims of discrimination produced by social structures that is comparable in form to that experienced by minorities.

This perspective is not intended to imply that either the dynamics of discrimination or its nature and degree are identical for women and minorities. But when a woman of any background seeks to compete with men of any group, she finds herself the victim of a discriminatory process. Regarding the similarities and differences between the discrimination experienced by women and minorities, one author has aptly stated:

> [W]hen two groups exist in a situation of inequality, it may be self-defeating to become embroiled in a quarrel over which is more unequal or the victim of greater oppression. The more salient question is how a condition of inequality for both is maintained and perpetuated — through what means is it reinforced?[31]

The following are additional examples of the interaction between social structures that affect minorities and women:

- The absence of minorities and women from executive, writing, directing, news reporting, and acting positions in television contributes to unfavorable stereotyping on the screen, which in turn reinforces existing stereotypes among the public and creates psychological roadblocks to progress in employment, education, and housing.[32]
- Living in inner-city high crime areas in disproportionate numbers, minorities, particularly minority youth, are more likely to be arrested and are more likely to go to jail than whites accused of similar offenses, and their arrest and conviction records are then often used as bars to employment.[33]
- Because of past discrimination against minorities and women, female and minority-headed businesses are often small and relatively new. Further disadvantaged by contemporary credit and lending practices, they are more

likely than white male–owned businesses to remain small and be less able to employ full-time specialists in applying for government contracts. Because they cannot monitor the availability of government contracts, they do not receive such contracts. Because they cannot demonstrate success with government contracts, contracting officers tend to favor other firms that have more experience with government contracts.[34]

Discriminatory actions by individuals and organizations are not only pervasive, occurring in every sector of society, but also cumulative with effects limited neither to the time nor the particular structural area in which they occur. This process of discrimination, therefore, extends across generations, across organizations, and across social structures in self-reinforcing cycles, passing the disadvantages incurred by one generation in one area to future generations in many related areas.[35]

These interrelated components of the discriminatory process share one basic result: the persistent gaps seen in the status of women and minorities relative to that of white males. These unequal results themselves have real consequences. The employer who wishes to hire more minorities and women may be bewildered by charges of racism and sexism when confronted by what appears to be a genuine shortage of qualified minority and female applicants. The guidance counselor who sees one promising minority student after another drop out of school or give up in despair may be resentful of allegations of racism when there is little he or she alone can do for the student. The banker who denies a loan to a female single parent may wish to do differently, but believes that prudent fiscal judgment requires taking into account her lack of financial history and inability to prove that she is a good credit risk. These and other decisionmakers see the results of a discriminatory process repeated over and over again, and those results provide a basis for rationalizing their own actions, which then feed into that same process.

When seen outside the context of the interlocking and intertwined effects of discrimination, complaints that many women and minorities are absent from the ranks of qualified job applicants, academically inferior and unmotivated, poor credit risks, and so forth, may appear to be justified. Decisionmakers like those described above are reacting to real social problems stemming from the process of discrimination. But many too easily fall prey to stereotyping and consequently disregard those minorities and women who have the necessary skills or qualifications. And they erroneously "blame the victims" of discrimination,[36] instead of examining the past and present context in which their own actions are taken and the multiple consequences of these actions on the lives of minorities and women.

The Process of Discrimination

Although discrimination is maintained through individual actions, neither individual prejudices nor random chance can fully explain the persistent national patterns of inequality and underrepresentation. Nor can these patterns be blamed on the persons who are at the bottom of our economic, political, and social order. Overt racism and sexism as embodied in popular notions of white and male supremacy have been widely repudiated, but our history of discrimination based on race, sex, and national origin has not been readily put aside. Past discrimination continues to have present effects. The task today is to identify those effects and the forms and dynamics of the discrimination that produced them.

Discrimination against minorities and women must now be viewed as an interlocking process involving the attitudes and actions of individuals and the organizations and social structures that guide individual behavior. That process, started by past events, now routinely bestows privileges, favors, and advantages on white males and imposes disadvantages and penalties on minorities and women. This process is also self-perpetuating. Many normal, seemingly neutral, operations of our society create stereotyped expectations that justify unequal results; unequal results in one area foster inequalities in opportunity and accomplishment in others; the lack of opportunity and accomplishment confirms the original prejudices or engenders new ones that fuel the normal operations generating unequal results.

As we have shown, the process of discrimination involves many aspects of our society. No single factor sufficiently explains it, and no single means will suffice to eliminate it. Such elements of our society as our history of *de jure* discrimination, deeply ingrained prejudices,[37] inequities based on economic and social class,[38] and the structure and function of all our economic, social, and political institutions[39] must be continually examined in order to understand their part in shaping today's decisions that will either maintain or counter the current process of discrimination.

It may be difficult to identify precisely all aspects of the discriminatory process and assign those parts their appropriate importance. But understanding discrimination starts with an awareness that such a process exists and that to avoid perpetuating it, we must carefully assess the context and consequences of our everyday actions. . . .

NOTES

1. Dred Scott v. Sanford, 60 U.S. (19 How.) 393, 408 (1857).

2. For a concise summary of this history, see U.S. Commission on Civil Rights, *Twenty Years After Brown*, pp. 4–29 (1975); *Freedom to the Free: 1863, Century of Emancipation* (1963).

3. The discriminatory conditions experienced by these minority groups have been documented in the following publications by the U.S. Commission on Civil Rights: *The Navajo Nation: An American Colony* (1975); *The Southwest Indian Report* (1973); *The Forgotten Minority: Asian Americans in New York City* (State Advisory Committee Report 1977); *Success of Asian Americans: Fact or Fiction?* (1980); *Stranger in One's Land* (1970); *Toward Quality Education for Mexican Americans* (1974); *Puerto Ricans in the Continental United States: An Uncertain Future* (1976).

4. Frontiero v. Richardson, 411 U.S. 677, 684–86 (1973), citing L. Kanowitz, *Women and the Law: The Unfinished Revolution*, pp. 5–6 (1970), and G. Myrdal, *An American Dilemma* 1073 (20th Anniversary Ed., 1962). Justice Brennan wrote the opinion of the Court, joined by Justices Douglas, White, and Marshall. Justice Stewart concurred in the judgment. Justice Powell, joined by Chief Justice Burger and Justice Blackmun, wrote a separate concurring opinion. Justice Rehnquist dissented. See also H. M. Hacker, "Women as a Minority Group," *Social Forces*, vol. 30 (1951), pp. 60–69; W. Chafe, *Women and Equality: Changing Patterns in American Culture* (New York: Oxford University Press, 1977).

5. Bradwell v. State, 83 U.S. (16 Wall) 130, 141 (1873) (Bradley, J., concurring), quoted in *Frontiero, supra* note 4.

6. U.S. Const. amend. XIX.

7. See U.S. Commission on Civil Rights, *Statement on the Equal Rights Amendment* (December 1978).

8. See, e.g., R. K. Merton, "Discrimination and the American Creed," in R. K. Merton, *Sociological Ambivalence and Other Essays* (New York: The Free Press, 1976), pp. 189–216. In this essay on racism, published for the first time more than 30 years ago, Merton presented a typology which introduced the notion that discriminatory actions are not always directly related to individual attitudes of prejudice. Merton's typology consisted of the following: Type I—the unprejudiced nondiscriminator; Type II—the unprejudiced discriminator; Type III—the prejudiced nondiscriminator; Type IV—the prejudiced discriminator. In the present context, Type II is crucial in its observation that discrimination is often practiced by persons who are not themselves prejudiced, but who respond to, or do not oppose, the actions of those who discriminate because of prejudiced attitudes (Type IV). See also D. C. Reitzes, "Prejudice and Discrimination: A Study in Contradictions," in *Racial and Ethnic Relations*, ed. H. M. Hughes (Boston: Allyn and Bacon, 1970), pp. 56–65.

9. See R. M. Kanter and B. A. Stein, "Making a Life at the Bottom," in *Life in Organizations, Workplaces as People Experience Them*, ed. Kanter and Stein (New York: Basic Books, 1976), pp. 176–90; also L. K. Howe, "Retail Sales Worker," ibid., pp. 248–51; also R. M. Kanter, *Men and Women of the Corporation* (New York: Basic Books, 1977).

10. See M. S. Granovetter, *Getting a Job: A Study of Contract and Careers* (Cambridge: Harvard University Press, 1974), pp. 6–11; also A. W. Blumrosen, *Black Employment and the Law* (New Brunswick, N.J.: Rutgers University Press, 1971), p. 232.

11. See U.S. Equal Employment Opportunity Commission, "Guidelines on Discrimination Because of Sex," 29 C.F.R. §1604.4 (1979); L. Farley, *Sexual Shakedown: The Sexual Harassment of Women on the Job* (New York: McGraw-Hill, 1978), pp. 92–96, 176–79; C. A. Mackinnon, *Sexual Harassment of Working Women* (New Haven: Yale University Press, 1979), pp. 25–55.

12. See R. Rosenthal and L. F. Jacobson, "Teacher Expectations for the Disadvantaged," *Scientific American*, 1968 (b) 218, 219–23; also D. Bar Tal, "Interactions of Teachers and Pupils," in *New Approaches to Social Problems*, ed. I. H. Frieze, D. Bar Tal, and J. S. Carrol (San Francisco: Jossey Bass, 1979), pp. 337–58; also U.S. Commission on Civil Rights, *Teachers and Students, Report V: Mexican American Education Study. Differences in Teacher Interaction with Mexican American and Anglo Students* (1973), pp. 22–23.

13. Ibid.

14. U.S. Department of Housing and Urban Development, "Measuring Racial Discrimination in American Housing Markets: The Housing Market Practices Survey" (1979); D. M. Pearce, "Gatekeepers and Home Seekers: Institutional Patterns in Racial Steering," *Social Problems*, vol. 26 (1979), pp. 325–42; "Benign Steering and Benign Quotas: The Validity of Race Conscious Government Policies to Promote Residential Integration," 93 *Harv. L. Rev.* 938, 944 (1980).

15. See M. N. Danielson, *The Politics of Exclusion* (New York: Columbia University Press, 1976), pp. 11–12; U.S. Commission on Civil Rights, *Equal Opportunity in Suburbia* (1974).

16. See L. L. Knowles and K. Prewitt, eds., *Institutional Racism in America* (Englewood Cliffs, N.J.: Prentice Hall, 1969), pp. 58–77, and E. D. Wright, *The Politics of Punishment* (New York: Harper and Row, 1973). Also, S. V. Brown, "Race and Parole Hearing Outcomes," in *Discrimination in Organizations*, ed. R. Alvarez and K. G. Lutterman (San Francisco: Jossey Bass, 1979), pp. 355–74.

17. Height and weight minimums that disproportionately exclude women without a showing of legitimate job requirement constitute unlawful sex discrimination. See Dothard v. Rawlinson, 433 U.S. 321 (1977); Bowe v. Colgate Palmolive Co., 416 F.2d 711 (7th Cir. 1969). Minimum height requirements used in screening applicants for employment have also been held to be unlawful where such a requirement excludes a significantly higher percentage of Hispanics than other national origin groups in the labor market and no job relatedness is shown. See Smith v. City of East Cleveland, 520 F.2d 492 (6th Cir. 1975).

18. U.S. Commission on Civil Rights, *Last Hired, First Fired* (1976); Tangren v. Wackenhut Servs., Inc., 480 F. Supp. 539 (D. Nev. 1979).

19. U.S. Commission on Civil Rights, *The Challenge Ahead, Equal Opportunity in Referral Unions* (1977), pp. 84–89.

20. A. Pifer, "Women Working: Toward a New Society," pp. 13–34, and D. Pearce, "Women, Work and Welfare: The Feminization of Poverty," pp. 103–24, both in K. A. Fernstein, ed., *Working Women and Families* (Beverly Hills: Sage Publications, 1979). Disproportionate numbers of single-parent families are minorities.

21. See Griggs v. Duke Power Company, 401 U.S. 424 (1971); U.S. Commission on Civil Rights, *Toward Equal Educational Opportunity: Affirmative Admissions Programs at Law and Medical Schools* (1978), pp. 10–12; I. Berg, *Education and Jobs: The Great Training Robbery* (Boston: Beacon Press, 1971), pp. 58–60.

22. See U.S. Commission on Civil Rights, *Toward Equal Educational Opportunity: Affirmative Admissions Programs at Law and Medical Schools* (1978), pp. 14–15.

23. See U.S. Commission on Civil Rights, *Mortgage Money: Who Gets It? A Case Study in Mortgage Lending Discrimination in Hartford, Conn.* (1974); J. Feagin and C. B. Feagin, *Discrimination American Style, Institutional Racism and Sexism* (Englewood Cliffs, N.J.: Prentice Hall, 1976), pp. 78–79.

24. See *Club Membership Practices by Financial Institutions: Hearing before the Comm. on Banking, Housing and Urban Affairs, United States Senate*, 96th Cong., 1st Sess. (1979). The Office of Federal Contract Compliance Programs of the Department of Labor has proposed a rule that would make the payment or reimbursement of membership fees in a private club that accepts or rejects persons on the basis of race, color, sex, religion, or national origin a prohibited discriminatory practice. 45 Fed. Reg. 4954 (1980) (to be codified in 41 C.F.R. §60–1.11).

25. See U.S. Commission on Civil Rights, *For All the People . . . By All the People* (1969), pp. 122–23.

26. See note 10.

27. See note 12.

28. See notes 14 and 15.

29. See Statement of Arthur S. Flemming, Chairman, U.S. Commission on Civil Rights, before the Subcommittee on Constitutional Rights of the Committee on the Judiciary of the U.S. Senate on S.407, S.903, and S.1279, Apr. 9, 1975, pp. 15–18, based on U.S. Commission on Civil Rights, *The Voting Rights Act: Ten Years After* (January 1975).

30. See, e.g., U.S. Commission on Civil Rights, *Equal Opportunity in Suburbia* (1974).

31. Chafe, *Women and Equality*, p. 78.

32. U.S. Commission on Civil Rights, *Window Dressing on the Set* (1977).

33. See note 16; Gregory v. Litton Systems, Inc., 472 F.2d 631 (9th Cir. 1972); Green v. Mo.-Pac. R.R., 523 F.2d 1290 (8th Cir. 1975).

34. See U.S. Commission on Civil Rights, *Minorities and Women as Government Contractors*, pp. 20, 27, 125 (1975).

35. See, e.g., A. Downs, *Racism in America and How to Combat It* (U.S. Commission on Civil Rights, 1970); "The Web of Urban Racism," in *Institutional Racism in America*, ed. Knowles and Prewitt (Englewood Cliffs, N.J.: Prentice Hall, 1969), pp. 134–76. Other factors in addition to race, sex, and national origin may contribute to these interlocking institutional patterns. In *Equal Opportunity in Suburbia* (1974), this Commission documented what it termed "the cycle of urban poverty" that confines minorities in central cities with declining tax bases, soaring educational and other public needs, and dwindling employment opportunities, surrounded by largely white, affluent suburbs. This cycle of poverty, however, started with and is fueled by discrimination against minorities. See also W. Taylor, *Hanging Together, Equality in an Urban Nation* (New York: Simon & Schuster, 1971).

36. The "self-fulfilling prophecy" is a well-known phenomenon. "Blaming the victim" occurs when responses to discrimination are treated as though they were the causes rather than the results of discrimination. See Chafe, *Women and Equality*, (pp. 76–78; W. Ryan, *Blaming the Victim* (New York: Pantheon Books, 1971).

37. See, e.g., J. E. Simpson and J. M. Yinger, *Racial and Cultural Minorities* (New York: Harper and Row, 1965), pp. 49–79; J. M. Jones, *Prejudice and Racism* (Reading, Mass.: Addison Wesley, 1972), pp. 60–111; M. M. Tumin, "Who Is Against Desegregation?" in *Racial and Ethnic Relations*, ed. H. Hughes (Boston: Allyn and Bacon, 1970), pp. 76–85; D. M. Wellman, *Portraits of White Racism* (Cambridge: Cambridge University Press, 1977).

38. See, e.g., D. C. Cox, *Caste, Class and Race: A Study in Social Dynamics* (Garden City, N.Y.: Doubleday, 1948); W. J. Wilson, *Power, Racism and Privilege* (New York: Macmillan, 1973).

39. H. Hacker, "Women as a Minority Group," *Social Forces*, vol. 30 (1951), pp. 60–69; J. Feagin and C. B. Feagin, *Discrimination American Style*; Chafe, *Women and Equality*; J. Feagin, "Indirect Institutionalized Discrimination," *American Politics Quarterly*, vol. 5 (1977), pp. 177–200; M. A. Chesler, "Contemporary Sociological Theories of Racism," in *Towards the Elimination of Racism*, ed. P. Katz (New York: Pergamon Press, 1976); P. Van den Berghe, *Race and Racism: A Comparative Perspective* (New York: Wiley, 1967); S. Carmichael and C. Hamilton, *Black Power* (New York: Random House, 1967); Knowles and Prewitt, *Institutional Racism in America*; Downs, *Racism in America and How to Combat It*.

2

DWB: *Driving While Black*

Robyn Meredith

DETROIT, July 15   The yuppie couple were driving home through the suburb of Royal Oak after dinner and a movie when a police car behind them turned on its lights and siren.

"I pulled over," Dennis W. Archer Jr. said, recalling the incident on Memorial Day. "Completely surrounding us there are six police cars."

Despite politely asking why they had been stopped, Mr. Archer said, he and his date were ordered out of the car without explanation. As an officer aimed a shotgun at him, Mr. Archer said, he was patted down and then pushed into the back seat of a police cruiser, where he watched as his date was handcuffed.

After about 15 minutes, he said, the officers let them go, acknowledging, with little apology, that the couple were unlikely to have committed a nearby armed robbery minutes earlier. Mr. Archer's date works as a county prosecutor. Mr. Archer, 30, is a lawyer and the eldest son of Detroit's Mayor, Dennis W. Archer.

The officers were white. Mr. Archer and his date are black.

For Mayor Archer, there was a sad familiarity. When his son called, the Mayor said, "I had flashbacks to when I was stopped."

That was 15 years ago, when police officers in Detroit pulled him over.

"They had pulled guns and put me in the back seat," the Mayor said. They went through his Cadillac Seville, looking for evidence that he was the drug dealer they were looking for, he said. But when the police rifled through his briefcase, they learned he was president of the State Bar Association.

In stopping the Mayor's son, the Royal Oak police said, officers responded appropriately and followed normal procedures for an investigation of a felony, rather than a simple traffic stop. Three minutes before stopping Mr. Archer, the police had received a report that a gunman robbed a convenience store nearby, then drove off with another person in a dark blue Jeep. Mr. Archer's Jeep Grand Cherokee is black, and carried two people.

"This is not a case of stopping a black driver for the sake of stopping a black driver," said Comdr. Thomas Wightman of the Royal Oak Police Department.

Originally published as "Near Detroit, a Familiar Sting in Being a Black Driver." From *The New York Times*, July 16, 1999. Copyright © 1999 by The New York Times Company. Reprinted by permission.

But the Mayor's son believes that the police would have given better treatment to a white couple, and he plans to file a complaint with the police department on Monday.

Minority members around the country say it is so common for them to be stopped for what they feel are slender reasons that they have a name for an imaginary crime: D. W. B., driving while black.

Last month, President Clinton ordered Federal law-enforcement agencies to compile data on the race and ethnicity of those they stop and challenged state and local police to do the same. Mr. Clinton called the practice of stopping of drivers because of the color of their skin "morally indefensible."

In April, New Jersey officials admitted that state troopers had unfairly singled out minority drivers.

And in New York, where the police shooting of an unarmed black man who was approached for questioning led to weeks of protests, Deputy Mayor Rudy Washington recently told of his own experience in being harassed by the police.

Here in Detroit, a city that is 76 percent black, the police are long past the days when squad cars carrying burly white officers would pull up to street corners and beat up blacks. In the 1967 riots here, white officers opened fire on a black uniformed rookie officer, Isaiah McKinnon, who later became the city's police chief.

Detroit's police force has been well integrated, and for more than 25 years the city has been run by black mayors.

But blacks—rich, middle-class and poor alike—still tell of being followed by the police when they drive into the primarily white suburbs or of being otherwise harassed when they encounter suburban police.

A black executive with General Motors sent his nephew to shop in his exclusive neighborhood, only to soon have the police interrupt a party at his house to investigate whether the youngster had stolen a can of vegetables. The receipt was produced and the police left, but the executive said he was still shaken.

The recent stop was the worst, but not the first, for the Mayor's son.

"I have been stopped before for what has been, in my opinion, no apparent reason," Mr. Archer said. "You cannot come across anyone who is African-American who has not at some point felt that they have been either subtly or very directly discriminated against because of their race, myself included."

Mayor Archer said the incident made him feel that society had gone "back in time, as opposed to moving forward where we can put these issues behind us and have a society based on mutual respect."

He sat with his son in the Mayor's office, under a print of the famous Norman Rockwell painting of bygone days, when United States marshals were needed to escort a young black girl to a once-white school, past a wall where someone had scrawled a racial epithet and thrown tomatoes.

His son's traffic stop was a curt reminder, Mayor Archer said, "that we happen to be people of color."

"It doesn't matter what your name happens to be, what your title happens to be, whatever the case may be," the Mayor said. "Doesn't matter."

3

Gender Bias on Wall Street

Ann Wozencraft

In October, Merrill Lynch & Company held an all-day marketing symposium at the Parker Meridien Hotel in Manhattan for more than 100 of its women brokers. At one session, panelists discussed an on-line forum, to begin the following week, in which investors could sign up to receive Merrill Lynch research if they agreed to be contacted by a broker. The program promised to generate thousands of solid client leads.

"How will these leads be distributed?" one woman asked.

The brokers "have already been chosen by their managers," a panelist said.

"Has anyone in this room been chosen?" another woman asked.

Not one woman raised her hand.

"There was almost an insurrection," said one woman who attended the meeting. "It was discrimination personified. We couldn't believe that all the leads were going to men."

Merrill says that women were in fact well represented among the brokers selected, but for many at the meeting, the lack of hands rankled deeply—if only because of the timing. Merrill was already embroiled in a sexual-discrimination suit. On Sept. 2, a Federal judge in Chicago had given final approval to a class-action settlement of a case filed by one current and seven former Merrill brokers who contended that the firm had discriminated against women in wages, promotions, account distributions, maternity leaves and other areas.

If anything, that October meeting helped build the numbers of women seeking redress. For even as Merrill Lynch was holding its symposium at the Parker

Meridien, plaintiffs' lawyers were holding their own meetings at the nearby Waldorf-Astoria.

"It was an awakening, and the beginning of a groundswell in the number of people deciding to file claims," said Linda Friedman of Stowell & Friedman, a Chicago law firm representing the plaintiffs. "We had expected a small turnout, but women kept coming over all day."

Tuesday is the last day women can file a claim, and at least 900 are doing so, or 31 percent of those eligible—a turnout far higher than expected, according to Mary Stowell, another lawyer representing the plaintiffs. Indeed, a typical response to a class-action call is about 3 percent, legal experts said.

The response has been strong at least in part because women at Merrill heard of the suit from co-workers; a consumer class action often involves a more disjointed group. And unlike some settlements, there is no limit to the amount the women can receive.

John L. Steffens, vice chairman of Merrill and head of its retail brokerage division, denied any pattern of discrimination at Merrill and said the firm had long been committed to improving its workplace. Many initiatives have benefited women, he said, including a 13-week paid maternity leave and a flexible telecommuting program. Since the end of 1997, two women have been named to the 18-member executive management committee.

"We are absolutely serious about making this a terrific place to work for a variety of diverse groups," he said. "It's a little difficult for me to comment precisely since I haven't seen any of the claims. Am I going to do something when I get the facts? You can bet on it."

Some do not regard the industry as terrific. "It's the last bastion of testosterone gone wild," said Marybeth Cremin, the lawsuit's original plaintiff. "This industry has been allowed to discriminate for years."

Ms. Cremin, of Wilmette, Ill., said that after getting her master's degree in business administration, she was drawn to the brokerage business by the potential for a high salary and the flexible hours. Instead, she said, she was paid less than male colleagues, not given high-revenue accounts even after she felt she earned them, not sent to training seminars, and penalized when she was on maternity leave.

She said she was dismissed in 1995 after her fourth child, Maryclare, was born, though she had often brought in close to $500,000 in business annually. She filed her suit in 1996, then was joined by seven others the following year.

"I don't expect the cards to be stacked in my favor, I just want it to be an even playing field," she said. "I hope Merrill and other firms will wake up and realize the resources they have in women employees and invest in training them."

Some women in the Merrill case charge harassment, but most focus on what they see as a pattern of economic disparity. Among their chief concerns are how accounts from departing brokers, walk-ins, leads and referrals are distributed.

Janna Brattain spent 10 years as a broker for Merrill in Anchorage and has filed a claim. She said that after she complained that women did not have the same access to top accounts, she was later dismissed.

"The top men brokers were fed the pick of the business, while everyone else got the crumbs," she said.

The suit has Wall Street paying attention, especially since it follows the infamous "boom-boom room" case involving the brokerage firm then known as Smith Barney. In 1996, three women from its office in Garden City, N.Y., filed a class-action suit charging the firm with sexual discrimination; the office, they said, maintained a fraternity-house culture in a basement where a toilet seat hung from the ceiling and Bloody Marys were served. The suit, also handled by Stowell & Friedman, now includes 22,500 former and current employees. A settlement became final in July, and the claims process began on Feb. 1.

"It was a wake-up call to the industry," said Michael Schlein, director of corporate development at what is now Salomon Smith Barney, a unit of Citigroup. "Smith Barney saw this as an opportunity to increase the momentum for change."

In 1995, 11 percent of its brokers were women; that rose to 15 percent by last year. The firm also agreed to a number of changes. It set a goal of having women make up a third of broker trainees hired—reaching 31 percent last year—and of raising the number of women and minorities in branch-manager posts.

Both lawsuits underscore how entrenched the obstacles still are for women on Wall Street. Women now account for about half the industry's work force, but relatively few have risen to top management.

"It's an old boys' network," said Patricia Ireland, president of the National Organization for Women. "Changing the culture of the securities industry doesn't just happen because of the passage of time. It comes because of the women who are willing to push hard and the men who are willing to support them." The large number of women brokers at Merrill claiming bias, she said, "gives the pendulum a big push."

According to Catalyst, a group that monitors how women are treated in the workplace, stereotypes have held the brokers back. "There's a perception that women are not aggressive or tough enough, that they're not business-getters," said Sheila Wellington, Catalyst's president. "As firms determine that women constitute important new markets for them, they'll realize that there is a sound business reason for diversity."

Under the settlement, the 2,897 women employed in Merrill's domestic retail brokerage business between Jan. 1, 1994, and June 18, 1998, can seek compensation. The process requires an investigation by the firm within 60 days and then mediation. If no settlement is reached, the claim will go to binding arbitration before a panel agreed to by both sides.

Merrill has long dominated the brokerage business, with 715 offices nationwide. But even as it has grown, the presence of women brokers has essentially remained steady. Of Merrill's 13,410 brokers in 1998, 2,114, or 15.8 percent, were women. In 1990, it was 1,609 of 10,464, or 15.4 percent.

Merrill has several "clubs" that recognize brokers producing more than $1 million, $1.75 million, or $2.5 million in annual revenue. In 1991, the firm said, women constituted 8.1 percent of the clubs' members; last year, the representation was up to 9.5 percent. Merrill, however, did not break out figures for how many women were in each club.

As part of the settlement, Merrill became the first firm to end mandatory arbitration for sexual discrimination and other civil rights claims. Employees with claims after July 1, 1998, may go to court. Paine Webber Group has adopted a similar policy.

"The securities industry has made an end run around civil rights laws by keeping its complaints out of the court system, so it's a step in the right direction," Ms. Friedman said.

About half of those filing claims are current employees, and many of those said they hoped to stay with Merrill. "We wouldn't be taking this kind of risk if it was just about the money," said one woman broker with more than 10 years of experience. "We want respect. And we're tired of going to work every day 10 steps behind all the men."

Not all the eligible women plan to file claims. Subha Barry, who runs Merrill's Plainsboro, N.J., office, said she had had great success working from within. When her second child was born, Merrill set up a terminal in her home and added telephone and fax lines.

"Certainly, there were incidents of golf outings and baseball games where women weren't included," Ms. Barry said. "So I went to my manager and said, 'Don't count me out just because I don't golf.' He ended up organizing golf lessons for the women."

For his part, Mr. Steffens said that the firm was committed to diversity and two-way communication. "I want to see us promote the best and the brightest," he said. "It's the only way we're going to be able to compete."

4

Homophobia Often Found in Schools, Data Show

James Brooke

DENVER, Oct. 13   Last Saturday morning, while Matthew Shepard lay co-matose from a beating, a college homecoming parade passed a few blocks from his hospital bed in Fort Collins, Colo. Propped on a fraternity float was a straw-haired scarecrow labeled in black spray paint, "I'm Gay."

Few people missed the message. Three days earlier, Mr. Shepard, a gay University of Wyoming freshman, was savagely beaten and tied to a ranch fence in such a position that a passer-by first mistook him for a scarecrow.

Today, officials at Colorado State University in Fort Collins reacted with out-rage, opening an investigation and disciplinary procedures against the fraternity, Pi Kappa Alpha. The fraternity chapter immediately suspended seven members and said they had acted independently.

But in a week when candlelight vigils for Mr. Shepard were being held on campuses across the nation, the scarecrow incident highlighted how hostility to-ward homosexuals often flourishes in high schools and universities, gay leaders said today.

"People would like to think that what happened to Matthew was an exception to the rule but, it was an extreme version of what happens in our schools on a daily basis," said Kevin Jennings, executive director of the Gay, Lesbian and Straight Education Network, a New York group dedicated to ending anti-gay bias in the schools.

Mr. Shepard, a slightly built 21-year-old, was beaten so severely that he died on Monday. He never regained consciousness after being discovered on Oct. 7, 18 hours after he was lashed to the fence. Two men, Russell A. Henderson, 21, and Aaron J. McKinney, 22, were arraigned on first degree murder charges late Monday night. Their girlfriends, Chasity V. Pasley, 20, and Kristen L. Price, 18, have been arraigned as accessories after the fact.

In response to the killing, about 50 candlelight vigils were scheduled this week, from Texas to Vermont, from Wayne, Neb., to New York City.

At the Poudre Valley Hospital in Fort Collins where Mr. Shepard was in intensive care for five days, his parents, Dennis and Judy Shepard, received about 6,000 electronic messages of condolences. Today, when funeral arrangements were announced for Friday in Casper, Wyo., the hospital Web site received 30,000 hits an hour.

University friends in Laramie, Wyo., have set up the Matthew Shepard Memorial Fund to raise money to pressure the state Legislature to pass legislation against hate crimes.

"I see his name going down in gay history as a catalyst for renewed activism," said Matt Foreman, a former Wyomingite who directs Empire State Pride Agenda, a gay political organization in New York.

From around the nation today, gay leaders emphasized that campus homophobia was not restricted to college towns in the Rocky Mountain West.

Last year, in a survey of almost 4,000 Massachusetts high school students, 22 percent of gay respondents said they had skipped school in the past month because they felt unsafe there, and 31 percent said they had been threatened or injured at school in the past year. These percentages were about five times greater than the percentages of heterosexual respondents. The survey was conducted at 58 high schools by the Massachusetts Department of Education.

In a separate study of nearly 500 community college students in the San Francisco area, 32 percent of male respondents said they had verbally threatened homosexuals and 18 percent said they had physically threatened or assaulted them. The study was conducted this year by Karen Franklin, a forensic psychologist who is a researcher at the University of Washington.

Surveys of gay college students conducted in the late 1980's at Yale University, Oberlin College, Rutgers University and Pennsylvania State University found that 16 percent to 26 percent had been threatened with violence, and that 40 percent to 76 percent had been verbally harassed, said the National Gay and Lesbian Task Force, a lobbying group based in Washington.

Last year, a Des Moines student group, Concerned Students, recorded hallway and classroom conversations at five high schools on 10 "homophobia recording days." They estimated that the average Des Moines high school student heard about 25 anti-gay remarks every day.

"Nine out of 10 'teaching tolerance' courses weed out gays," Mr. Foreman said. "There are a lot of people preaching anti-racism and [against] anti-Semitism. But it is still very much O.K. to make anti-gay jokes, to express anti-gay sentiments."

A survey of the nation's 42 largest school districts found that 76 percent did not train teachers on issues facing gay students and 42 percent lacked policies to protect students from discrimination based on sexual orientation, said the Gay, Lesbian and Straight Education Network, which did the study last month.

In Fort Collins, while the hospital officials struggled with an electronic avalanche of condolences, city police detectives were investigating a different kind of E-mail.

On Monday, hours after Mr. Shepard's death, two gay organizations, the Rainbow Chorus and the Lambda Community Center, received identical messages applauding the killing of Mr. Shepard. The messages closed with the words, "I hope it happens more often."

5

3 Blacks Win $1 Million in Bauer Store Incident

David Stout

WASHINGTON, Oct. 9   A Federal District Court jury in nearby Greenbelt, Md., ordered the Eddie Bauer company today to pay $1 million in damages over an incident in which three young black men were detained on suspicion of shoplifting.

One youth, who was forced to remove his shirt in the incident two years ago, Alonzo Jackson, received the bulk of the award: $850,000 in compensatory and punitive damages. His friends, Rasheed Plummer and Marco Cunningham, were awarded $75,000 each. All live in the Maryland suburbs of the capital.

"We're pleased," Donald Temple, a Washington lawyer for Mr. Jackson and Mr. Plummer, said today. "We've educated the public, and the country will benefit as a result."

The case attracted widespread attention as a civil rights issue, and prompted a public apology by Eddie Bauer, a giant clothing retailer based in Redmond, Wash., and a subsidiary of Spiegel Inc.

A statement issued by the company made no mention of an appeal. The company said it was pleased that the jury, while finding it negligent in supervising its people and liable for defamation of character, had not found that it had committed civil rights violations.

Mr. Jackson, now 18, Mr. Plummer, 19, and Mr. Cunningham, who is now 20, were shopping at a Bauer outlet store in Fort Washington, Md., a largely black and middle-class community, on Oct. 20, 1995, when they were confronted by two uniformed Prince Georges County police officers who were moonlighting as security guards.

Testimony revealed that one of the officers, Robert Sheehan, had become suspicious after noticing that Mr. Jackson's shirt looked new. In fact, it was: Mr. Jackson had bought it at the store the previous day.

Mr. Jackson could not immediately produce a receipt, so the shirt was confiscated, despite a cashier's recollection of selling a shirt to him the day before, according to testimony.

Mr. Plummer and Mr. Cunningham were detained about 10 minutes while their friend was being questioned, the jury was told. At one point, Mr. Cunningham was told, "Sit down or I'll lock you up," according to testimony.

Soon after the three were allowed to leave, Mr. Jackson returned to the store with the receipt to retrieve his shirt, but it was too late for the company to avert a major embarrassment.

The plaintiffs accused Eddie Bauer of "consumer racism" and said the incident was typical of the way black shoppers are regarded. At the time, Mr. Jackson was an honor student in high school who played basketball and held a part-time job.

Eddie Bauer's president, Rick Fersch, issued the apology and said the incident did not reflect the philosophy of the company, which made fair treatment of all customers a condition of employment.

Mr. Temple said today he regarded Mr. Fersch as "a good guy with good intentions." But the lawyer said Eddie Bauer's legal team had fought the plaintiffs at almost every step, initially offering a settlement, then taking the offer off the table.

The company's statement called the 1995 incident "an isolated event" and not representative of Eddie Bauer's commitment to respect the rights of all individuals.

The jury of four white and three black members deliberated for seven hours over two days before returning its verdict.

6

Another Day, Another 75 Cents

Ann Scott Tyson

WASHINGTON   Most nights, single mother Dolores Jones checks on her sleeping son, locks the door of her brick duplex, and drives down dark, pot-holed streets to a graveyard shift as a custodian on Capitol Hill.

For the past 11-1/2 years, Ms. Jones has worked until dawn dusting paper-strewn desktops, emptying trash, and pushing her husky Hoover sweeper through abandoned congressional suites—alone but for a few dogged staffers or lawmakers asleep behind "Do Not Disturb" signs.

But while she is resigned to the wearing job, Jones is no longer willing to tolerate what she sees as a blatant injustice: Men who perform essentially the same work as she does earn $1 more per hour.

"We are tired of the unfair treatment," says Jones, one of 52 women custodians who last July brought a class-action pay-equity suit against their employer.

Many US women today share Jones's exasperation. Indeed, decades after women began breaking into the labor force in record numbers, the No. 1 concern of America's 63 million working women is the stubborn male–female wage gap.

"Equal pay for equal work" is the top workplace issue for the vast majority of employed women (94 percent), according to a nationwide survey of 50,000 working women by the AFL-CIO last year. It is cited more often than child care (33 percent), sexual harassment (78 percent), or downsizing (72 percent).

The emphasis on fairness is justified by facts:

- Today, as a result of discrimination and other factors, women still earn only about 75 cents for every $1 that men make, according to the US Labor Department's median weekly wage figures for 1997.
- On average, women earn $24,000 a year, compared with $32,000 for men.
- If current wage patterns continue, the average 25-year-old woman who works full time year-round for 40 years will earn $400,000 to $500,000 less than her male peer, according to the Institute for Women's Policy Research (IWPR) in Washington.

From *The Christian Science Monitor,* July 17, 1998, pp. 7–8.

Especially hard hit by the gap are the 2 of every 5 working women who, like Jones, are the sole breadwinners in their homes. The toll is also heavy on minority women, as well as the expanding number of older women, whose retirement security is hurt by lower lifetime earnings.

"It's been hard on me in terms of keeping up with the mortgage," says Jones, who is divorced and supports her eight-year-old son and retired mother on $23,000 a year. Most of her female co-workers are heads of household, she says.

Moreover, even as women's participation in the labor force continues to grow—reaching nearly 60 percent last year—elimination of the wage gap is in no way assured, economists say.

Although the gap has narrowed slowly since 1980, when women's earnings averaged just 60 percent of men's, most of the change can be attributed to a backsliding by men rather than progress by women, says Heidi Hartmann, director of the IWPR. Falling wages for men account for about three-fifths of the shrinking of the wage gap since 1980.

But when men gain, as they did in the mid-1990s, the gap widens again. From 1993 to 1997, for example, men's wages rebounded as women's earnings stalled, leading to a wider gap.

* * *

Despite Significant Progress, Stubborn Wage Gap Persists

"Discrimination is clearly still a factor in the labor market today, and that is why enforcement efforts are very important," says [Secretary of Labor Alexis] Herman.

At least one-quarter of the wage gap is the result of differences in pay between men and women "working in similar jobs and establishments," according to a study published this year by economists of the National Bureau of Economic Research in Cambridge, Mass.

For example, Jones and other female "custodians" who vacuum and dust inside congressional suites contend that their work is the same as that of the male "laborers" who wash the hallways and polish the brass banisters outside. "We do just as much work as the men, and they get paid more," Jones says.

In addition to holding down women's pay, discrimination prevents women from being hired and promoted into better-paying jobs.

Finally, gender biases long entrenched in wage structures continue to hamper efforts to increase wages for what was once unpaid "women's work," such as child care, says Ellen Bravo, head of the 9 to 5 National Association of Working Women in Milwaukee. "Women's work has been devalued," she says.

7

I Don't Count as "Diversity"

Angelo Ragaza

When I left school for my first job nine years ago, I had no reason to believe I faced professional obstacles bigger than anyone else's. I was the child of middle-class professionals, grew up in a comfortable New Jersey suburb and held a degree from an Ivy League school. As an Asian-American, I was relieved that I belonged to a racial group that many equate with academic and professional success. But once in the workplace, I found myself slapped in the face for straddling the racial divide. In some situations, I was considered virtually white and not "minority" enough. In others, it was the other way round. I was temping at a national civil-rights organiza-tion when, a few months into the assignment, I was told that management was thinking about making my place there permanent. Interviewed by three different managers, I grew increasingly optimistic. At the last interview, the deputy director commended my performance and told me that I all but had the job. But the next day my hopes were dashed. Through the office grapevine, I found out that man-agement was under pressure from the community to diversify, and my replace-ment, an African-American women, filled the bill better than I.

The decision hit me, not in the hallowed realm of my ideals of inclusiveness, but in the hollow realm of my wallet. As an Asian, I thought I already was bringing diversity to the organization. But before I had a chance to morph from idealist to cynic, I left the nonprofit world for the world of publishing. When I compare the complexions of my colleagues with the staff of nonprofit organizations, I wonder whether I am indeed in America.

Some of my publishing friends say they've felt isolated and frustrated at being the only minorities on staff. Because of the homogeneity of editorial personnel, blatant stereotypes of Asian-Americans sometimes pass under the radar of other-wise exacting editors. And while some publications make a conscious effort to re-port on and hire minorities, I can't tell you the number of times I've pitched an Asian-American story to an editor, only to be told it wouldn't appeal to a "general" audience. Or the times an editor went through the motions of interviewing me, only to hire a friend. I don't want to insinuate that the people weren't qualified, but they did happen to share the editors' race, class and connections. The rank and file of magazine offices is filled with people who got their jobs because their

From *Newsweek*, February 8, 1999, p. 13.

parents put a call in to the higher-ups. Neither my mom nor my dad is in a position to do that, though in every way they—a biotechnologist and a computer engineer, respectively—should fit into the great American immigrant success story like a hand in a glove.

But don't look to my parents to jump on the backlash bandwagon. Over the course of her career, my mother has seen managers tailor job descriptions and manipulate the promotion process to install people with whom they felt "comfortable"—even if their choices' qualifications didn't hold a candle to hers. And my dad has struggled for years to be his own boss, partially because his accent, immigrant status and lack of connections were like dead weights on the corporate ladder.

It's easy to see why Asian-Americans make ideal poster faces for the affirmative-action backlash. Just yesterday we got "off the boat"; apparently overnight, we're driving Lexuses and sending our kids to Yale. We're proof that prejudice doesn't exist—and that affirmative action is unnecessary. Take the debate over college admissions, which routinely depicts schools like Harvard passing over Asian-American math whizzes for "less qualified" minority applicants. But what about Asian-Americans in the workforce? Here we cease to be useful to the foes of affirmative action. The few statistics that exist indicate that, despite having education and training to rival their white colleagues, Asian-Americans have not achieved parity in status and salary. An Asian-American is 60 percent more likely to hold a bachelor's degree than a white American but makes a lower median salary ($37,040 versus $42,050). And although Asian-Americans constitute 4 percent of the population, they occupy less than two tenths of 1 percent of the country's corporate directorships. In sports, the media, politics and entertainment, it would take a blindfold not to see our absence. Affirmative action's critics are wrong to forge an alliance with Asian-American Success. In fact, an Asian-American family is 20 percent more likely to be living in poverty than a white family. And in 1996, exit polls found that 73 percent of Asian-American Republicans and 79 percent of Asian-American Democrats voted against Proposition 209, the referendum that eliminated affirmative action in California.

Mainstream media ignored this finding. But it speaks volumes about Asian-American critics of affirmative action like "Illiberal Education" author Dinesh D'Souza, to whom the media have paid inordinate attention. These folks don't speak for all Asian-Americans. And they certainly don't speak for me, my mom or my dad.

8

The Border Patrol State

Leslie Marmon Silko

I used to travel the highways of New Mexico and Arizona with a wonderful sensation of absolute freedom as I cruised down the open road and across the vast desert plateaus. On the Laguna Pueblo reservation, where I was raised, the people were patriotic despite the way the U.S. government had treated Native Americans. As proud citizens, we grew up believing the freedom to travel was our inalienable right, a right that some Native Americans had been denied in the early twentieth century. Our cousin, old Bill Pratt, used to ride his horse 300 miles overland from Laguna, New Mexico, to Prescott, Arizona, every summer to work as a fire lookout.

In school in the 1950s, we were taught that our right to travel from state to state without special papers or threat of detainment was a right that citizens under communist and totalitarian governments did not possess. That wide open highway told us we were U.S. citizens; we were free. . . .

Not so long ago, my companion Gus and I were driving south from Albuquerque, returning to Tucson after a book promotion for the paperback edition of my novel *Almanac of the Dead.* I had settled back and gone to sleep while Gus drove, but I was awakened when I felt the car slowing to a stop. It was nearly midnight on New Mexico State Road 26, a dark, lonely stretch of two-lane highway between Hatch and Deming. When I sat up, I saw the headlights and emergency flashers of six vehicles—Border Patrol cars and a van were blocking both lanes of the highway. Gus stopped the car and rolled down the window to ask what was wrong. But the closest Border Patrolman and his companion did not reply; instead, the first agent ordered us to "step out of the car." Gus asked why, but his question seemed to set them off. Two more Border Patrol agents immediately approached our car, and one of them snapped, "Are you looking for trouble?" as if he would relish it.

I will never forget that night beside the highway. There was an awful feeling of menace and violence straining to break loose. It was clear that the uniformed men would be only too happy to drag us out of the car if we did not speedily comply with their request (asking a question is tantamount to resistance, it seems). So we

From Leslie Marmon Silko, *Yellow Woman and a Beauty of the Spirit: Essays on Native American Life Today.* Copyright © 1996 by Leslie Marmon Silko. Originally appeared in *The Nation,* October 17, 1994, pp. 412–416. Reprinted with the permission of Simon & Schuster.

stepped out of the car and they motioned for us to stand on the shoulder of the road. The night was very dark, and no other traffic had come down the road since we had been stopped. . . .

Two other Border Patrolmen stood by the white van. The one who had asked if we were looking for trouble ordered his partner to "get the dog," and from the back of the van another patrolman brought a small female German shepherd on a leash. The dog apparently did not heel well enough to suit him, and the handler jerked the leash. They opened the doors of our car and pulled the dog's head into it, but I saw immediately from the expression in her eyes that the dog hated them, and that she would not serve them. When she showed no interest in the inside of our car, they brought her around back to the trunk, near where we were standing. They half-dragged her up into the trunk, but still she did not indicate any stowed-away human beings or illegal drugs. . . .

Unfortunately, what happened to me is an everyday occurrence here now. Since the 1980s, on top of greatly expanding border checkpoints, the Immigration and Naturalization Service and the Border Patrol have implemented policies that interfere with the rights of U.S. citizens to travel freely within our borders. I.N.S. agents now patrol all interstate highways and roads that lead to or from the U.S.– Mexico border in Texas, New Mexico, Arizona and California. Now, when you drive east from Tucson on Interstate 10 toward El Paso, you encounter an I.N.S. check station outside Las Cruces, New Mexico. When you drive north from Las Cruces up Interstate 25, two miles north of the town of Truth or Consequences, the highway is blocked with orange emergency barriers, and all traffic is diverted into a two-lane Border Patrol checkpoint—ninety-five miles north of the U.S.– Mexico border.

I was detained once at Truth or Consequences, despite my and my companion's Arizona driver's licenses. Two men, both Chicanos, were detained at the same time, despite the fact that they too presented ID and spoke English without the thick Texas accents of the Border Patrol agents. While we were stopped, we watched as other vehicles—whose occupants were white—were waved through the checkpoint. White people traveling with brown people, however, can expect to be stopped on suspicion they work with the sanctuary movement, which shelters refugees. White people who appear to be clergy, those who wear ethnic clothing or jewelry and women with very long hair or very short hair (they could be nuns) are also frequently detained; white men with beards or men with long hair are likely to be detained, too, because Border Patrol agents have "profiles" of "those sorts" of white people who may help political refugees. (Most of the political refugees from Guatemala and El Salvador are Native American or mestizo because the indigenous people of the Americas have continued to resist efforts by invaders to displace them from their ancestral lands.) Alleged increases in illegal immigration by people of Asian ancestry means that the Border Patrol now routinely detains anyone who appears to be Asian or part Asian, as well.

Once your car is diverted from the Interstate Highway into the checkpoint area, you are under the control of the Border Patrol, which in practical terms exercises a power that no highway patrol or city patrolman possesses: They are willing to detain anyone, for no apparent reason. Other law-enforcement officers need a shred of probable cause in order to detain someone. On the books, so does the Border Patrol; but on the road, it's another matter. They'll order you to stop your car and step out; then they'll ask you to open the trunk. If you ask why or request a search warrant, you'll be told that they'll have to have a dog sniff the car before they can request a search warrant, and the dog might not get there for two or three hours. The search warrant might require an hour or two past that. They make it clear that if you force them to obtain a search warrant for the car, they will make you submit to a strip search as well.

Traveling in the open, though, the sense of violation can be even worse. Never mind high-profile cases like that of former Border Patrol agent Michael Elmer, acquitted of murder by claiming self-defense, despite admitting that as an officer he shot an "illegal" immigrant in the back and then hid the body, which remained undiscovered until another Border Patrolman reported the event. (Last month, Elmer was convicted of reckless endangerment in a separate incident, for shooting at least ten rounds from his M-16 too close to a group of immigrants as they were crossing illegally into Nogales in March 1992.) Or that in El Paso, a high school football coach driving a vanload of his players in full uniform was pulled over on the freeway and a Border Patrol agent put a cocked revolver to his head. (The football coach was Mexican-American, as were most of the players in his van; the incident eventually caused a federal judge to issue a restraining order against the Border Patrol.) We've a mountain of personal experiences like that which never make the newspapers. . . .

Just the other day, I mentioned to a friend that I was writing this article and he told me about his 73-year-old father, who is half Chinese and had set out alone by car from Tucson to Albuquerque the week before. His father had become confused by road construction and missed a turnoff from Interstate 10 to Interstate 25; when he turned around and circled back, he missed the turnoff a second time. But when he looped back for yet another try, Border Patrol agents stopped him and forced him to open his trunk. After they satisfied themselves that he was not smuggling Chinese immigrants, they sent him on his way. He was so rattled by the event that he had to be driven home by his daughter.

This is the police state that has developed in the southwestern United States since the 1980s. No person, no citizen, is free to travel without the scrutiny of the Border Patrol. In the city of South Tucson, where 80 percent of the respondents were Chicano or Mexicano, a joint research project by the University of Wisconsin and the University of Arizona recently concluded that one out of every five people there had been detained, mistreated verbally or nonverbally, or questioned by I.N.S. agents in the past two years.

9

Resegregation in American Schools

Gary Orfield and John T. Yun

This report focuses primarily upon four important trends. First, the American South is resegregating, after two and a half decades in which civil rights law broke the tradition of apartheid in the region's schools and made it the section of the country with the highest levels of integration in its schools. Second, the data shows continuously increasing segregation for Latino students, who are rapidly becoming our largest minority group and have been more segregated than African Americans for several years. Third, the report shows large and increasing numbers of African-American and Latino students enrolled in suburban schools, but serious segregation within these communities, particularly in the nation's large metropolitan areas. Since trends suggest that we will face a vast increase in suburban diversity, this raises challenges for thousands of communities. Fourth, we report a rapid on-going change in the racial composition of American schools and the emergence of many schools with three or more racial groups. The report shows that all racial groups except whites experience considerable diversity in their schools but whites are remaining in overwhelmingly white schools even in regions with very large non-white enrollments.

Though we usually think of segregation in racial and ethnic terms, it's important to also realize that the spreading segregation has a strong class component. When African-American and Latino students are segregated into schools where the majority of students are non-white, they are very likely to find themselves in schools where poverty is concentrated. This is of course not the case with segregated white students, whose majority-white schools almost always enroll high proportions of students from the middle class. This is a crucial difference, because concentrated poverty is linked to lower educational achievement. School level poverty is related to many variables that affect a school's overall chance at successfully educating students, including parent education levels, availability of advanced courses, teachers with credentials in the subject they are teaching, instability of enrollment, dropouts, untreated health problems, lower college-going rates and many other important factors. The nation's large program of compensatory education, Title I, has had great difficulty achieving gains in schools where poverty is highly concentrated. When school districts return to neighborhood schools, white students tend to sit next to middle class students but black and Latino students are likely to be next to impoverished students.

Therefore, while debates over the exact academic impact of desegregation continue, there is no question that black and Latino students in racially integrated schools are generally in schools with higher levels of average academic achievement than are their counterparts in segregated schools. Desegregation does not assure that students will receive the better opportunities in those schools—that depends on how the interracial school is run—but it does usually put minority students in schools which have better opportunities and better prepared peer groups. In a period in which mandatory state tests for graduation are being imposed, college admissions standards are rising, remedial courses in college are being cut back, and affirmative action has already been abolished in our two largest states, the harmful consequences for students attending less competitive schools are steadily increasing.

We are clearly in a period when many policymakers, courts, and opinion makers assume that desegregation is no longer necessary, or that it will be accomplished somehow without need of any deliberate plan. Polls show that most white Americans believe that equal educational opportunity is being provided. National political leaders have largely ignored the growth of segregation in the 1990s. Thus, knowledge of trends in segregation and its closely related inequalities is even more crucial now. For example, increased testing requirements for high school graduation, for passing from one grade to the next, and college entrance can only be fair if we offer equal preparation to children, regardless of skin color and language. Increasing segregation, however, pushes us in the opposite direction because it creates more unequal schools, particularly for low income minority children, who are the groups which most frequently receive low test scores. Educational policy decisions that do not take these realities into account will end up punishing students in inferior segregated schools, or even sending more children to such schools while simultaneously raising sanctions for those who do not achieve at a sufficiently high level.

In addition to its focus upon the trends of Southern resegregation, Latino student segregation and suburban segregation, this report documents basic national trends in enrollment and segregation for African-American students, Latinos, White and Asian students by region, by state, by community type—allowing comparison across the country. The final section offers recommendations on how to reverse the trend of rising segregation, concluding that there has been very little national leadership on this issue for the past quarter century, recalling the positive steps taken in the 1960s and 1970s, and suggesting a number of steps that would support successful desegregated schools.

10

Doctor Refuses to Treat Lesbian

Jane E. Allen

Michelle DuPont sat down in her new primary care doctor's office and was immediately put at ease by medical forms that listed "domestic partner" as a choice for marital status. She filled in the name of her partner of three years, Lisa, and thought to herself how pleasantly progressive the doctor seemed.

When Dr. Ronald Axtell asked her if she used birth control, DuPont says she responded, no, "I'm lesbian and therefore pregnancy isn't an issue."

After finishing a pelvic exam, Axtell suggested she make her next appointment with one of two other doctors in his Mission Viejo medical group. DuPont, 39, assumed he was sending her to a specialist for something he found during the examination.

Then, said DuPont, the "bombshell" hit. The doctor told her he didn't approve of her gay "lifestyle."

Still on the examining table, in a flimsy paper gown and feeling vulnerable because she'd revealed her need for antidepressants in the aftermath of childhood sexual abuse, she felt humiliated.

Axtell doesn't dispute offering opinions about DuPont's sexuality and referring her elsewhere during that June 1998 visit, says L.A. attorney Jeff Moffat, who represents the doctor in a discrimination lawsuit the American Civil Liberties Union filed on DuPont's behalf in state court May 13.

Moffat denies that Axtell discriminated against DuPont, saying the doctor did not refuse to treat her and made other arrangements for her to receive care.

DuPont, who now lives in the Oceanside area, has been openly gay since age 27 and her sexuality never before posed an issue, including with the Capistrano School District, where she formerly worked as a teaching assistant.

"I'm not Pollyanna, but I never would expect it from a doctor," says DuPont. But the impact of the event is that she waited nearly a year before seeking treatment for the anemia that brought her to Axtell in the first place.

DuPont's story illuminates a topic that is gaining attention: the health of gay women, long overlooked by medicine. Among the questions researchers are posing

Originally published as "Invisible Women: Many Lesbians Avoid Doctors for Fear of a Backlash from Judgmental Practitioners." From *The Los Angeles Times*, June 21, 1999. Copyright © 1999, The Times Mirror Company, Los Angeles Times. All rights reserved.

is whether lesbian health is suffering because of self-imposed exile from the doctor's office.

Like their heterosexual sisters, lesbians fear sexism in the examining room. But many also approach a medical appointment with the emotional baggage of experiences with judgmental, ignorant or homophobic doctors, experts in the field say.

* * *

Dr. Marki Knox, an obstetrician-gynecologist who works part time at the L.A. Gay and Lesbian Center's Lambda Medical Group, says she's examined many lesbians who reported going years without seeing a doctor. One woman said she had let 17 years pass. . . .

Sometimes the consequence is uterine fibroid tumors that grew. Knox treated two patients whose premalignant lesions were probably present about five years.

Knox says some women complain about having visited doctors who insisted they couldn't be lesbian "because they were too attractive or appeared too normal."

"I've had physicians tell them the problem was they had never had a normal sexual relationship and if they had, they obviously would be cured," Knox says. "These were in California. We're not talking Appalachia here." . . .

Some lesbians venture to a new medical office seeking signs the doctor will be "lesbian-friendly." They pray not to be asked repeatedly why they aren't using birth control if they're sexually active. Some would rather go home with unneeded birth control pills than "out" themselves to a stranger.

A 43-year-old animator from North Hollywood who asked only to be identified as "Nancy" recalled a visit to an older ob-gyn in Burbank. He told her some medical professionals consider homosexuality to be a form of mental illness. Her frustrated retort: "These are the things that make teenagers commit suicide when they're confused about their sexuality."

Suzanne Newman, a 34-year-old video producer-director from New York City, recalled telling a new doctor that she was a lesbian. He performed a painful pelvic exam. When she winced, he said: "What's the matter, missy, you can't take it?" Newman then paid out-of-pocket to see her former doctor.

* * *

As attention to lesbian health increases, the ACLU hopes DuPont's case, the first case of sexual discrimination in a doctor's office brought under the California Civil Rights Act, will draw more attention to treatment of gay women. ACLU attorney Taylor Flynn says the case is special because Axtell made specific notes in DuPont's file about her sexuality.

The notes included the following comments: "At the end of the visit, I told the [patient] that I felt uncomfortable treating her because of her lifestyle. I gave her the names of Dr. Tracy and Dr. Reuland to see in my place. The [patient] was very offended that I was prejudiced against her and was upset about that."

John L. Supple, an attorney for Bristol Park Medical Group, in which Axtell practices, says its policy "has always been and will continue to be to not discriminate . . . in providing medical care."

11

Grand-Slam Breakfast?

Emil Guillermo

Months after settling two major discrimination complaints, Denny's has more trouble brewing with a new Justice Department investigation. In April, a group of Asian Americans were denied service in a Syracuse restaurant, and then brutally beaten in the parking lot.

Early one morning, eight Syracuse University students—seven of them Asian Americans, including three Japanese nationals, and one Caucasian student—entered an off-campus Denny's and waited to be served. They waited. And waited.

"There were empty tables. And several whites who came later were seated ahead of them," says Elizabeth Ou Yang, an attorney with the Asian American Legal Defense and Education Fund, which is representing the students in both a criminal complaint and a possible federal civil suit against Denny's.

When the students complained, they were asked to leave. Two Denny's security guards escorted them. Once outside, Ou Yang says, one of the guards pushed the students. The students allege that a group of twenty white males came out of the restaurant, shouting racial epithets and looking for a fight.

Yuya Hasegawa, one of the international Japanese students, said he was attacked first. "I couldn't eat where I wanted to. I was beaten by whoever wanted to beat me. I am not welcome here," he said in a statement prepared by his attorneys.

Derrick Lizardo, a Filipino American student, came to Hasegawa's aid and was beaten unconscious. "I was never made to feel so helpless and so different in my entire life," he stated.

Yoshika Kusada, a Japanese American woman, also claims to have been knocked unconscious.

The two security guards, off-duty Onondaga County sheriff's deputies, did not intervene. They called for police backup instead. But Ou Yang claims their actions sparked the incident. "They needlessly pushed the Asian students outside, and caused others to come see what was going on," says Ou Yang.

The students have filed criminal charges with the Syracuse District Attorney's office. So far, the city has made no arrests. "If an arrest is not made shortly," Ou Yang said, "it will put doubt in the community's mind as to whether or not the D.A.'s office is vigorously investigating this case."

The Denny's franchise owner, Charles Davis, is African American. Davis says Denny's has become an easy target for discrimination charges. "I think if it wasn't Denny's, this charge probably would not have been brought up," he told a reporter for the *Syracuse Herald Journal.* Davis believes the restaurant and its staff will be exonerated once the Justice Department investigation is completed. He has apologized to the students for what has happened, saying if the charges are proven, he will fire the guilty parties.

"His apology is not sufficient," Ou Yang told a reporter. "He's sorry that his customers were inconvenienced, but seven people were attacked here."

The Justice Department's involvement in the case is due in part to Denny's history on race relations. In 1991, a group of eighteen African American teenagers at Denny's in San Jose, California, were asked to pay for their meals before the food arrived. In 1993, six African American Secret Service agents were denied service at a Denny's restaurant in Maryland. Both cases resulted in legal settlements that put Denny's and its franchises under a federal consent decree, whereby Denny's must report any allegations of discrimination to an independent civil rights monitor. To date, the Denny's chain, owned by Flagstar Cos. Inc. of Spartanburg, South Carolina, has paid more than $50 million to settle claims of discrimination at Denny's restaurants across the nation.

While the wait for justice may seem as interminable as the wait for a table, Ou Yang says the Asian American Legal Defense and Education Fund is conducting its own investigation. "We're proceeding with protecting our clients, rights every step of the way," she says.

In the meantime, Asian American students at Syracuse are wondering what will happen when school reconvenes in August. "The incident was a wakeup call for a lot of people that there's still a lot of racism around," says Chris Yuen, a Syracuse junior from Oakland, California. "I don't think people will forget when they get back on campus."

12

Supermarket Chain to Pay $81 Million to Settle a Bias Suit

Allen R. Myerson

One of the nation's largest supermarket chains agreed yesterday to pay $81.5 million to settle accusations that it systematically denied promotions, raises and preferred assignments to women.

The settlement, by Publix Supermarkets Inc., may be the largest workplace discrimination case in terms of the number of people it covers. The class-action lawsuit covers more than 100,000 women who worked since 1991 at Publix supermarkets in Florida, Georgia, South Carolina and Alabama.

Publix also agreed yesterday to a $3.5 million settlement with the Equal Employment Opportunity Commission over accusations that the company had similarly denied job opportunities to blacks.

The company admitted to no wrongdoing in either case, saying it was in full compliance with all fair-employment laws.

The settlements follow a number of other large employment bias settlements—including large sex discrimination cases at the Lucky Stores, Safeway and Albertson's supermarket chains. These cases are part of a new stage in the civil rights movement, transforming how many companies hire, pay and promote. Most prominent among them was an agreement by Texaco in November [1996] to pay $140 million to black employees who accused the company of denying them promotions because of their race.

At Publix, women make up about half the work force, but fewer than 5 percent of its 535 store managers, the women's lawyers said.

The discrimination suit was filed in Federal District Court in Tampa, Fla., in 1995 by 12 women who said they were concentrated at the cash registers, while men sold and stocked the merchandise—positions with more potential for advancement.

Women who received any promotions tended to do so in a few, traditionally female departments, like the bakery sections or especially the cashier staff, some said. The women said they were also often denied fair training, pay and full-time status. Publix said that the dozen women who initiated the case would receive about $90,000 each.

"The glass ceiling at Publix has been broken," said Eve Gambill Lowe, an E.E.O.C. lawyer. "Everyone can take pride in this outcome." The commission intervened to support the women's case and filed its own, parallel case regarding allegations of similar discrimination against black employees.

Several other grocery chains have also lost or settled major sex discrimination cases, including Lucky Stores for $107 million, covering 14,000 women, in 1994; Safeway for $7.5 million in 1994, and Albertson's for $29.4 million, covering female and Hispanic employees last year.

"There has been a major problem in the grocery store industry with regard to sex and often race," said Helen Norton, director of equal opportunity programs at the Women's Legal Defense Fund. "Women and blacks have been steered into deadend jobs." The Publix settlement shows both the persistence of discrimination and the effectiveness of large lawsuits in combating it, she said.

Still, Publix has had a reputation as a company that promotes from the lowest ranks. "Publix offers great opportunities to advance," asserts the 1993 edition of "The 100 Best Companies to Work for in America" (Currency-Doubleday), which includes Publix among the 100.

Publix has said that the relative absence of women from higher management reflects their lack of interest.

Howard M. Jenkins, the company's chief executive, said at a news conference that having spent millions fighting the suit already, the company wanted to avoid further distraction and expense.

"There was no finding or admission of wrongdoing," he said. "Today men make up the bulk of management. But we are rapidly increasing the number of females."

The company had collected sworn statements of support from more than 6,000 of its employees. But Judge Henry Lee Adams of the Federal court in Tampa noted that statements signed by current employees at the request of managers were suspect, Mr. Goldstein said. The judge also ordered the company to correct some of its statements to employees, including its portrayal of the suit as a labor union plot.

The company denied allegations that it had retaliated against women who had filed complaints and agreed not to do so in the future.

The company also agreed to have the women's lawyers and the Equal Employment Opportunity Commission monitor its pay and promotion practices for as long as seven years.

Judge Adams gave the $81.5 million settlement preliminary approval yesterday.

Publix, based in Lakeland, Fla., is Florida's largest private employer, with 100,000 workers. It is admired in the supermarket industry for its rapid growth around the Southeast.

"It's a top-notch operator, with strong expansion, strong management, and bright, clean, well-stocked stores," said Jonathan H. Ziegler, an analyst with Salomon Brothers. The settlement probably equals about half the chain's 1996 earnings, he said, on revenues of $10.5 billion.

The women employees will divide $63.5 million, generally receiving from $70 to $840 depending on their experience at Publix, according to the 120-page agreement.

Mr. Goldstein—of the law firm of Saperstein, Goldstein, Demchak & Baller in Oakland, Calif., which also handled the Lucky Stores case—said that in practice fewer women would probably receive larger settlements, depending on how many applied and qualified.

The other $18 million will go to the lawyers, including $2.5 million for monitoring the company's compliance. To be considered for promotions, employees, male and female, will have to file simple applications indicating their interest. The company promises to promote women in the same proportion as they meet some objective qualifications. Mr. Goldstein said that the resulting gains to women would be far greater than the settlement payouts.

The company, at the direction of the judge, had been meeting with mediators since June, with their meetings becoming more frequent in November. The case was set for trial next November.

The Publix case reflects the upswing in such employee suits. Federal class-action lawsuits, where large numbers of employees team up to complain of systematic corporate bias, have more than doubled in the last four years.

13

What Some Call Racist at American Eagle, Others Say Was in Jest

Scott McCartney

MIAMI In some ways, the dingy men's bathroom at the American Eagle airlines maintenance hangar here seemed like an abstract painting with a secret life of its own.

Light-blue walls were pocked with freshly painted dark-blue squares. Day by day, the Rothko-like squares would spread until, eventually, the process would begin all over again.

But rather than being part of some experiment in industrial aesthetics, the constant painting was meant to mask racial graffiti regularly penned by mechanics working at the AMR Corp. unit.

In interviews, company documents and court depositions, current and former employees say that racial slurs were as common as tire changes inside the hangar where turbo-prop planes for the American Airlines' commuter carrier were repaired.

In an era when blue-collar jokes and biting ethnic humor are as close as shock-jock radio, some white mechanics never imagined that their black co-workers might take offense. With both a diversity-training program and a raft of antidiscrimination policies in place, American Eagle executives contend that they certainly never heard or saw anything that merited an in-depth investigation.

How Far?

But a racial-discrimination lawsuit filed here in 1997 by former American Eagle mechanic Anthony Lee asks a federal court to decide whether the company should have looked more closely. The case, set for trial later this spring, raises questions about how far a corporation should and can go to police workplace biases.

From *The Wall Street Journal*, April 20, 1999.

Although high-profile cases of racial discrimination continue to plague corporate America, diversity trainers, human-resources executives and others say that companies' attentions have largely shifted to issues of sexual orientation and harassment. Indeed, after a female mechanic found pornographic material in an airplane cockpit in Albany, N.Y., in 1994, American Eagle launched an aggressive campaign that included mandatory sensitivity-training sessions and videos.

Like most companies today, AMR's American Eagle unit has adopted strong internal policies banning graffiti, disparaging comments or almost any other workplace behavior that smacks of racial or sexual discrimination. The company also conducts periodic diversity-training classes for most of its employees—though mechanics at the maintenance arm don't attend because they would have to be pulled off flight-line duty, an expensive proposition.

"Zero Tolerance"

"We have zero tolerance for unlawful harassment, and we have procedures in place to stop it," says Holly Elizabeth Stroud, Eagle's general counsel.

Prior to Mr. Lee's lawsuit, American Eagle's hangar in the northwest corner of Miami International Airport didn't attract much attention. Dirty, dank and infested with stray cats, it was only big enough to hold two turbo-prop planes at a time. Its work force of about 80 mechanics included a small number of blacks, younger Latinos and a core of older, white ex-strikers from Eastern Air Lines who were now earning just 50% of what they had made at their old employer.

Five years ago, American Eagle was in turmoil. The carrier, which feeds passengers to American Airlines flights, had suffered two fatal crashes in 1994 and was downsizing in Raleigh–Durham and Nashville. American Eagle also was beefing up its Miami staff in a bid to boost business in the Caribbean and Latin America. The results, Miami mechanics say, were heavy workloads at low pay with aging equipment and run-down facilities. (The company says "more difficult conditions" are a fact of life at commuter carriers, but that American Eagle has made a concerted effort to upgrade equipment and facilities.)

Doughnuts and Other Pranks

To ease the tension, there were daily pranks and stunts, like doing doughnuts on maintenance tractors. Shifts were punctuated by ethnic and sexual jokes, along with wisecracks involving everything from weight to religion. To white mechanic Jerome Rygiel, a jocular Eastern veteran, it didn't seem any worse than what you might hear on Howard Stern's radio show. "Some people made fun of people, but mostly we were making fun of stereotypes," says Mr. Rygiel, who was deposed in Mr. Lee's suit. "I never meant to ever be offensive."

But several employees, black and white, describe an increasingly racially charged workplace where most of the gibes were directed at blacks, many of whom kept quiet for fear of becoming targeted for more-hostile treatment or losing their jobs. "It was a very tough place for black people to work," says Christine Horne, a white mechanic who used to work at the commuter line.

Bulletin-board cartoons depicted black mechanics as gorillas or starving Somalians. Someone posted a jet-black, over-exposed Polaroid picture with four white dots on it and the names of two black mechanics "on the ramp at 10 p.m." Oswald Russell transferred off the busy overnight shift, where some of the worst antics were said to have occurred. "All of us, we felt this sense of hopelessness," he says.

He and other black mechanics say they complained about the atmosphere both to management and union officials. But, they say, some supervisors merely chuckled while others seemed afraid to discipline white instigators for fear of triggering a work slowdown.

"There was a group of employees that carried discriminatory practices too far," says Edgar Cerezo, Eagle's former maintenance base manager in Miami. "To them, it was all a joke." Mr. Cerezo, who was deposed in Mr. Lee's suit, says that during 1994, he repeatedly told his supervisors at American Eagle's regional headquarters in Nashville, Tenn., about racial problems and, at one point, even sent them a packet of cartoons and written slurs posted around the hangar. "I didn't get any help," he recalls in an interview. "Nashville paid attention to flight delays; they came down hard on you for that."

American Eagle denies receiving any such reports from Mr. Cerezo but acknowledges that, after a union official complained, Mr. Cerezo was ordered to post the company's discrimination policy. He was also told to repaint the graffiti-strewn bathroom.

Determined to Rise

Black mechanic Tony Lee was determined to ignore the insults and move up in the company. A former policeman and immigration officer in his native Jamaica, Mr. Lee, now 40 years old, came to the U.S. in 1985 to work as a baggage handler in New York. He eventually moved to Miami, took night classes and became the second black mechanic to work in American Eagle's maintenance hangar.

Despite friends' warnings that he might be exposing himself to harassment, Mr. Lee eventually became a crew chief, overseeing the work of up to 10 mechanics. "I thought it would put me in a position to foster better relations," he says.

Instead, a noose with the name "Tony" attached was hung by the time clock; in the locker room, one worker found a stuffed toy gorilla labeled "Tony Lee" with a noose around its neck, employees say in interviews and depositions. Meanwhile, mechanics recall that for weeks in 1994, the office that the crew chiefs shared was decorated with a life-size poster of a black basketball player with a mop on his head and a watermelon in hand. Tony Lee's name was written across his chest.

Mr. Lee says relations deteriorated with one of his superiors, mechanics supervisor Noel Franz, who began criticizing his crew's work. Mr. Cerezo, the base manager, says he talked to Mr. Franz for coming down harder on black employees than on whites, and criticized him for it in his 1993 performance review. He also warned him about telling racial jokes, which Mr. Cerezo says he personally heard.

No Record

Mr. Franz subsequently told American Eagle officials that he didn't recall such criticism, and American Eagle now says the 1993 performance review is missing. In recent court depositions, he denied every displaying racial bias, telling or hearing racial jokes or seeing graffiti around the hangar. Mr. Franz didn't return repeated calls requesting comment for this article.

Matters came to a head in May 1994, when Mr. Franz fired Mr. Lee after allegedly seeing him punch out the time card of a mechanic who had already gone home. Although Mr. Lee denies the allegation, several mechanics and crew chiefs on the overnight shift say mechanics were routinely allowed to leave before shift's end as a reward for getting their work done early.

"The day before Tony Lee was fired, I punched everybody out—sha-boom, sha-boom, sha-boom," says Ms. Horne, a former crew chief who now works as a computer trainer for the federal government. Mr. Cerezo was also fired over the incident: The company says he interfered with its investigation, while Mr. Cerezo maintains he was ousted for trying to defend Mr. Lee over what was common practice.

A few weeks after Mr. Lee was fired, he and five other black mechanics filed complaints with the Equal Employment Opportunity Commission, alleging racial discrimination in various matters involving firings, demotions and pay. A month after that, at a hearing before a state unemployment board, a former mechanic who is Latino mentioned seeing the nooses and cartoons.

First Notice?

American Eagle executives contend that the two instances were their first indications of any race-related problems in Miami. "You've got to know about it in order to deal with it," a company spokesman says.

But the warning signs should have been easy to spot, contends Mr. Lee's attorney, Ira Kurzban of Miami. Through the months, various Eagle executives and managers from other cities passed through the hangar themselves when racially charged material was hard to miss, current and former employees maintain. The life-size basketball player remained up for several weeks in a central office, employees say, and many of the cartoons were posted right by the time clock.

Under American Eagle's antidiscrimination policy, the EEOC filings did trigger a routine investigation by the company's personnel director, Cathy Janas. Still, tied up with other corporate issues such as base downsizings and a pair of crash investigations, she didn't talk to Miami employees until that September, more than four months after Mr. Lee was fired.

After interviewing 14 workers and taking five statements, Ms. Janas said in a January 1995 report that she couldn't find concrete evidence that the black mechanics had been treated any differently than their peers. Because of that conclusion, American Eagle says it decided not to implement her recommendation to hold a round of diversity-training classes at the Miami hangar.

Firing Offense

It did, however, send a letter to employees about harassment, warning that "we will not tolerate continuation of this conduct. To the extent we are able to identify any person who has engaged in this kind of behavior, we will consider it grounds for immediate termination of employment." The company never fired anyone at the hangar for harassment.

The EEOC ruled in August 1996 that there was "reasonable cause" to believe Mr. Lee's civil rights had been violated and he, in turn, filed his lawsuit in March 1997.

American Eagle still contends that Mr. Lee's firing involved a simple case of an employee falsifying a document in an arena where integrity is crucial. In court filings, company lawyers have argued that "there was no indication that either noose (if more than one) was racially motivated, regardless of whose name was on it." They add, "While Lee may have found some of the alleged conduct offensive, no conduct in this case was so exceedingly outrageous and reprehensible as to be beyond civilized standards." The company maintains the EEOC ruling was based on a "misunderstanding of facts."

Company executives also contend that the black mechanics should have been more aggressive about tearing down cartoons and posters themselves and taking their complaints to the proper officials in the human-relations department.

AMR recently demolished the old hangar and moved the commuter operation to its main American Airlines maintenance facility in Miami. Employees say that has improved the atmosphere, although some white mechanics contend that the Lee lawsuit has put everyone on edge.

"Freedom of expression is gone," says Mr. Rygiel, the white mechanic. "The good joking back and forth is gone."

14

Study Discerns Disadvantage for Blacks in Home Mortgages

Bill Dedman

CHICAGO, Nov. 13   When black and white homeowners refinance their mortgages—to fix a roof or pay off credit card bills or bring down their monthly payments—they often deal with vastly different lenders, according to a new study of lending in metropolitan Chicago.

Nine of 10 whites in Chicago borrow from top-drawer banks and mortgage companies, which the industry calls prime lenders. They lend to people with A credit ratings, making loans at competitive rates.

But even in the middle-income neighborhoods, 5 of 10 middle-income blacks are borrowing from "sub-prime" lenders. These companies say they lend only to people who have bad credit ratings (A– or B or C credit). They are allowed by law to charge for the higher risk of default.

This segregated mortgage market is described in the new study, called "Two Steps Back," which was based on reports that the lenders filed with the federal government form 1993 through 1998.

The study found that race was a stronger factor in predicting the pattern of loans than household income, home value, real estate debt, age of housing, education and location in city or suburb.

The study was done by the Woodstock Institute, a Chicago nonprofit group pushing for stronger enforcement of fair-lending laws, and paid for by the Ford Foundation and the MacArthur Foundation.

The racial pattern does not prove that lenders are discriminating, the researchers say. The federal data on which it is based show only the income of borrowers, not their credit history. And no one is suggesting that people with bad credit should borrow at the same terms as people with good credit.

From *The New York Times*, November 14, 1999. Copyright © 1999 by The New York Times Company. Reprinted by permission.

Still, the concentration of such lending in black neighborhoods of all incomes raises questions. Are blacks receiving the loans that fit them best? Or are they being singled out for more costly loans when they could qualify for cheaper ones?

To answer these questions, housing groups in 34 cities have organized a national test for racial discrimination in home-equity lending. The National Fair Housing Alliance gave notice to a group of subprime lenders on Thursday that tests have begun. Black, white and Hispanic homeowners with comparable credit scores will make loan applications to see if borrowers are treated equally.

In a few preliminary tests, the alliance says, creditworthy whites who approach subprime lenders are referred more often to the prime lender, where loans are made on more favorable terms. Creditworthy blacks were not given this advice.

"White testers were told, 'Oh, you shouldn't be talking to us. You should be talking to them,'" said Shanna L. Smith, executive director of the alliance. "Blacks were not told."

Groups that work in black neighborhoods around the country have contended that much of subprime lending is "predatory lending." Congress and state legislatures have heard testimony of high-pressure sales, especially to the elderly; high fees; and repeated refinancing.

Industry officials say they do not single out minorities, and are adding codes of ethics to stop abusive practices by a few lenders. They say they are performing a socially responsible function, extending credit to people who often have been ignored or rejected by banks.

"Nonprime lenders have brought democracy to credit markets," said Jeffrey L. Zeltzer, executive director of the National Home Equity Mortgage Association. "We've made a real difference in people's lives. We have no intention of apologizing for that."

Community groups contend that door-to-door loan sales are often followed by foreclosures. Foreclosures on properties with high-cost loans rose 500 percent in Chicago from 1993 to 1998, mostly in black neighborhoods, according to an earlier study by the National Training and Information Center, a community advocacy group.

"I've seen 300 cases," said Ira J. Rheingold, supervisory lawyer for the Legal Assistance Foundation of Chicago. "They're seniors; they have lots of equity; they're living on a fixed income; they need home repair; they need help with medical bills; they need some extra cash. They are the most vulnerable population out there."

Earlene DeBruce, 68, a black woman who lives on a pension, owned her home free and clear in the Austin neighborhood on Chicago's West Side.

When a man called to tell her she could get a lower rate on her loan, she invited him over for coffee.

Mrs. DeBruce got at least three loans from subprime lenders in the past five years. She owed $1,300 a month, more than her income. Now she is facing foreclosure.

"There's nights I can't sleep," she said, "because I'm so afraid of losing what I've had for 30 years."

The study, based on reports that the lenders in the Chicago area filed from 1993 through 1998, had these findings:

- Subprime lending is growing faster in black areas than in white areas. From 1993 to 1998, home-equity loans grew by 30 times in black areas, 2.5 times in white ones.
- A larger proportion of blacks than whites receive subprime loans. In 1998, 58 percent of home-equity loans in black areas were made by subprime lenders, compared with 10 percent in white areas.
- The pattern holds in middle-income areas. In similar black areas in 1998, the subprime lenders made 53 percent of the loans (2,090 out of 3,923), compared with 12 percent in middle-income white neighborhoods (5,537 out of 46,022).
- Lenders generally work more in areas of one race or another, but not in both. Of the 20 lenders who received the most applications in white areas, 17 were prime lenders. Eighteen of the top 20 lenders in black areas were subprime.
- When interest rates go down, many people refinance, to lock in lower monthly payments. When interest rates rise, refinancings slow. But in black areas, when interest rates rose, subprime lending rose.

In many cases, prime lenders and the subprime lenders are owned by the same companies.

Bank of America owns EquiCredit. The Money Store is owned by the First Union Corporation.

"Bank of America is an industry leader, if not the leader, in fair-lending practices across the board," said Dennis Wyss, a bank spokesman. He said it acquired loans through brokers, so did not know the race of most of its borrowers.

First Union has said it is changing its rules so people get the best terms for which they qualify no matter where they apply.

"We work hard to make sure that all of our customers get equitable treatment," said Virginia Stone Macklin, spokeswoman for First Union.

The Clinton administration has made homeownership among minorities a priority, with aggressive investigations of lending discrimination. Home buying by blacks and Hispanics rose more than twice as fast as by whites.

"In the last few years, however, abusive mortgage lending has grown to a scale that threatens to reverse the impact of these achievements," said Daniel W. Immgergluck, lead author of the Chicago study.

Community groups say the phenomenon has a new twist: often the homeowners who are approached by mortgage companies for high-cost loans are the same homeowners who already have low-cost loans through a community lending program.

Although Congress set some caps on fees in 1995, some states, including New York and Illinois, are considering stricter regulations.

The industry prefers self-regulation. "We need to root out any bad practices," said Mr. Zeltzer, of the lenders association. "Customers have to shop, shop, shop. The practicality is that most people don't shop."

15

Where Laborers Are Handy but Shunned

Matthew Purdy

BREWSTER, N.Y.   Depending on whom you talk to, Tony Hay is either the soul of a new suburban xenophobia or the last bulwark against Brewster as barrio.

The tiny Village of Brewster is in the outer suburbs where minivans are replacing tractors and immigrants come in handy to mow the lawn or build a stone wall. Sixty miles north of New York City, Brewster has taken on a distinctive Hispanic flavor. Taco Loco is one of Main Street's busiest restaurants, Manny's Taxi is owned by Manny Illescas, an Ecuadorean immigrant, and *El Diario* is available at Scally's Deli.

Like corners in Brooklyn and Queens, and the main drags of close-in suburbs like Mount Kisco and Glen Cove, the sidewalks here and in other semirural towns are now impromptu hiring halls where immigrants gather each morning waiting for contractors to hire them for the day.

There's plenty of work as land turns into lots in Putnam County, one of the fastest-growing counties in New York. But some of the fresh ground that the immigrants are manicuring has proved acidic.

Mr. Hay owns "Brewster's No. 1 discount beer supermarket," which he named On the Border back when the border on everyone's mind was the one between New York and Connecticut. He has tapped a keg of his strongest stuff and he is pouring it freely.

"There's a cultural difference between Americans and Latinos," he says. "We don't stand on the street looking for work. The average person will wake up at 8 o'clock and go to work. *They* wake up and go stand on the street corner and look for work. I call it visual pollution."

Mr. Hay is no trained cultural anthropologist, but neither is he simply a prominent beer distributor. He's the elected chairman of the Legislature in Putnam, a county that is 95 percent white.

In a proposed resolution, he asked federal immigration officials to address what he believes is an illegal immigration problem so "it will no longer return to plague our community." His vision is cataclysmic.

"The World Trade Center blew up, planes are blown out of the sky," he said. "I'm not saying it's Latinos, but they're all immigrants. The West Nile virus, they laugh at me, but we don't know where that came from. If Saddam Hussein shaved his mustache and spoke Spanish, he could come here and stand on the streets of Brewster. Muammar Qaddafi, he could come here."

No terrorism has hit Brewster. Nor has crime increased, said Sheriff Robert Thoubboron. But he said Mr. Hay had a point. The sheriff said that when his officers arrest illegal immigrants, overwhelmed immigration officials tell him to let them go.

"Either change the law so it's not on the books and it's not a crime, or beef up enforcement," he said.

Tom Opdyke, who owns the Bagel Depot opposite the train station, said, "Until Tony Hay made a statement, everybody else had their head in the sand." He said women are afraid of being harassed and some immigrant job seekers urinate in public. "This was always the country," he said. "Now we're a little like the city."

And as in cities, there are opposing viewpoints, strong ones. "It's big-time prejudice," said George Sclavounos, a refugee from earthquakes in Greece in the 1950's who owns the 3 Star Deli here. He said immigrants have revived a fading Main Street, and added: "We're not willing to cut our grass or climb up on our roofs to clean our gutters. We want them to do our chores, but we don't want them living around us."

At a legislative meeting last week, Mr. Hay's opponents came armed with a "Say No to Hate!" petition. Mr. Hay withdrew his resolution after immigration officials agreed to meet with Brewster officials.

But the anger continued. One man said, "when they jump the border down in Mexico, do they give them a map of Mount Kisco and Brewster?" A county employee told Mr. Hay she found his words "very hateful." Sam Oliverio Jr., another county legislator, said Mr. Hay's actions threaten "the constitutional rights that I, as a former serviceman, fought for."

Finally, Lone Hawk, of White Plains and the Gwich'in Nation, rose to say the debate grieved him. "This is our land," he said. "We lived in peace until the white man came."

Mr. Hawk was generous enough not to ask everyone to leave.

16

Lesbians and Gays Banned from St. Patrick's Parade

Patricia Lefevere

In what has become as sure a sign of St. Patrick's Day as corned beef and green beer, Irish gays and lesbians in New York were banned from yet another parade.

Since 1991 the city's Irish Gay and Lesbian Organization has been banned from marching in St. Patrick's Day parades. Successive court rulings have upheld the right of private groups sponsoring parades to select who can and cannot participate.

This year Brendan Fay, a Catholic gay activist, thought Irish-Catholic gays were on the way to victory. But by the time St. Patrick's Day arrived, Fay had been arrested for crashing a parade. Fay founded the Lavender and Green Alliance five years ago, a primarily Catholic group.

The first hopeful sign came when St. Paul the Apostle Church, the Paulist parish at Lincoln Center, invited the alliance to hold its annual St. Patrick's celebration at the church on March 10. Parish leaders advertised the dinner dance in the weekly bulletin and stood fast when some parishioners complained that a Catholic church should not be playing host to homosexuals.

About 300 gays and straights turned out for the dinner dance, some of them prominent New Yorkers. Priests and nuns danced and sang, as did parents who lost a son to AIDS.

Fay said the event represented "the true meaning of Eucharist." He was so overwhelmed by the inclusion that tears flowed as he announced the alliance's next victory. Members, he said, had been invited to march in the St. Patrick's Day parade in the Bronx, to be held on March 14. The event was the first St. Patrick's Day parade in the Bronx in 70 years.

Three days later, though, parade chairman Pat Devine rescinded the offer "regretfully" in response to pressure from some other groups marching in the parade.

Originally published as "As Sure as Shamrocks, Gays and Lesbians Banned from St. Patrick's Parade," *National Catholic Reporter*, March 26, 1999. Copyright © 1999 National Catholic Reporter Publishing Company.

Fay said Devine had told him that several church groups, including the Knights of Columbus and the Bronx's Ancient Order of Hibernians, had threatened to withdraw if the Lavender and Green were allowed to march under their banner.

Some 25 alliance members decided to march under their banner anyway. They were instantly met with shouts of "go home." Minutes after the parade began, police surrounded the gay marchers and requested they withdraw. Six refused. Police arrested Fay; teacher Jim McNulty; journalist Jim Van Bramer; attorney Donald Maher, who heads the Gay and Lesbian Coalition at St. Paul's; and two openly gay politicians, State Sen. Thomas Duane and Councilwoman Christine Quinn.

At least the alliance gained some new allies. As a result of the group's ouster from the parade, Bronx County President Fernando Ferrer refused to march as did city Comptroller Alan Hevesi and Public Advocate Mark Green. The trio represents New York City's three most prominent elected officials after Mayor Rudolph Giuliani who has long supported the court ban upholding parade sponsors' right to ban gay groups.

Fay remains optimistic. He said the dinner dance at St. Paul's proved that "inclusion is only a matter of time."

17

Lawsuits Depict a Police Culture of Sexual Harassment and Cover-Ups

Selwyn Raab

Twelve years ago, Stacey G. Maher became a rookie New York City police officer despite warnings from a cousin who was a seasoned police supervisor.

"He told me it was a horrible job for women," she recalled. "Every day at work you will be talked about, sized up and dissected like a frog in a lab."

Officer Maher now ruefully says that the relative, Michael J. Carney, who later became a deputy police inspector, was on the mark. Today, she is the central figure in two lawsuits that focus on issues that have roiled the Police Department: complaints of sexual harassment and laxity in internal investigations of police misconduct.

After coping silently for over a decade with what she characterized as the department's "insulated and cover-up culture," Officer Maher filed the suits against the city in Federal District Court in Manhattan because, she said, she believed her safety and the careers of several officers who supported her charges were imperiled.

In the suits and in interviews, Officer Maher depicts a police environment in which some supervisors expect sexual favors from female officers in return for better assignments, and an atmosphere that endangers the careers of officers who report possible police corruption.

"If you protest or make a formal complaint about anything in the department, you're squashed like a bug," she said in an interview.

The suit, accusing 11 department officials and supervisors of sexual harassment and violations of Federal laws against employment discrimination, was filed in March by Officer Maher, two other female officers and three male officers who support her claim that women on the police force were mistreated.

One of the male plaintiffs, Lieut. Lloyd D. Thompson, said he was removed last year as the commander of the Staten Island Task Force, a special boroughwide crime unit, because he refused to go along with a plan by other supervisors to retaliate against Officer Maher for filing a job bias and sexual harassment complaint with the department's Equal Employment Opportunity office.

In the second suit, filed in May, Officer Maher accused officials in Staten Island and in the department's Internal Affairs Bureau, which investigates police abuses and corruption, of endangering her safety by leaking confidential information about her to supervisors who were harassing her.

Jeffrey L. Goldberg, the lawyer for Officer Maher and the other plaintiffs, said they are each seeking damages of more than a million and a court order barring the department from retaliating against them in job assignments.

A Police Department spokesman, Lieut. Sean M. Crowley, said the allegations by Officer Maher and the other officers are being investigated, but he declined to give details. He said the department would not comment on Officer Maher's record as an officer. "Obviously," he added, "we didn't agree with her charges of bias and mistreatment of female officers."

The police force has about 5,700 female officers and supervisors, 15 percent of its strength of 37,700.

Paul Aronson, an assistant city corporation counsel, who represents the supervisors in both suits, denied the allegations in the sexual harassment case, which is not expected to go to trial until next year. He said the city was seeking a dismissal of the internal affairs suit on the ground that none of Officer Maher's constitutional rights were violated by the unit.

Officer Maher, 35, was 23 when she entered the Police Academy in 1986 and discovered what she maintained was a double standard of treatment for women recruits. "A female cop learns soon enough that you are going to be hit on left and right, whether you want it or not," she explained. "I made it very clear that I was not a player—and not a mark."

Warned by her cousin and armed with the practical experiences of growing up in gritty Brooklyn neighborhoods, the rookie officer had no qualms about warding off unwanted suitors. And she boasted of being an imposing 5 feet 11 inches tall and of having fast fists.

Her first difficult encounter, she said, came in January 1989, while she was still on probation, at the 84th Precinct in downtown Brooklyn. "My first day on the job, I was walking across the muster room," she recalled, "when a sergeant pointed to me and said out loud, 'That one, the blonde, is mine.'"

In her lawsuit, Officer Maher identified the sergeant as Joseph Monahan, who was her squad commander at the 84th Precinct. In the suit, Officer Maher asserted that after fighting off Sergeant Monahan's attempts to grope her, she was given "a punishment post" of foot patrol by herself on the Brooklyn Bridge in the dead of winter.

Officer Maher's cousin, Inspector Carney, who died last year, persuaded Sergeant Monahan, who is now a lieutenant, to reassign her to normal patrol duty, she said.

Sergeant Monahan, who was her squad commander for almost two years, never touched her again, she said. But, according to Officer Maher, from 1989 to last year, even when they worked at different precincts, Lieutenant Monahan continued to proposition her, although he knew she was married to a department detective, Stephen Gurniak.

A defendant in the sexual harassment and job bias suit, Lieutenant Monahan declined recently to respond to the specific allegations, but said that he was confident of being vindicated.

Officer Maher's dispute with the Internal Affairs Bureau stems from a tip she gave to the bureau about a police sergeant and her brother-in-law. Officer Maher's sister, Leslie, is married to Joseph C. Light, who, according to court records, has been convicted 10 times on charges including assault, possession of an unlicensed gun, larceny, possession of stolen property and resisting arrest.

In November 1996, Officer Maher said, she learned that Mr. Light, who has operated auto body repair shops in Brooklyn, had a business and social relationship with Police Sgt. Samuel Cosentino. Department regulations prohibit officers from consorting with known criminals.

Aware of the stigma attached to officers who are informers, Officer Maher said she was nevertheless duty bound to report the association between Sergeant Cosentino and Mr. Light to the Internal Affairs Bureau.

She contended in her complaint that bureau investigators violated police regulations by giving Sergeant Cosentino a confidential report naming her as the officer who linked him to Mr. Light. In her complaint, Officer Maher said that after she identified Sergeant Cosentino, she received several anonymous telephone calls at her home threatening her life and warning that if she did not desist, her home would be burned down.

In her complaint, Sergeant Cosentino is identified as having the improper relationship; however, he is not a defendant in the case.

At a departmental trial in July, Sergeant Cosentino pleaded not guilty to charges that he gave misleading statements to internal affairs investigators about his dealings with Mr. Light. The confidential findings of a hearing officer have been sent to Police Commissioner Howard Safir for a final ruling.

Alan I. Friess, Sergeant Cosentino's lawyer, said in an interview that Officer Maher falsely accused Sergeant Cosentino in an effort to damage Mr. Light's position in a legal battle over his children. Officer Maher's relatives are trying to gain custody of the children. Officer Maher denied that the custody battle influenced her decision to report Sergeant Cosentino.

Both issues of alleged harassment and leaks from the Internal Affairs Bureau exploded last year when Officer Maher was transferred from a Manhattan precinct to the 123d Precinct in Staten Island and later to the borough's task force.

She asserted that Lieutenant Monahan, who was a supervisor at the 123d Precinct, used his influence to vilify her because he feared that she might testify against him in a sexual harassment complaint filed with the department by another female officer.

"As soon as I arrived on Staten Island," she said in an interview, "I was branded as a rat and an informer who was spreading false rumors about bosses to get them in trouble." In her complaint, she asserted that an internal affairs investigator also gave supervisors at the task force confidential information about her cooperation in Sergeant Cosentino's case and about her private life.

Lieutenant Thompson, the former head of the task force, said in the suit that after Officer Maher complained late last year to the department's Equal Employment Opportunity office, he was ordered by Assistant Chief Eugene S. Devlin, the borough commander, to give her undesirable work shifts and to pressure her to transfer to another borough.

"It was retaliation at its worst, and the cover-up was phenomenal," Lieutenant Thompson, a 16-year police veteran who is also a lawyer, added in an interview.

Chief Devlin, who is a defendant in both suits, declined to comment, saying that the issues would be decided in court.

The two other male plaintiffs in the harassment suit, Officer Salvatore J. Bonaventura and Officer Vincent J. Giardiello, said they were ostracized by supervisors and other task force members after volunteering to be patrol partners with Officer Maher. Both officers said in the complaint that shortly before Officer Maher arrived at the task force, supervisors directed the unit's 100 officers to ostracize her.

"They said, 'Stay away from her—she's a rat and she's wearing a wire,'" Officer Bonaventura asserted in an interview.

Officer Maher, who is still on the task force, said she should have brought her original complaints to Federal authorities for independent investigations rather than going through Police Department channels. "This started out as a simple complaint against a lieutenant with free hands and a sergeant who might be doing something improper with a convicted felon," she said in an interview. "I was trying to do the right things by cops, and I'm living proof that the police can't police themselves."

18

No Means No

Robert Lockley used to enjoy his work as a prison guard at the Mid-State Correctional Facility in Fort Dix, N.J. "People look at you with respect when you have on a uniform," says Lockley. "It's a feeling I cherish to this day." But life on the job got complicated in 1990, when fellow guard Ronda Turner began flirting with him, then asked him out—repeatedly. Lockley, now 39, who had been at the prison since 1985, says he politely refused, telling her he was happily married.

According to witnesses, including other guards, Turner, now 38, only stepped up her advances, then began taunting Lockley, insisting he must be gay to refuse her. Lockley complained to superiors, to no avail, and became the butt of jokes in the prison. "Law enforcement is a very macho field," says Lockley, who lives with his wife, Sheryl, 36, and their two children in Willingboro, N.J. "I was basically being punished for not cheating on my wife."

Finally in 1994 he decided to sue. In a three-week trial this past spring, Turner testified that her comments to Lockley had been misunderstood. But a three-man, three-woman jury found that prison authorities had failed to protect Lockley from a hostile work environment and awarded him $3.75 million in damages—though he had originally asked for only $2,000 to cover his legal costs. (The court also ordered Turner transferred from Mid-State for six months.) The state is expected to appeal, but no matter what happens, Lockley believes his career at the prison is essentially over, even though he intends to keep working there. "I'd give the money back if I could just be secure at work," he says. "I've been there so long it's hard to imagine leaving."

From *People*, November 29, 1999, p. 230.

19

Racism at Texaco

Critics of affirmative action routinely argue that the effort is no longer necessary because discrimination is now dead. Nothing disproves that theory as emphatically as the emerging scandal at Texaco, where senior executives have been caught on tape deriding minority employees in racist terms—and plotting to destroy documents subpoenaed in a Federal discrimination case.

The tapes are excerpted in papers filed in Federal District Court in White Plains, where Texaco is based. The excerpts, reported this week by Kurt Eichenwald of *The Times*, come from a meeting held in August 1994 during which three senior executives discussed a class-action lawsuit filed by black employees who charged that Texaco had discriminated against them and created a racially hostile atmosphere. The Federal Equal Employment Opportunity Commission essentially validated the suit, ruling that there was reason to believe Texaco guilty of company-wide racial bias.

Transcripts of the August tapes leave little doubt about the atmosphere at the company. Senior executives, including Texaco's former treasurer Robert Ulrich, freely deride black employees as "niggers" and "black jelly beans."

Mr. Ulrich is quoted in the transcripts as belittling the interest of black employees in Kwanzaa, an Africanist celebration held in December. "I'm still having trouble with Hanukkah," Mr. Ulrich said. "Now we have Kwanzaa."

The tapes were made by Richard A. Lundwall, a senior personnel official at Texaco responsible for keeping minutes of the meetings, who made the tapes available to the plaintiffs after he was laid off. At several points on the tapes, the Texaco executives openly discuss destroying records to protect themselves in the discrimination case. Federal prosecutors in White Plains are investigating to determine whether the records were actually destroyed.

Peter I. Bijur, Texaco's chairman, has deplored the insensitivity of the taped remarks and placed the company's equal-opportunity programs under review. He issued a statement saying that discrimination is not the Texaco way. But plaintiffs say that the remarks were typical of what some of them experienced at the office.

The company has commissioned an investigation by an outside lawyer and has already punished one of the taped executives, Mr. Lundwall, by suspending certain payments to him. But that punishment might be seen as retribution for his releasing the tapes rather than as a penalty for discrimination.

When its investigations are complete, Texaco will need to make an example of all those who uttered racist comments at the meeting and make it clear that discrimination will no longer be tolerated. That is the only way to remove this ugly stain on Texaco's reputation.

20

A Teenager's Play for the Gay '90s?

Wendy Bounds

CHARLOTTE, N.C.   Scott Miller, artistic director for the Children's Theatre here, was friendly but firm. When Samantha Gellar, 17 years old, asked him if she should enter her play in his young playwright contest, he urged her to go ahead. But he also warned her he probably wouldn't produce her work if it won—because of its content. Undeterred, Ms. Gellar submitted "Life Versus the Paperback Romance," a short work about two adult women—one of whom is blind—who meet on a bus, become friends and ultimately fall in love.

The play did win the contest. And the Children's Theatre did refuse to put it on. And then the real drama began.

"I figured I might as well enter because of the $100 prize," says Ms. Gellar, a junior at Charlotte's Northwest School of the Arts. "It seemed like a nice thing to say, 'Yeah, my play won.'" The fairly certain prospect of not having her play produced "seemed a little disturbing," she says, but not terribly important.

That is, until Ms. Gellar actually did win the prize, along with four other students. While the other shows were performed two weeks ago for students and community members, as the contest winners' plays have been for three years, "Paperback Romance" became the first winning play to be suppressed. The

Children's Theatre decided a lesbian romance was inappropriate for an audience that would include 11-year-olds. The $100 check suddenly didn't seem adequate compensation any more, and Ms. Gellar began to question why her play—which has no nudity or sex other than a quick kiss—wasn't fit for the stage.

"I understand their reasons," the teenager says. "But I still consider it a form of discrimination. It's not a bad city; there are good people in it. It's just if they take a stand, they'll take the side of the people giving them money."

Ms. Gellar, as well as her parents, other artists and a community gay activist group called Time Out Youth, have decided they aren't going to let the Children's Theatre, which receives public money through the school system, prevent "Paperback Romance" from being produced. This Sunday, the play will get its first reading in a renovated church here called the Great Aunt Stella Center, a privately funded site devoted to public forums and performances. Following the reading will be a discussion—"Gay and Lesbian Youth: Do They Deserve to Have a Voice"— which the Stella Center hopes will address the controversy around the play.

Central to Ms. Gellar's conflict, of course, is the delicate line educators walk when it comes to children and matters of sexuality. While wanting to encourage free thought and creativity among youth, particularly in the arts, they also face backlash from parents who are taxpayers and often more conservative.

"It's definitely a difficult position," says Mr. Miller of the Children's Theatre. "We support her as a writer, not as a gay writer or Caucasian writer. But in this city and in many regions of the country, the use of homosexuality is considered very delicate. For us to present this onstage to a school audience and to do so without the delicate participation of parents would be indiscreet."

Certainly homosexual content has long triggered bitter conflict in the arts— particularly where children's eyes are involved. Yet the quandary promises to intensify as a growing number of youth feel freer to speak out about sexuality. They live in an era in which homosexuals are more visible and where pop culture regularly deals with gay and lesbian issues. Recently, a highschool-aged character on the hit Fox series "Dawson's Creek" came out as gay; "Melrose Place" and "Ellen" both included plots with gay characters as did mainstream movies like "My Best Friend's Wedding" and "Philadelphia."

Early exposure to homosexuality extends far beyond TV and cinema screens. An estimated 400 high schools now have student-run groups addressing the needs of gay teenagers and their straight friends, according to the fledgling Gay, Lesbian and Straight Education Network in New York. Gay proms are rising in number in cities like Lincoln, Neb., and Boston, and there are now schools—both public and private—in such cities as Dallas, New York and Los Angeles devoted to serving gay and lesbian students. Moreover, teachers increasingly are finding their classrooms peppered with children from homes with same-sex parents.

"I think this is something that is going to be an ever-increasing concern for society and schools," says Melissa Madura-Altmann, communications supervisor for Charlotte-Mecklenburg schools. "It's going to come up again and again in journal entries and short stories and play-writing competitions." She says the school system completely supports the Children's Theatre's decision not to produce Ms. Gellar's play.

It's worth noting that Ms. Gellar's drama is unfolding in a city already bitterly divided on this issue. Two years ago, the Mecklenburg County commissioners struck down funding for the arts because of objections to gay themes and characters in a roadshow production of Tony Kushner's Broadway hit about homosexuals with AIDS, "Angels in America." At the same time, the commissioners required county-funded counselors to get parental approval when a child sought help or answers about sex or sexuality.

Two weeks ago newly installed commissioners voted to overturn these measures. But as Ms. Gellar's predicament shows, the conflict is far from resolved in this Southern banking metropolis where many families still hold fundamentalist religious beliefs.

Ms. Gellar, who was born in Kansas and has four brothers and sisters, came out as a lesbian to her friends and family several years ago. She wrote "Paperback Romance" in about three days after watching a performance of William Gibson's "The Miracle Worker," the story of one teacher's struggle to communicate with a blind girl. Curiously, in Ms. Gellar's play, the protagonists' controversial relationship is overshadowed by the strength of the precisely detailed monologues spoken by Sarah, the blind character.

In one passage, Sarah mulls the virtues of a bus, where she first met Julie. "Public transit was never my favorite thing. In fact, I never really paid much attention to it. Now I see how it's become one of those few things left that brings strangers together. I know a lot of people who'd rather drive, but now I just go for the chance of meeting people, hearing the ways they breathe, smelling their deodorant, feeling their movement on the benches. It's fascinating how the mix of cologne, snoring, and body heat can fill a person's mind."

"We dealt with over 200 entries," explains Mr. Miller. "When reading a particular writer, you sometimes find someone with a voice who has mastered enough skills to register individuality. This writer does."

While her saga has been covered by the *Charlotte Observer*, the Associated Press, the BBC and local TV and radio, Ms. Gellar isn't sure she even wants to pursue theater.

Says the young playwright, who is squeezing in preparations for Sunday's performance between classes, homework and sleep: "I just want to go to college. Take a bunch of classes. Maybe do something that's a little less me-oriented."

21

From Mother to Suspect, in an Instant

Patricia Jones

A little more than a year ago, I had my first encounter with the police as a suspect. After my 2-year-old daughter's pediatrician appointment, while she was in the throes of a tantrum over doughnuts, she and I boarded a city bus. Soon her tirade became worse, the screaming louder, punctuated by protestations like "You take your hands off me!" and "I want to go home!"

After several embarrassing moments of trying to calm her while she pummeled me with her toddler's rage, I noticed that the driver had pulled the bus over between stops. He got off, and soon two white police officers boarded and asked me, very politely, very gently, to get off the bus.

I couldn't imagine why. I had certainly been subjected to the screams of other people's children many times, and their parents had never been asked to leave the bus. Nevertheless, I complied.

One of the officers then took my daughter, while the other began asking me questions about her crying. They remarked that she looked nothing like me. Well, that's true, but where's the crime in that? They looked at me and saw an obvious black woman, but I could tell that when they looked at her they were not quite certain of her ethnicity, since she looks very "other."

They began asking questions about my relationship with her. My initial thought was that they figured I had smacked her to induce the screaming, so I assumed I was defending myself against child abuse.

But then their questions were more about what she was saying than how loudly she was saying it. When it finally hit me that these cops thought I had snatched my daughter, I became so nervous and so scared of the possibility that this situation could go so terribly wrong that I just kept talking.

I'm not sure what I said—I just know that I didn't want to go to jail, or to be roughed up, or worse. And mostly, I wanted my daughter back in my arms. I don't know any mother so prepared that she travels with her child's birth certificate just in case she has to prove that she's the mother, but there I stood, suspect in their eyes.

So we were at an impasse. I with no proof that this screaming child was indeed my child, and they with the suspicion that I had abducted her. Then I remembered that I had stuck her prescription from the doctor in my pocket, so I handed it to one of the officers. He went to his car for several minutes and returned, simply saying, "Yeah, it's O.K."

The other officer handed me my daughter, who was still screaming but now at a fever pitch, and let us be on our way. It didn't strike me until much later that they never apologized for the mistake, or misunderstanding, or whatever they would have called it. And I never got their names or their precinct number.

When I told my friends and family about my ordeal, their reaction was the same. "I know you, of all people, didn't let them get away with that," my mother said. "I know you let them have it," a friend said.

The truth is, while ordinarily I speak my mind, this time I was forced to submit to my fear. Those officers got to see me in a way—docile and silenced—that I had rarely, if ever, seen myself. It was humiliating, and it stole from me, if only in that moment, a piece of my humanity.

As a mother, part of me can't help feeling that if my daughter had actually been abducted by someone, I would have expected the police to do nothing less than what they did. But as a black woman, I can't help being chilled to my very foundation by the thought of how things could have escalated.

This was my worst nightmare realized—being suspected by the police when I've done nothing wrong. When I see police officers cruising through the quiet streets of my neighborhood in Riverdale, when I'm driving down the West Side Highway, when I'm doing anything and see a cop, my first thought is not that protection is near.

My first impulse is to fear. I fear that I will be mistakenly identified as a felon. I fear that I will be pulled over just because I'm a black person driving a decent car. I fear that I will be shot because they think my purse, or candy bar, or my daughter's toy-anything, is a gun.

When I look back on that day, standing vulnerable and accused in front of two white cops who held my child, I think of what-ifs. What if they'd started shooting when I went into my pocket for the prescription? What if they'd mistaken my nervous chatter for a drug-induced frenzy? What if I had said one thing that rubbed them the wrong way?

It's frighteningly clear to me that compared with many others with black skin who have been stopped by the police, I was lucky.

22

Whistle-Blowing Marshal Tells of Long Harassment

Selwyn Raab

As a police officer and investigator, Stephen M. Zanowic Jr. spent 10 years on the streets, mainly chasing muggers and corrupt officers. In 1988, he thought he had found a prestigious law-enforcement niche when he was appointed a United States Deputy Marshal in Manhattan.

But Mr. Zanowic says that his promising career is now in a shambles because he, a white man, complained to Federal officials that white deputies were discriminating against black employees in the Marshal Service's Manhattan office. Mr. Zanowic claims that supervisors and other Deputy Marshals labeled him "a white rat" after he disclosed that about a dozen of them used a picture of the Rev. Dr. Martin Luther King Jr. for target practice and openly voiced racial slurs and threats against a black Deputy Marshal.

In a Federal lawsuit and in an interview, Mr. Zanowic (pronounced ZAN-oh-wick) asserted that officials in the Manhattan office responded to his whistle-blowing by blocking him from promotions and by assigning him to the least desirable marshal's job: guarding prisoners in a courthouse cellblock.

He said the hostility against him—even in an office that was monitored for security 24 hours a day by video cameras and guards—led to incidents in which his case files and his marshal's badge were stolen from his locker, a photograph of his wife that was on his desk was defaced, pornographic pictures of blacks were left on his desk, the word rat was scratched on his locker in six-inch-high letters, and a supervisor gave him a toy rat for Christmas.

Stress that he brought home from his job, Mr. Zanowic said, contributed to the breakup of his marriage. His wife of nine years obtained a divorce last year after he was denied a transfer to Florida.

"I found out the hard way what happens when you speak out against inherent racism in the Marshal Service," Mr. Zanowic said. "They don't investigate the charges. Instead they ostracize you as a weird malcontent and you become the target of harassment and internal investigations."

William T. Licatovich, a spokesman for the service, said that previous racism grievances filed by Mr. Zanowic were determined by the Justice Department to be unfounded. He said Federal rules prohibited him from commenting further on Mr. Zanowic's charges until the suit was resolved. Mr. Zanowic, who filed the Federal lawsuit in July, is seeking back pay for promotions he contends were unfairly denied him and an unspecified amount for alleged reprisals and abuses.

A spokeswoman for the Black Congressional Caucus, Marcella Howell, said that the caucus would review Mr. Zanowic's allegations on Nov. 5 at a hearing in Washington concerning charges of racial discrimination in the Marshal Service and in other Federal law-enforcement agencies.

Founded in 1789, the Marshal Service is the oldest Federal law-enforcement agency. Its 2,702 deputies and supervisors are responsible for protecting 700 courthouses, apprehending Federal fugitives, operating the Federal Witness Protection program, seizing property forfeited to the Government, investigating terrorists and guarding and transporting Federal defendants and prisoners.

The Manhattan office is the headquarters for the Southern District of New York State, which covers Manhattan, the Bronx and the northern suburbs and is considered by law-enforcement officials to be a prized assignment.

The service said its current records show that as of August, the Southern District had 93 Deputy Marshals and supervisors: 83 whites, 4 blacks, 5 of Hispanic origin and 1 Asian American. Nationally, 2,267, or 83.9 percent, of all deputies and supervisors are white; 195, or 7.2 percent, are black; 177, or 6.5 percent, are Hispanic; 45, or 1.7 percent, are Asian, and 18, or 0.7 percent, are native Americans.

Mr. Zanowic, 42, a sinewy, 6-foot-1-inch martial-arts enthusiast, grew up in Jersey City, served two years in the Army, mainly with the Military Police, and joined the Bayonne, N.J., Police Department in 1978.

In 1983, he switched to the New York City police force, where he was a patrol officer for two years and an investigator for three years in the Internal Affairs Bureau, which investigates misconduct by officers.

After passing a civil service test for the Marshal Service and completing a 13-week training course, Mr. Zanowic was assigned in the fall of 1988 to the Manhattan headquarters. "It was a good old boy's network," he said. "Most of the white guys deliberately separated themselves from the handful of African-American deputies and behind their backs always spoke derogatorily about them."

Many white deputies, he continued, frequently used ugly racial epithets and cautioned him against working with black deputies, especially William Scott, who in 1970 was the first black to be appointed a Deputy Marshal in the Southern District.

Mr. Zanowic said his background as a policeman drew him to Mr. Scott. "I could see from his confidence and demeanor that he was someone you could trust in a life-or-death situation," Mr. Zanowic said.

But befriending Mr. Scott and seeking permission to work with him on fugitive warrant cases soon drew the ire of about a dozen white deputies, Mr. Zanowic said. Once, he recalled, two deputies, who were unaware that he was observing them, pulled out their handguns when Mr. Scott walked by and pretended to shoot him in the back.

Mr. Scott, 57, who resigned in 1995 after 25 years as a Deputy Marshal and the higher rank of Inspector, said that Mr. Zanowic should be a role model for the Marshal Service. "There are very few people with the courage to stand up the way he did and risk his career and his life for principles," said Mr. Scott, who has also filed a civil rights lawsuit against the service.

Going through the chain of command, Mr. Zanowic said that in 1989 and 1990 he reported to several officials in the New York office the racist comments made about Mr. Scott and other black deputies. But no action was taken, he said.

By late 1989, Mr. Zanowic said, he was the target of a campaign by other deputies to intimidate him from making further complaints of racial bias. Many deputies, he said, refused to talk to or work with him.

Because of the job stress, Mr. Zanowic said he took an unpaid leave of absence in March from his $67,000-a-year job, and in July filed a civil rights discrimination suit in Federal District Court in Manhattan against the Marshal Service.

"I want justice and my career to get back on track," Mr. Zanowic said. "Most of all I want an apology and an admission that they close their eyes to the mistreatment of minorities."

23

Minority Private-School Students Claim Police Harassment

Kit R. Roane

Lorenzo Laboy was still in his school uniform—tan pants, neat white shirt, black tie, the gold script of Rice High School bold against his green V-neck sweater—as he headed one afternoon two weeks ago to his job at Resurrection Roman Catholic Church in Washington Heights.

But as Mr. Laboy, the senior class valedictorian, swiped his student Metrocard through the subway turnstile at St. Nicholas Avenue and 125th Street, several blocks from Rice, Harlem's only Roman Catholic High School, a police officer stopped him. The officer demanded identification and peppered him and a Rice classmate with questions about who they were and where they were going.

"He accused us of 'knitting' our school sweaters just so we could use student Metrocards," said Mr. Laboy, a lanky, Hispanic 18-year-old. "When we said that didn't make any sense, he went through our book bags before letting us go." The teen-ager, who hopes to enter Fordham University this fall, said he had no fear of being searched because the only things in his black knapsack were textbooks and a copy of Kafka's "Metamorphosis." But that did not diminish his anger; he had been similarly quizzed by officers on two other recent occasions.

Mr. Laboy and his classmates, who come to Rice from poor neighborhoods all over the city, expected that their school uniforms would draw taunts from local toughs, but they did not anticipate being stopped and sometimes frisked by police officers.

In the wake of the Amadou Diallo shooting, the Catholic order running the high school became so troubled about dozens of incidents reported to them by students over the last year that it has arranged a day of workshops with the police today at the school. The aim, school administrators said, was to prevent a possible tragedy.

"This has become a relatively common experience for our kids, and I think it's important that they learn to conduct themselves in the right way so they don't escalate the situation," said Brother John M. Walderman, the school's president.

Brother John said that complaints have come from good students with bright futures: nearly half of the approximately 300 teen-agers who attend the all-male school on 124th Street and Lenox Avenue have received scholarships. Ninety-nine percent of them graduate and 90 percent go on to college, Brother John said.

Orlando Gober, the school's principal, said that the complaints were a trickle when he first arrived five years ago, but that now at least 10 percent of the student body—which is three-fourths black and one-fourth Hispanic—has been stopped by the police in the last year.

"We have had many reports of these encounters," he said. "None of them have resulted in an arrest."

Deputy Inspector Michael Collins said that he knew of no reports of police harassment from students at Rice and that it was not police policy to search the bags of pedestrians.

The daylong session at the school will be led by community affairs officers from the 28th Precinct and by members of 100 Blacks in Law Enforcement Who Care, a group of minority police officers. The Bronx District Attorney, Robert T. Johnson, is also expected to address the conference, which will focus on police brutality and harassment.

"We want to make these young people aware of what things should be done and what things shouldn't when they are stopped by the police," said Officer Joel Ottley, a member of 100 Blacks from the 28th Precinct. "We want to bring their alertness up."

Officer Ottley said that in addition to answering questions, he planned to involve some of the teen-agers in role-playing, enacting various police encounters to teach them how to handle themselves if confronted.

"We just want to give them useful tips," he said, "like don't resist, or turn your dome light on in your car and roll down the tinted windows if you're stopped. We want them to understand that the street is no place to have a debate with the officer, and that if they feel they are being treated badly, there are other avenues, like filing a complaint or going to court."

Besides worrying that his students might be harmed during an encounter with police officers, Brother John said that the symposium was an important step in opening a dialogue between the police and the students, whose usual contact with law enforcement begins with a glare and sometimes ends in lengthy questioning.

"There is a level where it begins to affect them," Brother John said, "where they begin to say, 'What's wrong with me?', where they stop trying because, whatever they do, they are painted with the same broad brush by the police."

Terrance Thomas is one of those with big plans, hoping to go to college and become an electrical engineer or special effects master when he graduates from Rice in two years. But that, it seems, was not what police officers saw when they spotted the young man cooling off after a community-league basketball game on the Lower East Side early one night about a month ago. Much like the case of Amadou Diallo, an unarmed street peddler killed by Bronx street crimes officers in a hail of bullets on Feb. 4, Mr. Thomas—a sophomore at Rice—said he was seen only as a suspect.

He said he was told by the police that he fit the general profile of a man being sought in an apartment robbery, meaning he was young, black and wearing a dark sweatsuit.

"I was sitting there thirsty, when this cop came up and then a police van pulled up, too," he said of that night when he waited for some friends to finish their game inside the Henry Street Settlement around 8 P.M.

"At first I didn't do anything but put my head down because I was nervous. Then I heard 'Put your hands up' and when I looked up, there were about 10 cops and four of them had their guns pointed at me," he said. "Then they started asking me a lot of questions, like what I was doing there and stuff. They didn't let me go until some detectives arrived and said I wasn't the guy."

After apologizing, the police left. But the experience had a chilling effect on Mr. Thomas, who said he now had a very different view of the police in the city and how he fits into their lives.

"I was just so scared. I was shaking, thinking about the Diallo case and feeling like a criminal," he said. "Before, I just thought about police, like they were doing their job, you know. But they didn't have to pull guns on me like that. They don't have to think just because you're African-American, that you're a thief and up to no good."

Damarr McBean, a 15-year-old honors student, said he had been questioned and searched by the police more than five times in the last 18 months, sometimes in the hallway of his Hunts Point apartment building, other times as he walked to school in his uniform.

Tory Drakeford, an 18-year-old senior at the school, said he had been stopped so many times in the last year that he has lost count. After being stopped while using his student Metrocard in January, the honors student finally decided to assert himself and requested the officer's badge number. "The officer said he could tell I wasn't a student because of the way I swiped my card," Mr. Drakeford recounted. "Then he said I was trying to be a smart guy and just confiscated my school I.D."

It is not just the school's pupils being affected by the city's proactive approach to crime-fighting. Administrators said that Brother Tyrone Davis, who teaches business law at the school and is the executive director of the Archdiocese's office of black ministry, has grown so tired of being stopped by the police that he now rarely leaves work without donning his religious collar. Others, like Mr. McBean, say they just try to stay indoors.

"It just makes you feel really low, like you don't stand for anything," Mr. McBean said of his encounters with the police. "You just feel violated."

"That's why I like having this meeting, because you see all these other people having the same problems and it helps keep the self-esteem up and keeps you from getting down on yourself," he added, "because without self-esteem you won't succeed in anything in life."

24

Home Depot Pays $87.5 Million for Not Promoting More Women

Allen R. Myerson

Home Depot, the home improvement discount chain accused of parking women behind cash registers instead of putting them on the sales floor and promoting them, agreed yesterday to pay an $87.5 million settlement and reform its assignment and promotion practices.

The suit and the agreement, reached in mediation with a trial that was to have begun in San Francisco on Monday, directly applies to about 25,000 women who have worked for, or applied to, stores in the eight states of the chain's West Coast division. But Home Depot, with 118,000 employees and 569 stores, said that new procedures meant to advance women would take effect throughout the company.

Home Depot, admitting no wrongdoing, also agreed to settle three other sex discrimination suits for amounts the company refused to specify, beyond including them in $17 million of related costs.

Such cases are part of a new stage in the civil rights movement, transforming many companies' rules for hiring, pay scales and promotions. Federal lawsuits in which large numbers of employees team up to complain of systematic discrimination by their companies have more than doubled in four years.

The Home Depot agreement follows several large employment bias settlements—especially among retailers, including the Lucky Stores, Safeway and Albertson's supermarket chains—in recent years. In November, Texaco agreed to pay $140 million to black employees who accused the company of denying them promotions because of their race. Another of the nation's largest grocery chains, Publix Supermarkets, agreed in January to pay $81.5 million to settle accusations of sex bias and $3.5 million more over similar accusations of racial bias.

Home Depot, based in Atlanta, has rapidly spread its discount, warehouse-style stores across the country. The company has also gained a reputation as a prized employer and, in business surveys, one of the nation's most admired workplaces.

Home Depot prefers hiring salespeople with experience in the construction trades so they know their products and can better advise do-it-your-selfers. Women, however, complained that they were often confined to jobs with little prospect of advancement, even if they had the sort of construction experience that helped qualify men for the sales floors and promotions.

In a statement yesterday, the company said the settlement would preserve Home Depot's unique culture. "The Home Depot believes that entering into these agreements is in the best interest of our associates, customers and stockholders as it will allow the company to avoid distractions to our business," said Bernard Marcus, the company's chairman. "We are committed to putting these lawsuits behind us and focusing on what we do best."

The current class-action suit against Home Depot results from more than 60 individual complaints filed beginning in 1993.

The settlement includes $22.5 million in legal fees and expenses, among them the cost of overseeing the company's compliance over the coming five years. It was unclear, however, how the company's record would be assessed.

Suggestions for Further Reading

See daily papers as well as weekly and monthly national magazines for continuing accounts of discrimination and harassment.

The Economics of Race, Class, and Gender in the United States

ALTHOUGH IT IS FASHIONABLE TO DENY THE EXISTENCE of rich and poor and to proclaim all of us "middle class," class divisions are real and the gap between rich and poor in the United States is growing at an alarming rate. In fact, it is wider now than it has ever been since World War II. Being born into a particular class, racial/ethnic group, and sex has repercussions that affect every aspect of a person's life. In Part IV we attempt to understand something of their impact by turning our attention from lottery winners' windfalls and sports stars' salaries to statistics that reveal the economic realities faced by most ordinary people in their daily lives. Selection 1 by Holly Sklar, "Imagine a Country," provides a dramatic and thought-provoking introduction to this Part.

The 1990s was an incredible decade for economic growth. Thanks to the Internet revolution, new millionaires sprouted overnight and the media were quick to sing the praises of a stock market that seemed to know no direction but up. Lurking behind the giddy success of a small segment of the population during the last decade are some disturbing statistics that paint a different picture of what the decade meant for ordinary working people. For example, during the 1990s, corporate profits rose 108 percent, but workers' pay rose only 28 percent—and that was after two decades of real-wage decline. At the same time that workers' pay rose 28 percent, the pay of CEOs rose a whopping 481 percent.[1] No wonder the gap between rich and poor continues to grow.

The second article in Part IV takes a hard look at the U.S. economy at the beginning of the twenty-first century and finds that the top 1 percent of households have more wealth than the entire bottom 95 percent. Unsurprisingly, it reports that many households are deeper in debt than they were a decade ago, that (after adjusting for inflation) average workers are still earning less than they did when Richard Nixon was president, and that large numbers of Americans are unable to pay their mortgages, rent, or utility bills, or get enough to eat. And, again unsurprisingly, studies make it clear that there is a high correlation between economic status, health, and longevity.

Selection 3 takes a look at one family that has not benefited from the stock market boom of the last decade. Craig and Susan Miller of Overland Park, Kansas, are fairly typical of the working families who have seen their life-style and their life chances plummet as a result of changes in the job market—changes that have resulted from the introduction of new technologies and the decisions made by corporations to move jobs abroad in search of a cheaper, nonunionized work force. The financial choices the Millers must make each day are in sharp contrast to those faced by Patricia Duff as she contemplates life as a single parent after her divorce from billionaire Ronald O. Perelman. As Selection 5 reports, Ms. Duff, herself a millionaire, believes that she will require child support in the amount of $4,400 *a day* over the next 14 years to raise her 4-year-old daughter. The budget items specified in this newspaper story provide an interesting look at how "the other half" lives and testify to the dramatic differences in life-style that result from the differences in income and wealth that we are examining.

But even those families who continue to qualify as "middle class," based on their family income, face different realities once race/ethnicity is factored in as a variable. Selection 5, "Persistent Racial Segregation Mars Suburbs' Green Dream," illustrates why it is impossible to separate issues of class from issues of race and ethnicity. According to author Diana Jean Schema, persistent segregation in housing often results in members of certain racial/ethnic groups spending more on housing and property taxes than their white counterparts, at the same time that those groups are consigned to communities with inferior housing, inadequate schools, and poorly maintained or nonexistent parks and recreational facilities, libraries, and other amenities. (For an interesting account of the role government policies played in creating residential segregation immediately following World War II, see the article by Karen Brodkin in Part I.) In addition, African American and other "minority"-group families are more likely to be called upon to support a large extended family with their middle-class earnings than are whites. Ironically, because of the effects of long-term racism and long-term discrimination, black middle-class families are often less likely to have the financial assets that whites (whose families have been middle class for several generations) can count on. In the end, studies suggest that what it means to be "middle class," even what it means to be "rich," differs dramatically for members of different racial/ethnic groups.

Dalton Conley addresses some of these issues head-on in his piece entitled "Being Black, Living in the Red: Wealth Matters." Conley and an increasing number of other social scientists are turning their attention to differences in accumulated wealth to explain the differences in standard of living and quality of life enjoyed by different racial/ethnic groups. (Selection 2 touches on this point as well). Conley points out that in the United States, "at all income, occupational, and education levels, black families on average have drastically lower levels of wealth than similar white families." This he believes accounts for the persistence of black–white inequality.

Selection 7 relies on charts and graphs to present an overview of the way in which differences in race/ethnicity and sex affect occupation and earnings in the United States today. This material graphically illustrates the persistence of a wage gap between women and men over many years and then goes on to provide specific information about pay differentials in a number of occupations. If you have already read some of the newspaper accounts of cases of discrimination included in Part III, these data may not come as such a surprise. But other data provided by the National Committee on Pay Equity may well surprise you. Current statistics that highlight differences in earnings correlated with sex and race/ethnicity tell us that female college graduates in general earn $14,574 a year *less* than male graduates and that similar inequities are to be found when we compare earnings for women and men by race/ethnicity at different levels of educational achievement. Taken together, the material in this selection documents a persistent wage gap, based on race and sex, over many years and suggests that racism and sexism, not ability or qualifications, have determined which jobs women and men do and how much worth is attached to their work.

In Selection 8, Randy Albelda and Chris Tilly look at some of the reasons behind the wage gap and behind the high poverty rates experienced by women, especially single women with children. They explain women's economic situation by analyzing some of the economic and social changes in the United States that have a particularly deleterious impact on women and spend time examining some of the prevailing political thinking about women, families, and poverty—thinking that they believe will exacerbate the situation by creating a series of no-win, double-bind choices for women (and, increasingly, for some men, too.)

As Katherine S. Newman points out in Selection 9, one of the most dramatic responses to recent changes in the U.S. economy has been the move to end welfare as we know it. But according to Newman, "dismantling the welfare system is not the way to solve the problem of persistent poverty." Like Albelda and Tilly, she views the current attack on the poor and their children as an attempt to find a convenient scapegoat for problems that are far more systemic. (Some would argue that this kind of thinking provides yet another illustration of "blaming the victim," a phenomenon that William Ryan describes in his essay of the same title in Part VII.) Both Selection 8 and Selection 9 ask readers to take a long, hard look at poverty in U.S. society and ask us to bring a critical eye to some contemporary proposals that seek to end poverty by making war on its victims.

NOTE

1. *A Decade of Executive Excess: The 1990s,* Sixth Annual Executive Compensation Survey, Institute for Policy Studies and United for a Fair Economy, September 1, 1999.

1

Imagine a Country

Holly Sklar

Imagine a country where one out of four children is born into poverty, and wealth is being redistributed upward. The top 1 percent of families doubled their share of the nation's wealth from 21 percent in 1972 to 42 percent in 1992. Since 1975, the percentage of children living in extreme poverty has also doubled.

Highlighting growing wage inequality, the nation's leading business newspaper acknowledges, "The rich really are getting richer, and the poor really are getting poorer."

Imagine a country where the top 1 percent of families have about the same amount of wealth as the bottom 95 percent. Where the poor and middle class are told to tighten their belts to balance a national budget bloated with bailouts and subsidies for the well-off.

It's not Mexico.

Imagine a country which demands that people work for a living while denying many a living wage.

Imagine a country where wages have fallen for average workers, adjusting for inflation, despite significant growth in the economy. Real per capita GDP (gross domestic product) rose 33 percent from 1973 to 1994, yet real weekly wages fell 19 percent for nonsupervisory workers, the vast majority of the workforce.

It's not Chile.

Imagine a country where the stock market provides "payoffs for layoffs."

Imagine a country where workers are downsized while corporate profits and executive pay are upsized. The average CEO (chief executive officer) of a major corporation was paid as much as 40 factory workers in 1965, 60 factory workers in 1978, 122 factory workers in 1989, and 173 factory workers in 1995.

A leading business magazine says, "People who worked hard to make their companies competitive are angry at the way the profits are distributed. They think it is unfair, and they are right."

It's not England.

Imagine a country where living standards are falling for younger generations despite the fact that many households have two wage earners, have fewer children,

An earlier version of this article appeared in Z *Magazine*, November 1992. Reprinted by permission of the author.

and are better educated than their parents. Since 1973, the share of workers without a high school degree has been cut in half. The share of workers with at least a four-year college degree has doubled.

The entry-level hourly wages of male high school graduates fell 27.3 percent between 1979 and 1995, and the entry-level wages of women high school graduates fell 18.9 percent. A college degree is increasingly necessary, but not necessarily sufficient to earn a decent income. Between 1989 and 1995, the entry-level wages of male college graduates fell 9.5 percent, and the entry-level wages of women college graduates fell 7.7 percent.

Imagine a country where the percentage of young full-time workers (ages 18–24) earning low wages doubled from 23 percent in 1979 to 47 percent in 1992. Where families with household heads age 25 to 34 had 1994 incomes that were $4,611 less than their 1979 counterparts.

It's not Russia.

Imagine a country where leading economists consider it "full employment" when the official unemployment rate is 6 percent (over 7 million people). To be counted in the official unemployment rate you must have searched for work in the past four weeks. The government doesn't count people as "unemployed" if they are so discouraged from long and fruitless job searches that they have given up looking. It doesn't count as "unemployed" those who couldn't look for work in the past month because they had no child care, for example. If you need a full-time job but you're working part-time—whether 1 hour or 34 hours—because that's all you can find, you're counted as employed.

A leading business magazine observes, "Increasingly the labor market is filled with surplus workers who are not being counted as unemployed."

Imagine a country where there is a shortage of jobs, not a shortage of work. Millions of people need work and urgent work needs people—from creating affordable housing, to repairing bridges and building mass transit, to cleaning up pollution and converting to renewable energy, to staffing after-school programs and community centers.

Imagine a country where for more and more people a job is not a ticket out of poverty, but into the ranks of the working poor. Between 1979 and 1992, the proportion of full-time workers paid low wages jumped from 12 percent to 18 percent—nearly one in every five full-time workers.

Imagine a country where one out of four officially poor children live in families in which one or more parents work full-time, year round. The official poverty line is set well below the actual cost of minimally adequate housing, health care, food, and other necessities.

Imagine a country where more workers are going back to the future of sweatshops and day labor. Corporations are replacing full-time jobs with disposable "contingent workers." They include temporary employees, contract workers, and "leased" employees—some of them fired and then "rented" back at a large discount by the same company—and involuntary part-time workers, who want permanent full-time work.

It's not Spain.

How do workers increasingly forced to migrate from job to job, at low and variable wage rates, without health insurance or paid vacation, much less a pension, care for themselves and their families, own a home, pay for college, save for retirement, plan a future, build strong communities?

Imagine a country where after mass layoffs and union-busting, only 14 percent of workers were unionized as of 1995. One out of three workers were union members in 1955.

Imagine a country where the concerns of working people are dismissed as "special interests" and the profit-making interests of globe-trotting corporations substitute for the "national interest."

Imagine a country whose government negotiates "free trade" agreements that help corporations trade freely on cheap labor at home and abroad.

One ad financed by the country's agency for international development showed a Salvadoran woman in front of a sewing machine. It told corporations, "You can hire her for 33 cents an hour. Rosa is more than just colorful. She and her co-workers are known for their industriousness, reliability and quick learning. They make El Salvador one of the best buys." The country that financed the ad intervened militarily to make sure El Salvador would stay a "best buy" for corporations.

It's not Canada.

Imagine a country where more than half of all women with children under age 6, and three-fourths of women with children ages 6–17, are in the paid workforce, but affordable child care and after-school programs are scarce. (Families with incomes below the poverty line spend nearly one-fifth of their incomes on child care.) Kids are apparently expected to have three parents: two parents with jobs to pay the bills, and another parent to be home in mid-afternoon when school lets out—as well as all summer.

Imagine a country where women working year round, full-time earn 71 cents for every dollar men earn. Women don't pay 71 cents on a man's dollar for their college degrees or 71 percent as much to feed or house their children.

Imagine a country where instead of rooting out discrimination, many policy makers are busily blaming women for their disproportionate poverty. Back in 1977, a labor department study found that if working women were paid what similarly qualified men earn, the number of poor families would decrease by half. A 1991 government study found that even "if all poor single mothers obtained [full-time] jobs at their potential wage rates," given their educational and employment background and prevailing wages, "the percentage not earning enough to escape from poverty would be 35 percent."

Two out of three workers who earn the miserly minimum wage are women. Full-time work at minimum wage pays below the official poverty line for a family of two.

Imagine a country where discrimination against women is pervasive from the bottom to the top of the payscale, and it's not because women are on the "mommy track." In the words of a leading business magazine, "at the same level of management, the typical woman's pay is lower than her male colleague's—even when she has the exact same qualifications, works just as many years, relocates just as often, provides the main financial support for her family, takes no time off for personal reasons, and wins the same number of promotions to comparable jobs."

It's not Japan.

Imagine a country where the awful labeling of children as "illegitimate" has again been legitimized. Besides meaning born out of wedlock, illegitimate also means illegal, contrary to rules and logic, misbegotten, not genuine, wrong—to be a bastard. The word "illegitimate" has consequences. It helps make people more disposable. Single mothers and their children have become prime scapegoats for illegitimate economics.

Imagine a country where violence against women is so epidemic it is their leading cause of injury. So-called domestic violence accounts for more visits to hospital emergency departments than car crashes, muggings, and rapes combined. About a third of all murdered women are killed by husbands, boyfriends and ex-partners (less than a tenth are killed by strangers). Researchers say that "men commonly kill their female partners in response to the woman's attempt to leave an abusive relationship."

The country has no equal rights amendment.

It's not Algeria.

Imagine a country where homicide is the second-largest killer of young people, ages 15–24; "accidents," many of them drunk-driving fatalities, are first. Increasingly lethal weapons designed for hunting people are produced for profit by major manufacturers and proudly defended by a politically powerful national rifle association. Half the homes in the country contain firearms, and guns in the home greatly increase the risk of murder and suicide for family members and close acquaintances.

Informational material from a national shooting sports foundation asks, "How old is old enough?" to have a gun, and advises parents:

> Age is not the major yardstick. Some youngsters are ready to start at 10, others at 14. The only real measures are those of maturity and individual responsibility. Does your youngster follow directions well? Would you leave him alone in the house for two or three hours? Is he conscientious and reliable? Would you send him to the grocery store with a list and a $20 bill? If the answers to these questions or similar ones are "yes," then the answer can also be "yes" when your child asks for his first gun.

Imagine a country where children are taught that violence is the way to resolve conflict through popular wars and media "entertainment." "In the media world, brutality is portrayed as ordinary and amusing" and often merged with sex, observes a prominent public health educator. Not only do the screen "good guys" use violence as a first resort, but total war is the only response to the dehumanized "bad guys" who often speak with foreign accents. War cartoons and violent "superhero" shows are created expressly to sell toys to children. Video and computer games showcase increasingly graphic and participatory "virtual" violence. The strong consensus of private and government research is that on-screen violence contributes to off-screen violence.

It's not Australia.

Imagine a country whose school system is rigged in favor of the already-privileged with lower caste children tracked by race and income into the most deficient and demoralizing schools and classrooms. Public school budgets are heavily determined by private property taxes, allowing higher income districts to spend much more than poor ones. In one large state in 1991–92, spending per pupil ranged from $2,337 in the poorest district to $56,791 in the wealthiest.

In rich districts kids take well-stocked libraries, laboratories, and state-of-the-art computers for granted. In poor schools they are rationing out-of-date textbooks and toilet paper. Rich schools often look like country clubs—with manicured sports fields and swimming pools. Poor schools often look more like jails—with concrete grounds and grated windows. College prep courses, art, music, physical education, field trips, and foreign languages are often considered necessities for the affluent, luxuries for the poor.

Wealthier citizens argue that lack of money isn't the problem in poorer schools—family values are—until proposals are made to make school spending more equitable. Then money matters greatly for those who already have more.

It's not India.

Imagine a country where Black unemployment and infant mortality is more than twice that of whites, and Black life expectancy is seven years less. The government subsidized decades of segregated suburbanization for whites while the inner cities left to people of color were treated as outsider cities—separate, unequal, and disposable. Recent studies have documented continuing discrimination in employment, banking, and housing.

Imagine a country whose constitution once defined Black slaves as worth three-fifths of a human being. Today, median Black per capita income is three-fifths that of whites.

It's not South Africa.

Imagine a country which pretends that anyone who needs a job can find one, while its federal reserve board enforces slow growth economic policies that keep millions of people unemployed, underemployed, and underpaid.

Imagine a country with full prisons instead of full employment. The prison population has more than doubled since 1980. The nation is Number One in the world when it comes to locking up its own people.

Imagine a country where prison labor is a growth industry and so-called corrections spending is the fastest-growing part of state budgets. Apparently, the government would rather spend $25,000 a year to keep someone in prison than on cost-effective programs of education, community development, addiction treatment, and employment to keep them out. In the words of a national center on institutions and alternatives, this nation has "replaced the social safety net with a dragnet."

Imagine a country that has been criticized by human rights organizations for expanding rather than abolishing use of the death penalty—despite documented racial bias and numerous cases of innocents being put to death.

It's not China.

Imagine a country that imprisons Black men at a rate nearly five times more than apartheid South Africa. One out of three Black men in their twenties are either in jail, on probation, or on parole. Meanwhile, one out of three Black men and women ages 16–19 are officially unemployed, as are nearly one out of five ages 20–24. Remember, to be counted in the official unemployment rate you must be actively looking for a job and not finding one. "Surplus" workers are increasingly being criminalized.

A 1990 justice department report observed, "The fact that the legal order not only countenanced but sustained slavery, segregation, and discrimination for most of our Nation's history—and the fact that the police were bound to uphold that order—set a pattern for police behavior and attitudes toward minority communities that has persisted until the present day." A 1992 newspaper article is titled, "GUILTY . . . of being black: Black men say success doesn't save them from being suspected, harassed and detained."

Imagine a country waging a racially biased "War on Drugs." More than three out of four drug users are white, but Blacks and Latinos are much more likely to be arrested and convicted for drug offenses and receive much harsher sentences. Almost 90 percent of those sentenced to state prison for drug possession in 1992 were Black and Latino.

A study in a prominent medical journal found that drug and alcohol rates were slightly higher for pregnant white women than pregnant Black women, but Black women were about ten times more likely to be reported to authorities by private doctors and public health clinics—under a mandatory reporting law. Poor women were also more likely to be reported.

It is said that truth is the first casualty in war, and the "War on Drugs" is no exception. Contrary to stereotype, "The typical cocaine user is white, male, a high school graduate employed full time and living in a small metropolitan area or suburb," says the nation's former drug czar. A leading newspaper reports that law officers and judges say, "Although it is clear that whites sell most of the nation's cocaine and account for 80 percent of its consumers, it is blacks and other minorities who continue to fill up [the] courtrooms and jails, largely because, in a political climate that demands that something be done, they are the easiest people to arrest." They are the easiest to scapegoat.

Imagine a country which intervenes in other nations in the name of the "War on Drugs," while it is the number one exporter of addictive, life-shortening tobacco. It is also number four in the world in alcohol consumption—the drug most associated in reality with violence and death—and number one in drunk-driving fatalities per capita. Those arrested for drunk driving are overwhelmingly white and male and typically are treated much more leniently than illicit drug offenders.

It's not France.

Imagine a country where the cycle of unequal opportunity is intensifying. Its beneficiaries often slander those most systematically undervalued, underpaid, underemployed, underfinanced, underinsured, underrated, and otherwise underserved and undermined—as undeserving, "underclass," impoverished in moral and social values, and lacking the proper "work ethic." The oft-heard stereotype of deadbeat poor people masks the growing reality of dead-end jobs and disposable workers.

Imagine a country abolishing aid to families with dependent children while maintaining aid for dependent corporations.

Imagine a country slashing assistance to its poorest people, disabled children, and elderly refugees to close a budget deficit produced by excessive military spending and tax cuts for corporations and the rich. Wealthy people—whose tax rates are among the lowest in the world—not only benefited from deficit spending and tax breaks, they earn interest on the debt as government bond holders.

Imagine a country with a greed surplus and justice deficit. According to a former secretary of labor, "were the tax code as progressive as it was even as late as 1977," the top 10 percent of income earners "would have paid approximately $93 billion more in taxes" than they paid in 1989. How much is $93 billion? About the same amount as the combined 1989 government budget for all these programs for low-income persons: aid to families with dependent children, supplemental security income, general assistance, food and nutrition benefits, housing, jobs and employment training, and education aid from preschool to college loans.

Imagine a country where state and local governments are rushing to expand lotteries, video poker, and other government-promoted gambling to raise revenues, disproportionately from the poor, which they should be raising from a fair tax system.

Imagine a country whose military budget continues consuming resources at nearly average Cold War levels although the Soviet Union no longer exists. In the post–Cold War world, the "Peace Dividend" means the congress gives the military more than it asks for. This nation also leads the world in arms exports.

Imagine a country that ranks first in the world in wealth and military power, and 26th in child mortality (under age 5). If the government were a parent it would be guilty of child abuse. Thousands of children die preventable deaths.

Imagine a country where health care is managed for maximum profit. In many countries health care is a right, but in this one 42 million people have no health insurance and another 29 million are underinsured, according to the nation's college of physicians. Lack of health insurance is associated with a 25 percent higher risk of death.

Imagine a country where descendants of its first inhabitants live on reservations strip-mined of natural resources. Life expectancy averages in the forties—not the seventies. Infant mortality is seven times higher than the national average, and a higher proportion of people live in poverty than any other ethnic group. An Indian leader is the country's best-known political prisoner.

Imagine a country where 500 years of plunder and lies are masked in expressions like "Indian giver." Where the military still dubs enemy territory "Indian country."

Imagine a country which has less than 5 percent of the world's population, but uses 25 percent of the world's oil resources. Only 3 percent of the public's trips are made by public transportation. It has felled more trees since 1978 than any other country. It is the number one contributor to acid rain and global warming.

It's not Brazil.

Imagine a country where half the eligible voters don't vote. The nation's house of representatives is not representative of the nation. It is overwhelmingly male and disproportionately white. The senate is representative of millionaires.

Imagine a country where white men who are "falling down" the economic ladder are being encouraged to believe they are falling because women and people of color are climbing over them to the top or dragging them down from the bottom. That way, they will blame women and people of color rather than the system. They will buy the myth of "reverse discrimination." Never mind that white males hold 95 percent of senior management positions (vice president and above).

Imagine a country where on top of discrimination comes insult. It's common for people of color to get none of the credit when they succeed—portrayed as undeserving beneficiaries of affirmative action and "reverse discrimination"—and all of the blame when they fail. A study of the views of 15- to 24-year-olds found that 49 percent of whites believe that it is more likely that "qualified whites lose out on scholarships, jobs, and promotions because minorities get special preferences" than "qualified minorities are denied scholarships, jobs, and promotions because of racial prejudice." Only 34 percent believed that minorities are more likely to lose out.

Imagine a country where scapegoating thrives on misinformation. The majority of whites in a national 1995 survey said that average Blacks held equal or better jobs than average whites. Survey respondents also wrongly estimated the white share of the population to be under 50 percent—rather than 74 percent.

Imagine a country where a former presidential press secretary boasted to reporters: "You can say anything you want in a debate, and 80 million people hear it. If reporters then document that a candidate spoke untruthfully, so what? Maybe 200 people read it, or 2,000 or 20,000."

Imagine a country where a far-right television commentator-turned-presidential candidate—whose heroes include Senator Joe McCarthy, Spanish dictator Franco, and Chilean dictator Pinochet—told the national convention of one of the two major parties: "There is a religious war going on in this country. It is a cultural war." Delegates waved signs saying "Gay Rights Never"—the '90s version of segregation forever. Referring to recent rioting in a major city following the acquittal of police officers who had severely beaten a Black man, the once and future candidate said: "I met the troopers of the 18th Cavalry, who had come to save the city. . . . And as those boys took back the streets of [that city], block by block, my friends, we must take back our cities and take back our culture and take back our country."

It's not the former Yugoslavia.

Imagine a country where scapegoating fuels fear and fear fuels scapegoating. The list of scapegoats grows rapidly with homeless people, women and children receiving welfare, people of color, gays and lesbians, Jews, undocumented immigrants, longtime legal immigrants, people with disabilities. More and more children are declared illegitimate. More and more people are treated as disposable.

It's not Germany.

It's the disUnited States.

Decades ago Martin Luther King Jr. warned, in *Where Do We Go from Here: Chaos or Community?* (Harper & Row, 1967), "History is cluttered with the wreckage of nations and individuals who pursued [the] self-defeating path of hate." King declared:

> A true revolution of values will soon cause us to question the fairness and justice of many of our past and present policies. We are called to play the good samaritan on life's roadside; but . . . one day the whole Jericho road must be transformed so that men and women will not be beaten and robbed as they make their journey through life. . . .
>
> A true revolution of values will soon look uneasily on the glaring contrast of poverty and wealth. . . . There is nothing but a lack of social vision to prevent us from paying an adequate wage to every American citizen whether he be a hospital worker, laundry worker, maid or day laborer. There is nothing except shortsightedness to prevent us from guaranteeing an annual minimum—and *livable*—income for every American family. There is nothing, except a tragic death wish, to prevent us from reordering our priorities, so that the pursuit of peace will take precedence over the pursuit of war.

SELECTED SOURCES

Donald L. Barlett and James B. Steele, *America: Who Really Pays the Taxes?* (New York: Touchstone, 1994).

Business Week, annual report on executive pay, April 22, 1996; "The Real Truth about the Economy," November 7, 1994.

Ira J. Chasnoff, et al., "The Prevalence of Illicit-Drug or Alcohol Use during Pregnancy and Discrepancies in Mandatory Reporting in Pinellas County, Florida," *New England Journal of Medicine*, April 26, 1990.

Children's Defense Fund and Northeastern University's Center for Labor Market Studies, *Vanishing Dreams: The Economic Plight of America's Young Families* (Washington, DC: Children's Defense Fund, 1992).

Steven B. Duke and Albert C. Gross, *America's Longest War: Rethinking Our Tragic Crusade against Drugs* (New York: Jeremy P. Tarcher/Putnam, 1993).

Economic Policy Institute: Lawrence Mishel, Jared Bernstein, and John Schmitt, *The State of Working America 1996–97* (Washington, DC: Economic Policy Institute, 1996).

Anne B. Fisher, "When Will Women Get to the Top?" *Fortune*, September 21, 1992.

Susan Glick and Josh Sugarmann, "Why Johnny Can Shoot," *Mother Jones*, January/February 1995, excerpted from Violence Policy Center (Washington, DC), *Use the Schools: How Federal Tax Dollars Are Spent to Market Guns to Kids*.

Ron Harris, "Blacks Feel Brunt of Drug War," *Los Angeles Times*, April 22, 1990.

Arthur L. Kellermann and James A. Mercy, "Men, Women, and Murder: Gender-Specific Differences in Rates of Fatal Violence and Victimization," *Journal of Trauma* 33:1, July 1992.

Arthur L. Kellermann, et al., "Gun Ownership as a Risk Factor for Homicide in the Home," and Jerome P. Kassirer, "Guns in the Household" (editorial), *New England Journal of Medicine*, October 7, 1993.

Jonathan Kozol, *Savage Inequalities: Children in America's Schools* (New York: Crown Publishers, 1991).

Peter Medoff and Holly Sklar, *Streets of Hope: The Fall and Rise of an Urban Neighborhood* (Boston: South End Press, 1994).

Richard Morin, "Across the Racial Divide," *Washington Post Weekly*, October 16–22, 1995.

National Center on Institutions and Alternatives, *Hobbling a Generation: Baltimore, Maryland* (September 1992).

National Labor Committee Education Fund in Support of Worker and Human Rights in Central America (New York), *Free Trade's Hidden Secrets: Why We Are Losing Our Shirts* (November 1993) and *Paying to Lose Our Jobs* (September 1992).

People for the American Way, *Democracy's Next Generation II: A Study of American Youth on Race* (Washington, DC: 1992).

Michael M. Phillips, "The Outlook: Inequality May Grow for Lifetime Earnings," *Wall Street Journal*, December 23, 1996.

Deborah Prothrow-Stith, *Deadly Consequences: How Violence Is Destroying Our Teenage Population and a Plan to Begin Solving the Problem* (New York: Harper Perennial, 1991/1993).

Robert B. Reich, *The Work of Nations* (New York: Alfred A. Knopf, 1991).

Albert J. Reiss Jr. and Jeffrey A. Roth, eds., National Research Council, *Understanding and Preventing Violence* (Washington, DC: National Academy Press, 1993).

Jeffrey A. Roth, "Psychoactive Substances and Violence," U.S. Department of Justice, National Institute of Justice, *Research in Brief*, February 1994.

John E. Schwarz and Thomas J. Volgy, *The Forgotten Americans: Thirty Million Working Poor in the Land of Opportunity* (New York: W.W. Norton, 1992).

The Sentencing Project: Marc Mauer and Tracy Huling, *Young Black Americans and the Criminal Justice System: Five Years Later* (Washington, DC: Sentencing Project, 1995); Cathy Shine and Marc Mauer, *Does the Punishment Fit the Crime? Drug Users and Drunk Drivers: Questions of Race and Class* (Washington, DC: Sentencing Project, 1993).

Andrew L. Shapiro, *We're Number One: Where America Stands—and Falls—in the New World Order* (New York: Vintage Books, 1992).

Holly Sklar, *Chaos or Community? Seeking Solutions, Not Scapegoats for Bad Economics* (Boston: South End Press, 1995).

Carol Stocker and Barbara Carton, "GUILTY . . . of Being Black," *Boston Globe*, May 7, 1992.

John J. Sweeney, *America Needs a Raise* (Boston: Houghton Mifflin, 1996).

Lester Thurow, *The Future of Capitalism* (New York: William Morrow, 1996).

Margery Austin Turner, et al., *Opportunities Denied, Opportunities Diminished: Racial Discrimination in Hiring* (Washington, DC: Urban Institute Press, 1991).

United Nations Children's Fund, *The State of the World's Children: 1996* (New York: UNICEF/Oxford University Press, 1996).

U.S. Bureau of the Census, *Statistical Abstract of the United States: 1995; Money Income in the United States: 1995; Poverty in the United States: 1995;* "The Earnings Ladder: Who's at the Bottom? Who's at the Top?" *Statistical Brief,* March 1994.

U.S. Department of Health and Human Services, National Institute on Drug Abuse (NIDA), *National Household Survey on Drug Abuse,* various reports.

U.S. Department of Justice, Bureau of Justice Statistics, various reports.

U.S. Department of Labor, Bureau of Labor Statistics, *Employment and Earnings* (monthly).

U.S. General Accounting Office, *Mother-Only Families: Low Earnings Will Keep Many Children in Poverty* (April 1991); *Workers at Risk: Increased Numbers in Contingent Employment Lack Insurance, Other Benefits* (March 1991).

Hubert Williams and Patrick V. Murphy, "The Evolving Strategy of Police: A Minority View," *Perspectives on Policing,* U.S. Department of Justice (January 1990).

Edward N. Wolff, "Time for a Wealth Tax?" Boston Review, February–March 1996; *Top Heavy: A Study of the Increasing Inequality of Wealth in America* (New York: Twentieth Century Fund, 1995).

2

The Growing Wealth Gap

Holly Sklar, Chuck Collins, and Betsy Leondar-Wright

The booming economy has been a bust for millions of Americans. Most households have lower inflation-adjusted net worth now than they did in 1983, when the Dow was still at 1,000.

The top 1 percent of households have soared while most Americans have been working harder to stay in place, if they have not fallen further behind. Since the 1970s, the top 1 percent of households have doubled their share of the national wealth to 40 percent. The top 1 percent of households have more wealth than the

From Z *Magazine,* May 1999, pp. 47–52.

This article is based on the authors' new book, *Shifting Fortunes: The Perils of the Growing American Wealth Gap,* published by the Boston-based United for a Fair Economy; www.stw.org.

entire bottom 95 percent. Financial wealth is even more concentrated. The top 1 percent of households have nearly half of all financial wealth (net worth minus net equity in owner-occupied housing), says economist Edward Wolff of New York University. Wealth is further concentrated at the top of the top 1 percent. The richest 0.5 percent of households have 42 percent of the financial wealth.

The total net worth of the median American household just about matches the projected sticker price of Ford's new supersized sports utility vehicle, the Excursion. Adjusting for inflation, the net worth of the household in the middle (the median household) fell from $54,600 in 1989 to $49,900 in 1997. Median financial wealth fell from $13,000 in 1989 to $11,700 in 1997.

The percentage of households with zero or negative net worth (greater debts than assets) increased from 15.5 percent in 1983 to 18.5 percent in 1995—nearly one out of five households. That's nearly double the rate in 1962 when the comparable figure was 9.8 percent—one out of ten households. The net worth of the poorest fifth of households averaged –$5,600 in 1997. That's down from –$3,000 in 1983.

Many households are deeper in debt. Debt as a percentage of personal income rose from 58 percent in 1973 to 76 percent in 1989 to an estimated 85 percent in 1997.

The growth in household debt has helped keep the economy growing despite wage stagnation at home and economic turmoil abroad—at a significant cost to many families and the nation's long-term economic health. "The unsustainable growth in debt," says John Schmitt of the Economic Policy Institute, "undermines the stability of the recovery and threatens to magnify the impact of any downturn." A rise in interest rates "could put some newly-indebted households over the edge. Even a mild increase in unemployment could produce a substantial rise in bad debts, private bankruptcies, and mortgage foreclosures."

The stock market boom has sent the fortunes of some Americans soaring while leaving many others in the dust. At a 15 percent annual return—big by historical standards—investments double about every five years. The recent stock market has done much better than that.

From 1983 to 1998, the Standard & Poor's 500 Index (S & P 500), a much broader gauge of the stock market than the Dow, grew a cumulative 1,336 percent with dividends reinvested. If you had put $10,000 in the stock market in 1983, you could have more than $143,000 today. Unfortunately, most Americans didn't have the $10,000 to invest then, and they don't have it today. A million dollars invested by a wealthy American in S&P 500 index stocks in 1983 would have ballooned to $14.4 million by the end of 1998.

Between 1983 and 1995, the S&P 500 delivered a huge cumulative return of 582 percent (with dividends reinvested). At the same time, the median household net worth dropped 11 percent and the bottom 40 percent lost an incredible 80 percent. The top 1 percent, meanwhile, gained 17 percent.

Between 1995 and 1998, S&P 500 stocks had an annualized return of 30 percent. Most of it went to the top 10 percent of households.

Four out of ten households now own stock directly and indirectly, but most still don't own much. Almost 90 percent of the value of all stocks and mutual funds owned by households is in the hands of the top 10 percent. According to Edward Wolff, an estimated 42 percent of the benefits of the increase in the stock market between 1989 and 1997 went to the richest 1 percent alone. The bottom 80 percent of households split 11 percent of the gains.

The Wage Gap

Nine years into the longest peacetime expansion in U.S. history, average workers are still earning less, adjusting for inflation, than they did when Richard Nixon was president. Despite long-overdue wage growth since 1996, hourly wages for average workers in 1998 were still 6.2 percent below 1973, adjusting for inflation; weekly wages were 12 percent lower than in 1973. Nonfarm business productivity grew nearly 33 percent in the same period, according to the Economic Policy Institute.

What if wages had kept rising with productivity? What if they were 33 percent higher in 1998 than they were in 1973? The average hourly wage in 1998 would have been $18.10, rather than $12.77. That's a difference of $5.33 an hour—more than $11,000 for a full-time, year-round worker. The 30 cents workers gained in their hourly wages between 1997 and 1998 pales by comparison.

The place of recent wage growth has already slowed despite tight labor markets in many parts of the country. The cumulative wages lost since 1973 will never be recovered—much less their lost investment potential.

The minimum wage has become a poverty wage. It was 19 percent lower in 1998 at $5.15 than it was in 1979, when it was worth $6.39, adjusted for inflation. The minimum wage used to bring a family of three, with a full-time worker, above the official poverty line. Now it doesn't bring a full-time worker with one child above the official poverty line.

Many Americans can't make ends meet today, much less build assets for the future. A recent study by the Urban Institute, *Snapshots of America's Families*, found that many families with incomes up to 200 percent of the federal poverty level—which they call lower-income families—had trouble supporting themselves and their families. Nearly three in ten lower-income families were unable to pay the mortgage, rent or utility bills at some point in the prior year. Nearly half of lower-income families reported worrying about or having difficulty affording food.

Low-income workers are turning increasingly to food banks and homeless shelters, which cannot keep up with the rising demand. In its 1998 survey of 30 major cities, the U.S. Conference of Mayors found that requests for emergency shelter by homeless families had risen 15 percent during the past year; 30 percent of the requests went unmet. The mayors also found that more than one-fifth of the urban homeless were employed. The mayors found that requests for emergency food increased an average of 14 percent during the past year. One out of five requests for food assistance went unmet.

A survey by Second Harvest, the nation's largest private network of food charities, found that nearly 40 percent of the households who received Second Harvest food in 1997 had at least one employed person. Recent visitors to a Greenwich, Connecticut food bank included "a cook from a local French restaurant, a construction worker, housekeepers from nearby estates who made the minimum wage, $5.15 an hour, and a woman who cared for the children of housekeepers" (*New York Times*, February 26, 1999).

According to the Washington-based Wider Opportunities for Women and the Boston-based Women's Educational and Industrial Union, the self-sufficiency standard (the level of income necessary to meet all basic needs, including taxes) for an adult and preschooler in high-cost Boston is $32,279—nearly twice the official poverty line for a family of four. In lower-cost Berkshire County, Massachusetts it's $24,678. No wonder many low-income workers—including growing numbers of former welfare recipients—can't make ends meet. Recent studies of former recipients and those combining work and welfare have found they typically earn between $8,000 and $10,800 annually. Most do not receive paid vacation, sick leave, or health benefits from their employers.

Retired people's incomes have long been said to rest on a "three-legged stool" of Social Security (and Medicare), private savings, and employer pensions. The stool is wobbling for some retirees and collapsing for others, as savings decline and pension coverage deteriorates.

Fewer than half of all workers (47 percent) were covered by pensions in 1996—down from 51 percent in 1979. To make matters worse, there has been a shift away from traditional "defined benefit" pension plans, which guarantee workers fixed retirement payments based on pre-retirement wages and years of service, toward "defined contribution" plans, such as 401(k)s, that take a chunk out of workers' paychecks and saddle employees with all the investment risk. According to the Economic Policy Institute, defined contribution plans accounted for 42 percent of all pension plans in 1997, up from 13 percent in 1975.

Lower-wage workers are far less likely than high-wage workers to be covered by any employer-sponsored retirement plan, further exacerbating the wealth gap. Only 16 percent of the lowest wage workers (the bottom fifth by income) were covered by employer-provided pension plans in 1996, versus 73 percent of workers in the top fifth. In addition to placing the investment risk on employees, defined contribution plans require employee contributions in order to receive company matching contributions, if offered. Many low-wage workers faced with the dilemma of choosing between feeding and housing their family today and saving for retirement in the future, do not participate in defined contribution plans even when given the option.

Home $weet Home

As the Children's Defense Fund observes, "Homeownership has long been a central part of the American dream. It is also a major source of financial security and stability for young families, and an essential means of accumulating the equity that has enabled countless families later to borrow money in order to stave off a crisis, send a child to college, or help start a family business."

Fueled by low mortgage interest rates, the U.S. homeownership rate hit a record 66 percent in 1998, but for people under age 55, the rates were actually lower in 1998 than in 1982.

The biggest government support for home-ownership comes in the form of the tax deduction for mortgage interest on owner-occupied first and second homes. Unfortunately, much of the tax write-off goes to higher-income families. The more you can already afford to spend, the more the government subsidizes you. As the *New York Times* reports (January 10, 1999), for each dollar in tax savings from the mortgage-interest deduction "going to the average taxpayer making $200,000 or more, the average taxpayer in all lower income groups combined saves just 6 cents."

For the fiscal year ending September 30, 1999, the mortgage deduction will add up to about $53.7 billion. That's $23 billion more than total 1998 federal spending by the Department of Housing and Urban Development (under $31 billion). The mortgage deduction cost 23 times as much as the credit for low-income housing investment ($2.3 billion).

While tax subsidies for affluent homeowners remained high, federal funding for low-income housing was cut by 80 percent from 1978 to 1991, adjusting for inflation. Not surprisingly, shortages of affordable housing have increased greatly.

The Racial Wealth Gap

While the racial income gap is terribly wide, the racial wealth gap is even worse. According to Edward Wolff, the median black household had a net worth of just $7,400 in 1995—about 12 percent of the $61,000 in median wealth for whites. Median black financial wealth (net worth minus home equity) was just $200—a mere 1 percent of the $18,000 in median financial wealth for whites. In the same year, nearly one out of three black households had zero or negative net worth, twice the rate among whites.

Hispanic households have even less wealth than blacks. The median Hispanic household had a net worth of only $5,000 in 1995—just 8 percent of whites. Median financial wealth was actually zero.

Because of employment, housing, insurance, and other discrimination, black and Latino families are far less likely than whites to own the homes in which they live. In 1995, the homeownership rate was 47 percent for blacks and 44 percent for Hispanics, about two-thirds the rate for white households (69 percent).

In 1999, the *Kansas City Star* analyzed mortgage applications taken by more than 500 area banks and mortgage companies from 1992 to 1997. As reported by Ted Sickinger, a former commercial loan officer, "lenders still reject minority mortgage applicants for more frequently than they do whites. Even high-income minorities are rejected more frequently than whites with lower incomes."

Moreover, "most loans made in minority neighborhoods refinance existing debt and are made by companies that often charge higher interest rates and fees. In white neighborhoods, by contrast, most loans are made at market rates and go to buy homes—the kind of lending that helps borrowers build wealth." Unlike the overt redlining of the past, the *Kansas City Star* found "discrimination with a smile."

Melvin Oliver and Thomas Shapiro analyzed the asset gap in their book, *Black Wealth/White Wealth*. Even if differences in income, occupation, education, and other factors are removed from the equation, a difference of $43,143 in average net worth remained in 1988. They call it "the costs of being black." For married couples, the difference was greater: $46,294. Housing discrimination is a major factor. Inheritance is another. White parents generally have far greater resources to pay for their children's college education, help them with their first home purchase, and bequeath them assets at death.

As Oliver and Shapiro observe, "Wealth signifies the command over financial resources that a family has accumulated over its lifetime along with those resources that have been inherited across generations."

Inequality is a matter of life and death—and not just for the poor. In the words of the University of Washington International Health Program and Health Alliance International, "the greater the income differences within populations (whether of whole countries or of cities or larger administrative areas within countries), the worse their health. This helps explain why the United States, the richest and most powerful country in the world (spending more than any other on health care), ranks below 25th in the league of countries ordered by life expectancy. Income differences between rich and poor are bigger in the United States than in any other developed nation."

A July 1998 report in the *American Journal of Public Health* found that higher income inequality is associated with increased mortality at all per capita income levels. "Given the mortality burden associated with income inequality," the report concludes, "business, private, and public sector initiatives to reduce economic inequalities should be a high priority."

Closing the Wealth Gap

Increased inequality is not the result of natural phenomena like sun spots or shifting winds. It is the result of over two decades of public policies and private corporate practices that have benefitted asset owners at the expense of wage earners.

Where are we headed? "The Atlanta-based Affluent Market Institute predicts that by 2005 America's millionaires will control 60 percent of the nation's purchasing dollars," notes Jeff Gates in *The Ownership Solution*.

"Money makes money," said Adam Smith, author of *The Wealth of Nations*, long ago. Immediate steps are needed to enable low- and moderate-income families to earn, save, and invest more money, and build asset security.

3

Family Struggles to Make Do after Fall from Middle Class

Dirk Johnson

KANSAS CITY, Mo.—With two cars in the garage and a swing set in the backyard, Craig Miller and his family fell easily into the suburban rhythms of Johnson County.

He was a sheet-metal worker for T.W.A. His middle-class status was stamped on the pay stub: $15.65 an hour. And the shopping mall clerks didn't care if the paying customer wore steel-toe boots or tasseled loafers.

But the airline was troubled, and it laid off Mr. Miller in the summer of 1992. When he began to search for another job, he quickly learned the market value of a blue-collar worker with a strong back and a good work ethic but few special skills: about $5 an hour.

Mr. Miller, a 37-year-old father of four, now works behind the counter in a McDonald's, hustling orders for Quarter Pounders and chicken fahjitas and deferring to teen-age customers with "Yes, sir" and "Thank you, ma'am."

Mr. Miller also drives a school bus. And on the side he has started a small business, changing furnace filters. He printed up cards for the venture, "Sani-Max," but there hasn't been much demand for his service.

For the last eight years his wife, Susan, 34, has worked part time as a stock clerk at Toys "R" Us at night, when her husband can watch the children. She recently got a raise and now makes $5.95 an hour.

In most ways, the nation's economy seems to be racing ahead, evident here in the spiffy shops of Country Club Plaza and the big new crop of $200,000 houses sprouting in the corn fields on the outskirts of town.

New Jobs, but Not Enough

Throughout the country, some two million new jobs were created last year. But for people like Craig and Susan Miller, who lack college degrees as well as coveted skills, the statistics on an increasing number of jobs offer little comfort.

"Sure, we've got four of them," Mr. Miller said, managing a chuckle. "So what? So you can work like a dog for $5 an hour."

In nearly three years since the 1990–91 recession, employers nationwide have taken on three million workers, but that is less than half as many as they hired after the 1981–82 recession. And many of the new jobs are part time or temporary.

At the same time, the number of manufacturing jobs has fallen 8.3 percent from 1989 through February 1994. Tens of thousands of jobs have moved abroad; advances in technology have taken others.

As the Millers gaze into the future from their brick-and-frame house in Overland Park, Kan., they see an employment landscape shaped like a barbell. At one end are bankers and lawyers and accountants exulting in the high-flying stock market; at the other end are countermen at fast-food franchises and clerks at big discount stores struggling to pay the bills. The solid, working-class middle ground, where the Millers once stood, has meanwhile grown narrow—and slippery.

Counting all their part-time jobs, the Millers will make about $18,000 this year, less than half what Mr. Miller earned as a union sheet-metal worker. They have found the fall difficult to fathom, and even harder to accept. They could probably qualify for food stamps but refuse to consider applying.

"We're middle-class people," Mr. Miller said. "It's just that we have a lower-class income."

The Daily Routine

The work day starts in darkness. Mr. Miller, an Army veteran, crawls out of bed about 6 A.M., careful not to wake his youngest child, 3-year-old Amanda, who shares her parent's bedroom. By 7 A.M. he is behind the wheel of a school bus, stopping and going along tree-lined suburban streets of Overland Park. He will do it again in the late afternoon. The daily pay is $35, no benefits.

After completing the morning bus route, he stops back at his house to change into his blue McDonald's uniform with his "Craig" name-plate pinned onto it. His restaurant job starts at 9:30 A.M., in a strip mall on Highway 69.

The pay in a fast-food restaurant is low, but the work is relentless. Customers are often lined up six deep. Mr. Miller, a man who once fixed dents in the fuselages of jets and felt pride in his craft whenever a plane soared overhead, darts between the counter and the food pickup shelf, back and forth, a hundred times a day, careful not to misfill an order.

In the slower moments, he comes around the counter, dips a mop in a bucket and drags it across the floor. With the customers, he always tries to wear a polite smile, but he doesn't always meet their eyes.

"I still have some pride, you know," he said. "But what am I going to do? I think the needs of my children are a little more important than my ego."

When he took the job, Mr. Miller expected to be the oldest worker at McDonald's. He was surprised to find several people past 30.

Still wearing the McDonald's uniform, he climbs back in the school bus at 2:30 P.M. for the afternoon run. About 5, he arrives home.

Dinner is served right away, often pasta with ground turkey. The Millers never buy beef anymore.

Just before 6, Mrs. Miller leaves for her job, six hours of bending and lifting to stock the shelves with toys. It will be midnight by the time she returns home. She also works one day a week at the same McDonald's as her husband.

Battle with Bills

Every time the telephone rings, the Millers instinctively fear that a bill collector is calling. They are $3,000 behind in medical bills. Mrs. Miller's part-time job provides health benefits, with the company paying 80 percent of medical bills and the employee 20 percent. But with four children, even paying just 20 percent adds up. And one child recently had surgery.

When a bill collector got huffy on the phone the other day, Mrs. Miller told him wearily, "Oh, get in line."

The couple buy one newspaper a week, for the food coupons, and only one light burns in the house at a time. When a child forgets to flip off the switch, Mrs. Miller chides gently: "Have you got stock in the electric company? Well, neither do I."

Not so long ago, such worries would have seemed absurd. The Millers were saving so they could exchange their rented house for one of their own. At backyard barbecues and church picnics they moved comfortably in a social circle that included college graduates, people who wore suits to work and were therefore deemed "professional" but who often earned no more than the Millers.

When a child in school boasted of a parent who was a doctor or a lawyer, 7-year-old Peter Miller was known to reply, "My daddy can fix planes so they can fly high in the sky."

A quarter century ago, Mr. Miller remembers feeling the same kind of pride in his own blue-collar father. But the rules and rewards were simple then: if a man wasn't afraid to sweat, he could succeed.

Mr. Miller had watched his father make good on the bargain, a factory worker who provided a two-story house, a decent savings account and summer vacations to the California redwoods and Yellowstone National Park.

"I Miss It a Lot"

That was the kind of life that Mr. Miller had always planned for his own family. But now there doesn't seem to be much point in even talking about it.

"Oh, yeah, I miss it a lot," he said, referring to the old job, and perhaps to the old rules.

He clings to the hope that the fortunes of T.W.A. will improve and that the company will then re-call him and others who were laid off.

One recent evening, Mr. Miller pulled out some old work tools, grasping them in hands that are now much smoother, and explained the purpose of each.

On the floor next to the sofa was a two-year-old airline magazine, with a cover article titled, "How to make good landings." On the wall, an art print carried a quote from Isaiah: "We grope for the wall like the blind."

Mr. Miller doesn't care to talk much about McDonald's. He sat in the living room with a visitor for two hours one evening, never taking off the jacket that covered his McDonald's shirt. Finally, for a brief moment, he unsnapped the buttons to reveal the uniform.

"There, you see it," he said, with a blush of embarrassment and perhaps a glint of rage. Then he closed the jacket again.

Sad Stories Abound

Now and then, Mr. Miller checks with some of his old buddies from the T.W.A. hangar, men who used to talk about rushing yardage and batting averages on coffee breaks. Now they share rumors about the latest threatened corporate "downsizing."

One of the men, Joe Tomczuk, could not find a job that paid more than $6 an hour. He moved back home with his parents, at age 39, and wondered if he should abandon the hope of ever getting married and starting a family.

"Women are just like me; they want security," Mr. Tomczuk said. "What are they going to see in me?"

Another former colleague is now a janitor in a school. Others seem to have disappeared.

In the months after T.W.A. laid off several hundred workers like Mr. Miller, some marriages collapsed. Alcohol took a toll. And union officials say perhaps a dozen men peered into the bleakness of the future and committed suicide.

Mr. Miller said some friends had encouraged him to move to a city where good blue-collar jobs were more plentiful. But where was that? Even at his father's old factory, in Muscatine, Iowa, a ketchup plant, technology was phasing out workers.

Keeping Up for the Children

But moving is simply not an option. The Millers' eldest child, 11-year-old Jeremiah, has severe learning disabilities but has been making significant progress, which his parents credit to the top-notch teachers at the affluent Blue Valley School District. The couple will not consider risking Jeremiah's future in a mediocre school; nor are they willing to put him through the emotional strain of starting over in strange surroundings even if the schools were superior.

"We try not to tell the kids too much," Mr. Miller said. "This belongs on our shoulders, not theirs."

But some things are difficult to avoid. Not long ago, Jeremiah asked if he could take his friends to a restaurant for his birthday, a custom with many children at his school.

"We'll have to talk about that," Mr. Miller told the boy.

Mrs. Miller glanced toward the children and shook her head.

"I hope they choose their careers carefully," she said later, "Everything is geared to the college people anymore. If your job isn't sitting in front of a computer, watch out."

Mrs. Miller said she and her husband should have seen the writing on the wall. But when times were good, they seemed like they would last forever. Now she has scant hope that those days will ever return.

"For people like us," she said. "I'm afraid the good times are gone for good."

4

Billionaire's Ex-Wife Wants $4,400 a Day to Raise Daughter

David Rohde

Patricia Duff unveiled for the first time yesterday exactly how much child support she says she needs from her billionaire ex-husband, Ronald O. Perelman, to raise their 4-year-old daughter—$4,400 a day for the next 14 years.

Ms. Duff's request, which totals $22.3 million, came as she concluded her phase of a snail-like custody trial in State Supreme Court in Manhattan. Ms. Duff, a prominent Democratic fund-raiser who is worth $23 million, and Mr. Perelman, the majority owner of Revlon Inc. who is worth an estimated $6 billion, have been locked in an ugly custody and child support battle over their daughter, Caleigh, for the last three years.

If Ms. Duff is awarded the amounts that she requested, Mr. Perelman will pay $1.6 million a year in child support, in addition to $1.3 million in alimony, to Ms.

Duff until Caleigh turns 18. Ms. Duff's supporters contend that such a settlement is piddling to a multibillionaire like Mr. Perelman.

On the witness stand yesterday, Ms. Duff presented a detailed budget listing Caleigh's monthly living expenses. According to Ms. Duff, she spends $9,953 each month on travel expenses for Caleigh and her nanny. A total of $3,175 a month is spent on clothing for Caleigh, and $3,585 on "recreational" activities, she said. The cost of Caleigh's personal domestic employees—apparently nannies and maids—is $30,098 a month, and the 4-year-old dines out at a cost of $1,450 a month, Ms. Duff said.

As they have throughout the trial, Mr. Perelman's representatives ridiculed the figures and suggested that Ms. Duff was trying to use her daughter to pad her income. "In her testimony, Ms. Duff was only able to estimate actual expenses for Caleigh of $5,000 a month, or $60,000 a year," said Allen Rubenstein, a spokesman for Mr. Perelman. "These numbers speak for themselves."

In a June 1998 affidavit, Ms. Duff estimated her monthly child support needs at $87,000 a month. The figure that she proposed yesterday was $132,000 a month.

She also included a request that Mr. Perelman pay part of Caleigh's housing costs. The cost of the Upper East Side apartment and the Connecticut and East Hampton, N.Y., homes that Ms. Duff is proposing would range from $1 million a year to $750,000 a year, she said. She also estimated $1.3 million to $2 million in initial first-year start-up costs.

Ms. Duff's time on the witness stand was not as contentious as in recent days, when she was repeatedly reprimanded by Justice Franklin R. Weissberg for failing to answer questions. When asked whether Caleigh's nanny also flew first-class on four weekend trips to Florida in 1997, she replied, "Absolutely."

After her testimony, Ms. Duff repeated the argument of her lawyer, Richard D. Emery, that Caleigh should enjoy the same standard of living as Mr. Perelman's children from previous marriages. She said the life style that she was requesting paled in comparison to the type of luxury that Mr. Perelman lived in.

"It's not private jets," she said. "It's not a big yacht. It's rough parity with an Upper East Side family. It's a privileged life, no question about it."

5

Persistent Racial Segregation Mars Suburbs' Green Dream

Diana Jean Schemo

ROOSEVELT, L.I. When Marshella Atkinson's parents decided to leave Brooklyn for Long Island, the enthusiasm of friends and teachers made her smile with anticipation.

Perhaps they pictured the swimming pools of nearby Levittown, or the shopping centers of Garden City, or the well-stocked library and spotless corridors of Plainview–Old Bethpage High School. Ms. Atkinson is not sure.

But four years later, the 16-year-old does know one thing: They could not have meant Roosevelt, where boarded-up houses dot the walk home from high school and people complain that their streets are last to be plowed by the Town of Hempstead, where Roosevelt is the most troubled section.

"I think they set it up so that when a black family moves here, it ends up in Roosevelt," said Ms. Atkinson, a junior at Roosevelt High School. She glanced at a hole in her classroom ceiling where tiles had been ripped away. Graffiti scarred the walls. "I thought it was going to be a dream place," she said.

Drawn by the promise of escape from inner-city congestion and violence, more and more families like the Atkinsons are moving to America's suburbs. Like the white middle class before them, they come for a home of their own, good schools, open spaces and relative safety, everything that the suburbs symbolize in the American narrative.

But segregation is not declining as black and Hispanic people move to the suburbs, according to John R. Logan, a sociologist at the State University of New York at Albany, who has studied segregation around 10 major cities. Nationally, one black person in three now lives in the suburbs, but even those with middle-class incomes usually end up in middle-class pockets of poorer neighborhoods.

Lily-white communities tend not to become integrated but to remain largely lily-white, with the addition of well-defined minority precincts. On Long Island, 95 percent of black residents are concentrated in 5 percent of the census tracts. According to census data, the likelihood of a white resident of Nassau living in the same census tract as a black or Hispanic person is only 8 percent, and the chance that white children will find black youngsters in school with them is just 9 percent.

In New York City, by contrast, the comparable likelihood is 18 percent on either score, or more than twice the degree of integration, said Dr. Andrew A. Beveridge, director of the Program of Applied Social Research at Queens College of the City University of New York, who analyzed the data.

Suffolk, slightly less segregated than Nassau, is more like suburbs around the country, Professor Beveridge said.

Laws Have No Effect

"Both within cities and suburbs, Hispanics and blacks are segregated, and they're forced to locate in the least desirable communities," Professor Logan said. "And I see no evidence that any change in civil rights laws or fair housing legislation is having any effect."

Of course, some blacks choose to live in black neighborhoods. Others opted for integrated areas that white flight has since rendered mostly black. Still others can afford only the cheapest suburban housing. But a great many blacks complain they are never shown the full range of housing choices or are discouraged from buying in predominantly white communities.

Once they arrive, blacks find that the suburban landscape and the suburban way of life increase racial isolation: The tendency to restrict parks, libraries and other amenities to local residents; to rely on cars rather than on mass transit; and to emphasize home rule in government promote a segregated existence, no matter what the intent.

White Flight: Integration, Then Racial Isolation

While the Long Island suburbs, in their postwar expansion, were providing the blueprint for an America of the automobile age, the plan accepted white prejudices of the day, typically restricting the emerging communities to "members of the Caucasian race."

Federal laws now bar discrimination, but mechanisms of segregation endure. James Thomas landed in the Suffolk County hamlet of Bellport after a thwarted attempt to buy a house in white Port Jefferson 33 years ago. Mr. Thomas's mailman, who was white, offered to sell Mr. Thomas his Cape Cod in Bellport for $10,500. "You have to take where you can get," the retired factory supervisor said.

For 20 years, Bellport remained a "solid, good community." But what he thought was steady integration turned out to be a white hemorrhage. A decade ago, Mr. Thomas realized that the people moving in were no longer working class or middle class but getting by on government aid. Bellport became as blighted as any city neighborhood, its streets lined with prostitutes and certain corners given over to drug dealing.

Mr. Thomas looked across the hedges at a house that had burned down several months before: a jungle of exposed wires and half-fallen floors. For him, the delay in razing the house, since removed, was sure proof of the Town of Brookhaven's disregard for blacks. "You can't tell me that this would be left to stand this way in a white neighborhood," he said.

Services Dwindle

Whites who bought homes in the suburbs typically began a lifelong climb up the social and economic ladder. Many blacks are forced to watch their investment decline as whites flee, poorer minorities move in and services dwindle. Homeowners like Ed Larson of the North Amityville Taxpayers Association meet to enlist police against drug peddlers, prostitutes and street crime, problems that seldom preoccupy their white counterparts.

"If the American dream is to buy a house in the suburbs, send your kid to a good school and have some grass, yes, it's the American dream," said Hugh A. Wilson, director of the Institute for Suburban Studies at Adelphi University. "If it's also to do that in an integrated setting, then for blacks, it's not fulfilling the dream."

Some blacks complain that isolation feeds a quiet acceptance of racism. Alton Williams, first vice president of the Nassau County Guardians, which represents black police officers, said he was shocked to see a white supremacist flyer on another officer's bulletin board. It showed a smiling blond child with the caption "MISSING: A future for white children in America."

"The fear is that if people from the inner city come out to this pristine land, it will be ruined," said Melvin Boone, president of the Guardians. "And by saying 'people from the inner city,' who are they talking about?"

"They're talking about me," Mr. Williams replied.

Mr. Boone nodded. "And about me," he said.

Fragmented Power: Regressive Taxes Punish Blacks

In Roosevelt, 70 of the 92 members of the volunteer fire department are black. But last week the New York State Attorney General disclosed that for 26 years blacks had been kept out of a fraternal group that provided insurance for Roosevelt firefighters. The group was ordered to open its doors and pay $53,000 in retroactive benefits.

While overt racism is not the norm, many experts say that political and institutional barriers work against minority residents.

For example, the tax system on Long Island appears to penalize minorities. According to an analysis of Census data, blacks on Long Island and in many other suburbs pay higher rates of property taxes than homeowners in more affluent white communities. Poorer blacks in effect subsidize wealthier whites.

In Suffolk County, blacks pay 17.6 percent higher property taxes than whites on homes of comparable market value, while in Nassau the figure is 5.6 percent. The data, which compared homes bought by blacks and whites in the 1980's, may actually understate the disparity by not including property taxes for longtime homeowners.

Tax experts say the disparity reflects voter pressure that protects the status quo and deters governments from reassessing properties in a timely fashion. As real estate values in many white communities soared throughout the 1980's, homes were seldom reassessed. When growing numbers of minority families were funneled into suburban neighborhoods where values dropped as whites began to flee, their homes were not reassessed downward either.

Overtaxing minority communities contributes to the higher number of foreclosures in these areas, said George Peterson of the Urban Institute. Money that homeowners could have spent on upkeep goes instead to pay bloated tax bills, planning officials say. Roosevelt's residents, like Sheila Caballero, executive director of the I Am Corporation, a nonprofit group that works to build self-esteem among black youngsters, say the neighborhood has only become more run down with the years.

No Blacks Elected Countywide

Neither Nassau nor Suffolk has ever elected a black to countywide office. Nassau is under a court order to overhaul its form of government for failing adequately to represent the county's minority residents, 14 percent of its population.

At the town level, officials are typically elected at large, making it difficult for black or Hispanic people to be elected or to win support for issues important to their neighborhoods.

Ms. Caballero, who has campaigned for a youth center in Roosevelt, says the Hempstead Town Board, which elected its first black member last year, is consistently more attuned to the wealthier voters of Garden City. "Everywhere we turn, we're in a box, and we can't figure out how to get out of that box," she said.

The Next Generation: Patchwork Quilt of School Districts

In the public schools, too, many minority residents say they are ill served by a patchwork of school districts that protects local control over enrollment, programs and curriculum. The combination replicates in suburbia the disparities that the New York State Department of Education recently said most glaringly divide school districts in white, middle class suburbs from minority, low-income urban districts.

Recently, Raymond Mattry, a program coordinator for I Am, took some Roosevelt students to Plainview–Old Bethpage High School, where the New York Civil Liberties Union had come for an anti-hate workshop. Akilah Watkins, a junior from Roosevelt, seemed shocked by the contrast between her own high school and Plainview, with its almost all-white student body.

At Roosevelt, library books from the 1930's describe the Treaty of Versailles as the last word in arms limitation. The football team works out in a cramped room lighted by a bare bulb, on equipment that Joseph Vito confesses he borrowed from his town's recreation center. ("I don't think they noticed it's gone," the gym teacher said, ducking his head in embarrassment.)

At Plainview, the science chairman, Saul Reine, shows off his newest addition: a dedicated computer network that he was able to buy despite budget tightening.

"There's a misconception that affluent communities don't have problems," Mr. Reine said. "They do. It's just we have a safety net to catch the children, to help them when they fall."

At Plainview–Old Bethpage, student officers were discussing several proposals at a recent meeting: establishing an anti-vandalism fund, sectioning off a lounge in the cafeteria, helping the environmental club.

None of the youths expressed any defeatism until the subject was race. The students said they missed contact with black and Hispanic people, but suggested such exposure should have begun in elementary school.

"I think it would be a good thing, but I can't see it happening," said Shari Glockner, student vice president. "I feel so sheltered in this community."

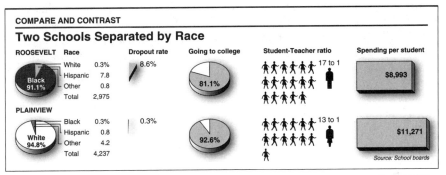

COMPARE AND CONTRAST

Two Schools Separated by Race

ROOSEVELT	Race		Dropout rate	Going to college	Student-Teacher ratio	Spending per student
Black 91.1%	White	0.3%	8.6%	81.1%	17 to 1	$8,993
	Hispanic	7.8				
	Other	0.8				
	Total	2,975				
PLAINVIEW						
White 94.8%	Black	0.3%	0.3%	92.6%	13 to 1	$11,271
	Hispanic	0.8				
	Other	4.2				
	Total	4,237				*Source: School boards*

The New York Times

6

Being Black, Living in the Red: *Wealth Matters*

Dalton Conley

If I could cite one statistic that inspired this study, it would be the following: in 1994, the median white family had assets worth more than seven times those of the median nonwhite family. Even when we compare white and minority families at the same income level, whites enjoy a huge advantage in wealth. For instance, at the lower end of the income spectrum (less than $15,000 per year), the median African American family has no assets, while the equivalent white family holds $10,000 worth of equity. At upper income levels (greater than $75,000 per year), white families have a median net worth of $308,000, almost three times the figure for upper-income African American families ($114,600).[1]

Herein lie the two motivating questions of this study. First, why does this wealth gap exist and persist over and above income differences? Second, does this wealth gap explain racial differences in areas such as education, work, earnings, welfare, and family structure? In short, this study examines where race *per se* really matters in the post–civil rights era and where race simply acts as a stand-in for that dirty word of American society: class. The answers to these questions have important implications for the debate over affirmative action for social policy in general.

An alternative way to conceptualize what this article is about is to contrast the situations of two hypothetical families. Let's say that both households consist of married parents, in their thirties, with two young children.[2] Both families are low-income—that is, the total household income of each family is approximately the amount that the federal government has "declared" to be the poverty line for a family of four (with two children). In 1996, this figure was $15,911.

Brett and Samantha Jones (family 1) earned about $12,000 that year. Brett earned this income from his job at a local fast-food franchise (approximately two thousand hours at a rate of $6 per hour). He found himself employed at this low-wage job after being laid off from his relatively well-paid position as a sheet metal worker at a local manufacturing plant, which closed because of fierce competition from companies in Asia and Latin America. After six months of unemployment,

From Dalton Conley, *Being Black, Living in the Red: Race, Wealth, and Social Policy in America* (Los Angeles: University of California Press, 1999), pp. 1–11.

the only work Brett could find was flipping burgers alongside teenagers from the local high school.

Fortunately for the Jones family, however, they owned their own home. Fifteen years earlier, when Brett graduated from high school, married Samantha, and landed his original job as a sheet metal worker, his parents had lent the newlyweds money out of their retirement nest egg that enabled Brett and Samantha to make a 10 percent down payment on a house. With Samantha's parents cosigning—backed by the value of their own home—the newlyweds took out a fifteen-year mortgage for the balance of the cost of their $30,000 home. Although money was tight in the beginning, they were nonetheless thrilled to have a place of their own. During those initial, difficult years, an average of $209 of their $290.14 monthly mortgage payment was tax deductible as a home mortgage interest deduction. In addition, their annual property taxes of $800 were completely deductible, lowering their taxable income by a total of $3,308 per year. This more than offset the payments they were making to Brett's parents for the $3,000 they had borrowed for the down payment.

After four years, Brett and Samantha had paid back the $3,000 loan from his parents. At that point, the total of their combined mortgage payment ($290.14), monthly insurance premium ($50), and monthly property tax payment ($67), minus the tax savings from the deductions for mortgage interest and local property taxes, was less than the $350 that the Smiths (family 2) were paying to rent a unit the same size as the Joneses' house on the other side of town.

That other neighborhood, on the "bad" side of town, where David and Janet Smith lived, had worse schools and a higher crime rate and had just been chosen as a site for a waste disposal center. Most of the residents rented their housing units from absentee landlords who had no personal stake in the community other than profit. A few blocks from the Smiths' apartment was a row of public housing projects. Although they earned the same salaries and paid more or less the same monthly costs for housing as the Joneses did, the Smiths and their children experienced living conditions that were far inferior on every dimension, ranging from the aesthetic to the functional (buses ran less frequently, large supermarkets were nowhere to be found, and class size at the local school was well over thirty).

Like Brett Jones, David Smith had been employed as a sheet metal worker at the now-closed manufacturing plant. Unfortunately, the Smiths had not been able to buy a home when David was first hired at the plant. With little in the way of a down payment, they had looked for an affordable unit at the time, but the real estate agents they saw routinely claimed that there was just nothing available at the moment, although they promised to "be sure to call as soon as something comes up. . . " The Smiths never heard back from the agents and eventually settled into a rental apartment.

David spent the first three months after the layoffs searching for work, drawing down the family's savings to supplement unemployment insurance—savings that were not significantly greater than those of the Joneses, since both families had more or less the same monthly expenses. After several months of searching, David managed to land a job. Unfortunately, it was of the same variety as the job Brett

Jones found: working as a security guard at the local mall, for about $12,000 a year. Meanwhile, Janet Smith went to work part time, as a nurse's aide for a home health care agency, grossing about $4,000 annually.

After the layoffs, the Joneses experienced a couple of rough months, when they were forced to dip into their small cash savings. But they were able to pay off the last two installments of their mortgage, thus eliminating their single biggest living expense. So, although they had some trouble adjusting to their lower standard of living, they managed to get by, always hoping that another manufacturing job would become available or that another company would buy out the plant and re-open it. If worst came to worst, they felt that they could always sell their home and relocate in a less expensive locale or an area with a more promising labor market.

The Smiths were a different case entirely. As renters, they had no latitude in reducing their expenses to meet their new economic reality, and they could not afford their rent on David's reduced salary. The financial strain eventually proved too much for the Smiths, who fought over how to structure the family budget. After a particularly bad row when the last of their savings had been spent, they decided to take a break; both thought life would be easier and better for the children if Janet moved back in with her mother for a while, just until things turned around economically—that is, until David found a better-paying job. With no house to anchor them, this seemed to be the best course of action.

Several years later, David and Janet Smith divorced, and the children began to see less and less of their father, who stayed with a friend on a "temporary" basis. Even though together they had earned more than the Jones family (with total incomes of $16,000 and $12,000, respectively), the Smiths had a rougher financial, emotional, and family situation, which, we may infer, resulted from a lack of property ownership.

What this comparison of the two families illustrates is the inadequacy of relying on income alone to describe the economic and social circumstances of families at the lower end of the economic scale. With a $16,000 annual income, the Smiths were just above the poverty threshold. In other words, they were not defined as "poor," in contrast to the Joneses, who were.[3] Yet the Smiths were worse off than the Joneses, despite the fact that the U.S. government and most researchers would have classified the Jones family as the one who met the threshold of neediness, based on that family's lower income.

These income-based poverty thresholds differ by family size and are adjusted annually for changes in the average cost of living in the United States. In 1998, more than two dozen government programs—including food stamps, Head Start, and Medicaid—based their eligibility standards on the official poverty threshold. Additionally, more than a dozen states currently link their needs standard in some way to this poverty threshold. The example of the Joneses and the Smiths should tell us that something is gravely wrong with the way we are measuring economic hardship—poverty—in the United States. By ignoring assets, we not only give a distorted picture of life at the bottom of the income distribution but may even create perverse incentives.

Of course, we must be cautious and remember that the Smiths and the Joneses are hypothetically embellished examples that may exaggerate differences. Perhaps the Smiths would have divorced regardless of their economic circumstances. The hard evidence linking modest financial differences to a propensity toward marital dissolution is thin; however, a substantial body of research shows that financial issues are a major source of marital discord and relationship strain.[4] It is also possible that the Smiths, with nothing to lose in the form of assets, might have easily slid into the world of welfare dependency. A wide range of other factors, not included in our examples, affect a family's well-being and its trajectory. For example, the members of one family might have been healthier than those of the other, which would have had important economic consequences and could have affected family stability. Perhaps one family might have been especially savvy about using available resources and would have been able to take in boarders, do under-the-table work, or employ another strategy to better its standard of living. Nor do our examples address educational differences between the two households.

But I have chosen not to address all these confounding factors for the purpose of illustrating the importance of asset ownership *per se*. Of course, homeownership, savings behavior, and employment status all interact with a variety of other measurable and unmeasurable factors. This interaction, however, does not take away from the importance of property ownership itself.

The premise of this study is a relatively simple and straightforward one: in order to understand a family's well-being and the life chances of its children—in short, to understand its class position—we not only must consider income, education, and occupation but also must take into account accumulated wealth (that is, property, assets, or net worth—terms that I will use interchangeably). While the importance of wealth is the starting point of the study, its end point is the impact of the wealth distribution on racial inequality in America. As you might have guessed, an important detail is missing from the preceding description of the two families: the Smiths are black and have fewer assets than the Joneses, who are white.

At all income, occupational, and education levels, black families on average have drastically lower levels of wealth than similar white families. The situation of the Smiths may help us to understand the reason for this disparity of wealth between blacks and whites. For the Smiths, it was not discrimination in hiring or education that led to a family outcome vastly different from that of the Joneses; rather, it was a relative lack of assets from which they could draw. In contemporary America, race and property are intimately linked and form the nexus for the persistence of black–white inequality.

Let us look again at the Smith family, this time through the lens of race. Why did real estate agents tell the Smiths that nothing was available, thereby hindering their chances of finding a home to buy? This well-documented practice is called "steering," in which agents do not disclose properties on the market to qualified African American home seekers, in order to preserve the racial makeup of white communities—with an eye to maintaining the property values in those neighborhoods. Even if the Smiths had managed to locate a home in a predominantly

African American neighborhood, they might well have encountered difficulty in obtaining a home mortgage because of "redlining," the procedure by which banks code such neighborhoods "red"—the lowest rating—on their loan evaluations, thereby making it next to impossible to get a mortgage for a home in these districts. Finally, and perhaps most important, the Smiths' parents were more likely to have been poor and without assets themselves (being black and having been born early in the century), meaning that it would have been harder for them to amass enough money to loan their children a down payment or to cosign a loan for them. The result is that while poor whites manage to have, on average, net worths of over $10,000, impoverished blacks have essentially no assets whatsoever.[5]

Since wealth accumulation depends heavily on intergenerational support issues such as gifts, informal loans, and inheritances, net worth has the ability to pick up both the current dynamics of race and the legacy of past inequalities that may be obscured in simple measures of income, occupation, or education. This thesis has been suggested by the work of sociologists Melvin Oliver and Thomas Shapiro in their recent book *Black Wealth/White Wealth.*[6] They claim that wealth is central to the nature of black–white inequality and that wealth—as opposed to income, occupation, or education—represents the "sedimentation" of both a legacy of racial inequality as well as contemporary, continuing inequities. Oliver and Shapiro provide a textured description of the divergence of black–white asset holdings. They touch on some of the causal factors leading to this growing gap, such as differential mortgage interest rates paid by black and white borrowers. . . .

It is the hypothesis of this study that certain tenacious racial differences—such as deficits in education, employment, wages, and even wealth itself among African Americans—will turn out to be indirect effects, mediated by class differences. In other words, it is not race *per se* that matters directly; instead, what matters are the wealth levels and class positions that are associated with race in America. In this manner, racial differences in income and asset levels have come to play a prominent role in the perpetuation of black–white inequality in the United States.

This is not to say that race does not matter; rather, it maps very well onto class inequality, which in turn affects a whole host of other life outcomes. In fact, when class is taken into consideration, African Americans demonstrate significant net *advantages* over whites on a variety of indicators (such as rates of high school graduation, for instance). In this fact lies the paradox of race and class in contemporary America.

❊　❊　❊

Is It All Black and White?

Throughout this introduction, I have spoken only of blacks and whites when addressing the issue of race. America is no longer a biracial society, however. So why examine the impact of wealth and property issues with respect to blacks and whites exclusively? One reason for this strategy is technical. It is very difficult to find useful, longitudinal data on assets for the American population; this is particularly true for minorities who make up a small percentage of the population, even when their numbers are growing rapidly. . . .

That said, there are other reasons why this shortcoming should not be so troubling. Perhaps the most important is that on almost all measures—including property ownership—blacks and whites demonstrate the greatest disparities of all racial groups in the United States.[7] This holds true for indicators ranging from residential segregation to wages to academic achievement. In other words, what is true for Latinos in terms of hindered life chances appears even more true for African Americans. Further, within the Hispanic population, wide variation exists in wealth and other factors. Certain groups such as Cubans and Spaniards tend to fall close to whites for a variety of indicators, whereas other groups such as Mexicans, Puerto Ricans, and Dominicans more resemble the African American population by socioeconomic and family measures. In short, the Hispanic population demonstrates much variation but largely falls between blacks and whites (closer to African Americans on average). Even more interesting, skin color within the Hispanic population is a good predictor of where on the spectrum between blacks and whites an individual is likely to fall. In other words, the "blacker" a Hispanic person looks, the morel likely he or she is to resemble the African American demographic profile; the "whiter" a Hispanic person appears, the more he or she will resemble the demographic profile of European ethnic groups.[8]

What about Asian Americans, the so-called "model minority" (that is, a group that has been socioeconomically successful despite its minority status)? At one time in American history, Jews were considered the "model minority" and were pointed to as an example of how "anyone can make it in America" (the implied question asking why blacks could not do the same thing). Interestingly, Jews today are no longer generally considered a separate race but instead form part of the white community. In fact, sociologist Andrew Hacker claims that there are only two races in America, white and nonwhite; therefore, for instance, Pakistanis with very dark skin can be considered symbolically "white" in his scheme. He argues that today Asian Americans fall under the "white umbrella" as an "in-group"—in other words, they are not systematically excluded from reaping the benefits of American capitalism, as are those under the "black umbrella," the "out-group." Correspondingly, today the role of model minority has been largely taken over by Asian Americans.[9]

The issue of entrepreneurship also comes into play when making comparisons. If many Chinese and Koreans, for example, can come to the United States with nothing and manage to excel in school and start businesses with little formal capital, why cannot African Americans do the same? The answer to this question may lie in a long cultural history of entrepreneurship among these Asian ethnic groups—or perhaps in their very status as immigrants. "Immigrants in the United States, Canada and Australia," write Ivan Light and Carol Rosenstein in *Race, Ethnicity, and Entrepreneurship in Urban America*, "continued to manifest higher rates of self-employment than the native born, a proclivity they have displayed for at least a century."[10] By definition, immigrants are the world's overachievers, so they do not form a valid comparison group for the native black or white communities. The act of migrating itself is an important causal factor to be reckoned with before any judgments are made about the relative proclivities of ethnic groups toward entrepreneurial activity.

Research has supported this immigrant exceptionalism argument, finding in one case, for instance, "that successive generations of white ethnics [in Providence] evidence successively lower rates of self-employment."[11] Another study found that when "human capital" (education) is held constant, Asian American and African American entrepreneurship rates are essentially the same.[12] Other work contradicts this finding, however, finding a net lower rate of self-employment among blacks even after factoring out a variety of other variables.[13]

Theories of entrepreneurship may offer some explanation. One theory holds that a group's rate of self-employment will be high when it faces disadvantage in the rest of the labor market.[14] Thus, the fact that Asian Americans get a "low" return on their educational credentials could help to explain their higher rates of entrepreneurship. But what about African Americans? As we have already seen, black Americans receive lower wages than the majority group (whites) at the same education levels. According to the theory, we should then expect African Americans to have a higher than average rate of self-employment; instead, the rate is lower (3.7 percent in 1993, compared to 9.0 percent for whites). These rates may indicate that this theory of "labor market disadvantage" is missing an important component: group resources (that is, levels of human capital). It is one thing to have high levels of education (as Asian Americans do) and not be adequately rewarded for them. It is quite a different situation to have lower than average education levels (as African Americans do) and receive still lower returns on these years of schooling. In other words, the labor market equilibrium will balance itself in favor of self-employment only when the resources are there to begin with.[15]

Consumer racism has also been shown to have a role in depressing the rate of black entrepreneurship.[16] If nonblack consumers—who obviously form the largest part of the market—automatically prefer a white electrician or barber to a black one, for instance, this discourages African American self-employment. It is also important to realize that the rates of entrepreneurial activity for one group are not independent of the rates for other groups. While there has been no evidence to show that Asian American businesses have "prevented" black ones from forming, we do have evidence that rates of Asian entrepreneurship increase in communities with a high percentage of black residents (net of the size of the Asian population).[17] In other words, Koreans, for example, may not be displacing black businesses, but they are filling a consumer need in black communities that otherwise would have gone untended since African Americans may lack the financial and educational resources to start such enterprises. Entrepreneurship is related to immigration, labor market prospects, and wealth endowments in complex ways. Thus, even if the data were available, comparing Asian immigrants with native-born black Americans is neither simple nor fruitful. The clearer comparison is between blacks and whites, the vast majority of whom are native-born.

NOTES

1. Data from the Panel Study of Income Dynamics (PSID), 1994 Wealth Supplement. The PSID is an ongoing study conducted by the Survey Research Center, Institute for Social Research, at the University of Michigan; see the PSID Web site at *www.isr.umich.edu/src/psid.*

2. These family descriptions were extrapolated from profiles of specific families who were interviewed for this study. The age, racial, income, family size, wealth, housing tenure, and divorce descriptions of these families come directly from cases 4348 and 1586 of the PSID 1984 wave (inflation-adjusted to 1996 dollars). The names and other details are fictitious but are in line with previous research that would suggest such profiles.

3. Neither family received health insurance from an employer. Since the Smiths' income was under 185 percent of the poverty line, their children were eligible for Medicaid. (In most states, the Joneses' children would also have been eligible for Medicaid since that family's wealth was in the form of a home, which is excluded from the asset limits of many states.)

4. See, e.g., G. Levinger and O. Moles, eds., *Divorce and Separation: Contexts, Causes, and Consequences* (New York: Basic Books, 1979); and R. Conger, G.H. Elder, et al., "Linking Economic Hardship to Marital Quality and Instability," *Journal of Marriage and the Family* 52 (1990): 643–56.

5. Throughout this study, the terms "black" and "African American" are used interchangeably, as are the terms "Hispanic" and "Latino." Black people of Caribbean origin make up a negligible portion of the data sample.

6. M. Oliver and T. Shapiro, *Black Wealth/White Wealth: A New Perspective on Racial Inequality* (New York: Routledge, 1995).

7. There are two general exceptions to this statement. First, Native Americans, who make up a very small portion of the population, tend to be more socioeconomically disadvantaged than blacks (although this varies by nation/tribe). Second, educational data show that some Latino groups (particularly those with limited English literacy on average) do more poorly than blacks on some measures.

8. For a discussion of skin tone and stratification, see, e.g., V.M. Keith and C. Herring, "Skin Tone and Stratification in the Black Community," *American Journal of Sociology* 97 (1991): 760–78.

9. A. Hacker, *Two Nations: Black and White, Separate, Hostile, and Unequal* (New York: Ballantine, 1992).

10. I. Light and C. Rosenstein, *Race, Ethnicity, and Entrepreneurship in Urban America* (New York: Aldine de Gruyter, 1995), p.17.

11. Ibid., p.18.

12. R.L. Boyd, "Black and Asian Self-Employment in Large Metropolitan Areas: A Comparative Analysis," *Social Problems* 37 (1990): 258–73.

13. Light and Rosenstein, *Race, Ethnicity, and Entrepreneurship.*

14. H.W. Aurand, "Self Employment: Last Resort of the Unemployed," *International Social Science Review* 58 (1983): 7–11.

15. Light and Rosenstein, *Race, Ethnicity, and Entrepreneurship.*

16. G.J Borjas and S.G. Bronars, "Consumer Discrimination and Self-Employment," *Journal of Political Economy* 97 (1989): 581–605.

17. Ibid.

7

The Wage Gap:
Myths and Facts

National Committee on Pay Equity

The Wage Gap: 1998

1998 Median Annual Earnings Year-Round, Full-Time Workers

Wage Gap: 73%

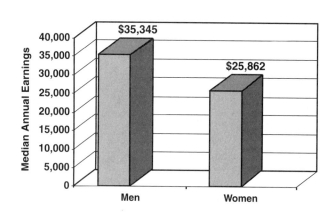

1998 Median Annual Earnings by Race and Sex

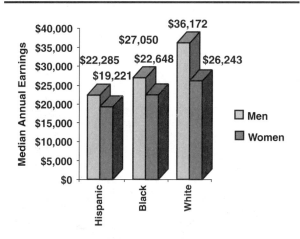

The Wage Gap: 1998 by Race and Sex

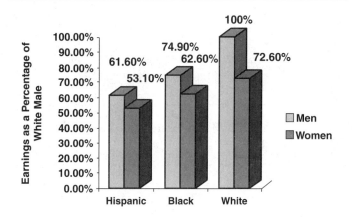

NOTES

- The wage gap is a statistical indicator often used as an index of the status of women's earnings relative to men's. It is also used to compare the earnings of people of color to those of White men.
- The wage gap is expressed as a percentage (for example, in 1998, women earned 73 percent as much as men) and is calculated by dividing median annual earnings for women by median annual earnings for men.
- To calculate the wage gap for each race/sex group, median annual earnings are divided by those of White males, who are not subject to race- or sex-based wage discrimination.

- Individual earnings data for Asian/Pacific Islanders and Native Americans are available, yet they are from a very small sample and thus are not as reliable.
- Statistics are from the Census Bureau *Current Population Reports*, Series P-60, U.S. Commerce Department.

Changes in the Wage Gap, 1970–1998

Median annual earnings of black men and women, Hispanic men and women, and white women as a percentage of white men's median annual earnings.

Year	White Men	Black Men	Hispanic Men	White Women	Black Women	Hispanic Women
1970	100%	69.00%	N/A	58.70%	48.20%	N/A
1975	100%	74.30%	72.10%	57.50%	55.40%	49.30%
1980	100%	70.70%	70.80%	58.90%	55.70%	50.50%
1985	100%	69.70%	68.00%	63.00%	57.10%	52.10%
1990	100%	73.10%	66.30%	69.40%	62.50%	54.30%
1992	100%	72.60%	63.35%	70.00%	64.00%	55.40%
1994	100%	75.10%	64.30%	71.60%	63.00%	55.60%
1995	100%	75.90%	63.30%	71.20%	64.20%	53.40%
1996	100%	80.00%	63.90%	73.30%	65.10%	56.60%
1997	100%	75.10%	61.40%	71.90%	62.60%	53.90%
1998	100%	74.90%	61.60%	72.60%	62.60%	53.10%

The Wage Gap Since 1960: 38 Years Later, Still 27 Percent Behind

Median Earnings of Year-Round, Full-Time Workers by Sex: 1960 to 1998

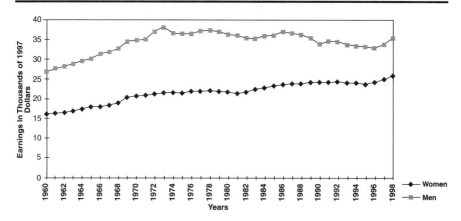

Over a 38 year period, the gap, in 1998 dollars, between women's and men's earnings has closed by less than $2,000.

Source: Data from the Census Bureau, 1998.

The Wage Gap by Education: 1998

Following are wages reflecting the median earnings in 1998 for full-time, year-round workers, 25 years and older.

	H.S. Grad	B.A. Degree	Master's	Doctorate
All Men	$30,868	$49,982	$60,168	$69,188
White	$31,562	$50,614	$60,177	$71,715
Black	$25,203	$41,310	$42,323	—
Hispanic	$25,602	$38,078	$61,928	—

	H.S. Grad	B.A. Degree	Master's	Doctorate
All Women	$21,963	$35,408	$42,002	$52,167
White	$22,438	$35,408	$42,002	$51,662
Black	$19,381	$35,339	$40,766	—
Hispanic	$19,826	$32,289	$42,400	—

Source: U.S. Bureau of the Census.

KEY FINDINGS

- Female college graduates are behind male college graduates by **$14,574.**
- A black college-educated female earns **$15,275** less annually than the college-educated white male.
- A Hispanic college-educated female makes **$18,325** less annually than the college-educated white male.

The Wage Gap over Time

In Real Dollars, Women See Little Change

Since 1963, when the Equal Pay Act was signed, the wage gap has been closing at a very slow rate. In 1963, women made 59 cents for every dollar that men earned; in 1998, women earn 73 cents to the dollar. That means the wage gap has narrowed by less than a half penny per year!

Over 36 years, the real median earnings of women have fallen short by a total of $464,200.

Thus, on an annual basis, the average woman earns approximately $12,894 less than the average man.

The wage gap narrowed from 64 percent in 1986 to 73 percent in 1998, but some of this is due to a decrease in men's real wages, rather than an increase in women's real wages. Although men's real wages did increase last year, their 1998 real wages are still approximately 6 percent lower than in 1986. Women's real wages, however, have increased by only about 7 percent.

Year	Women's Earnings	Men's Earnings	Dollar Difference	Percent
1998	$25,862	$35,345	$9,483	73
1997	25,362	34,199	8,837	74
1996	24,632	33,394	8,762	74
1995	24,062	33,687	9,625	71
1994	24,423	33,935	9,512	72
1993	24,531	34,300	9,769	72
1992	24,833	35,083	10,250	71
1991	24,597	35,210	10,613	70
1990	24,721	34,518	9,797	72
1989	24,672	35,927	11,255	69
1988	24,258	36,728	12,470	66
1987	24,265	37,229	12,964	65
1986	24,141	37,561	13,420	64
1985	23,668	36,652	12,984	65
1984	23,187	36,425	13,238	64
1983	22,773	35,809	13,036	64
1982	22,189	35,937	13,748	62
1981	21,711	36,652	14,941	59
1980	22,176	36,862	14,686	60
1979	22,360	37,477	15,117	60
1978	22,579	37,985	15,406	59
1977	22,227	37,722	15,495	59
1976	22,225	36,922	14,697	60
1975	21,764	37,003	15,239	59
1974	21,890	37,258	15,368	59
1973	21,877	38,630	16,753	57
1972	21,671	37,453	15,782	58
1971	21,152	35,546	14,394	60
1970	21,008	35,386	14,378	59
1969	20,590	34,979	14,389	59
1968	19,270	33,136	13,866	58
1967	18,635	32,250	13,977	58
1966	18,273	31,748	13,475	58
1965	18,245	30,446	12,201	60
1964	17,746	30,003	12,257	59
1963	17,255	29,271	12,016	59
1962	16,956	28,595	11,639	59
1961	16,626	28,061	11,435	59
1960	16,487	27,173	10,686	61

Source: Census Bureau, March *Current Population Survey.*
Note: All figures in 1998 dollars.

Profile of the Wage Gap by Selected Occupations

According to an analysis of data provided by the U.S. Department of Labor's Bureau of Labor Statistics, women are paid less in almost every occupational classification for which data is available.[1]

Even in job categories where women make up the majority of workers, women are paid less. Only in two categories, miscellaneous food preparation and legal assistant, do women make more money. The women in miscellaneous food preparation average $6 more per week than men in the same occupation. They earn 102 percent of men's earnings. Female legal assistants earn 104 percent of the earnings of comparable men; they earn $20 more per week.

Below are median earnings for women and men in selected occupations. The earnings gap and earnings ratio (as a percentage) are shown, as well as the percentage of workers in each occupation who are women.

Table I
Occupations with Estimated Earnings of under $20,000*

Occupation	Percent Women	Men's Wages	Women's Wages	Earnings Gap	Earnings Ratio (%)
Waiter/Waitress	72%	$343	$282	$61	82%
Cleaning & Building Service Occupations	29%	$358	$288	$70	80%
Bartender	55%	$379	$293	$86	77%
Dry Cleaning Machine Operators	55%	$301	$270	$31	90%

*Approximate annual earnings categories were estimated by multiplying median weekly wages for men by 52 weeks.

Table II
Occupations with Estimated Earnings between $20,000 and $33,000

Occupation	Percent Women	Men's Wages	Women's Wages	Earnings Gap	Earnings Ratio (%)
Bus Driver	41%	$476	$352	$124	74%
Sales Worker; Retail & Personal	56%	$412	$272	$140	66%
Mechanics & Repairers	4%	$599	$519	$ 80	87%
Admin. Support, incl. clerical	76%	$518	$418	$100	81%
Construction Trades	2%	$545	$408	$137	75%

[1]Data was analyzed using 1998 Household Data Annual Averages, Bureau of Labor Statistics.

Table III
Occupations with Estimated Earnings above $33,000

Occupation	Percent Women	Men's Wages	Women's Wages	Earnings Gap	Earnings Ratio (%)
Accountants & Auditors	60%	$ 821	$618	$203	75%
Securities & Financial Services Sales	31%	$ 930	$598	$332	64%
Pharmacists	42%	$1,146	$985	$161	86%
Engineers	10%	$1,011	$831	$180	82%
Physicians	32%	$1,255	$966	$289	77%
Teachers, College & Univ.	37%	$ 998	$769	$229	77%
Lawyers	34%	$1,350	$951	$399	70%
Editors and Reporters	44%	$ 812	$616	$196	76%

Table IV
Other Occupations in Which the Majority of Workers Are Women

Occupation	Percent Women	Men's Wages	Women's Wages	Earnings Gap	Earnings Ratio (%)
Registered Nurse	91%	$774	$734	$40	95%
Social Worker	65%	$609	$568	$41	93%
Elementary School Teacher	84%	$749	$677	$72	90%
Secretaries, Stenographers, & Typists	98%	$484	$436	$48	90%
Cashiers	75%	$302	$259	$43	86%

African American Women in the Workplace*

Labor Force Participation—62.8 percent

- In 1998, 8.4 million black women were in the labor force, with a participation rate of 62.8 percent (Bureau of Labor Statistics).
- The Bureau of Labor Statistics predicts that by 2006, 9.2 million black women will be in the labor force.

*Sources: Census Bureau, Bureau of Labor Statistics, Women's Bureau of the Department of Labor

Earnings

The Wage Gap by Gender and Race/Hispanic Origin

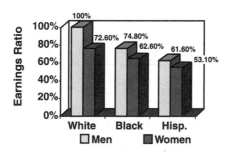

- According to the Census Bureau, in 1998, black women's median earnings ($22,648) were only 62.6 percent of the earnings of white men ($36,172).
- In one year, the average black woman earns $13,524 less than the average white man. Over a thirty-year career, this adds up to a $405,720 loss!

Black Women by Occupation

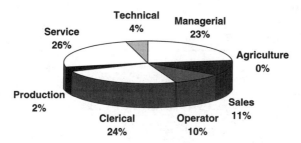

Source: Bureau of Labor Statistics.

Job Description	Women's Median Weekly Earnings
Administrative Support	$419
Sales	$372
Service	$296
All Occupations	$456

Source: Bureau of Labor Statistics.

- The median weekly earnings for all women are $456, a substantially greater amount than what women in administrative support, sales, or service occupations are paid. Since 60 percent of black working women are in those jobs, they are disproportionately affected by the low wages of these industries.

- Black women can find help in unions. While the median weekly earnings in 1998 for black women who are protected by a union is $537, those who are nonunion average $376 per week (BLS).

Education

Education Obtained by Black Women

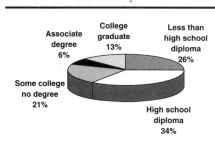

Source: U.S. Department of Labor.

- Seventy-four percent of black women have completed high school, while 13 percent have completed at least a bachelor's degree.
- Education, however, does not guarantee that the wage gap will disappear. Black women still make less even with the same amount of education.

Income and Education

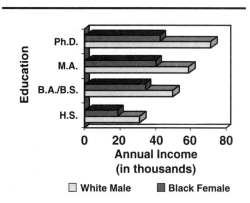

- Black women with bachelor's degrees make only a few thousand more than white males who have only completed high school (Census Bureau).

Family Life

- Black women head 29.8 percent of all female-headed households in the U.S. These women have a median income of $16,770 annually, while single white male householders have a median income of $37,798 (Census Bureau).

Unemployment

1998 Unemployment by Race and Gender

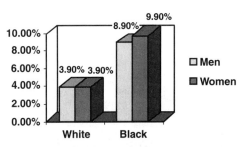

Source: Bureau of Labor Statistics.

- The unemployment rate for black women in 1998 was higher than for black men, and it was more than twice that of white women.

Unequal Pay for Equal Work

- Women, including African Americans, continue to receive unequal pay for equal work despite laws prohibiting this wage discrimination.
- In one of the largest wage disparity settlements in more than 30 years, Corestates, a financial corporation, recently provided back pay to 238 workers (at least 70 of whom were minority women). The lump sum of the settlement was approximately $1.48 million.

Implications

- This pattern of substantially lower lifetime earnings affects the quality of life for African American women and their families, limits their opportunity for promotion, and contributes to decreased savings, pensions, and Social Security payments for African American women in their senior years.

Women of Hispanic Origin in the Workplace*

Labor Force Participation Rate—56 percent

- In 1998, 10.3 million Hispanic women over the age of 16 lived in the United States. Fifty-six percent (or 5.7 million) were in the labor force (Bureau of Labor Statistics).
- The Bureau of Labor Statistics projects that in 2005, 6.9 million Hispanic women will be in the labor force.

Sources: Bureau of Labor Statistics (U. S. Department of Labor); Census Bureau (U. S. Department of Commerce); Women's Bureau of the Department of Labor.

Earnings

The Wage Gap by Gender and Race/Hispanic Origin

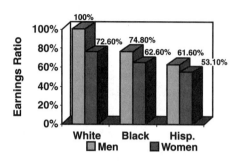

- According to the Census Bureau, in 1998, the median earnings for Hispanic women were $19,221, only 53.1 percent of the median earnings of white men ($36,172).
- In one year, the average Hispanic woman earns $16,951 less than the average white man. Over a 30-year career, that adds up to a $508,530 loss! (Census).

Occupational Segregation

Hispanic Women by Occupation

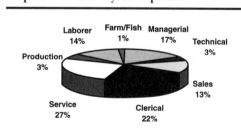

Source: Bureau of Labor Statistics.

Job Description	Women's Median Weekly Earnings
Administrative Support	$418
Sales	$372
Service	$296
All Occupations	$456

Source: Bureau of Labor Statistics, 1998.

- Sixty-two percent of Hispanic women are employed in administrative support, sales, or service occupations, which are traditionally low paying.

Family Life

- In 1998, 13.5 percent of all female-headed households were Hispanic (Census Bureau).
- The median income of a single female Hispanic householder is only $16,532. Single white male householders have an income of $37,798 (Census Bureau).

Education

Education of Hispanic Women in 1998

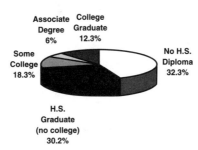

Source: Bureau of Labor Statistics—1998.

- Thirty-two percent of Hispanic women have not completed high school, and only 12 percent hold a college degree or higher.

Income and Education in 1998

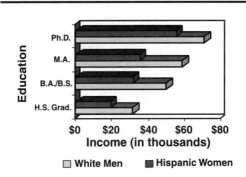

- Hispanic women with a high school diploma earn $19,826. That is 37.2 percent less than white men with the same level of education (Census Bureau).

Unions

- While the median weekly earnings for Hispanic women who were members of a union in 1998 is $478, those who are nonunion average $322 per week (Bureau of Labor Statistics).

Unemployment

Unemployment Rate of Women in 1998

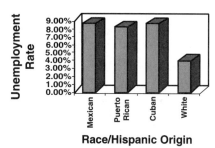

Source: Bureau of Labor Statistics.

- In 1998, the unemployment rates of women of Cuban, Puerto Rican, and Mexican descent were more than twice as high as those for white women.

Poverty Rates

Poverty Rates by Race/Hispanic Origin

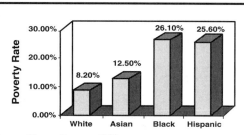

Source: Census Bureau, 1998.

- The poverty rate for Hispanics (25.6 percent) is over three times the poverty rate for whites (8.2 percent).

Implications

- This pattern of substantially lower lifetime earnings affects the quality of life for Hispanic women and their families, limits their access to education and health care, and contributes to decreased retirement security for Hispanic women in their senior years.

8

Women, Income, and Poverty:
There's a Family Connection

Randy Albelda and Chris Tilly

The More Things Change . . .

Women's lives have changed dramatically over the last forty years. Women find themselves in jobs, educational institutions, and public offices they never would have dreamed of in the 1950s. New social freedoms and economic opportunities mean that a woman living without a man is no longer considered an oddity.

But other things haven't changed so much. The American economic and political system has yet to catch up to the social and cultural strides women have made. Women's earnings are considerably lower than men's, approximately 70 cents to every man's dollar. Women are still primarily responsible for providing or finding child care and taking care of domestic chores. Thus, most women's economic fortunes still depend far too much on men's fortunes.

After four decades of economic, political, and social changes, women are by no means equal partners with men in economic or family life. Women, especially those with children, who have moved up the corporate ladder hit the "glass ceiling"—that invisible barrier to further advancement—and are shunted off to the "mommy track." Many more women—particularly single mothers—with limited skills or support are stuck in a "bottomless pit" of poverty. While these two groups of women may seem a world apart, they have much in common—their economic opportunities are restricted because of their gender.

Aside from the few born to wealth, people in this country get their income from three main sources: sharing the income of other family members, earning income themselves in the labor market, and receiving income from the government. Earnings occupy the central place among the three, since they far exceed government-provided income and constitute the main source of income to be shared within families. But discrimination and job segregation limit women's access to labor

From Randy Albelda and Chris Tilly, *Glass Ceilings and Bottomless Pits: Women's Work, Women's Poverty* (Boston: South End Press, 1997), pp. 1–17.

market earnings. Child care demands additionally constrain many women's possibilities for paid work.

This inequity is particularly disastrous for single women with children. Half of all single mothers in the United States have incomes below the poverty line. Single mothers face the same obstacles as other women *plus* the lack of a spouse's income—leaving many of them dependent on government-provided income.

As inflation eats away at cash benefits, and as state and federal legislators impose stringent requirements designed to thin the welfare rolls, poverty looks more and more like a bottomless pit. Sensible welfare reform, based on understanding the actual needs and capabilities of mothers, can give women a leg up out of poverty. But before we tackle the issues of poverty and welfare reform, it is important to place women's economic situation in a larger context. A good starting place is a brief look at four major economic trends affecting women, and many men as well.

A Different World Than Our Mothers Faced: Four Trends

Trend 1: The Declining Marriage Rate

For a variety of reasons, marriage is not for everyone. Fewer and fewer women are getting or staying married (see Figure 1). As of 1995, close to 45 percent of women were *not* currently married.[1] (Annual Census Bureau surveys, unfortunately, do not make it possible to tell how many of these live with partners). Not staying married is an important part of this picture: about two-thirds of all first marriages (and an even higher proportion of remarriages) end in separation or divorce.[2]

Figure 1
More Women Are Not Married
Percentage of adult women who are unmarried, 1960–1995

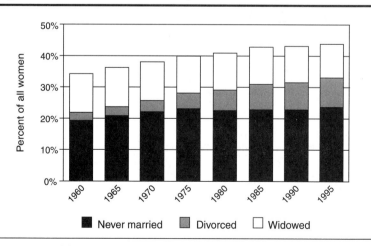

Source: U.S. Bureau of the Census, Household and Family Characteristics, various years.

But just because fewer women are married doesn't mean they aren't raising children. One-half of all females over sixteen have custody of a child under the age of eighteen. And of those women with children, one out of every three is not married. This means that *one woman out of six is a single mother.*

Trend 2: The Growing Labor Market

Work, both unpaid and paid, can be an important way to interact with the world and a source of pride. Increasingly, women are doing *both* kinds of work— unpaid work in the home and work for pay outside the home. More and more women—and especially more and more mothers—are in the paid labor force (see Figure 2). Two out of every three mothers also have a paid job outside the home.

In 1947, a woman was only 38 percent as likely to be working or looking for work as a man. By 1996, that percentage had more than doubled to 79 percent. Of course, these patterns differed by race: for example, black women have always been more likely to work than white or Latina women. But the overall trend prevails across racial boundaries. Black women were 54 percent as likely to be in the paid labor force as black men in 1954, and 88 percent as likely in 1996.

More work for women has not translated into equal pay. Women usually don't work as many hours a week outside the home as men do, and for every hour they

Figure 2
More Women and Fewer Men Are in the Paid Labor Force
Labor force participation rates* of men and women sixteen years of age and older, 1955–1995

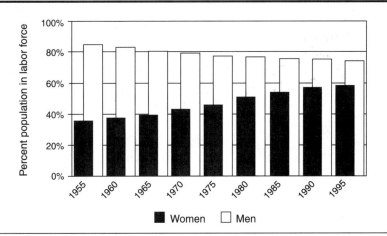

*The labor force participation rate is equal to the numbers of those employed plus those looking for work divided by the adult population. That number is multiplied by 100 to get a percentage.

Source: Economic Report of the President, 1996.

Figure 3
Women's Earnings Still Lag behind Men's
Median earnings* of year-round, full-time male and female workers in 1995 dollars in the United States, 1955–1995

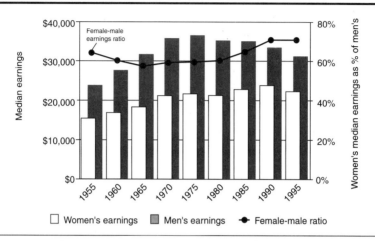

*Median earnings is the earnings level where 50% earn more and 50% earn less than that amount.

Source: U. S. Bureau of the Census, *Current Population Reports,* series P60, various years.

do work, women earn less than men. Nationwide in 1995, a woman working full-time, year-round earned 64 percent as much as her male counterpart. Women actually fell further behind during the 1960s and 1970s, and then gained some ground in the 1980s and 1990s, leaving them with 71 percent of male earnings in 1995—only slightly better than in 1955 (see Figure 3).

Although women make two-thirds of what men do for every hour they work, because women work fewer hours a year than men do—mostly because of family-care responsibilities—women's average *annual* earnings stand at one-half those of men, even among those who are heads and spouses. Among all heads and spouses employed, men averaged $28,690 per year in 1993; women averaged only $14,120 a year.[3]

Trend 3: The Decline of Manufacturing Work

While more women are in the labor force and more jobs are open to women today than they were thirty years ago, other changes in the structure of the economy have also had important impacts on men and women. One of those changes is the steady decline of manufacturing jobs—especially high-paying jobs in heavy industries such as auto, steel, and aircraft—and the corresponding steady increase in the percentage of service jobs. The phenomenon, popularly referred to as the "deindustrialization" of America, is easy to see in Figure 4.[4] In 1955, one-third of

Figure 4
More Service and Fewer Manufacturing Jobs in the Economy
Percentage of persons employed in manufacturing and in service and retail industry jobs,
1955–1995

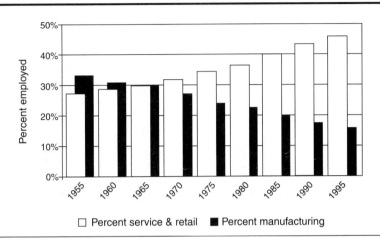

Source: *Economic Report of the President*, table B-42, 1996.

all jobs were in manufacturing; by 1995, the figure had fallen to one-sixth. Conversely, in 1955, the service and retail industries accounted for about one-quarter of all jobs; by 1995, they represented almost one-half. And while not all jobs in the manufacturing sector pay high wages, and not all jobs in the service sector pay low wages, there is a strong correlation between pay and industry sector. In 1995, the average weekly paycheck from a manufacturing job was $514, 85 percent higher than the average pay in the service and retail industries.[5]

Those particularly hurt by the decline in manufacturing jobs are younger workers without a college education. Also, since men have historically held the vast majority of manufacturing jobs, deindustrialization has had a profoundly negative effect on their earnings, which can be seen in Figure 3. Although women are concentrated in the growing service sector, deindustrialization has not helped women's wages either—with the possible exception of women with higher levels of education.

While the reasons for the change in the structure of the economy are complex, rapid technological changes, increased international competition, and concerted corporate strategies to maximize profits all play important roles. The impact on families has been clear. Men's earning power has declined—especially that of men who are not in high levels of management. The days when the majority of middle-class men could support an entire family on their paychecks are pretty much gone. Middle-class women's entry into the labor force is partly due to increased desires to have more economic independence and partly due to financial necessity.

Figure 5
The Feminization of Poverty
Poor persons in female-headed families as a percentage of all poor persons, 1960–1995

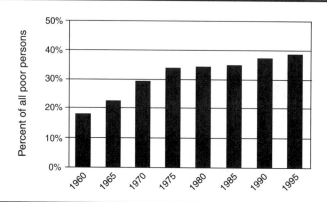

Source: U.S. Bureau of the Census, *Poverty in the United States: 1995*, P60–194, 1996.

Trend 4: The Poverty Trap

With the marriage rate declining and men's incomes falling, more and more women rely less and less on men's income for support. Unfortunately, the labor market has taken up only some of the income slack. Therefore, it is not surprising to find more women and their families slipping into poverty. Even though women are now more likely to work for pay, many do not earn enough to support themselves and a family. For the growing number of families headed by women only, the end result is financial disaster. In 1995, almost two out of every five people who were poor lived in families consisting of a single woman plus dependents. This is more than twice the rate in 1960 (see Figure 5).

In 1993, 16 percent of all families and lone individuals were poor. At the same time, 52 percent of single-mother families—or *one out of every two*—were poor. Compare this to an 11 percent (or one out of every ten) poverty rate for two-adult families with children.

Poverty is most definitely a women's issue, and it has been for a long time. Of all poor adults, two-thirds are women. Poverty is also a children's issue: one out of every four children in this country lives in a poor family—most likely a family with only a woman to support him or her. And that makes government policies toward the poor and poor families a women's issue, as certainly as equal pay or freedom of choice.

Pretzel Logic: Contradictory Values about Work and Family

Four contradictions cloud political thinking about women, families, and poverty.

Contradiction 1: Family Values vs. Valuing Families

In the early 1990s, when Vice President Dan Quayle attacked television character Murphy Brown (portrayed by Candice Bergen) for choosing to have a child without a husband, the resulting political flap energized a discussion over what constitutes family values. That discussion continues today. In a display of uncommon unity, most people agree on the importance of care and concern for family and community, hard work, commitment, and instilling moral and spiritual values in children. But fewer agree on what a *family is* or *should be.* Further, the debate highlights an important contradiction in the thinking of most Americans:

- *On the one hand,* we are a country that says we should value families and, above all else, children. After all, everyone agrees that children are the future of our country. *On the other hand,* we are a country that doesn't value the *work* of taking care of children.

In the United States, childcare is every individual family's responsibility. Typically, the burden falls on women. Mothers take care of children for free, while childcare workers are paid embarrassingly low wages.

Contradiction 2: The Obligation to Work vs. the Opportunity to Work

The nationwide recession in the early 1990s showed that almost all of us are potentially vulnerable to economic downturns. The lackluster recovery and rampant corporate downsizing painfully demonstrate that even in the midst of historic profit levels and what appear to be positive economic indicators, for most employees job security is by no means assured. The icy hand of unemployment has even touched people who thought they had a job for life—middle managers and midcareer professionals at large companies like IBM and AT&T. These experiences serve as a chilly reminder of the second contradiction:

- *On the one hand,* we believe that able-bodied adults have an obligation to work. Many sing the praises of the hardworking people in the working and middle classes, implicitly or explicitly scorning the idle rich and—especially—the shiftless poor. Horatio Alger's vision of upward mobility through diligence, resourcefulness, and thrift still dominates. *On the other hand,* as a nation, we make no commitment to ensure that jobs are there for those willing and able to work. Indeed, the federal government has backed further and further away from any commitments to pursue full employment, and the average unemployment rate has climbed decade by decade.

Without available jobs, the principle of an obligation to work rings hollow.

Contradiction 3: Having a Job vs. Having a Living Wage

The number of people who work yet are still poor is at its highest in decades. In 1995, 10 percent of adult workers below the poverty line (and a full 12 percent of poor adults under age sixty-five) actually held a *year-round, full-time* job (see Figure 6).[6] The growth in low-wage jobs and the erosion of the minimum wage in inflation-adjusted dollars means that many employed people don't earn enough to buy the basic necessities for themselves or their families. This highlights a contradiction that many thought this country had eradicated thirty years ago:

- *On the one hand*, we believe that a job is the best way out of poverty. Those with the opportunity to hold a job can and should be self-sufficient. Able-bodied adults are expected to take care of themselves because hard work pays off in the labor market. *On the other hand*, as a nation, we give no assurance that people with jobs will earn enough to support themselves, nor any guarantee of health insurance or even steady work.

Without jobs that pay living wages, the current emphasis on work as a ticket out of poverty is a cruel joke.

Figure 6
Working but Poor
Percentage of poor adults who worked year-round, full-time, 1966–1995

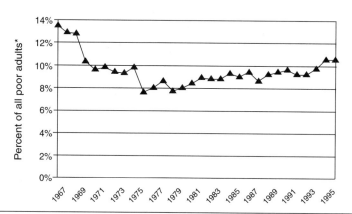

*Between 1966 and 1978, includes persons fourteen years of age and older. Between 1979 and 1989, includes persons fifteen years of age and older. From 1990 onward, includes persons sixteen years of age and older.

Source: For 1966–1994, Center on Budget and Policy Priorities, *Poverty and Income Trends,* 1994 (using *Current Population Reports*), p. 77. For 1995, U.S. Bureau of the Census, *Poverty in the United States: 1995,* P60–194, p. 17.

Contradiction 4: Legitimate vs. Illegitimate Dependencies

The commonly held notion of the "undeserving poor" points to yet another contradiction:

- *On the one hand,* dependency within the family is considered natural. When a breadwinner provides for his or her family, we don't question the moral fiber of those dependent on the primary wage earner. Indeed, when one spouse stays home to cook, clean, and care for the children, this represents *inter*dependence—a division of labor. *On the other hand,* many denounce dependency on the government as pitiable at best, reprehensible at worst. A woman who stays home to cook, clean, and care for her children *without* a husband is often viewed as taking unfair advantage of government generosity. But why not recognize this as another kind of *inter*dependence at the level of the community or the whole society?

As these four contradictions play themselves out, women—especially women with children and women of color—and increasing numbers of men are feeling the squeeze.

Scapegoating Poor Women and Their Children

Politicians and pundits have targeted social safety net programs, particularly welfare programs directed toward single mothers and their children, as wasteful and even as the *cause* of poverty in this country. They have scapegoated poor women and their children. By playing on people's economic insecurity, these policymakers have avoided addressing the contradictions just outlined—promoting instead state and national surges to decimate the programs that support poor families. This is not only a morally repugnant strategy, it is also economically bankrupt. It avoids dealing with the most basic economic issues facing women today and will result in more poverty, not less.

There are many things wrong with the welfare system, but it has always served as an absolutely vital lifeline for many families. And some form of public assistance for women raising children alone has always been necessary in an economy that makes wage-earning the most important source of income.

* * *

Women Are Poor for a Reason

Half of all single-mother families in this country are poor—but not because they are lazy, lack initiative, or are unlucky. The primary reason is because it is difficult for one adult to support a family, and even harder if that adult is female. Mothers must do unpaid work, limiting their time to do paid work, and when they do paid work, they are paid significantly less than men.

Childcare responsibilities affect women at all income levels. As women with children know, it is very hard to work full-time and care for children as well. Part-time jobs rarely pay enough for one person to live on, let alone an entire family. Most of the good full-time jobs that pay enough to support an entire family assume there's a "wife" at home, and accordingly, make large demands on the worker's time and flexibility. Highly paid women who choose to be mothers (and cannot simply turn their lives over to the company) face the second-class status of being on the horizontal "mommy track" rather than the vertical job ladder many male or childless women workers climb to higher pay and prestige.

Finding childcare is a problem for any family. And all women face the reality of lower pay than men. But for single mothers, these issues collide in a devastating combination. Welfare policies that inadequately address these issues implicitly and explicitly deny and devalue what women contribute to their families, workplaces, and communities in the form of unpaid labor.

*   *   *

NOTES

1. U.S. Bureau of the Census, *Marital Status and Living Arrangements: March 1994*, P20–484, table 1 (1996).

2. Teresa Castro Martin and Larry L. Bumpass, "Recent Trends in Marital Disruption," *Demography*, vol. 26, no. 1 (1989): 37–51.

3. Calculated by authors from the March 1994 Current Population Survey. (The Current Population Survey is a monthly survey of a sample of U.S. households, conducted by the U.S. Bureau of the Census. Every March the Census Bureau asks households more detailed questions about their income in the previous year.) A primary earner is either the head of a household or the spouse of the head.

4. This term was made popular by Barry Bluestone and Bennett Harrison in their book *The Deindustrialization of America* (New York: Basic Books, 1982).

5. Calculated by authors from U.S. Bureau of Labor Statistics, *Employment and Earnings* (January 1996), tables B-1 and B-2. Much of the weekly pay difference results from the fact that service and retail workers are more likely to work part-time. The hourly manufacturing wage, however, is still 29 percent above the hourly wage in service and retail.

6. U.S. Bureau of the Census, *Poverty in the United States: 1995*, P60–194 (Washington, D.C.: Government Printing Office, 1996), table 3, p. 17.

9

What Scholars Can Tell Politicians about the Poor

Katherine S. Newman

Welfare reform is a lightning rod for the discontented American middle class, which has been shaken by levels of economic insecurity that were hard to imagine a mere 20 years ago. The years of corporate buyouts, hostile takeovers, mergers, bankruptcies, and downsizing have left the average American with stagnant wages, increasing pressure to work greater hours, and the nagging sense that this scenario is no longer temporary. It is hardly surprising that, in this climate and in the panic over the nation's deficit, the search for scapegoats has taken on a new sense of urgency.

Welfare mothers seem to fill the bill nicely. Conservatives argue that the nation's economy is sagging under the burden of supporting the poor. Cutting off welfare benefits, we are told, is the best medicine: It will eliminate the incentives that reward dependency and replace them with the traditional work ethic. We may lose a few poor people or their children along the way, but ultimately this social-Darwinist strategy is supposed to pay off as the poor straighten up and fly into the labor market.

The recipe is appealing, because it taps into tenets of American culture that date to Benjamin Franklin: belief in the work ethic, hostility toward sloth, and conviction that individuals are the masters of their own fate. And it resonates with voters because conservative welfare reformers have convinced them that there are, in fact, lots of jobs going begging.

For the past two years, my research team has studied a real inner-city labor market, to discover how people go about finding jobs in a depressed area, how much competition exists for employment, and what those who have jobs do with the money they earn. This study of workers in the fast-food industry, in New York City's Harlem, is one-half of a comparative project; the other half is under way in Oakland, Cal., where Carol B. Stack, a professor of education at the University of California at Berkeley, has followed a comparable sample of fast-food workers.

The project was born out of a desire to expand on a much-discussed body of research on the urban underclass. It was spurred largely by the work of the

Originally published in *The Chronicle of Higher Education*, June 23, 1995, pp. B1–B2. Reprinted by permission of the author. Katherine Newman is Professor of Public Policy at Harvard University.

sociologist William Julius Wilson at the University of Chicago. In his landmark 1987 book, *The Truly Disadvantaged: The Inner City, the Underclass, and Public Policy,* Mr. Wilson argues that the decline of manufacturing jobs and the growth of service-industry jobs that demand strong academic credentials have created a massive population of jobless poor in the urban North who are geographically and socially segregated from the mainstream working population. He and other theorists of the underclass maintain that minorities' social isolation removes role models, destroys access to social networks crucial for employment, and undercuts belief in the value of schooling. These negative features of life among the unemployed are said to characterize inner-city ghettos as a whole.

The emphasis on the jobless poor has, however, obscured what I believe is an equally important population: the working poor. These are the people who go to work every day, as Jesse Jackson has said—the people who make beds in hospitals, make change in stores, and serve hamburgers in fast-food restaurants. Academic researchers who study poverty have spent relatively little time examining the lives and struggles of ghetto dwellers who participate in the mainstream economy at its bottom level. So it should not surprise us that policy makers and members of the public think of the poor as distinctly different from working people.

Yet even in some of our most economically depressed inner cities, working for a living remains a key norm. In central Harlem, where my research was conducted, about 40 percent of the population exist on incomes below the poverty line, 29 percent live on public assistance, and 18 percent are officially unemployed. But many people do participate in the mainstream world of work. In fact, 67 percent of the households in this part of New York include at least one full-time worker.

The literature on the underclass emphasizes the social isolation of the poor— the geographic separation of the jobless from the stable working population and their exclusion from vital social networks. Far from being segregated from one another, however, the working and non-working poor in Harlem live together. Because the service-industry employees in our study work for the minimum wage, they are not able to escape from the inner city. They continue to live in some of the city's most depressed neighborhoods, even though they go to work every day and bring their wages home as one contribution (among many) to the support of poverty-level households. They participate in lateral social networks that do, indeed, facilitate job hunting, but since the networks are composed largely of other minimum-wage workers, they do not foster upward mobility.

However, these service workers are also well acquainted with people who live in much better parts of the city and in the suburbs. Their well-off acquaintances constitute a vertical network composed largely of older friends and family members, beneficiaries of the better employment opportunities of the past. These more-fortunate people were able to leave the ghetto when they got a job in manufacturing in the 1960s or later in the public sector (public transit, local utilities, the post office) or in the military.

Because public-sector and military jobs are getting scarcer, and many manufacturing jobs have disappeared, these middle-class friends and relatives cannot do much to help their younger relatives move up in the world. But they do constitute a network of people who present examples of success to nephews, nieces, and grandchildren locked into low-wage jobs. Thus people in the inner city do have role models in these vertical networks, although that's not enough to set them on the path of upward mobility.

In some respects, however, the low-wage earners we have studied are the lucky ones in central Harlem, where jobs are in extremely short supply. In the fast-food industry, where most jobs pay only the minimum wage, and opportunities for significant advancement are modest, the competition for jobs is nonetheless fierce. During the five-month period in 1993 when we tracked this labor market, we found that the ratio of job seekers to job-finders was 14 to 1. That is, 14 people applied for every job opening at $4.25 per hour. When we interviewed the rejected job seekers a year later, we discovered that 73 percent of them were still unemployed, even though they had continued to pound the pavement. There simply were not enough jobs to go around.

We found that people under the age of 20 had a much harder time getting fast-food jobs than did their older counterparts. Restaurant jobs are the stereotypical form of entry-level employment, and in suburban communities boasting many different kinds of jobs, they remain a major mechanism for introducing young people to the world of work. But in the inner city they have become "real" jobs, which adults are taking to try to support their families. This simultaneously removes the opportunity for young people to get a foot in the door and places enormous pressure on households struggling to make ends meet on $4.25 an hour.

African Americans are finding the going particularly rough, even in neighborhoods such as central Harlem, where they constitute a majority of the residents. Although almost 70 percent of the "new hires" in our study were African Americans, black job applicants were more likely than Latinos to be rejected. The applicant pool in Harlem is overwhelmingly composed of blacks, but Latino job seekers enjoy disproportionate success. Only 13.6 percent of African-American applicants for the jobs we studied were hired, while 38 percent of other minority applicants—primarily Latinos—were hired.

We also found that immigrants had an advantage. Employers apparently believe that immigrants from poor countries are better candidates for low-wage jobs because they look upon our minimum wage as a relatively good salary, while native-born job seekers see it as the bottom of the barrel.

Thus competition among members of minority groups struggling for a foothold on the employment ladder is growing, as is the social tension that the competition produces on the street and behind the counter. Although politicians point to the economic success of unschooled immigrants as proof that native-born members of minority groups have retreated to the comforts of the welfare system, our research shows no such thing. Instead, the people we studied are battling for the declining number of opportunities available, with some gaining and most losing.

What we found in Harlem should, at one level, be heartwarming, even to the most conservative policy maker: a strong commitment to the work ethic, a persistent effort to find jobs, and a realistic sense of the rewards of the low-wage world. On the "values" end of this debate, then, much evidence exists to support the notion that the inner-city labor force is eager to join the mainstream. The problem lies in the lack of opportunity—a fact that legislators and other national policy makers ignore or are not aware of.

This is particularly unfortunate for those who need a job to help pay for their education. Fifty-eight percent of the African Americans working in Harlem's fast-food industry have a high-school diploma, and most of the rest are still enrolled in school. More than half of the workers—black and Latino—who have finished high school are taking courses in vocational schools, junior colleges, or regular colleges. Minimum-wage jobs are vital sources of "financial aid" for working poor students. Without this employment, many would find it impossible to continue their schooling.

The country desperately needs more employment opportunities, even at the entry level, to accommodate the demand for work among inner-city residents. This is particularly true if we hope to absorb welfare recipients into the work force—which is going to be much more difficult than most policy makers suggest. Long-term welfare recipients are less qualified for employment in terms of academic credentials and work experience than are today's average job seekers in Harlem. Those forced off the welfare rolls and into the labor market are going to find the competition stiff and their own prospects dim.

Policy makers, as well as scholars, must realize that, in addition to the persistently jobless population described in research literature on the underclass, the United States is blessed with a significant number of responsible poor people who want, above all, to participate in the mainstream economy. Despite their poverty, the working poor continue to believe that education provides the best way out, that getting a job is important, and that people who don't work are not to be admired.

The working poor are, however, faced with the fact that few jobs of any kind are available to them, much less those that can support a family.

Dismantling the welfare system is not the way to solve the problem of persistent poverty. That problem can't be wished away, nor can the inner-city residents who scramble for the few jobs available. Scholars must press policy makers to take into account the persistent efforts of ghetto dwellers to find work, and to reward that diligence with real job opportunities, not mere rhetoric urging them to do exactly what they already are trying to do—find employment.

Suggestions for Further Reading

AFL-CIO and Institute for Women's Policy Research. *Equal Pay for Working Families.* Washington, DC, 1999.

Albelda, Randy. *Economics and Feminism: Disturbances in the Field.* New York: Twayne, 1996.

Amott, Theresa, and Dorothy Amott. *Caught in the Crisis: Women and the U.S. Economy.* New York: Monthly Review Press, June 1993.

Amott, Theresa L., and Julie Atthaei. *Race, Gender, and Work: A Multicultural History of Women in the U.S.* Boston: South End Press, 1991.

Anderson, Sarah, et al. *A Decade of Executive Excess: The 1990s.* Boston: United for a Fair Economy, 1999.

Bartlett, Donald L., and James B. Steele. *America: What Went Wrong.* Kansas City: Andrews and McMeel, 1992.

Brouwer, Steve. *Sharing the Pie.* New York: Henry Holt, 1998.

Children's Defense Fund. *The State of America's Children.* Washington, DC:. Children's Defense Fund, 20001 (published annually).

Danziger, Sheldon, and Peter Gottschalk, eds. *Uneven Tides Rising: Inequality in America.* New York: Russell Sage Foundation, 1993.

DeMott, Benjamin. *The Imperial Middle.* New York: William Morrow, 1990.

Domhoff, G. William. *Who Rules America Now?* New York: Simon & Schuster, 1983.

Estes, Ralph W. *Who Pays? Who Profits? The Truth about the American Tax System.* Washington, DC: Institute for Policy Studies, 1993.

Gans, Herbert J. *The War against the Poor.* New York: Basic Books, 1995.

Hacker, Andrew. *Two Nations.* New York: Scribner's, 1992.

Hacker, Andrew. *Money: Who Has How Much and Why.* New York: Touchstone Books, 1998.

Hartman, Chester. *Double Exposure: Poverty & Race in America.* Armonk, NY: M.E. Sharpe, 1997.

Kahlenberg, D. Richard. *The Remedy: Class, Race and Affirmative Action*, a New Republic Book. New York: Basic Books, 1996.

Kozol, Jonathan. *Savage Inequalities: Children in America's Schools.* New York: Crown Publishers, 1991.

Lav, Iris J., et al. *The States and the Poor: How Budget Decisions Affected Low Income People in 1992.* Washington, DC: Center on Budget and Policy Priorities; and Albany, NY: Center for the Study of the States, 1993.

Newman, Katherine S. *Falling from Grace: The Experience of Downward Mobility in the American Middle Class.* New York: Vintage Books, 1989.

Phillips, Kevin. *The Politics of the Rich and the Poor.* New York: Random House, 1990.

Polakrow, Valerie. *Lives on the Edge: Single Women and Their Children in the Other America.* Chicago: University of Chicago Press, 1993.

Rix, Sara E., for the Women's Research and Education Institute. *The American Woman, 1993–94 Status Report.* New York: W.W. Norton, 1994.

Schwarz, John E., and Thomas J. Volgy. *The Forgotten Americans: Thirty Million Working Poor in the Land of Opportunity.* New York: W.W. Norton, 1992.

Sidel, Ruth. *Keeping Women and Children Last.* New York: Penguin Books, 1996.

Turner, Margery Austin, et al. *Opportunities Denied, Opportunities Diminished: Racial Discrimination in Hiring.* Washington, DC: Urban Institute Press, 1991.

Yates, Michael. *Longer Hours, Fewer Jobs: Employment and Unemployment in the United States.* New York: Monthly Review Press, 1993.

In addition to these books, the following organizations are good sources for obtaining current statistics analyzed in terms of race, class, and gender:

The Association for American Indian Affairs, 432 Park Avenue South, New York, NY 10016.

United for a Fair Economy, 37 Temple Place, Boston, MA 02111.

National Jobs for All Coalition, 475 Riverside Drive, New York, NY 10115.

Institute for Women's Policy Research, 1400 20th Street NW, Suite 104, Washington DC 20036.

Institute for Gay and Lesbian Strategic Studies, P.O. Box 2603, Amherst, MA.

The National Urban League, Inc., 500 East 62nd Street, New York, NY 10021.

The National Committee on Pay Equity, 1201 Sixteenth Street NW, Room 422, Washington, DC 20036.

Southern Regional Council, Inc., 60 Walton NW, Atlanta, GA 30303.

PART V

Many Voices, Many Lives: Some Consequences of Racial, Gender, and Class Inequality

STATISTICS CAN TELL US A GREAT DEAL ABOUT LIFE in any given society, yet they paint only part of the picture. They can tell us that more than 110,000 Japanese Americans were herded into relocation camps during World War II, but they can tell us little of the lives lived in those camps or of the repercussions on those lives years later. They can tell us that every day four women die in this country as a result of domestic violence, but they cannot convey what it means to live in an abusive relationship. Statistics can tell us a story with numbers, but they cannot translate those numbers into lived experience. For that, we must turn to stories about people's lives.

Who will tell these stories? For many years, and not so long ago, the voices of the majority of people in our society were missing from the books in libraries and on our course reading lists. The experiences of women from all racial and ethnic groups, regardless of their class position, were missing, as was the history, culture, and experience of many men. In their place were the writings and teachings of a relatively small group—predominantly privileged, white, and male—who offered their experience and their perspective as if they were universal. Ironically, even books about breast-feeding and childbirth were written exclusively by male "experts" who defined and described a reality they had never known. White sociologists, psychologists, and anthropologists set themselves up as experts on American Indian, Hispanic, Black, and Asian experience and culture, offering elaborate, critical accounts of the family structure and life-style of each group. Novels chronicling the growth to manhood of young white males from the upper or middle class were routinely assigned in high school and college English courses and examined for "universal themes," while novels about the experiences of men of color, working people, and women of all groups were relegated to "special interest" courses and treated as marginal. In short, by definition, serious scholarship, "real" science, and "great" literature were what had been produced by well-to-do white males and often focused exclusively on their experiences; accounts of the lives of other groups, if available at all, were rarely written by members of those groups.

However, more accounts of the lives of ordinary people have recently become available, thus filling in some of the gaps in the limited experience each of us brings to our study of race, class, gender, and sexuality. The selections in Part V are offered as a way of fleshing out the bare-bones facts provided in Part IV. They provide us with an opportunity to move outside the limits of our particular identity, at least for a few minutes, and to find out what the world looks like from someone else's perspective. In Part V we get a glimpse of what it was like to be a Japanese American growing up on the West Coast during World War II as Yuri Kochiyama shares his experiences, first in California and then in a relocation camp in Jerome, Arkansas. We listen as Sonia Shah talks about what it means to be an Asian American in the United States and see how the socially constructed stereotypes and categories imbedded in that term look through her eyes. We listen as Delina D. Pryce, a Costa Rican–born, self-proclaimed Black Latina, talks about her anger and frustration over being asked to chose which part of her identity she will embrace—Black or Latina—a choice she refuses to make. We stand on a cardboard box down the street from his junior high school with Dave Grossman as the seventh-grader proudly announces that he is gay. And we walk the streets of Brooklyn, New York, with June Jordan as she reflects upon her own childhood and the childhood boxer Mike Tyson knew a 25-minute bus ride from her house. Each of these essays, and the others in Part V as well, provide us with unique opportunities to look at everyday life in the United States using the lenses of race, gender, class, and sexuality to see things we may not have noticed before. In addition, they broaden our range of vision to include some of the other factors that can have significant impact on life choices: among them are religion, age, physical condition, and geographical location. Some of these factors are touched upon or highlighted as well in these readings. In some contexts, these factors play a major role in shaping the way others treat us, in determining how much we are paid, what kinds of educational opportunities are available to us, and where and how we live. In other contexts, these variables may well be irrelevant. Reading about them adds another dimension to our understanding of the complex set of additional factors that interact with issues of race, class, gender, and sexuality.

But even as we acknowledge how much there is to learn from looking at the lives and experiences of many different people, there is also a danger in this project—the danger of overgeneralizing. It is easy to take the particular experience of one member of a group and attribute it to all members of that group. Many students who are members of a religious, racial, or ethnic minority have had the uncomfortable experience of being asked to speak for all members of that minority group at some point in their college experience. Failing to see members of minority groups as individuals is typical of a society in which stereotyping flourishes. On the other hand, for the purposes of studying issues of race, class, gender, and sexuality, it is often necessary to look beyond individual differences and generalize about "Native Americans" or "Chicanas" or "men" in order to highlight aspects of their experience that are more typical of that group's experience than of the experience of other groups. As we have already seen, it would be naive to think that the individual exists in a vacuum, untouched by the racism, sexism, heterosexism, and class bias in society. Unless we understand something about the ways different *groups* experience life in the United States, we will never adequately understand the particular experiences of individual people.

The essays in this part have been selected because they give a sense of the diversity of life experience in the United States while they reflect some of the consequences of the inequalities documented in Part IV. For the most part, these articles, poems, and essays need no introduction. They speak for themselves.

1

Racial and Ethnic Minorities:
An Overview

*Beth B. Hess, Elizabeth W. Markson,
and Peter J. Stein*

Native Americans

The Native American tribes that populated North America before the arrival of Europeans were quickly defined as biologically and morally "inferior" to the more "civilized" newcomers who were only doing God's will in conquering the natives and taking their land. All Native Americans were categorized as "Indians" and their widely varying cultures treated with equal contempt. In addition to their losses in battle with the settlers, the tribes were also ravaged by diseases brought by the Europeans, against which they had no biological defenses (Thornton, 1987).

These ethnocentric assumptions followed the westward flow of white settlers, continually displacing the native tribes and absorbing their lands on the basis of treaties that were not intended to be taken seriously. During the late 1800s, entire tribes were forcibly relocated to reservations in sparsely populated areas with few natural resources—certainly not the farming or grazing lands that had been the basis of their traditional way of life. Here, too, disease and economic hardship followed, and the Native American population fell from several million to roughly 250,000 in 1900 (Thornton, 1987). By this time, also, an unknown number of Native Americans had joined the industrial labor force, intermarried, and disappeared into the multicultural urban population. In the 1950s and 1960s, many more left the reservations to live and work in cities, but rather than melt into the urban masses, these newcomers often formed cohesive communities in which diverse Native American traditions were maintained but also modified to fit the city environment (Weibel-Orlando, 1991).

Today, there are about two million Americans of native ancestry, including Eskimo and Aluet populations in Alaska. Slightly over one-third live on reservations or other designated areas held in trust by the federal government and administered by the Bureau of Indian Affairs (BIA) as part of the nineteenth-century treaties whereby tribal land was exchanged for protection of Indian rights. Although the treaties promised adequate housing, education, and health care, the history of the BIA has been one of almost total neglect and goal displacement, in which the billions allocated to the tribes have gone mostly to maintaining the bureaucracy that administers the funds. Not one of the more than 300 treaties between the tribes and the government of the United States has been honored (Richardson, 1993).

As a consequence of this pattern of *internal colonialism*, whereby native populations are treated as if they were foreign colonies, life on the reservation remains grim, marked by high rates of poverty and its consequences: homicide, suicide, family violence, school failure, infant mortality, alcohol-related diseases, diabetes, and tuberculosis (Bachman, 1992). Because relative poverty also characterizes Native Americans outside the reservations, their life expectancy is the lowest of all subpopulations in the United States.

Yet, the past decade has also been one of great hope for Native Americans. Court cases requiring compliance with the treaties have resulted in favorable judgments for many tribes, including 300,000 acres of prime land in Maine returned to the Penobscot and Passamaquoddy, and fishing rights restored to Great Lakes tribes. College graduation rates are inching upward, although they remain much lower than for Asian and white students (Cage, 1993). And changes at the federal level have encouraged self-determination in spending priorities on the reservations, bypassing the BIA (Richardson, 1993).

The major factor in the improving economic status of American Indians, however, has been the introduction of gambling casinos on the reservations. The original treaties guaranteed tribal rights to local resources as well as freedom from control by the state governments. These conditions brought great wealth to the Oklahoma reservations, where oil deposits had been discovered earlier. More recently, the tribes have invoked the same treaty rights to exempt the reservations from state-level prohibitions against gambling establishments. As a result, casinos have been opened on several Indian reservations, bringing jobs and millions of dollars in profits to formerly poverty stricken tribes. For example, the Pequot Indian casino in Connecticut has been so successful that tribal leaders are negotiating to acquire thousands of additional acres from local landowners. The casino is one of the largest employers in the state and its proposed expansion will make the facility one of the largest in the world (Johnson, 1993). This has prompted Donald Trump to file a lawsuit arguing that the Indians are taking unfair advantage of honest businesspersons such as himself.

There has also been a revival of Indian cultural pride and an increasing interest in preserving the diversity of tribal history, customs, and crafts. Perhaps all these trends together will finally bring hope and help to the tens of thousands of Native Americans still trapped in the cycle of poverty and violence.

African Americans

The history of slavery in America raises many important questions about the construction of difference. How can one group of humans treat another as if they were not human? Only by defining "the other" as so very different as to be "nonhuman." Obviously, this process is easiest when the "other" has little resemblance to "us," as in the case of black African tribal peoples compared to the European Christians on this continent who bought and sold them. Within the overall system of dehumanization and degradation, the actual conditions of slave life varied greatly from colony to colony, by the type of agriculture involved, and over time as the black population increased and the mix between African- and American-born slave changed (Kolchin, 1993).

Of all enslaved Africans brought to the Americas, only about 10 percent or 650,000 were sold to owners in the North American colonies, the remainder going to South America. But because the living and working conditions for slaves in the colonies were somewhat better than elsewhere, this relatively small population expanded rapidly, so that the number of native-born Blacks made further trade with Africa unnecessary (Kolchin, 1993). Thus, by 1860, most of the three million Blacks in the United States were American-born and racial stereotypes changed to reflect the paternalistic view of slaves as children rather than as untamed savages.

Over time, African-American slaves developed a unique culture, blended from native elements and those imposed by their owners, within which some degree of *autonomy* (self-direction) could be exercised. The subculture of slavery, as with any other, provided a supportive environment, alternative definitions of reality, a basis for positive self-image, and a strength necessary for survival. Although whites were of two minds about introducing Christianity to the slaves, the idea of converting "heathen" won out over the definitions of Blacks as unredeemable. Not only did Christianity spread rapidly among the slaves, but it was reworked in such a way as to become a force for ultimately challenging the system of slavery itself.

Not all African Americans lived as slaves in the South; many made their way to the North and West where they also met with prejudice and discrimination, but were at least free from everyday controls. Similarly, the formal end of slavery in 1865 brought one kind of freedom but left former slaves under the control of a range of "Jim Crow" laws designed to limit their choices of jobs, residential location, right to vote, and so forth. It was these limitations, written into law, that created the system of de jure segregation that was dismantled only in the 1960s.

Today, African Americans compose about 12 percent of the U.S. population, but remain disadvantaged along many dimensions of social stratification. Blacks are overrepresented at the lower end of the income and occupation hierarchies, and underrepresented in positions of political and economic power. In addition, the employment and income gaps that had been narrowing between 1965 and 1980 began to widen once again, as the Reagan and Bush administrations cut programs that assisted racial minorities and failed to enforce regulations designed to reduce discrimination in housing and jobs. The result has been labeled *American apartheid* to refer to the systematic residential segregation of African Americans in areas where employment opportunities are almost nonexistent (Massey and Denton, 1993). Unlike the experience of other urban minorities, the isolation of Blacks has been more intense over a longer period of time while the kinds of jobs available to earlier waves of immigrants have been moved to where the labor force is whiter (Neckerman and Kirschenman, 1991). Even Atlanta, Georgia, once thought to be a symbol of Black political and economic progress, is experiencing the effects of the new apartheid (Orfield and Ashkinaze, 1991).

Institutionalized racism remains a powerful determinant of the life chances of African Americans. In 1992, for example, rejection rates for mortgage and home improvement loans were twice as high for Blacks as for whites *at the same income level* (Quint, 1992). Employers continue to prefer hiring immigrant workers who do not speak English rather than American-born Blacks willing to work for lower wages (Massey and Denton, 1993). Social Security disability benefits are refused more often to African Americans than to whites at similar levels of physical impairment (Labaton, 1992). Blacks are twice as likely as whites to be fired from the U.S. Postal Service, even when their work records and educational backgrounds are identical (Zwerling and Silver, 1992). Even middle-class African Americans continue to face hostile treatment in restaurants and stores (Feagin, 1991).

The employment and income gulf between whites and Blacks will grow even larger as Americans demand that the federal government cut its own labor force as a deficit reduction measure. This is so because minority groups have always found the government a more willing employer than private businesses. Thus, any reduction in public employment will have its most negative impact on African Americans. As a consequence, the proportion of Blacks attaining middle-class occupational status will also decline, reversing one of the more favorable statistical trends of the past three decades.

What happens when immigrants are also Black? Their fate depends on the skills they bring, their family structure, and whether or not they speak English. Thus, French-speaking unskilled Black Haitians are intercepted at sea and turned back. In contrast, English-speaking, relatively well-educated Blacks from the Caribbean region have enjoyed unusual economic and political success in New York City, but only within the limits to upward mobility set by race as a "master status" (Kasinitz, 1992). Despite the obvious influence of skin color, most white Americans continue to interpret racial inequality in terms of personal variables — less ability, less willingness to learn — rather than situational factors such as discrimination (Sigelman and Welch, 1993).

Asian Americans

Asian Americans represent at least a dozen distinct cultures and language groups, yet a tendency to classify all Asians together has dominated immigration policy and popular attitudes. In fact, the Pan-Asian (*pan*, or *all*) community is not only increasingly varied, but its composition has changed dramatically between 1970 and 1990, as shown in Figure 1. Whereas Americans of Japanese origin were the largest Asian subgroup in 1970, today they rank below Americans of Chinese and Filipino ancestry. The recent wave of immigrants from Southeast Asia has added diversity and numbers to the Pan-Asian population.

In general, Asian Americans are considered to be examples of a *model minority* for having fulfilled the American Dream of upward mobility as a result of hard work. And indeed, poverty rates for most Asian subgroups are lower than for the nation as a whole; average family incomes are even slightly above that of non-Hispanic whites; and educational achievement the highest of any race/ethnic subgroup (Lott and Felt, 1991). These global numbers, however, hide great variation between and within various Asian populations.

Chinese Americans

In both the United States and Canada, in the mid nineteenth century, young Chinese men were imported (often forcibly put on ships in the Chinese city of Shanghai—hence, "shanghaied") to work on the transcontinental railroad. Not allowed to become citizens and forbidden to send for a wife or marry an American, those who remained formed an almost exclusively male community in West Coast cities in the United States and Canada. The gambling, opium smoking, and prostitution that characterized these segregated all-male communities only reinforced the socially constructed image of Chinese as anti-family and immoral (Anderson, 1991).

Chinese neighborhoods were targets of white mob violence as racial fears were periodically fanned by politicians up until the outbreak of World War II in 1941, when the Chinese suddenly became the "good" Asians in contrast to the "evil Japs."

Restrictive immigration laws were greatly revised in 1965, by which time many Chinese were finally granted citizenship and allowed to bring family members to North America. Over the past three decades, the Chinese American community has grown in size and wealth. The educational success of Chinese American youth has been exceptional, in part due to the traditional high value placed on learning in Chinese culture. The more important influence, however, appears to be the achievement motivation derived from their parents' involvement in family-owned small businesses such as restaurants, laundries, garment manufacturing, and tourist stores in Chinatowns (Sanchirico, 1991).

Studies of the assimilation patterns of minority groups often focus on the degree to which the group has carved out a special place in the urban economy—an *ethnic/racial enclave*—in which they control local businesses and establish a protective subculture, often reinforced by discrimination and other segregating forces. The enclave nurtures economic stability and serves as a springboard to upward mobility. In the case of Chinese Americans, various Chinatowns have served this purpose well, thanks in large part to an influx of money from Hong Kong, Taiwan, and other "offshore" territories. As a result, banks and mortgage companies are able to provide loans for new businesses and homes, ultimately encouraging assimilation among the children and grandchildren of immigrants who move up and out to the suburbs (Zhou and Logan, 1991; Zhou, 1992).

Despite the general prosperity of the community, many Chinese who remain in the enclave and most new immigrants live in poverty and are exploited at work. In addition, with so much offshore money entering the enclave, the line between legitimate and illegitimate business is often blurred.

Local merchants today are targets for gangs of young Asians involved in the protection racket, as well as drugs, gambling, and prostitution—in the grand tradition of organized crime in America.

Figure 1
Distribution of Asian American Population, 1970–1990

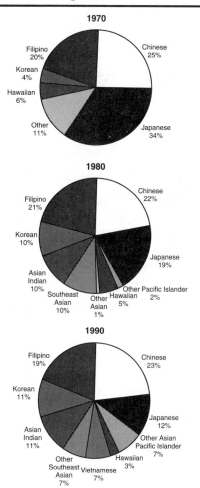

Source: U.S. Bureau of the Census, *We, the Asian Americans* (Washington, D.C.: GPO, 1973), p. 2; U.S. Bureau of the Census, *We, the Asian and Pacific Islander Americans* (Washington, D.C.: GPO, 1988), p. 2; *Statistical Abstract of the United States, 1992*, p. 21.

Japanese Americans

The path to structural assimilation for Japanese Americans has also been marked by discrimination, prejudice, segregation, and official violence. Lacking the numbers and resources to form an enclave of the size and influence of a Chinatown, Japanese communities on the West Coast were located in areas where members enjoyed great success as farmers and gardeners. Like all Asians, Japanese immigrants were forbidden to own land or become citizens; they had, however, been able to emigrate as husband and wife, and because their children were born in the United States, the second generation, which soon outnumbered the first, were American citizens.

Nonetheless, following the Japanese attack on Pearl Harbor and the outbreak of World War II in 1941, all Japanese Americans living on the West Coast were forcibly rounded up and sent to detention camps for the duration of the war. Although the reason given for this forced evacuation was "national security," the more powerful motives were economic and emotional. Japanese agricultural successes had long been envied by their white neighbors, who eagerly took over the property that had been confiscated without compensation. Emotionally, the social construction of the Japanese as untrustworthy Asians could go unchallenged because of their relative isolation. In contrast, in Hawaii, where national security really was at stake, the Japanese had become so integrated into mainstream institutions that they were able to avoid such fear and mistrust (Parrillo, 1994).

The experience of the detention camps had several long-term effects on the Japanese American community, primarily through the erosion of power of men over women and of elders over juniors (Fugita and O'Brien, 1991). Many of the younger detainees were able to leave the camps to attend school elsewhere in the United States or to serve in the armed forces. This weakening of traditional authority speeded up the process of assimilation once the war ended and the camps were emptied.

No longer tied to agricultural occupations or to an ethnic enclave, native-born Japanese Americans were both geographically and socially mobile, attending college in large numbers, moving into white collar jobs in electronics and engineering, and marrying outside the Asian community. Few are left who remember the camps, and only in 1988 did Congress approve legislation that officially apologized for the forced detention and that offered a tax-free payment of $20,000 to surviving victims — very little and extremely late.

Other Asians

Policy changes in the 1980s led to the lifting of other restrictions on immigration from various parts of Asia. The outcome, as shown in Figure 1, has been a large influx of people from Southeast Asia: Cambodia, Thailand, Laos, and Vietnam, representing dozens of ethnic groups, each with its unique language and culture. Many of these new immigrants are from rural areas, with minimal education and job skills, and little knowledge of English—traits likely to arouse fear and hostility as well as inhibit economic integration. In addition, the most recent arrivals have faced greater than usual resentment because of growing competition for jobs among workers at the lower end of the occupational system. It does not take a crystal ball to predict that their assimilation will be slower and more problematic than that of earlier Asian immigrants.

In contrast, Asians from the Indian subcontinent entered the United States with educational credentials and technical skills, and have found their economic foothold in the pharmaceutical industry and health-care facilities. Although they, too, have experienced discrimination, their economic success allows greater choice of where to live. Recent arrivals from the Philippine Islands are also relatively well educated, with professional degrees in medicine, law, and engineering, even though most have had to settle for less prestigious jobs. Immigrants from Korea lack the educational background of the Asian Indians and Filipinos, but compensate with a powerful commitment to self-employment for the entire family. Koreans have been successful in operating small grocery stores in urban neighborhoods, although this often brings them into conflict with other minority groups resentful of the Koreans' presence.

The New Ethnics

The "old ethnics" refers to the waves of immigrants from Europe. The "new ethnics," and fastest growing subgroups, come from South and Central America and from the Middle East.

Latinos

The Census categories of "Hispanic," "Spanish Origin," and the more recently preferred "Latino/a," are umbrella terms that cover a diverse although largely Catholic population. The four major subgroups of Spanish origin Americans, shown in Figure 2, are very different from one another in racial/ethnic ancestry, immigrant history, and current status. Together, however, they currently compose 10 percent of the population of the United States and are expected to outnumber African Americans as the nation's largest minority group by 2010. Their political influence, however, is diluted by the many divisions within this population, which is also stratified by socioeconomic status and skin color (Knouse et al., 1992).

MEXICAN AMERICANS (CHICANO/AS)   The largest Latino subgroup (62 percent) is of Mexican origin. Some are descendents of people who had settled in the Southwest territories before that area was annexed by the United States in 1848; others have lived in the United States for several generations; and many have entered more recently in response to employment opportunities in American factories close to the border.

Figure 2
Subgroups within the Hispanic Population of the United States, 1991

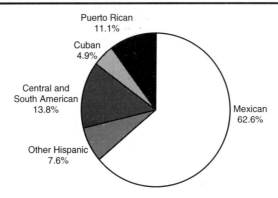

Source: U.S. Bureau of the Census, Series P20–455, "The Hispanic Population of the United States: March 1991," (Washington D.C.: GPO, 1991), p. 2.

Most Mexican Americans continue to live in the Southwest and in distinctly Mexican neighborhoods, or *barrios*. While language and culture set the Chicano community apart from the world of European Americans ("Anglos"), appearance also has an impact on their employment and earnings. Mexican American men with dark skin and/or Native American features receive significantly lower earnings than their more Anglo-looking peers, all other characteristics being equal. Although the stereotype of the Mexican farmhand persists, about 90 percent live in urban areas where the men typically find work as laborers and machine operators and the women as domestic servants or office cleaners.

Despite the fact that the great majority are legal residents, the social construction of "illegal alien" is often applied to all Chicanos (and even to all Latinos). As a consequence of economic discrimination and social isolation, upward mobility has been severely limited. Family income and educational attainment remain below the U.S. average, while family size is higher. Although the traditional extended family network continues to be a major source of economic and emotional support, many aspects of family life have undergone change, particularly with respect to the power of men and of elders. As Mexican American women become acculturated, educated, and part of the labor force, their power in the family and marriage is enhanced (Segura, 1993). Similarly, the children who are educated in America often have an advantage over their parents.

PUERTO RICANS   American citizens since 1917, Puerto Ricans arrived on the North American mainland in large numbers in the 1950s because of the collapse of the sugar industry on their island. The majority have settled in the Northeast, especially the New York/New Jersey/Connecticut area, where they have found employment in low-skill, low-pay service jobs. The ethnic enclave has not yet generated the kind of resources or opportunities for self-employment of many Asian communities. Nor has the overall economy produced the type of jobs that could serve as a springboard to upward mobility.

Puerto Ricans are characterized by a mixture of Spanish, Indian, and African ancestry, which subjects them to racial as well as ethnic barriers to upward mobility. Although the poverty rate for Puerto Rican Americans is close to 60 percent, and labor force participation rates for both men and women are below those for the population as a whole, their expectations of success are higher than are those of persons remaining on the Island.

There are some signs of positive upward movement in high school and college graduation rates, political influence, representation in the arts, and community control. On the negative side, dropout and unemployment rates remain high, and four in ten families are headed by a single parent (U.S. Bureau of the Census, P20–455, 1991).

CUBAN AMERICANS   The first wave of Cuban immigrants consisted of relatively well-educated and affluent people fleeing the revolution that brought Fidel Castro to power in the mid-1950s. This cultural and social elite, many of whom were descended from European Spaniards, settled in Miami, Florida, where a very successful ethnic enclave was established, which has gradually accumulated great political influence. Cuban Americans are better educated, wealthier, and more assimilated than the other subgroups. In contrast to other Latinos, this is an extremely conservative population, highly favored under the Reagan and Bush administrations that openly encouraged the Cubans' desire to overthrow the Castro regime and reestablish their power on the island.

Nonetheless, Miami Anglos remain mistrustful of their Spanish-speaking neighbors, especially after Castro expelled another wave of immigrants in 1980 who were much poorer and less educated, and included former prisoners and inmates. Various attempts by Anglos to impose "English only" rules on the city government have ultimately failed in the courts. The primary opposition to Cuban American power today comes from local African Americans who feel that authorities have favored Latino immigrants over native-born Blacks.

In general, the success of the Cuban immigrants was largely due to the resources with which they entered, and later to the degree to which their conservative politics fit the spirit of the 1980s.

Middle Easterners

In recent years, a new group of immigrants has emerged as a visible urban minority: newcomers from the Middle Eastern countries of Egypt, Syria, Jordan, Lebanon, Iran, and Iraq. Relatively light-skinned, they bring many diverse cultures, languages, and religions to America. Some are ethnic Arabs, others not; most are Moslem, but not all; many are from affluent families, but others are working class youth; some are political refugees, but the majority seek economic opportunities (Parrillo, 1994). Their common denominator is the geographic area from which they come, and up until the 1990s their presence had not been a matter of public concern. The best estimates are that between three and four million Middle Easterners, primarily Moslem, currently reside in the United States. But because this is primarily a young adult population from countries with traditionally high fertility, the number could soon exceed six million, surpassing the size of the American Jewish population (Bernstein, 1993).

Assimilation has been made difficult by the demands of the Moslem religion, particularly the need to stop other activity and pray at particular hours during the day, and to observe many dietary (eating) rules. Family relationships and the role of women are also very different from those of the surrounding culture. But these typical problems of any new minority in America have been compounded in the 1990s by international events such as the war against Iraq and the emergence of terrorist groups on American soil. All "Arabs" have become objects of fear and hostility, although very few are a danger to public safety. This reaction is similar to the "yellow menace" scares that led to anti-Asian riots in California in the 1920s and to detention camps for Japanese Americans in the 1940s.

In reality, the Middle Eastern populations have in many ways fit the pattern of "model minorities," establishing ethnic/religious enclaves that provide employment and funding for businesses within the community. Middle Eastern communities depart from the model, however, in that their goal may not be assimilation but, rather, maintaining a unique heritage in the face of modernizing influences. The key institution here is the religious center, called a mosque, which serves as a unifying element and source of shared identity, reinforcing traditional customs and power relationships. It remains to be seen whether exposure to the modernizing influences of American culture, especially on the part of youth and women, will produce a major challenge to these traditions.

REFERENCES

Anderson, Kay J. *Vancouver's Chinatown: Racial Discourse in Canada, 1875–1980.* Montreal: McGill–Queen's University Press, 1991.

Bachman, Ronet. *Death and Violence on the Reservation: Homicide, Family Violence, and Suicide in American Indian Populations.* New York: Auburn House, 1992.

Bernstein, Richard. "A Growing Islamic Presence: Balancing Sacred and Secular." *New York Times,* May 2, 1993: 1 ff.

Cage, Mary Crystal. "Graduation Rates of American Indians and Blacks Improve, Lag behind Others'." *Chronicle of Higher Education,* May 26, 1993: A29.

Feagin, Joe R. "The Continuing Significance of Race: Anti-Black Discrimination in Public Places." *American Sociological Review* 56 (1991): 101–116.

Fugita, Stephen S., and David J. O'Brien. *Japanese American Ethnicity: The Persistence of Community.* Seattle: University of Washington Press, 1991.

Johnson, Kirk. "Indians' Casino Money Pumps Up the Volume." *New York Times,* September 1, 1993: B1.

Kasinitz, Philip. *Caribbean New York: Black Immigrants and the Politics of Race.* Ithaca, N.Y.: Cornell University Press, 1992.

Knouse, Stephen P., Paul Rosenfeld, and Amy L. Culbertson (Eds.). *Hispanics in the Workplace.* Newbury Park, Calif.: Sage, 1992.

Kolchin, Peter. *American Slavery, 1619–1877.* New York: Hill & Wang, 1993.

Labaton, Stephen. "Benefits Are Refused More Often to Disabled Blacks, Study Finds." *New York Times,* May 11, 1992: 1 ff.

Lott, Juanita Tamayo, and Judy C. Felt. "Studying the Pan-Asian Community." *Population Today* 19 (2) (1991): 6–8.

Massey, Douglas S., and Nancy A. Denton. *American Apartheid: Segregation and the Making of the Underclass.* Cambridge, Mass: Harvard University Press, 1993.

Neckerman, Kathryn M., and Joleen Kirschenman. "Hiring Strategies, Racial Bias, and Inner-City Workers." *Social Problems* 38 (1991): 433–452.

Orfield, Gary, and Carole Ashkinaze. *The Closing Door: Conservative Policy and Black Opportunity.* Chicago: University of Chicago Press, 1991.

Parrillo, Vincent N. *Strangers to These Shores: Race and Ethnic Relations in the United States,* 4th ed. New York: Macmillan, 1994.

Quint, Michael. "Anti-Black Bias Still Found in Mortgage Applications." *New York Times,* October 2, 1992: D1.

Richardson, Bill. "More Power to the Tribes." *New York Times,* July 7, 1993: A15.

Sanchirico, Andrew. "The Importance of Small-Business Ownership in Chinese American Educational Achievement." *Sociology of Education* 64 (1991): 293–304.

Segura, Denise A. "Chicanas in White Collar Jobs: Gender/Race-Ethnic Dilemmas and Affirmations." Paper presented at the annual meeting of the American Sociological Association, Miami, Fla., August 1993.

Sigelman, Lee, and Susan Welch. "The Contact Hypothesis Revisited: Black-White Interaction and Positive Racial Attitudes." *Social Forces* 71 (1993): 781–795.

Telles, Edward E. "Residential Segregation by Skin Color in Brazil." *American Sociological Review* 57 (1992): 186–197.

Thornton, Russell. *American Indian Holocaust and Survival: A Population History since 1492.* Norman: University of Oklahoma Press, 1987.

U.S. Bureau of the Census. "The Hispanic Population of the United States: March 1991." *Current Population Reports,* P20–455. Washington, D.C.: U.S. Government Printing Office, 1991.

Weibel-Orlando, Joan. *Indian Country, L.A.: Maintaining Ethnic Community in Complex Society.* Urbana: University of Illinois Press, 1991.

Zhou, Min. *Chinatown: The Socioeconomic Potential of an Urban Enclave.* Philadelphia: Temple University Press, 1992.

Zhou, Min, and John R. Logan. "In and Out of Chinatown: Residential Mobility and Segregation of New York City's Chinese." *Social Forces* 70 (1991): 387–407.

Zwerling, Craig, and Hilary Silver. "Race and Job Dismissals in a Federal Bureaucracy." *American Sociological Review* 57 (1992): 651–660.

2

On Being South Asian in North America

Chandra Talpade Mohanty

My local newspaper tells me that worldwide migration is at an all-time high in the early 1990s. Folks are moving from rural to urban areas in all parts of the Third World, and from Asia, Africa, the Caribbean and Latin America to Europe, North America and selected countries in the Middle East. Apparently two percent of the world's population no longer lives in the country in which they were born. Of course, the newspaper story primarily identifies the "problems" (for Europe and the USA) associated with these transnational migration trends. One such "problem" is taking jobs away from "citizens." I am reminded of a placard carried by Black and Third World people at an anti-racism rally in London: We Are Here Because You Were There. My location in the USA, then, is symptomatic of large numbers of migrants, nomads, immigrants, workers across the globe for whom notions of home, identity, geography and history are infinitely complicated in the late twentieth century. Questions of nation(ality), and of "belonging" (witness the situation of South Asians in Africa), are constitutive of the Indian diaspora. This essay is a personal, anecdotal meditation on the politics of gender and race in the construction of South Asian identity in North America.

On a TWA flight on my way back to the U.S. from a conference in the Netherlands, the professional white man sitting next to me asks: (a) which school do I go to? and (b) when do I plan to go home?—all in the same breath. I put on my most professorial demeanor (somewhat hard in crumpled blue jeans and cotton T-shirt—this uniform only works for white male professors, who of course could command authority even in swimwear!) and inform him that I teach at a small liberal arts college in upstate New York, and that I have lived in the U.S. for fifteen years. At this point, my work is in the U.S., not in India. This is no longer entirely true—my work is also with feminists and grassroots activists in India, but he doesn't need to know this. Being "mistaken" for a graduate student seems endemic to my existence in this country—few Third World women are granted professional (i.e., adult) and/or permanent (one is always a student!) status in the U.S., even if we exhibit clear characteristics of adulthood, like grey hair and facial lines. He ventures a further question: what do you teach? On hearing "women's studies," he becomes quiet and we spend the next eight hours in polite silence. He has decided that I do not fit into any of his categories, but what can you expect from a *Feminist* (an *Asian* one!) anyway? I feel vindicated and a little superior— even though I know he doesn't really feel "put in his place." Why should he? He has a number of advantages in this situation: white skin, maleness and citizenship privileges. From his enthusiasm about expensive "ethnic food" in Amsterdam, and his J. Crew clothes, I figured class difference (economic or cultural) wasn't exactly an issue in our interaction. We both appeared to have similar social access as "professionals."

I have been asked the "home" question (when are you going home) periodically for fifteen years now. Leaving aside the subtly racist implications of the question (go home—you don't belong), I am still not satisfied with my response. What is home? The place I was born? Where I grew up? Where my parents live? Where I live and work as an adult? Where I locate my community—my people? Who are "my people"? Is home a geographical space, an historical space, an emotional, sensory space? Home is always so crucial to immigrants and migrants—I even write about it in scholarly texts, perhaps to avoid addressing it as an issue that is also very personal. Does two percent of the world's population think about these questions pertaining to home? This is not to imply that the other ninety-eight percent does not think about home. What interests me is the meaning of home for immigrants and migrants. I am convinced that this question—how one understands and defines home—is a profoundly political one.

Since settled notions of territory, community, geography, and history don't work for us, what does it really mean to be "South Asian" in the USA? Obviously I was not South Asian in India—I was Indian. What else could one be but "Indian" at a time when a successful national independence struggle had given birth to a socialist democratic nation-state? This was the beginning of the decolonization of the Third World. Regional geographies (South Asia) appeared less relevant as a mark of identification than citizenship in a post-colonial independent nation on the cusp of economic and political autonomy. However, in North America, identification as South Asian (in addition to Indian, in my case) takes on its own logic. "South Asian" refers to folks of Indian, Pakistani, Sri Lankan, Bangladeshi, Kashmiri, and Burmese origin. Identifying as South Asian rather than Indian adds numbers and hence power within the U.S. State. Besides, regional differences among those from different South Asian countries are often less relevant than the commonalities based on our experiences and histories of immigration, treatment and location in the U.S.

Let me reflect a bit on the way I identify myself, and the way the U.S. State and its institutions categorize me. Perhaps thinking through the various labels will lead me back to the question of home and identity. In 1977, I arrived in the USA on an F1 visa—a student visa. At that time, my definition of myself—a graduate student in Education at the University of Illinois, and the "official" definition of me (a student allowed into the country on an F1 visa) obviously coincided. Then I was called a "foreign student," and expected to go "home" (to India—even though my parents were in Nigeria at the time) after getting my Ph.D. Let's face it, this is the assumed trajectory for a number of Indians, especially the post-independence (my) generation, who come to the U.S. for graduate study.

However, this was not to be my trajectory. I quickly discovered that being a foreign student, and a woman at that, meant being either dismissed as irrelevant (the quiet Asian woman stereotype), treated in racist ways (my teachers asked if I understood English and if they should speak slower and louder so that I could keep up—this in spite of my inheritance of the Queen's English and British colonialism!), or celebrated and exoticized (you are so smart! your accent is even better than that of Americans—a little Anglophilia at work here, even though all my Indian colleagues insist we speak English the Indian way!).

The most significant transition I made at that time was the one from "foreign student" to "student of color." Once I was able to "read" my experiences in terms of race, and to read race and racism as it is written into the social and political fabric of the U.S., practices of racism and sexism became the analytic and political lenses through which I was able to anchor myself here. Of course, none of this happened in isolation—friends, colleagues, comrades, classes, books, films, arguments, and dialogues were constitutive of my political education as a woman of color in the U.S.

In the late 1970s and early 1980s feminism was gaining momentum on American campuses—it was in the air, in the classrooms, on the streets. However, what attracted me wasn't feminism as the mainstream media and white Women's Studies departments defined it. Instead, it was a very specific kind of feminism, the feminism of U.S. women of color and Third World women, that spoke to me. In thinking through the links between gender, race and class in their U.S. manifestations, I was for the first time enabled to think through my own gendered, classed post-colonial history. In the early 1980s, reading Audre Lorde, Nawal el Sadaawi, Cherríe Moraga, bell hooks, Gloria Joseph, Paula Gunn Allen, Barbara Smith, Merle Woo and Mitsuye Yamada, among others, generated a sort of recognition that was intangible but very inspiring. A number of actions, decisions and organizing efforts at that time led me to a sense of home and community in relation to women of color in the U.S. Home not as a comfortable, stable, inherited and familiar space, but instead as an imaginative, politically charged space where the familiarity and sense of affection and commitment lay in shared collective analysis of social injustice, as well as a vision of radical transformation. Political solidarity and a sense of family could be melded together imaginatively to create a strategic space I could call "home." Politically, intellectually and emotionally I owe an enormous debt to feminists of color—and especially to the sisters who have sustained me over the years. . . .

For me, engagement as a feminist of color in the U.S. made possible an intellectual and political genealogy of being Indian that was radically challenging as well as profoundly activist. Notions of home and community began to be located within a deeply political space where racialization and gender and class relations and histories became the prism through which I understood, however partially, what it could mean to be South Asian in North America. Interestingly, this recognition also forced me to re-examine the meanings attached to home and community in India.

What I chose to claim, and continue to claim, is a history of anti-colonialist, feminist struggle in India. The stories I recall, the ones that I retell and claim as my own, determine the choices and decisions I make in the present and the future. I did not want to accept a history of Hindu chauvinist (bourgeois) upward mobility (even though this characterizes a section of my extended family). We all choose partial, interested stories/histories—perhaps not as deliberately as I am making it sound here. But consciously, or unconsciously, these choices about our past(s) often determine the logic of our present.

Having always kept my distance from conservative, upwardly mobile Indian immigrants for whom the South Asian world was divided into green-card holders and non-green-card holders, the only South Asian links I allowed and cultivated were with Indians with whom I shared a political vision. This considerably limited my community. Racist and sexist experiences in graduate school and after made it imperative that I understand the U.S. in terms of its history of racism, imperialism and patriarchal relations, specifically in relation to Third World immigrants. After all, we were into the Reagan-Bush years, when the neo-conservative backlash made it impossible to ignore the rise of racist, anti-feminist, and homophobic attitudes, practices and institutions. Any purely culturalist or nostalgic/sentimental definition of being "Indian" or "South Asian" was inadequate. Such a definition fueled the "model minority" myth. And this subsequently constituted us as "outsiders/foreigners" or as interest groups who sought or had obtained the American dream.

In the mid-1980s, the labels changed: I went from being a "foreign student" to being a "resident alien." I have always thought that this designation was a stroke of inspiration on the part of the U.S. State, since it accurately names the experience and status of immigrants—especially immigrants of color. The flip side of "resident alien" is "illegal alien," another inspired designation. One can be either a resident or illegal immigrant, but one is always an alien. There is no confusion here—no melting pot ideology or narratives of assimilation—one's status as an "alien" is primary. Being legal requires identity papers. (It is useful to recall that the "passport"—and by extension the concept of nation-states and the sanctity of their borders—came into being after World War I.)

One must be stamped as legitimate (that is, not-gay-or-lesbian and not-communist!) by the Immigration and Naturalization Service (INS). The INS is one of the central disciplinary arms of the U.S. State. It polices the borders and controls all border crossings—especially those into the U.S. In fact, the INS is also one of the primary forces which institutionalizes race differences in the public arena, thus regulating notions of home, legitimacy and economic access to the "American dream" for many of us. For instance, carrying a green card documenting resident alien status in the U.S. is clearly very different from carrying an American passport, which is proof of U.S. citizenship. The former allows one to enter the U.S. with few hassles; the latter often allows one to breeze through the borders and ports of entry of other countries, especially countries which happen to be trading partners (much of Western Europe and Japan, among others) or in an unequal relationship with the U.S. (much of the noncommunist Third World). At a time when notions of a capitalist free-market economy seem (falsely) synonymous with the values attached to democracy, an American passport can open many doors. However, just carrying an American passport is no insurance against racism and unequal and unjust treatment within the U.S. It would be important to compare the racialization of first-generation immigrants from South Asia to the racialization of second-generation South Asian Americans. For example, one significant difference between these two generations would be between experiencing racism as a phenomenon specific to the U.S., versus growing up in the ever-present shadow of racism in the case of South Asians born in the U.S. This suggests that the psychic effects of racism would be different for these two constituencies. In addition, questions of home, identity and history take on very different meanings for South Asians born in North America. But to be fair, this comparison requires a whole other reflection that is beyond the scope of this essay.

Rather obstinately, I have refused to give up my Indian passport and have chosen to remain as a resident alien in the U.S. for the last decade or so. Which leads me to reflect on the complicated meanings attached to holding Indian citizenship while making a life for myself in the USA. In India, what does it mean to have a green card—to be an expatriate? What does it mean to visit Bombay every two to four years, and still call it home? Why does speaking in Marathi (my mother-tongue) become a measure and confirmation of home? What are the politics of being a part of the majority and the "absent elite" in India, while being a minority and a racialized "other" in the U.S.? And does feminist politics, or advocating feminism, have the same meanings and urgencies in these different geographical and political contexts?

Some of these questions hit me smack in the face during my last visit to India, in December 1992—post-Ayodhya (the infamous destruction of the Babri Masjid in Ayodhya by Hindu fundamentalists on 6 December 1992). In earlier, rather infrequent visits (once every four or five years was all I could afford), my green card designated me as an object of envy, privilege and status within my extended family. Of course the same green card has always been viewed with suspicion by left and feminist friends who (quite understandably) demand evidence of my ongoing commitment to a socialist and democratic India. During this visit, however, with emotions running high within my family, my green card marked me as an outsider who couldn't possibly understand the "Muslim problem" in India. I was made aware of being an "outsider" in two profoundly troubling shouting matches with my uncles, who voiced the most incredibly hostile sentiments against Muslims. Arguing that India was created as a secular state and that democracy had everything to do with equality for all groups (majority and minority) got me nowhere. The very fundamentals of democratic citizenship in India were/are being undermined and redefined as "Hindu."

Bombay was one of the cities hardest hit with waves of communal violence following the events in Ayodhya. The mobilization of Hindu fundamentalists, even paramilitary organizations, over the last half century and especially since the mid-1980s had brought Bombay to a juncture where the most violently racist discourse about Muslims seemed to be woven into the fabric of acceptable daily life. Racism was normalized in the popular imagination such that it became almost impossible to publicly raise questions about the ethics or injustice of racial/ethnic/religious discrimination. I could not assume a distanced posture towards religion any more. Too many injustices were being done in my name.

Although born a Hindu, I have always considered myself a non-practicing one—religion had always felt rather repressive when I was growing up. I enjoyed the rituals but resisted the authoritarian hierarchies of organized Hinduism. However, the Hinduism touted by fundamentalist organizations like the RSS (Rashtriya Swayamsevak Sangh, a paramilitary Hindu fundamentalist organization founded in the 1930s) and the Shiv Sena (a Maharashtrian chauvinist, fundamentalist, fascist political organization that has amassed a significant voice in Bombay politics and government) was one that even I, in my ignorance, recognized as reactionary and distorted. But this discourse was real—hate-filled rhetoric against Muslims appeared to be the mark of a "loyal Hindu." It was unbelievably heart-wrenching to see my hometown become a war zone with whole streets set on fire, and a daily death count to rival any major territorial border war. The smells and textures of Bombay, of home, which had always comforted and nurtured me, were violently disrupted. The scent of fish drying on the lines at the fishing village in Danda was submerged in the smell of burning straw and grass as whole bastis (chawls) were burned to the ground. The very topography, language and relationships that constituted "home" were quietly but surely exploding. What does community mean in this context? December 1992 both clarified as well as complicated for me the meanings attached to being an Indian citizen, a Hindu, an educated woman/feminist, and a permanent resident in the U.S. in ways that I have yet to resolve. After all, it is often moments of crisis that make us pay careful attention to questions of identity. Sharp polarizations force one to make choices (not in order to take sides, but in order to accept responsibility) and to clarify our own analytic, political and emotional topographies. . . .

Let me now circle back to the place I began: the meanings I have come to give to home, community and identity. By exploring the relationship between being a South Asian immigrant in America and an expatriate Indian citizen in India, I have tried, however partially and anecdotally, to clarify the complexities of home and community for this particular feminist of color/South Asian in North America.

The genealogy I have created for myself here is partial, interested and deliberate. It is a genealogy that I find emotionally and politically enabling—it is part of the genealogy that underlies my self-identification as an educator involved in a pedagogy of liberation. Of course, my history and experiences are far messier and not at all as linear as this narrative makes them sound. But then the very process of constructing a narrative for oneself—of telling a story—imposes a certain linearity and coherence that is never entirely there. But that is the lesson, perhaps, especially for us immigrants and migrants: i.e., that home, community and identity all fall somewhere between the histories and experiences we inherit and the political choices we make through alliances, solidarities and friendships.

One very concrete effect of my creating this particular space for myself has been my recent involvement in two grassroots organizations, one in India and the other in the U.S. The former, an organization called *Awareness*, is based in Orissa and works to empower the rural poor. Their focus is political education (similar to Paolo Friere's notion of "conscientization"), and they have recently begun to very consciously organize rural women. *Grassroots Leadership of North Carolina* is the U.S. organization I work with. It is a multiracial group of organizers (largely African American and White) working to build a poor and working peoples movement in the American South. While the geographical, historical and political contexts are different in the case of these two organizations, my involvement in them is very similar, as is my sense that there are clear connections to be made between the work of the two organizations. In addition, I think that the issues, analyses and strategies for organizing for social justice are also quite similar. This particular commitment to work with grassroots organizers in the two places I call home is not accidental. It is very much the result of the genealogy I have traced here. After all, it has taken me over a decade to make these commitments to grassroots work in both spaces. In part, I have defined what it means to be South Asian by educating myself about, and reflecting on, the histories and experiences of African American, Latina, West Indian, African, European American, and other constituencies in North America. Such definitions and understandings do provide a genealogy, but a genealogy that is always relational and fluid as well as urgent and necessary.

This essay is dedicated to the memory of Lanubai and Gauribai Vijaykar, maternal grandaunts, who were single, educated, financially independent, and tall (over six feet) at a time when it was against the grain to be any one of these things; and to Audre Lorde, teacher, sister, friend, whose words and presence continue to challenge, inspire, and nurture me.

3

Then Came the War

Yuri Kochiyama

I was red, white, and blue when I was growing up. I taught Sunday school, and was very, very American. But I was also very provincial. We were just kids rooting for our high school.

My father owned a fish market. Terminal Island was nearby, and that was where many Japanese families lived. It was a fishing town. My family lived in the city proper. San Pedro was very mixed, predominantly white, but there were blacks also.

I was nineteen at the time of the evacuation. I had just finished junior college. I was looking for a job, and didn't realize how different the school world was from the work world. In the school world, I never felt racism. But when you got into the work world, it was very difficult. This was 1941, just before the war. I finally did get a job at a department store. But for us back then, it was a big thing, because I don't think they had ever hired an Asian in a department store before. I tried, because I saw a Mexican friend who got a job there. Even then they didn't hire me on a regular basis, just on Saturdays, summer vacation, Easter vacation, and Christmas vacation. Other than that, I was working like the others—at a vegetable stand, or doing part-time domestic work. Back then, I only knew of two Japanese American girl friends who got jobs as secretaries—but these were in Japanese companies. But generally you almost never saw a Japanese American working in a white place. It was hard for Asians. Even for Japanese, the best jobs they felt they could get were in Chinatowns, such as in Los Angeles. Most Japanese were either in some aspect of fishing, such as in the canneries, or went right from school to work on the farms. That was what it was like in the town of San Pedro. I loved working in the department store, because it was a small town, and you got to know and see everyone. The town itself was wonderful. People were very friendly. I didn't see my job as work—it was like a community job.

Everything changed for me on the day Pearl Harbor was bombed. On that very day—December 7—the FBI came and they took my father. He had just come home from the hospital the day before. For several days we didn't know where they

From Joann Faung Jean Lee, *Asian American Experiences in the United States: Oral Histories of First to Fourth Generation Americans from China, the Philippines, Japan, India, the Pacific Islands, Vietnam and Cambodia.* © 1991 Joann Faung Jean Lee. Reprinted by permission of McFarland & Company, Inc., Publishers, Jefferson, NC 28640.

had taken him. Then we found out that he was taken to the federal prison at Terminal Island. Overnight, things changed for us. They took all men who lived near the Pacific waters, and had nothing to do with fishing. A month later, they took every fisherman from Terminal Island, sixteen and over, to places—not the regular concentration camps—but to detention centers in places like South Dakota, Montana, and New Mexico. They said that all Japanese who had given money to any kind of Japanese organization would have to be taken away. At that time, many people were giving to the Japanese Red Cross. The first group was thirteen hundred Isseis—my parents' generation. They took those who were leaders of the community, or Japanese school teachers, or were teaching martial arts, or who were Buddhist priests. Those categories which would make them very "Japanesey," were picked up. This really made a tremendous impact on our lives. My twin brother was going to the University at Berkeley. He came rushing back. All of our classmates were joining up, so he volunteered to go into the service. And it seemed strange that here they had my father in prison, and there the draft board okayed my brother. He went right into the army. My other brother, who was two years older, was trying to run my father's fish market. But business was already going down, so he had to close it. He had finished college at the University of California a couple of years before.

They took my father on December 7th. The day before, he had just come home from the hospital. He had surgery for an ulcer. We only saw him once, on December 13. On December 20th they said he could come home. By the time they brought him back, he couldn't talk. He made guttural sounds and we didn't know if he could hear. He was home for twelve hours. He was dying. The next morning, when we got up, they told us that he was gone. He was very sick. And I think the interrogation was very rough. My mother kept begging the authorities to let him go to the hospital until he was well, then put him back in the prison. They did finally put him there, a week or so later. But they put him in a hospital where they were bringing back all these American Merchant Marines who were hit on Wake Island. So he was the only Japanese in that hospital, so they hung a sheet around him that said, Prisoner of War. The feeling where he was was very bad.

You could see the hysteria of war. There was a sense that war could actually come to American shores. Everybody was yelling to get the "Japs" out of California. In Congress, people were speaking out. Organizations such as the Sons and Daughters of the Golden West were screaming "Get the 'Japs' out." So were the real estate people, who wanted to get the land from the Japanese farmers. The war had whipped up such a hysteria that if there was anyone for the Japanese, you didn't hear about it. I'm sure they were afraid to speak out, because they would be considered not only just "Jap" lovers, but unpatriotic.

Just the fact that my father was taken made us suspect to people. But on the whole, the neighbors were quite nice, especially the ones adjacent to us. There was already a six AM to six PM curfew and a five mile limit on where we could go from our homes. So they offered to do our shopping for us, if we needed.

Most Japanese Americans had to give up their jobs, whatever they did, and were told they had to leave. The edict for 9066—President Roosevelt's edict* for evacuation—was in February 1942. We were moved to a detention center that April. By then the Japanese on Terminal Island were just helter skelter, looking for anywhere they could go. They opened up the Japanese school and Buddhist churches, and families just crowded in. Even farmers brought along their chickens and chicken coops. They just opened up the places for people to stay until they could figure out what to do. Some people left for Colorado and Utah. Those who had relatives could do so. The idea was to evacuate all the Japanese from the coast. But all the money was frozen, so even if you knew where you wanted to go, it wasn't that simple. By then, people knew they would be going into camps, so they were selling what they could, even though they got next to nothing for it.

We were fortunate, in that our neighbors, who were white, were kind enough to look after our house, and they said they would find people to rent it, and look after it till we got back. But these neighbors were very, very unusual.

We were sent to an assembly center in Arcadia, California, in April. It was the largest assembly center on the West Coast, having nearly twenty thousand people. There were some smaller centers with about six hundred people. All along the West Coast—Washington, Oregon, California—there were many, many assembly centers, but ours was the largest. Most of the assembly centers were either fair-grounds, or race tracks. So many of us lived in stables, and they said you could take what you could carry. We were there until October.

Even though we stayed in a horse stable, everything was well organized. Every unit would hold four to six people. So in some cases, families had to split up, or join others. We slept on army cots, and for mattresses they gave us muslin bags, and told us to fill them with straw. And for chairs, everybody scrounged around for carton boxes, because they could serve as chairs. You could put two together and it could be a little table. So it was just makeshift. But I was amazed how, in a few months, some of those units really looked nice. Japanese women fixed them up. Some people had the foresight to bring material and needles and thread. But they didn't let us bring anything that could be used as weapons. They let us have spoons, but no knives. For those who had small children or babies, it was rough. They said you could take what you could carry. Well, they could only take their babies in their arms, and maybe the little children could carry something, but it was pretty limited.

I was so red, white, and blue, I couldn't believe this was happening to us. America would never do a thing like this to us. This is the greatest country in the world. So I thought this is only going to be for a short while, maybe a few weeks or something, and they will let us go back. At the beginning no one realized how long this would go on. I didn't feel the anger that much because I thought maybe

---

*Executive Order No. 9066 does not mention detention of Japanese specifically, but was used exclusively against the Japanese. Over 120,000 Japanese were evacuated from the West Coast.

this was the way we could show our love for our country, and we should not make too much fuss or noise, we should abide by what they asked of us. I'm a totally different person now than I was back then. I was naïve about so many things. The more I think about it, the more I realize how little you learn about American history. It's just what they want you to know.

At the beginning, we didn't have any idea how temporary or permanent the situation was. We thought we would be able to leave shortly. But after several months they told us this was just temporary quarters, and they were building more permanent quarters elsewhere in the United States. All this was so unbelievable. A year before we would never have thought anything like this could have happened to us—not in this country. As time went by, the sense of frustration grew. Many families were already divided. The fathers, the heads of the households, were taken to other camps. In the beginning, there was no way for the sons to get in touch with their families. Before our group left for the detention camp, we were saying goodbye almost every day to other groups who were going to places like Arizona and Utah. Here we finally had made so many new friends—people who we met, lived with, shared the time, and got to know. So it was even sad on that note and the goodbyes were difficult. Here we had gotten close to these people, and now we had to separate again. I don't think we even thought about where they were going to take us, or how long we would have to stay there. When we got on the trains to leave for the camps, we didn't know where we were going. None of the groups knew. It was later on that we learned so and so ended up in Arizona, or Colorado, or some other place. We were all at these assembly centers for about seven months. Once they started pushing people out, it was done very quickly. By October, our group headed out for Jerome, Arkansas, which is on the Texarkana corner.

We were on the train for five days. The blinds were down, so we couldn't look out, and other people couldn't look in to see who was in the train. We stopped in Nebraska, and everybody pulled the blinds to see what Nebraska looked like. The interesting thing was, there was a troop train stopped at the station too. These American soldiers looked out, and saw all these Asians, and they wondered what we were doing on the train. So the Japanese raised the windows, and so did the soldiers. It wasn't a bad feeling at all. There was none of that "you Japs" kind of thing. The women were about the same age as the soldiers—eighteen to twenty-five, and we had the same thing on our minds. In camps, there wasn't much to do, so the fun thing was to receive letters, so on our train, all the girls who were my age, were yelling to the guys, "Hey, give us your address where you're going, we'll write you." And they said, "Are you sure you're going to write?" We exchanged addresses and for a long time I wrote to some of those soldiers. On the other side of the train, I'll never forget there was this old guy, about sixty, who came to our window and said, "We have some Japanese living here. This is Omaha, Nebraska." This guy was very nice, and didn't seem to have any ill feelings for Japanese. He had calling cards, and he said "Will any of you people write to me?" We said, "Sure," so he threw in a bunch of calling cards, and I got one, and I wrote to him for years. I wrote to him about what camp was like, because he said, "Let me know what it's like wherever you end up." And he wrote back, and told me what was happening in Omaha, Nebraska. There were many, many interesting experiences too. Our mail was generally not censored, but all the mail from the soldiers was. Letters meant everything.

When we got to Jerome, Arkansas, we were shocked because we had never seen an area like it. There was forest all around us. And they told us to wait till the rains hit. This would not only turn into mud, but Arkansas swamp lands. That's where they put us — in swamp lands, surrounded by forests. It was nothing like California.

I'm speaking as a person of twenty who had good health. Up until then, I had lived a fairly comfortable life. But there were many others who didn't see the whole experience the same way. Especially those who were older and in poor health and had experienced racism. One more thing like this could break them. I was at an age where transitions were not hard — the point where anything new could even be considered exciting. But for people in poor health, it was hell.

There were army-type barracks, with two hundred to two hundred and five people to each block and every block had its own mess hall, facility for washing clothes, showering. It was all surrounded by barbed wire, and armed soldiers. I think they said only seven people were killed in total, though thirty were shot, because they went too close to the fence. Where we were, nobody thought of escaping because you'd be more scared of the swamps — the poisonous snakes, the bayous. Climatic conditions were very harsh. Although Arkansas is in the South, the winters were very, very cold. We had a pot bellied stove in every room and we burned wood. Everything was very organized. We got there in October, and were warned to prepare ourselves. So on our block, for instance, males eighteen and over could go out in the forest to chop down trees for wood for the winter. The men would bring back the trees, and the women sawed the trees. Everybody worked. The children would pile up the wood for each unit.

They told us when it rained, it would be very wet, so we would have to build our own drainage system. One of the barracks was to hold meetings, so block heads would call meetings. There was a block council to represent the people from different areas.

When we first arrived, there were some things that weren't completely fixed. For instance, the roofers would come by, and everyone would hunger for information from the outside world. We wanted to know what was happening with the war. We weren't allowed to bring radios; that was contraband. And there were no televisions then. So we would ask the workers to bring us back some papers, and they would give us papers from Texas or Arkansas, so for the first time we would find out about news from the outside.

Just before we went in to the camps, we saw that being a Japanese wasn't such a good thing, because everybody was turning against the Japanese, thinking we were saboteurs, or linking us with Pearl Harbor. But when I saw the kind of work they did at camp, I felt so proud of the Japanese, and proud to be Japanese, and wondered why I was so white, white when I was outside, because I was always with white folks. Many people had brothers or sons who were in the military and Japanese American servicemen would come into the camp to visit the families, and we felt so proud of them when they came in their uniforms. We knew that it would only be a matter of time before they would be shipped overseas. Also what made us feel proud was the forming of the 442 unit.*

I was one of these real American patriots then. I've changed now. But back then, I was all American. Growing up, my mother would say we're Japanese. But I'd say, "No, I'm American." I think a lot of Japanese grew up that way. People would say to them, "You're Japanese," and they would say, "No, we're Americans." I don't even think they used the hyphenated term "Japanese-American" back then. At the time, I was ashamed of being Japanese. I think many Japanese Americans felt the same way. Pearl Harbor was a shameful act, and being Japanese Americans, even though we had nothing to do with it, we still somehow felt we were blamed for it. I hated Japan at that point. So I saw myself at that part of my history as an American, and not as a Japanese or Japanese American. That sort of changed while I was in the camp.

I hated the war, because it wasn't just between the governments. It went down to the people, and it nurtured hate. What was happening during the war were many things I didn't like. I hoped that one day when the war was over there could be a way that people could come together in their relationships.

Now I can relate to Japan in a more mature way, where I see its faults and its very, very negative history. But I also see its potential. Scientifically and technologically it has really gone far. But I'm disappointed that when it comes to human rights she hasn't grown. The Japan of today—I feel there are still things lacking. For instance, I don't think the students have the opportunity to have more leeway in developing their lives.

We always called the camps "relocation centers" while we were there. Now we feel it is apropos to call them concentration camps. It is not the same as the concentration camps of Europe; those we feel were death camps. Concentration camps were a concentration of people placed in an area, and disempowered and disenfranchised. So it is apropos to call what I was in a concentration camp. After two years in the camp, I was released.

Going home wasn't much of a problem for us because our neighbors had looked after our place. But for most of our Japanese friends, starting over again was very difficult after the war.

I returned in October of 1945. It was very hard to find work, at least for me. I wasn't expecting to find anything good, just something to tide me over until my boyfriend came back from New York. The only thing I was looking for was to work in a restaurant as a waitress. But I couldn't find anything. I would walk from one end of the town to the other, and down every main avenue. But as soon as they found out I was Japanese, they would say no. Or they would ask me if I was in the

---

*American soldiers of Japanese ancestry were assembled in two units: the 442 Regimental Combat Team and the 100th Infantry Battalion. The two groups were sent to battle in Europe. The 100th Battalion had over 900 casualties and was known as the Purple Heart Battalion. Combined, the units received 9,486 purple hearts and 18,143 individual decorations.

union, and of course I couldn't be in the union because I had just gotten there. Anyway, no Japanese could be in the union, so if the answer was no I'm not in the union, they would say no. So finally what I did was go into the rough area of San Pedro—there's a strip near the wharf—and I went down there. I was determined to keep the jobs as long as I could. But for a while, I could last maybe two hours, and somebody would say "Is that a 'Jap'?" And as soon as someone would ask that, the boss would say, "Sorry, you gotta go. We don't want trouble here." The strip wasn't that big, so after I'd go the whole length of it, I'd have to keep coming back to the same restaurants, and say, "Gee, will you give me another chance." I figure, all these servicemen were coming back and the restaurants didn't have enough waitresses to come in and take these jobs. And so, they'd say "Okay. But soon as somebody asks who you are, or if you're a 'Jap,' or any problem about being a 'Jap,' you go." So I said, "Okay, sure. How about keeping me until that happens?" So sometimes I'd last a night, sometimes a couple of nights that no one would say anything. Sometimes people threw cups at me or hot coffee. At first they didn't know what I was. They thought I was Chinese. Then someone would say, "I bet she's a 'Jap'." And I wasn't going to say I wasn't. So as soon as I said "Yeah," then it was like an uproar. Rather than have them say, "Get out," I just walked out. I mean, there was no point in fighting it. If you just walked out, there was less chance of getting hurt. But one place I lasted two weeks. These owners didn't want to have to let me go. But they didn't want to have problems with the people.

And so I did this until I left for New York, which was about three months later. I would work the dinner shift, from six at night to three in the morning. When you are young you tend not to take things as strongly. Everything is like an adventure. Looking back, I felt the people who were the kindest to me were those who went out and fought, those who just got back from Japan or the Far East. I think the worst ones were the ones who stayed here and worked in defense plants, who felt they had to be so patriotic. On the West Coast, there wasn't hysteria anymore, but there were hostile feelings towards the Japanese, because they were coming back. It took a while, but my mother said that things were getting back to normal, and that the Japanese were slowly being accepted again. At the time, I didn't go through the bitterness that many others went through, because it's not just what they went through, but it is also what they experienced before that. I mean, I happened to have a much more comfortable life before, so you sort of see things in a different light. You see that there are all kinds of Americans, and that they're not all people who hate Japs. You know too that it was hysteria that had a lot to do with it.

All Japanese, before they left camp, were told not to congregate among Japanese, and not to speak Japanese. They were told by the authorities. There was even a piece of paper that gave you instructions. But then people went on to places like Chicago where there were churches, so they did congregate in churches. But they did ask people not to. I think psychologically the Japanese, having gone through a period where they were so hated by everyone, didn't even want to admit they were Japanese, or accept the fact that they were Japanese. Of course, they would say they were Japanese Americans. But I think the psychological damage of the wartime period, and of racism itself, has left its mark. There is a stigma to being Japanese. I think that is why such a large number of Japanese, in particular Japanese American women, have married out of the race. On the West Coast I've heard people say that sixty to seventy percent of the Japanese women have married, I guess, mostly whites. Japanese men are doing it too, but not to that degree. I guess Japanese Americans just didn't want to have that Japanese identity, or that Japanese part. There is definitely some self-hate, and part of that has to do with the racism that's so deeply a part of this society.

Historically, Americans have always been putting people behind walls. First there were the American Indians who were put on reservations, Africans in slavery, their lives on the plantations, Chicanos doing migratory work, and the kinds of camps they lived in, and even, too, the Chinese when they worked on the railroad camps where they were almost isolated, dispossessed people—disempowered. And I feel those are the things we should fight against so they won't happen again. It wasn't so long ago—in 1979—that the feeling against the Iranians was so strong because of the takeover of the U.S. embassy in Iran, where they wanted to deport Iranian students. And that is when a group called Concerned Japanese Americans organized, and that was the first issue we took up, and then we connected it with what the Japanese had gone through. This whole period of what the Japanese went through is important. If we can see the connections of how often this happens in history, we can stem the tide of these things happening again by speaking out against them.

Most Japanese Americans who worked years and years for redress never thought it would happen the way it did. The papers have been signed, we will be given reparation, and there was an apology from the government. I think the redress movement itself was very good because it was a learning experience for the Japanese people; we could get out into our communities and speak about what happened to us and link it with experiences of other people. In that sense, though, it wasn't done as much as it should have been. Some Japanese Americans didn't even learn that part. They just started the movement as a reaction to the bad experience they had. They don't even see other ethnic groups who have gone through it. It showed us, too, how vulnerable everybody is. It showed us that even though there is a Constitution, that constitutional rights could be taken away very easily.

4

Asian American?

Sonia Shah

I was recently asked to write about Asian American History Month, which, since 1979, has been observed during the month of May.

Despite the fact that I write about Asian American issues on a fairly regular basis, and in many ways consider myself an Asian American, it wasn't easy to figure. The very term, "Asian American History," makes our presence here sound so official, so natural.

Yet the term "Asian America" itself is problematic. Most of the people whom others would characterize as "Asian American" most emphatically don't think of themselves that way. (And many, including most of those in my family, would be almost offended: they are Gujuratis, thank you very much!) Our particular histories, ethnicities, and nationalities are one million times more visceral and meaningful in our lives than pan-Asianness (and what would that be, one wonders: "fusion" cooking?).

The push to unify the disparate peoples and histories of Chinese, Japanese, Vietnamese, Hmong, Pakistanis, Thais, and Indians, among others, comes from both right and left. Of course it would be easier for the U.S. census, but also for the radicals who started the "Yellow Power" movement in the 1960s, among others. But unlike other diverse ethnic/racial groups, such as African Americans and Native Americans, Asian Pacific Americans share no common historical trauma like slavery or colonization. We share no "Asian" language or ethnicity or nation or color. What we have in common, most of us would rather forget.

There is an undeniable strategic value in our unity. Americans know so little about Asian cultures, in general, that the stereotypes and fantasies projected upon any one group bleed over onto the next. We have those in common, and it wouldn't do any good to resist some and not the others. As a group, Asians have sometimes been held up as "model minorities" and at other times pilloried as spies and interlopers, but always, it seems, we are held at a distance, no matter how "American" we may become. This is at least partly because our role in American society is largely defined not by our unique contributions per se, but by our assigned roles in the unfolding drama between American labor and capital, and between blacks and whites.

ZNet Commentary, April 26, 1999.

Each wave of Asian immigration to American shores has been triggered by U.S. immigration policy or military interventions in Asia. When American labor has gotten too expensive, due to union organizing victories and the like, immigration laws have strategically shifted to import workers from Asia, whether poor Chinese laborers in the 1800s to build the railroads or professional Asians in the 1960s to service the then-growing welfare state. U.S. military interventions in the Philippines, Korea, Vietnam, and elsewhere likewise resulted in floods of Asian refugees at American gates. Today, the workers, farmers, and small landowners in Asia whose livelihoods have been crushed by the demands of U.S. multinational companies—now freer than ever to do business abroad—are being smuggled illegally into the country.

Predictably, backlashes against these workers have followed in each case. Laws excluding Chinese from becoming citizens, owning property, marrying, or attending public schools with whites were enacted in the mid- to late-1800s. In 1942, the U.S. government stripped 110,000 Japanese Americans of their homes, possessions, and savings and forced them into concentration camps; upon their release—jobless, penniless—the government served as an employment agency, fielding the many requests for servants.

The 1980s economy sparked another wave of anti-Asian violence: in 1982, Chinese American Vincent Chin was beaten to death with a baseball bat by unemployed auto workers who thought he was Japanese (and who served not a single day in jail). In 1987, Navraz Mody was beaten to death by a gang of youths in New Jersey, home of the infamous "dotbusters" (a vicious reference to the Indian bindhi).

Today, many Asian workers serve as a sort of middle-tier wedge between blacks and whites, and between corporate elites and workers—most tragically in Los Angeles during the 1992 riots. Even the much-lauded professional Asians are harassed and excluded on the basis of their accents, their degrees often devalued and held to higher-than-usual standards. For all the fanfare regarding their success, most of them still make less money than whites with comparable educations. Undocumented Asian workers take the jobs nobody else will tolerate, toiling in sweatshops and factories. In one particularly egregious case, dozens of Thai workers were recently found to have been held against their will in a barbed-wire-enclosed southern California sweatshop between 1990 and 1997.

The model minority myth—consciously encouraged by embattled elites in Asian communities—likewise inserts Asians into the larger drama about blacks and whites. While an education can be had and a living made based on model minority myths (at least for some), it is at the cost of indulging the racist delusion that there can be some "good minorities" in implicit contrast to those other "bad minorities," who have only themselves to blame.

Part of the double-bind of Asian Americans is that retaining our Asian heritages can be almost as difficult as becoming American. The American media continues to be fascinated with Asian misery and senseless oppression. When Americans gain a peek into life in Asia, it is invariably a horror scene: Indonesians eating bark; Chinese women drinking pesticides; Thai prostitutes chained to their beds; dead bodies in rivers, contaminated blood supplies, mudslides, train wrecks, massacres. Non-Asians may be strangely comforted by these tales of distant woe. But what could anyone with ties to those countries feel, beside sorrow, shame, rage, alienation, or: Thank God we're here and not there!

The story of Asian American history, in these ways, is a story of not belonging, of alienation from America and Asia. Yet, despite all this ambivalence and contradiction about our place in U.S. society, Asian Americans have played upon the broader American stage and have made lives and history change as a result.

People such as the human rights advocate Yuri Kochiyama; the feminist activist Anannya Bhattacharjee; the queer activist Urvashi Vaid; the radical poet Janice Mirikitani; the public intellectuals Glenn Omatsu, Peter Kwong; and Mari Matsuda; the filmmakers Richard Fung and Renee Tajima to name just a few, among many others, are building an inspired, radical Asian left to improve all of our lives.

Their legacy—the future of history—are today's vibrant Asian American immigrant worker movements, the growing institution of Asian American Studies in universities, a flourishing Asian American arts community, and more. These people and the institutions they have built, against the odds, are the Asian makers of American history. They have and will continue to force America to reckon with the realities of a diverse, multilingual, yellow and brown, ever-more-vocal Asianized America.

5

TV Arabs

Jack G. Shaheen

America's bogyman is the Arab. Until the nightly news brought us TV pictures of Palestinian boys being punched and beaten, almost all portraits of Arabs seen in America were dangerously threatening. Arabs were either billionaires or bombers— rarely victims. They were hardly ever seen as ordinary people practicing law, driving taxis, singing lullabies or healing the sick. Though TV news may portray them more sympathetically now, the absence of positive media images nurtures suspicion and stereotype. As an Arab-American, I have found that ugly caricatures have had an enduring impact on my family.

Jack G. Shaheen, a CBS News Consultant on Middle East Affairs, is Professor of Mass Communications Emeritus at Southern Illinois University.

I was sheltered from prejudicial portraits at first. My parents came from Lebanon in the 1920s; they met and married in America. Our home in the steel city of Clairton, Pa., was a center for ethnic sharing—black, white, Jew and gentile. There was only one major source of media images then, at the State movie theater where I was lucky enough to get a part-time job as an usher. But in the late 1940s, Westerns and war movies were popular, not Middle Eastern dramas. Memories of World War II were fresh, and the screen heavies were the Japanese and the Germans. True to the cliché of the times, the only good Indian was a dead Indian. But when I mimicked or mocked the bad guys, my mother cautioned me. She explained that stereotypes blur our vision and corrupt the imagination. "Have compassion for all people, Jackie," she said. "This way, you'll learn to experience the joy of accepting people as they are, and not as they appear in films. Stereotypes hurt."

Mother was right. I can remember the Saturday afternoon when my son, Michael, who was seven, and my daughter, Michele, six, suddenly called out: "Daddy, Daddy, they've got some bad Arabs on TV." They were watching that great American morality play, TV wrestling. Akbar the Great, who liked to hear the cracking of bones, and Abdullah the Butcher, a dirty fighter who liked to inflict pain, were pinning their foes with "camel locks." From that day on, I knew I had to try to neutralize the media caricatures.

It hasn't been easy. With my children, I have watched animated heroes Heckle and Jeckle pull the rug from under "Ali Boo-Boo, the Desert Rat," and Laverne and Shirley stop "Sheik Ha-Mean-Ie" from conquering "the U.S. and the world." I have read comic books like the "Fantastic Four" and "G.I. Combat" whose characters have sketched Arabs as "lowlifes" and "human hyenas." Negative stereotypes were everywhere. A dictionary informed my youngsters that an Arab is a "vagabond, drifter, hobo and vagrant." Whatever happened, my wife wondered, to Aladdin's good genie?

To a child, the world is simple: good versus evil. But my children and others with Arab roots grew up without ever having seen a humane Arab on the silver screen, someone to pattern their lives after. Is it easier for a camel to go through the eye of a needle than for a screen Arab to appear as a genuine human being?

Hollywood producers must have an instant Ali Baba kit that contains scimitars, veils, sunglasses and such Arab clothing as *chadors* and *kufiyahs*. In the mythical "Ay-rabland," oil wells, tents, mosques, goats and shepherds prevail. Between the sand dunes, the camera focuses on a mock-up of a palace from "Arabian Nights"—or a military air base. Recent movies suggest that Americans are at war with Arabs, forgetting the fact that out of 21 Arab nations, America is friendly with 19 of them. And in "Wanted Dead or Alive," a movie that starred Gene Simmons, the leader of the rock group Kiss, the war comes home when an Arab terrorist comes to the United States dressed as a rabbi and, among other things, conspires with Arab-Americans to poison the people of Los Angeles. . . .

The Arab remains American culture's favorite whipping boy. In his memoirs, Terrel Bell, Ronald Reagan's first secretary of education, writes about an "apparent bias among mid-level, right-wing staffers at the White House" who dismissed Arabs as "sand niggers." Sadly, the racial slurs continue. At a recent teacher's conference, I met a woman from Sioux Falls, S.D., who told me about the persistence of discrimination. She was in the process of adopting a baby when an agency staffer warned her that the infant had a problem. When she asked whether the child was mentally ill, or physically handicapped, there was silence. Finally, the worker said: "The baby is Jordanian."

To me, the Arab demon of today is much like the Jewish demon of yesterday. We deplore the false portrait of Jews as a swarthy menace. Yet a similar portrait has been accepted and transferred to another group of Semites—the Arabs. Print and broadcast journalists have started to challenge this stereotype. They are now revealing more humane images of Palestinian Arabs, a people who traditionally suffered from the myth that Palestinian equals terrorist. Others could follow that lead and retire the stereotypical Arab to a media Valhalla.

It would be a step in the right direction if movie and TV producers developed characters modeled after real-life Arab-Americans. We could then see a White House correspondent like Helen Thomas, whose father came from Lebanon, in "The Golden Girls," a heart surgeon patterned after Dr. Michael DeBakey on "St. Elsewhere," or a Syrian-American playing tournament chess like Yasser Seirawan, the Seattle grandmaster.

Politicians, too, should speak out against the cardboard caricatures. They should refer to Arabs as friends, not just as moderates. And religious leaders could state that Islam, like Christianity and Judaism, maintains that all mankind is one family in the care of God. When all image makers rightfully begin to treat Arabs and all other minorities with respect and dignity, we may begin to unlearn our prejudices.

6

The Myth of the Latin Woman:
I Just Met a Girl Named María

Judith Ortiz Cofer

On a bus trip to London from Oxford University where I was earning some graduate credits one summer, a young man, obviously fresh from a pub, spotted me and as if struck by inspiration went down on his knees in the aisle. With both hands over his heart he broke into an Irish tenor's rendition of "María" from *West Side Story.* My politely amused fellow passengers gave his lovely voice the round of gentle applause it deserved. Though I was not quite as amused, I managed my version of an English smile: no show of teeth, no extreme contortions of the facial muscles—I was at this time of my life practicing reserve and cool. Oh, that British control, how I coveted it. But María had followed me to London, reminding me of a prime fact of my life: you can leave the Island, master the English language, and travel as far as you can, but if you are a Latina, especially one like me who so obviously belongs to Rita Moreno's gene pool, the Island travels with you.

This is sometimes a very good thing—it may win you that extra minute of someone's attention. But with some people, the same things can make *you* an island—not so much a tropical paradise as an Alcatraz, a place nobody wants to visit. As a Puerto Rican girl growing up in the United States and wanting like most children to "belong," I resented the stereotype that my Hispanic appearance called forth from many people I met.

Our family lived in a large urban center in New Jersey during the sixties, where life was designed as a microcosm of my parents' casas on the island. We spoke in Spanish, we ate Puerto Rican food bought at the bodega, and we practiced strict Catholicism complete with Saturday confession and Sunday mass at a church where our parents were accommodated into a one-hour Spanish mass slot, performed by a Chinese priest trained as a missionary for Latin America.

As a girl I was kept under strict surveillance, since virtue and modesty were, by cultural equation, the same as family honor. As a teenager I was instructed on how to behave as a proper señorita. But it was a conflicting message girls got, since the Puerto Rican mothers also encouraged their daughters to look and act like women and to dress in clothes our Anglo friends and their mothers found too "mature" for our age. It was, and is, cultural, yet I often felt humiliated when I appeared at an American friend's party wearing a dress more suitable to a semiformal than to a playroom birthday celebration. At Puerto Rican festivities, neither the music nor the colors we wore could be too loud. I still experience a vague sense of letdown when I'm invited to a "party" and it turns out to be a marathon conversation in hushed tones rather than a fiesta with salsa, laughter, and dancing—the kind of celebration I remember from my childhood.

I remember Career Day in our high school, when teachers told us to come dressed as if for a job interview. It quickly became obvious that to the barrio girls, "dressing up" sometimes meant wearing ornate jewelry and clothing that would be more appropriate (by mainstream standards) for the company Christmas party than as daily office attire. That morning I had agonized in front of my closet, trying to figure out what a "career girl" would wear because, essentially, except for Marlo Thomas on TV, I had no models on which to base my decision. I knew how to dress for school: at the Catholic school I attended we all wore uniforms; I knew how to dress for Sunday mass, and I knew what dresses to wear for parties at my relatives' homes. Though I do not recall the precise details of my Career Day outfit, it must have been a composite of the above choices. But I remember a comment my friend (an Italian-American) made in later years that coalesced my impressions of that day. She said that at the business school she was attending the Puerto Rican girls always stood out for wearing "everything at once." She meant, of course, too much jewelry, too many accessories. On that day at school, we were simply made the negative models by the nuns who were themselves not credible fashion experts to any of us. But it was painfully obvious to me that to the others, in their tailored skirts and silk blouses, we must have seemed "hopeless" and "vulgar." Though I now know that most adolescents feel out of step much of the time, I also know that for the Puerto Rican girls of my generation that sense was intensified. The way our teachers and classmates looked at us that day in school was just a taste of the culture clash that awaited us in the real world, where prospective employers and men on the street would often misinterpret our tight skirts and jingling bracelets as a come-on.

Mixed cultural signals have perpetuated certain stereotypes—for example, that of the Hispanic woman as the "Hot Tamale" or sexual firebrand. It is a one-dimensional view that the media have found easy to promote. In their special vocabulary, advertisers have designated "sizzling" and "smoldering" as the adjectives of choice for describing not only the foods but also the women of Latin America. From conversations in my house I recall hearing about the harassment that Puerto Rican women endured in factories where the "boss men" talked to them as if sexual innuendo was all they understood and, worse, often gave them the choice of submitting to advances or being fired.

It is custom, however, not chromosomes, that leads us to choose scarlet over pale pink. As young girls, we were influenced in our decisions about clothes and colors by the women—older sisters and mothers who had grown up on a tropical island where the natural environment was a riot of primary colors, where showing your skin was one way to keep cool as well as to look sexy. Most important of all, on the island, women perhaps felt freer to dress and move more provocatively, since, in most cases, they were protected by the traditions, mores, and laws of a Spanish/ Catholic system of morality and machismo whose main rule was: *You may look at my sister, but if you touch her I will kill you.* The extended family and church structure could provide a young woman with a circle of safety in her small pueblo on the island; if a man "wronged" a girl, everyone would close in to save her family honor.

This is what I have gleaned from my discussions as an adult with older Puerto Rican women. They have told me about dressing in their best party clothes on Saturday nights and going to the town's plaza to promenade with their girlfriends in front of the boys they liked. The males were thus given an opportunity to admire the women and to express their admiration in the form of *piropos*: erotically charged street poems they composed on the spot. I have been subjected to a few piropos while visiting the Island, and they can be outrageous, although custom dictates that they must never cross into obscenity. This ritual, as I understand it, also entails a show of studied indifference on the woman's part; if she is "decent," she must not acknowledge the man's impassioned words. So I do understand how things can be lost in translation. When a Puerto Rican girl dressed in her idea of what is attractive meets a man from the mainstream culture who has been trained to react to certain types of clothing as a sexual signal, a clash is likely to take place. The line I first heard based on this aspect of the myth happened when the boy who took me to my first formal dance leaned over to plant a sloppy overeager kiss painfully on my mouth, and when I didn't respond with sufficient passion said in a resentful tone: "I thought you Latin girls were supposed to mature early"—my first instance of being thought of as a fruit or vegetable—I was supposed to *ripen*, not just grow into womanhood like other girls.

It is surprising to some of my professional friends that some people, including those who should know better, still put others "in their place." Though rarer, these incidents are still commonplace in my life. It happened to me most recently during a stay at a very classy metropolitan hotel favored by young professional couples for their weddings. Late one evening after the theater, as I walked toward my room with my new colleague (a woman with whom I was coordinating an arts program), a middle-aged man in a tuxedo, a young girl in satin and lace on his arm, stepped directly into our path. With his champagne glass extended toward me, he exclaimed, "Evita!"

Our way blocked, my companion and I listened as the man half-recited, half-bellowed "Don't Cry for Me, Argentina." When he finished, the young girl said: "How about a round of applause for my daddy?" We complied, hoping this would bring the silly spectacle to a close. I was becoming aware that our little group was attracting the attention of the other guests. "Daddy" must have perceived this too, and he once more barred the way as we tried to walk past him. He began to shout-sing a ditty to the tune of "La Bamba"—except the lyrics were about a girl named María whose exploits all rhymed with her name and gonorrhea. The girl kept saying "Oh, Daddy" and looking at me with pleading eyes. She wanted me to laugh along with the others. My companion and I stood silently waiting for the man to end his offensive song. When he finished, I looked not at him but at his daughter. I advised her calmly never to ask her father what he had done in the army. Then I walked between them and to my room. My friend complimented me on my cool handling of the situation. I confessed to her that I really had wanted to push the jerk into the swimming pool. I knew that this same man—probably a corporate executive, well educated, even worldly by most standards—would not have been likely to regale a white woman with a dirty song in public. He would perhaps have checked his impulse by assuming that she could be somebody's wife or mother, or at least *somebody* who might take offense. But to him, I was just an Evita or a María: merely a character in his cartoon-populated universe.

Because of my education and my proficiency with the English language, I have acquired many mechanisms for dealing with the anger I experience. This was not true for my parents, nor is it true for the many Latin women working at menial jobs who must put up with stereotypes about our ethnic group such as: "They make good domestics." This is another facet of the myth of the Latin woman in the United States. Its origin is simple to deduce. Work as domestics, waitressing, and factory jobs are all that's available to women with little English and few skills. The myth of the Hispanic menial has been sustained by the same media phenomenon that made "Mammy" from *Gone with the Wind* America's idea of the black woman for generations; María, the housemaid or counter girl, is now indelibly etched into the national psyche. The big and the little screens have presented us with the picture of the funny Hispanic maid, mispronouncing words and cooking up a spicy storm in a shiny California kitchen.

This media-engendered image of the Latina in the United States has been documented by feminist Hispanic scholars, who claim that such portrayals are partially responsible for the denial of opportunities for upward mobility among Latinas in the professions. I have a Chicana friend working on a Ph.D. in philosophy at a major university. She says her doctor still shakes his head in puzzled amazement at all the "big words" she uses. Since I do not wear my diplomas around my neck for all to see, I too have on occasion been sent to that "kitchen," where some think I obviously belong.

One such incident that has stayed with me, though I recognize it as a minor offense, happened on the day of my first public poetry reading. It took place in Miami in a boat-restaurant where we were having lunch before the event. I was nervous and excited as I walked in with my notebook in my hand. An older woman motioned me to her table. Thinking (foolish me) that she wanted me to autograph a copy of my brand new slender volume of verse, I went over. She ordered a cup of coffee from me, assuming that I was the waitress. Easy enough to mistake my poems for menus, I suppose. I know that it wasn't an intentional act of cruelty, yet of all the good things that happened that day, I remember that scene most clearly, because it reminded me of what I had to overcome before anyone would take me seriously. In retrospect I understand that my anger gave my reading fire, that I have almost always taken doubts in my abilities as a challenge—and that the result is, most times, a feeling of satisfaction at having won a convert when I see the cold, appraising eyes warm to my words, the body language change, the smile that indicates that I have opened some avenue for communication. That day I read to that woman and her lowered eyes told me that she was embarrassed at her little faux pas, and when I willed her to look up at me, it was my victory, and she graciously allowed me to punish her with my full attention. We shook hands at the end of the reading, and I never saw her again. She has probably forgotten the whole thing but maybe not.

Yet I am one of the lucky ones. My parents made it possible for me to acquire a stronger footing in the mainstream culture by giving me the chance at an education. And books and art have saved me from the harsher forms of ethnic and racial prejudice that many of my Hispanic *compañeras* have had to endure. I travel a lot around the United States, reading from my books of poetry and my novel, and the reception I most often receive is one of positive interest by people who want to know more about my culture. There are, however, thousands of Latinas without the privilege of an education or the entrée into society that I have. For them life is a struggle against the misconceptions perpetuated by the myth of the Latina as whore, domestic, or criminal. We cannot change this by legislating the way people look at us. The transformation, as I see it, has to occur at a much more individual level. My personal goal in my public life is to try to replace the old pervasive stereotypes and myths about Latinas with a much more interesting set of realities. Every time I give a reading, I hope the stories I tell, the dreams and fears I examine in my work, can achieve some universal truth which will get my audience past the particulars of my skin color, my accent, or my clothes.

I once wrote a poem in which I called us Latinas "God's brown daughters." This poem is really a prayer of sorts, offered upward, but also, through the human-to-human channel of art, outward. It is a prayer for communication, and for respect. In it, Latin women pray "in Spanish to an Anglo God/with a Jewish heritage," and they are "fervently hoping/that if not omnipotent,/at least He be bilingual."

7

Black Latina

Delina D. Pryce

I always thought of former major-league baseball player Ruben Sierra as the sexiest man in the world. His dark, chocolaty skin, spicy Puerto Rican accent, and cocky attitude—together with his home runs and $6 million contract—always made for an enjoyable day at the ballpark. But during my monologue of praise, nothing dampened my mood quicker than hearing, "Ruben's not black; he's Puerto Rican." It was a grim reminder of the ignorance that I've had to deal with ever since I was old enough to fully understand the truth.

If I received a dollar for every time I heard, "You're not black, you're Hispanic" or "You're not Hispanic, you're black," I'd be well on my way to equaling Ruben's small fortune. To a lot of people, and to the majority of the people I've met, "black" and "Latino" are mutually exclusive terms. Reality couldn't be further from the truth.

Many people don't realize that slave ships dropped Africans off not only in the United States but also in the Caribbean, Mexico, Central America, and South America. Blacks in this country share a common history with those in the Caribbean and Latin America. Yet, because historical circumstances have created a variety of cultures within the black community in the Americas, people, including blacks themselves, are quick to make distinctions.

It saddens me that those with an obviously African ancestry refuse to acknowledge it, clinging instead to a lone term, "Hispanic" or "Latino." Being labeled "black" in the United States carries a heavy burden of stereotypes that many black Latinos would rather not deal with. In my view, if you're being followed in a store or beaten by the police, it doesn't really matter what you check on a census form. To a racist you're still a nigger.

Because I was born in Costa Rica, people want me to choose. "What are you?" they ask. When I was growing up, sometimes I'd check "Hispanic," sometimes I'd check "black," sometimes I'd check both. Administrators at my school, I was told, didn't like that. It made their statistics a little less scientific.

I was born in Costa Rica, moved to Mexico when I was two years old, and have been living in Texas for almost fourteen years. Yes, my upbringing was unlike most of my black friends in the States. Still, I am more like them than I'm like my Hispanic friends from various countries. We listen to the same music, enjoy the same churches, use the same hair stylists, and experience the same strain of racism. In a lot of ways it's easier for my black friends to comprehend that there is an African Diaspora. They see the fact that I speak Spanish as an asset ("Can you help me with my Spanish homework?"). If anything has been harder for me to explain to them, it's that I'm not "mixed with Hispanic."

On the other hand, my Latino friends see my race as a liability. "You're not black, like the African Americans in the United States," one told me recently. It bothers me that to accept me they want to distance me from being black, which carries negative connotations in the Americas. Some even have the audacity to tell me why they despise "those black people." They even wait for me to agree.

In Peru, blacks are still being used as ornamental images—chauffeurs, pallbearers, valets, and servants. In Brazil, blacks are considered marginal members of society. In countless other Latin American countries, blacks are shut out of government and positions of power. Television shows, news programs, and beauty magazines omit dark faces. The denial of racial diversity in the media, government and business is much like what the United States faced 30 years ago. "We are looking for ways to improve our self-esteem because the society conveys to blacks that we are nothing. We want to let people know that we are not only there to cook and play football [soccer]," said Piedad Cordoba de Castro, the first black woman to become senator in Colombia, in a 1995 *Dallas Morning News* article. This is why I think it is foolish for black Latinos to overlook their blackness and believe they are Hispanic like their countrymen of European ancestry. "The effort to build a black consciousness movement in Latin America has been hobbled by the low level of racial identification among blacks," Cordoba de Castro said. A hierarchy exists within Latin American countries. Those of European ancestry are at the top and those of African heritage are at the bottom, one notch below indigenous people. Those of mixed race—mestizos (indigenous and Caucasian) and malattos (indigenous and Negroid)—fall somewhere in between. Many blacks are eager to point out their Indian blood, thus elevating themselves above black.

I realize the inaccuracy and silliness of racial and ethnic categories in this day and age. Contrary to neo-Nazi belief, no one is really any one thing anymore. What still remains, inequality and power, all over the world, is defined and determined in racial terms. For this reason, racial identification should be used to unite and struggle together for equality. The stupidity of useless racial identification stems from the ignorance of racism. Black Latinos, who don't identify themselves as such, try to be exceptions to the rules and stereotypes that govern blacks. But racists don't care if you're bilingual and international. The very nature of prejudice does not allow for exceptions; it looks at group traits, not at individuals. Racism is prejudice combined with power. Until black Hispanics believe this, they will continue to be happily oppressed, and not even realize it (and even deny it).

It's time to know and celebrate who you really are. I know black culture in Costa Rica. I know black culture in the United States. I also know they both stem from the same place. Being Latina and black are not mutually exclusive, but mutually complementary. Being black and Latina has influenced and shaped my views, my thoughts, my experiences—who I am. Never would I deny either because they're both me. And I like me. Why don't others agree?

8

Latinos Gain Visibility in Cultural Life of U.S.

Mireya Navarro

HOUSTON   Lucy Lopez is 72 years old, but she still remembers the name of her kindergarten teacher: Miss Jones. On the first day of school, Miss Jones put Lucy in a corner for not knowing how to count to four in English.

So when she had children, Lucy and her husband, Gabriel, both born in Texas of Mexican parents, gave some of them non-Hispanic names like Debra Susan and Adam Floyd. They spoke to the children only in English.

But for the third Lopez generation, there is less pressure to choose between two cultures. Sofia Angela Lopez, 16, a granddaughter, postponed her quinceañera, the traditional 15th birthday celebration, so she could have a Sweet 16 party instead. She sings alternative rock in English, and hymns at Mass in Spanish. When she debates history with her father, he sounds like a Mexican in Texas and she sounds like a Texan of Mexican descent.

"He sees America as, 'This was Mexico, this was our land,' that kind of attitude," she said. "I feel it was Mexico, but to tell you the truth, I don't really know how Mexico is. I'm more like, 'This is America now.'"

The America of Sofia Lopez is an increasingly Hispanic nation, home to 31 million people of Latin ancestry, a rapidly growing number that in the next five years is expected to surpass African-Americans as the largest minority group and will most likely make up a fourth of the nation's population in 50 years, a demographic trend that has provoked both debate and celebration. Even as Californians vote to end bilingual education, news magazines proclaim and applaud the Latinization of popular culture.

But what the growth has also done is help "Latinize" many Hispanic people who are finding it easier to affirm their heritage. And as they find strength in numbers, as younger generations grow up with more ethnic pride and as a Latin influence starts permeating fields like entertainment, advertising and politics, Latinos are becoming visible in ways that offer glimpses of what their larger presence may mean for the United States.

So right does Carlos J. Guerrero, 34, a Houston businessman and Texas native, feel about his heritage these days that he just ordered his first guayabera shirt, through the Internet. So right it feels to be Latino, said Nestor Rodriguez, 51, co-director of the University of Houston's Center for Immigration Research, that he no longer regards tacos as a "peasant's meal."

"It's not that we're regaining our culture," Mr. Rodriguez said. "It's that now tacos are everybody's meal."

Jose Alberto Medrano, 24, a political science student at the University of Houston and a legislative aide, has even stopped going by Albert, the name he used in grade school.

"It just didn't feel threatening to be Jose anymore," the Chicago-born Mr. Medrano said. "I used to feel I would be discriminated against, that it wouldn't be socially acceptable. It's cool to be Hispanic now." (Last year Jose replaced Michael as the most popular newborn boy's name in Texas and California.)

At Youth Engaged in Service College Preparatory School, the charter school Sofia attends in Houston, a group of classmates discussed what they rejected of their parents' culture. They tended to identify attitudes and beliefs: deep religiousness, or the sexism that limits the aspirations of girls.

"My mom thinks girls should not play sports," said Elvia Flores, 16, who came to the United States from Mexico at age 6 and who plays soccer.

At the same time, however, there was no trace of shame, no fear of appearing foreign for embracing other parts of the culture. They all spoke Spanish, although some of them admitted to speaking poorly. Sofia, who aspires to be "a lawyer or F.B.I. agent," said she planned to pass on to her children what she termed "sentimental" traditions, like observing the Day of the Dead. And they all find inspiration in the achievements of any Latino, whether Jennifer Lopez, the Puerto Rican movie star, or Sammy Sosa, the Dominican home run star.

Such comfort level with heritage is far higher than that of the previous generation. John Lantigua, a Miami journalist and novelist whose father was a Cuban immigrant and whose mother was a Puerto Rican, said his parents pursued the

American dream in the 1950's by moving from the Bronx to the New Jersey suburbs and forbidding him to speak Spanish.

"I used to find scrapbooks in my house from the days before I was born, when my parents would go out to the Palladium and the Copacabana," Mr. Lantigua, 51, said. "I knew my parents had had this other life that I wasn't encouraged to have."

Many members of Mr. Lantigua's generation reacted by trying to recover what had been denied them, self-consciously immersing themselves in Latin culture.

"As I was planning my life, I knew I didn't want to live like that, with that lack of connection to a community," Mr. Lantigua said. "I've spent my whole adult life going back to it, to reconnect with that culture."

David E. Hayes-Bautista, 53, a Mexican-American who is director of the Center for the Study of Latino Health at the University of California at Los Angeles, also grew up with parents who "thought the best they could do was to protect us from being Latino."

"The Chicano movement was a reaction to that," Mr. Hayes-Bautista said. "We used to worry about whether a true Chicano would eat a hamburger. My children would say, 'What? That's crazy. Eat a burger if you're hungry.'

"They don't worry about losing anything. They are surrounded by people like them."

So much so that in the age of "Livin' La Vida Loca" and "Yo quiero Taco Bell," when the Hispanic presence is increasingly prominent in the popular culture, Sofia Lopez's parents worry that their daughter, who is growing up in a mostly Hispanic neighborhood and attends a mostly Hispanic school, will end up too Americanized.

"Our culture gets lesser and lesser as times change," said Sofia's mother, Oralia Lopez.

The phenomenon of assimilation alongside cultural affirmation is not unlike that experienced by other ethnic groups as they set roots in this country, some experts say. But the Hispanic population is likely to make its presence more deeply felt, these experts say, because Latinos make up the largest ethnic and linguistic group to arrive; they retain ties to their geographically close countries of origin, and the migration is continuing. All those factors reinforce Hispanic culture and the Spanish language while at the same time, assimilation dilutes them.

But because Hispanic people fall under many categories, many sociologists said, it is far from certain what kind of imprint their growth will make on the nation or how exactly they will broaden what it means to be an "American." With origins in 22 countries, some Latinos are English speakers and others are Spanish speakers; some are Americans with centuries-old roots here and others have just arrived.

What it means to be "Hispanic," a Census Bureau label as much as anything, is a matter of opinion. Today among the Lopezes here, in an extended family of more than 50 members, some describe themselves as white, some as Mexican, some as American Tex-Mex. So diverse is the Hispanic population—in race, color and ethnic background, among other things—that statistics on income and education are misleading, demographers say.

And despite a persistent image of Latinos as poor, Spanish-speaking immigrants, census figures show that more than 60 percent speak English fluently and are native born, and market researchers classify 75 percent of Hispanic households as middle or upper class. Latinos make up about 11 percent of the nation's total population, with Mexican-Americans accounting for more than 60 percent of them.

Many sociologists say that all evidence points to continuing assimilation, and some see no major changes beyond an expansion of the visibility that large Hispanic populations already have in the 10 states where they are concentrated.

But these states, particularly California, Texas, New York, Florida and Illinois, are also pivotal in Presidential elections. That fact helps explain why candidates like Vice President Al Gore and Gov. George W. Bush of Texas find themselves struggling to speak Spanish. As the Hispanic population numbers translate into votes, some Hispanic organizations predict, issues like quality of education and wage minimums, which disproportionately affect Latinos because of their high percentages of young people and large families, will become more prominent.

Yet for all the media attention and the rapid growth of Spanish-language media, Hispanic organizations and business leaders still express frustration, saying that Latinos seem invisible in the mainstream culture.

As the media rave over pop stars like Ricky Martin, who is Puerto Rican, several Latino groups are calling for a boycott of network television this month to protest the absence of Latinos in major roles.

"It's black and white, white and black—it's not black, brown and white," said Jeff Valdez, a Los Angeles television producer who is negotiating with investors to form a cable network for English-speaking Latinos to fill what he calls "a huge void." He added, "The reality is that there are more opportunities, but it's still got a long way to go."

Cecilia Munòz, policy director for the National Council of La Raza, a civil rights organization, said Latinos ultimately need economic and educational equality, which she said she hoped would come with increased integration.

"We've been discovered again," she said. "One hopes we reach a point when we're no longer being discovered anymore."

In San Antonio, Mike U. Villareal, 28, a computer company owner with a master's degree from Harvard University, is running for Texas state representative in the Democratic primary next March. As he walked the streets of his district recently on a "listening tour" of voters, Mr. Villareal said he wanted to be part of what he expected to be Texas's transition from "a Republican, Anglo-dominant" state to one that is more inclusive of the state's entire population, currently 28 percent Hispanic, 12 percent non-Hispanic black and 58 percent non-Hispanic white.

The country he envisions 50 years from now is not a lot different from that of today, he said, except for "different characters at the decision-making table."

"The growth of the Latino population is a wrench thrown into our system that will require us to make positive adjustments," Mr. Villareal said. "Issues that are on our minds will be in the minds of the rest of the country because we're all in the same boat."

9

What I Learned about Jews

Joe Wood

The preacher begins his tale, then reads some history: You are black and proud and you will remember that somewhere along the way some of the people in our line were made very low and not tough at all. I recall: We laughed at the whites when their backs were turned, and our mother spit out the lemon seeds under the porch because she said someday a tree with its natty leaves would lick light there long after we moved to the city. We were slaves then and maybe we are still today, slaves, our blackness a badge of terrifying knowledge, a certificate of human accomplishment, its possibility and strength, like a god or a flame inside cupped hands, not something to flee from like a dead body or a bad smell.

While Jews, along with Italians and the Irish, have in most of the century's renderings of American history been assigned the role of "immigrant," and as such are permitted a history before America, Negroes were made in America. That left us with a blank place where a history should be: no place to put our peoplehood and few ways to understand the situation. So we patched our wounds with the pages of the Bible. So in church, our hospital, we tell the tale over and over again; how much we resemble the ancient Jews, how we too are slaves awaiting deliverance. We hold this tale more dear than did the pilgrims who made us slaves—but what of the Jews, who would certainly want their story back?

It was simple and plain. You'd heard that the Jews controlled jazz, the media, the Democratic Party, the civil rights movement and Harlem real estate, and you wondered. You knew this didn't explain why the police beat you up or why the public education system was a mess or why your neighborhood was without cable and regular garbage pickup, but still you wondered.

"Don't let them call you an anti-Semite, sista," he said. "You'll never work again."

"Jewish people run Hollywood, just like they do *The New York Times*," you said.

"Definitely," he said.

"If that's the way it works, why can't I say it?"

"You know why," he said. "The Jews got it sewed up, and refuse to admit it. I'm tired of reading about Israel and the Holocaust. And about how they worked in the civil rights movement. My theory is they produced the civil rights movement and they pumped up King and all them preachers as a public relations diversion so no one would notice them buying mortgages."

"Well . . . ," you said, scratching your nose. You felt guilty whenever someone talked about "the Jews."

He picked up the slack. "I read where the Anti-Defamation League said the whiteboys are the ones writing 'Heil Hitler' and 'Jewboy' and stuff like that on the synagogues. Niggas got better sense than that."

"True," you said.

There was a silence.

"The Jews," he said, pausing. "My theory is the Holocaust messed them up. No matter how comfortable life starts to feel, they always bring back the Nazis. Or use them as an excuse to beat down niggas."

"Six million is a lot of million," you said, in a light voice.

"I'm telling you, Holocaust got them psychotic. But I want to hear them talk about how many million of us died getting here. Six million's only a drop in the ocean compared to what we went through. I want to know how many of us died on their slave ships. They never teach about that Holocaust."

Then he continued. "You don't hate them sometimes?"

Very quickly you said, "No."

"Good. Well I do. I'll be honest. I hate them sometimes. Because they were the minstrels. Al Jolson was a Jew and the Beastie Boys are Jews. Somebody even told me Elvis was a Jew. They bought our stuff for a dime and made a mint off it. Fats Waller to Chuck Berry to all them rappers—it's the Jews making the money. They act like your friend, but they're the No. 1 pimps of niggas. You got to admit that."

"Jewish people definitely don't have a monopoly on that."

"But the Jews were the ones who made Hollywood: Selznick and Goldwyn and Mayer—Jews. It's a fact. Undeniable. Now it's to the point where they don't even have to slander us anymore. They got their Negro minstrels to say what they want in their papers and magazines and they give 'em a dollar and a prize and it's nothing but Negro smiles. You know what I'm saying—they hate niggas because they know we got their number."

You felt the pull of the words. Down. And then you felt guilty inside, because you wanted to say something more, to separate yourself, and you couldn't, so you smiled—even though you knew there was a limit to your solidarity with the brotha. James Baldwin got it right when he wrote about the special disappointment you've reserved for the Jews—also ex-slaves, but that's where your complicity ended. You knew Jewish people didn't cause more black problems than other whites did. You remembered the preacher's story of the mother and her lemon tree, our collective selfhood. This was the real story, and it actually had very little to do with Jews. You

remembered, and you comforted yourself by saying your blackness and his blackness was why you smiled, but suddenly you felt the urge to spit something out.

I read a lot as a kid. I was a curious and obedient boy who paid close attention
to his parents' exhortations about the improvement of the race. I had a role to play.
My parents were determined to see their children become doctors or lawyers or
captains of industry or something to help black people to be proud, so I tried hard,
very hard—I brought all my books to bed. My mother drove my sister and me to
the library, and my father drove us to private school, and when I lay down I would
open the books: the Bible, Edith Wharton, Malcolm X, *The New Republic*, James
Joyce, Yukio Mishima, Gerard Manley Hopkins, James Baldwin, Spiderman, Tom
Wolfe, *Playboy*, Maya Angelou, John le Carré, Kurt Vonnegut.

I also read Norman Mailer's tales and Saul Bellow's stories and Norman
Podhoretz's "My Negro Problem—and Ours." Podhoretz's essay described and
tried to defend a racist Jew's racism. I still think of that piece whenever I hear talk
of black anti-Semitism. But as I bring my own Jewish story to light now, I will re-
frain from harping on any "Jewish problem"; I will instead try to tell the truth,
which is more complicated than words like "problem" allow.

For I grew up feeling a little like a Jew. Most of the children at Riverdale School
in the Bronx were Jewish, and I went there for 10 years. I tried to fit in and did. I listened to the same music and wore the same clothes and laughed at Woody Allen
movies for the same reasons as my peers. I lived on the other side of town, but I
knew the difference between the words "meshugga" and "zaftig"—I spoke the language of my environment. I even adopted my classmates' views of the world.

I shared, for instance, my Jewish schoolmates' dislike of WASP's even though I
hadn't met many. The WASP's mainly went to Collegiate and places outside the city
like Hotchkiss or Andover, and only the dumbest of their children came to
Riverdale. Most of the school's administrators were of Anglo heritage, and this was a
problem for many of the Jewish parents. My peers followed their parents' lead. I remember them saying the goyim "ruled the country," then saying "You're a Jew" during a dispute about money; or fawning over Nordic facial features, making fun of the
WASP's with Jewish noses. This perspective resembled the distaste for whites expressed around my neighborhood, a blend of vocal contempt and private admiration.

Our parents didn't particularly care for whites, but they weren't hostile in an
active way. No one would have acted funny or said anything to any of the block's
remaining few, the ones who hadn't moved to Jersey or Westchester. Mostly, you
heard talk about Jamaicans or the islanders we derisively called 'Ricans. The
whites usually discussed were the Italians, who still had some shops in the area.
They were reputedly mafia and were to be avoided if possible, though they were
admired for their sense of family and their piety.

But there wasn't much talk of Jews, even in church. I remember a Catholic
friend saying they were the ones who betrayed Christ, and it made sense. We had
all learned that Jews were the ones who had inhabited the long dark before the

coming of the Lord. But no preacher or Sunday school teacher ever said anything directly against Jewish people when I was around, except that we were oppressed, like the blood of Abraham.

When our parents talked about Jews, the topic was usually commerce. You might be able to go to Delancey Street and "Jew down" a shopkeeper, it was said, but you'd probably fail, because they're too smart with money. The Jew doesn't care about anybody but himself. The Jew keeps money and power inside the Jewish community. If you hire a Jewish accountant, he's going to recommend a Jewish lawyer. *Believe me.* Black people, our parents emphasized, need to learn how to stick together the way the Jews do.

This casual collection of attitudes hardened over time at school, where I encountered Jews every day. No matter how Jewish I felt, I could not completely ignore my difference. Lines between black people and Jews were partly hidden, but they were always there. I remember an outraged conversation about the Holocaust among some of the older children on the bus ride back to our side of town. One of the Jewish students had the nerve to argue that the Holocaust was far worse than slavery, and everyone agreed the kid was *arrogant*. From then on I used this word often—I began to record all events that proved it. There was the pity in the voices of otherwise lovely people when the subject of black America came up. There were the patronizing parents who wanted their daughter to date me because, "Why should it matter?" There was the outright racism of certain vicious classmates. In ninth grade, Scott W. told me in the library that I should be glad I'm not still in Africa—if it weren't for Europe I would still be chucking spears. Another classmate said that while black people were gifted at sports and music, Jews had provided the world with intellectual genius. As proof, he ticked off three names: Freud, Einstein, Marx. I got very angry.

For a long time I wondered whether the Jews were really chosen by God, as one of my Jewish classmates suggested. The argument seemed watertight. Wherever Jews were given the chance they have shown themselves to be smarter than anyone else. *Look at how well we've done in America and everywhere else we've gone. Look at the Jews. Look.*

This was reinforced by Riverdale's unofficial story: There exists a WASP-Jewish-black hierarchy, and it is the real ordering structure of the world. It explained our school, the paltry numbers of blacks, the predominance of Jewish students, the continuing dominance of WASP administrators. Everything we saw seemed natural. The blacks were an undiscussed underclass, the Jews were the electorate, the WASP's democracy's vanishing counsel. Each group seemed chosen for its role by nature and God.

But things shifted drastically when I went to college. On entering Yale I studied my Jewish peers, and kept a firm eye on the school's pretensions to Oxford and Cambridge, the way students were asked to call some administrators "Master," as if slavery never happened. Yale was, to say the least, a problematic institution for black students, a cold place that required all sorts of submission, but it was also difficult for Jewish students, and to a degree I hadn't expected.

What I saw challenged any belief I had in Jewish chosenness. For the first time in my life I found myself in a school where Jews were simply one smart group of many. There were also smart people who were blacks and had grown up like me in the rarefied precincts of middle-class whiteness. Black students from cities with high concentrations of Jewish people were familiar with Jewish anxieties about "old" wealth and other WASP virtues, and we also considered anti-Semitism to be a very bad thing. It is fair, however, to say that most of us felt a decidedly grudging admiration for Jewish people. My ideas about Jewish supremacy remained a mix of anger and belief until I witnessed so many of my Jewish classmates folding in the face of Yale's anti-Semitism. I guess I had never had the secret stake my Jewish high-school classmates had in admiring WASP's; seeing Jewish peers genuflect removed any illusions of Jewish chosenness.

Dan and I roomed together during our junior and senior years at Yale. We became close friends even though we competed a lot over grades and once over a woman's affections. We love each other like brothers. Our kinship is not simple. There is the difference in class: Dan is from Wisconsin and his mother is a judge, his father a geneticist; I am from the Bronx and my parents are social workers. While Dan is a serious cyclist and hiker, I am the sort who watches movies and reads. Also, differences lurk within our similarities. In high school, I was one of a very small number of black people at a school of Jews; Dan was a Jew among many Christians. I'm not a nationalist, cultural or otherwise, and Dan is not religious. But alienation has had radically different effects on our lives. While I find more to despise about America each day, Dan's outsider status hasn't affected his love of the country; he believes in this place. There are many divisions between us, and they are real. But so is our bond.

The summer after junior year Dan went to South Africa to monitor what the Government called trials. I remember him working on the application at my desk; I still have a print he gave me of black and white figures tearing down a great house of cards, "Rise and Destruction of Power." Dan took humanism to South Africa and brought me back a distant blackness, as he did when he gave me Miles Davis or Billie Holiday records to check out. There is a passage in John Edgar Wideman's *Brothers and Keepers* in which the author describes wanting to beat down a whiteboy for knowing more about the blues than he did. I understand his rage, but I hardly felt it. Mostly I loved learning about what I didn't know, sometimes covering up how much I was learning, sometimes questioning my friend's authority or authenticity, but always in the main feeling thankful. I believe it is the same mix of sensations Dan felt for me when I talked. I had, after all, grown up among a lot of Jewish people, and he hadn't; his parents had moved from New York to the Midwest. The references I brought from the city contained a curious and appealing atavism: I was a strange native informant reporting on his ancestral home, and he was a native alien of mine.

If Dan was "black" in any way, it was in precisely the same way that I was a "Jew." Our lives were shaped by cross-cultural consumption and the force of political sympathies, neither of which, in the end, necessarily makes you a real group member. Suburban Jewish guys who like black culture—it's a common enough phenomenon, I suppose, as were black kids in the old ghettos who grew up knowing a little Yiddish. Still, our ethnic "guest appearances" counted for something, since they did help make us who we were. Dan and I had chosen each other, after all, because we understood.

Last spring I went to visit Dan in Seattle, where he was clerking for a Federal judge. There was almost no news in that green and fragrant city about blacks and Jews and how we like to fight. It was only Dan and me and my thoughts and the smell of fruit blossoms wafting in through the open window.

I wondered how Dan came to be my brother. Brother. It means something else now. As with the word "immigrant," which in New York no longer means Jews or Italians so much as Dominicans and Haitians and Mexicans and Southeast Asians. Who is a "real" immigrant today, and who is an alien? Who deserves to become a member of the American tribe?

There is a line, a neoconservative "political correctness," on this question. Richard Cohen of *The Washington Post*, for example, had this to say about the boycotts of Asian grocers by blacks: "What a diversion all this picketing and boycotting is. And what a tragedy to boot. In New York, Washington and other cities, certain blacks talk about Asians as if they were involved in a conspiracy against them: Where do they get the money to buy these stores? Certain black leaders curse Asians or, just for good measure, Jews. They are constantly on the lookout for scapegoats. They have so thoroughly accepted the ethic of victimization that they blame others for a situation that they themselves can rectify: open some stores." I think the president of a Korean grocers' group was more to the point when he told a reporter, "We are no different than the Jews, Italians and other Europeans."

Family is made of the people family says are family. Folks like Cohen and the store owner are clearly trying to embrace each other, and leave Negroes outside. They say, *Look at those hard-working Jewish immigrants and sullen, menacing Negroes and remember: the story hasn't changed. Put Dominicans and Haitians and Mexicans here on the problem side, away, and let in the huddled Koreans and Eastern Europeans and (white) Cubans—the good ones. They are most like the "model" immigrants who came here early in the century. They deserve to be American. They should be family.*

It is as stupid a story as the Rev. Louis Farrakhan's foolishness about Jews, and certainly more dangerous. If family is made of the people family says are family, and if "family" and "immigrant" do not include people who are deemed problematic, collective responsibility for crime, segregated housing, the failure of public education—for all of which blacks are routinely blamed—just disappears. The paradigm is old and familiar.

Dan and I come from better traditions. Today, he is a death penalty defense lawyer. Once in a while, he and I get to talking about pooling our talents to elect him senator from Wisconsin or something. It would make sense: we want more people to get a better deal, especially the most despised, who are so often black.

Somehow along the way, Dan and I grew up and examined the stories we'd been told. Thus far, our research has helped usher Dan, the progressive Jew, and me, the progressive black, into the same camp.

But I don't mean to mislead you about my thinking. Politics and the other crossings of our heritages are only part of what Dan and I share. Our brotherhood is made of ethnic sympathies, but it also has nothing to do with our being black or Jewish or any of that, and I love Dan not because he's Jewish or, in some sense, black, and not because I am black or, in some sense, Jewish. While our tribes, and their memories, and their stories, did make us, they also have nothing to do with it. The heart, after all, is raised on a mess of stories, and then it writes its own.

10

Pigskin, Patriarchy, and Pain

Don Sabo

I am sitting down to write as I've done thousands of times over the last decade. But today there's something very different. I'm not in pain.

A half-year ago I underwent back surgery. My physician removed two disks from the lumbar region of my spine and fused three vertebrae using bone scrapings from my right hip. The surgery is called a "spinal fusion." For seventy-two hours I was completely immobilized. On the fifth day, I took a few faltering first steps with one of those aluminum walkers that are usually associated with the elderly in nursing homes. I progressed rapidly and left the hospital after nine days completely free of pain for the first time in years.

How did I, a well-intending and reasonably gentle boy from western Pennsylvania, ever get into so much pain? At a simple level, I ended up in pain because I played a sport that brutalizes men's (and now sometimes women's) bodies. *Why* I played football and bit the bullet of pain, however, is more complicated. Like a young child who learns to dance or sing for a piece of candy, I played for rewards and payoffs. Winning at sport meant winning friends and carving a place for myself within the male pecking order. Success at the "game" would make me less like myself and more like the older boys and my hero, Dick Butkus. Pictures of his hulking and snarling form filled my head and hung over my bed, beckoning me

From Michael A. Messner and Donald F. Sabo, eds., *Sex, Violence and Power in Sports: Rethinking Masculinity* (Freedom, CA: The Crossing Press). © 1994. Reprinted by permission.

forward like a mythic Siren. If I could be like Butkus, I told myself, people would adore me as much as I adored him. I might even adore myself. As an adolescent I hoped sport would get me attention from the girls. Later, I became more practical-minded and I worried more about my future. What kind of work would I do for a living? Football became my ticket to a college scholarship which, in western Pennsylvania during the early 'sixties, meant a career instead of getting stuck in the steelmills.

The Road to Surgery

My bout with pain and spinal "pathology" began with a decision I made in 1955 when I was 8 years old. I "went out" for football. At the time, I felt uncomfortable inside my body—too fat, too short, too weak. Freckles and glasses, too! I wanted to change my image, and I felt that changing my body was one place to begin. My parents bought me a set of weights, and one of the older boys in the neighborhood was solicited to demonstrate their use. I can still remember the ease with which he lifted the barbell, the veins popping through his bulging biceps in the summer sun, and the sated look of strength and accomplishment on his face. This was to be the image of my future.

That Fall I made a dinner-table announcement that I was going out for foot-ball. What followed was a rather inauspicious beginning. First, the initiation rites. Pricking the flesh with thorns until blood was drawn and having hot peppers rubbed in my eyes. Getting punched in the gut again and again. Being forced to wear a jockstrap around my nose and not knowing what was funny. Then came what was to be an endless series of proving myself: calisthenics until my arms ached; hitting hard and fast and knocking the other guy down; getting hit in the groin and not crying. I learned that pain and injury are "part of the game."

I "played" through grade school, co-captained my high school team, and went on to become an inside linebacker and defensive captain at the NCAA Division I level. I learned to be an animal. Coaches took notice of animals. Animals made first team. Being an animal meant being fanatically aggressive and ruthlessly com-petitive. If I saw an arm in front of me, I trampled it. Whenever blood was spilled, I nodded approval. Broken bones (not mine of course) were secretly seen as little victories within the bigger struggle. The coaches taught me to "punish the other man," but little did I suspect that I was devastating my own body at the same time. There were broken noses, ribs, fingers, toes and teeth, torn muscles and ligaments, bruises, bad knees, and busted lips, and the gradual pulverizing of my spinal col-umn that, by the time my jock career was long over at age 30, had resulted in seven years of near-constant pain. It was a long road to the surgeon's office.

Now surgically freed from its grip, my understanding of pain has changed. Pain had gnawed away at my insides. Pain turned my awareness inward. I blamed myself for my predicament; I thought that I was solely responsible for every twinge and sleepless night. But this view was an illusion. My pain, each individual's pain, is really an expression of a linkage to an outer world of people, events, and forces. The origins of our pain are rooted *outside*, not inside, our skins.

The Pain Principle

Sport is just one of the many areas in our culture where pain is more important than pleasure. Boys are taught that to endure pain is courageous, to survive pain is manly. The principle that pain is "good" and pleasure is "bad" is crudely evident in the "no pain, no gain" philosophy of so many coaches and athletes. The "pain principle" weaves its way into the lives and psyches of male athletes in two fundamental ways. It stifles men's awareness of their bodies and limits our emotional expression. We learn to ignore personal hurts and injuries because they interfere with the "efficiency" and "goals" of the "team." We become adept at taking the feelings that boil up inside us—feelings of insecurity and stress from striving so hard for success—and channeling them in a bundle of rage which is directed at opponents and enemies. This posture toward oneself and the world is not limited to "jocks." It is evident in the lives of many nonathletic men who, as tough guys, deny their authentic physical or emotional needs and develop health problems as a result.

Today, I no longer perceive myself as an *individual* ripped off by athletic injury. Rather, I see myself as just *one more man among many men* who got swallowed up by a social system predicated on male domination. Patriarchy has two structural aspects. First, it is an hierarchical system in which men dominate women in crude and debased, slick and subtle ways. Feminists have made great progress exposing and analyzing this dimension of the edifice of sexism. But it is also a system of *intermale dominance*, in which a minority of men dominates the masses of men. This intermale dominance hierarchy exploits the majority of those it beckons to climb its heights. Patriarchy's mythos of heroism and its morality of power-worship implant visions of ecstasy and masculine excellence in the minds of the boys who ultimately will defend its inequities and ridicule its victims. It is inside this institutional framework that I have begun to explore the essence and scope of "the pain principle."

Taking It

Patriarchy is a form of social hierarchy. Hierarchy breeds inequity and inequity breeds pain. To remain stable, the hierarchy must either justify the pain or explain it away. In a patriarchy, women and the masses of men are fed the cultural message that pain is inevitable and that pain enhances one's character and moral worth. This principle is expressed in Judeo-Christian beliefs. The Judeo-Christian god inflicts or permits pain, yet "the Father" is still revered and loved. Likewise, a chief disciplinarian in the patriarchal family, the father has the right to inflict pain.

The "pain principle" also echoes throughout traditional western sexual morality; it is better to experience the pain of *not* having sexual pleasure than it is to have sexual pleasure.

Most men learn to heed these cultural messages and take their "cues for survival" from the patriarchy. The Willie Lomans of the economy pander to the prophets of profit and the American Dream. Soldiers, young and old, salute their neo-Hun generals. Right-wing Christians genuflect before the idols of righteousness, affluence, and conformity. And male athletes adopt the visions and values that coaches are offering: to take orders, to take pain, to "take out" opponents, to take the game seriously, to take women, and to take their place on the team. And if they can't "take it," then the rewards of athletic camaraderie, prestige, scholarship, pro contracts, and community recognition are not forthcoming.

Becoming a football player fosters conformity to male-chauvinistic values and self-abusing lifestyles. It contributes to the legitimacy of a social structure based on patriarchal power. Male competition for prestige and status in sport and elsewhere leads to identification with the relatively few males who control resources and are able to bestow rewards and inflict punishment. Male supremacists are not born, they are made, and traditional athletic socialization is a fundamental contribution to this complex social-psychological and political process. Through sport, many males, indeed, learn to "take it"—that is, to internalize patriarchal values which, in turn, become part of their gender identity and conception of women and society.

My high school coach once evoked the pain principle during a pregame pep talk. For what seemed an eternity, he paced frenetically and silently before us with fists clenched and head bowed. He suddenly stopped and faced us with a smile. It was as though he had approached a podium to begin a long-awaited lecture. "Boys," he began, "people who say that football is a 'contact sport' are dead wrong. Dancing is a contact sport. Football is a game of pain and violence! Now get the hell out of here and kick some ass." We practically ran through the wall of the locker room, surging in unison to fight the coach's war. I see now that the coach was right but for all the wrong reasons. I should have taken him at his word and never played the game!

11

He Defies You Still:
The Memoirs of a Sissy

Tommi Avicolli

You're just a faggot
No history faces you this morning
A faggot's dreams are scarlet
Bad blood bled from words that scarred[1]

Scene One

A homeroom in a Catholic high school in South Philadelphia. The boy sits quietly in the first aisle, third desk, reading a book. He does not look up, not even for a moment. He is hoping no one will remember he is sitting there. He wishes he were invisible. The teacher is not yet in the classroom so the other boys are talking and laughing loudly.

Suddenly, a voice from beside him:

"Hey, you're a faggot, ain't you?"

The boy does not answer. He goes on reading his book, or rather pretending he is reading his book. It is impossible to actually read the book now.

"Hey, I'm talking to you!"

The boy still does not look up. He is so scared his heart is thumping madly; it feels like it is leaping out of his chest and into his throat. But he can't look up.

"Faggot, I'm talking to you!"

To look up is to meet the eyes of the tormentor.

Suddenly, a sharpened pencil point is thrust into the boy's arm. He jolts, shaking off the pencil, aware that there is blood seeping from the wound.

"What did you do that for?" he asks timidly.

"Cause I hate faggots," the other boy says, laughing. Some other boys begin to laugh, too. A symphony of laughter. The boy feels as if he's going to cry. But he must not cry. Must not cry. So he holds back the tears and tries to read the book again. He must read the book. Read the book.

From *Radical Teacher* 24: 4–5. Copyright © 1985 by Tommi Avicolli. Reprinted by permission of *Radical Teacher*, P.O. Box 383316, Cambridge, MA 02238.

When the teacher arrives a few minutes later, the class quiets down. The boy does not tell the teacher what has happened. He spits on the wound to clean it, dabbing it with a tissue until the bleeding stops. For weeks he fears some dreadful infection from the lead in the pencil point.

Scene Two

The boy is walking home from school. A group of boys (two, maybe three, he is not certain) grab him from behind, drag him into an alley and beat him up. When he gets home, he races up to his room, refusing dinner ("I don't feel well," he tells his mother through the locked door) and spends the night alone in the dark wishing he would die. . . .

These are not fictitious accounts—I *was* that boy. Having been branded a sissy by neighborhood children because I preferred jump rope to baseball and dolls to playing soldiers, I was often taunted with "hey sissy" or "hey faggot" or "yoo hoo honey" (in a mocking voice) when I left the house.

To avoid harassment, I spent many summers alone in my room. I went out on rainy days when the street was empty.

I came to like being alone. I didn't need anyone, I told myself over and over again. I was an island. Contact with others meant pain. Alone, I was protected. I began writing poems, then short stories. There was no reason to go outside anymore. I had a world of my own.

> *In the schoolyard today*
> *they'll single you out*
> *Their laughter will leave your ears ringing*
> *like the church bells*
> *which once awed you. . . .*[2]

School was one of the more painful experiences of my youth. The neighborhood bullies could be avoided. The taunts of the children living in those endless repetitive row houses could be evaded by staying in my room. But school was something I had to face day after day for some two hundred mornings a year.

I had few friends in school. I was a pariah. Some kids would talk to me, but few wanted to be known as my close friend. Afraid of labels. If I was a sissy, then he had to be a sissy, too. I was condemned to loneliness.

Fortunately, a new boy moved into our neighborhood and befriended me; he wasn't afraid of the labels. He protected me when the other guys threatened to beat me up. He walked me home from school; he broke through the terrible loneliness. We were in third or fourth grade at the time.

We spent a summer or two together. Then his parents sent him to camp and I was once again confined to my room.

Scene Three

High school lunchroom. The boy sits at a table near the back of the room. Without warning, his lunch bag is grabbed and tossed to another table. Someone opens it and confiscates a package of Tastykakes; another boy takes the sandwich. The empty bag is tossed back to the boy who stares at it, dumbfounded. He should be used to this; it has happened before.

Someone screams, "faggot," laughing. There is always laughter. It does not annoy him anymore.

There is no teacher nearby. There is never a teacher around. And what would he say if there were? Could he report the crime? He would be jumped after school if he did. Besides, it would be his word against theirs. Teachers never noticed anything. They never heard the taunts. Never heard the word, "faggot." They were the great deaf mutes, pillars of indifference; a sissy's pain was not relevant to history and geography and god made me to love honor and obey him, amen.

Scene Four

High school Religion class. Someone has a copy of *Playboy*. Father N. is not in the room yet; he's late, as usual. Someone taps the boy roughly on the shoulder. He turns. A finger points to the centerfold model, pink fleshy body, thin and sleek. Almost painted. Not real. The other asks, mocking voice, "Hey, does she turn you on? Look at those tits!"

The boy smiles, nodding meekly; turns away.

The other jabs him harder on the shoulder, "Hey, whatsamatter, don't you like girls?"

Laughter. Thousands of mouths; unbearable din of laughter. In the Arena: thumbs down. Don't spare the queer.

"Wanna suck my dick? Huh? That turn you on, faggot!"

The laughter seems to go on forever. . . .

Behind you, the sound of their laughter
echoes a million times
in a soundless place
They watch how you walk/sit/stand/breathe. . . .[3]

What did being a sissy really mean? It was a way of walking (from the hips rather than the shoulders); it was a way of talking (often with a lisp or in a high-pitched voice); it was a way of relating to others (gently, not wanting to fight, or hurt anyone's feelings). It was being intelligent ("an egghead" they called it sometimes); getting good grades. It meant not being interested in sports, not playing football in the street after school; not discussing teams and scores and playoffs. And it involved not showing fervent interest in girls, not talking about scoring with tits or *Playboy* centerfolds. Not concealing naked women in your history book; or porno books in your locker.

On the other hand, anyone could be a "faggot." It was a catch-all. If you did something that didn't conform to what was the acceptable behavior of the group, then you risked being called a faggot. If you didn't get along with the "in" crowd, you were a faggot. It was the most commonly used put-down. It kept guys in line. They became angry when somebody called them a faggot. More fights started over someone calling someone else a faggot than anything else. The word had power. It toppled the male ego, shattered his delicate facade, violated the image he projected. He was tough. Without feeling. Faggot cut through all this. It made him vulnerable. Feminine. And feminine was the worst thing he could possibly be. Girls were fine for fucking, but no boy in his right mind wanted to be like them. A boy was the opposite of girl. He was not feminine. He was not feeling. He was not weak.

Just look at the gym teacher who growled like a dog; or the priest with the black belt who threw kids against the wall in rage when they didn't know their Latin. They were men, they got respect.

But not the physics teacher who preached pacifism during lectures on the nature of atoms. Everybody knew what he was—and why he believed in the anti-war movement.

My parents only knew that the neighborhood kids called me names. They begged me to act more like the other boys. My brothers were ashamed of me. They never said it, but I knew. Just as I knew that my parents were embarrassed by my behavior.

At times, they tried to get me to act differently. Once my father lectured me on how to walk right. I'm still not clear on what that means. Not from the hips, I guess, don't "swish" like faggots do.

A nun in elementary school told my mother at Open House that there was "something wrong with me." I had draped my sweater over my shoulders like a girl, she said. I was a smart kid, but I should know better than to wear my sweater like a girl!

My mother stood there, mute. I wanted her to say something, to chastise the nun; to defend me. But how could she? This was a nun talking—representative of Jesus, protector of all that was good and decent.

An uncle once told me I should start "acting like a boy" instead of like a girl. Everybody seemed ashamed of me. And I guess I was ashamed of myself, too. It was hard not to be.

Scene Five

Priest: Do you like girls, Mark?
Mark: Uh-huh.

Priest: I mean *really* like them?

Mark: Yeah—they're okay.

Priest: There's a role they play in your salvation. Do you understand it, Mark?

Mark: Yeah.

Priest: You've got to like girls. Even if you should decide to enter the seminary, it's important to keep in mind God's plan for a man and a woman. . . .[4]

Catholicism of course condemned homosexuality. Effeminacy was tolerated as long as the effeminate person did not admit to being gay. Thus, priests could be effeminate because they weren't gay.

As a sissy, I could count on no support from the church. A male's sole purpose in life was to father children—souls for the church to save. The only hope a homosexual had of attaining salvation was by remaining totally celibate. Don't even think of touching another boy. To think of a sin was a sin. And to sin was to put a mark upon the soul. Sin—if it was a serious offense against god—led to hell. There was no way around it. If you sinned, you were doomed.

Realizing I was gay was not an easy task. Although I knew I was attracted to boys by the time I was about eleven, I didn't connect this attraction to homosexuality. I was not queer. Not I. I was merely appreciating a boy's good looks, his fine features, his proportions. It didn't seem to matter that I didn't appreciate a girl's looks in the same way. There was no twitching in my thighs when I gazed upon a beautiful girl. But I wasn't queer.

I resisted that label—queer—for the longest time. Even when everything pointed to it, I refused to see it. I was certainly not queer. Not I.

We sat through endless English classes, and History courses about the wars between men who were not allowed to love each other. No gay history was ever taught. No history faces you this morning. You're just a faggot. Homosexuals had never contributed to the human race. God destroyed the queers in Sodom and Gomorrah.

We learned about Michelangelo, Oscar Wilde, Gertrude Stein—but never that they were queer. They were not queer. Walt Whitman, the "father of American poetry," was not queer. No one was queer. I was alone, totally unique. One of a kind. Were there others like me somewhere? Another planet, perhaps?

In school, they never talked of the queers. They did not exist. The only hint we got of this other species was in religion class. And even then it was clouded in mystery—never spelled out. It was sin. Like masturbation. Like looking at *Playboy* and getting a hard-on. A sin.

Once a progressive priest in senior year religion class actually mentioned homosexuals—he said the word—but was into Erich Fromm, into homosexuals as pathetic and sick. Fixated at some early stage; penis, anal, whatever. Only heterosexuals passed on to the nirvana of sexual development.

No other images from the halls of the Catholic high school except those the other boys knew: swishy faggot sucking cock in an alley somewhere, grabbing asses in the bathroom. Never mentioning how much straight boys craved blowjobs, it was part of the secret.

It was all a secret. You were not supposed to talk about the queers. Whisper maybe. Laugh about them, yes. But don't be open, honest; don't try to understand. Don't cite their accomplishments. No history faces you this morning. You're just a faggot   faggot   no history   just a faggot

Epilogue

The boy marching down the Parkway. Hundreds of queers. Signs proclaiming gay pride. Speakers. Tables with literature from gay groups. A miracle, he is thinking. Tears are coming loose now. Someone hugs him.

> *You could not control*
> *the sissy in me*
> *nor could you exorcise him*
> *nor electrocute him*
> *You declared him illegal illegitimate*
> *insane and immature*
> *But he defies you still.*[5]

NOTES

1. From the poem "Faggot" by Tommi Avicolli, published in *GPU News*, September 1979.

2. Ibid.

3. Ibid.

4. From the play *Judgment of the Roaches* by Tommi Avicolli, produced in Philadelphia at the Gay Community Center, the Painted Bride Arts Center and the University of Pennsylvania; aired over WXPN-FM, in four parts; and presented at the Lesbian/Gay Conference in Norfolk, VA, July 1980.

5. From the poem "Sissy Poem," published in *Magic Doesn't Live Here Anymore* (Philadelphia: Spruce Street Press, 1976).

12

With No Immediate Cause

Ntozake Shange

every 3 minutes a woman is beaten
every five minutes a
woman is raped/every ten minutes
a lil girl is molested
yet i rode the subway today
i sat next to an old man who
may have beaten his old wife
3 minutes ago or 3 days/30 years ago
he might have sodomized his
daughter but i sat there
cuz the young men on the train
might beat some young women
later in the day or tomorrow
i might not shut my door fast
enuf/push hard enuf
every 3 minutes it happens
some woman's innocence
rushes to her cheeks/pours from her mouth
like the betsy wetsy dolls have been torn
apart/their mouths
menses red & split/every
three minutes a shoulder
is jammed through plaster and the oven door/
chairs push thru the rib cage/hot water or
boiling sperm decorate her body
i rode the subway today
& bought a paper from a
man who might
have held his old lady onto
a hot pressing iron/i dont know
maybe he catches lil girls in the
park & rips open their behinds

with steel rods/i can't decide
what he might have done i only
know every 3 minutes
every 5 minutes every 10 minutes/so
i bought the paper
looking for the announcement
the discovery/of the dismembered
woman's body/the
victims have not all been
identified/today they are
naked and dead/refuse to
testify/one girl out of 10's not
coherent/i took the coffee
& spit it up/i found an
announcement/not the woman's
bloated body in the river/floating
not the child bleeding in the
59th street corridor/not the baby
broken on the floor/

> "there is some concern
> that alleged battered women
> might start to murder their
> husbands & lovers with no
> immediate cause"

i spit up i vomit i am screaming
we all have immediate cause
every 3 minutes
every 5 minutes
every 10 minutes
every day
women's bodies are found
in alleys & bedrooms/at the top of the stairs
before i ride the subway/buy a paper/drink
coffee/i must know/
have you hurt a woman today
did you beat a woman today
throw a child across a room
> are the lil girl's panties
> in yr pocket
did you hurt a woman today

i have to ask these obscene questions
the authorities require me to
establish
immediate cause

13

Requiem for the Champ

June Jordan

Mike Tyson comes from Brooklyn. And so do I. Where he grew up was about a twenty-minute bus ride from my house. I always thought his neighborhood looked like a war zone. It reminded me of Berlin—immediately after World War II. I had never seen Berlin except for black-and-white photos in *Life* magazine, but that was bad enough: Rubble. Barren. Blasted. Everywhere you turned your eyes recoiled from the jagged edges of an office building or a cathedral, shattered, or the tops of apartment houses torn off, and nothing alive even intimated, anywhere. I used to think, "This is what it means to fight and really win or really lose. War means you hurt somebody, or something, until there's nothing soft or sensible left."

For sure I never had a boyfriend who came out of Mike Tyson's territory. Yes, I enjoyed my share of tough guys and/or gang members who walked and talked and fought and loved in quintessential Brooklyn ways: cool, tough, and deadly serious. But there was a code as rigid and as romantic as anything that ever made the pages of traditional English literature. A guy would beat up another guy or, if appropriate, he'd kill him. But a guy talked different to a girl. A guy made other guys clean up their language around "his girl." A guy brought ribbons and candies and earrings and tulips to a girl. He took care of her. He walked her home. And if he got serious about that girl, and even if she was only twelve years old, then she became his "lady." And woe betide any other guy stupid enough to disrespect that particular young Black female.

But none of the boys—none of the young men—none of the young Black male inhabitants of my universe and my heart ever came from Mike Tyson's streets or avenues. We didn't live someplace fancy or middle-class, but at least there were ten-cent gardens, front and back, and coin Laundromats, and grocery stores, and soda parlors, and barber shops, and Holy Roller churchfronts, and chicken shacks, and dry cleaners, and bars-and-grills, and a takeout Chinese restaurant, and all of that usable detail that does not survive a war. That kind of seasonal green turf and daily-life supporting pattern of establishments to meet your needs did not exist inside the gelid urban cemetery where Mike Tyson learned what he thought he needed to know.

I remember when the City of New York decided to construct a senior housing project there, in the childhood world of former heavyweight boxing champion Mike Tyson. I remember wondering, "Where in the hell will those old people have to go in order to find food? And how will they get there?"

I'm talking godforsaken. And much of living in Brooklyn was like that. But then it might rain or it might snow and, for example, I could look at the rain forcing forsythia into bloom or watch how snowflakes can tease bare tree limbs into temporary blossoms of snow dissolving into diadems of sunlight. And what did Mike Tyson ever see besides brick walls and garbage in the gutter and disintegrating concrete steps and boarded-up windows and broken car parts blocking the sidewalk and men, bitter, with their hands in their pockets, and women, bitter, with their heads down and their eyes almost closed?

In his neighborhood, where could you buy ribbons for a girl, or tulips?

Mike Tyson comes from Brooklyn. And so do I. In the big picture of America, I never had much going for me. And he had less. I only learned, last year, that I can stop whatever violence starts with me. I only learned, last year, that love is infinitely more interesting, and more exciting, and more powerful, than really winning or really losing a fight. I only learned, last year, that all war leads to death and that all love leads you away from death. I am more than twice Mike Tyson's age. And I'm not stupid. Or slow. But I'm Black. And I come from Brooklyn. And I grew up fighting. And I grew up and I got out of Brooklyn because I got pretty good at fighting. And winning. Or else, intimidating my would-be adversaries with my fists, my feet, and my mouth. And I never wanted to fight. I never wanted anybody to hit me. And I never wanted to hit anybody. But the bell would ring at the end of another dumb day in school and I'd head out with dread and a nervous sweat because I knew some jackass more or less my age and more or less my height would be waiting for me because she or he had nothing better to do than to wait for me and hope to kick my butt or tear up my books or break my pencils or pull hair out of my head.

This is the meaning of poverty: when you have nothing better to do than to hate somebody who, just exactly like yourself, has nothing better to do than to pick on you instead of trying to figure out how come there's nothing better to do. How come there's no gym/no swimming pool/no dirt track/no soccer field/no ice-skating rink/ no bike/no bike path/no tennis courts/no language arts workshop/no computer science center/no band practice/no choir rehearsal/no music lessons/no basketball or baseball team? How come neither one of you has his or her own room in a house where you can hang out and dance and make out or get on the telephone or eat and drink up everything in the kitchen that can move? How come nobody on your block and nobody in your class has any of these things?

I'm Black. Mike Tyson is Black. And neither one of us was ever supposed to win anything more than a fight between the two of us. And if you check out the mass-media material on "us," and if you check out the emergency-room reports on "us," you might well believe we're losing the fight to be more than our enemies have decreed. Our enemies would deprive us of everything except each other: hungry and furious and drug-addicted and rejected and ever convinced we can never be beautiful or right or true or different from the beggarly monsters our enemies envision and insist upon, and how should we then stand, Black man and Black woman, face to face?

Way back when I was born, Richard Wright had just published *Native Son* and, thereby, introduced white America to the monstrous produce of its racist hatred.

Poverty does not beautify. Poverty does not teach generosity or allow for sucker attributes of tenderness and restraint. In white America, hatred of Blackfolks has imposed horrible poverty upon us.

And so, back in the thirties, Richard Wright's Native Son, Bigger Thomas, did what he thought he had to do: he hideously murdered a white woman and he viciously murdered his Black girlfriend in what he conceived as self-defense. He did not perceive any options to these psychopathic, horrifying deeds. I do not believe he, Bigger Thomas, had any other choices open to him. Not to him, he who was meant to die like the rat he, Bigger Thomas, cornered and smashed to death in his mother's beggarly clean space.

I never thought Bigger Thomas was okay. I never thought he should skate back into my, or anyone's, community. But I did and I do think he is my brother. The choices available to us dehumanize. And any single one of us, Black in this white country, we may be defeated, we may become dehumanized, by the monstrous hatred arrayed against us and our needy dreams.

And so I write this requiem for Mike Tyson: international celebrity, millionaire, former heavyweight boxing champion of the world, a big-time winner, a big-time loser, an African-American male in his twenties, and, now, a convicted rapist.

Do I believe he is guilty of rape?

Yes I do.

And what would I propose as appropriate punishment?

Whatever will force him to fear the justice of exact retribution, and whatever will force him, for the rest of his damned life, to regret and to detest the fact that he defiled, he subjugated, and he wounded somebody helpless to his power.

And do I therefore rejoice in the jury's finding?

I do not.

Well, would I like to see Mike Tyson a free man again?

He was never free!

And I do not excuse or condone or forget or minimize or forgive the crime of his violation of the young Black woman he raped!

But did anybody ever tell Mike Tyson that you talk different to a girl? Where would he learn that? Would he learn that from U.S. Senator Ted Kennedy? Or from hotshot/scot-free movie director Roman Polanski? Or from rap recording star Ice Cube? Or from Ronald Reagan and the Grenada escapade? Or from George

Bush in Panama? Or from George Bush and Colin Powell in the Persian Gulf? Or from the military hero flyboys who returned from bombing the shit out of civilian cities in Iraq and then said, laughing and proud, on international TV: "All I need, now, is a woman"? Or from the hundreds of thousands of American football fans? Or from the millions of Americans who would, if they could, pay surrealistic amounts of money just to witness, up close, somebody like Mike Tyson beat the brains out of somebody?

And what could which university teach Mike Tyson about the difference between violence and love? Is there any citadel of higher education in the country that does not pay its football coach at least three times as much as the chancellor and six times as much as its professors and ten times as much as its social and psychological counselors?

In this America where Mike Tyson and I live together and bitterly, bitterly, apart, I say he became what he felt. He felt the stigma of a priori hatred and intentional poverty. He was given the choice of violence or violence: the violence of defeat or the violence of victory. Who would pay him to rehabilitate innercity housing or to refurbish a bridge? Who would pay him what to study the facts of our collective history? Who would pay him what to plant and nurture the trees of a forest? And who will write and who will play the songs that tell a guy like Mike Tyson how to talk to a girl?

What was America willing to love about Mike Tyson? Or any Black man? Or any man's man?

Tyson's neighborhood and my own have become the same no-win battleground. And he has fallen there. And I do not rejoice. I do not.

14

Out of the Closet, but Not Out of Middle School

Libby Copeland

On the last day of seventh grade, Dave Grossman mounted some cardboard boxes down the street from his junior high school and held a one-boy rally.

I'm sick of pretending, he announced into a cheap loudspeaker.

From *The Washington Post*, June 29, 1999.

I'm gay.

The affair was a bit botched. Dave's principal, fearing a "disruption," asked him to move his makeshift stage and rainbow flags away from school grounds. The event caused barely an eye-roll from his peers, who scattered from school eager to inaugurate summer.

Still, there was Dave with his loudspeaker and his conviction. Like a soap opera character haunted by a secret past, he had been living two lives. In school, he was a straight kid with straight A's. After classes, he rode the Metro downtown and hung with gay friends past dinner time. He says few people could believe that at 13, he was so certain he was gay.

Two years later, Dave puts it like this: "It was a lot of built-up frustration over everyone saying, 'You're too young, you're too young, you're too young.'"

In the national debate about gay and bisexual identity, age is a volatile fault line along which schools are being forced to pick sides. Gay-youth advocacy groups say the average age of kids who "come out" has decreased substantially in recent years. Whereas once a teenager might have come out in senior year with a burn-your-bridges disinhibition, now that same teenager is making his homosexuality public in middle school or ninth grade.

Puberty is a roulette wheel of biding time and spurting growth. One preteen is sexually active while her classmate is still collecting stickers. American girls are hitting puberty far earlier than they were a century ago, and there's growing awareness of a disconnection between physical and mental maturity. Add the perennial dilemmas of sex education—how much kids should learn, how soon, from whom—and you have a recipe for controversy.

What happens when a middle school student—in braces, in a training bra, inexperienced—announces that she's gay?

It's happening. Ritch Savin-Williams, a developmental psychologist at Cornell University, used data from nine independent studies conducted over the last 20 years to conclude that the average age at which young men label their same-sex attractions as gay dropped from almost 20 in 1979 to just 13 in 1998. They may not, however, definitively call themselves gay until a few years later.

"Every time we sample these kids, the average age is getting younger," says Savin-Williams. "What's different is that now gay kids are becoming like straight kids—they know that they're gay before they have sex."

At Longfellow Middle School in Falls Church, Dave Grossman forced the issue that advocacy groups, educators and mental health providers have been debating for several years: Should the nation's struggle over sex and morality play out inside schools, involving kids in a debate that can be loudspeaker loud? Or should such issues be fought at the ballot box, from church pulpits and at home?

Longfellow's principal, Gail Womble, respected Dave's desire to come out, if not his venue. In the end, she was relieved that Dave said his piece without causing an uproar.

"I did have concerns about how middle school students would meet that kind of disclosure," says Womble, who has since moved to Rachel Carson Middle

School in Fairfax. "At this age, we have kids who are old enough to be exploring those feelings and other kids who are still playing with Barbie dolls."

Dave's mother was disgusted by what she felt were "outrageous" banishing dictums imposed on her son, like making Dave move his stage across the street. Donna Brown Grossman says Womble also asked Dave to cover a T-shirt reading "Nobody Knows I'm Gay," and would not let him pass out homemade pamphlets promoting his rally.

"Her reaction was one thing that made me feel that I had to take my child out of the public school system," says Grossman, 48, who subsequently transferred her son to Thornton Friends, a private Quaker school. As school systems debate whether to allow gay support groups, or pass anti-harassment policies on behalf of gays, or show their faculty the controversial documentary "It's Elementary: Talking About Gay Issues in School," proponents on both sides point to the tender age of the youngsters as evidence of the rectitude of their positions.

Gay-rights advocacy groups and much of the mental health community cite 12-year-old gay youngsters as proof that being homosexual is "natural." Christian conservative groups argue that young adolescents bombarded by hormones and pop images of sexuality are especially susceptible to gay "recruiting."

"Those kids are incredibly impressionable, and I think certainly the younger the age, the more they can be swayed," says Peter LaBarbera, editor of the Lambda Report on Homosexuality, which argues that the declining age at which youngsters are coming out is largely the product of gay propaganda inside schools.

"There's different gradations. Love, sexuality: It's a very tangled web."

This is Ellen Sweeney, 18, an assured young woman who was co-leader of the gay discussion group at Sidwell Friends, a private school in Northwest Washington, during this, her senior year. She began to question her own sexuality in seventh grade, joined the discussion group in high school, and recently, has taught workshops to middle school students on gay issues. Incidentally, Sweeney is straight. But, she says, "I question myself up until this day."

This open attitude toward sexuality is a splinter in the skin of many who oppose gay discussion groups. They ask, what if youngsters who would otherwise be straight are encouraged to question, and ultimately, to declare themselves gay?

In the last few years in the Washington area, at least 15 gay discussion groups have cropped up in high schools and one middle school. The majority of the groups are in Montgomery County, where, amid a storm of controversy three years ago, the school board added gay students and teachers to the list of people protected from discrimination. The groups, which range from sanctioned clubs to informal lunch gatherings, serve as sounding boards—to examine homophobia, for example, or the feelings of a member who says she has been "questioning."

The problem with such discussions, opponents say, is that they don't offer an alternative to open-armed acceptance of homosexuality. Janet Folger, national director of the Center for Reclaiming America, an arm of Coral Ridge Ministries, says if gay issues must be part of the school climate, youngsters should at least be exposed to "ex-gays" and told of the health risks of homosexuality.

As things stand, "there is no balance," Folger says. "There is no message of hope . . . that you can walk away from it."

Like many area private schools, Edmund Burke School in the District doesn't see it that way. When a gay-issues discussion group was created there this year, middle school students were included in the weekly lunch meetings. Hugh Taft-Morales, the group's faculty adviser, said the group has "no agenda."

"They are already talking about this," he says. "What we're doing is taking responsibility as adults to raise the level of the discussion."

Although no exhaustive data can be found on discussion groups in schools, the New York-based Gay, Lesbian and Straight Educational Network keeps tabs on clubs that register with it. Its national list has blossomed from roughly 150 high school "Gay/Straight Alliances" last year to about 400 this year, concentrated mainly in Massachusetts, California and the New York City area. In Maryland and Virginia, there are seven registered high school alliances.

"Some people feel it's not our job," says Pamela Latt, principal of Centreville High School, which is on track to become the third high school in Virginia with a registered gay/straight alliance. Centreville has had a gay counseling group for two years, but a few students have been pushing for more.

"Having a counseling group sort of sends the wrong message," says Caroline Zuscheck, 17, a straight student involved in the effort. "It's like if you have an eating disorder or a problem with depression."

But although the principal supports starting an alliance next year, she also has reservations. On one hand, she says, it will contribute to a healthier environment for gay teenagers, a high-risk group. But Latt knows she is treading on important toes in conservative Centreville, where some School Board and community members have already voiced discomfort with a school-sanctioned club. "I don't blame people for being very cautious and careful," she says.

Latt is conflicted for other reasons. She is Catholic and has puzzled over whether homosexuality is wrong (she doesn't think so) and what causes it (she doesn't know). At any rate, she says, the alliance is about "saving lives," not promoting homosexuality. But perhaps in an ideal world, this messy moral stew wouldn't fall into the principal's lap.

"This really shouldn't be a part of my job," Latt says finally. "But I don't think I have a choice."

Amy Levy and her son remember the moment differently. The way Will tells it, his mom was nagging him, Why don't you have a girlfriend? The way Levy tells it, Will's confession came straight out of the clear blue sky.

Never mind why. That moment changed everything. One minute, the mother is dropping her son off in the car. The next, he tells her, "I'm gay," and hops out.

He is 14.

For Levy, 50, that belly-flop into reality challenged a lot of rules. Will was the first openly gay student at his tiny Bethesda private school, which has no specific policies on the issue. In an attempt to carve a comfortable space for himself, Will, now 16, met with teachers. Levy met with teachers. Teachers met with other teachers.

Levy says Will's coming out made them all dissect their feelings about homosexuality. "Do you really believe in what you thought you believed in when it becomes part of your life?" she wonders. (To protect her son, Levy asked that Will's last name, which is different from hers, not be published.)

Gay-rights advocates say this type of discussion is a door slowly creaking open, a departure from past decades when an unofficial "don't ask, don't tell" policy reigned in high schools and middle schools.

At a recent meeting for gay Montgomery County youths, two adults leading the session reminisced about how different it once was: one man, one woman, both in their forties or fifties, both of whom married at 23, both of whom divorced, both of whom realized only in adulthood that they were, in fact, gay.

They listened to the teenagers and then ticked off each belated milestone in their own closeted lives, as if to say, All those years lost.

Dave Grossman is a slight, blue-eyed youth with an energy and intelligence that sometimes gets the better of him. He skipped eighth grade, and, after ninth, went to Simon's Rock, a college in Great Barrington, Mass., designed for kids of high school age. Now he's transferring to American University, entering his second year of college at 15.

While he was growing up, Dave says, instinct told him he liked other boys. He just knew, natural as corn. In fourth grade, he says, "I came to my senses. I was just staring benignly at the boy across from me."

At 11, Dave found online chat rooms and located the gay bulletin board in short order.

At 12, he told his parents, because there was no reason not to, because now he knew for sure, and the knowledge pressed in on him. It was after synagogue on a late summer night. The date sticks in his mind—August 30, 1996. He recalls his mother crying with the shock and the strangeness. "She was like, 'Wow, I didn't even know you had a sexuality.'"

And Dave started his journey, because he saw himself as a young man with a sexuality and an image to build, and he shed his baby fat, his glasses and his gawky hair and hatched a plan to let people know that he had found himself. A stage, a loudspeaker, a grand announcement.

"I was going to do something," he says. "Something that was extravagant."

A showdown of sorts—even if there were few people around to watch. A showdown, at the very least, with the person who mattered.

15

More and More Young Women Choose Surgical "Perfection"

Ann Gerhart

This is what people see when they look at Lucie Lukesova: A classic Eastern European beauty, ample and soft, with flawless skin, naturally rosy cheeks and sparkling blue eyes.

This is what Lukesova sees when she looks at herself: Fat chin. Big belly. Padded hips.

So a few weeks ago, she had liposuction. She describes it as one of the happiest days of her life. The 3½-hour surgery corrected what she perceived as flaws. Whether it corrected her self-image remains to be seen.

Lukesova is 19.

Teenagers and young women are going under the knife in record numbers, and they're not just getting nose jobs anymore. Last year, cosmetic surgeons performed some 25,000 elective procedures on teens, according to national figures from the American Society of Plastic and Reconstructive Surgeons—a nearly 100 percent increase over 1992. They put breast implants in nearly 2,000 girls. They sucked the fat out of 1,645.

In the Washington area, home to nearly 100 plastic surgeons, a mini tummy tuck and a new chest are just the thing to wear down the graduation aisle under the cap and gown, at least in a certain set. For some cosseted children of perfection-seeking boomers, a Cross pen doesn't pass muster anymore.

Roger Friedman, the head of plastic surgery at Suburban Hospital in Bethesda, did a breast augmentation on an 18-year-old last month.

"She was 5-foot-9 and 125 pounds, and she had breasts like a man," he says. "She was graduating and wanted this done in time for the next step."

And he had done her mother's implants, 10 years ago.

At Suburban Hospital, which has a hefty 46 plastic surgeons on staff, a 19-year-old gets a breast reduction and throws in some abdominal liposuction for good measure; a 14-year-old gets a chin implant; a dozen twentysomethings opt for bigger breasts, all in a week.

Originally published as "Nipped in the Bud: More and More Young Women Choose Surgical 'Perfection.'" From *The Washington Post*, June 23, 1999.

In Gaithersburg, Gregory Dick sees about four teenagers each month on the prowl for liposuction or breast augmentation; that's a fourfold increase over eight years ago. He sends nearly half of those away.

"The trouble with adolescent surgery is it's a tricky business," Dick says. "Many times the teenager doesn't know what he or she wants and is responding to peer or media pressure." Several surgeons said they are reluctant to make permanent alterations during the transitional teenage years. "Teenagers' images change as fast as their body," says Mark Mausner, a Chevy Chase surgeon who does about 400 procedures a year. "One day, the dress looks terrific, and the next day, it isn't fitting right."

One 22-year-old Columbia woman says she has been yearning for liposuction for some years. "I have always had a weight problem," she says. Always means ever since she was 13 or 14. "Even when I had lost some weight, there was this one stubborn area where it wouldn't go away," on her stomach and hips, she says. A recent college graduate waiting to hear about her medical school applications, she took $5,000 of her savings and just spent it on a mini tummy tuck and liposuction.

That was her graduation gift to herself. She is five feet tall and weighs about 125 pounds.

Now why wouldn't the nation's capital be a hotbed of plastic, elastic surgical activity? It is a center of image-making. And its affluent, educated, savvy adolescents are keenly aware that their driven, ambitious parents are prodding, shaping, bobbing and tweezing the visuals on themselves.

"In New York, you go to a cocktail party and they'll tell you where they had surgery. In L.A., you go to a party and they'll show you where they had surgery," says Mausner. "In Washington, nobody talks, but everybody has surgery." Add to that all of the following: an obsessive quest for perfection; a fusillade of slender but busty advertising images; a parade of celebrities with cosmetic enhancements in full jiggle, including the 17-year-old pop sensation Britney Spears, now appearing on MTV with her new, improved breasts; cheaper, safer procedures marketed aggressively.

And, in a weird and paradoxical way, feminism itself shares the blame: If a girl can be anything she wants to be—a Citadel rat, a Web millionaire, a professional basketball player—then why can't she carve out a different body for herself? Body Addition and Subtraction At Six Flags America in Largo, a trio of 13-year-olds, taut and already tan in their bathing suits, wait in line for pizza and discuss what offending body lump they will remove first, when they get their liposuction. "I'm fine with my nose. I wouldn't pay the money for the nose. I'm going first for this," says one girl, and she reaches up and grabs the skin where her shoulder meets her back. There is no fat there.

The Big Adult Voice has been sounding the alarm for some years over girls and their poor body image, but eating disorders and depression continue to rise. The increase in elective aesthetic surgery among the young is but the latest manifestation, an extreme and quick fix helped along by a booming economy and overindulgent parents.

Dismay over body image starts for girls even before puberty. Some 40 percent of 9-year-old girls told researchers they feared getting fat; 81 percent of 10-year-olds said the same thing. "All the self-consciousness with body image has filtered down to the very young. I hear a greater preoccupation every year, and most of it is focused on weight," says Rita Freedman, a New York psychologist and author. Young girls and older teens are "convinced that unless they approximate whatever image is touted in the media, they will have no chance of being socially successful."

And the prized female form in fashion ads remains rail-thin, without womanly hips and rump. In the rest of the popular culture, it's skinny while nearly toppling from big breasts. "You are a victim of this crazy ideal body image that is impossible to achieve unless you create it yourself," says L. Kris Gowen, a psychologist and former researcher at the Stanford University Center on Adolescence. "And it's fake. Hey, breasts are fat. To have very large breasts and a skinny body is really counter to the norm." It's the big and glossy norm in the magazine plastic surgery ads, however.

"I don't know anybody who is satisfied with the body," says Lukesova. "I want to add a piece here, cut a piece there." "I find it very hard to find a woman who is happy with her breasts. They are too big, too small, too saggy," says Susan Otero, a reconstructive breast surgeon at Washington Hospital Center. "Everybody has something about them."

The earlier onset of this dissatisfaction, researchers suggest, is because our culture is drenched in visuals.

"We are in a period in time when the myth-making has increased tremendously because of the amount of imagery in our lives," says Freedman, "computers, videos." Children are photographed ceaselessly, almost from the moment of conception. First come the ultrasounds, then the preschool graduations, followed by those pesky professional photographers lurking around the Little League games. At the same time, the marketing to kids is ever more specific. "There is such a commercialization of their bodies—what they should eat, what they should buy, what they should wear," says Freedman. "There is a lot of money to be made by persuading 15-year-olds that their lip color should be blue instead of red."

Sex fogs up this picture most of all. Teenagers and even young women are not old enough to make permanent decisions about changing their bodies through liposuction or breast surgery, the psychologists argue, because their sexual identity is still in flux. The surgeons say they tend to agree, but some among them are wielding the scalpels and pushing up the statistics.

"The breast carries tremendous psychological overlays," says Mausner, whose clients are "everyone, from secretaries to maids to the people you see on television." Sexy is healthy, but "what is considered looking healthy? Being tan and having big breasts. It's ridiculous." Teenagers and women in their early twenties, he says, rarely understand their developing sexuality.

Otero notices that, as a female surgeon who does mostly reconstructive work after mastectomies, "my views of women's breasts are very much different." She's learned with experience that her own aesthetic sense of "what looks natural and pretty" doesn't jibe with her clients who often want the "Playboy breast, with the nipples looking up into the air." She smiles a little, then allows: "It's hard to be a feminist and do breast surgery."

Despite physicians' reluctance to put breast implants in teenagers, the American Society for Aesthetic Plastic Surgery has guidelines on teen surgery that are timidly encouraging. "When one breast significantly differs from the other in terms of either size or shape, surgery can help girls as young as 16," one of the guidelines suggests. And breast reductions are widely accepted as appropriate for girls of 16—and even covered by insurance—even though many times the surgeon must remove and reset the nipples, damaging nerve endings and milk ducts in the process.

The woman from Columbia has a newly minted degree in psychology—and a preliposuction 27-inch waist. She comes from a deeply religious culture that disapproves of too much attention paid to personal appearance. In her studies, she has been thoroughly exposed to the academic research on body-image sickness in girls and young women. So how does she reconcile what she knows to what she feels?

"See, this is the funny thing. I kind of agree with all that," she says, slowly, "but then I succumb to it myself."

Family Dynamics

The parents are often the worst. Dick calls it the "JonBenet Ramsey Syndrome." Overintense, wanting their children to be perfect, baby boomers who refuse to age without a fight, they drag their sons and daughters into the doctor's office and make demands. They wave the checks. Their children sit slumped in the chair, not speaking. Every surgeon has these horror stories.

Gregory Dick: "A mother brought in the daughter because the breasts are deformed, one was one size, and one the other. The daughter didn't seem to mind so much. I said, 'Any pressure from boyfriends?' The parent scoffed. 'What boy would be interested in a girl with breasts like that?' I almost fell out of my chair."

Steven Hopping: "I had a mother; she lost weight and had liposuction, and she had a short, heavy daughter, 15. She had a bad complexion. She was under psychiatric care. The mother pleaded with me and my staff, and reluctantly, I did the lipo. And now, a year later, her weight is up. She's not any happier. That was a mistake I made. You would love to help these people and be the one to save them. I'm a surgeon; I love quick changes myself. But I didn't solve any problems. I just moved it around."

Mark Mausner: "The woman who didn't have perfect breasts as a child wants her daughter to do it. You always have to be aware of the family dynamic and listen carefully to who is talking. Half of the job is psychiatry."

Even mothers who would never dream of sanctioning plastic surgery for their daughters unconsciously hand down a legacy of obsession.

Rita Freedman is treating a 16-year-old girl who has a weight problem. "Her mother is weight-obsessed, and she had lipo. The girl looks at a mother who is much thinner than she used to be, and who is much thinner than herself, and she feels judged. The mother is trying to relax and remove herself from how she feels about her heavy daughter. It's all very difficult." $1,666 PER INCH

"I did this for myself," insists the 22-year-old after her tummy tuck and liposuction. Her parents, who are from the Philippines, never knew until afterward. "I don't think they really understand why I did it."

Plastic surgery is generally accepted now, she says, but she's still a little embarrassed, and doesn't want her name used.

"I know that spending this money on your looks is supposed to be wasteful, but I had saved it up and I didn't really miss it," she says. When the swelling goes down, she says, her surgeon told her the 27-inch waist will be 24 inches. That's the goal: Only $1,666 per inch.

For Lucie Lukesova, having liposuction was "a dream come true."

"I love my body," she says, "but it's a pressure from the friends and acquaintances. They say, 'You should lose some weight.'" She said she has tried, "but I don't have the willpower. I can keep it for two weeks, and then its bye-bye."

She saved some money from her job taking care of her toddler niece, and then she met up with Hopping, a surgeon at Columbia Hospital for Women who is somewhat of a trendsetter in these procedures. He offered to waive his fee if he could use her to demonstrate new liposuction techniques in front of other doctors.

"All the big body is gone," she says excitedly, the week after her procedure. "I'm still swollen, but it looks much smaller." She is thrilled with the way her neck looks, where Hopping removed her flab. Nothing hurts very much. She is doing her normal duties.

Before her fat cells were sucked away, she carefully ticked off her faults in an interview. "I think you are lovely," said the reporter. Lukesova smiled a little, lowered her big, blue eyes and murmured "thank you," but she shook her head. And now? "I am very happy," she says.

"Now, I am looking in the mirror all the time."

16

When Money Is Everything, Except Hers

Dirk Johnson

DIXON, Ill.   Watching classmates strut past in designer clothes, Wendy Williams sat silently on the yellow school bus, wearing a cheap belt and rummage-sale slacks.

One boy stopped and yanked his thumb, demanding her seat.

"Move it, trailer girl," he sneered.

It has never been easy to live on the wrong side of the tracks. But in the economically robust 1990's, with sprawling new houses and three-car garages sprouting like cornstalks on the Midwestern prairie, the sting that comes with scarcity gets rubbed with an extra bit of salt.

Seen through the eyes of a 13-year-old girl growing up at Chateau Estates, a fancy name for a tin-plain trailer park, the rosy talk about the nation's prosperity carries a certain mocking echo.

The everyday discussion in the halls of Reagan Middle School in this city about 100 miles west of Chicago touches on computer toys that can cost $1,000, family vacations to Six Flags or Disney World and stylish clothes that bear a Nike emblem or Tommy Hilfiger's coveted label.

Unlike young people a generation ago, those today must typically pay fees to play for the school sports teams or band. It costs $45 to play in the youth summer soccer league. It takes money to go skating on weekends at the White Pines roller rink, to play laser tag or rock-climb at the Plum Hollow Recreation Center, to mount a steed at the Horseback Riding Club, to gaze at Leonardo DiCaprio and Kate Winslet at the Plaza Cinemas, to go shopping for clothes at Cherryvale Mall.

To be without money, in so many ways, is to be left out.

"I told this girl: 'That's a really awesome shirt. Where did you get it?'" said Wendy, explaining that she knew it was out of her price range, but that she wanted to join the small talk. "And she looked at me and laughed and said, 'Why would you want to know?'"

A lanky, soft-spoken girl with large brown eyes, Wendy pursed her lips to hide a slight overbite that got her the nickname Rabbit, a humiliation she once begged her mother and father to avoid by sending her to an orthodontist.

For struggling parents, keenly aware that adolescents agonize over the social pecking order, the styles of the moment and the face in the mirror, there is no small sense of failure in telling a child that she cannot have what her classmates take for granted.

"Do you know what it's like?" asked Wendy's mother, Veronica Williams, "to have your daughter come home and say, 'Mom, the kids say my clothes are tacky,' and then walk off with her head hanging low."

This is not the desperate poverty of Chicago housing projects, where the plight of empty pockets is worsened by the threat of gangs and gunfire. Wendy lives in relative safety in a home with both parents. Her father, Wendell Provow, earns $9 an hour as a welder. Her mother works part-time as a cook for Head Start, the Federal education program.

Unlike students in some urban pockets, isolated from affluence, Wendy receives the same education as a girl from a $300,000 house in the Idle Oaks subdivision. The flip side of that coin is the public spectacle of economic struggle. This is a place small enough where people know the personal stories, or, at least, repeat them as if they did.

Even in this down-to-earth town, where a poor boy nicknamed Dutch grew up to become President, young people seem increasingly enchanted with buying, having, spending and status.

R. Woodrow (Woody) Wasson, the principal at Reagan Middle School, makes it a point to sit down with every child and ask them about their hopes and dreams.

"They want to be doctors, lawyers, veterinarians and, of course, professional athletes," said Mr. Wasson, whose family roots here go back to the 19th century. "I don't remember the last time I heard somebody say they wanted to be a police officer or a firefighter. They want to do something that will make a lot of money and have a lot of prestige."

He said a teacher in a nearby town has been trying to recruit high school students for vocational studies to become tool-and-die artisans, a trade that can pay $70,000 a year.

"The teacher can't fill the slots," Mr. Wasson said. "Nobody's interested in that kind of work."

It is not surprising that children grow up believing that money is so important, given the relentless way they are targeted by marketers.

"In the past, you just put an ad in the magazine," said Michael Wood, the director of research for Teen-Age Research Unlimited, a marketing consultant in suburban Chicago. "Now savvy marketers know you must hit them at all angles—Web sites, cable TV shows, school functions, sporting events."

He noted the growth of cross-promotions, like the deal in which actors on the television show "Dawson's Creek," which is popular among adolescents, wear clothes by J. Crew and appear in its catalogue.

But young people get cues in their everyday lives. Some spending habits that would once have been seen as ostentatious—extravagant parties for small children, new cars for teenagers—have become familiar trappings of middle-class comfort.

The stock market, although it is sputtering now, has made millionaires of many people in Main Street towns. Building developers here recently won approval to build a gated community, which will be called Timber Edge.

"Wendy goes to school around these rich kids," her mother said, "and wonders why she can't have things like they do."

A bright girl with a flair for art, writing and numbers, Wendy stays up late most nights, reading books. "The Miracle Worker" was a recent favorite.

But when a teacher asked her to join an elevated class for algebra, she politely declined. "I get picked on for my clothes and living in the trailer park," said Wendy, who never brings anyone home from school. "I don't want to get picked on for being a nerd, too."

Her mother, who watched three other daughters drop out of school and have babies as teen-agers, has told Wendy time and again: "Don't lose your self-esteem."

One time a boy at school was teasing Wendy about her clothes—"They don't even match," he laughed—and her humble house in the trailer park.

She listened for a while. He kept insulting her. So she lifted a leg—clothed as it was in discount jeans from the Farm & Fleet store—and kicked him in the shins.

He told the authorities. She got the detention.

It became clear to Wendy that the insults were not going to stop. It also became clear that shin-kicking, however deserved, was not going to be the solution.

She went to a guidance counselor, Cynthia Kowa Basler, a dynamic woman who keeps close tabs on the children, especially girls who fret about their weight and suddenly stop eating lunch.

"I am large," she tells the girls, "and I have self-esteem."

Wendy, who knew that Mrs. Basler held sessions with students to increase their self-confidence, went to the counselor. "I feel a little down," Wendy told her. The counselor gathered eight students, including other girls like Wendy, who felt embarrassed about their economic station.

In this school named for Ronald Reagan, the students were told to study the words of Eleanor Roosevelt.

One of her famous quotations was posted above the counselor's desk: "No one can make you feel inferior without your consent."

As a group, the students looked up the definition of inferior and consent.

And then they read the words out loud.

"Again," the counselor instructed.

"Louder," the counselor insisted.

Again and again, they read the inspirational words.

In role-playing exercises, the children practiced responses to taunts, which sometimes called for nothing more than a shrug.

"Mrs. Basler told us to live up to our goals—show those kids," Wendy said. "She told us that things can be a lot different when you're grown up. Maybe things will be the other way around then."

Wendy smiled at the notion.

Life still has plenty of bumps. When Wendy gets off the school bus—the trailer park is the first stop, so everyone can see where she lives—she still looks at her shoes.

She still pulls her shirt out to hide a belt that does not quite make the grade. And she still purses her lips to hide an overbite. But her mother has noticed her smiling more these days. And Wendy has even said she might consider taking an advanced course in math, her favorite subject.

"I want to go to college," Wendy said the other day. "I want to become a teacher."

One recent day, she popped in to the counselor's office, just to say hello, then walked back down the halls, her arms folded around her schoolbooks.

Mrs. Basler stood at the doorway and watched her skip away, a student with so much promise, and so many obstacles.

For the girl from Chateau Estates, it is a long way from the seventh grade to college.

"She's going to make it," the counselor said, with a clenched fist and a voice full of hope.

17

Her Son/Daughter

Kate Bornstein

"Who are you?" asks the third blue-haired lady, peering up at me through the thick lenses of her rhinestone cat glasses. Only it comes out in one word: "Hoowahyoo?" I'm wearing black; we all are. It's my mother's funeral service, after all, and the little old ladies are taking inventory of the mourners. Me, I have to take inventory of my own identities whenever someone asks me who I am, and the answer that tumbles out of my mouth is rarely predictable. But this is my mother's funeral, and I am devastated, and to honor the memory of my mom, I'm telling each of them the who of me I know they can deal with.

"I'm Kate Bornstein," I answer her in this quiet-quiet voice of mine, "Mildred's daughter."

From *The New York Times Magazine*, 1999. Copyright © 1999 by The New York Times Company. Reprinted by permission.

"Daughter?!" She shoots back incredulously the same question each of her predecessors had asked, because everyone knew my mother had two sons.

"Mildred never mentioned she had a daughter." The eyes behind those glasses are dissecting my face, looking for family resemblances. When I was a boy, I looked exactly like my father. Everyone used to say so. Then, when I went through what people would call my sex change, they would say, "You know, you look just like your mother." Except I'm tall. Nearly six feet of me in mourning for the passing of my mother, and I'm confronting this brigade of matrons whose job seems to be to protect my mother from unwanted visitors on this morning of her funeral on the Jersey Shore.

"You're her daughter? So who's your father? It's not Paul, am I right?" Now there would be a piece of gossip these women could gnaw on over their next mahjongg game. "Mildred had another child," they'd say after calling two bams. "A daughter no less! And Paul, God rest his soul, he never knew."

My mother was raised in a nearly orthodox Jewish household. She lived her life measuring her self-worth by the presence of the men in her life. Her father, a successful merchant, died a year before I was born. Her husband, a successful doctor, died a year before I told her that one of her two sons was about to become a dyke. She preferred the word "lesbian." "My son, the lesbian," she would tell her close friends.

My mother was there the night the rabbi asked me who I was. I was a senior in college, a real hippie: beard, beads and suede knee-high moccasins with fringe hanging down past my calves. I was home for some holiday or other, and my parents wanted to show off their son who was going to Brown. I had always enjoyed Friday night services. To this day, I don't remember what about the rabbi's sermon outraged me, but there I was, jumping to my feet in the middle of the sermon, arguing some point of social justice.

My father was grinning. (He had never been bar mitzvahed, having kicked his rabbi in the shins the first day of Hebrew school.) My mother had her hand over her mouth to keep from laughing. She was never very fond of our rabbi, not since the time he refused to make a house call to console my father the night my grandfather died. So there we were, the rabbi and the hippie, arguing rabbinical law and social responsibility. He finally dismissed me with a nod. I dismissed him with a chuckle, and the service continued. On the way out of the synagogue, we had to file by the rabbi, who was shaking everyone's hand.

"Albert," he said to me, peering up through what would later be known as John Lennon glasses. "Hoowahyoo? You've got the beard, so now you're Jesus Christ?"

I've done my time as an evangelist. Twelve years in the Church of Scientology, and later, when I had escaped Hubbard's minions, four or five years as a reluctant poster child for the world's fledgling transgender movement.

My mother never heard the blue-haired ladies ask "Hoowahyoo?" of the tall-tall woman with mascara running down her cheeks. She never heard a producer from the Ricki Lake show ask me, "Who are you?" when I told her I wasn't a man or a woman. My mother never heard the Philadelphia society matron ask me the same question when I tried to attend her private women-only Alcoholics Anonymous group.

My mother only once asked me, "Who are you?" It was about a week before she died. "Hoowahyoo, Albert?" she asked anxiously, mixing up names and pronouns in the huge dose of morphine. "Who are you?"

I told her the truth: I was her baby, I always would be. I told her I was her little boy, and the daughter she never had. I told her I loved her.

"Ha!" she exclaimed, satisfied with my proffered selection of whos. "That's good. I didn't want to lose any of you, ever."

18

"We Are Who You Are":
Feminism and Disability

Bonnie Sherr Klein

It all begins in 1987. I am 46 years old, and enjoying an athletic and sexy vacation with my husband, Michael. On a hot day, we bicycle ten miles to the town tennis courts. I feel weak and nauseated, and play badly. We think it must be junk-food poisoning.

Within several hours, I am staggering and slurring my speech. I have double vision. Michael, a family physician, recognizes the signs of central nervous system damage. At midnight, he speeds me home to Montreal, to the emergency room of the hospital where he works.

Diagnostic tests are inconclusive. We are shocked and scared, but I begin to stabilize. Within a few days, I am released from the intensive care unit, and take a few steps with a walker. After two weeks, we celebrate our twentieth anniversary in the hospital with our children. I feel blessed and happy to be alive.

The next day I become totally paralyzed. Semiconscious, I am "locked in" and unable to speak. A respirator breathes for me. A magnetic resonance test (MRI) reveals that a congenital malformation at the base of my brain stem has bled, resulting in several strokes. It is like a time bomb waiting to explode again. Local specialists declare it inoperable because of its inaccessible location. Close family and friends come to say goodbye.

From *Ms. Magazine*, November–December 1992, pp. 70–74. © 1992. Reprinted by permission of *Ms. Magazine*.

Michael refuses to accept this fatal verdict. He locates a surgeon who is prepared to remove the malformation.

I am jet-ambulanced on a respirator to London, Ontario. By my bed, the surgeon posts a newspaper clipping: a picture of me with Kate Millett from my documentary *Not a Love Story*. I overhear a staff remark: "She used to be a filmmaker." I remain in intensive care for several months. Michael stays with me, acting as husband, family doctor, nurse, and advocate. He will not resume work for several months.

As I come back to life but cannot move, speak, or breathe, I have frequent panic attacks. Only Michael can talk me down. He breathes with me until I fall asleep. The literal meaning of "conspire" is to breathe together. We are in a conspiracy for my life. This becomes the metaphor of our partnership. This *is* a love story.

Recovery

Back in Montreal, I spend more months in the hospital, and then in a rehabilitation institute. Like a helpless baby, I learn how to swallow, speak, sit upright, use the toilet, stand.

(Memory Journal: When I am sufficiently recovered, I get bathing privileges twice a week. A male orderly transfers me to a gurney and wheels me down the hall. I am "wrapped" diaper-fashion in a rubber sling, and with a horrible-sounding grind, winched into a tub where a nurse bathes and shampoos me. The soothing warm water is one of the few nice body sensations I have. But it is frightening to be winched. I can hear older women screaming and moaning, and all I can think of—as in my nightmares—is a concentration camp.)

But I am never abandoned to institutional care. I am supported and nursed every day by Michael and our daughter, Naomi—then 17. Our son, Seth, 19, begins attending the University of Toronto shortly after my surgery. He studies on the five-hour train commute each way; his enthusiastic comments about my dramatic changes since the previous weekend are like a transfusion. Naomi is just emerging from a difficult adolescence. Conflicted by her mother's highly visible feminism, she has asserted her individuality by learning the skills of femininity. Now she does the intimate niceties for me—shaving the underarms; bleaching the facial hairs darkened by steroids mistakenly prescribed. My skin is blotched, my features lopsided, but my daughter makes me feel pretty. Not surprisingly, Naomi also fails her semester at school.

Several months after the stroke, as soon as I can use a pencil, the occupational therapist helps me to copy circles and squares like a schoolgirl. My first communication is an illegible letter to Naomi, in which I share my fear about how slow recovery may be, an admission I make to no one else. Once I can write, I begin my journal, which becomes a tool for my survival. I use it to process the strange and troubling events happening in my body, to record thoughts I cannot trust my damaged mind to remember, to remind myself how far I have come.

The Long Haul: Rehabilitation

After seven months in the hospital, I am at home over the next two and a half years, in the long process of rehabilitation. I have conventional physical, occupational, and speech therapy. As I gradually improve, I remember my old feminist wisdom that I know my body better than anyone else. I take control. I experiment with so-called alternative approaches like acupuncture. Michael and I dance and play, in whatever motivating ways we can invent to push my physical limits. And I learn to rest. In my prestroke life, this was never easy for me, juggling the three F's: family, filmmaking, and feminism. Now I have no choice. My body's messages are nonnegotiable.

The anguish is profound when I let it emerge, and it comes out at the slightest invitation.

(*Journal, March 1, 1989: This evening, when Michael and I dance, I am weepy. Because he's been outside playing basketball, my girlhood sport, while I am curled up inside in bed. And because I can hardly dance, and dancing was one of the things we did together, starting the day we met 22 years ago. I want to kick up my heels, and they won't go, dammit! But strange as it may sound, I also experience the euphoria of just being alive. It is not a cover-up, it is real. I laugh out loud when the leaves riot with autumn colors. I am living on the edge, with no script guides or maps, inventing every moment as I live it.*)

The stroke hit me in the middle of editing a film. The producer and editor bring the film to the hospital and my home so we can work on it together. *Mile Zero* is the story of four teenagers—one of whom is Seth—who are organizing against nuclear arms. The premiere, 16 months after my stroke, is the most triumphant moment in my rehabilitation. I have reclaimed the important piece of myself that was a filmmaker.

Yet I still do not accept myself as disabled; disability is "a stage I am just passing through." For the premiere, I reject a fully accessible educational institution and choose a glamorous cinema with inaccessible bathrooms—even though I am in a wheelchair.

I long to hold on to the acute appreciation of life engendered by survival and rebirth, but euphoria does not last indefinitely. My mother dies after a long struggle with Alzheimer's disease. This loss is compounded by Naomi's departure for the University of Toronto. I want to be generous about letting her go, but losses are interconnected: I mourn my mother, my daughter, myself.

In June 1989, almost two years poststroke, I receive a last-minute invitation to participate in a festival of Canadian women's films abroad. Two of my films are featured. My immediate response is "Impossible! I can't travel without personal assistance." The travel money is quickly offered to another filmmaker. When Naomi discovers me crying, she offers to quit work to accompany me. We go off together at great personal expense, and greater trepidation.

The women who had organized the festival—also Canadian filmmakers—had promised to "accommodate" me, but they make no provision for my needs. I am expected to fit in and keep up. They schedule my films late at night when I am too tired; they do not include me in panel discussions or press conferences; they arrange social events in inaccessible places. I miss the informal personal exchanges catalyzed by the shared film experience.

I can no longer move in what had been my world. I feel I have been used for my films, but neglected and made invisible as a person. I feel as if my colleagues are ashamed of me because I am no longer the image of strength, competence, and independence that feminists, including myself, are so eager to project. There is clearly a conflict between feminism's rhetoric of inclusion and failure to include disability. My journals reveal that this is the only moment in which I think of suicide.

I am coming up against multiple barriers, personal and social. I cannot return to my former life, and I do not know what my life will be now. Even feminism has betrayed me. It seems too narrow a lens for the new realities of my life. I also feel an unresolved conflict between feminism and my increased dependence on—and appreciation for—Michael.

About two and a half years poststroke, I have an experience that begins to clarify my thinking about feminism. We spend the winter in Beersheba, Israel, where Michael is working to help me escape Montreal's ice and snow. A woman from the local chapter of the Israel Women's Network phones: as a visiting feminist, would I speak on any "women's issue" of my choosing at their next meeting? Again my first reaction is negative: "I am no longer engaged with women's issues; I have been so self-obsessed with my stroke that's all I could possibly talk about." Her response is quick: "That's exactly what we want to hear about, but were too shy to ask!"

I have forgotten how wonderful it is to share intimately with a group of women! I read bits from my journal, and my story prompts theirs. One woman says, "My relationship with my husband is fine as long as I'm healthy, capable, and available sexually, but I don't know what would happen if I were incapacitated." She hadn't read the United Nations statistic that disabled women are twice as likely to get divorced or separated as disabled men. We realize that we rarely talk about illness, disability, and dying, though we will all confront these realities.

Every issue is a woman's issue; relationships, dependence, and autonomy are as much a part of feminism as day care and violence. I have undersold feminism. I slowly recognize that the way I am living my stroke has everything to do with myself as a feminist—as well as with implications for feminism itself.

"Coming Out" Disabled

I feel comfortable and stimulated in this group of Israeli women; they are middle-class, middle-aged, married Jewish women like me. But no one else there is disabled. I am "other." I desperately need company.

I had first heard of DAWN (the DisAbled Women's Network, Canada) years earlier when it approached Studio D to make our screenings more accessible. We appreciated being sensitized, favored wheelchair-accessible venues, and enjoyed the aesthetics of sign language interpretation with our movies. But sometimes DAWN's demands seemed "excessive"; our meager resources were already exhausted by items on our agenda that seemed to affect *most* women. But in retrospect, I know that as a not-yet-disabled woman I was afraid of disability.

As soon as I return to Canada, I dig DAWN's phone number out of a feminist newsletter. I realize that its agenda is identical to mine (and feminism's): dependence and autonomy, image and self-esteem, powerlessness, isolation, violence, and vulnerability; equality and access; sexuality. Three years after my stroke, I go to my first DAWN meeting at the local YWCA.

I feel apologetic, illegitimate, because I was not born disabled, and am not as severely disabled as many other people. I feel guilty about my privileges of class, profession (including my disability pension), and family. I am a newcomer to the disability movement; I have not paid my dues. (Doesn't this litany sound "just like a woman"?)

Our talk keeps moving between the personal and the political, because disability—like gender, race, age, and sexuality—is a social as well as a biological construct. The DAWN members, typical of disabled women, are mostly unemployed, poor, and living alone. It is like the early days of consciousness-raising in the women's movement: sharing painful (and funny) experiences, "clicks!" of recognition; swapping tips for coping with social service bureaucracies and choosing the least uncomfortable tampons for prolonged sitting. It is exhilarating to cry and laugh with other women again.

Here I am not other, because everyone is other. It is the sisterhood of disability. The stroke has connected me with women who were not part of my world before—working-class women with little education, women with intellectual and psychiatric disabilities, women with physical "abnormalities" from whom I would have averted my eyes in polite embarrassment. All women like me.

"We are women. We are women with disabilities. We are women who are abused. We are your sisters. . . . Your issues are our issues, and each of our issues is also your issue. We are who you are." (From "Meeting Our Needs: An Access Manual for Transition Houses," DAWN, June 1991.)

I discover it is easier for me to be a disabled feminist than a disabled person. Feminism means loving myself as I am. After three long years, I am finally ready to accept myself as permanently, irrevocably disabled: acceptance is not an event but an ongoing process. I learn more about the disability rights movement. I meet other women with disabilities, who become my buddies, sisters, teachers, and "rolling" models. I learn, not surprisingly, that women are leaders in the disability movement.

(Journal, October 1990: Boston's first Disability Pride Day. I usually dislike the rhetoric of rallies, the solicited mass response. But today I want my tape recorder. A gutsy, nervous young woman with the thick drawl of cerebral palsy is emcee. Not

only is her speech different, but there is a new language being spoken here. I feel like a privileged eavesdropper at first, but she is speaking for me and about me. Or is she? She cues us for a chant: "Disabled and . . ." The crowd responds: PROUD! My throat jams on the word mid-chant. Is this honest? Who am I trying to fool? It's one thing to accept, but another to be proud. I'm proud of surviving and adapting maybe, but am I proud of being disabled? But it feels good to be shouting with hundreds of other bodies, looking happy despite—because of?—their "deformities." Or is the word "differences"? Or is it "our"?)

Happily, the timing of my personal journey is synchronous with the women's movement. The Canadian Research Institute for the Advancement of Women (CRIAW) announces the theme for its 1990 national conference: "The More We Get Together . . ." on women and disability. I decide to go, alone, to Prince Edward Island. Thanks to the joint efforts of CRIAW and DAWN, this historic event is not only totally accessible but empowering—for both the women with disabilities and those without. Every woman with disability is paired with a "sister" who gives us whatever assistance we need—and who learns firsthand about disability.

It is a coming-out experience for many of us. For me, it is the first time I identify myself publicly as a woman with disability, and revel in the company of so many others. Because women with disabilities are often isolated, for many this is their first conference. They learn from the experience of longtime feminists.

Many of the so-called nondisabled women come out as well. Kay Macpherson, 79, and Muriel Duckworth, 83, are well-known Canadian peace activists and feminists. But we have never considered them "disabled." Now, for the first time, Kay talks about what it means to be losing her sight. She talks loudly because her close friend Muriel has learned to be assertive about her increasing deafness. Muriel and Kay describe their support networks of friends who look after each other by sharing meals, and house keys in case of falls. Our stories lead us to discover the continuum from "ability" to "disability." My stroke has given me a telescope on aging. We are all disabled under the skin—each of us has vulnerabilities, visible or not, and they are part of us. We are interdependent. Feminism is strongest when it includes its "weakest."

I leave CRIAW with a new sense of purpose and continuity. No longer illegitimate among either feminists or people with disabilities, I feel I have a particular contribution to make: perhaps I can help to bridge the gap between our two cultures. After all, my life's work has been about telling each other our stories.

Where Am I Now?

After five years, my physical condition is still evolving—but almost imperceptibly. I feel constantly imbalanced. I stand and walk with two canes, slowly and unsteadily. For longer distances, I drive my electric three-wheeled scooter, Gladys, but she can only be transported in a lift-equipped van, and furthermore is stopped by the smallest step. I am often dependent on someone to push Manny, my portable manual wheelchair. I do not drive a car alone—yet.

I need to exercise and nap every day, and I get weekly massages, acupuncture, and chiropractic to maximize my fluidity and minimize my pain. With only one functioning vocal chord, I choke frequently, but my speech is intelligible (and my voice as breathlessly sexy as I always wanted). I tire easily and tolerate stress badly.

Being forced to slow down is not all negative. The rhythm of my life has changed dramatically. Before, it was governed by the calendar and the clock. Now I follow the natural pace of my body. The tasks of everyday living take me much longer. I have become patient, as have those around me. I have to ration my limited energy and choose carefully who I see and what I do. I have no time to waste on bullshit, but I do have time to smell the flowers. I cherish my solitude, and enjoy the fullness of the company of intimate friends and family.

But I need to be useful and connected, to feel once again that I am contributing to making this a better world. I don't know if I will ever make films again, but I am writing a book about my experience, and spending time with other people with disabilities. As with my walking, it all comes to balance. Some people look at me suspiciously when I hint at the gifts of the stroke. I would never deny the pain of dependence, the grieving for lost freedoms, the fear for the future. Would I take an immediate cure if offered? Probably. But would I want to undo it, as if it never happened? Absolutely not. It has become part of my identity. It is who I am now.

In retrospect, the "clicks!" in my consciousness about disability paralleled my coming to feminist consciousness two decades earlier. For a long time, I denied I was disabled, and kept my distance from other "cripples" in the hospital gym because I was an exception to the rule. Later, I was sure I could "overcome" it; I would be supercrip (superwoman); I would support the rights of other people with disabilities, but *I* was not oppressed. As time passed, I experienced with great pain the ways in which other people's attitudes and societal barriers disempowered me. At first, I internalized the oppression and lost all self-esteem. Then, as I reconnected with feminism and discovered my commonality with other women (and men) with disabilities, I began to see more clearly. With solidarity came strength.

Between writing this piece and correcting the galleys, I have taken a giant step in my journey. I went to Independence 92 in Vancouver, an international conference on disability—more than 2,000 of us from more than 100 countries! For one week, I had the heady feeling that we were taking over the world. Even better—we were remaking it, creating a world in which difference is not the problem but part of the solution.

It is a feast for this disabled filmmaker's eyes: a gridlock of wheelchairs on a freight elevator, a shoulder chain of the blind leading the blind, signing singing, nursing babies in wheelchairs—images we have not seen because we disabled are invisible, even to each other; images so rare and precious they have not yet been co-opted or trivialized.

Somehow, I think I will be making films again.

19

The Case of Sharon Kowalski and Karen Thompson:
Ableism, Heterosexism, and Sexism

Joan L. Griscom

In November 1983, in Minnesota, Sharon Kowalski was in a head-on collision with a drunk driver. Her four-year-old niece died soon after; her seven-year-old nephew survived; and she suffered a severe brain-stem injury. As a result, she was paralyzed and lost the ability to speak. Kowalski was living in a committed partnership with Karen Thompson, although only their closest friends knew. Soon after the accident, serious conflict developed between Thompson and Kowalski's parents, which erupted in a series of lawsuits that lasted for eight years. Thompson fought in the courts to secure adequate rehabilitation for Sharon as well as access to friends and family of her choice. In July 1985, acting under Minnesota guardianship laws, Sharon's father placed her in a nursing home that lacked adequate rehabilitation facilities and prohibited Thompson and other friends from visiting her. If Thompson had not continued the legal struggle, Kowalski would probably still be locked away in this home. In January 1989, she was finally transferred to an appropriate rehabilitation center and reunited with lover and friends; and in 1991 she was finally allowed her choice to live with Karen.

In this article I tell the story of Sharon Kowalski and Karen Thompson and show how prejudices deeply entrenched in our medical and legal systems intertwined to deny Kowalski the fullest quality of life. Among these modes of oppression are ableism, discrimination against disabled persons; heterosexism, the belief structured into our institutions that only heterosexual relationships are legitimate; and sexism, discrimination against women.

A History of the Events

By November 1983, Sharon Kowalski and Karen Thompson had lived in partnership for almost four years. Karen was thirty-six years old, an assistant professor of physical education at St. Cloud State University in Minnesota, devoutly religious,

Reprinted by permission of the author.

conservative in social outlook. Three years earlier she had refused to join a class action sex discrimination suit at her university. Sharon was twenty-seven years old, an outstanding athlete who had graduated from St. Cloud in physical education and had just accepted a job coaching golf at St. Cloud for the next spring. She had grown up in the Iron Mine area of northern Minnesota, a conservative world where women are expected to marry young. Defying such expectations, she became the first member of her family to attend college, earning her own tuition by working part-time in the mines. After she and Karen fell in love, they exchanged rings, bought a house together, and vowed a lifetime commitment.

After the accident, it was unclear if Sharon would live. For weeks she lay in a coma, and Karen spent as many as eight hours a day talking to her, reading the Bible, massaging and stretching her neck, shoulders, and hands. As medical staff explained, it is essential to massage and stretch brain-injured patients in a coma, for they tend to curl up tightly and permanently damage their muscles in the process. Doctors were pessimistic about Sharon's recovery. However, in January 1984, Karen noticed that Sharon was moving her right index finger, and discovered that Sharon could indicate yes-and-no answers to questions by moving her finger. Later she began to tap her fingers, and then slowly learned to write letters and words.

The Kowalski parents became suspicious of the long hours Karen was spending with her, and increasingly Karen feared they would take steps to exclude her from Sharon's life. Initially the parents stayed at Karen's and Sharon's home but subsequently moved out without telling her; and one evening Donald Kowalski told her she was visiting too often, that only family could really love Sharon. After consulting a hospital psychologist, Karen wrote the parents a letter explaining their love, in hopes they would understand her need to be with Sharon and her importance to Sharon. The Kowalskis reacted with shock, denial, and rage. As the nightmare deepened, Karen consulted an attorney and learned she had no legal rights, unless she won guardianship. In March 1984, she therefore filed for guardianship, and Donald Kowalski immediately counterfiled.

The results of the hearing at first appeared positive. In an out-of-court settlement, guardianship was awarded to Donald Kowalski, but Karen was granted equal access to medical and financial information and full visitation rights. She participated in both the physical and occupational therapy. Sharon continued to improve slowly, responding more often than before and more fully. Karen made her an alphabet board, and Sharon began to spell out answers to questions. Subsequently she began to communicate by using a typewriter, and in August she spoke a few words. But conflicts continued. The day after the hearing, Donald Kowalski incorrectly told Karen she did not have visitation rights. Later, when it became necessary to move Sharon to another institution, he tried to cancel Karen's arrangements to work with Sharon and her therapists. When Karen and other friends took Sharon out on day passes, to church and other events, he objected, and subsequently testified in court that he did not want her out in public. In October 1984, by court order, Sharon was moved further away to Duluth, and Kowalski filed a motion to gain full power as guardian and deny Karen visitation. Karen counter-filed to remove him as guardian.

The hearings on these motions took months to complete. During this period Sharon was moved several times, regressed in her skills, and became clinically depressed. By this time the Minnesota Civil Liberties Union (MCLU) had entered the case, arguing that under the First Amendment Sharon's rights of free speech and free association were being violated. The Handicap Services Program of Tri-County Action Programs, Inc., submitted lengthy testimony of Sharon's capacity to communicate, including a long conversation with her in which she stated that she was gay and Karen was her lover. At Sharon's request, the MCLU asked for the right to represent her and suggested she might eventually testify for herself. Ultimately the court refused both requests. It found that Sharon lacked sufficient understanding to make decisions for herself, and wrote that the elimination of the conflict between the Kowalskis and Karen was in her best interest. Accordingly, on July 23, 1985, the court awarded Donald Kowalski full guardianship, including the right to determine visitation. Within a day he denied visitation to Karen, other friends of Sharon, the MCLU, various disability rights groups, and others. In two days he transferred her to a nursing home near his home with only minimal rehabilitation facilities. In August 1985, Karen saw Sharon for what would be the last time for over three years.

As this summary indicates, the medical system had failed Sharon in at least three respects. First, it failed to supply her with necessary rehabilitation in the years when it was vital to her recovery. Following brain-stem injury, the initial months and years are crucial in rehabilitation; the longer the incapacity lasts, the more permanent the damage. As the legal battles wore on, her chances of rehabilitation diminished. Stark in the medical record is the fact that this woman who was starting to stand and starting to feed herself was locked away for over three years with an implanted feeding tube, insufficiently stretched and exercised so that muscles that were starting to work curled back on themselves again. Second, she was deprived of the bombardment of emotional and physical stimulation needed to regenerate her cognitive faculties. For example, once she was in the nursing home, the regenerative outside excursions were forbidden. Third, although medical staff often recognized Sharon's unusual response to Karen, they failed to explain to her parents the importance of maintaining the connection. There was an urgent need for counseling to assist the parents, but except for one court-mandated session, none took place.

The failure of the medical system was consistently supported by the legal system. Initially the court ruled that Sharon must be in a nursing home with a young adult rehabilitation ward. But once Donald Kowalski was awarded full guardianship, he was able to move her to a nursing home without such a ward. Another contradiction occurred in late 1985 when the Minnesota Office of Health Facility Complaints investigated Sharon's right to have visitors of her choice, a right guaranteed under the Minnesota Patient Bill of Rights. They found that indeed her right was being violated. However, the state appeals court held that visitation rights under the Patient Bill of Rights were inapplicable to this case, since the healthcare facility was not restricting the right of visitation, the guardian was.

The deficiencies of guardianship law are a key problem throughout this case. First, a guardian can restrict a patient's rights, and there is no legal recourse. As is often said, under present laws a guardian can lock up a person and throw away the key. This is a national problem, affecting disabled people, elderly people, and others who are presumed incompetent for any number of reasons. Second, guardians are inadequately supervised. Under Minnesota statutes, a guardian is required to have the ward tested annually for competency. Donald Kowalski never did so, and for over three years the courts did not require him to do so. As early as December 1985, Karen filed a motion in district court to hold the guardian in contempt for failure to arrange competency testing and for failure to heed Sharon's "reliably expressed" wishes for visitation. The courts routinely rejected such motions until 1988.

Between 1985 and 1988 Karen and the Minnesota Civil Liberties Union pursued repeated appeals to various Minnesota courts, and all were denied. By now, since the legal system had failed her, Karen had begun to seek help from the media, disability rights groups, gay and lesbian groups, and women's groups. She recognized that the legal precedents set in this case could be devastating for others: gay/lesbian couples, unmarried heterosexual people, or people living in communities of choice. Karen, the reserved, closeted, conservative professor, was slowly transformed into a passionate public speaker in her quest to secure freedom and adequate rehabilitation for Sharon; and slowly she gained national attention. The alternative press, in particular, responded; national groups such as the National Organization for Women passed resolutions of support; the National Committee to Free Sharon Kowalski formed with regional chapters. Finally the mainstream media, initially hostile, began publishing supportive articles; Karen appeared on national TV programs; and significant politicians, including Jesse Jackson, began to express concern and support. Meanwhile Sharon remained in the nursing home, cut off from many former friends, physically regressing and psychologically depressed.

In September 1987, Karen filed a new request to have Sharon tested for competency. February 1988 brought the first break in the case; the judge ruled the testing should be done, and finally, in July, he ordered it. In January 1989, Sharon was moved to the Miller-Dwan Medical Center in Duluth for a 60-day evaluation. Through his attorney, Donald Kowalski unsuccessfully argued against both the move and the testing. At Miller-Dwan, Sharon immediately expressed her wish to see Karen, as well as her awareness that her father would disapprove. On February 2, 1989, Karen visited her for the first time in three and a half years, an event that made banner headlines in the alternative press across the nation. She was, however, highly depressed, and there were numerous physical changes: for example, her feet had curled up so tightly that she was no longer able to stand. A more significant issue was her cognitive ability; her short-term memory loss remains considerable.

The competency evaluation nevertheless demonstrated that she could communicate on an adult level and that she had significant potential for rehabilitation. As a long-term goal Miller-Dwan recommended "her return to pre-morbid home environment" and added:

> We believe Sharon has shown areas of potential and ability to make rational choices in many areas of her life. She has consistently indicated a desire to return home and, by that, [she] means to St. Cloud to live with Karen Thompson again.

Soon after the release of this report, Donald Kowalski resigned as guardian, for both financial and health reasons, and the parents stopped attending medical conferences. In June 1989, Sharon was transferred to Travilla, a long-term rehabilitation center in Minneapolis for brain-injured young adults. Here she had extensive occupational, physical, and speech therapy. Karen again was able to spend many hours with her, taking her out on passes. She had surgery on her legs, feet, toes, left shoulder and arm to reverse the results of three years of inadequate care. She began to use a speech synthesizer and a motorized wheelchair.

Karen subsequently filed for guardianship, and Sharon's court-appointed attorney and medical staff from Miller-Dwan and Travilla testified positively in favor of their relationship. The medical personnel testified unanimously that Sharon is capable of deciding for herself what kinds of relationships she wants and with whom, and that she responds more to Karen than to anyone else. Further, they testified that Sharon is capable of living outside an institution, that returning home to St. Cloud would be best for her, and that Karen is best qualified to care for her in a home environment. However, witnesses for the Kowalskis opposed the petition. According to one report, they stated they would not continue to see Sharon if Karen became her guardian. The judge appeared increasingly uncomfortable with the national publicity generated by the case. While in August 1990 he allowed Sharon and Karen to fly out to San Francisco for the national convention of the National Organization for Women, where they each received a Woman of Courage award, in October he denied permission for Sharon to attend the first Disability Pride Day in Boston. He issued a gag order against Karen, which was overturned on appeal. Finally, in April 1991 he denied guardianship to Karen and awarded it to a supposedly "neutral third party," a former classmate of Sharon who lives near the Kowalski parents and who testified against Karen in a 1984 hearing. The judge based his decision in part on the Kowalskis' opposition, in part on his belief that although Sharon is capable of expressing wishes for visitation, her expressed wish to live with Karen in St. Cloud is "not tantamount to a preference of who should be her guardian." Karen appealed this decision.

In December 1991, the appeals court reversed the judge's ruling and granted guardianship of Sharon to Karen. The decision was based primarily on two factors: the medical testimony that Sharon is capable of making her own choices, and the fact that the two women are "a family of affinity" that deserves respect. This decision sets important precedents for disability rights and gay/lesbian families. Sharon now lives with Karen.

The Three Modes of Oppression

Sharon Kowalski was denied the fullest quality of life by three interacting systems of oppression: ableism, heterosexism, and sexism. These are not simply prejudices held by individuals; they also pervade social structures such as the medical and legal systems and thus become modes of oppression. Originally Karen believed that the difficulties she and Sharon were experiencing were merely personal problems. She had believed all her life that the institutions of our society are basically fair and reasonable and support the rights of individuals. In the book[1] she co-authored with her St. Cloud colleague Julie Andrzejewski, she documented the development of her awareness that widespread social and political forces were involved in their supposedly personal problems and that the oppression they have experienced is systemic.

Ableism has been rampant throughout this case. Sharon's inability to speak has often been construed as a lack of competence, and her particular kinds of communication have not been recognized. Quite early Karen noticed that some people did not speak to Sharon, some raised their voices as if she were deaf, and others spoke to her as if she were a child. One doctor spoke about Sharon in her presence as if she were not there. When Karen later asked her how she felt about this, Sharon typed out, "Shitty." Probably one reason Sharon has responded to Karen more than anyone else is that from the start Karen has talked extensively to her, read to her, played music for her, and consulted her wishes at every point. Although the MCLU and the Handicap Services Program submitted extensive transcripts of conversations with Sharon, the courts did not accept these as evidence of competence, relying instead on the testimony of people who had much less interaction with her. In a major article in the St. Paul *Pioneer Press* (1987), the reporter described the Kowalskis visiting the room "where their eerily silent daughter lies trapped in her twisted body." Eerily silent? This is the person who typed out "columbine" when asked what her favorite flower is, answered arithmetical questions correctly, and responded to numerous questions about her life, her feelings, and her wishes? She also communicates nonverbally in many ways: gestures, facial expressions, smiles, tears, and laughter.

Thanks to ableism, Sharon has often been stereotyped as helpless. The presumption of helplessness "traps" her far more severely than her "twisted body." Once a person is stereotyped as helpless, then there is no need to consult her wishes; her testimony is unnecessary; her written communications can be ignored. When Sharon was transferred to Miller-Dwan in 1989 for competency testing, Karen reported with joy that the staff was giving her full information and allowing her to make choices, even if her choice was to do nothing. Most seriously, if a person is seen as helpless, then there is no potential for rehabilitation. As Ellen Bilofsky[2] has written, Sharon was presumed "incompetent until proven competent." If the courts had not accepted Karen's 1987 motion for competency testing, Sharon might have remained in the nursing home indefinitely, presumed incompetent.

Finally, ableism can lead to keeping disabled people hidden, literally out of sight. This is clearly illustrated in Donald Kowalski's responses to his daughter. He argued strenuously against day passes and resented Karen's efforts to take her out. He testified that he would not take Sharon to a shopping center or to church because he did not wish to put her "on display . . . in her condition." Although it was clear to medical staff that outside excursions provided Sharon with important pleasure and stimulation, both vital for rehabilitation, they often cooperated with the father in denying her the possibility. According to an article in the Washington *Post*, Kowalski once said, "What the hell difference does it make if she's gay or lesbian or straight or anything because she's laying there in diapers? . . . let the poor kid rest in peace." Invisible in the nursing home to which he had moved her, cut off from lover and friends, there was little chance for Sharon to demonstrate competence. The wonder is that after three and a half years of loss, loneliness, and lack of proper care, she was able to emerge from her depression and respond to her examiners. To retain her capacity for response, through such an experience, suggests a strong spirit.

The second mode of oppression infusing this case is homophobia, the fear and dislike of homosexuality, and heterosexism, the structuring of our institutions so that only heterosexual relationships are legitimated. Glaringly apparent throughout is the failure to recognize committed gay/lesbian partnerships. Donald Kowalski has consistently denied the possibility. When Karen first arrived at the hospital after the accident, the first on the scene, she was not allowed access to Sharon or even to any information because she was not "family." Seeing her anguish, a Roman Catholic priest interceded, brought information, and arranged for a doctor to speak with her. Although the two women considered themselves married, in law they were not, and therefore lacked any social or legal rights as a couple. As a couple, there would have been no denial of visitation, and the long nightmare of the three-and-a-half year separation would have been avoided. While unmarried heterosexual partners might still have trouble securing guardianship, there would be little problem for a married partner.

Because of heterosexism, Sharon's obvious emotional need for her partner and Karen's rehabilitative effect on her were not honored. Since it was clear that Sharon responded actively to Karen, she was often included in the therapeutic work. Yet, prior to 1989, medical staff often were unwilling to testify to this positive effect, even when they had privately noted it to Karen. Perhaps they feared condoning the same-sex relationship if they reported positively about it; perhaps they did not wish to be involved in the conflict. One neurologist, Dr. Keith Larson, did testify, although he stipulated that he spoke as a friend of the court, not as one of Karen's witnesses. His testimony is worth looking at in detail.

> The reason I'm here today is . . . to deliver an observation that I have agonized over, and thought a great deal about, and prayed a little bit . . . I cannot help but say that Sharon's friend, Karen, can get out of Sharon physical actions, attempts at vocalization, and longer periods of alertness and attention than can really any of our professional therapists.

Why was it necessary to "agonize" over this testimony? To pray about it? Why such a tremendous effort? Clearly, had one of the partners been male, Larson would have had no such difficulty. He simply would have reported the obvious fact: the patient responded far more to her partner than to anyone else. Some medical staff did testify to Karen's positive effects: psychologists, nurses, occupational therapists. And since 1989 the testimony of medical personnel from Miller-Dwan and Travilla has been strong and unanimous. However, in repeated decisions, the courts ignored this testimony.

Finally, heterosexism is evident in a consistent tendency to exaggerate the role of sex in same-sex relationships. In general our society believes that the lives of gay/lesbian people revolve around sex, although evidence from all social-psychological research is that homosexual people are no more sexually active than heterosexual people. Further, gay/lesbian sex is often perceived as sexual exploitation rather than an appropriate expression of mutual caring. The final denial of Karen's visitation rights was based on the charge that she might sexually abuse Sharon. A physician hired by the Kowalskis, Dr. William L. Wilson, leveled this charge as follows:

> It has come to my attention that Karen Thompson has been involved in bathing Sharon Kowalski behind a closed door for a prolonged period of time. It has also come to my attention that Ms. Thompson has alleged a sexual relationship with Sharon Kowalski that existed prior to the accident. Based on this knowledge and my best medical judgment concerning Sharon and her welfare, I feel that visits by Karen Thompson at this time would expose Sharon Kowalski to a high risk of sexual abuse.

Accordingly, as Sharon's physician, Wilson directed the nursing home staff not to permit Karen to visit. Even though under legal statute Karen could have continued her visits while the various decisions were under appeal, the nursing home was obliged to obey the doctor's order.

In this instance, ableism and heterosexism merge. Had Sharon and Karen been unmarried heterosexual partners, sexual abuse probably would have not been an issue. Had they been married, the issue would not exist. Ableism often denies disabled persons their sexuality. However, a person does not lose her sexuality simply because she becomes disabled. Furthermore, a person who loses the capacity to speak has a special need for touching. What are Sharon's sexual rights? Karen has written that when Sharon was starting to emerge from the coma, she once reached out and touched Karen's breast, and later placed Karen's hand on her breast. At the time Karen did not dare to ask medical advice for fear of revealing their relationship; and she recognized that if they were a heterosexual couple, she could have. Even to raise such questions might have exposed her to further charges of sexual abuse. Thus ableism and heterosexism combined to deny both Sharon and Karen the chance to explore such questions.

Heterosexism dictates that only heterosexual partnership can form the basis for a family. While same-sex partnerships are often called "anti-family" in our homophobic society, actually such relationships create family, in that they create stable emotional and economic units. *Family*, in this sense, may be defined as a kin-like unit of two or more persons who are related by blood, marriage, adoption, or primary commitment, and who usually share the same household. Sharon and Karen considered themselves married. Karen's long pilgrimage over almost nine years is testimony to an extraordinary depth of commitment; she would not permit her loved one to be locked away without rehabilitation. Sharon, similarly, has consistently said that she is gay, Karen is her lover, and she wishes to live again with her in St. Cloud. While marriage has historically occurred between two sexes, we cannot determine our definition from history. In United States history, for example, marriage between black and white persons was forbidden for centuries. In 1967, when the Supreme Court finally declared miscegenation laws unconstitutional, there were still such laws on the books in sixteen states.

Sexism is sufficiently interfused with heterosexism that it is difficult to separate them. Heterosexism often enforces a social role on women in which they are subordinated to men. For example, women in the social world of the area in Minnesota where Sharon grew up were expected to marry young and submit to the authority of their husbands, a model that is intrinsically sexist. From the perspective of this model, Sharon's partnership with Karen was illegitimate. Sexism is also apparent in the awarding of full guardianship to the father. In a sexist society, it is appropriate to assign a woman to her male parent; had Sharon been a man rather than a twenty-eight-year-old "girl," such a decision might have been less possible. In a sexist society, women are not encouraged to take responsibility for their sexuality, just as society denies sexual rights to the disabled and elderly. Finally, our society devalues friendship, especially between women. Soon after the accident, a doctor advised Karen to go away and forget Sharon. The gist of his remarks was that "Sharon's parents will always be her parents. They have to deal with this, but you don't. Maybe you should go back to leading your own life." Friendship between the two women was considered unimportant. Ableism as well as sexism is apparent in this advice.

It is sometimes impossible to separate the modes of oppression even for the purpose of analysis. This case makes clear that all the issues work simultaneously and cannot be isolated from each other. Like Audre Lorde,[3] I argue that "there is no hierarchy of oppressions." Admittedly, any individual's perspective on the case is likely to reflect the issue most central to his or her own life: e.g., the gay press emphasizes heterosexism, and the disability rights press emphasizes ableism. Unfortunately, each all too often slights or omits the other. While working in coalition on the case, some women were ill at ease with disability rights activists, and some disability rights groups were anxious about associating themselves with gay/lesbian issues. But the fact is that there are lesbians and gays in the disabled community, and disabled folks in the women's community. Karen experienced the inseparability of the issues on one occasion when she was invited to speak to a Presbyterian disability rights concerns group. They asked her to speak only about ableism, since they had already "done" gay concerns. She tried, but found it nearly impossible; she had to censor her material, ignore basic facts, and leave out crucial connections.

What the three modes of oppression have in common is that in each case one group of people takes power over another. Disabled people, women, gay men and lesbians are all to some degree denied their full personhood by the structures of our society. Their self-determination is limited; their choices can be denied. Their sexuality is controlled. On the basis of ableism, heterosexism, and sexism, Sharon Kowalski's opportunity for the fullest quality of life was permanently taken from her. She was denied proper medical care, legal counsel of her choice, and access to the people she wished to see. As the Minnesota Civil Liberties Union put it, "The convicted criminal loses only his or her liberty; Sharon Kowalski has lost the right to choose who she may see, who she may like, and who she may love." Even her right to be tested for competency was denied for years. Once she secured access to good medical treatment and the people she loves, she was still denied the right to live where she chooses.

Conclusion

Many activists and coalition groups became involved nationally in the struggle to provide rehabilitation for Sharon Kowalski and bring her home. These included disability rights activists, gays and lesbians, feminists and their male supporters, and civil rights workers. In addition there have been many hundreds, perhaps thousands, of people who were drawn to this case by the dimension of human rights. After all, any of us could be hit by a drunk driver, become disabled, and in the process lose our legal and medical rights. The Kowalski/Thompson case stands as a warning that in our deeply divided society, freedom is still a privilege and rights are fragile.

People living in nontraditional families—whether gay/lesbian, unmarried heterosexuals, or communities of choice—need legal protection to secure their legal and medical rights. Karen Thompson has stressed the importance of making your relationships known to your family of birth, if possible, and informing them of your wishes in case of accident. Also, it is essential to execute a durable power of attorney, a document in which you stipulate a person to make medical and financial decisions for you in case you are incapacitated. Copies should be given to your physicians. While requirements vary from state to state and such powers of attorney are not always enforceable, they may serve to protect your rights. Information about how to execute them may be found in your public library, in consultation with a competent lawyer, or in Appendix B of the book *Why Can't Sharon Kowalski Come Home?*[4]

NOTES

1. Karen Thompson and Julie Andrzejewski. *Why Can't Sharon Kowalski Come Home?* San Francisco: Spinster/Aunt Lute, 1988.

2. Ellen Bilofsky. "The Fragile Rights of Sharon Kowalski." *Health/PAC Bulletin*, 1989, 19, 4–16.

3. Audre Lorde. "There Is No Hierarchy of Oppressions." *Interracial Books for Children Bulletin*, 1983, *14*, 9. See also "Age, Race, Class, and Sex: Women Redefining Difference" in *Sister Outsider*. Trumansburg, New York: Crossing Press, 1984.

4. Thompson and Andrezejewski, *op cit*.

20

Race Is a Four-Letter Word

Teja Arboleda

I've been called *nigger* and a neighbor set the dogs on us in Queens, New York.

I've been called *spic* and was frisked in a plush neighborhood of Los Angeles.

I've been called *Jap* and was blamed for America's weaknesses.

I've been called *Nazi* and the neighborhood G.I. Joes had me every time.

I've been called *Turk* and was sneered at in Germany.

I've been called *Stupid Yankee* and was threatened in Japan.

I've been called *Afghanistani* and was spit on by a Boston cab driver.

I've been called *Iraqi* and Desert Storm was America's pride.

I've been called *mulatto, criollo, mestizo, simarron, Hapahaoli, masala, exotic, alternative, mixed-up, messed-up, half-breed,* and *in between.* I've been mistaken for Moroccan, Algerian, Egyptian, Lebanese, Iranian, Turkish, Brazilian, Argentinean, Puerto Rican, Cuban, Mexican, Indonesian, Nepalese, Greek, Italian, Pakistani, Indian, Black, White, Hispanic, Asian, and being a Brooklynite. I've been mistaken for Michael Jackson and Billy Crystal on the same day.

I've been ordered to get glasses of water for neighboring restaurant patrons. I've been told to be careful mopping the floors at the television station where I was directing a show. Even with my U.S. passport, I've been escorted to the "aliens only" line at Kennedy International Airport. I've been told I'm not dark enough. I've been told I'm not White enough. I've been told I talk American real good. I've been told, "Take your humus and your pita bread and go back to Mexico!" I've been ordered to "Go back to where you belong, we don't like *your* kind here!"

I spent too much time and energy as a budding adult abbreviating my identity and rehearsing its explanation. I would practice quietly by myself, reciting what my father always told me: "Filipino-German." He never smiled when he said this.

From *in the shadow of race*, Teja Arboleda (Mahwah, NJ: Lawrence Erlbaum Associates, 1998), pp. 1–5.

My father's dark skin told many stories that his stern face and anger-filled tension couldn't translate. My mother's light skin could never spell empathy—even suntanning only made her turn bright red. My brother Miguel and I became curiosity factors when we appeared in public with her. During the past 34 years, my skin has lightened, somewhat, but then in the summers (even in New England where summers happen suddenly, and disappear just as quickly), I can darken several degrees in a matter of hours. This phenomena seems a peculiar paradigm to which people's perceptions of my culture or race alter with the waning and waxing of my skin tone. I can almost design others' perceptions by counting my minutes in the sun. My years in Japan, the United States, Germany, and the numerous countries, cities, and towns through which I've traveled, have proven that my flesh is irrelevant to the language I speak, to the way I walk and talk, or the way I jog or mow my lawn or to the fact that I often use chopsticks to eat. It is irrelevant to *who* or *what* I married, my political viewpoints, my career, my hopes, desires and fears.

I don't remember being taught by my parents never to *question* skin color, yet when I compare the back of my hand to these pages, I cannot help myself—I must know. Like a sickness coursing through my veins with the very blood that makes me who I am, I ask: What color am I? And, what color was I yesterday? Tomorrow? There is also that pesky, familiar feeling I get when, in the corner of my eye, I catch passing strangers with judgments written on their brows. Maybe paranoia, maybe vanity, but the experiences and memories of too often being "different" or "undefinable" have left me with a weary sense of instant verdict on my part. And sometimes I study their thousands of faces, hoping somehow to connect. I know that they ask themselves the same questions, as they are plagued by the same epidemic, asking and reasking themselves, ourselves, "Who and what are we?"

Overadapting to new environments has become second nature to me, as my father and my mother eagerly fed me culture. As a child I felt like I was being dragged to different corners of the planet with my parents, filling their need for exploration and contact, and teaching us the value and beauty of difference. Between packing suitcases and wandering through unfamiliar territory, all I had ever wanted was to be "the same."

They were successful in some respects—I do believe I am liberal in my thinking—but inevitably there was a price to pay. With each step, each move, each landing through the thick and tenuous atmosphere of a new culture, my feet searched for solid ground, for something familiar. The concept of home, identity, and place become ethereal, like a swirl of gases circling in orbit, waiting for gravity to define their position.

In a sense, I have been relegated to ethnic benchwarmer, on a hunt for simplicity in a world of confusing words that deeply divide us all. In response, I learned to overcompensate. New places and new faces have rarely threatened me, but I have a desperate need to belong to whatever group I'm with at any particular moment. I soak in the surrounding elements to cope with what my instincts oblige, and deliver a new temporary self. I am out of bounds, transcending people and places. I carry within my blood the memories of my heritage connected in the web of my mind, the marriage of history and biology. I breathe the air of my ancestors as if it were fresh from the sunrises of their past. I am illogical, providing argument to traditional categories of race, culture, and ethnicity. I am a cultural chameleon, adapting out of necessity only to discover, yet again, a new Darwinism at the frontiers of identity.

"What are you, anyway?" sometimes demandingly curious Americans like to ask. "I'm Filipino-German," I used to say. I have never been satisfied with abbreviating my identity to the exclusion of all the other puzzle pieces that would then be lost forever in shadowy corners where no one ever looks.

Do I throw a nod at a Black brother who passes me on the street? And if I did so, would he understand why I did? Do I even call him "brother"? Does *he* call *me* "brother"? If not, should he call me a "half-brother," or throw me a half nod? In the United States do I nod or bow to Japanese nationals in a Japanese restaurant? Would they know to bow with me? In Jamaica Plain, Massachusetts, if a Hispanic male gestures hello to me, is it a simple greeting, or a gesture of camaraderie because I might be Hispanic? Do I dress up to go to a country club because, in the eyes of its rich White men, I would otherwise live up their idea of the stereotypical minority? Should I dance well, shaking and driving my body like Papa's family afforded me, or should I remain appropriately conservative to preserve the integrity of a long-gone Puritan New England? Do I shave for the silver hallways of white-collar high-rises so as not to look too "ethnic"? Do I agree to an audition for a commercial when I know the reason I'm there is just to fill in with some skin color for an industry quota?

"I know you're *something*," someone once said. "You have some Black in you," another offered. "He must be ethnic or something," I've overheard. "I've got such a boring family compared to yours," another confided. "You're messed-up," an elementary school girl decided. "Do you love your race?" her classmate wondered. "*What* did you marry?" I've been asked. "*Who* did you marry?" I've been asked. "Is she just like you?" I've been asked. "You are the quintessential American," someone decided.

* * *

America continues to struggle through its identity crisis, and the simple, lazy, bureaucratic checklist we use only serves to satisfy an outdated four-letter word—*race*. Like the basic food groups, it is overconsumed and digested, forming a hemorrhoid in the backside of the same old power struggle. I am only one of many millions of Americans, from this "League of Outsiders," demanding a change in the way we are designed, routed, cattle-called, herded, and shackled into these simplified classifications.

The United States is going through growing pains. The immigrants coming to the United States and becoming citizens are no longer primarily of European origin. But let's not fool ourselves into thinking that America is only now becoming multicultural.

In 1992, *Time* magazine produced a special issue entitled, "The New Face of America" with the subtitle, "How immigrants are shaping the world's first multicultural society." The cover featured a picture of a woman's face. Next to the face was a paragraph that suggested her image was the result of a computerized average of faces of people of several different races.

The operative words on the cover are "races," "culture," and "first." Race and culture are very different words. Race in America is predominantly determined by skin color. Culture is determined by our experiences and our interactions within a society, large or small.

Then there is this idea of being "first." Are we to say that this continent was never populated by a mix of people? Are we to say that the Lacota and Iroquois were of exactly the same culture? What about the different Europeans who settled here later on? Of course, African slaves were not all from the same tribe, and they certainly were not of the same culture as the slave traders.

In the middle of the magazine, there was a compilation, more like a chart of photographs of people from all over the world. The editor and computer artist scanned all the pictures into a computer. Then, by having the computer average the faces together, they produced a variety of facial combinations. Remember, however, they said on the cover, "People from different *races* … to form the world's first *multicultural* society." But in the body of the article and its accompanying pictures, many people were not identified by their *race*, but rather by their *nationalities*—such as Italian and Chinese—in other words *citizenship*, a very different word.

Through it all, *Time* was trying to educate us, but at the same time, we're miseducated. The world—not just this country—has always been and always will be a multicultural environment. So what is it about the words *multicultural* or *diversity* that is confusing or overwhelming?

In the next 20 years, the average American will no longer be technically White. This will have to be reflected in the media, in the workplace, and in the schools, not out of charitable interest, but out of necessity. More people are designating themselves as multiracial or multicultural. People continue to marry across religious, cultural, and ethnic barriers. A definition for "mainstream society" is harder to find.

* * *

My mother's father, Opa, died a year after Oma passed away. The day after the funeral in Germany, my mother's relatives told her, for the first time, that her father was not really her father (i.e., biologically). All the people who knew the true identity of her father have long since passed away. So, if my mother's biological father was, let's say, Italian or Russian, does that make her German-Italian or German-Russian? She says no. German, only German, because that's how she was raised.

My brother, Miguel, married a Brazilian. (*Pause*) Do you have an image in your head of what she looks like? I did when he first told me about her over the phone. Well, she is Brazilian by culture and citizenship, but her parents are

Japanese nationals who moved to Brazil in their early 20s to escape poverty in Japan after World War II. So she *looks stereotypically* Japanese. But she speaks Portuguese and doesn't interact socially like most Japanese do.

✻ ✻ ✻

I offer myself as a case study in transcending the complex maze of barriers, pedestals, doors, and traps that form the boundaries that confine human beings to dominant and minority groups.

I am tired. I am exhausted. I am always looking for new and improved definitions for my identity. My very-mixed heritage, culture, and international experiences seem like a blur sometimes, and I long for a resting place. A place where I can breathe like I did in my mother's womb: without having to open my mouth.

Suggestions for Further Reading

Abbott, Franklin, ed. *New Men, New Minds.* Freedom, CA: Crossing Press, 1993.

Anguilar-San Juan, Karin. *The State of Asian America.* Boston: South End Press, 1994.

Anzaldua, Gloria, ed. *Making Faces, Making Soul: Creative and Critical Perspectives by Women of Color.* San Francisco: Aunt Lute Books, 1990.

Azoulay, Katya Gibel. *Black, Jewish, and Interracial.* Durham, NC: Duke University Press, 1997.

Bean, Joseph. *In the Life: A Black Gay Anthology.* Boston: Alyson Publications, 1986.

Brown, R.M. *RubyFruit Jungle.* New York: Bantam, 1977.

Chinese Historical Society of Southern California. *Linking Our Lives: Chinese American Women of Los Angeles.* Los Angeles: Chinese Historical Society of Southern California, 1984.

Clausen, Jan. *Apples and Oranges: My Journey to Sexual Identity.* Houghton Mifflin, 1999.

Cofer, Judith Ortiz. *The Latin Deli.* Athens: University of Georgia Press, 1993.

Crozier-Hogle, Lois, et al. *Surviving in Two Worlds: Contemporary Native American Voices.* University of Texas Press, 1997.

Danticat, Edwidge. *Breath, Eyes, Memory.* New York: Vintage Books, 1994.

Davis, Lennard. *The Disability Reader.* Routledge, 1997.

Delgado, Richard, and Jean Stefancic. *The Latino/a Condition: A Critical Reader.* New York: New York University Press, 1998.

Findlen, Barbara. *Listen Up: Voices from the Next Feminist Generation.* Seal Press, 1995.

Flores, Angel, and Kate Flores. *The Defiant Muse: Hispanic Feminist Poems from the Middle Ages to the Present.* New York: Feminist Press, 1986.

Geary, Hobson, ed. *The Remembered Earth: An Anthology of Contemporary Native American Literature.* Albuquerque: University of New Mexico Press, 1981.

Gwaltney, J. *Drylongso: A Self-Portrait of Black America.* New York: Vintage Books, 1981.

Haley, Alex. *The Autobiography of Malcolm X*. New York: Grove Press, 1964.

Holmes, Sarah, ed. *Testimonies: A Collection of Lesbian Coming Out Stories*. Boston: Alyson Publications, 1988.

James, M. Annette. *The State of Native Americans*. Boston: South End Press, 1993.

Jen, Gish. *Typical American*. New York: Penguin, 1992.

Kim, Elaine H., and Lilia V. Villanueva. *Making More Waves: New Writings by Asian American Women*. Boston: Beacon Press, 1997.

Kimmel, Michael S., and Michael A. Messner, eds. *Men's Lives*. New York: Macmillan, 1997.

Kingston, M.H. *The Woman Warrior*. New York: Vintage Books, 1981.

Lee, Joann Faung Jean, ed. *Asian Americans*. New York: New Press, 1991.

Moody, A. *Coming of Age in Mississippi*. New York: Dell, 1968.

Native Americans 500 Years After. Photographs by Joseph C. Farner, text by Michael Dorris. New York: Thomas Crowell, 1975.

Ng, Fae Myenne. *Bone*. New York: Harper Perennial, 1994.

Pemberton, Gayle. *The Hottest Water in Chicago*. New York: Doubleday/Anchor, 1992.

Rebollendo, Tey Diana, and Eliana S. Rivero, eds. *Infinite Divisions: An Anthology of Chicana Literature*. Tucson: University of Arizona Press, 1993.

Reid, John. *The Best Little Boy in the World*. New York: G.P. Putnam's Sons, 1973.

Rivera, E. *Family Installments: Memories of Growing Up Hispanic*. New York: Penguin, 1983.

Rubin, L.B. *Worlds of Pain: Life in the Working Class Family*. New York: Basic Books, 1976.

Santiago, Esmeralda. *When I Was Puerto Rican*. New York: Vintage Books, 1993.

Shulman, A.K. *Memoirs of an Ex-Prom Queen*. New York: Knopf, 1972.

Silko, L.M. *Ceremony*. New York: New American Library, 1972.

Smith, B., ed. *Home Girls: A Black Feminist Anthology*. New York: Kitchen Table/Women of Color Press, 1983.

Tan, Amy. *The Joy Luck Club*. New York: Ivy Books, 1990.

Tatum, Charles, ed. *New Chicana/Chicano Writing 2*. Tucson: University of Arizona Press, 1992.

Thompson, Karen, and Julie Andrzejewski. *Why Can't Sharon Kowalski Come Home?* San Francisco: Spinsters/Aunt Lute, 1988.

Turkel, Studs. *Working*. New York: Avon Books, 1972.

Warshaw, Robin. *I Never Called It Rape*. New York: Harper & Row, 1988.

Winged Words: American Indian Writers Speak. Lincoln: University of Nebraska Press, 1990.

Zahava, Irene, ed. *Speaking for Ourselves: Short Stories by Jewish Lesbians*. Freedom, CA: Crossing Press, 1990.

PART VI

How It Happened: Race and Gender Issues in U.S. Law

HISTORY HOLDS THE KEY TO BOTH THE PAST AND THE PRESENT. By studying history we can understand how what happened in the past is reflected in the present, and we can distinguish between discriminatory or unjust contemporary policies and practices that represent accidental or aberrant abridgement of rights and those that are part of a pattern of racism and sexism. But whose history shall we study?

History can be written from many different perspectives. The life stories of so-called great men will vary greatly, depending on whether the biographers are their mothers, their wives, their lovers, their peers, their children, or their servants. Each perspective contributes something unique and essential to the portrait. Furthermore, historians now ask why history should be the study of "great men" exclusively, as they increasingly turn their attention to the lives of ordinary people in order to produce a more inclusive and hence more accurate account of the past.

We can even question who decides what counts as history. It was once the case that the war diaries of generals were regarded as important historical documents, whereas the diaries written by women giving an account of their daily lives were ignored or discarded. What made one document invaluable and the other irrelevant? Traditional historians adopted a fairly narrow, Eurocentric perspective on the past and used it as the basis for writing what was then alleged to provide an "objective" and "universal" picture of the past. These texts left out important information and consigned the majority of people in U.S. society to the margins of history. This approach failed to reflect the ways in which women, people of all colors, and working people created the wealth and culture of this country.

It is commonly believed that history involves collecting and studying facts. But what counts as a "fact," and who decides which facts are important? Whose interests are served or furthered by these decisions? For many years, one of the first "facts" that grade-school children learned was that Christopher Columbus discovered America. Yet this "history" is neither clear nor incontrovertible. It is a piece of the past examined from the point of view of white Europeans; it is in their interest to persuade others to believe it, since this "fact" undermines the claims of others. Native Americans might well ask how Columbus could have discovered America in 1492 if they had already been living here for thousands of years. Teaching children that bit of fiction about Columbus served to render Native Americans invisible and thus tacitly excused or denied the genocide carried out by European settlers.

During the contemporary period, many new approaches to history have arisen to remedy the omissions and distortions of the past. Women's history, black history, lesbian and gay history, ethnic history, labor history, and others all propose to transform traditional history so that it more accurately reflects the reality of people's lives, both past and present.

Part VI does not attempt to provide a comprehensive history of the American Republic since its beginning. Rather, it traces the legal status of people of color and women since the first Europeans came to this land. After a preliminary reading (Selection 1) that represents an overview of legal issues as they apply to Native Americans in particular, this Part proceeds by presenting legal documents that highlight developments in legal status. In a few cases, these documents are supplemented with materials that help paint a clearer picture of the issues involved or their implications.

Much is left out by adopting this framework for our study. Most significantly, discussions of the actual political and social movements that brought about the changes in the legal realm are omitted. For this reason, students are urged to supplement their study of the legal documents with the rich accounts of social history from the *Suggestions for Further Reading* at the end of Part VI.

However, the legal documents themselves are fascinating. They make it possible to reduce the record of hundreds of years of history to a manageable size. We can thus form a picture of the rights and status of many so-called minority groups in this country, a picture that contrasts sharply with the one usually offered in high school social studies classes. Most importantly, the documents can help us answer the question raised by material in the first five parts of this text: How did it happen that all women and all people of color came to have such limited access to power and opportunity?

The readings here show that, from the country's inception, the laws and institutions of the United States were designed to create and maintain the privileges of wealthy white males. The discrimination documented in the early parts of this book is no accident. It has a long and deliberate history. Understanding this history is essential if we are to create a more just and democratic society.

On July 4, 1776, the thirteen colonies set forth a declaration of independence from Great Britain. In that famous document, the founders of the Republic explained their reasons for separating from the homeland and expressed their hopes for the new Republic. In lines that are rightly famous and often quoted, the signatories proclaimed that "all Men are created equal, that they are endowed by their Creator with certain unalienable Rights, that among these are Life, Liberty and the Pursuit of Happiness." They went on to assert that "to secure these Rights, Governments are instituted among Men, deriving their just Powers from the Consent of the Governed." When these words were written, however, a large portion of the population of the United States had no legal rights whatsoever. Native Americans, women, indentured servants, poor white men who did not own property, and, of course, Negroes held as slaves could not vote, nor were they free to exercise their liberty or pursue their happiness in the same way that white men with property could. When the authors of the Declaration of Independence proclaimed that all men were created equal and endowed with unalienable rights, they meant "men" quite literally and white men specifically. Negroes held in slavery, as it turned out, were worth "three fifths of all other Persons," a figure stipulated in Article 1, Section 2, of the United States Constitution (see Selection 3). This section of the Constitution, which is often referred to as the "three-fifths compromise," undertook to establish how slaves would be counted for the purposes of determining taxes as well as for calculating representation of the states in Congress.

Faced with the need for an enormous work force to cultivate the land, the European settlers first tried to enslave the American Indian population. Later, the settlers brought over large numbers of "indentured workers" from Europe. These workers were poor white men, women, and children, some serving prison sentences at home, who were expected to work in the colonies for a certain period of time and then receive their freedom. When neither of these populations proved suitable, the settlers began importing African Negroes to serve their purposes.

Records show that the first African Negroes were brought to this country as early as 1526. Initially, the Negroes appear to have had the same status as indentured servants, but the laws reflect a fairly rapid distinction between the two groups. Maryland law made this distinction as early as 1640; Massachusetts legally recognized slavery in 1641; Virginia passed a law making Negroes slaves for life in 1661; and so it went until the number of slaves grew to roughly 600,000 at the time of the signing of the Declaration of Independence.[1] Numerous legal documents, such as An Act for the Better Ordering and Governing of Negroes and Slaves, passed in South Carolina in

1712 and excerpted in Selection 2, prescribed the existence of the slaves, as did the acts modeled on An Act Prohibiting the Teaching of Slaves to Read, a North Carolina statute reprinted here in Selection 4.

When the early European settlers came to this country, there were approximately 2.5 million Native Americans living on the land that was to become the United States. These peoples were divided among numerous separate and autonomous tribes, each with its own highly developed culture and history. The white settlers quickly lumped these diverse peoples into a single and inferior category, "Indians," and set about destroying their culture and seizing their lands. The Indian Removal Act of 1830 was fairly typical of the kinds of laws that were passed to carry out the appropriation of Indian lands. Believing the Indians to be inherently inferior to whites, the U.S. government had no hesitation about legislating the removal of the Indians from valuable ancestral lands to ever more remote and barren reservations. The dissolution of the Indian tribal system was further advanced by the General Allotment Act (Dawes Act) of 1887, which divided tribal landholdings among individual Indians and thereby successfully undermined the tribal system and the culture of which it was a part. In addition, this act opened up lands within the reservation area for purchase by the U.S. government, which then made those lands available to white settlers for homesteading. Many supporters of the allotment policy, who were considered "friends" of the Indians, argued that the benefits of individual ownership would have a "civilizing effect" on them.[2] Instead, it ensured a life of unrelenting poverty for most because it was usually impossible for a family to derive subsistence from the use of a single plot of land, without the support of the tribal community.

While John Adams was involved in writing the Declaration of Independence, his wife, Abigail Adams, took him to task for failing to accord women the same rights and privileges as men: "I cannot say that you are very generous to the ladies; for whilst you are proclaiming peace and good will to men, emancipating all nations, you insist upon retaining an absolute power over wives."[3] Although law and custom consistently treated women as if they were physically and mentally inferior to men, the reality of women's lives was very different. Black female slaves were forced to perform the same inhuman fieldwork as black male slaves and were expected to do so even in the final weeks of pregnancy. They were routinely beaten and abused without regard for the supposed biological fragility of the female sex. White women settlers gave birth to large numbers of children, ten and twelve being quite common and as many as twenty births not being unusual. And they did so in addition to working side by side with men to perform all those duties necessary to ensure survival in a new and unfamiliar environment. When her husband died, a woman often assumed his responsibilities as well. It was not until well into the 1800s, primarily as a result of changes brought about by the Industrial Revolution, that significant class differences began to affect the lives and work of white women.

As women, both black and white, became increasingly active in the anti-slavery movement during the 1800s, many noticed certain similarities between the legal status of women and the legal status of people held as slaves. Participants at the first women's rights convention, held in Seneca Falls, New York, in 1848, listed women's grievances and specified their demands. At this time, married women were regarded as property of their husbands and had no direct legal control over their own wages, their property, or even their children. The Declaration of Sentiments issued in Seneca Falls was modeled on the Declaration of Independence in the hope that men would extend the declaration's rights to women. It is reprinted in this Part (as Selection 5) along with readings from a variety of sources from the period that reflect the most typical male responses to women's demand for the vote and other rights (see Selection 6). Similar emotional attacks are still used today to ridicule and then dismiss contemporary feminist demands.

The abysmal legal status of women and people of color in the United States during the nineteenth century is graphically documented in a series of court decisions reproduced in this Part. In *People* v. *Hall,* 1854 (excerpted in Selection 7), the California Supreme Court decided that a California statute barring Indians and Negroes from testifying in court cases involving whites also applied to Chinese Americans. The judges asserted that the Chinese are "a race of people whom nature has marked as inferior, and who are incapable of progress or intellectual development beyond a certain point." The extent of anti-Chinese feeling in parts of the United States can be further inferred from portions of the California Constitution adopted in 1876 (see Selection 14).

In a more famous case, *Dred Scott* v. *Sandford,* 1857 (Selection 8), the United States Supreme Court was asked to decide whether Dred Scott, a Negro, was a citizen of the United States with the rights that that implied. Scott, a slave who had been taken from Missouri, a slave state, into the free state of Illinois for a period of time, argued that because he was free and had been born in the United States, he was therefore a citizen. The Court ruled that this was not the case and, using reasoning that strongly parallels *People* v. *Hall,* offered a survey of U.S. law and custom to show that Negroes were never considered a part of the people of the United States. In *Bradwell* v. *Illinois,* 1873 (summarized in Selection 12), the Supreme Court ruled that women could not practice law and used the opportunity to carefully distinguish the rights and prerogatives of women from those of men. The Court maintained that "civil law, as well as nature herself, has always recognized a wide difference in the respective spheres and destinies of man and woman" and went on to argue that women belong in the "domestic sphere."

During the period in which these and other court cases were brought, the United States moved toward and ultimately fought a bloody civil war. It was allegedly fought "to free the slaves," but much more was at stake. The Civil War reflected a struggle to the death between the Southern aristocracy, whose wealth was based on land and whose power rested on a kind of feudal economic-political order, and the Northern capitalists, who came into being by virtue of the Industrial Revolution and who wished to restructure the nation's economic-political institutions to better serve the needs of the new industrial order. Chief among these needs was a large and mobile work force for the factories in the North. Hundreds of thousands of soldiers died in the bloody conflict, while other men purchased army deferments and used the war years to amass tremendous personal wealth. On the Confederate side, men who owned fifty or more slaves were exempted from serving in the army, whereas wealthy Northern men were able to purchase deferments from the Union for the sum of $300. Among those who purchased deferments and went on to become millionaires as a result of war profiteering were John D. Rockefeller, Andrew Carnegie, J. Pierpont Morgan, Philip Armour, James Mellon, and Jay Gould.[4]

In September 1862, President Abraham Lincoln signed the Emancipation Proclamation (Selection 9) as part of his efforts to bring the Civil War to an end by forcing the Southern states to concede. It did not free all slaves; it freed only those in states or parts of states in rebellion against the federal government. Only in September 1865, after the conclusion of the war, were all people held as slaves freed by the Thirteenth Amendment (Selection 10). However, Southern whites did not yield their privileges easily. Immediately after the war, the Southern states began to pass laws known as "The Black Codes," which attempted to reestablish the relations of slavery. Some of these codes are described in this Part in Selection 11, written by the distinguished historian W. E. B. Du Bois.

In the face of such efforts to deny the rights of citizenship to black men, Congress passed the Fourteenth Amendment (Selection 10) in July 1868. This amendment, which continues to play a major role in contemporary legal battles over discrimination, includes a number of important provisions. It explicitly extended citizenship to all those born or naturalized in the United States and guaranteed all citizens "due process" and "equal protection" of the law. In addition, it canceled all debts incurred by the Confederacy in its unsuccessful rebellion while recognizing the validity of the debts incurred by the federal government. This meant that wealthy Southerners who had extended large sums of money or credit to the Confederacy would lose it, whereas wealthy Northern industrialists would be repaid.

Southern resistance to extending the rights and privileges of citizenship to black men persisted, and the Southern states used all their powers, including unbridled terror and violence, to subvert the intent of the Thirteenth and Fourteenth Amendments. The Fifteenth Amendment (Selection 10), which explicitly granted the vote to black men, was passed in 1870 but was received by the Southern states with as little enthusiasm as had greeted the Thirteenth and Fourteenth Amendments.

As the abolitionist movement grew and the Civil War became inevitable, many women's rights activists, also active in the struggle to end slavery, argued that the push for women's rights should temporarily defer to the issue of slavery. In fact, after February 1861, no women's rights conventions were held until the end of the war. Although black and white women had long worked together in both movements, the question of which struggle took precedence created serious splits among women's rights activists, including such strong black allies as Frederick Douglass and Sojourner Truth. Some argued that the evils of slavery were so great that they took precedence over the legal discrimination experienced by middle-class white women. They resented attempts by Elizabeth Cady Stanton and others to equate the condition of white women with that of Negroes held in slavery and argued, moreover, that the women's rights movement had never been concerned with the extraordinary suffering of black women or the special needs of working women. The explicitly racist appeals made by some white women activists as they sought white men's support for women's suffrage did nothing to bridge this schism. While black men received the vote in 1868, at least on paper, women would have to continue their fight until the passage of the Nineteenth Amendment (Selection 17) in 1920. As a result, many women and blacks saw each other as adversaries or obstacles in their struggle for legal equality, deflecting their attention from the privileged white men who provoked the conflict and whose power was reinforced by it.

One special cause for bitterness was the Fourteenth Amendment's reference to "male inhabitants" and the right to vote. This was the first time that voting rights had explicitly been rendered gender-specific. The Fourteenth Amendment was tested in 1875 by *Minor* v. *Happersett* (Selection 13), in which the Court was asked to rule directly on the question of whether women had the vote by virtue of their being citizens of the United States. The Court ruled unanimously that women did not have the vote, arguing that women, like criminals and mental defectives, could legitimately be denied the vote by the states.[5] In a somewhat similar case, *Elk* v. *Wilkins,* 1884 (Selection 15), John Elk, an American Indian who had left his tribe and lived among whites, argued that he was a citizen by virtue of the Fourteenth Amendment and should not be denied the right to vote by the state of Nebraska. The Supreme Court ruled that neither the Fourteenth nor the Fifteenth Amendment applied to Elk. Native Americans became citizens of the United States three years later, under one of the provisions of the Dawes Act of 1887.

Unsuccessful in their attempts to reinstate some form of forced servitude by passage of "The Black Codes," Southern states began to legalize the separation of the races in all aspects of public and private life. In *Plessy* v. *Ferguson,* 1896 (Selection 16), the Supreme Court was asked to rule on whether segregation by race in public facilities violated the Thirteenth and Fourteenth Amendments. In a ruling that was to cruelly affect several generations of black

Americans, the Supreme Court decided that restricting Negroes to the use of "separate but equal" public accommodations did not deny them equal protection of the law. This decision remained in effect for almost sixty years until *Brown* v. *Board of Education of Topeka,* 1954 (Selection 19). In the historic *Brown* decision, the Court ruled, in effect, that "separate" could not possibly be "equal." Nonetheless, abolishing segregation on paper was one thing; actually bringing about the integration of public facilities was another. The integration of public schools, housing, and employment in both the North and the South has been a long and often bloody struggle that continues to this day.

The racist attitudes toward Chinese Americans, reflected in the nineteenth-century California statutes and constitution, as we have already seen, extended toward Japanese Americans as well. This racism erupted during the twentieth century after the bombing of Pearl Harbor by Japan on December 7, 1941. Anti-Japanese feelings ran so high that President Franklin Roosevelt issued an executive order allowing the military to designate "military areas" from which it could then exclude any persons it chose. On March 2, 1942, the entire West Coast was designated as such an area, and within a few months everyone of Japanese ancestry (defined as those having as little as one-eighth Japanese blood) was evacuated. More than 110,000 people of Japanese descent, most of them American citizens, were forced to leave their homes and jobs and to spend the war years in so-called relocation camps behind barbed wire.[6] Although the United States was also at war with Germany, no such barbaric treatment was afforded German Americans. The military evacuation of Japanese Americans was challenged in *Korematsu* v. *United States,* 1944. In its decision, excerpted in Selection 18, the Supreme Court upheld the forced evacuation.

The twentieth century has seen the growth of large and diverse movements for race and gender justice. These movements precipitated the creation of a number of commissions and government agencies that were to research and enforce equal treatment for people of color and women, the passage of a number of statutes to this end, and a series of Supreme Court decisions. For women, one of the most significant Court decisions of the recent past was *Roe* v. *Wade,* 1973 (Selection 20), which, for the first time, gave women the right to terminate pregnancy by abortion. Rather than affirming a woman's right to control her body, however, the *Roe* decision is based on the right to privacy. The impact of *Roe* was significantly blunted by *Harris* v. *McRae,* 1980, in which the Court ruled that the right to privacy did not require public funding of medically necessary abortions for women who could not afford them. In practice, this meant that middle-class women who chose abortion could exercise their right but that many poor white women and women of color could not. The single biggest defeat for the women's movement of this period was the failure to pass the much misunderstood Equal Rights Amendment, which is reprinted in Selection 21.

More recently, the Supreme Court was asked to rule on the constitutionality of homosexual intercourse when Michael Hardwick, a practicing homosexual, brought suit challenging the constitutionality of Georgia's sodomy law. In *Bowers* v. *Hardwick,* 1986 (Selection 22), the Court upheld that law. In a broad decision that could have disturbing implications for many different kinds of private sexual conduct between consenting adults, the Supreme Court ruled that it is not unconstitutional to legislate against certain forms of sexual activity. The prohibition against sodomy, as well as other legal issues that might impact directly on lesbians and gay men, are surveyed in Selection 23,"Confronting Obstacles to Lesbian and Gay Equality."

NOTES

1. W. Z. Foster, *The Negro People in American History* (New York: International Publishers, 1954), p. 37.

2. U.S. Commission on Civil Rights, *Indian Tribes: A Continuing Quest for Survival,* a report of the United States Commission on Civil Rights, June 1981, p. 34.

3. Letter to John Adams, May 7, 1776.

4. H. Wasserman, *Harvey Wasserman's History of the United States* (New York: Harper & Row, 1975), p. 3.

5. E. Flexner, *Century of Struggle* (Cambridge, MA: Harvard University Press, 1976), p. 172.

6. R. E. Cushman and R. F. Cushman, *Cases in Constitutional Law* (New York: Appleton-Century-Crofts, 1958), p. 127.

1

Indian Tribes:
A Continuing Quest for Survival

U.S. Commission on Human Rights

Traditional civil rights, as the phrase is used here, include those rights that are secured to individuals and are basic to the United States system of government. They include the right to vote and the right to equal treatment without discrimination on the basis of race, religion, or national origin, among others, in such areas as education, housing, employment, public accommodations, and the administration of justice.

In order to understand where American Indians stand today with respect to these rights, it is important to look at historical developments of the concept of Indian rights along with the civil rights movement in this country. The consideration given to these factors here will not be exhaustive, but rather a brief look at some of the events that are most necessary to a background understanding of this area.

A basic and essential factor concerning American Indians is that the development of civil rights issues for them is in reverse order from other minorities in this country. Politically, other minorities started with nothing and attempted to obtain a voice in the existing economic and political structure. Indians started with everything and have gradually lost much of what they had to an advancing alien civilization. Other minorities have had no separate governmental institutions. Their goal primarily has been and continues to be to make the existing system involve them and work for them. Indian tribes have always been separate political entities interested in maintaining their own institutions and beliefs. Their goal has been to prevent the dismantling of their own systems. So while other minorities have sought integration into the larger society, much of Indian society is motivated to retain its political and cultural separateness.

Although at the beginning of the colonization process Indian nations were more numerous and better adapted to survival on this continent than the European settlers, these advantages were quickly lost. The colonization period saw the rapid expansion of non-Indian communities in numbers and territory covered and a shift in the balance of strength from Indian to non-Indian communities and

Indian Tribes: A Continuing Quest for Survival, a report of the United States Commission on Civil Rights, June 1981, p. 34. Reprinted by permission.

governments. The extent to which Indians intermingled with non-Indian society varied by time period, geographical location, and the ability of natives and newcomers to get along with one another. As a general matter, however, Indians were viewed and treated as members of political entities that were not part of the United States. The Constitution acknowledges this by its separate provision regarding trade with the Indian tribes.[1] Indian tribes today that have not been forcibly assimilated, extinguished, or legally terminated still consider themselves to be, and are viewed in American law, as separate political units.

The Racial Factor

An important element in the development of civil rights for American Indians today goes beyond their legal and political status to include the way they have been viewed racially. Since colonial times Indians have been viewed as an "inferior race"; sometimes this view is condescendingly positive—the romanticized noble savage—at other times this view is hostile—the vicious savage—at all times the view is racist. All things Indian are viewed as inherently inferior to their counterparts in the white European tradition. Strong racist statements have appeared in congressional debates, Presidential policy announcements, court decisions, and other authoritative public utterances. This racism has served to justify a view now repudiated, but which still lingers in the public mind, that Indians are not entitled to the same legal rights as others in this country. In some cases, racism has been coupled with apparently benevolent motives, to "civilize" the "savages," to teach them Christian principles. In other cases, the racism has been coupled with greed; Indians were "removed" to distant locations to prevent them from standing in the way of the development of the new Western civilization. At one extreme the concept of inferior status of Indians was used to justify genocide; at the other, apparently benevolent side, the attempt was to assimilate them into the dominant society. Whatever the rationale or motive, whether rooted in voluntary efforts or coercion, the common denominator has been the belief that Indian society is an inferior lifestyle.

> It sprang from a conviction that native people were a lower grade of humanity for whom the accepted cannons [*sic*] of respect need not apply; one did not debase oneself by ruining a native person. At times, this conviction was stated explicitly by men in public office, but whether expressed or not, it generated decision and action.[2]

Early assimilationists like Thomas Jefferson proceeded from this assumption with benevolent designs.

> Thus, even as they acknowledged a degree of political autonomy in the tribes, their conviction of the natives' cultural inferiority led them to interfere in their social, religious, and economic practices. Federal agents to the tribes not only negotiated

treaties and tendered payments; they pressured husbands to take up the plow and wives to learn to spin. The more conscientious agents offered gratuitous lectures on the virtues of monogamy, industry, and temperance.

The same underlying assumption provided the basis for Andrew Jackson's attitude. "I have long viewed treaties with the Indians an absurdity not to be reconciled to the principles of our government," he said. As President he refused to enforce the decisions of the U.S. Supreme Court upholding Cherokee tribal autonomy, and he had a prominent role in the forced removal of the Cherokees from Georgia and the appropriation of their land by white settlers. Other eastern tribes met a similar fate under the Indian Removal Act of 1830.[3]

Another Federal Indian land policy, enacted at the end of the 19th century and followed until 1934, that shows the virulent effect of racist assumptions was the allotment of land parcels to individual Indians as a replacement for tribal ownership. Many proponents of the policy were considered "friends of the Indians," and they argued that the attributes of individual land ownership would have a great civilizing and assimilating effect on American Indians. This action, undertaken for the benefit of the Indians, was accomplished without consulting them. Had Congress heeded the views of the purported beneficiaries of this policy, allotment might not have been adopted. Representatives of 19 tribes met in Oklahoma and unanimously opposed the legislation, recognizing the destructive effect it would have upon Indian culture and the land base itself, which was reduced by 90 million acres in 45 years.

An important principle established by the allotment policy was that the Indian form of land ownership was not "civilized," and so it was the right of the Government to invalidate that form. It is curious that the principle of the right to own property in conglomerate form for the benefit of those with a shareholder's undivided interest in the whole was a basis of the American corporate system, then developing in strength. Yet a similar form of ownership when practiced by Indians was viewed as a hallmark of savagery. Whatever the explanation for this double standard, the allotment policy reinforced the notion that Indians were somehow inferior, that non-Indians in power knew what was best for them, and that these suppositions justified the assertion that non-Indians had the power and authority to interfere with the basic right to own property.

Religion is another area in which non-Indians have felt justified in interfering with Indian beliefs. The intent to civilize the natives of this continent included a determined effort to Christianize them. Despite the constitutional prohibition, Congress, beginning in 1819, regularly appropriated funds for Christian missionary efforts. Christian goals were visibly aligned with Federal Indian policy in 1869 when a Board of Indian Commissioners was established by Congress under President Grant's administration. Representative of the spectrum of Christian denominations, the independently wealthy members of the Board were charged by the Commissioner of Indian Affairs to work for the "humanization, civilization and Christianization of the Indians." Officials of the Federal Indian Service were supposed to cooperate with this Board.

The benevolent support of Christian missionary efforts stood in stark contrast to the Federal policy of suppressing tribal religions. Indian ceremonial behavior was misunderstood and suppressed by Indian agents. In 1892 the Commissioner of Indian Affairs established a regulation making it a criminal offense to engage in such ceremonies as the sun dance. The spread of the Ghost Dance religion, which promised salvation from the white man, was so frightening to the Federal Government that troops were called in to prevent it, even though the practice posed no threat to white settlers.

The judiciary of the United States, though it has in many instances forthrightly interpreted the law to support Indian legal claims in the face of strong, sometimes violent opposition, has also lent support to the myth of Indian inferiority. For example, the United States Supreme Court in 1883, in recognizing the right of tribes to govern themselves, held that they had the exclusive authority to try Indians for criminal offenses committed against Indians. In describing its reasons for refusing to find jurisdiction in a non-Indian court in such cases, the Supreme Court said:

> It [the non-Indian court] tries them, not by their peers, nor by the customs of their people, nor the law of their land, but by *superiors* of a different race, according to the law of a social state of which they have an imperfect conception, and which is opposed to the traditions of their history, to the habits of their lives, to the strongest prejudices of their *savage nature*; one which measures the red man's revenge by the maxims of the white man's morality.[4] (emphasis added)

In recognizing the power of the United States Government to determine the right of Indians to occupy their lands, the Supreme Court expressed the good faith of the country in such matters with these words: "the United States will be governed by such considerations of justice as will control a Christian people in their treatment of an ignorant and dependent race."[5]

Another example of racist stereotyping to be found in the courts is this example from the Supreme Court of Washington State:

> The Indian was a child, and a dangerous child, of nature, to be both protected and restrained. . . . True, arrangements took the form of treaty and of terms like "cede," "relinquish," "reserve." But never were these agreements between equals . . . [but rather] that "between a superior and an inferior."[6]

This reasoning, based on racism, has supported the view that Indians are wards of the Government who need the protection and assistance of Federal agencies and it is the Government's obligation to recreate their governments, conforming them to a non-Indian model, to establish their priorities, and to make or approve their decisions for them.

Indian education policies have often been examples of the Federal Government having determined what is "best" for Indians. Having judged that assimilation could be promoted through the indoctrination process of white schools, the Federal Government began investing in Indian education. Following the model established by army officer Richard Pratt in 1879, boarding schools were established where Indian children were separated from the influences of tribal and home life. The boarding schools tried to teach Indians skills and trades that would be useful in white society, utilizing stern disciplinary measures to force assimilation. The tactics used are within memory of today's generation of tribal leaders who recall the policy of deterring communication in native languages. "I remember being punished many times for . . . singing one Navajo song, or a Navajo word slipping out of my tongue just in an unplanned way, but I was punished for it."

Federal education was made compulsory, and the policy was applied to tribes that had sophisticated school systems of their own as well as to tribes that really needed assistance to establish educational systems. The ability of the tribal school to educate was not relevant, given that the overriding goal was assimilation rather than education.

Racism in Indian affairs has not been sanctioned recently by political or religious leaders or other leaders in American society. In fact, public pronouncements over the last several decades have lamented past evils and poor treatment of Indians.[7] The virulent public expressions of other eras characterizing Indians as "children" or "savages" are not now acceptable modes of public expression. Public policy today is a commitment to Indian self-determination. Numerous actions of Congress and the executive branch give evidence of a more positive era for Indian policy.[8] Beneath the surface, however, the effects of centuries of racism still persist. The attitudes of the public, of State and local officials, and of Federal policymakers do not always live up to the positive pronouncements of official policy. Some decisions today are perceived as being made on the basis of precedents mired in the racism and greed of another era. Perhaps more important, the legacy of racism permeates behavior and that behavior creates classic civil rights violations. . . .

NOTES

1. U.S. Const. Art. 1, §8.

2. D'Arcy McNickel, *Native American Tribalism* (New York: Oxford University Press, 1973), p. 56.

3. Act of May 28, 1830, ch. 148, 4 Stat. 411.

4. *Ex Parte Crow Dog*, 109 U.S. 556, 571 (1883).

5. *Missouri, Kansas, and Texas Railway Co.* v. *Roberts*, 152 U.S. 114, 117 (1894).

6. *State* v. *Towessnute*, 154 P. 805, 807 (Wash. Sup. Ct. 1916), quoting *Choctaw Nation* v. *United States*, 119 U.S. 1, 27 (1886).

7. See, e.g., President Nixon's July 8, 1970, Message to the Congress, Recommendations for Indian Policy, H. Doc. No. 91–363, 91st Cong., 2d sess.

8. Ibid; Indian Self-Determination and Education Assistance Act, Pub. L. No. 93–638, 88 Stat. 2203 (1975); Indian Child Welfare Act of 1978, Pub. L. No. 95–608, 92 Stat. 3096; U.S. Department of the Interior, *Report on the Implementation of the Helsinki Final Act* (1979).

2

An Act for the Better Ordering and Governing of Negroes and Slaves, South Carolina, 1712

Colonial America had a role for the Negro. But the presence of a servile population, presumably of inferior stock, made it necessary to adopt measures of control. As might be expected, the southern colonies had the most highly developed codes governing Negroes. In 1712 South Carolina passed "An Act for the better ordering and governing of Negroes and Slaves." This comprehensive measure served as a model for slave codes in the South during the colonial and national periods. Eight of its thirty-five sections are reproduced below.

Whereas, the plantations and estates of this province cannot be well and sufficiently managed and brought into use, without the labor and service of negroes and other slaves; and forasmuch as the said negroes and other slaves brought unto the people of this Province for that purpose, are of barbarous, wild, savage natures, and such as renders them wholly unqualified to be governed by the laws, customs, and practices of this Province; but that it is absolutely necessary, that such other constitutions, laws and orders, should in this Province be made and enacted, for the good regulating and ordering of them, as may restrain the disorders, rapines and inhumanity, to which they are naturally prone and inclined, and may also tend to the safety and security of the people of this Province and their estates; to which purpose,

I. *Be it therefore enacted,* by his Excellency William, Lord Craven, Palatine, and the rest of the true and absolute Lords and Proprietors of this Province, by and with the advice and consent of the rest of the members of the General Assembly, now met at Charlestown, for the South-west part of this Province, and by the authority of the same, That all negroes, mulatoes, mustizoes or Indians, which at any time heretofore have been sold, or now are held or taken to be, or hereafter shall

From Thomas Cooper and David J. McCord, eds., *Statutes at Large of South Carolina* (10 vols., Columbia, 1836–1841), VII, 352–357.

be bought and sold for slaves, are hereby declared slaves; and they, and their children, are hereby made and declared slaves, to all intents and purposes; excepting all such negroes, mulatoes, mustizoes or Indians, which heretofore have been, or hereafter shall be, for some particular merit, made and declared free, either by the Governor and council of this Province, pursuant to any Act or law of this Province, or by their respective owners or masters; and also, excepting all such negroes, mulatoes, mustizoes or Indians, as can prove they ought not to be sold for slaves. And in case any negro, mulatoe, mustizoe or Indian, doth lay claim to his or her freedom, upon all or any of the said accounts, the same shall be finally heard and determined by the Governor and council of this Province.

II. And for the better ordering and governing of negroes and all other slaves in this Province, *Be it enacted* by the authority aforesaid, That no master, mistress, overseer, or other person whatsoever, that hath the care and charge of any negro or slave, shall give their negroes and other slaves leave, on Sundays, hollidays, or any other time, to go out of their plantations, except such negro or other slave as usually wait upon them at home or abroad, or wearing a livery; and every other negro or slave that shall be taken hereafter out of his master's plantation, without a ticket, or leave in writing, from his master or mistress, or some other person by his or her appointment, or some white person in the company of such slave, to give an account of his business, shall be whipped; and every person who shall not (when in his power) apprehend every negro or other slave which he shall see out of his master's plantation, without leave as aforesaid, and after apprehended, shall neglect to punish him by moderate whipping, shall forfeit twenty shillings, the one half to the poor, to be paid to the church wardens of the Parish where such forfeiture shall become due, and the other half to him that will inform for the same, within one week after such neglect; and that no slave may make further or other use of any one ticket than was intended by him that granted the same, every ticket shall particularly mention the name of every slave employed in the particular business, and to what place they are sent, and what time they return; and if any person shall presume to give any negro or slave a ticket in the name of his master or mistress, without his or her consent, such person so doing shall forfeit the sum of twenty shillings; one half to the poor, to be disposed of as aforesaid, the other half to the person injured, that will complain against the person offending, within one week after the offence committed. And for the better security of all such persons that shall endeavor to take any runaway, or shall examine any slave for his ticket, passing to and from his master's plantation, it is hereby declared lawful for any white person to beat, maim or assult, and if such negro or slave cannot otherwise be taken, to kill him, who shall refuse to shew his ticket, or, by running away or resistance, shall endeavor to avoid being apprehended or taken.

III. *And be it further enacted* by the authority aforesaid, That every master, mistress or overseer of a family in this Province, shall cause all his negro houses to be searched diligently and effectually, once every fourteen days, for fugitive and runaway slaves, guns, swords, clubs, and any other mischievous weapons, and finding any, to take them away, and cause them to be secured; as also, for clothes, goods, and any other things and commodities that are not given them by their master, mistress, commander or overseer, and honestly come by; and in whose custody they find any thing of that kind, and suspect or know to be stolen goods, the same they shall seize and take into their custody, and a full and ample description of the particulars thereof, in writing, within ten days after the discovery thereof, either to the provost marshall, or to the clerk of the parish for the time being, who is hereby required to receive the same, and to enter upon it the day of its receipt, and the particulars to file and keep to himself; and the clerk shall set upon the posts of the church door, and the provost marshall upon the usual public places, or places of notice, a short brief, that such lost goods are found; whereby, any person that hath lost his goods may the better come to the knowledge where they are; and the owner going to the marshall or clerk, and proving, by marks or otherwise, that the goods lost belong to him, and paying twelve pence for the entry and declaration of the same, if the marshall or clerk be convinced that any part of the goods certified by him to be found, appertains to the party inquiring, he is to direct the said party inquiring to the place and party where the goods be, who is hereby required to make restitution of what is in being to the true owner; and every master, mistress or overseer, as also the provost marshall or clerk, neglecting his duty in any the particulars aforesaid, for every neglect shall forfeit twenty shillings.

IV. And for the more effectual detecting and punishing such persons that trade with any slave for stolen goods, *Be it further enacted* by the authority aforesaid, That where any person shall be suspected to trade as aforesaid, any justice of the peace shall have power to take from him suspected, sufficient recognizance, not to trade with any slave contrary to the laws of this Province; and if it shall afterwards appear to any of the justices of the peace, that such person hath, or hath had, or shipped off, any goods, suspected to be unlawfully come by, it shall be lawful for such justice of the peace to oblige the person to appear at the next general sessions, who shall there be obliged to make reasonable proof, of whom he brought, or how he came by, the said goods, and unless he do it, his recognizance shall be forfeited. . . .

VII. And *whereas*, great numbers of slaves which do not dwell in Charlestown, on Sundays and holidays resort thither, to drink, quarrel, fight, curse and swear, and profane the Sabbath, and using and carrying of clubs and other mischievous weapons, resorting in great companies together, which may give them an opportunity of executing any wicked designs and purposes, to the damage and prejudice of the inhabitants of this Province; for the prevention whereof, *Be it enacted* by the authority aforesaid, That all and every the constables of Charlestown, separately on every Sunday, and the holidays at Christmas, Easter and Whitsonside, together with so many men as each constable shall think necessary to accompany him, which he is hereby empowered for that end to press, under the penalty of twenty shillings to the person that shall disobey him, shall, together with such persons, go through all or any the streets, and also, round about Charlestown, and as much further on the neck as they shall be informed or have reason to suspect any meeting or concourse of any such negroes or slaves to be at that time, and to enter into any house, at

Charlestown, or elsewhere, to search for such slaves, and as many of them as they can apprehend, shall cause to be publicly whipped in Charlestown, and then to be delivered to the marshall, who for every slave so whipped and delivered to him by the constable, shall pay the constable five shillings, which five shillings shall be re-paid the said marshall by the owner or head of that family to which the said negro or slave, doth belong, together with such other charges as shall become due to him for keeping runaway slaves; and the marshall shall in all respects keep and dispose of such slave as if the same was delivered to him as a runaway, under the same penalties and forfeiture as hereafter in that case is provided; and every constable of Charlestown which shall neglect or refuse to make search as aforesaid, for every such neglect shall forfeit the sum of twenty shillings. . . .

IX. *And be it further enacted* by the authority aforesaid, That upon complaint made to any justice of the peace, of any heinous or grievous crime, committed by any slave or slaves, as murder, burglary, robbery, burning of houses, or any lesser crimes, as killing or stealing any meat or other cattle, maiming one the other, steal-ing of fowls, provisions, or such like trespasses or injuries, the said justice shall issue out his warrant for apprehending the offender or offenders, and for all per-sons to come before him that can give evidence; and if upon examination, it prob-ably appeareth, that the apprehended person is guilty, he shall commit him or them to prison, or immediately proceed to tryal of the said slave or slaves, accord-ing to the form hereafter specified, or take security for his or their forthcoming, as the case shall require, and also to certify to the justice next to him, the said cause, and to require him, by virtue of this Act, to associate himself to him, which said justice is hereby required to do, and they so associated, are to issue their summons to three sufficient freeholders, acquainting them with the matter, and appointing them a day, hour and place, when and where the same shall be heard and deter-mined, at which day, hour and place, the said justices and freeholders shall cause the offenders and evidences to come before them, and if they, on hearing the mat-ter, the said freeholders being by the said justices first sworn to judge uprightly and according to evidence, and diligently weighing and examining all evidences, proofs and testimonies (and in case of murder only, if on violent presumption and circumstances), they shall find such negro or other slave or slaves guilty thereof, they shall give sentence of death, if the crime by law deserve the same, and forth-with by their warrant cause immediate execution to be done, by the common or any other executioner, in such manner as they shall think fit, the kind of death to be inflicted to be left to their judgment and discretion; and if the crime committed shall not deserve death, they shall then condemn and adjudge the criminal or criminals to any other punishment, but not extending to limb or disabling him, without a particular law directing such punishment, and shall forthwith order exe-cution to be done accordingly.

X. And in regard great mischiefs daily happen by petty larcenies committed by negroes and slaves of this Province, *Be it further enacted* by the authority aforesaid, That if any negro or other slave shall hereafter steal or destroy any goods, chattels, or provisions whatsoever, of any other person than his master or mistress, being under the value of twelve pence, every negro or other slave so offending, and being brought before some justice of the peace of this Province, upon complaint of the party injured, and shall be adjudged guilty by confession, proof, or probable circumstances, such negro or slave so offending, excepting children, whose punishment is left wholly to the discretion of the said justice, shall be adjudged by such justice to be publicly and severely whipped, not exceeding forty lashes; and if such negro or other slave punished as aforesaid, be afterwards, by two justices of the peace, found guilty of the like crimes, he or they, for such his or their second offence, shall either have one of his ears cut off, or be branded in the forehead with a hot iron, that the mark thereof may remain; and if after such punishment, such negro or slave for his third offence, shall have his nose slit; and if such negro or other slave, after the third time as aforesaid, be accused of petty larceny, or of any of the offences before mentioned, such negro or other slave shall be tried in such manner as those accused of murder, burglary, *etc.* are before by this Act provided for to be tried, and in case they shall be found guilty a fourth time, of any of the offences before mentioned, then such negro or other slave shall be adjudged to suffer death, or other punishment, as the said justices shall think fitting; and any judgment given for the first offence, shall be a sufficient conviction for the first offence; and any after judgment after the first judgment, shall be a sufficient conviction to bring the offender within the penalty of the second offence, and so for inflicting the rest of the punishments; and in case the said justices and freeholders, and any or either of them, shall neglect or refuse to perform the duties by this Act required of them, they shall severally, for such their defaults, forfeit the sum of twenty-five pounds. . . .

XII. *And it is further enacted* by the authority aforesaid, That if any negroes or other slaves shall make mutiny or insurrection, or rise in rebellion against the authority and government of this Province, or shall make preparation of arms, powder, bullets or offensive weapons, in order to carry on such mutiny or insurrection, or shall hold any counsel or conspiracy for raising such mutiny, insurrection or rebellion, the offenders shall be tried by two justices of the peace and three freeholders, associated together as before expressed in case of murder, burglary, *etc.*, who are hereby empowered and required to try the said slaves so offending, and inflict death, or any other punishment, upon the offenders, and forthwith by their warrant cause execution to be done, by the common or any other executioner, in such manner as they shall think fitting; and if any person shall make away or conceal any negro or negroes, or other slave or slaves, suspected to be guilty of the beforementioned crimes, and not upon demand bring forth the suspected offender or offenders, such person shall forfeit for every negro or slave so concealed or made away, the sum of fifty pounds; *Provided, nevertheless*, that when and as often as any of the beforementioned crimes shall be committed by more than one negro, that shall deserve death, that then and in all such cases, if the Governor and council of this Province shall think fitting, and accordingly shall order, that only one or more of the said criminals should suffer death as exemplary, and the rest to be returned to the owners, that then, the owners of the negroes so offending, shall bear proportionably the loss of the said negro or negroes so put to death, as shall be allotted them by the said justices and freeholders; and if any person shall refuse his part so allotted him, that then, and in all such cases, the said justices and freeholders are hereby required to issue out their warrant of distress upon the goods and chattels of the person so refusing, and shall cause the same to be sold by public outcry, to satisfy the said money so allotted him to pay, and to return the overplus, if any be, to the owner; *Provided, nevertheless*, that the part allotted for any person to pay for his part or proportion of the negro or negroes so put to death, shall not exceed one sixth part of his negro or negroes so excused and pardoned; and in case that shall not be sufficient to satisfy for the negro or negroes that shall be put to death, that the remaining sum shall be paid out of the public treasury of this Province.

3

The "Three-Fifths Compromise":
The U.S. Constitution, Article I, Section 2

One of the major debates in the Constitutional Convention hinged on the use of slaves in computing taxes and fixing representation. Southern delegates held that slaves should be computed in determining representation in the House, but that they should not be counted in determining a state's share of the direct tax burden. The northern delegates' point of view was exactly the opposite. A compromise was reached whereby three-fifths of the slaves were to be counted in apportionment of representation and in direct taxes among the states. Thus the South was victorious in obtaining representation for its slaves, even though delegate Luther Martin might rail that the Constitution was an insult to the Deity "who views with equal eye the poor African slave and his American master." The "three-fifths compromise" appears in Article I, Section 2.

Representatives and direct Taxes shall be apportioned among the several States which may be included within this Union, according to their respective Numbers, which shall be determined by adding to the whole Number of free Persons, including those bound to Service for a Term of Years, and excluding Indians not taxed, three fifths of all other Persons.

4

An Act Prohibiting the Teaching of Slaves to Read

To keep the slaves in hand, it was deemed necessary to keep them innocent of the printed page. Otherwise, they might read abolitionist newspapers that were smuggled in, become dissatisfied, forge passes, or simply know too much. Hence most states passed laws prohibiting anyone from teaching slaves to read or write. The North Carolina statute was typical.

An Act to Prevent All Persons from Teaching Slaves to Read or Write, the Use of Figures Excepted

Whereas the teaching of slaves to read and write, has a tendency to excite dissatisfaction in their minds, and to produce insurrection and rebellion, to the manifest injury of the citizens of this State:

Therefore,

Be it enacted by the General Assembly of the State of North Carolina, and it is hereby enacted by the authority of the same, That any free person, who shall hereafter teach, or attempt to teach, any slave within the State to read or write, the use of figures excepted, or shall give or sell to such slave or slaves any books or

From *Acts Passed by the General Assembly of the State of North Carolina at the Session of 1830–1831* (Raleigh, 1831), 11.

pamphlets, shall be liable to indictment in any court of record in this State having jurisdiction thereof, and upon conviction, shall, at the discretion of the court, if a white man or woman, be fined not less than one hundred dollars, nor more than two hundred dollars, or imprisoned; and if a free person of color, shall be fined, imprisoned, or whipped, at the discretion of the court, not exceeding thirty-nine lashes, nor less than twenty lashes.

II. *Be it further enacted,* That if any slave shall hereafter teach, or attempt to teach, any other slave to read or write, the use of figures excepted, he or she may be carried before any justice of the peace, and on conviction thereof, shall be sentenced to receive thirty-nine lashes on his or her bare back.

III. *Be it further enacted,* That the judges of the Superior Courts and the justices of the County Courts shall give this act in charge to the grand juries of their respective counties.

5

Declaration of Sentiments and Resolutions, Seneca Falls Convention, 1848

The Declaration of Sentiments, adopted in July 1848 at Seneca Falls, New York, at the first woman's rights convention, is the most famous document in the history of feminism. Like its model, the Declaration of Independence, it contains a bill of particulars. Some people at the meeting thought the inclusion of disfranchisement in the list of grievances would discredit the entire movement, and when the resolutions accompanying the Declaration were put to a vote, the one calling for the suffrage was the only one that did not pass unanimously. But it did pass and thus inaugurated the woman's suffrage movement in the United States.

Declaration of Sentiments

When, in the course of human events, it becomes necessary for one portion of the family of man to assume among the people of the earth a position different from that which they have hitherto occupied, but one to which the laws of nature and of nature's God entitle them, a decent respect to the opinions of mankind requires that they should declare the causes that impel them to such a course.

We hold these truths to be self-evident: that all men and women are created equal; that they are endowed by their Creator with certain inalienable rights; that among these are life, liberty, and the pursuit of happiness; that to secure these rights governments are instituted, deriving their just powers from the consent of the governed. Whenever any form of government becomes destructive of these ends, it is the right of those who suffer from it to refuse allegiance to it, and to insist upon the institution of a new government, laying its foundation on such principles, and organizing its powers in such form, as to them shall seem most likely to effect their safety and happiness. Prudence, indeed, will dictate that governments long established should not be changed for light and transient causes; and accordingly all experience hath shown that mankind are more disposed to suffer, while evils are sufferable, than to right themselves by abolishing the forms to which they were accustomed. But when a long train of abuses and usurpations, pursuing invariably the same object, evinces a design to reduce them under absolute despotism, it is their duty to throw off such government, and to provide new guards for their future security. Such has been the patient sufferance of the women under this government, and such is now the necessity which constrains them to demand the equal station to which they are entitled.

The history of mankind is a history of repeated injuries and usurpations on the part of man toward woman, having in direct object the establishment of an absolute tyranny over her. To prove this, let facts be submitted to a candid world.

He has never permitted her to exercise her inalienable right to the elective franchise.

He has compelled her to submit to laws, in the formation of which she had no voice.

He has withheld from her rights which are given to the most ignorant and degraded men—both natives and foreigners.

Having deprived her of this first right of a citizen, the elective franchise, thereby leaving her without representation in the halls of legislation, he has oppressed her on all sides.

He has made her, if married, in the eye of the law, civilly dead.

He has taken from her all right in property, even to the wages she earns.

He has made her, morally, an irresponsible being, as she can commit many crimes with impunity, provided they be done in the presence of her husband. In the covenant of marriage, she is compelled to promise obedience to her husband, he becoming, to all intents and purposes, her master—the law giving him power to deprive her of her liberty, and to administer chastisement.

He has so framed the laws of divorce, as to what shall be the proper causes, and in case of separation, to whom the guardianship of the children shall be given, as to be wholly regardless of the happiness of women—the law, in all cases, going upon the false supposition of the supremacy of man, and giving all power into his hands.

After depriving her of all rights as a married woman, if single, and the owner of property, he has taxed her to support a government which recognizes her only when her property can be made profitable to it.

He has monopolized nearly all the profitable employments, and from those she is permitted to follow, she receives but a scanty remuneration. He closes against her all the avenues to wealth and distinction which he considers most honorable to himself. As a teacher of theology, medicine, or law, she is not known.

He has denied her the facilities for obtaining a thorough education, all colleges being closed against her.

He allows her in Church, as well as State, but a subordinate position, claiming Apostolic authority for her exclusion from the ministry, and, with some exceptions, from any public participation in the affairs of the Church.

He has created a false public sentiment by giving to the world a different code of morals for men and women, by which moral delinquencies which exclude women from society, are not only tolerated, but deemed of little account in man.

He has usurped the prerogative of Jehovah himself, claiming it as his right to assign for her a sphere of action, when that belongs to her conscience and to her God.

He has endeavored, in every way that he could, to destroy her confidence in her own powers, to lessen her self-respect, and to make her willing to lead a dependent and abject life.

Now, in view of this entire disfranchisement of one-half the people of this country, their social and religious degradation—in view of the unjust laws above mentioned, and because women do feel themselves aggrieved, oppressed, and fraudulently deprived of their most sacred rights, we insist that they have immediate admission to all the rights and privileges which belong to them as citizens of the United States.

In entering upon the great work before us, we anticipate no small amount of misconception, misrepresentation, and ridicule; but we shall use every instrumentality within our power to effect our object. We shall employ agents, circulate tracts, petition the State and National legislatures, and endeavor to enlist the pulpit and the press in our behalf. We hope this Convention will be followed by a series of Conventions embracing every part of the country.

Resolutions

WHEREAS, The great precept of nature is conceded to be, that "man shall pursue his own true and substantial happiness." Blackstone in his Commentaries remarks, that this law of Nature being coeval with mankind, and dictated by God himself, is of course superior in obligation to any other. It is binding over all the globe, in all countries and at all times; no human laws are of any validity if contrary to this, and such of them as are valid, derive all their force, and all their validity, and all their authority, mediately and immediately, from this original; therefore,

Resolved, That such laws as conflict, in any way, with the true and substantial happiness of woman, are contrary to the great precept of nature and of no validity, for this is "superior in obligation to any other."

Resolved, That all laws which prevent woman from occupying such a station in society as her conscience shall dictate, or which place her in a position inferior to that of man, are contrary to the great precept of nature, and therefore of no force or authority.

Resolved, That woman is man's equal—was intended to be so by the Creator, and the highest good of the race demands that she should be recognized as such.

Resolved, That the women of this country ought to be enlightened in regard to the laws under which they live, that they may no longer publish their degradation by declaring themselves satisfied with their present position, nor their ignorance, by asserting that they have all the rights they want.

Resolved, That inasmuch as man, while claiming for himself intellectual superiority, does accord to woman moral superiority, it is pre-eminently his duty to encourage her to speak and teach, as she has an opportunity, in all religious assemblies.

Resolved, That the same amount of virtue, delicacy, and refinement of behavior that is required of woman in the social state, should also be required of man, and the same transgressions should be visited with equal severity on both man and woman.

Resolved, That the objection of indelicacy and impropriety, which is so often brought against woman when she addresses a public audience, comes with a very ill-grace from those who encourage, by their attendance, her appearance on the stage, in the concert, or in feats of the circus.

Resolved, That woman has too long rested satisfied in the circumscribed limits which corrupt customs and a perverted application of the Scriptures have marked out for her, and that it is time she should move in the enlarged sphere which her great Creator has assigned her.

Resolved, That it is the duty of the women of this country to secure to themselves their sacred right to the elective franchise.

Resolved, That the equality of human rights results necessarily from the fact of the identity of the race in capabilities and responsibilities.

Resolved, therefore, That, being invested by the Creator with the same capabilities, and the same consciousness of responsibility for their exercise, it is demonstrably the right and duty of woman, equally with man, to promote every righteous cause by every righteous means; and especially in regard to the great subjects of morals and religion, it is self-evidently her right to participate with her brother in teaching them, both in private and in public, by writing and by speaking, by any instrumentalities proper to be used, and in any assemblies proper to be held; and this being a self-evident truth growing out of the divinely implanted principles of human nature, any custom or authority adverse to it, whether modern or wearing the hoary sanction of antiquity, is to be regarded as a self-evident falsehood, and at war with mankind.

[All the preceding resolutions had been drafted by Elizabeth Cady Stanton. At the last session of the convention Lucretia Mott offered the following, which, along with all the other resolutions except the ninth, was adopted unanimously.—*Ed.*]

Resolved, That the speedy success of our cause depends upon the zealous and untiring efforts of both men and women, for the overthrow of the monopoly of the pulpit, and for the securing to woman an equal participation with men in the various trades, professions, and commerce.

6

The Antisuffragists:
Selected Papers, 1852–1887

Editorial, New York *Herald* (1852)

The farce at Syracuse has been played out. . . .

Who are these women? What do they want? What are the motives that impel them to this course of action? The *dramatis personae* of the farce enacted at Syracuse present a curious conglomeration of both sexes. Some of them are old maids, whose personal charms were never very attractive, and who have been sadly slighted by the masculine gender in general; some of them women who have been badly mated, whose own temper, or their husbands', has made life anything but agreeable to them, and they are therefore down upon the whole of the opposite sex; some, having so much of the virago in their disposition, that nature appears to have made a mistake in their gender—mannish women, like hens that crow; some of boundless vanity and egotism, who believe that they are superior in intellectual ability to "all the world and the rest of mankind," and delight to see their speeches and addresses in print; and man shall be consigned to his proper sphere—nursing the babies, washing the dishes, mending stockings, and sweeping the house. This is "the good time coming." Besides the classes we have enumerated, there is a class

From "The Woman's Rights Convention—The Last Act of the Drama," editorial, New York *Herald*, September 12, 1852.

of wild enthusiasts and visionaries—very sincere, but very mad—having the same vein as the fanatical Abolitionists, and the majority, if not all of them, being, in point of fact, deeply imbued with the anti-slavery sentiment. Of the male sex who attend these Conventions for the purpose of taking part in them, the majority are henpecked husbands, and all of them ought to wear petticoats. . . .

How did woman first become subject to man as she now is all over the world? By her nature, her sex, just as the negro is and always will be, to the end of time, inferior to the white race, and, therefore, doomed to subjection; but happier than she would be in any other condition, just because it is the law of her nature. The women themselves would not have this law reversed. . . .

What do the leaders of the Woman's Rights Convention want? They want to vote, and to hustle with the rowdies at the polls. They want to be members of Congress, and in the heat of debate to subject themselves to coarse jests and indecent language. . . . They want to fill all other posts which men are ambitious to occupy—to be lawyers, doctors, captains of vessels, and generals in the field. How funny it would sound in the newspapers, that Lucy Stone, pleading a cause, took suddenly ill in the pains of parturition, and perhaps gave birth to a fine bouncing boy in court! Or that Rev. Antoinette Brown was arrested in the middle of her sermon in the pulpit from the same cause, and presented a "pledge" to her husband and the congregation; or, that Dr. Harriot K. Hunt, while attending a gentleman patient for a fit of the gout or *fistula in ano*, found it necessary to send for a doctor, there and then, and to be delivered of a man or woman child—perhaps twins. A similar event might happen on the floor of Congress, in a storm at sea, or in the raging tempest of battle, and then what is to become of the woman legislator?

New York State Legislative Report (1856)*

Mr. Foote, from the Judiciary Committee, made a report on Women's rights that set the whole House in roars of laughter:

"The Committee is composed of married and single gentlemen. The bachelors on the Committee, with becoming diffidence, having left the subject pretty much to the married gentlemen, they have considered it with the aid of the light they have before them and the experience married life has given them. Thus aided, they are enabled to state that the ladies always have the best place and choicest titbit at the table. They have the best seat in the cars, carriages, and sleighs; the warmest place in the winter, and the coolest place in the summer. They have their choice on which side of the bed they will lie, front or back. A lady's dress costs three times as much as that of a gentleman; and, at the present time, with the prevailing fashion, one lady occupies three times as much space in the world as a gentleman.

*This Report on Woman's Rights, made to the New York State Legislature and concerning a petition for political equality for women, was printed in an Albany paper in March 1856.

"It has thus appeared to the married gentlemen of your Committee, being a majority (the bachelors being silent for the reason mentioned, and also probably for the further reason that they are still suitors for the favors of the gentler sex), that, if there is any inequality or oppression in the case, the gentlemen are the sufferers. They, however, have presented no petitions for redress; having, doubtless, made up their minds to yield to an inevitable destiny. . . ."

Orestes A. Brownson, The Woman Question (1869 and 1873)*

The conclusive objection to the political enfranchisement of women is, that it would weaken and finally break up and destroy the Christian family. The social unit is the family, not the individual; and the greatest danger to American society is, that we are rapidly becoming a nation of isolated individuals, without family ties or affections. The family has already been much weakened, and is fast disappearing. We have broken away from the old homestead, have lost the restraining and purifying associations that gathered around it, and live away from home in hotels and boarding-houses. We are daily losing the faith, the virtues, the habits, and the manners without which the family cannot be sustained; and when the family goes, the nation goes too, or ceases to be worth preserving. . . .

Extend now to women suffrage and eligibility; give them the political right to vote and to be voted for; render it feasible for them to enter the arena of political strife, to become canvassers in elections and candidates for office, and what remains of family union will soon be dissolved. The wife may espouse one political party, and the husband another, and it may well happen that the husband and wife may be rival candidates for the same office, and one or the other doomed to the mortification of defeat. Will the husband like to see his wife enter the lists against him, and triumph over him? Will the wife, fired with political ambition for place or power, be pleased to see her own husband enter the lists against her, and succeed at her expense? Will political rivalry and the passions it never fails to engender increase the mutual affection of husband and wife for each other, and promote domestic union and peace, or will it not carry into the bosom of the family all the strife, discord, anger, and division of the political canvass? . . .

Woman was created to be a wife and a mother; that is her destiny. To that destiny all her instincts point, and for it nature has specially qualified her. Her proper sphere is home, and her proper function is the care of the household, to manage a family, to take care of children, and attend to their early training. For this she is

---

*This document consists of two articles by Orestes A. Brownson: "The Woman Question. Article I [from the *Catholic World*, May 1869]," in Henry F. Brownson, ed., *The Works of Orestes A. Brownson*, XVIII (Detroit, 1885), 388–89; and "The Woman Question. Article II [a review of Horace Bushnell, *Women's Suffrage: The Reform against Nature* (New York, 1869), from *Brownson's Quarterly Review* for October 1873]," in Henry F. Brownson, *op. cit.*, p. 403.

endowed with patience, endurance, passive courage, quick sensibilities, a sympathetic nature, and great executive and administrative ability. She was born to be a queen in her own household, and to make home cheerful, bright, and happy.

We do not believe women, unless we acknowledge individual exceptions, are fit to have their own head. The most degraded of the savage tribes are those in which women rule, and descent is reckoned from the mother instead of the father. Revelation asserts, and universal experience proves that the man is the head of the woman, and that the woman is for the man, not the man for the woman; and his greatest error, as well as the primal curse of society is that he abdicates his headship, and allows himself to be governed, we might almost say, deprived of his reason, by woman. It was through the seductions of the woman, herself seduced by the serpent, that man fell, and brought sin and all our woe into the world. She has all the qualities that fit her to be a help-meet of man, to be the mother of his children, to be their nurse, their early instructress, their guardian, their life-long friend; to be his companion, his comforter, his consoler in sorrow, his friend in trouble, his ministering angel in sickness; but as an independent existence, free to follow her own fancies and vague longings, her own ambition and natural love of power, without masculine direction or control, she is out of her element, and a social anomaly, sometimes a hideous monster, which men seldom are, excepting through a woman's influence. This is no excuse for men, but it proves that women need a head, and the restraint of father, husband, or the priest of God.

Remarks of Senator George G. Vest in Congress (1887)*

Mr. VEST. . . . If this Government, which is based on the intelligence of the people, shall ever be destroyed it will be by injudicious, immature, or corrupt suffrage. If the ship of state launched by our fathers shall ever be destroyed, it will be by striking the rock of universal, unprepared suffrage. . . .

The Senator who last spoke on this question refers to the successful experiment in regard to woman suffrage in the Territories of Wyoming and Washington. Mr. President, it is not upon the plains of the sparsely settled Territories of the West that woman suffrage can be tested. Suffrage in the rural districts and sparsely settled regions of this country must from the very nature of things remain pure when corrupt everywhere else. The danger of corrupt suffrage is in the cities, and those masses of population to which civilization tends everywhere in all history. Whilst the country has been pure and patriotic, cities have been the first cancers to appear upon the body-politic in all ages of the world.

---

*The remarks of Senator George G. Vest (Democrat, Missouri) may be found in the *Congressional Record*, 49th Cong., 2d sess., January 25, 1887, p. 986.

Wyoming Territory! Washington Territory! Where are their large cities? Where are the localities in those Territories where the strain upon popular government must come? The Senator from New Hampshire [Henry W. Blair—*Ed.*], who is so conspicuous in this movement, appalled the country some months since by his ghastly array of illiteracy in the Southern States. . . . That Senator proposes now to double, and more than double, that illiteracy. He proposes now to give the negro women of the South this right of suffrage, utterly unprepared as they are for it.

In a convention some two years and a half ago in the city of Louisville an intelligent negro from the South said the negro men could not vote the Democratic ticket because the women would not live with them if they did. The negro men go out in the hotels and upon the railroad cars. They go to the cities and by attrition they wear away the prejudice of race; but the women remain at home, and their emotional natures aggregate and compound the race-prejudice, and when suffrage is given them what must be the result? . . .

I pity the man who can consider any question affecting the influence of woman with the cold, dry logic of business. What man can, without aversion, turn from the blessed memory of that dear old grandmother, or the gentle words and caressing hand of that dear blessed mother gone to the unknown world, to face in its stead the idea of a female justice of the peace or township constable? For my part I want when I go to my home—when I turn from the arena where man contends with man for what we call the prizes of this paltry world—I want to go back, not to be received in the masculine embrace of some female ward politician, but to the earnest, loving look and touch of a true woman. I want to go back to the jurisdiction of the wife, the mother; and instead of a lecture upon finance or the tariff, or upon the construction of the Constitution, I want those blessed, loving details of domestic life and domestic love.

. . . I speak now respecting women as a sex. I believe that they are better than men, but I do not believe they are adapted to the political work of this world. I do not believe that the Great Intelligence ever intended them to invade the sphere of work given to men, tearing down and destroying all the best influences for which God has intended them.

The great evil in this country to-day is in emotional suffrage. The great danger to-day is in excitable suffrage. If the voters of this country could think always coolly, and if they could deliberate, if they could go by judgment and not by passion, our institutions would survive forever, eternal as the foundations of the continent itself; but massed together, subject to the excitements of mobs and of these terrible political contests that come upon us from year to year under the autonomy of our Government, what would be the result if suffrage were given to the women of the United States?

Women are essentially emotional. It is no disparagement to them they are so. It is no more insulting to say that women are emotional than to say that they are delicately constructed physically and unfitted to become soldiers or workmen under the sterner, harder pursuits of life.

What we want in this country is to avoid emotional suffrage, and what we need is to put more logic into public affairs and less feeling. There are spheres in which feeling should be paramount. There are kingdoms in which the heart should reign supreme. That kingdom belongs to woman. The realm of sentiment, the realm of love, the realm of the gentler and the holier and kindlier attributes that make the name of wife, mother, and sister next to that of God himself.

I would not, and I say it deliberately, degrade woman by giving her the right of suffrage. I mean the word in its full signification, because I believe that woman as she is to-day, the queen of the home and of hearts, is above the political collisions of this world, and should always be kept above them. . . .

It is said that the suffrage is to be given to enlarge the sphere of woman's influence. Mr. President, it would destroy her influence. It would take her down from that pedestal where she is to-day, influencing as a mother the minds of her offspring, influencing by her gentle and kindly caress the action of her husband toward the good and pure.

7

People v. *Hall,* 1854

Bias against Chinese and other colored "races" was endemic in nineteenth-century California, but perhaps no single document so well demonstrates that bias as this majority opinion handed down by the Chief Justice of the California Supreme Court. Since Chinese miners lived in small, segregated groups, the practical effect of this decision was to declare "open season" on Chinese, since crimes against them were likely to be witnessed only by other Chinese.

The People, Respondent, v.
George W. Hall, Appellant

The appellant, a free white citizen of this State, was convicted of murder upon the testimony of Chinese witnesses.

The point involved in this case, is the admissibility of such evidence.

The 394th section of the Act Concerning Civil Cases, provides that no Indian or Negro shall be allowed to testify as a witness in any action or proceeding in which a White person is a party.

The 14th section of the Act of April 16th, 1850, regulating Criminal Proceedings, provides that "No Black, or Mulatto person, or Indian, shall be allowed to give evidence in favor of, or against a white man."

The true point at which we are anxious to arrive, is the legal signification of the words, "Black, Mulatto, Indian and White person," and whether the Legislature adopted them as generic terms, or intended to limit their application to specific types of the human species.

Before considering this question, it is proper to remark the difference between the two sections of our Statute, already quoted, the latter being more broad and comprehensive in its exclusion, by use of the word "Black," instead of Negro.

Conceding, however, for the present, that the word "Black," as used in the 14th section, and "Negro," in 394th, are convertible terms, and that the former was intended to include the latter, let us proceed to inquire who are excluded from testifying as witnesses under the term "Indian."

When Columbus first landed upon the shores of this continent, in his attempt to discover a western passage to the Indies, he imagined that he had accomplished the object of his expedition, and that the Island of San Salvador was one of those Islands of the Chinese sea, lying near the extremity of India, which had been described by navigators.

Acting upon this hypothesis, and also perhaps from the similarity of features and physical conformation, he gave to the Islanders the name of Indians, which appellation was universally adopted, and extended to the aboriginals of the New World, as well as of Asia.

From that time, down to a very recent period, the American Indians and the Mongolian, or Asiatic, were regarded as the same type of human species. . . .

. . . That this was the common opinion in the early history of American legislation, cannot be disputed, and, therefore, all legislation upon the subject must have borne relation to that opinion. . . .

. . . In using the words, "No Black, or Mulatto person, or Indian shall be allowed to give evidence for or against a White person," the Legislature, if any intention can be ascribed to it, adopted the most comprehensive terms to embrace every known class or shade of color, as the apparent design was to protect the White person from the influence of all testimony other than that of persons of the same caste. The use of these terms must, by every sound rule of construction, exclude every one who is not of white blood. . . .

. . . We have carefully considered all the consequences resulting from a different rule of construction, and are satisfied that even in a doubtful case we would be impelled to this decision on grounds of public policy.

The same rule which would admit them to testify, would admit them to all the equal rights of citizenship, and we might soon see them at the polls, in the jury box, upon the bench, and in our legislative halls.

This is not a speculation which exists in the excited and overheated imagination of the patriot and statesman, but it is an actual and present danger.

The anomalous spectacle of a distinct people, living in our community, recognizing no laws of this State except through necessity, bringing with them their prejudices and national feuds, in which they indulge in open violation of law; whose mendacity is proverbial; a race of people whom nature has marked as inferior, and who are incapable of progress or intellectual development beyond a certain point, as their history has shown; differing in language, opinions, color, and physical conformation; between whom and ourselves nature has placed an impassible difference, is now presented, and for them is claimed, not only the right to swear away the life of a citizen, but the further privilege of participating with us in administering the affairs of our Government. . . .

. . . For these reasons, we are of opinion that the testimony was inadmissible. . . .

8

Dred Scott v. *Sandford,* 1857

The question is simply this: Can a negro, whose ancestors were imported into this country, and sold as slaves, become a member of the political community formed and brought into existence by the Constitution of the United States, and as such become entitled to all the rights, and privileges, and immunities, guarantied by that instrument to the citizen? One of which rights is the privilege of suing in a court of the United States in the cases specified in the Constitution.

It will be observed, that the plea applies to that class of persons only whose ancestors were negroes of the African race, and imported into this country, and sold and held as slaves. The only matter in issue before this court, therefore, is whether the descendants of such slaves, when they shall be emancipated, or who are born of parents who had become free before their birth, are citizens of a State, in the sense in which the word citizen is used in the Constitution of the United States. And this being the only matter in dispute on the pleadings, the court must be understood as speaking in his opinion of that class only, that is, of those persons who are the descendants of Africans who were imported into this country, and sold as slaves.

From Benjamin C. Howard, *Report of the Decision of the Supreme Court of the United States in the Case Dred Scott* . . . (Washington, 1857), 9, 13–14, 15–17, 60.

It becomes necessary, therefore, to determine who were citizens of the several States when the Constitution was adopted. And in order to do this, we must recur to the Governments and institutions of the thirteen colonies, when they separated from Great Britain and formed new sovereignties, and took their places in the family of independent nations. We must inquire who, at that time, were recognised as the people or citizens of a State, whose rights and liberties had been outraged by the English Government; and who declared their independence, and assumed the powers of Government to defend their rights by force of arms.

In the opinion of the court, the legislation and histories of the times, and the language used in the Declaration of Independence, show, that neither the class of persons who had been imported as slaves, nor their descendants, whether they had become free or not, were then acknowledged as a part of the people, nor intended to be included in the general words used in that memorable instrument.

It is difficult at this day to realize the state of public opinion in relation to that unfortunate race, which prevailed in the civilized and enlightened portions of the world at the time of the Declaration of Independence, and when the Constitution of the United States was formed and adopted. But the public history of every European nation displays it in a manner too plain to be mistaken.

They had for more than a century before been regarded as beings of an inferior order, and altogether unfit to associate with the white race, either in social or political relations; and so far inferior, that they had no rights which the white man was bound to respect; and that the negro might justly and lawfully be reduced to slavery for his benefit. He was bought and sold, and treated as an ordinary article of merchandise and traffic, whenever a profit could be made by it. This opinion was at that time fixed and universal in the civilized portion of the white race. It was regarded as an axiom in morals as well as in politics, which no one thought of disputing, or supposed to be open to dispute; and men in every grade and position in society daily and habitually acted upon it in their private pursuits, as well as in matters of public concern, without doubting for a moment the correctness of this opinion.

And in no nation was this opinion more firmly fixed or more uniformly acted upon than by the English Government and English people. They not only seized them on the coast of Africa, and sold them or held them in slavery for their own use, but they took them as ordinary articles of merchandise to every country where they could make a profit on them, and were far more extensively engaged in this commerce than any other nation in the world.

The opinion thus entertained and acted upon in England was naturally impressed upon the colonies they founded on this side of the Atlantic. And, accordingly, a negro of the African race was regarded by them as an article of property, and held, and bought and sold as such, in every one of the thirteen colonies which united in the Declaration of Independence, and afterwards formed the Constitution of the United States. The slaves were more or less numerous in the different colonies, as slave labor was found more or less profitable. But no one seems to have doubted the correctness of the prevailing opinion of the time.

The legislation of the different colonies furnishes positive and indisputable proof of this fact.

The language of the Declaration of Independence is equally conclusive:

It begins by declaring that, "when in the course of human events it becomes necessary for one people to dissolve the political bands which have connected them with another, and to assume among the powers of the earth the separate and equal station to which the laws of nature and nature's God entitle them, a decent respect for the opinions of mankind requires that they should declare the causes which impel them to the separation."

It then proceeds to say: "We hold these truths to be self-evident: that all men are created equal; that they are endowed by their Creator with certain unalienable rights; that among them is life, liberty, and the pursuit of happiness; that to secure these rights, Governments are instituted, deriving their just powers from the consent of the governed."

The general words above quoted would seem to embrace the whole human family, and if they were used in a similar instrument at this day would be so understood. But it is too clear for dispute, that the enslaved African race were not intended to be included, and formed no part of the people who framed and adopted this declaration; for if the language, as understood in that day, would embrace them, the conduct of the distinguished men who framed the Declaration of Independence would have been utterly and flagrantly inconsistent with the principles they asserted; and instead of the sympathy of mankind, to which they so confidently appealed, they would have deserved and received universal rebuke and reprobation.

Yet the men who framed this declaration were great men—high in literary acquirements—high in their sense of honor, and incapable of asserting principles inconsistent with those on which they were acting. They perfectly understood the meaning of the language they used, and how it would be understood by others; and they knew that it would not in any part of the civilized world be supposed to embrace the negro race, which, by common consent, had been excluded from civilized Governments and the family of nations, and doomed to slavery. They spoke and acted according to the then established doctrines and principles, and in the ordinary language of the day, and no one misunderstood them. The unhappy black race were separated from the white by indelible marks, and laws long before established, and were never thought of or spoken of except as property, and when the claims of the owner or the profit of the trader were supposed to need protection.

The state of public opinion had undergone no change when the Constitution was adopted, as is equally evident from its provisions and language.

This brief preamble sets forth by whom it was formed, for what purposes, and for whose benefit and protection. It declares that it is formed by the *people* of the United States; that is to say, by those who were members of the different political communities in the several States; and its great object is declared to be to secure the blessings of liberty to themselves and their posterity. It speaks in general terms of the *people* of the United States, and of *citizens* of the several States, when it is providing for the exercise of the powers granted or the privileges secured to the citizen. It does not define what description of persons are intended to be included under these terms, or who shall be regarded as a citizen and one of the people. It uses them as terms so well understood, that no further description or definition was necessary.

But there are two clauses in the Constitution which point directly and specifically to the negro race as a separate class of persons, and show clearly that they were not regarded as a portion of the people or citizens of the Government then formed.

One of these clauses reserves to each of the thirteen States the right to import slaves until the year 1808, if it thinks proper. And the importation which it thus sanctions was unquestionably of persons of the race of which we are speaking, as the traffic in slaves in the United States had always been confined to them. And by the other provision the States pledge themselves to each other to maintain the right of property of the master, by delivering up to him any slave who may have escaped from his service, and be found within their respective territories. By the first above-mentioned clause, therefore, the right to purchase and hold this property is directly sanctioned and authorized for twenty years by the people who framed the Constitution. And by the second, they pledge themselves to maintain and uphold the right of the master in the manner specified, as long as the Government they then formed should endure. And these two provisions show, conclusively, that neither the description of persons therein referred to, nor their descendants, were embraced in any of the other provisions of the Constitution, for certainly these two clauses were not intended to confer on them or their posterity the blessings of liberty, or any of the personal rights so carefully provided for the citizen

Upon the whole, therefore, it is the judgment of this court, that it appears by the record before us that the plaintiff in error is not a citizen of Missouri, in the sense in which that word is used in the Constitution; and that the Circuit Court of the United States, for that reason, had no jurisdiction in the case, and could give no judgment in it. Its judgment for the defendant must, consequently, be reversed, and a mandate issued, directing the suit to be dismissed for want of jurisdiction.

9

The Emancipation Proclamation

Abraham Lincoln

Emancipation Proclamation by the President of the United States of America: A Proclamation

January 1, 1863

Whereas, on the twenty-second day of September, in the year of our Lord one thousand eight hundred and sixty two, a proclamation was issued by the President of the United States, containing, among other things, the following, to wit:

"That on the first day of January, in the year of our Lord one thousand eight hundred and sixty-three, all persons held as slaves within any State or designated part of a State, the people whereof shall then be in rebellion against the United States, shall be then, thenceforward, and forever free; and the Executive Government of the United States, including the military and naval authority thereof, will recognize and maintain the freedom of such persons, and will do no act or acts to repress such persons, or any of them, in any efforts they may make for their actual freedom.

"That the Executive will, on the first day of January aforesaid, by proclamation, designate the States and parts of States, if any, in which the people thereof, respectively, shall then be in rebellion against the United States; and the fact that any State, or the people thereof, shall on that day be, in good faith, represented in the Congress of the United States by members chosen thereto at elections wherein a majority of the qualified voters of such State shall have participated, shall, in the absence of strong countervailing testimony, be deemed conclusive evidence that such State, and the people thereof, are not then in rebellion against the United States."

Now, therefore I, Abraham Lincoln, President of the United States, by virtue of the power in me vested as Commander-in-Chief, of the Army and Navy of the United States in time of actual armed rebellion against authority and government of the United States, and as a fit and necessary war measure for suppressing said rebellion, do, on this first day of January, in the year of our Lord one thousand eight hundred and sixty-three, and in accordance with my purpose so to do publicly proclaimed for the full period of one hundred days, from the day first above mentioned, order and designate as the States and parts of States wherein the people thereof respectively, are this day in rebellion against the United States, the following, to wit:

Arkansas, Texas, Louisiana (except the Parishes of St. Bernard, Plaquemines, Jefferson, St. Johns, St. Charles, St. James[,] Ascension, Assumption, Terrebonne, Lafourche, St. Mary, St. Martin, and Orleans, including the City of New-Orleans), Mississippi, Alabama, Florida, Georgia, South-Carolina, North-Carolina, and Virginia (except the forty-eight counties designated as West Virginia, and also the counties of Berkley, Accomac, Northampton, Elizabeth-City, York, Princess Ann, and Norfolk, including the cities of Norfolk & Portsmouth [)]; and which excepted parts are, for the present, left precisely as if this proclamation were not issued.

And by virtue of the power, and for the purpose aforesaid, I do order and declare that all persons held as slaves within said designated States, and parts of States, are, and henceforward shall be free; and that the Executive Government of the United States, including the military and naval authorities thereof, will recognize and maintain the freedom of said persons.

And I hereby enjoin upon the people so declared to be free to abstain from all violence, unless in necessary self-defence; and I recommend to them that, in all cases when allowed, they labor faithfully for reasonable wages.

And I further declare and make known, that such persons of suitable condition, will be received into the armed service of the United States to garrison forts, positions, stations, and other places, and to man vessels of all sorts in said service.

And upon this act, sincerely believed to be an act of justice, warranted by the Constitution, upon military necessity, I invoke the considerate judgment of mankind, and the gracious favor of Almighty God.

In witness whereof, I have hereunto set my hand and caused the seal of the United States to be affixed.

Done at the City of Washington, this first day of January, in the year of our Lord one thousand eight hundred and sixty-three, and of the Independence of the United States of America the eighty-seventh.

By the President:
Abraham Lincoln

William H. Steward,
Secretary of State

10

United States Constitution:
Thirteenth (1865), Fourteenth (1868), and Fifteenth (1870) Amendments

Amendment XIII (Ratified December 6, 1865). *Section 1.* Neither slavery nor involuntary servitude, except as a punishment for crime whereof the party shall have been duly convicted, shall exist within the United States, or any place subject to their jurisdiction.

Section 2. Congress shall have power to enforce this article by appropriate legislation.

Amendment XIV (Ratified July 9, 1868). *Section 1.* All persons born or naturalized in the United States, and subject to the jurisdiction thereof, are citizens of the United States and of the state wherein they reside. No State shall make or enforce any law which shall abridge the privileges or immunities of citizens of the United States; nor shall any State deprive any person of life, liberty, or property, without due process of law; nor deny to any person within its jurisdiction the equal protection of the laws.

Section 2. Representatives shall be apportioned among the several states according to their respective numbers, counting the whole number of persons in each state, excluding Indians not taxed. But when the right to vote at any election for the choice of Electors for President and Vice-President of the United States, Representatives in Congress, the executive and judicial officers of a State, or the members of the Legislature thereof, is denied to any of the male inhabitants of such State, being twenty-one years of age, and, citizens of the United States, or in any way abridged, except for participation in rebellion, or other crime, the basis of representation therein shall be reduced in the proportion which the number of such male citizens shall bear to the whole number of male citizens twenty-one years of age in such State.

Section 3. No person shall be a Senator or Representative in Congress, or elector of President and Vice-President, or hold any office, civil or military, under the United States, or under any State, who, having previously taken an oath, as a member of Congress, or as an officer of the United States, or as an executive or judicial officer of any State, to support the Constitution of the United States, shall have engaged in insurrection or rebellion against the same, or given aid or comfort to the enemies thereof. But Congress may by a vote of two-thirds of each House, remove such disability.

Section 4. The validity of the public debt of the United States, authorized by law, including debts incurred for payment of pensions and bounties for services in suppressing insurrection or rebellion, shall not be questioned. But neither the United States nor any State shall assume or pay any debt or obligation incurred in aid of insurrection or rebellion against the United States, or any claim for the loss or emancipation of any slave; but all such debts, obligations, and claims, shall be held illegal and void.

Section 5. The Congress shall have power to enforce, by appropriate legislation, the provisions of this article.

Amendment XV (Ratified February 3, 1870). *Section 1.* The right of citizens of the United States to vote shall not be denied or abridged by the United States or by any State on account of race, color, or previous condition of servitude.

Section 2. The Congress shall have power to enforce this article by appropriate legislation.

11

The Black Codes

W. E. B. Du Bois

The whole proof of what the South proposed to do to the emancipated Negro, unless restrained by the nation, was shown in the Black Codes passed after [President Andrew] Johnson's accession, but representing the logical result of attitudes of mind existing when Lincoln still lived. Some of these were passed and enforced. Some were passed and afterward repealed or modified when the reaction of the North was realized. In other cases, as for instance, in Louisiana, it is not clear just which laws were retained and which were repealed. In Alabama, the Governor induced the legislature not to enact some parts of the proposed code which they overwhelmingly favored.

From W.E.B. Du Bois, *Black Reconstruction* (New York: Harcourt Brace, 1935). Reprinted by permission of David G. Du Bois.

The original codes favored by the Southern legislatures were an astonishing affront to emancipation and dealt with vagrancy, apprenticeship, labor contracts, migration, civil and legal rights. In all cases, there was plain and indisputable attempt on the part of the Southern states to make Negroes slaves in everything but name. They were given certain civil rights: the right to hold property, to sue and be sued. The family relations for the first time were legally recognized. Negroes were no longer real estate.

Yet, in the face of this, the Black Codes were deliberately designed to take advantage of every misfortune of the Negro. Negroes were liable to a slave trade under the guise of vagrancy and apprenticeship laws; to make the best labor contracts, Negroes must leave the old plantations and seek better terms; but if caught wandering in search of work, and thus unemployed and without a home, this was vagrancy, and the victim could be whipped and sold into slavery. In the turmoil of war, children were separated from parents, or parents unable to support them properly. These children could be sold into slavery, and "the former owner of said minors shall have the preference." Negroes could come into court as witnesses only in cases in which Negroes were involved. And even then, they must make their appeal to a jury and judge who would believe the word of any white man in preference to that of any Negro on pain of losing office and caste.

The Negro's access to the land was hindered and limited; his right to work was curtailed; his right of self-defense was taken away, when his right to bear arms was stopped; and his employment was virtually reduced to contract labor with penal servitude as a punishment for leaving his job. And in all cases, the judges of the Negro's guilt or innocence, rights and obligations were men who believed firmly, for the most part, that he had "no rights which a white man was bound to respect."

Making every allowance for the excitement and turmoil of war, and the mentality of a defeated people, the Black Codes were infamous pieces of legislation.

Let us examine these codes in detail.[1] They covered, naturally, a wide range of subjects. First, there was the question of allowing Negroes to come into the state. In South Carolina the constitution of 1865 permitted the Legislature to regulate immigration, and the consequent law declared "that no person of color shall migrate into and reside in this State, unless, within twenty days after his arrival within the same, he shall enter into a bond, with two freeholders as sureties . . . in a penalty of one thousand dollars, conditioned for his good behavior, and for his support."

Especially in the matter of work was the Negro narrowly restricted. In South Carolina, he must be especially licensed if he was to follow on his own account any employment, except that of farmer or servant. Those licensed must not only prove their fitness, but pay an annual tax ranging from $10–$100. Under no circumstances could they manufacture or sell liquor. Licenses for work were to be granted by a judge and were revokable on complaint. The penalty was a fine double the amount of the license, one-half of which went to the informer.

Mississippi provided that "every freedman, free Negro, and mulatto shall on the second Monday of January, one thousand eight hundred and sixty-six, and annually thereafter, have a lawful home or employment, and shall have written evidence thereof . . . from the Mayor . . . or from a member of the board of police . . . which licenses may be revoked for cause at any time by the authority granting the same."

Detailed regulation of labor was provided for in nearly all these states.

Louisiana passed an elaborate law in 1865, to "regulate labor contracts for agricultural pursuits." Later, it was denied that this legislation was actually enacted but the law was published at the time and the constitutional convention of 1868 certainly regarded this statute as law, for they formally repealed it. The law required all agricultural laborers to make labor contracts for the next year within the first ten days of January, the contracts to be in writing, to be with heads of families, to embrace the labor of all the members, and to be "binding on all minors thereof." Each laborer, after choosing his employer, "shall not be allowed to leave his place of employment, until the fulfillment of his contract, unless by consent of his employer, or on account of harsh treatment, or breach of contract on the part of the employer; and if they do so leave, without cause or permission, they shall forfeit all wages earned to the time of abandonment. . . .

"In case of sickness of the laborer, wages for the time lost shall be deducted, and where the sickness is feigned for purposes of idleness, . . . and also should refusal to work be continued beyond three days, the offender shall be reported to a justice of the peace, and shall be forced to labor on roads, levees, and other public works, without pay, until the offender consents to return to his labor. . . .

"When in health, the laborer shall work ten hours during the day in summer, and nine hours during the day in winter, unless otherwise stipulated in the labor contract; he shall obey all proper orders of his employer or his agent; take proper care of his work mules, horses, oxen, stock; also of all agricultural implements; and employers shall have the right to make a reasonable deduction from the laborer's wages for injuries done to animals or agricultural implements committed to his care, or for bad or negligent work. Bad work shall not be allowed. Failing to obey reasonable orders, neglect of duty and leaving home without permission, will be deemed disobedience. . . . For any disobedience a fine of one dollar shall be imposed on the offender. For all lost time from work hours, unless in case of sickness, the laborer shall be fined twenty-five cents per hour. For all absence from home without leave, the laborer will be fined at the rate of two dollars per day. Laborers will not be required to labor on the Sabbath except to take the necessary care of stock and other property on plantations and do the necessary cooking and household duties, unless by special contract. For all thefts of the laborers from the employer of agricultural products, hogs, sheep, poultry or any other property of the employer, or willful destruction of property or injury, the laborer shall pay the employer double the amount of the value of the property stolen, destroyed or injured, one half to be paid to the employer, and the other half to be placed in the general fund provided for in this section. No live stock shall be allowed to laborers without the permission of the employer. Laborers shall not receive visitors during work hours. All difficulties arising between the employers and laborers, under this section, shall be settled, and all fines be imposed, by the former; if not satisfactory to the laborers, an appeal may be had to the nearest justice of the peace and two freeholders, citizens, one of said citizens to be selected by the employer and the other by the laborer; and all fines imposed and collected under this section shall be deducted from the wages due, and shall be placed in a common fund, to be divided among the other laborers employed on the plantation at the time when their full wages fall due, except as provided for above."

Similar detailed regulations of work were in the South Carolina law. Elaborate provision was made for contracting colored "servants" to white "masters." Their masters were given the right to whip "moderately" servants under eighteen. Others were to be whipped on authority of judicial officers. These officers were given authority to return runaway servants to their masters. The servants, on the other hand, were given certain rights. Their wages and period of service must be specified in writing, and they were protected against "unreasonable" tasks, Sunday and night work, unauthorized attacks on their persons, and inadequate food.

Contracting Negroes were to be known as "servants" and contractors as "masters." Wages were to be fixed by the judge, unless stipulated. Negroes of ten years of age or more without a parent living in the district might make a valid contract for a year or less. Failure to make written contracts was a misdemeanor, punishable by a fine of $5 to $50; farm labor to be from sunrise to sunset, with intervals for meals; servants to rise at dawn, to be careful of master's property and answerable for property lost or injured. Lost time was to be deducted from wages. Food and clothes might be deducted. Servants were to be quiet and orderly and to go to bed at reasonable hours. No night work or outdoor work in bad weather was to be asked, except in cases of necessity, visitors not allowed without the master's consent. Servants leaving employment without good reason must forfeit wages. Masters might discharge servants for disobedience, drunkenness, disease, absence, etc. Enticing away the services of a servant was punishable by a fine of $20 to $100. A master could command a servant to aid him in defense of his own person, family or property. House servants at all hours of the day and night, and at all days of the weeks, "must answer promptly all calls and execute all lawful orders. . . ."

Mississippi provided "that every civil officer shall, and every person may, arrest and carry back to his or her legal employer any freedman, free Negro, or mulatto who shall have quit the service of his or her employer before the expiration of his or her term of service without good cause; and said officer and person shall be entitled to receive for arresting and carrying back every deserting employee aforesaid the sum of five dollars, and ten cents per mile from the place of arrest to the place of delivery, and the same shall be paid by the employer and held as a set-off for so much against the wages of said deserting employee."

It was provided in some states, like South Carolina, that any white man, whether an officer or not, could arrest a Negro. "Upon view of a misdemeanor committed by a person of color, any person present may arrest the offender and take him before a magistrate, to be dealt with as the case may require. In case of a misdemeanor committed by a white person toward a person of color, any person may complain to a magistrate, who shall cause the offender to be arrested, and according to the nature of the case, to be brought before himself, or be taken for trial in the district court."

On the other hand, in Mississippi, it was dangerous for a Negro to try to bring a white person to court on any charge. "In every case where any white person has been arrested and brought to trial, by virtue of the provisions of the tenth section of the above recited act, in any court in this State, upon sufficient proof being made to the court or jury, upon the trial before said court, that any freedman, free Negro or mulatto has falsely and maliciously caused the arrest and trial of said white person or persons, the court shall render up a judgment against said freedman, free Negro or mulatto for all costs of the case, and impose a fine not to exceed fifty dollars, and imprisonment in the county jail not to exceed twenty days; and for a failure of said freedman, free Negro or mulatto to pay, or cause to be paid, all costs, fines and jail fees, the sheriff of the county is hereby authorized and required, after giving ten days' public notice, to proceed to hire out at public outcry, at the courthouse of the county, said freedman, free Negro or mulatto, for the shortest time to raise the amount necessary to discharge said freedman, free Negro or mulatto from all costs, fines, and jail fees aforesaid."

Mississippi declared that: "Any freedman, free Negro, or mulatto, committing riots, routs, affrays, trespasses, malicious mischief and cruel treatment to animals, seditious speeches, insulting gestures, language or acts, or assaults on any person, disturbance of the peace, exercising the functions of a minister of the gospel without a license from some regularly organized church, vending spirituous or intoxicating liquors, or committing any other misdemeanor, the punishment of which is not specifically provided for by law, shall, upon conviction thereof, in the county court, be fined not less than ten dollars, and not more than one hundred dollars, and may be imprisoned, at the discretion of the court, not exceeding thirty days. . . ."

The most important and oppressive laws were those with regard to vagrancy and apprenticeship. Sometimes they especially applied to Negroes; in other cases, they were drawn in general terms but evidently designed to fit the Negro's condition and to be enforced particularly with regard to Negroes.

The Virginia Vagrant Act enacted that "any justice of the peace, upon the complaint of any one of certain officers therein named, may issue his warrant for the apprehension of any person alleged to be a vagrant and cause such person to be apprehended and brought before him; and that if upon due examination said justice of the peace shall find that such person is a vagrant within the definition of vagrancy contained in said statute, he shall issue his warrant, directing such person to be employed for a term not exceeding three months, and by any constable of the county wherein the proceedings are had, be hired out for the best wages which can be procured, his wages to be applied to the support of himself and his family. The said statute further provides, that in case any vagrant so hired shall, during his term of service, run away from his employer without sufficient cause, he shall be apprehended on the warrant of a justice of the peace and returned to the custody of his employer, who shall then have, free from any other hire, the services of such vagrant for one month in addition to the original term of hiring, and that the employer shall then have power, if authorized by a justice of the peace, to work such vagrant with ball and chain. The said statute specified the persons who shall be considered vagrants and liable to the penalties imposed by it. Among those declared to be vagrants are all persons who, not having the wherewith to support their families, live idly and without employment, and refuse to work for the usual and common wages given to other laborers in the like work in the place where they are."

In Florida, January 12, 1866: "It is provided that when any person of color shall enter into a contract as aforesaid, to serve as a laborer for a year, or any other specified term, on any farm or plantation in this State, if he shall refuse or neglect to perform the stipulations of his contract by willful disobedience of orders, wanton impudence or disrespect to his employer, or his authorized agent, failure or refusal to perform the work assigned to him, idleness, or abandonment of the premises or the employment of the party with whom the contract was made, he or she shall be liable, upon the complaint of his employer or his agent, made under oath before any justice of the peace of the county, to be arrested and tried before the criminal court of the county, and upon conviction shall be subject to all the pains and penalties prescribed for the punishment of vagrancy."

In Georgia, it was ruled that "All persons wandering or strolling about in idleness, who are able to work, and who have no property to support them; all persons leading an idle, immoral, or profligate life, who have no property to support them and are able to work and do not work; all persons able to work having no visible and known means of a fair, honest, and respectable livelihood; all persons having a fixed abode, who have no visible property to support them, and who live by stealing or by trading in, bartering for, or buying stolen property; and all professional gamblers living in idleness, shall be deemed and considered vagrants, and shall be indicated as such, and it shall be lawful for any person to arrest said vagrants and have them bound over for trial to the next term of the county court, and upon conviction, they shall be fined and imprisoned or sentenced to work on the public works, for not longer than a year, or shall, in the discretion of the court, be bound over for trial to the next term of the county court, and upon conviction, they shall be fined and imprisoned or sentenced to work on the public works, for not longer than a year, or shall, in the discretion of the court, be bound out to some person for a time not longer than one year, upon such valuable consideration as the court may prescribe."

Mississippi provided "That all freedmen, free Negroes, and mulattoes in this state over the age of eighteen years, found on the second Monday in January, 1866, or thereafter, with no lawful employment or business, or found unlawfully assembling themselves together, either in the day or night time, and all white persons so assembling with freedmen, free Negroes or mulattoes, or usually associating with freedmen, free Negroes or mulattoes on terms of equality, or living in adultery or fornication with a freedwoman, free Negro or mulatto, shall be deemed vagrants, and on conviction thereof shall be fined in the sum of not exceeding, in the case of a freedman, free Negro or mulatto, fifty dollars, and a white man two hundred dollars and imprisoned, at the discretion of the court, the free Negro not exceeding ten days, and the white men not exceeding six months."

Sec. 5 provides that "all fines and forfeitures collected under the provisions of this act shall be paid into the county treasury for general county purposes, and in case any freedman, free Negro or mulatto, shall fail for five days after the imposition of any fine or forfeiture upon him or her, for violation of any of the provisions of this act to pay the same, that it shall be, and is hereby made, the duty of the Sheriff of the proper county to hire out said freedman, free Negro or mulatto, to any person who will, for the shortest period of service, pay said fine or forfeiture and all costs; *Provided*, a preference shall be given to the employer, if there be one, in which case the employer shall be entitled to deduct and retain the amount so paid from the wages of such freedman, free Negro or mulatto, then due or to become due; and in case such freedman, free Negro or mulatto cannot be hired out, he or she may be dealt with as a pauper. . . ."

In Alabama, the "former owner" was to have preference in the apprenticing of a child. This was true in Kentucky and Mississippi.

Mississippi "provides that it shall be the duty of all sheriffs, justices of the peace, and other civil officers of the several counties in this state to report to the probate courts of their respective counties semi-annually, at the January and July terms of said courts, all freedmen, free Negroes and mulattoes, under the age of eighteen, within their respective counties, beats, or districts, who are orphans, or whose parent or parents have not the means, or who refuse to provide for and support said minors, and thereupon it shall be the duty of said probate court to order the clerk of said court to apprentice said minors to some competent and suitable person, on such terms as the court may direct, having a particular care to the interest of said minors; *Provided*, that the former owner of said minors shall have the preference when, in the opinion of the court, he or she shall be a suitable person for that purpose. . . ."

"Capital punishment was provided for colored persons guilty of willful homicide, assault upon a white woman, impersonating her husband for carnal purposes, raising an insurrection, stealing a horse, a mule, or baled cotton, and housebreaking. For crimes not demanding death Negroes might be confined at hard labor, whipped, or transported; 'but punishments more degrading than imprisonment shall not be imposed upon a white person for a crime not infamous.'"[2]

In most states Negroes were allowed to testify in courts but the testimony was usually confined to cases where colored persons were involved, although in some states, by consent of the parties, they could testify in cases where only white people were involved. . . .

Mississippi simply reenacted her slave code and made it operative so far as punishments were concerned. "That all the penal and criminal laws now in force in this State, defining offenses, and prescribing the mode of punishment for crimes and misdemeanors committed by slaves, free Negroes or mulattoes, be and the same are hereby reenacted, and declared to be in full force and effect, against freedmen, free Negroes, and mulattoes, except so far as the mode and manner of trial and punishment have been changed or altered by law."

North Carolina, on the other hand, abolished her slave code, making difference of punishment only in the case of Negroes convicted of rape. Georgia placed the fines and costs of a servant upon the master. "Where such cases shall go against the servant, the judgment for costs upon written notice to the master shall operate as a garnishment against him, and he shall retain a sufficient amount for the payment thereof, out of any wages due to said servant, or to become due during the period of service, and may be cited at any time by the collecting officer to make answer thereto."

The celebrated ordinance of Opelousas, Louisiana, shows the local ordinances regulating Negroes. "No Negro or freedman shall be allowed to come within the limits of the town of Opelousas without special permission from his employer, specifying the object of his visit and the time necessary for the accomplishment of the same.

"Every Negro freedman who shall be found on the streets of Opelousas after ten o'clock at night without a written pass or permit from his employer, shall be imprisoned and compelled to work five days on the public streets, or pay a fine of five dollars.

"No Negro or freedman shall be permitted to rent or keep a house within the limits of the town under any circumstances, and anyone thus offending shall be ejected, and compelled to find an employer or leave the town within twenty-four hours.

"No Negro or freedman shall reside within the limits of the town of Opelousas who is not in the regular service of some white person or former owner, who shall be held responsible for the conduct of said freedman.

"No Negro or freedman shall be permitted to preach, exhort, or otherwise declaim to congregations of colored people without a special permission from the Mayor or President of the Board of Police, under the penalty of a fine of ten dollars or twenty days' work on the public streets.

"No freedman who is not in the military service shall be allowed to carry firearms, or any kind of weapons within the limits of the town of Opelousas without the special permission of his employer, in writing, and approved by the Mayor or President of the Board.

"Any freedman not residing in Opelousas, who shall be found within its corporate limits after the hour of 3 o'clock, on Sunday, without a special permission from his employer or the Mayor, shall be arrested and imprisoned and made to work two days on the public streets, or pay two dollars in lieu of said work."[3]

Of Louisiana, Thomas Conway testified February 22, 1866: "Some of the leading officers of the state down there—men who do much to form and control the opinions of the masses—instead of doing as they promised, and quietly submitting to the authority of the government, engaged in issuing slave codes and in promulgating them to their subordinates, ordering them to carry them into execution, and this to the knowledge of state officials of a higher character, the governor and others. And the men who issued them were not punished except as the military authorities punished them. The governor inflicted no punishment on them while I was there, and I don't know that, up to this day, he has ever punished one of them. These codes were simply the old black code of the state, with the word 'slave' expunged, and 'Negro' substituted. The most odious features of slavery were preserved in them. . . ."[4]

NOTES

1. Quotations from McPherson, *History of United States during Reconstruction*, pp. 29–44.
2. Simkins and Woody, *South Carolina during Reconstruction*, pp. 49, 50.
3. Warmoth, *War, Politics and Reconstruction*, p. 274.
4. *Report on the Joint Committee on Reconstruction*, 1866, Part IV, pp. 78–79.

12

Bradwell v. *Illinois*, 1873

Mid-nineteenth century feminists, many of them diligent workers in the cause of abolition, looked to Congress after the Civil War for an express guarantee of equal rights for men and women. Viewed in historical perspective, their expectations appear unrealistic. A problem of far greater immediacy faced the nation. Moreover, the common law heritage, ranking the married woman in relationship to her

From Herma Hill Kay, ed., *Kay's Text Cases and Materials on Sex-Based Discrimination*, 2nd ed. *American Casebook Series.* Copyright © 1993 by Herma Hill Kay. Reprinted with the permission of the West Publishing Company.

husband as "something better than his dog, a little dearer than his horse,"[1] was just beginning to erode. Nonetheless, the text of the fourteenth amendment appalled the proponents of a sex equality guarantee. Their concern centered on the abortive second section of the amendment, which placed in the Constitution for the first time the word "male." Threefold use of the word "male," always in conjunction with the term "citizens," caused concern that the grand phrases of the first section of the fourteenth amendment would have, at best, qualified application to women.[2]

For more than a century after the adoption of the fourteenth amendment, the judiciary, with rare exceptions, demonstrated utmost deference to sex lines drawn by the legislature. . . .

The Court's initial examination of a woman's claim to full participation in society through entry into a profession traditionally reserved to men came in 1873 in Bradwell v. Illinois.[3] Myra Bradwell's application for a license to practice law had been denied by the Illinois Supreme Court solely because she was a female. The Supreme Court affirmed this judgment with only one dissent, recorded but not explained, by Chief Justice Chase. Justice Miller's opinion for the majority was placed on two grounds: (1) since petitioner was a citizen of Illinois, the privileges and immunities clause of article IV, section 2 of the Federal Constitution[4] was inapplicable to her claim; and (2) since admission to the bar of a state is not one of the privileges and immunities of United States citizenship, the fourteenth amendment did not secure the asserted right. Justice Bradley, speaking for himself and Justices Swayne and Field, chose to place his concurrence in the judgment on broader grounds. He wrote[5]:

[T]he civil law, as well as nature herself, has always recognized a wide difference in the respective spheres and destinies of man and woman. Man is, or should be, woman's protector and defender. The natural and proper timidity and delicacy which belongs to the female sex evidently unfits it for many of the occupations of civil life. The constitution of the family organization, which is founded in the divine ordinance, as well as in the nature of things, indicates the domestic sphere as that which properly belongs to the domain and functions of womanhood. The harmony, not to say identity, of interests and views which belong, or should belong, to the family institution is repugnant to the idea of a woman adopting a distinct and independent career from that of her husband. So firmly fixed was this sentiment in the founders of the common law that it became a maxim of that system of jurisprudence that a woman had no legal existence separate from her husband, who was regarded as her head and representative in the social state and, notwithstanding some recent modifications of this civil status, many of the special rules of law flowing from and dependent upon this cardinal principle still exist in full force in most States. One of these is, that a married woman is incapable, without her husband's consent, of making contracts which shall be binding on her or him. This very incapacity was one circumstance which the Supreme Court of Illinois deemed important in rendering a married woman incompetent fully to perform the duties and trusts that belong to the office of an attorney and counsellor.

It is true that many women are unmarried and not affected by any of the duties, complications, and incapacities arising out of the married state, but these are exceptions to the general rule. The paramount destiny and mission of woman are to fulfil the noble and benign offices of wife and mother. This is the law of the Creator. And the rules of civil society must be adapted to the general constitution of things, and cannot be based upon exceptional cases.

The humane movements of modern society, which have for their object the multiplication of avenues for woman's advancement, and of occupations adapted to her condition and sex, have my heartiest concurrence. But I am not prepared to say that it is one of her fundamental rights and privileges to be admitted into every office and position, including those which require highly special qualifications and demanding special responsibilities. In the nature of things it is not every citizen of every age, sex, and condition that is qualified for every calling and position. It is the prerogative of the legislator to prescribe regulations founded on nature, reason, and experience for the due admission of qualified persons to professions and callings demanding special skill and confidence. This fairly belongs to the police power of the State; and, in my opinion, in view of the peculiar characteristics, destiny, and mission of woman, it is within the province of the legislature to ordain what offices, positions, and callings shall be filled and discharged by men, and shall receive the benefit of those energies and responsibilities, and that decision and firmness which are presumed to predominate in the sterner sex.

Although the method of communication between the Creator and the judge is never disclosed, "divine ordinance" has been a dominant theme in decisions justifying laws establishing sex-based classifications.[6] Well past the middle of the twentieth century laws delineating "a sharp line between the sexes"[7] were sanctioned by the judiciary on the basis of lofty inspiration as well as restrained constitutional interpretation. . . .

NOTES

1. Alfred, Lord Tennyson, *Locksley Hall* (1842); see Johnston, Sex and Property: The Common Law Tradition, The Law School Curriculum, and Developments Toward Equality, 47 N.Y.U.L. Rev. 1033, 1044–1070 (1972).
2. E. Flexner, *Century of Struggle* 142–55 (1959).
3. 83 U.S. (16 Wall.) 130, 21 L. Ed. 442 (1873).
4. Article IV, section 2 reads: "The Citizens of each State shall be entitled to all Privileges and Immunities of Citizens in the several States."
5. 83 U.S. (16 Wall.) at 141–42.
6. E.g., *State v. Heitman*, 105 Kan. 139, 146–47, 181 P. 630. 633–34 (1919); *State v. Bearcub*, 1 Or. App. 579, 580, 465 P. 2d 252, 253 (1970).
7. *Goesaert v. Cleary*, 335 U.S. 464, 466, 69 S. Ct. 198, 199, 93 L. Ed. 163, 165 (1948). *Goesaert* was disapproved in *Craig v. Boren*, 429 U.S. 190, 210 n. 23, 97 S. Ct. 451, 463, 50 L. Ed. 2d 397, 414 (1976).

13

Minor v. *Happersett,* 1875

In this case the court held that although women were citizens, the right to vote was not a privilege or immunity of national citizenship before adoption of the 14th Amendment, nor did the amendment add suffrage to the privileges and immunities of national citizenship. Therefore, the national government could not require states to permit women to vote.

14

California Constitution, 1876

In 1876, at the height of the anti-Chinese movement, California adopted a new constitution. Its anti-Chinese provisions, largely unenforceable, represent an accurate measure of public feeling.

Article XIX

Section 1. The Legislature shall prescribe all necessary regulations for the protection of the State, and the counties, cities, and towns thereof, from the burdens and evils arising from the presence of aliens, who are or may become vagrants, paupers, mendicants, criminals, or invalids afflicted with contagious or infectious diseases, and from aliens otherwise dangerous or detrimental to the well-being or

Selection 13 from *Congressional Quarterly's Guide to the U.S. Supreme Court,* 1979, p. 631.

peace of the State, and to impose conditions upon which such persons may reside in the State, and to provide means and mode of their removal from the State upon failure or refusal to comply with such conditions; provided, that nothing contained in this section shall be construed to impair or limit the power of the Legislature to pass such police laws or other regulations as it may deem necessary.

Section 2. No corporation now existing or hereafter formed under the laws of this State, shall, after the adoption of this Constitution, employ, directly or indirectly, in any capacity, any Chinese or Mongolian. The Legislature shall pass such laws as may be necessary to enforce this provision.

Section 3. No Chinese shall be employed on any State, county, municipal, or other public work, except in punishment for crime.

Section 4. The presence of foreigners ineligible to become citizens of the United States is declared to be dangerous to the well-being of the State, and the Legislature shall discourage their immigration by all the means within its power. Asiatic coolieism is a form of human slavery, and is forever prohibited in this State; and all contracts for coolie labor shall be void. All companies or corporations, whether formed in this country or any foreign country, for the importation of such labor, shall be subject to such penalties as the Legislature may prescribe. The Legislature shall delegate all necessary power to the incorporated cities and towns of this State for the removal of Chinese without the limits of such cities and towns, or for their location within prescribed portions of those limits; and it shall also provide the necessary legislation to prohibit the introduction into this State of Chinese after the adoption of this Constitution. This section shall be enforced by appropriate legislation.

15

Elk v. *Wilkins*, November 3, 1884

John Elk, an Indian who had voluntarily separated himself from his tribe and taken up residence among the whites, was denied the right to vote in Omaha, Nebraska, on the grounds that he was not a citizen. The Supreme Court considered the question of whether Elk had been made a citizen by the Fourteenth Amendment and decided against him.

From *Elk* v. *Wilkins,* 112 *United States Reports: Cases Adjudged in the Supreme Court* (New York: Banks & Brothers).

. . . The plaintiff, in support of his action, relies on the first clause of the first section of the Fourteenth Article of Amendment of the Constitution of the United States, by which "all persons born or naturalized in the United States, and subject to the jurisdiction thereof, are citizens of the United States and of the State wherein they reside"; and on the Fifteenth Article of Amendment, which provides that "the right of citizens of the United States to vote shall not be denied or abridged by the United States or by any State on account of race, color, or previous condition of servitude." . . .

The petition, while it does not show of what Indian tribe the plaintiff was a member, yet, by the allegations that he "is an Indian, and was born within the United States," and that "he had severed his tribal relation to the Indian tribes," clearly implies that he was born a member of one of the Indian tribes within the limits of the United States, which still exists and is recognized as a tribe by the government of the United States. Though the plaintiff alleges that he "had fully and completely surrendered himself to the jurisdiction of the United States," he does not allege that the United States accepted his surrender, or that he has ever been naturalized, or taxed, or in any way recognized or treated as a citizen, by the State or by the United States. Nor is it contended by his counsel that there is any statute or treaty that makes him a citizen.

The question then is, whether an Indian, born a member of one of the Indian tribes within the United States, is, merely by reason of his birth within the United States, and of his afterwards voluntarily separating himself from his tribe and taking up his residence among white citizens, a citizen of the United States, within the meaning of the first section of the Fourteenth Amendment of the Constitution. . . .

Indians born within the territorial limits of the United States, members of, and owing immediate allegiance to, one of the Indian tribes (an alien, though dependent, power), although in a geographical sense born in the United States, are no more "born in the United States and subject to the jurisdiction thereof," within the meaning of the first section of the Fourteenth Amendment, than the children of subjects of any foreign government born within the domain of that government, or the children born within the United States, of ambassadors or other public ministers of foreign nations.

This view is confirmed by the second section of the Fourteenth Amendment, which provides that "representatives shall be apportioned among the several States according to their respective numbers, counting the whole number of persons in each State, excluding Indians not taxed." Slavery having been abolished, and the persons formerly held as slaves made citizens, this clause fixing the apportionment of representatives has abrogated so much of the corresponding clause of the original Constitution as counted only three-fifths of such persons. But Indians not taxed are still excluded from the count, for the reason that they are not citizens. Their absolute exclusion from the basis of representation, in which all other persons are now included, is wholly inconsistent with their being considered citizens. . . .

The plaintiff, not being a citizen of the United States under the Fourteenth Amendment of the Constitution, has been deprived of no right secured by the Fifteenth Amendment, and cannot maintain this action.

16

Plessy v. Ferguson, 1896

After the collapse of Reconstruction governments, Southern whites began gradually to legalize the informal practices of segregation which obtained in the South. One such law was passed by the Louisiana legislature in 1890 and provided that "all railway companies carrying passengers . . . in this State shall provide separate but equal accommodations for the white and colored races."

Plessy v. Ferguson tested the constitutionality of this recent trend in Southern legislation. Plessy was a mulatto who, on June 7, 1892, bought a first-class ticket on the East Louisiana Railway for a trip from New Orleans to Covington, Louisiana, and sought to be seated in the "white" coach. Upon conviction of a violation of the 1890 statute, he appealed to the Supreme Court of Louisiana, which upheld his conviction, and finally to the U.S. Supreme Court, which pronounced the Louisiana law constitutional, on May 18, 1896. The defense of Plessy and attack on the Louisiana statute was in the hands of four men, the most famous of whom was Albion W. Tourgée. M. J. Cunningham, attorney general of Louisiana, was assisted by two other lawyers in defending the statute. The majority opinion of the Court was delivered by Justice Henry B. Brown. John Marshall Harlan dissented and Justice David J. Brewer did not participate, making it a 7–1 decision.

In his dissent to this decision Harlan asserted that "Our Constitution is color-blind, and neither knows nor tolerates classes among citizens. In respect of civil rights, all citizens are equal before the law." He offered the prophecy that "the judgment rendered this day will, in time, prove to be quite as pernicious as the decision made by this tribunal in the Dred Scott *case."*

The constitutionality of this act is attacked upon the ground that it conflicts both with the Thirteenth Amendment of the Constitution, abolishing slavery, and the Fourteenth Amendment, which prohibits certain restrictive legislation on the part of the States.

From *Plessy v. Ferguson,* 163 U.S. 537 *United States Reports: Cases Adjudged in the Supreme Court* (New York, Banks & Brothers, 1896).

1. That it does not conflict with the Thirteenth Amendment, which abolished slavery and involuntary servitude, except as a punishment for crime, is too clear for argument. Slavery implies involuntary servitude—a state of bondage: the owner-ship of mankind as a chattel, or at least the control of the labor and services of one man for the benefit of another, and the absence of a legal right to the disposal of his own person, property and services. . . .

A statute which implies merely a legal distinction between the white and col-ored races—a distinction which is founded in the color of the two races, and which must always exist so long as white men are distinguished from the other race by color—has no tendency to destroy the legal equality of the two races, or reestablish a state of involuntary servitude. Indeed, we do not understand that the Thirteenth Amendment is strenuously relied upon by the plaintiff in error in this connection.

2. By the Fourteenth Amendment, all persons born or naturalized in the United States, and subject to the jurisdiction thereof, are made citizens of the United States and of the State wherein they reside; and the States are forbidden from making or enforcing any law which shall abridge the privileges or immunities of citizens of the United States, or shall deprive any person of life, liberty or prop-erty without due process of law, or deny to any person within their jurisdiction the equal protection of the laws. . . .

The object of the amendment was undoubtedly to enforce the absolute equal-ity of the two races before the law, but in the nature of things it could not have been intended to abolish distinctions based upon color, or to enforce social, as dis-tinguished from political equality, or a commingling of the two races upon terms unsatisfactory to either. Laws permitting, and even requiring, their separation in places where they are liable to be brought into contact do not necessarily imply the inferiority of either race to the other, and have been generally, if not univer-sally, recognized as within the competency of the state legislatures in the exercise of their police power. The most common instance of this is connected with the es-tablishment of separate schools for white and colored children, which has been held to be a valid exercise of the legislative power even by courts of States where the political rights of the colored race have been longest and most earnestly en-forced. . . .

While we think the enforced separation of the races, as applied to the internal commerce of the State, neither abridges the privileges or immunities of the col-ored man, deprives him of his property without due process of law, nor denies him the equal protection of the laws, within the meaning of the Fourteenth Amendment, we are not prepared to say that the conductor, in assigning passen-gers to the coaches according to their race, does not act at his peril, or that the pro-vision of the second section of the act, that denies to the passenger compensation in damages for a refusal to receive him into the coach in which he properly be-longs, is a valid exercise of the legislative power. Indeed, we understand it to be conceded by the State's attorney, that such part of the act as exempts from liability the railway company and its officers is unconstitutional. The power to assign to a particular coach obviously implies the power to determine to which race the passenger belongs, as well as the power to determine who, under the laws of the particular State, is to be deemed a white, and who a colored person. . . .

It is claimed by the plaintiff in error that, in any mixed community, the reputation of belonging to the dominant race, in this instance the white race, is *property*, in the same sense that a right of action, or of inheritance, is property. Conceding this to be so, for the purposes of this case, we are unable to see how this statute deprives him of, or in any way affects his right to, such property. If he be a white man and assigned to a colored coach, he may have his action for damages against the company for being deprived of his so called property. Upon the other hand, if he be a colored man and be so assigned, he has been deprived of no property, since he is not lawfully entitled to the reputation of being a white man.

In this connection, it is also suggested by the learned counsel for the plaintiff in error that the same argument that will justify the state legislature in requiring railways to provide separate accommodations for the two races will also authorize them to require separate cars to be provided for the people whose hair is of a certain color, or who are aliens, or who belong to certain nationalities, or to enact laws requiring colored people to walk upon one side of the street, and white people upon the other, or requiring white men's houses to be painted white, and colored men's black, or their vehicles or business signs to be of different colors, upon the theory that one side of the street is as good as the other, or that a house or vehicle of one color is as good as one of another color. The reply to all this is that every exercise of the police power must be reasonable, and extend only to such laws as are enacted in good faith for the promotion for the public good, and not for the annoyance or oppression of a particular class. . . .

We consider the underlying fallacy of the plaintiff's argument to consist in the assumption that the enforced separation of the two races stamps the colored race with a badge of inferiority. If this be so, it is not by reason of anything found in the act, but solely because the colored race chooses to put that construction upon it. The argument necessarily assumes that if, as has been more than once the case, and is not unlikely to be so again, the colored race should become the dominant power in the state legislature, and should enact a law in precisely similar terms, it would thereby relegate the white race to an inferior position. We imagine that the white race, at least, would not acquiesce in this assumption. The argument also assumes that social prejudices may be overcome by legislation, and that equal rights cannot be secured to the negro except by an enforced commingling of the two races. We cannot accept this proposition. If the two races are to meet upon terms of social equality, it must be the result of natural affinities, a mutual appreciation of each other's merits and a voluntary consent of individuals.

17

United States Constitution:
Nineteenth Amendment (1920)

Amendment XIX (ratified August 18, 1920). *Section 1.* The right of citizens of the United States to vote shall not be denied or abridged by the United States or by any State on account of sex.

Section 2. Congress shall have power to enforce this Article by appropriate legislation.

18

Korematsu v. *United States,* 1944

The present case involved perhaps the most alarming use of executive military authority in our nation's history. Following the bombing of Pearl Harbor in December 1941, the anti-Japanese sentiment on the West Coast brought the residents of the area to a state of near hysteria; and in February 1942, President Roosevelt issued an executive order authorizing the creation of military areas from which any or all persons might be excluded as the military authorities might decide. On March 2, the entire West Coast to a depth of about forty miles was designated by the commanding general as Military Area No. 1, and he thereupon proclaimed a curfew in that area for all persons of Japanese ancestry. Later he ordered the compulsory evacuation from the area of all persons of Japanese ancestry, and by the middle of the summer most of these people had been moved inland to "War Relocation Centers," the American equivalent of concentration camps. Congress subsequently made it a crime to violate these military orders. Of the 112,000 persons of Japanese ancestry involved, about 70,000 were native-born American citizens, none of whom had been specifically accused of disloyalty. Three cases were brought to the Supreme Court as challenging the right of the government to override in this manner the customary civil rights of these citizens. In Hirabayashi v. United States, 320 U.S. 81 (1943), the Court upheld the curfew regulations as a valid military measure to prevent espionage and sabotage. "Whatever views we may entertain regarding the loyalty to this country of the citizens of Japanese ancestry, we cannot reject as unfounded the judgment of the military authorities and of Congress that there were disloyal members of that population, whose number and strength could not be precisely and quickly ascertained. We cannot say that the war-making branches of the Government did not have grounds for believing that in a critical hour such persons could not readily be isolated and separately dealt with, and constituted a menace to the national defense and safety. . . ." While emphasizing that distinctions based on ancestry were "by their very nature odious to a free people," the Court nonetheless felt "that in time of war residents having ethnic affiliations with an invading enemy may be a greater source of danger than those of a different ancestry."

While the Court, in the present case, held valid the discriminatory mass evacuation of all persons of Japanese descent, it also held in Ex parte Endo, 323 U.S. 283 (1944), that an American citizen of Japanese ancestry whose loyalty to this country had been established could not constitutionally be held in a War Relocation Center but must be unconditionally released. The government had allowed persons to leave the Relocation Centers under conditions and restrictions that aimed to guarantee that there should not be "a dangerously disorderly migration of unwanted people to unprepared communities." Permission to leave was granted only if the applicant had the assurance of a job and a place to live, and wanted to go to a place "approved" by the War Relocation Authority. The Court held that the sole purpose of the evacuation and detention program was to protect the war effort against sabotage and espionage. "A person who is concededly loyal presents no problem of espionage or sabotage. . . . He who is loyal is by definition not a spy or a saboteur." It therefore follows that the authority to detain a citizen of Japanese ancestry ends when his loyalty is established. To hold otherwise would be to justify his detention not on grounds of military necessity but purely on grounds of race.

Although no case reached the Court squarely challenging the right of the government to incarcerate citizens of Japanese ancestry pending a determination of their loyalty, the tenor of the opinions leaves little doubt that such action would have been sustained. The present case involved only the right of the military to evacuate such persons from the West Coast. Justice Murphy, one of the three dissenters, attacked the qualifications of the military to make sociological judgments about the effects of ancestry, and pointed out that the time consumed in evacuating these persons (eleven months) was ample for making an orderly inquiry into their individual loyalty.

Mr. Justice Black delivered the opinion of the Court, saying in part:

The petitioner, an American citizen of Japanese descent, was convicted in a federal district court for remaining in San Leandro, California, a "Military Area," contrary to Civilian Exclusion Order No. 34 of the Commanding General of the Western Command, U.S. Army, which directed that after May 9, 1942, all persons of Japanese ancestry should be excluded from that area. No question was raised as to petitioner's loyalty to the United States. The Circuit Court of Appeals affirmed, and the importance of the constitutional question involved caused us to grant certiorari.

It should be noted, to begin with, that all legal restrictions which curtail the civil rights of a single racial group are immediately suspect. That is not to say that all such restrictions are unconstitutional. It is to say that courts must subject them to the most rigid scrutiny. Pressing public necessity may sometimes justify the existence of such restrictions; racial antagonism never can.

In the instant case prosecution of the petitioner was begun by information charging violation of an Act of Congress, of March 21, 1942, 56 Stat. 173, which provides that ". . . whoever shall enter, remain in, leave, or commit any act in any military area or military zone prescribed, under the authority of an Executive order of the President, by the Secretary of War, or by any military commander designated by the Secretary of War, contrary to the restrictions applicable to any such area or zone or contrary to the order of the Secretary of War or any such military commander, shall, if it appears that he knew or should have known of the existence and extent of the restrictions or order and that his act was in violation thereof, be guilty of a misdemeanor and upon conviction shall be liable to a fine of not to exceed $5,000 or to imprisonment for not more than one year, or both, for each offense."

Exclusion Order No. 34, which the petitioner knowingly and admittedly violated, was one of a number of military orders and proclamations, all of which were substantially based upon Executive Order No. 9066, 7 Fed. Reg. 1407. That order, issued after we were at war with Japan, declared that "the successful prosecution of the war requires every possible protection against espionage and against sabotage to national-defense material, national-defense premises, and national-defense utilities. . . ."

One of the series of orders and proclamations, a curfew order, which like the exclusion order here was promulgated pursuant to Executive Order 9066, subjected all persons of Japanese ancestry in prescribed West Coast military areas to remain in their residences from 8 P.M. to 6 A.M. As is the case with the exclusion order here, that prior curfew order was designed as a "protection against espionage and against sabotage." In Kiyoshi Hirabayashi v. United States, 320 U.S. 81, we sustained a conviction obtained for violation of the curfew order. The Hirabayashi conviction and this one thus rest on the same 1942 Congressional Act and the same basic executive and military orders, all of which orders were aimed at the twin dangers of espionage and sabotage.

The 1942 Act was attacked in the Hirabayashi case as an unconstitutional delegation of power; it was contended that the curfew order and other orders on which it rested were beyond the war powers of the Congress, the military authorities and of the President, as Commander in Chief of the Army; and finally that to apply the curfew order against none but citizens of Japanese ancestry amounted to a constitutionally prohibited discrimination solely on account of race. To these questions, we gave the serious consideration which their importance justified. We upheld the curfew order as an exercise of the power of the government to take steps necessary to prevent espionage and sabotage in an area threatened by Japanese attack.

In the light of the principles we announced in the Hirabayashi case, we are unable to conclude that it was beyond the war power of Congress and the Executive to exclude those of Japanese ancestry from the West Coast war area at the time they did. True, exclusion from the area in which one's home is located is a far greater deprivation than constant confinement to the home from 8 P.M. to 6 A.M. Nothing short of apprehension by the proper military authorities of the gravest imminent danger to the public safety can constitutionally justify either. But exclusion from a threatened area, no less than curfew, has a definite and close relationship to the prevention of espionage and sabotage. The military authorities, charged with the primary responsibility of defending our shores, concluded that curfew provided inadequate protection and ordered exclusion. They did so, as pointed out in our Hirabayashi opinion, in accordance with Congressional authority to the military to say who should, and who should not, remain in the threatened areas.

In this case the petitioner challenges the assumptions upon which we rested our conclusions in the Hirabayashi case. He also urges that by May 1942, when Order No. 34 was promulgated, all danger of Japanese invasion of the West Coast had disappeared. After careful consideration of these contentions we are compelled to reject them.

Here, as in the Hirabayashi case, ". . . we cannot reject as unfounded the judgment of the military authorities and of Congress that there were disloyal members of that population, whose number and strength could not be precisely and quickly ascertained. We cannot say that the warmaking branches of the Government did not have ground for believing that in a critical hour such persons could not readily be isolated and separately dealt with, and constituted a menace to the national defense and safety, which demanded that prompt and adequate measures be taken to guard against it."

Like curfew, exclusion of those of Japanese origin was deemed necessary because of the presence of an unascertained number of disloyal members of the group, most of whom we have no doubt were loyal to this country. It was because we could not reject the finding of the military authorities that it was impossible to bring about an immediate segregation of the disloyal from the loyal that we sustained the validity of the curfew order as applying to the whole group. In the instant case, temporary exclusion of the entire group was rested by the military on the same ground. The judgment that exclusion of the whole group was for the same reason a military imperative answers the contention that the exclusion was in the nature of group punishment based on antagonism to those of Japanese origin.

That there were members of the group who retained loyalties to Japan has been confirmed by investigations made subsequent to the exclusion. Approximately five thousand American citizens of Japanese ancestry refused to swear unqualified allegiance to the United States and to renounce allegiance to the Japanese Emperor, and several thousand evacuees requested repatriation to Japan.

We uphold the exclusion order as of the time it was made and when the petitioner violated it. . . . In doing so, we are not unmindful of the hardships imposed by it upon a large group of American citizens. . . . But hardships are part of war, and war is an aggregation of hardships. All citizens alike, both in and out of uniform, feel the impact of war in greater or lesser measure. Citizenship has its responsibilities as well as its privileges, and in time of war the burden is always heavier. Compulsory exclusion of large groups of citizens from their homes, except under circumstances of direst emergency and peril, is inconsistent with our basic governmental institution. But when under conditions of modern warfare our shores are threatened by hostile forces, the power to protect must be commensurate with the threatened danger. . . .

[The Court dealt at some length with a technical complication that arose in the case. On May 30, the date on which Korematsu was charged with remaining unlawfully in the prohibited area, there were two conflicting military orders outstanding, one forbidding him to remain in the area, the other forbidding him to leave but ordering him to report to an assembly center. Thus, he alleged, he was punished for doing what it was made a crime to fail to do. The Court held the orders not to be contradictory, since the requirement to report to the assembly center was merely a step in an orderly program of compulsory evacuation from the area.]

It is said that we are dealing here with the case of imprisonment of a citizen in a concentration camp solely because of his ancestry, without evidence or inquiry concerning his loyalty and good disposition towards the United States. Our task would be simple, our duty clear, were this a case involving the imprisonment of a loyal citizen in a concentration camp because of racial prejudice. Regardless of the true nature of the assembly and relocation centers—and we deem it unjustifiable to call them concentration camps with all the ugly connotations that term implies—we are dealing specifically with nothing but an exclusion order. To cast this case into outlines of racial prejudice, without reference to the real military dangers which were presented, merely confuses the issue. Korematsu was not excluded from the Military Area because of hostility to him or his race. He was excluded because we are at war with the Japanese Empire, because the properly constituted military authorities feared an invasion of our West Coast and felt constrained to take proper security measures, because they decided that the military urgency of the situation demanded that all citizens of Japanese ancestry be segregated from the West Coast temporarily, and finally, because Congress reposing its confidence in this time of war in our military leaders—as inevitably it must—determined that they should have the power to do just this. There was evidence of disloyalty on the part of some, the military authorities considered that the need for action was great, and time was short. We cannot—by availing ourselves of the calm perspective of hindsight—now say that at that time these actions were unjustified.

Affirmed.

Mr. Justice Frankfurter wrote a concurring opinion. Justices Roberts, Murphy, and Jackson each wrote a dissenting opinion.

19

Brown v. *Board of Education of Topeka,* 1954

Mr. Chief Justice Warren delivered the opinion of the Court.

These cases come to us from the States of Kansas, South Carolina, Virginia, and Delaware. They are premised on different facts and different local conditions, but a common legal question justifies their consideration together in this consolidated opinion.[1]

In each of the cases, minors of the Negro race, through their legal representatives, seek the aid of the courts in obtaining admission to the public schools of their community on a nonsegregated basis. In each instance, they had been denied admission to schools attended by white children under laws requiring or permitting segregation according to race. This segregation was alleged to deprive the plaintiffs of the equal protection of the laws under the Fourteenth Amendment. In each of the cases other than the Delaware case, a three-judge federal district court denied relief to the plaintiffs on the so-called "separate but equal" doctrine announced by this Court in Plessy v. Ferguson, 163 U.S. 537. Under that doctrine, equality of treatment is accorded when the races are provided substantially equal facilities, even though these facilities be separate. In the Delaware case, the Supreme Court of Delaware adhered to that doctrine, but ordered that the plaintiffs be admitted to the white schools because of their superiority to the Negro schools.

The plaintiffs contend that segregated public schools are not "equal" and cannot be made "equal," and that hence they are deprived of the equal protection of the laws. Because of the obvious importance of the question presented, the Court took jurisdiction.[2] Argument was heard in the 1952 Term, and reargument was heard this Term on certain questions propounded by the Court. . . .[3]

In approaching this problem, we cannot turn the clock back to 1868 when the Amendment was adopted, or even to 1896 when Plessy v. Ferguson was written. We must consider public education in the light of its full development and its present place in American life throughout the Nation. Only in this way can it be determined if segregation in public schools deprives these plaintiffs of the equal protection of the laws.

Today, education is perhaps the most important function of state and local governments. Compulsory school attendance laws and the great expenditures for education both demonstrate our recognition of the importance of education to our democratic society. It is required in the performance of our most basic public responsibilities, even service in the armed forces. It is the very foundation of good citizenship. Today it is a principal instrument in awakening the child to cultural values, in preparing him for later professional training, and in helping him to adjust normally to his environment. In these days, it is doubtful that any child may reasonably be expected to succeed in life if he is denied the opportunity of an education. Such an opportunity, where the state has undertaken to provide it, is a right which must be made available to all on equal terms.

We come then to the question presented: Does segregation of children in public schools solely on the basis of race, even though the physical facilities and other "tangible" factors may be equal, deprive the children of the minority group of equal educational opportunities? We believe that it does.

In Sweatt v. Painter, in finding that a segregated law school for Negroes could not provide them equal educational opportunities, this Court relied in large part on "those qualities which are incapable of objective measurement but which make for greatness in a law school." In McLaurin v. Oklahoma State Regents, the Court, in requiring that a Negro admitted to a white graduate school be treated like all other students, again resorted to intangible considerations: ". . . his ability to study, to engage in discussions and exchange views with other students, and in general, to learn his profession." Such considerations apply with added force to children in grade and high schools. To separate them from others of similar age and qualifications solely because of their race generates a feeling of inferiority as to their status in the community that may affect their hearts and minds in a way unlikely ever to be undone. The effect of this separation on their educational opportunities was well stated by a finding in the Kansas case by a court which nevertheless felt compelled to rule against the Negro plaintiffs:

> Segregation of white and colored children in public schools has a detrimental effect upon the colored children. The impact is greater when it has the sanction of the law; for the policy of separating the races is usually interpreted as denoting the inferiority of the negro group. A sense of inferiority affects the motivation of a child to learn. Segregation with the sanction of law, therefore, has a tendency to [retard] the educational and mental development of negro children and to deprive them of some of the benefits they receive in a racial[ly] integrated school system.[4]

Whatever may have been the extent of psychological knowledge at the time of Plessy v. Ferguson, this finding is amply supported by modern authority.[5] Any language in Plessy v. Ferguson contrary to this finding is rejected.

We conclude that in the field of public education the doctrine of "separate but equal" has no place. Separate educational facilities are inherently unequal. Therefore, we hold that the plaintiffs and others similarly situated for whom the actions have been brought are, by reason of the segregation complained of, deprived of the equal protection of the laws guaranteed by the Fourteenth Amendment. This disposition makes unnecessary any discussion whether such segregation also violates the Due Process Clause of the Fourteenth Amendment.

Because these are class actions, because of the wide applicability of this decision, and because of the great variety of local conditions, the formulation of decrees in these cases presents problems of considerable complexity. On reargument, the consideration of appropriate relief was necessarily subordinated to the primary question—the constitutionality of segregation in public education. We have now announced that such segregation is a denial of the equal protection of the laws. In order that we may have the full assistance of the parties in formulating decrees, the cases will be restored to the docket, and the parties are requested to present further argument on Questions 4 and 5 previously propounded by the Court for the reargument this Term.[6] The Attorney General of the United States is again invited to participate. The Attorneys General of the states requiring or permitting segregation in public education will also be permitted to appear as amici curiae upon request to do so by September 15, 1954, and submission of the briefs by October 1, 1954.

It is so ordered.

NOTES

1. In the Kansas case, Brown v. Board of Education, the plaintiffs are Negro children of elementary school age residing in Topeka. They brought this action in the United States District Court for the District of Kansas to enjoin enforcement of a Kansas statute which permits, but does not require, cities of more than 15,000 population to maintain separate school facilities for Negro and white students. Kan. Gen. Stat. §72-1724 (1949). Pursuant to that authority, the Topeka Board of Education elected to establish segregated elementary schools. Other public schools in the community, however, are operated on a nonsegregated basis. The three-judge District Court, convened under 28 U.S.C. §§2281 and 2284, found that segregation in public education has a detrimental effect upon Negro children, but denied relief on the ground that the Negro and white schools were substantially equal with respect to buildings, transportation, curricula, and educational qualifications of teachers. 98 F. Supp. 797. The case is here on direct appeal under 28 U.S.C. §1253. [The Topeka, Kansas, case would be analogous to a northern school case inasmuch as the school segregation that existed in Topeka was not mandated by state law, and some of the system was integrated. It would be eighteen years before the Court would accept another such case for review. Keyes v. School District No. 1, Denver, 445 F.2d 990 (10th Cir. 1971), *cert. granted,* 404 U.S. 1036 (1972)].

In the South Carolina case, Briggs v. Elliot, the plaintiffs are Negro children of both elementary and high school age residing in Clarendon County. They brought this action in the United States District Court for the Eastern District of South Carolina to enjoin enforcement of provisions in the state constitution and statutory code which require the segregation of Negroes and whites in public schools. S.C. Const., Art. XI, §7; S.C. Code §5377 (1942). The three-judge District Court, convened under 28 U.S.C. §§2281 and 2284, denied the requested relief. The court found that the Negro schools were inferior to the white schools and ordered the defendants to begin immediately to equalize the facilities. But the court sustained the validity of the contested provisions and denied the plaintiffs admission to the white schools during the equalization program. 98 F. Supp. 529. This Court vacated the District Court's judgment and remanded the case for the purpose of obtaining the court's views on a report filed by the defendants concerning the progress made in the equalization program. 342 U.S. 350. On remand, the District Court found that substantial equality had been achieved except for buildings and that the defendants were proceeding to rectify this inequality as well. 103 F. Supp. 920. The case is again here on direct appeal under 28 U.S.C. §1253.

In the Virginia case, Davis v. County School Board, the plaintiffs are Negro children of high school age residing in Prince Edward County. They brought this action in the United States District Court for the Eastern District of Virginia to enjoin enforcement of provisions in the state constitution and statutory code which require the segregation of Negroes and whites in public schools. Va. Const., §140; Va. Code §22-221 (1950). The three-judge District Court, convened under 28 U.S.C. §§2281 and 2284, denied the requested relief. The court found the Negro school inferior in physical plant, curricula, and transportation, and ordered the defendants forthwith to provide substantially equal curricula and transportation and to "proceed with all reasonable diligence and dispatch to remove" the inequality in physical plant. But, as in the South Carolina case, the court sustained the validity of the contested provisions and denied the plaintiffs admission to the white schools during the equalization program. 103 F. Supp. 337. The case is here on direct appeal under 28 U.S.C. §1253.

In the Delaware case, Gebhart v. Belton, the plaintiffs are Negro children of both elementary and high school age residing in New Castle County. They brought this action in the Delaware Court of Chancery to enjoin enforcement of provisions in the state constitution and statutory code which require the segregation of Negroes and whites in public schools. Del. Const., Art. X, §2; Del. Rev. Code §2631 (1935). The Chancellor gave judgment for the plaintiffs and ordered their immediate admission to schools previously attended only by white children, on the ground that the Negro schools were inferior with respect to teacher training, pupil-teacher ratio, extracurricular activities, physical plant, and time and distance involved in travel. 87 A.2d 862. The Chancellor also found that segregation itself results in an inferior education for Negro children (see note 4, infra), but did not rest his decision on that ground. Id., at 865. The Chancellor's decree was affirmed by the Supreme Court of Delaware, which intimated, however, that the defendants might be able to obtain a modification of the decree after equalization of the Negro and white schools had been accomplished. 91 A.2d 137, 152. The defendants, contending only that the Delaware courts had erred in ordering the immediate admission of the Negro plaintiffs to the white schools, applied to this Court for certiorari. The writ was granted, 344 U.S. 891. The plaintiffs, who were successful below, did not submit a cross-petition.

2. 344 U.S. 1, 141, 891.

3. 345 U.S. 972. The Attorney General of the United States participated both Terms as amicus curiae.

4. A similar finding was made in the Delaware case: "I conclude from the testimony that in our Delaware Society, State-imposed segregation in education itself results in the Negro children, as a class, receiving educational opportunities which are substantially inferior to those available to white children otherwise similarly situated." 87 A.2d 862, 865.

5. K. B. Clark, Effect of Prejudice and Discrimination on Personality Development (Midcentury White House Conference on Children and Youth, 1950); Witmer and Kotinsky, Personality in the Making (1952), c. VI; Deutscher and Chein, The Psychological Effects of Enforced Segregation: A Survey of Social Science Opinion, 26 J. Psychol. 259 (1948); Chein, What Are the Psychological Effects of Segregation Under Conditions of Equal Facilities?, 3 Int. J. Opinion and Attitude Res. 229 (1949); Brameld, Educational Costs, in Discrimination and National Welfare (MacIver, ed., 1949), 44–48; Frazier, The Negro in the United States (1949), 674–681. And see generally Myrdal, An American Dilemma (1944).

6. "4. Assuming it is decided that segregation in public schools violates the Fourteenth Amendment

"(a) would a decree necessarily follow providing that, within the limits set by normal geographic school districting, Negro children should forthwith be admitted to schools of their choice, or

"(b) may this Court, in the exercise of its equity powers, permit an effective gradual adjustment to be brought about from existing segregated systems to a system not based on color distinctions?

"5. On the assumption on which questions 4(a) and (b) are based, and assuming further that this Court will exercise its equity powers to the end described in question 4(b),

"(a) should this Court formulate detailed decrees in these cases;

"(b) if so, what specific issues should the decrees reach;

"(c) should this Court appoint a special master to hear evidence with a view to recommending specific terms for such decrees;

"(d) should this Court remand to the courts of first instance with directions to frame decrees in these cases, and if so what general directions should the decrees of this Court include and what procedures should the courts of first instance follow in arriving at the specific terms of more detailed decrees?"

20

Roe v. *Wade,* 1973

This historic decision legalized a woman's right to terminate her pregnancy by abortion. The ruling was based upon the right of privacy founded on both the Fourteenth and Ninth Amendments to the Constitution. The Court ruled that this right of privacy protected the individual from interference by the state in the decision to terminate a pregnancy by abortion during the early portion of the pregnancy. At the same time, it recognized the interest of the state in regulating decisions concerning the pregnancy during the latter period as the fetus developed the capacity to survive outside the woman's body.

21

The Equal Rights Amendment (Defeated)

Section 1. Equality of Rights under the law shall not be denied or abridged by the United States or any state on account of sex.

Section 2. The Congress shall have the power to enforce, by appropriate legislation, the provisions of this article.

Section 3. This amendment shall take effect two years after the date of ratification.

First introduced in Congress in 1923, the ERA was finally passed in 1972. However, because it failed to be ratified by the requisite number of states by its July 1982 deadline, the ERA never became part of the Constitution.

22

Bowers v. *Hardwick,* 1986

Justice White delivered the opinion of the Court.

In August 1982, respondent Hardwick (hereafter respondent) was charged with violating the Georgia statute criminalizing sodomy by committing that act with another adult male in the bedroom of respondent's home. After a preliminary hearing, the District Attorney decided not to present the matter to the grand jury unless further evidence developed.

Respondent then brought suit in the Federal District Court, challenging the constitutionality of the statute insofar as it criminalized consensual sodomy. He asserted that he was a practicing homosexual, that the Georgia sodomy statute, as administered by the defendants, placed him in imminent danger of arrest, and that the statute for several reasons violates the Federal Constitution. . . .

[2] This case does not require a judgment on whether laws against sodomy between consenting adults in general, or between homosexuals in particular, are wise or desirable. It raises no question about the right or propriety of state legislative decisions to repeal their laws that criminalize homosexual sodomy, or of state-court decisions invalidating those laws on state constitutional grounds. The issue presented is whether the Federal Constitution confers a fundamental right upon homosexuals to engage in sodomy and hence invalidates the laws of the many States that still make such conduct illegal and have done so for a very long time. The case also calls for some judgment about the limits of the Court's role in carrying out its constitutional mandate.

We first register our disagreement with the Court of Appeals and with respondent that the Court's prior cases have construed the Constitution to confer a right of privacy that extends to homosexual sodomy and for all intents and purposes have decided this case. . . .

Accepting the decisions in these cases . . . we think it evident that none of the rights announced in those cases bears any resemblance to the claimed constitutional right of homosexuals to engage in acts of sodomy that is asserted in this case. No connection between family, marriage, or procreation on the one hand and homosexual activity on the other has been demonstrated, either by the Court of Appeals or by respondent. Moreover, any claim that these cases nevertheless stand for the proposition that any kind of private sexual conduct between consenting adults is constitutionally insulated from state proscription is unsupportable. Indeed, the Court's opinion in Carey twice asserted that the privacy right, which the Griswold line of cases found to be one of the protections provided by the Due Process Clause, did not reach so far. . . .

Precedent aside, however, respondent would have us announce, as the Court of Appeals did, a fundamental right to engage in homosexual sodomy. This we are quite unwilling to do. It is true that despite the language of the Due Process Clauses of the Fifth and Fourteenth Amendments, which appears to focus only on the processes by which life, liberty, or property is taken, the cases are legion in which those Clauses have been interpreted to have substantive content, subsuming rights that to a great extent are immune from federal or state regulation or proscription. Among such cases are those recognizing rights that have little or no textual support in the constitutional language. Meyer, Prince, and Pierce fall in this category, as do the privacy cases from Griswold to Carey.

Striving to assure itself and the public that announcing rights not readily identifiable in the Constitution's text involves much more than the imposition of the Justices' own choice of values on the States and the Federal Government, the Court has sought to identify the nature of the rights qualifying for heightened judicial protection. In Palko v. Connecticut . . . (1937), it was said that this category includes those fundamental liberties that are "implicit in the concept of ordered liberty," such that "neither liberty nor justice would exist if [they] were sacrificed." A different description of fundamental liberties appeared in Moore v. East Cleveland . . . (1977) (opinion of POWELL, J.), where they are characterized as those liberties that are "deeply rooted in this Nation's history and tradition.". . .

It is obvious to us that neither of these formulations would extend a fundamental right to homosexuals to engage in acts of consensual sodomy. Proscriptions against that conduct have ancient roots. . . . Sodomy was a criminal offense at common law and was forbidden by the laws of the original thirteen States when they ratified the Bill of Rights. In 1868, . . . the 24 States and the District of Columbia continued to provide criminal penalties for sodomy performed in private and between consenting adults. . . . Against this background, to claim that a right to engage in such conduct is "deeply rooted in this Nation's history and tradition" or "implicit in the concept of ordered liberty" is, at best, facetious.

[3] Nor are we inclined to take a more expansive view of our authority to discover new fundamental rights imbedded in the Due Process Clause. The Court is most vulnerable and comes nearest to illegitimacy when it deals with judge-made constitutional law having little or no cognizable roots in the language or design of the Constitution. . . .

Respondent, however, asserts that the result should be different where the homosexual conduct occurs in the privacy of the home. He relies on Stanley v. Georgia, . . . (1969), where the Court held that the First Amendment prevents conviction for possessing and reading obscene material in the privacy of one's home: "If the First Amendment means anything, it means that a State has no business telling a man, sitting alone in his house, what books he may read or what films he may watch." . . .

Stanley did protect conduct that would not have been protected outside the home, and it partially prevented the enforcement of state obscenity laws; but the decision was firmly grounded in the First Amendment. The right pressed upon us here has no similar support in the text of the Constitution, and it does not qualify for recognition under the prevailing principles for construing the Fourteenth Amendment. Its limits are also difficult to discern. Plainly enough, otherwise illegal conduct is not always immunized whenever it occurs in the home. Victimless crimes, such as the possession and use of illegal drugs, do not escape the law where they are committed at home. Stanley itself recognized that its holding offered no protection for the possession in the home of drugs, firearms, or stolen goods. . . . And if respondent's submission is limited to the voluntary sexual conduct between consenting adults, it would be difficult, except by fiat, to limit the claimed right to homosexual conduct while leaving exposed to prosecution adultery, incest, and other sexual crimes even though they are committed in the home. We are unwilling to start down that road.

[4] Even if the conduct at issue here is not a fundamental right, respondent asserts that there must be a rational basis for the law and that there is none in this case other than the presumed belief of a majority of the electorate in Georgia that homosexual sodomy is immoral and unacceptable. This is said to be an inadequate rationale to support the law. The law, however, is constantly based on notions of morality, and if all laws representing essentially moral choices are to be invalidated under the Due Process Clause, the courts will be very busy indeed. Even respondent makes no such claim, but insists that majority sentiments about the morality of homosexuality should be declared inadequate. We do not agree, and are unpersuaded that the sodomy laws of some 25 States should be invalidated on this basis.

Accordingly, the judgment of the Court of Appeals is
Reversed.

23

Confronting Obstacles to Lesbian and Gay Equality

Paula L. Ettelbrick

Lesbian and gay citizens differ little from others in their aspirations and expectations. They aspire to a life in which they can reach their full potential—a satisfying job, a loving family life, a chance to participate openly in social and political worlds, and a safe, secure place to live. They expect, along the way, to be treated fairly and to be valued for who they are, rather than demonized for what they are not.

Such goals, even in a democratic and pluralistic society, are not easily accomplished. The law, either explicitly or implicitly, has treated lesbians and gay men differently from other citizens or, at best, has ignored them altogether. Politicians, always fearful that tolerant views about sexuality will not play well with their constituents, are more likely to give way to the anti-gay minority than the fair-minded majority. Courts are more likely than not to credit stereotypical presentations over fact-based evidence. And much of the public, caught between American cultural ideals of fair treatment on the one hand, and well-developed religiously based views about sexuality on the other, assumes, with regard to lesbians and gay men, that the acceptance of the first equals the destruction of the second.

To date, the lesbian and gay community has made little headway in seeking true sexual equality. The idea that they are the sexual equals of straight citizens is appalling to even progressive heterosexuals. As a result, such appeals as the basis for equality are readily rejected by courts and legislatures around the country. This, of course, is not solely the dilemma of the lesbian and gay community. Do most white people actually believe that people of any color are truly their equals? Do men really believe that women are their peers? That people who are poor are as important as those who are rich? Although sexual, racial, gender, and class equality may be the ultimate goal of those who are oppressed within these classes, they require a lifelong, successive generational commitment. Usually minimal economic equality of the type conferred through civil rights laws is the substitute for true equality: the basic right to a job, a home, access to a public institution regardless of one's race, sex, religion, or other protected category. While sexual equality for lesbians and gay men remains elusive, the foundation has been set toward attaining baseline economic equality.

Reprinted by permission of the author.

But the promise of economic equality must be always guarded. Of the many fronts on which the lesbian and gay community seeks equality, two best illustrate the ebb and flow of economic equality as the fundamental basis of equality. They are (1) the efforts to include sexual orientation as a protected class within existing civil rights laws, and (2) the public debate generated by the legal challenge brought by three gay couples in Hawaii who want the right to marry.

Civil Rights Protection for Lesbians and Gay Men

Each year since 1971 a bill has been introduced into the New York State legislature to amend existing human rights laws to include two words: sexual orientation. Similar bills, for similar lengths of time, have languished in Congress and many other states' legislatures only to be passed over or voted down. If passed, these bills would ban discrimination against any individual because of his or her sexual orientation in employment, housing, public accommodations, and other areas.

Thirty-five years after the passage of federal civil rights legislation, the idea of equal treatment under the law is hardly controversial. Yet many lesbian and gay advocates and their supporters have wondered why it is still so difficult to include lesbians and gay men in this promise. The bills proposed by lesbian and gay advocates merely add two words to existing federal and state frameworks of civil rights protection: sexual orientation.[1]

Passing laws to protect lesbians and gay men has been difficult for two reasons: the lingering hostility toward lesbians and gay men, and the incitement of renewed hostility toward civil rights laws in general. Without a response to both directed hostilities, the prospect for lesbian and gay economic equality through civil rights protections will remain dim.

Dismantling stereotypes and legal obstacles is one of the early steps in the process of seeking economic equality under civil rights laws. For lesbians and gay men it has required unraveling the scientific, criminal, and religious views of homosexuality that have shaped public opinion. For years, both the American Psychological Association and the American Psychiatric Association listed homosexuality in their diagnostic manuals as a mental illness. Thus, it was considered to be a medical and scientific fact that homosexuality is a pathological state that alters the ability of those who engage in homosexual sexual activity to function in the world. Because of this diagnosis, federal law denied entry to non-U.S. citizens who were thought to be gay or lesbian. The stigma of mental illness hung over most lesbians and gay men until later in this century, preventing them from coming to terms with their sexuality and leading to successful or attempted suicides and alienation from family. Even nearly 25 years after the repeal of this designation, the view that gay people are "sick" lingers and the treatment of homosexuality as a mental illness is practiced by a small but vocal band within the medical profession.

The existence and enforcement of certain criminal sexual laws have promoted the concept of lesbians and gay men as criminals and disenfranchised them from entitlement to equal treatment. The mere existence of sodomy laws, which outlaw oral and anal sexual activity (sexual practices that are hardly the exclusive domain of lesbians and gay men), has fostered the automatic presumption that those who identify as gay have broken the law. Though the vast majority of individuals who engage in oral or anal sex are not gay, the stigma of criminality hangs around the necks only of lesbians and gay men. Sodomy laws have long been the cornerstone for systematic discrimination against lesbians and gay men in employment, military service, professional licensing, and custody of their children.

Attempts in the last 10 years to overturn sodomy laws through legal challenge or legislative repeal have been unsuccessful, largely as a result of the United States Supreme Court decision in the 1986 case of *Bowers* v. *Hardwick.* There, the Court was asked to strike down Georgia's sodomy law on the grounds that the right of lesbians and gay men to engage in sexual activity with their partners was being denied. The constitutional right of privacy, it was argued, should extend to the right of an adult to engage in private, consensual sexual activity with another adult. The premise of the challenge was the right of all adults, including lesbians and gay men, to engage in sexual activity. However, clearly unwilling to equate lesbian and gay sexual activity with heterosexual sexual activity, the Court rejected the gay advocates' arguments as "at best, factious" and left standing the Georgia sodomy law as well as those still in force in other states. Of the 26 states that still had sodomy laws at the time of the *Hardwick* decision, few have had the courage to extend equal sexual rights to lesbians and gay men.

Finally, religious opposition to homosexuality has held hostage most attempts to pass laws banning discrimination against lesbians and gay men. A number of religions and religious leaders have deemed homosexuality to be sinful and immoral, though the religious community is decidedly split on civil rights laws and most of its members support equal treatment of lesbians and gay men. Unlike criminal laws, religious justifications cannot be repealed or ruled unconstitutional. Nor do they have a scientific or medical basis that can be disproved. They are, simply, a belief system. Though nothing in the civil rights protections proposed in any state or by the federal government deprives individuals of believing what they will about the morality of lesbians and gay men, religious opponents argue that extending legal recognition to this community is tantamount to promoting sinful behavior. Efforts to pass sexual orientation amendments to civil rights laws have been stymied primarily by this argument. Despite the constitutional separation of religion and the state, most legislators do not like to be viewed as voting against religious principles.

The perception—so firmly reinforced by such major institutions as medicine, law, and religion—that gay people are either mentally ill, criminals, or immoral has taken years to overcome. Although most scientific justifications against homosexuality have been refuted, more than 20 states still outlaw same-sex, consensual sexual conduct, a small but visible portion of the psychiatric community purports to "treat" homosexuality, and a few politically persuasive religious groups still oppose legal protections for lesbians and gay men.

However, though hostility to lesbians and gay men accounts for some of the roadblocks this effort has encountered, of equal culpability is the growing hostility toward civil rights laws in general. The fomenting of hostility toward affirmative action and the derogatory connotation attached to the word "quota" have played a significant role in slowing down this effort. To the extent that the public has been led to believe that civil rights laws provide an unequal economic advantage to certain protected groups of people (namely women and racial minorities), a substantial roadblock is created to lesbian and gay economic equality. Fears that employers might be required to hire a certain number of gay people, coupled with the misperception that all gay people are middle class and have no need for economic protection, have become difficult hurdles in the passage of these laws.

Politicians have taken great advantage of the increased hostility toward civil rights laws at the same time that they have astutely noted the predominant public view that people should not be denied a job because of their sexual orientation. Many nonreligious lobbyists and political advocates have steered away from the typical homophobic ranting. In New York State, for instance, the Conservative party, which staunchly opposes the state's sexual orientation nondiscrimination bill, has informed lawmakers that the bill is unnecessary. Lesbians and gay men, they claim, are already protected under state law. Aside from the blatant untruth of this claim, the argument is notable for two reasons: it inherently accepts the notion that protection should be afforded to this community, and it does not promote gross stereotypes of lesbians and gay men.

Economic equality is still a mainstay in the view of most Americans. The promotion of the idea that one group has or is getting a better deal than another has been extremely effective in fanning opposition to civil rights laws. This has worked against lesbians and gay men in significant ways.

Radical right wing groups have adroitly coined the term "special rights" as their rhetorical rallying cry against lesbian and gay equality. In 1992 the right wing's campaign, which asserted that lesbians and gay men were seeking "special rights," effectively led the majority of voters in Colorado to pass an amendment to the state constitution banning the adoption of any law protecting lesbians and gay men from discrimination. Though the United States Supreme Court struck down the amendment on the grounds that members of a group cannot be exempt from constitutional protection because of the majority's hatred of them, the special rights rhetoric of the radical right is still used to fight against lesbian and gay equality.

In referring to the lesbian and gay movement as one that seeks "special rights," two distinct ideas are conveyed. First, it implies that lesbians and gay men are seeking protections beyond what anyone else has, and it taps into people's "gut" instinct that no one person should be advantaged over another person. It also pulls forth a homophobic reaction in that if anyone *should* receive special rights, it should certainly *not* be a gay person.

The second, more covert, message conveyed by the special rights rhetoric is that civil rights laws are bad. By supplementing the special rights message with inflammatory references to quotas, a direct pitch is made to provoke hostility toward civil rights laws in general, and women and people of color in particular. The message is most compelling to the working-class white man who feels that everyone gets a better break than he does.

Opponents have also effectively halted lesbian and gay efforts by reinterpreting the purpose of civil rights laws as addressing only discrimination against those who, as a class, are economically disadvantaged. To promote the idea that lesbians and gay men are not entitled to legal protection, they claim that lesbians and gay men are in fact economically advantaged as a class. Lesbians and gay men are presented as being more educated and having no family responsibilities to tie them down, allowing them a level of "disposable" income and privilege not enjoyed by straight people. The fact that lesbian and gay families are both invisible and economically disadvantaged, or that civil rights laws are intended to eliminate all discrimination against groups who historically have encountered unequal treatment—whether it results in economic disadvantage or simply the harm of being denied access—is ignored. In addition, this perception is supported by the media's attention to only a small portion of the gay community—especially middle-class, white gay men who are political activists—as being representative of the entire community. Just as the public is made ceaselessly aware of the black welfare mother, but not the well-educated African American teenage boy, the media never brings into view the working-class Asian lesbian and her children or the transgendered Latin youth who works three jobs to care for his grandmother. Such false presentations of lesbian and gay economic privilege pits that community against those already protected by the law.

With only 10 states that have passed laws providing for economic equality for lesbians and gay men, and no federal law, lesbians and gay men are still a long way from equal treatment in the workplace, housing market, and other important public spheres. Although homophobia is clearly a culprit, the racist and misogynist rhetorical campaign of the radical right also threatens the whole structure of civil rights protections.

Marriage and Family Recognition for Lesbians and Gay Men

In 1993 the nearly unthinkable occurred—the Hawaii Supreme Court became the first court in the country, perhaps the world, to rule that the exclusion of lesbian and gay couples from the state's marriage laws violated the state constitutional guarantee against sex discrimination. Whereas the sex discrimination provision of the Hawaii constitution prohibits the state from adopting legal classifications based on sex unless there is a compelling reason to do so, it was unconstitutional for the state to adopt a law allowing, for instance, a woman to marry a man, but not another woman. Such a classification, clearly based on the sex of the parties, is unallowable.

The court's rationale was not based on the premise that the protection of lesbian and gay relationships is as important to the fabric of society as the protection afforded heterosexual marriage. Far from it. In fact, the court denounced any argument that came close to asserting that the basis for the request is that lesbian and gay relationships are equal to heterosexual relationships. Rather, the court was compelled by the sheer weight of the economic equality argument. Insofar as marriage carries with it a number of economic benefits granted by the state, lesbian and gay couples should not be economically disadvantaged by the state's denial of access to legal marriage.

Although same-sex marriage in Hawaii will not be allowed until yet another ruling by the state's Supreme Court,[2] the decision set off a minor firestorm in the rest of the country. The radical right took advantage of election-year Republican primaries to force all but one Republican presidential candidate to sign a statement or commit publicly to denouncing the right of lesbians and gay men to marry. State legislatures (and the U.S. Congress) quickly drafted laws to defend the institution of marriage from encroachment in their states by individuals (lesbian and gay couples) for whom marriage was never intended. To date, 18 states have adopted laws prohibiting the performance of same-sex marriages or the recognition of same-sex marriages performed in Hawaii or any other state that might be so bold as to allow them. The U.S. Congress, in a heated election year, passed the Defense of Marriage Act (DOMA), which purports to allow states to prohibit same-sex marriages and to deny the extension of any federal benefits to legitimately married lesbian and gay couples, should any state allow it. Since marriage has always been a matter of state, not federal, law, DOMA represented aberrant behavior even by Congress, as it had never before in the history of the nation attempted to define marriage.

Even though there is a legal component to the question of same-sex marriage, marriage is very much a religious institution. Marriage regulates sexuality by being the marker between "moral" sex (sex engaged in by two people who are married to each other) and "immoral" sex (sex engaged in by everyone else). As both a legal and religious matter, marriage has created a sexual hierarchy between men and women. Through law, practice, and social tolerance, men have always enjoyed greater power and privilege within the institution of marriage.

Marriage is one of a handful of forums that defines the sexual roles between men and women. Married men are fathers who work outside the home and provide for the financial well-being of their families. Women are mothers who care for their children, their husbands, and their homes. If they work outside the home, many women ironically find no support for their central role as mothers (such as flex time, day care, or paid parenting leave); this reinforces the social pressure to remain at home and out of the public forums inhabited by men. The image of the ideal marriage also firmly enforces middle-class values.

Marriage has been viewed traditionally as the correct and only institution within which to raise healthy, morally responsible children. Single parents, unmarried couples, lesbian and gay couples, and anyone else whose lives do not conform to the cultural view of family put their children at peril. Concerns about depriving children of immediate male role models and appropriate moral guidance predominate as arguments against nonconformist childrearing. Not surprisingly, the only nonconformists who are idolized are single male parents who by definition exhibit the requisite selfless devotion to children that all should emulate. In a male-dominated world, there is little concern for appropriate female role models.

The legal ability to marry is also a test of one's full citizenship. Laws that once banned marriage to Jews in Germany or between white people and people of color here in the United States were intended to send an unequivocal message about full equality. Unlike these earlier miscegenation laws, current marriage laws were never adopted with the goal of depriving lesbian and gay couples of that right. However, the resistance to providing them the right to marry certainly reinforces their lack of social status.

Within this context, imagine the concerns many people have when faced with the real possibility that lesbian and gay couples may one day soon be allowed to "legitimize" their relationships through marriage. Marriage has for so long been treated like a private club for the morally responsible straight couple that the prospect of same-sex marriage creates integration-related anxiety. Though they would never have to actually meet or know each other, straight married couples and lesbian married couples would be forced to mingle within matrimony. This fear generates incomprehensible concerns about the prospect that same-sex marriage will diminish the meaning of marriage and that marriage as an institution must be defended against others who wish to marry. Whereas at one time many people were concerned about outside attacks on marriage waged by straight couples who had the option, but not the desire, to marry, concern has clearly shifted. At the same time, many feel caught between a modern-day view of marriage as an institution for those who love one another and wish to build a life together, and the traditional meaning of marriage essentialized by religious and civil law as an institution strictly reserved for a man and a woman.

The Hawaii marriage decision in combination with the two-decade-long movement for recognition of lesbian and gay families through domestic partnership, adoption, custody and contract law, and feminist critique of marriage and the family, which provided the historical possibility for the Hawaii court's decision, has generated an important debate about the late twentieth-century role of marriage and views of family. Straight and lesbian feminist critiques have concentrated on challenging the strict sexual roles enforced through marriage and the legitimacy of marriage as the central definitional component of family. Lesbian and gay critiques have built on these two critical points and challenged the exclusivity of heterosexuality to the definition of marriage. An inevitable outcome of these combined critiques may well be legal and social structures that respect and recognize both nonmarital family structures for people of any sexual orientation and same-sex inclusive marriage. To do justice under the law, it is essential to separate the central structures of marriage by distinguishing marriage as a civil contract from marriage as a religious institution.

For nearly two decades, lesbian and gay advocates have argued that the civil benefits and privileges that accrue through marriage should not be provided exclusively to those who marry. The premise for extending only to married couples benefits such as health insurance, tax breaks, Social Security benefits, access to adoption of children, and thousands of other legal and social benefits has been to support those who share family responsibilities to care for one another. But sharing family responsibilities is not the sole domain of married couples. For example, thousands of lesbian couples share equally in the parenting responsibility for children, though only one member of each couple is the biological parent. Yet under the law only the biological parent has any recognized right or responsibility to care for the child. As a result, the children may not have access to the family health benefits, property, or decision-making authority of the nonbiological parent. Most states do not allow the other mother to adopt the child in order to secure the family relationship. Should the biological mother die or become disabled, the child's relationship with her other mother is put into legal limbo, and she may be removed from the home of the only other parent she has known. Insofar as they function as family, these families should receive the same legal and social support as that conferred to family members through adoption or marriage.

As a result of this advocacy, a growing number of employers now provide family health benefits to domestic partners and the children of an employee's domestic partner, most hospitals no longer exclude unmarried partners from intensive care units, and respect for the right of lesbian and gay parents to secure their family relationships has increased.

Although lesbian and gay families are far from obtaining equal family benefits, the obstacles they face are more visible and the response of policy makers is more forthcoming. This movement has questioned the legitimacy of the state in depriving many families of the family benefits conferred through civil marriage. Is it legitimate for the state to use marriage as the dividing line between those families who receive the state's full economic and legal support, and those who do not? Although most people are still uneasy about conferring marriage rights to lesbian and gay couples, even conservative commentators and legislators have proposed that lesbian and gay couples should be given all the benefits of marriage, but not the right to call themselves married. They seem to recognize that marriage should not be the sole distribution point for civil benefits and privileges, although as an institution it must remain the domain of heterosexual unions. Thus, they separate the religious from the civil aspects of marriage.

This separation is further highlighted by the changed cultural attitude toward marriage. When New Jersey governor Christine Todd Whitman recently commented that she supports domestic partner benefits for gay couples but believes that marriage is the proper institution for raising children, she received a public response not just from gay people but from straight women as well. They pointed out to their governor that they did not marry their husbands in order to be vessels for a man's children, but because they loved them. This response highlighted a fundamental cultural change in the way women, and men, view the institution of marriage. Historically marriage was used to formalize property distribution, to confer legitimacy to children, and to conform to religious propriety; romantic views of love and emotional commitment played little or no role in why people married. Marriage now serves primarily as the most visible means by which people can express their love and commitment to one another, and the other factors play a less significant role in the motivation for marriage.

Given the decidedly romantic purpose for which marriage exists culturally, and the cultural consciousness of the desirability of equal treatment, what can be the reason for denying marriage to a lesbian or gay couple who love one another and are willing to take on the commitment and responsibility this culture expects of married people? Given the vast economic advantages that only families joined by marriage receive, what can be the reason for economically disadvantaging those who cannot or choose not to marry? It may well be that cultural beliefs in economic equality, rather than the claim that lesbian and gay relationships are the sexual equals of heterosexual relationships, will force the issue of how to extend economic equality to people in all families and relationships that exhibit a commitment to caring for one another. The clear economic advantages of civil marriage make the case self-evident: no family, whether married or not, should be denied the benefits of marriage.

NOTES

1. In recent years the federal bill banning sexual orientation discrimination, known as the Employment Non-Discrimination Bill (ENDA), has been substantially rewritten and, in the opinion of some, watered down to dodge the criticisms of moderate and conservative politicians who have an ever-growing list of why they do not favor including lesbians and gay men in the laws banning discrimination. For example, the federal bill covers only employment, fully exempts religious institutions, and exempts employers from having to provide equal employment benefits to lesbian and gay workers, a right to which every other employee is currently entitled.

2. After the 1993 ruling, the case was sent back to the trial court to determine whether the state could prove a compelling reason for continuing to prohibit lesbian and gay marriages. At trial, the state argued that the sole compelling reason for denying marriage to lesbian and gay couples was because heterosexual marriage is the best forum for raising children. Because the data overwhelmingly prove that being raised by loving, attentive parents is the best forum for children—regardless of the sexual orientation, sex, or marital status of the parent or parents—in late 1996 the trial court rejected the state's argument. The case is again on appeal.

Suggestions for Further Reading

Anderson, Karen. *Changing Women: A History of Racial Ethnic Women in Modern America.* Oxford University Press, 1996.

Acuna, Rudolpho. *Occupied America: A History of Chicanos.* New York: Harper & Row, 1987.

Aptheker, B. *Woman's Legacy: Essays on Race, Sex, and Class in American History.* Amherst: University of Massachusetts Press, 1982.

Baxendall, R., L. Gordon, and S. Reverby. *America's Working Women: A Documentary HIstory—1600 to the Present.* New York: Random House, 1976.

Berlin, Ira. *Free at Last?* Boston: Little, Brown, 1991.

Berry, M.F., and J.W. Blassingame. *Long Memory: The Black Experience in America.* New York: Oxford University Press, 1982.

Boyer, R.O., and H. Morais. *Labor's Untold Story.* New York: United Electrical, Radio and Machine Workers of America, 1972.

Cluster, D., ed. *They Should Have Served That Cup of Coffee.* Boston: South End Press, 1979.

Cott, Nancy F. *Root of Bitterness: Documents of the Social History of American Women.* Boston: Northeastern Press, 1986.

Deitz, James L. *Economic History of Puerto Rico: Institutional Change and Capitalist Development.* Princeton, NJ: Princeton University Press, 1986.

Duberman, Martin Baum, Martha Vicinus, and George Chauncey, Jr. *Hidden from History: Reclaiming the Gay and Lesbian Past.* New York: New American Library, 1989.

DuBois, Ellen, and Vicki Ruis. *Unequal Sisters.* New York: Routledge & Kegan Paul, 1990.

Flexner, Eleanor. *Century of Struggle.* Cambridge, MA: Harvard University Press, 1976.

Gee, E., ed. *Counterpoint: Perspectives on Asian Americans.* Los Angeles: Asian American Studies Center, University of California, Los Angeles, 1976.

Giddings, P. *When and Where I Enter: The Impact of Black Women on Race and Sex in America.* New York: Bantam Books, 1976.

Jacobs, P., and S. Landau, eds. *To Serve the Devil. Vol. 1, Natives and Slaves; Vol. 2, Colonials and Sojourners: A Documentary Analysis of America's Racial History and Why It Has Been Kept Hidden.* New York: Vintage Books, 1971.

Katz, Jonathan. *Gay American History: Lesbians and Gay Men in the U.S.: A Documentary History.* New York: Avon Books, 1984.

Konig, Hans. *The Conquest of America: How the Indian Nations Lost Their Continent.* New York: Monthly Review Press, 1993.

Mintz, Sidney. *Caribbean Transformations.* Baltimore: Johns Hopkins Press, 1974.

Perez, Emma. *The Decolonial Imaginary: Writing Chicanas into History.* Bloomington: Indiana University Press, 1999.

Robson, Ruthann. *Lesbian (Out)Law: Survival under the Rule of Law.* Ithaca, NY: Firebrand Books, 1992.

Stampp, K. M. *The Peculiar Institution: Slavery in the Ante-Bellum South.* New York: Vintage Books, 1956.

Takaki, Ronald. *A Different Mirror: Multicultural American History.* Boston: Little, Brown, 1993.

Takaki, Ronald. *From Different Shores: Perspectives on Race and Culture in America.* New York: Oxford University Press, 1987.

United States Commission on Human Rights. *Indian Tribes: A Continuing Quest for Survival.* Washington, DC: United States Commission on Human Rights, 1981.

Wagenheim, K., and O. J. Wagenheim, eds. *The Puerto Ricans: A Documentary History.* New York: Praeger, 1973.

PART VII

Maintaining Race, Class, and Gender Hierarchies: Social Control

THE MOST EFFECTIVE FORMS OF SOCIAL CONTROL are always invisible. Tanks in the streets and armed militia serve as constant reminders that people are not free; further, they provide a focus for anger and an impetus for rebellion. More effective by far are the beliefs and attitudes a society fosters to rationalize and reinforce prevailing distributions of power and opportunity. It is here that stereotypes and ideology have an important role to play. They shape how we see ourselves and others, they affect how we define social issues, and they determine whom we hold responsible for society's ills. They play a part in persuading people that differences in wealth, power, and opportunity are reflections of natural differences among people, not the results of the economic and political organization of society. If stereotypes, ideology, and language are truly effective, they go beyond rationalizing inequality to rendering it invisible. Once again we find that the social construction of gender, race, and class as hierarchy, which has been examined throughout this book, is at the heart of the belief system that makes the prevailing distribution of wealth and opportunity appear natural and inevitable rather than arbitrary and alterable. In U.S. society the stereotypes and values transmitted through education and the media have played a critical role in perpetuating racism, sexism, and class privilege, even at those times when the law has been used as a vehicle to fight discrimination rather than maintain it.

The selections in Part VII examine some of the ways in which our unconscious beliefs about ourselves and others reinforce existing social roles and class positions and blunt social criticism. Stereotypes and beliefs are perpetuated by the institutions within which we live and grow. In addition to providing us with information and values, education, religion, and the family, along with the media, encourage us to adopt a particular picture of the world and our place in it. These institutions shape our perceptions of others and give us a sense of our own future. The curriculum from elementary school through college and beyond presents a world view that is firmly anchored in white male European traditions and knowledge. Rather than identifying and contextualizing its perspective, the core of the traditional curriculum offers this narrow view of the past and present as if it were reality. In addition to severely limiting our understanding of the past and present in this way, the curriculum defines what counts as knowledge and culture in ways that are capable of obliterating the contributions of all but a few.

The mass media selectively provide information, promote certain values, and teach us who and what we should regard as important. Along with other institutions, they shape our definition of community, painting a picture of society divided between "us" and "them." By making inequities and suffering appear to be the result of personal or group deficiency rather than the consequences of injustice, stereotypes and ideology reconcile people to the status quo and prevent them from seeking change. Violence and the threat of violence reinforce ideology and threaten with pain or death those who challenge the prevailing system or its conventions and prescriptions.

In addition to creating and maintaining mistaken beliefs about the causes of unequal distribution of privilege, stereotypes can play an important role in reconciling individuals to discriminatory treatment. If stereotypes are truly effective, they can prevent the individual not only from recognizing discrimination but even from encountering it, by ensuring that he or she does not seek opportunities that are unavailable to members of his or her group.

In Selection 1, "Self-Fulfilling Stereotypes," Mark Snyder uses examples from psychological research to show how important people's expectations are in shaping their perceptions of others and in determining how they behave. In particular, these studies raise serious questions about the "objectivity" of interviewers' evaluations of job candidates and applicants for admission to educational programs; the studies suggest that how we see others often says more about our own unconscious stereotyping and expectations than about the individuals being evaluated. As Snyder points out, some of the most interesting studies in the field of education show that teachers' expectations are at least as important as a child's innate ability in determining how well young children do in school. Taken together, Snyder's essay and Selection 2 by Richard Mohr on gay stereotypes make it clear that the stereotypes people harbor can have powerful consequences for the life chances and well-being of others.

While some stereotyping is so crude that it can be easily dismissed, advertising has become extremely sophisticated in its ability to shape and manipulate unconscious attitudes and values. In "White Lies," Maurice Berger examines the portrayal of a "prototypical" Black man in an ad campaign by one of America's more successful designers. After offering a subtle and thought-provoking analysis of the way in which Black masculinity is constructed in the ad, Berger goes on to generalize about the relationship between such portrayals and the maintenance of prevailing relations of dominance and subordination in society. He argues that the cultural and social institutions that are controlled by white people continue to operate to protect white privilege.

Although men in our society continue to be judged by the jobs they hold and the amount of money they earn, women continue to be judged according to a narrow and rigid standard of beauty. The messages that bombard young women from an early age continue to foster the belief that having a tiny waist is infinitely more important than earning an advanced degree or learning a technical skill. Although many women have made considerable strides in the world of work, the prevailing ideology continues to assert that being attractive (read "thin") enough to capture the right man is the real way to success. Aside from its heterosexist bias, this emphasis on physical appearance (and consequently on unhealthy standards for body weight) is simply one more way in which society keeps women in their place. In Selection 4, "Am I Thin Enough Yet?", Sharlene Hesse-Biber explores some of the consequences of the ways in which women have been encouraged to internalize an artificial and unattainable standard of beauty.

In Selection 5, William Chafe examines the impact of both race and gender stereotypes and ideology by drawing an analogy between sex and race. He argues persuasively that racism and sexism function analogously as forms of social control. Although Chafe suggests that he is comparing the experiences of white women with those of African Americans, a careful reading of his essay suggests that he is really comparing the experiences of white women with those of black men. The reader might be interested in exploring whether Chafe's claim about racism, sexism, and social control holds up equally well when we construct similar accounts of the experiences of African American women, as well as members of other racial/ethnic groups discussed in this book. Chafe begins by analyzing how stereotypes, ideology, and language can distort expectations, perceptions, and experience, and then proceeds to ask whose interests are served by this distortion.

While prevailing definitions of femininity suggest that women are most desirable when they are neither powerful, successful, nor independent, men are pressured to be economically successful and physically powerful. In

Selection 6, "Pulling Train," Peggy Sanday discusses the role of gang rape in the social construction of masculinity, thereby providing another insight into the process of gender socialization. Reading Sanday's essay in conjunction with Selection 3 in this section, Selections 10, 11, and 13 in Part V, and Selection 8 in Part VIII can provide the opportunity for an extended discussion of how masculinity is constructed in contemporary society.

Returning to Part VII, Selections 7, 8, and 9 examine some of the ways in which education and the media construct images and expectations about race, class, and gender that reinforce the ideology of difference. Expectations as to how girls and boys will perform in the early grades, along with different treatment in the classroom on the basis of gender and race, can have tragic consequences. Although residential segregation throughout the country generally results in segregated schooling, even those schools that appear to have a diverse student body often track students on the basis of race and class. This results in school buildings that are integrated but classes that are segregated, with college prep programs and advanced placement courses virtually off limits to many. Not only do the media play a major role in fostering gender stereotypes, as Gregory Manstios argues in Selection 9, "Media Magic: Making Class Invisible," their programming and perspective impact on our ability to "see" class at all. "By ignoring the poor and blurring the lines between working people and the upper class," he writes, "the news media creates a universal middle class." By adopting the perspective of those most privileged, it distorts the realities of daily life and encourages most of us to identify with the needs and interests of a privileged few.

In Selection 10, William Ryan considers how stereotyping and ideology reinforce the status quo by directing people's attention away from the economic and social arrangements that perpetuate unequal treatment and by encouraging people to blame the victims of these institutions for their own misery. Ryan's essay introduces a technique he calls "blaming the victim," which effectively allows people to recognize injustice without either assuming responsibility for it or acknowledging the need to make fundamental changes in social and economic institutions.

Often, people become overwhelmed and discouraged when they realize how much their unconscious images and beliefs affect their ways of seeing each other and the world; as a result, they fail to go on to analyze the consequences of ideology. Believing that people are naturally prejudiced and can't change is one more bit of ideology that prevents us from questioning prevailing social and economic arrangements and asking whether they serve the best interests of all. By dividing us from each other and confusing us about who profits from these arrangements, ideology and stereotypes imprison us in a false world. In Part VIII of this book, a number of thinkers offer their suggestions about how to move beyond race, class, and gender divisions.

1

Self-Fulfilling Stereotypes

Mark Snyder

Gordon Allport, the Harvard psychologist who wrote a classic work on the nature of prejudice, told a story about a child who had come to believe that people who lived in Minneapolis were called monopolists. From his father, moreover, he had learned that monopolists were evil folk. It wasn't until many years later, when he discovered his confusion, that his dislike of residents of Minneapolis vanished.

Allport knew, of course, that it was not so easy to wipe out prejudice and erroneous stereotypes. Real prejudice, psychologists like Allport argued, was buried deep in human character, and only a restructuring of education could begin to root it out. Yet many people whom I meet while lecturing seem to believe that stereotypes are simply beliefs or attitudes that change easily with experience. Why do some people express the view that Italians are passionate, blacks are lazy, Jews materialistic, and lesbians mannish in their demeanor? In the popular view, it is because they have not learned enough about the diversity among these groups and have not had enough contact with members of the groups for their stereotypes to be challenged by reality. With more experience, it is presumed, most people of good will are likely to revise their stereotypes.

My research over the past decade convinces me that there is little justification for such optimism—and not only for the reasons given by Allport. While it is true that deep prejudice is often based on the needs of pathological character structure, stereotypes are obviously quite common even among fairly normal individuals. When people first meet others, they cannot help noticing certain highly visible and distinctive characteristics: sex, race, physical appearance, and the like. Despite people's best intentions, their initial impressions of others are shaped by their assumptions about such characteristics.

What is critical, however, is that these assumptions are not merely beliefs or attitudes that exist in a vacuum; they are reinforced by the behavior of both prejudiced people and the targets of their prejudice. In recent years, psychologists have collected considerable laboratory evidence about the processes that strengthen stereotypes and put them beyond the reach of reason and good will.

My own studies initially focused on first encounters between strangers. It did not take long to discover, for example, that people have very different ways of treating those whom they regard as physically attractive and those whom they consider physically unattractive, and that these differences tend to bring out precisely those kinds of behavior that fit with stereotypes about attractiveness.

In an experiment that I conducted with my colleagues Elizabeth Decker Tanke and Ellen Berscheid, pairs of college-age men and women met and became acquainted in telephone conversations. Before the conversations began, each man received a Polaroid snapshot, presumably taken just moments before, of the woman he would soon meet. The photograph, which had actually been prepared before the experiment began, showed either a physically attractive woman or a physically unattractive one. By randomly choosing which picture to use for each conversation, we insured that there was no consistent relationship between the attractiveness of the woman in the picture and the attractiveness of the woman in the conversation.

By questioning the men, we learned that even before the conversations began, stereotypes about physical attractiveness came into play. Men who looked forward to talking with physically attractive women said that they expected to meet decidedly sociable, poised, humorous, and socially adept people, while men who thought that they were about to get acquainted with unattractive women fashioned images of rather unsociable, awkward, serious, and socially inept creatures. Moreover, the men proved to have very different styles of getting acquainted with women whom they thought to be attractive and those whom they believed to be unattractive. Shown a photograph of an attractive woman, they behaved with warmth, friendliness, humor, and animation. However, when the woman in the picture was unattractive, the men were cold, uninteresting, and reserved.

These differences in the men's behavior elicited behavior in the women that was consistent with the men's stereotyped assumptions. Women who were believed (unbeknown to them) to be physically attractive behaved in a friendly, likeable, and sociable manner. In sharp contrast, women who were perceived as physically unattractive adopted a cool, aloof, and distant manner. So striking were the differences in the women's behavior that they could be discerned simply by listening to tape recordings of the woman's side of the conversations. Clearly, by acting upon their stereotyped beliefs about the women whom they would be meeting, the men had initiated a chain of events that produced *behavioral confirmation* for their beliefs.

Similarly, Susan Anderson and Sandra Bem have shown in an experiment at Stanford University that when the tables are turned—when it is women who have pictures of men they are to meet on the telephone—many women treat the men according to their presumed physical attractiveness, and by so doing encourage the men to confirm their stereotypes. Little wonder, then, that so many people remain convinced that good looks and appealing personalities go hand in hand.

Sex and Race

It is experiments such as these that point to a frequently unnoticed power of stereotypes: the power to influence social relationships in ways that create the illusion of reality. In one study, Berna Skrypnek and I arranged for pairs of previously unacquainted students to interact in a situation that permitted us to control the information that each one received about the apparent sex of the other. The two people were seated in separate rooms so that they could neither see nor hear each other. Using a system of signal lights that they operated with switches, they negotiated a division of labor, deciding which member of the pair would perform each of several tasks that differed in sex-role connotations. The tasks varied along the dimensions of masculinity and femininity: sharpen a hunting knife (masculine), polish a pair of shoes (neutral), iron a shirt (feminine).

One member of the team was led to believe that the other was, in one condition of the experiment, male; in the other, female. As we had predicted, the first member's belief about the sex of the partner influenced the outcome of the pair's negotiations. Women whose partners believed them to be men generally chose stereotypically masculine tasks; in contrast, women whose partners believed that they were women usually chose stereotypically feminine tasks. The experiment thus suggests that much sex-role behavior may be the product of other people's stereotyped and often erroneous beliefs.

In a related study at the University of Waterloo, Carl von Baeyer, Debbie Sherk, and Mark Zanna have shown how stereotypes about sex roles operate in job interviews. The researchers arranged to have men conduct simulated job interviews with women supposedly seeking positions as research assistants. The investigators informed half of the women that the men who would interview them held traditional views about the ideal woman, believing her to be very emotional, deferential to her husband, home-oriented, and passive. The rest of the women were told that their interviewer saw the ideal woman as independent, competitive, ambitious, and dominant. When the women arrived for their interviews, the researchers noticed that most of them had dressed to meet the stereotyped expectations of their prospective interviewers. Women who expected to see a traditional interviewer had chosen very feminine-looking makeup, clothes, and accessories. During the interviews (videotaped through a one-way mirror) these women behaved in traditionally feminine ways and gave traditionally feminine answers to questions such as "Do you have plans to include children and marriage with your career plans?"

Once more, then, we see the self-fulfilling nature of stereotypes. Many sex differences, it appears, may result from the images that people create in their attempts to act out accepted sex roles. The implication is that if stereotyped expectations about sex roles shift, behavior may change, too. In fact, statements by people who have undergone sex-change operations have highlighted the power of such expectations in easing adjustment to a new life. As the writer Jan Morris said in recounting the story of her transition from James to Jan: "The more I was treated as a woman, the more woman I became."

The power of stereotypes to cause people to confirm stereotyped expectations can also be seen in interracial relationships. In the first of two investigations done at Princeton University by Carl Word, Mark Zanna, and Joel Cooper, white undergraduates interviewed both white and black job applicants. The applicants were actually confederates of the experimenters, trained to behave consistently from interview to interview, no matter how the interviewers acted toward them.

To find out whether or not the white interviewers would behave differently toward white and black job applicants, the researchers secretly videotaped each interview and then studied the tapes. From these, it was apparent that there were substantial differences in the treatment accorded blacks and whites. For one thing, the interviewers' speech deteriorated when they talked to blacks, displaying more errors in grammar and pronunciation. For another, the interviewers spent less time with blacks than with whites and showed less "immediacy," as the researchers called it, in their manner. That is, they were less friendly, less outgoing, and more reserved with blacks.

In the second investigation, white confederates were trained to approximate the immediate or the nonimmediate interview styles that had been observed in the first investigation as they interviewed white job applicants. A panel of judges who evaluated the tapes agreed that applicants subjected to the nonimmediate styles performed less adequately and were more nervous than job applicants treated in the immediate style. Apparently, then, the blacks in the first study did not have a chance to display their qualifications to the best advantage. Considered together, the two investigations suggest that in interracial encounters, racial stereotypes may constrain behavior in ways to cause both blacks and whites to behave in accordance with those stereotypes.

Rewriting Biography

Having adopted stereotyped ways of thinking about another person, people tend to notice and remember the ways in which that person seems to fit the stereotype, while resisting evidence that contradicts the stereotype. In one investigation that I conducted with Seymour Uranowitz, student subjects read a biography of a fictitious woman named Betty K. We constructed the story of her life so that it would fit the stereotyped images of both lesbians and heterosexuals. Betty, we wrote, never had a steady boyfriend in high school, but did go out on dates. And although we gave her a steady boyfriend in college, we specified that he was more of a close friend than anything else. A week after we had distributed this biography, we gave our subjects some new information about Betty. We told some students that she was now living with another woman in a lesbian relationship; we told others that she was living with her husband.

To see what impact stereotypes about sexuality would have on how people remembered the facts of Betty's life, we asked each student to answer a series of questions about her life history. When we examined their answers, we found that the students had reconstructed the events of Betty's past in ways that supported their own stereotyped beliefs about her sexual orientation. Those who believed that Betty was a lesbian remembered that Betty had never had a steady boyfriend in high school, but tended to neglect the fact that she had gone out on many dates in college. Those who believed that Betty was now a heterosexual tended to remember that she had formed a steady relationship with a man in college, but tended to ignore the fact that this relationship was more of a friendship than a romance.

The students showed not only selective memories but also a striking facility for interpreting what they remembered in ways that added fresh support for their stereotypes. One student who accurately remembered that a supposedly lesbian Betty never had a steady boyfriend in high school confidently pointed to the fact as an early sign of her lack of romantic or sexual interest in men. A student who correctly remembered that a purportedly lesbian Betty often went out on dates in college was sure that these dates were signs of Betty's early attempts to mask her lesbian interests.

Clearly, the students had allowed their preconceptions about lesbians and heterosexuals to dictate the way in which they interpreted and reinterpreted the facts of Betty's life. As long as stereotypes make it easy to bring to mind evidence that supports them and difficult to bring to mind evidence that undermines them, people will cling to erroneous beliefs.

Stereotypes in the Classroom and Work Place

The power of one person's beliefs to make other people conform to them has been well demonstrated in real life. Back in the 1960s, as most people well remember, Harvard psychologist Robert Rosenthal and his colleague Lenore Jacobson entered elementary-school classrooms and identified one out of every five pupils in each room as a child who could be expected to show dramatic improvement in intellectual achievement during the school year. What the teachers did not know was that the children had been chosen on a random basis. Nevertheless, something happened in the relationships between teachers and their supposedly gifted pupils that led the children to make clear gains in test performance.

It can also do so on the job. Albert King, now a professor of management at Northern Illinois University, told a welding instructor in a vocational training center that five men in his training program had unusually high aptitude. Although these five had been chosen at random and knew nothing of their designation as high-aptitude workers, they showed substantial changes in performance. They were absent less often than were other workers, learned the basics of the welder's trade in about half the usual time, and scored a full 10 points higher than other trainees on a welding test. Their gains were noticed not only by the researcher and by the welding instructor, but also by other trainees, who singled out the five as their preferred coworkers.

Might not other expectations influence the relationships between supervisors and workers? For example, supervisors who believe that men are better suited to some jobs and women to others may treat their workers (wittingly or unwittingly) in ways that encourage them to perform their jobs in accordance with stereotypes about differences between men and women. These same stereotypes may determine who gets which job in the first place. Perhaps some personnel managers allow stereotypes to influence, subtly or not so subtly, the way in which they interview job candidates, making it likely that candidates who fit the stereotypes show up better than job-seekers who do not fit them.

Unfortunately, problems of this kind are compounded by the fact that members of stigmatized groups often subscribe to stereotypes about themselves. That is what Amerigo Farina and his colleagues at the University of Connecticut found when they measured the impact upon mental patients of believing that others knew their psychiatric history. In Farina's study, each mental patient cooperated with another person in a game requiring teamwork. Half of the patients believed that their partners knew they were patients, the other half believed that their partners thought they were nonpatients. In reality, the nonpatients never knew a thing about anyone's psychiatric history. Nevertheless, simply believing that others were aware of their history led the patients to feel less appreciated, to find the task more difficult, and to perform poorly. In addition, objective observers saw them as more tense, more anxious, and more poorly adjusted than patients who believed that their status was not known. Seemingly, the belief that others perceived them as stigmatized caused them to play the role of stigmatized patients.

Consequences for Society

Apparently, good will and education are not sufficient to subvert the power of stereotypes. If people treat others in such a way as to bring out behavior that supports stereotypes, they may never have an opportunity to discover which of their stereotypes are wrong.

I suspect that even if people were to develop doubts about the accuracy of their stereotypes, chances are they would proceed to test them by gathering precisely the evidence that would appear to confirm them.

The experiments I have described help to explain the persistence of stereotypes. But, as is so often the case, solving one puzzle only creates another. If by acting as if false stereotypes were true, people lead others, too, to act as if they were true, why do the stereotypes not come to *be* true? Why, for example, have researchers found so little evidence that attractive people are generally friendly, sociable, and outgoing and that unattractive people are generally shy and aloof?

I think that the explanation goes something like this: Very few among us have the kind of looks that virtually everyone considers either very attractive or very unattractive. Our looks make us rather attractive to some people but somewhat less attractive to other people. When we spend time with those who find us attractive, they will tend to bring out our more sociable sides, but when we are with those who find us less attractive, they will bring out our less sociable sides. Although our actual physical appearance does not change, we present ourselves quite differently to our admirers and to our detractors. For our admirers we become attractive people, and for our detractors we become unattractive. This mixed pattern of behavior will prevent the development of any consistent relationship between physical attractiveness and personality.

Now that I understand some of the powerful forces that work to perpetuate social stereotypes, I can see a new mission for my research. I hope, on the one hand, to find out how to help people see the flaws in their stereotypes. On the other hand, I would like to help the victims of false stereotypes find ways of liberating themselves from the constraints imposed on them by other members of society.

2

Anti-Gay Stereotypes

Richard D. Mohr

A . . . Gallup poll found that only one in five Americans reports having a gay acquaintance.[1] This finding is extraordinary given the number of practicing homosexuals in America. Alfred Kinsey's 1948 study of the sex lives of 5000 white males shocked the nation: 37 percent had at least one homosexual experience to orgasm in their adult lives; an additional 13 percent had homosexual fantasies to orgasm; 4 percent were exclusively homosexual in their practices; another 5 percent had virtually no heterosexual experience; and nearly 20 percent had at least as many homosexual as heterosexual experiences.[2] With only slight variations, these figures held across all social categories: region, religion, political belief, class, income, occupation, and education.

Two out of five men one passes on the street have had orgasmic sex with men. Every second family in the country has a member who is essentially homosexual, and many more people regularly have homosexual experiences. Who are homosexuals? They are your friends, your minister, your teacher, your bankteller, your doctor, your mailcarrier, your secretary, your congressional representative, your sibling, parent, and spouse. They are everywhere, virtually all ordinary, virtually all unknown.

What follows? First, the country is profoundly ignorant of the actual experience of gay people. Second, social attitudes and practices that are harmful to gays have a much greater overall negative impact on society than is usually realized. Third, most gay people live in hiding—in the closet—making the "coming out" experience the central fixture of gay consciousness and invisibility the chief social characteristic of gays.

Society's ignorance of gay people is, however, not limited to individuals' lack of personal acquaintance with gays. Stigma against gay people is so strong that even discussions of homosexuality are taboo. This taboo is particularly strong in academe, where it is reinforced by the added fear of the teacher as molester. So even within the hearth of reason irrational forces have held virtually unchallenged and largely unchallengeable sway. The usual sort of clarifying research that might be done on a stigmatized minority has with gays only just begun—haltingly—in history, literature, sociology, and the sciences.

Yet ignorance about gays has not stopped people from having strong opinions about them. The void which ignorance leaves has been filled with stereotypes. Society holds chiefly two groups of anti-gay stereotypes; the two are an oddly contradictory lot. One set of stereotypes revolves around alleged mistakes in an individual's gender identity: lesbians are women that want to be, or at least look and act like, men—bulldykes, diesel dykes; while gay men are those who want to be, or at least look and act like, women—queens, fairies, limp-wrists, nellies. Gays are "queer," which, remember, means at root not merely weird but chiefly counterfeit—"he's as queer as a three dollar bill." These stereotypes of mismatched or fraudulent genders provide the materials through which gays and lesbians become the butts of ethnic-like jokes. These stereotypes and jokes, though derisive, basically view gays and lesbians as ridiculous.

Another set of stereotypes revolves around gays as a pervasive, sinister, conspiratorial, and corruptive threat. The core stereotype here is the gay person as child molester and, more generally, as sex-crazed maniac. These stereotypes carry with them fears of the very destruction of family and civilization itself. Now, that which is essentially ridiculous can hardly have such a staggering effect. Something must be afoot in this incoherent amalgam.

Sense can be made of this incoherence if the nature of stereotypes is clarified. Stereotypes are not *simply* false generalizations from a skewed sample of cases examined. Admittedly, false generalizing plays a part in most stereotypes a society holds. If, for instance, one takes as one's sample homosexuals who are in psychiatric hospitals or prisons, as was done in nearly all early investigations, not surprisingly one will probably find homosexuals to be of a crazed and criminal cast. Such false generalizations, though, simply confirm beliefs already held on independent grounds, ones that likely led the investigator to the prison and psychiatric ward to begin with. Evelyn Hooker, who in the mid-fifties carried out the first rigorous studies to use nonclinical gays, found that psychiatrists, when presented with results of standard psychological diagnostic tests—but with indications of sexual orientation omitted—were able to do no better than if they had guessed randomly in their attempts to distinguish gay files from nongay ones, even though the psychiatrists believed gays to be crazy and supposed themselves to be experts in detecting craziness.[3] These studies proved a profound embarrassment to the psychiatric establishment, the financial well-being of which was substantially enhanced by "curing" allegedly insane gays. Eventually the studies contributed to the American Psychiatric Association's dropping homosexuality from its registry of mental illnesses in 1973.[4] Nevertheless, the stereotype of gays as sick continues apace in the mind of America.

False generalizations *help maintain* stereotypes; they do not *form* them. As the history of Hooker's discoveries shows, stereotypes have a life beyond facts. Their origin lies in a culture's ideology—the general system of beliefs by which it lives—and they are sustained across generations by diverse cultural transmissions, hardly any of which, including slang and jokes, even purport to have a scientific basis. Stereotypes, then, are not the products of bad science, but are social constructions that perform central functions in maintaining society's conception of itself.

On this understanding, it is easy to see that the anti-gay stereotypes surrounding gender identification are chiefly means of reinforcing still powerful gender roles in society. If, as this stereotype presumes (and condemns), one is free to choose one's social roles independently of gender, many guiding social divisions, both domestic and commercial, might be threatened. The socially gender-linked distinctions would blur between breadwinner and homemaker, protector and protected, boss and secretary, doctor and nurse, priest and nun, hero and whore, saint and siren, lord and helpmate, and God and his world. The accusations "fag" and "dyke" (which recent philology has indeed shown to be rooted in slang referring to gender-bending, especially cross-dressing)[5] exist in significant part to keep women in their place and to prevent men from breaking ranks and ceding away theirs.

The stereotypes of gays as child molesters, sex-crazed maniacs, and civilization destroyers function to displace (socially irresolvable) problems from their actual source to a foreign (and so, it is thought, manageable) one. Thus, the stereotype of child molester functions to give the family unit a false sheen of absolute innocence. It keeps the unit from being examined too closely for incest, child abuse, wife-battering, and the terrorism of constant threats. The stereotype teaches that the problems of the family are not internal to it, but external.

Because this stereotype has this central social function, it could not be dislodged even by empirical studies, paralleling Hooker's efforts, that showed heterosexuals to be child molesters to a far greater extent than the actual occurrence of heterosexuals in the general population.[6] But one need not even be aware of such debunking empirical studies in order to see the same cultural forces at work in the social belief that gays are molesters as in its belief that they are crazy. For one can see them now in society's and the media's treatment of current reports of violence, especially domestic violence. When a mother kills her child or a father rapes his daughter—regular Section B fare even in major urban papers—this is never taken by reporters, columnists, or pundits as evidence that there is something wrong with heterosexuality or with traditional families. These issues are not even raised.

But when a homosexual child molestation is reported it is taken as confirming evidence of the way homosexuals are. One never hears of heterosexual murders, but one regularly reads of "homosexual" ones. Compare the social treatment of Richard Speck's sexually motivated mass murder in 1966 of Chicago nurses with that of John Wayne Gacy's serial murders of Chicago youths. Gacy was in the culture's mind taken as symbolic of gay men in general. To prevent the possibility that The Family was viewed as anything but an innocent victim in this affair, the mainstream press knowingly failed to mention that most of Gacy's adolescent victims were homeless hustlers, even though this was made obvious at his trial.[7] That knowledge would be too much for the six o'clock news and for cherished beliefs.

The stereotype of gays as sex-crazed maniacs functions socially to keep individuals' sexuality contained. For this stereotype makes it look as though the problem of how to address one's considerable sexual drives can and should be answered with repression, for it gives the impression that the cyclone of dangerous psychic forces is *out there* where the fags are, not within one's own breast. With the decline of the stereotype of the black man as raping pillaging marauder (found in such works as *Birth of a Nation, Gone with the Wind,* and *Soul on Ice*), the stereotype of gay men as sex-crazed maniacs has become more aggravated. The stereotype of the sex-crazed threat seems one that society desperately needs to have somewhere in its sexual cosmology.

For the repressed homosexual, this stereotype has an especially powerful allure—by hating it consciously, he subconsciously appears to save himself from himself, at least as long as the ruse does not exhaust the considerable psychic energies required to maintain it, or until, like ultraconservative Congressmen Robert E. Bauman (R-Md.) and Jon C. Hinson (R-Miss.), he is caught importuning hustlers or gentlemen in washrooms.[8] If, as Freud and some of his followers thought, everyone feels an urge for sex partners of both genders, then the fear of gays works to show us that we have not "met the enemy and he is us."[9]

By directly invoking sex acts, this second set of stereotypes is the more severe and serious of the two—one never hears child-molester jokes. These stereotypes are aimed chiefly against men, as in turn stereotypically the more sexed of the genders. They are particularly divisive for they create a very strong division between those conceived as "us" and those conceived as "them." This divide is not so strong in the case of the stereotype of gay men as effeminate. For women (and so the woman-like) after all do have their place. Nonstrident, nonuppity useful ones can even be part of "us," indeed, belong, like "our children," to "us." Thus, in many cultures with overweening gender-identified social roles (like prisons, truckstops, the armed forces, Latin America, and the Islamic world) only passive partners in male couplings are derided as homosexual.[10]

Because "the facts" largely do not matter when it comes to the generation and maintenance of stereotypes, the effects of scientific and academic research and of enlightenment generally will be, at best, slight and gradual in the changing fortunes of gays. If this account of stereotypes holds, society has been profoundly immoral. For its treatment of gays is a grand scale rationalization and moral sleight-of-hand. The problem is not that society's usual standards of evidence and procedure in coming to judgments of social policy have been misapplied to gays, rather when it comes to gays, the standards themselves have simply been ruled out of court and disregarded in favor of mechanisms that encourage unexamined fear and hatred.

Partly because lots of people suppose they do not know a gay person and partly through their willful ignorance of society's workings, people are largely unaware of the many ways in which gays are subject to discrimination in consequence of widespread fear and hatred. Contributing to this social ignorance of discrimination is the difficulty for gay people, as an invisible minority, even to complain of discrimination. For if one is gay, to register a complaint would suddenly target one as a stigmatized person, and so, in the absence of any protections against discrimination, would in turn invite additional discrimination.

Further, many people, especially those who are persistently downtrodden and so lack a firm sense of self to begin with, tend either to blame themselves for their troubles or to view their troubles as a matter of bad luck or as the result of an innocent mistake by others—as anything but an injustice indicating something wrong with society. Alfred Dreyfus went to his grave believing his imprisonment for treason and his degradation from the French military, in which he was the highest ranking Jewish officer, had all just been a sort of clerical error, merely requiring recomputation, rather than what it was—lightning striking a promontory from out of a storm of national bigotry.[11] The recognition of injustice requires doing something to rectify wrong; the recognition of systematic injustices requires doing something about the system, and most people, especially the already beleaguered, simply are not up to the former, let alone the latter.

For a number of reasons, then, discrimination against gays, like rape, goes seriously underreported. What do they experience? First, gays are subject to violence and harassment based simply on their perceived status rather than because of any actions they have performed. A[n] . . . extensive study by the National Gay and Lesbian Task Force found that over 90 percent of gays and lesbians had been victimized in some form on the basis of their sexual orientation.[12] More than one in five gay men and nearly one in ten lesbians had been punched, hit, or kicked; a quarter of all gays had had objects thrown at them; a third had been chased; a third had been sexually harassed and 14 percent had been spit on—all just for being perceived to be gay.

The most extreme form of anti-gay violence is queerbashing—where groups of young men target another man who they suppose is gay and beat and kick him unconscious and sometimes to death amid a torrent of taunts and slurs. Such seemingly random but in reality socially encouraged violence has the same social origin and function as lynchings of blacks—to keep a whole stigmatized group in line. As with lynchings . . . the police and courts have routinely averted their eyes, giving their implicit approval to the practice.

Few such cases with gay victims reach the courts. Those that do are marked by inequitable procedures and results. Frequently judges will describe queerbashers as "just All-American Boys." In 1984, a District of Columbia judge handed suspended sentences to queerbashers whose victim had been stalked, beaten, stripped at knife point, slashed, kicked, threatened with castration, and pissed on, because the judge thought the bashers were good boys at heart—after all they went to a religious prep school.[13]

In the summer of 1984, three teenagers hurled a gay man to his death from a bridge in Bangor, Maine. Though the youths could have been tried as adults and normally would have been, given the extreme violence of their crime, they were tried rather as children and . . . [were to] be back on the streets again automatically when they turn[ed] twenty-one.[14]

Further, police and juries simply discount testimony from gays.[15] They typically construe assaults on and murders of gays as "justified" self-defense—the killer need only claim his act was a panicked response to a sexual overture.[16] Alternatively, when guilt seems patent, juries will accept highly implausible insanity or other "diminished capacity" defenses. In 1981 a former New York City Transit Authority policeman, later claiming he was just doing the work of God, machine-gunned down nine people, killing two, in two Greenwich Village gay bars. His jury found him innocent due to mental illness.[17] The best known example of a successful "diminished capacity" defense is Dan White's voluntary manslaughter conviction for the 1978 assassination of openly gay San Francisco city councilman Harvey Milk—Hostess Twinkies, his lawyer successfully argued, made him do it.[18]

These inequitable procedures and results collectively show that the life and liberty of gays, like those of blacks, simply count for less than the life and liberty of members of the dominant culture. . . .

NOTES

1. "Public Fears—And Sympathies," *Newsweek*, August 12, 1985, p. 23.

2. Alfred C. Kinsey, et al., *Sexual Behavior in the Human Male* (Philadelphia: Saunders, 1948), pp. 650–51. On the somewhat lower incidences of lesbianism, see Alfred C. Kinsey, et al., *Sexual Behavior in the Human Female* (Philadelphia: Saunders, 1953), pp. 472–75.

3. Evelyn Hooker, "The Adjustment of the Male Overt Homosexual," *Journal of Projective Techniques* (1957) 21:18–31, reprinted in Hendrik M. Ruitenbeck, ed., *The Problem of Homosexuality*, pp. 141–61, epigram quote from p. 149 (New York: Dutton, 1963).

4. See Ronald Bayer, *Homosexuality and American Psychiatry* (New York: Basic Books, 1981).

5. See Wayne Dynes, *Homolexis: A Historical and Cultural Lexicon of Homosexuality* (New York: Gay Academic Union, Gai Saber Monograph No. 4, 1985), s.v. dyke, faggot.

6. For studies showing that gay men are no more likely—indeed, are less likely—than heterosexuals to be child molesters and that the most widespread and persistent sexual abusers of children are the children's fathers, stepfathers or mother's boyfriends, see Vincent De Francis, *Protecting the Child Victim of Sex Crimes Committed by Adults* (Denver: The American Humane Association, 1969), pp. vii, 38, 69–70; A. Nicholas Groth, "Adult Sexual Orientation and Attraction to Underage Persons," *Archives of Sexual Behavior* (1978) 7:175–81; Mary J. Spencer, "Sexual Abuse of Boys," *Pediatrics* (July 1986) 78(1):133–38.

7. See Lawrence Mass, "Sanity in Chicago: The Trial of John Wayne Gacy and American Psychiatry," *Christopher Street* [New York] (June 1980) 4(7):26. See also Terry Sullivan, *Killer Clown* (New York: Grosset & Dunlap), 1983, pp. 219–25, 315–16; Tim Cahill, *Buried Dreams* (Toronto: Bantam Books, 1986), pp. 318, 352–53, 368–69.

8. For Robert Bauman's account of his undoing, see his autobiography, *The Gentleman from Maryland* (New York: Arbor House, 1986).

9. On Freud, see Timothy F. Murphy, "Freud Reconsidered: Bisexuality, Homosexuality, and Moral Judgment," *Journal of Homosexuality* (1984) 9(2–3):65–77.

10. On prisons, see Wayne Wooden and Jay Parker, *Men Behind Bars: Sexual Exploitation in Prison* (New York: Plenum, 1982). On the armed forces, see George Chauncey Jr., "Christian Brotherhood or Sexual Perversion? Homosexual Identities and the Construction of Sexual Boundaries in the World War One Era," *Journal of Social History* (1985) 19: 189–211.

11. See Jean-Denis Bredin, *The Affair: The Case of Alfred Dreyfus*, trans. Jeffrey Mehlman (1983; New York: George Braziller, 1986), pp. 486–96.

12. National Gay and Lesbian Task Force, *Anti-Gay/Lesbian Victimization* (New York: National Gay and Lesbian Task Force, 1984). See also "Anti-Gay Violence," Subcommittee on Criminal Justice, Committee on the Judiciary, House of Representatives, 99th Congress, 2nd Session, October 9, 1986, serial no. 132.

13. "Two St. John's Students Given Probation in Assault on Gay," *The Washington Post*, May 15, 1984, p. I.

The 1980 Mariel boatlift, which included thousands of gays escaping Cuban internment camps, inspired U.S. Federal District Judge A. Andrew Hauk in open court to comment of a Mexican illegal alien caught while visiting his resident alien daughter: "And he isn't even a fag like all these faggots we're letting in." *The Advocate* [Los Angeles], November 27, 1980, no. 306, p. 15. Cf. "Gay Refugees Tell of Torture, Oppression in Cuba," *The Advocate*, August 21, 1980, no. 299, pp. 15–16.

14. See *The New York Times*, September 17, 1984, p. D17, and October 6, 1984, p. 6.

15. John D'Emilio writes of the trial of seven police officers caught in a gay bar shakedown racket: "The defense lawyer cast aspersions on the credibility of the prosecution witnesses . . . and deplored a legal system in which 'the most notorious homosexual may testify against a policeman.' Persuaded by this line of argument, the jury acquitted all of the defendants." *Sexual Politics, Sexual Communities: The Making of a Homosexual Minority in the United States, 1940–1970* (Chicago: University of Chicago Press, 1983), p. 183.

16. See for discussion and examples, Pat Califia, "'Justifiable' Homicide?" *The Advocate*, May 12, 1983, no. 367, p. 12; and Robert G. Bagnall, et al., "Burdens on Gay Litigants and Bias in the Court System: Homosexual Panic, Child Custody, and Anonymous Parties," *Harvard Civil Rights–Civil Liberties Law Review* (1984) 19:498–515.

17. *The New York Times*, July 25, 1981, p. 27, and July 26, 1981, p. 25.

18. See Randy Shilts, *The Mayor of Castro Street: The Life and Times of Harvey Milk* (New York: St. Martin's, 1982), pp. 308–25.

3

White Lies

Maurice Berger

On the left-hand side of the two-page advertisement in *The New York Times Magazine* is a regal head shot of a polo pony framed against a bright-blue background. His neck is long and muscular. Bound in the leather straps of the bridle, his head is a deep mahogany, with a strip of white running down the snout. His mane is closely cropped. His ears are small and rigid. His eyes glisten like black marbles. His nostrils flare. His closed mouth appears almost to be grinning.

On the right-hand side of this advertisement (for Ralph Lauren Polo shirts) is a human counterpart to the majestic horse. The man is strikingly beautiful. His head looks to the left, a perfect pendant to the right-facing horse. His skin is a deep mahogany. His elegant, shaved pate has just a hint of black stubble. His small ears curve upward and slightly away from his head. His eyes are dark and dramatic. His nostrils appear to be slightly flared; white light bounces off the bridge of his nose. His full, luscious lips seem almost to be breaking into a smile. His bright-blue shirt nearly blends into the background, giving the effect of a head and neck that graphically float, naked and powerful, against a sea of blue.

It is strange to see a black man representing a company that made its mark appealing to the American middle-class fascination with WASP wealth and taste—even if the man is Tyson Beckford, the first African American male supermodel. Beckford has been the designer's "Polo man" since March 1995, which suggests, in part, that Lauren is reaching out to prospective black customers. But juxtaposing a picture of a black man to one of an animal—the model is not wearing polo gear and is not even in the same space as the horse, suggesting that the two, rather than interacting, are being compared to each other—is an unfortunate ploy. Intentionally or otherwise, the ad replays a long-standing racist fantasy about black people: no matter how beautiful, smart, or talented, they are in some ways always exotic and animal-like.

This fantasy allows white people to feel superior to black people who they suspect may be more beautiful, more talented, or better endowed than they are. It may explain why black models are rarely seen on the cover of fashion and women's and men's magazines and why images of violent black men and irresponsible black mothers abound in the media. Positive images of black men often center on

From Maurice Berger, *White Lies: Race and the Myths of Whiteness* (New York: Farrar, Straus & Giroux, 1999), pp. 133–138.

their physicality or athleticism: "Athletes, more than rappers, are more like national heroes," says Beckford's agent, Bethann Hardison. "But also, when it comes down to black men's bodies, historically it's been about how strong and well defined they are—that's what's had value. It's the same old story." The press release for a recent show of menswear by the designer John Bartlett, unusual in that it featured six black models, celebrated the special prowess of black men: "They just have a certain natural masculinity to them," Bartlett observes.

The association between blackness and innate physicality, masculinity, or naturalness often relegates black men to a less-than-human status in the media. In 1988, for example, TV sportscaster Jimmy "the Greek" Snyder offered this on-air explanation of black athletic gifts: "[T]he slave owner would breed his big black with his big black woman so that he could have a big black kid. . . . The black is a better athlete to begin with because he's been bred to be that way because of his thigh size and his big size. [Blacks can] jump higher and run faster." (Snyder was later fired by CBS Sports.)

Like Lauren's vision of the black man as polo pony, such stereotypes deny the intellectual and human dimension of blackness just as surely as they systematically ascribe to black people bestial traits that are rarely applied to whites (the Marlboro Man, after all, is riding *on* his majestic horse). Sometimes this belittling of blackness is more subtle, though by no means free of the prejudices of racial biology. In 1994, for example, golfer Jack Nicklaus told an interviewer that black men have "different muscles that react in different ways" and thus were anatomically unsuited to play golf. (A few years later, of course, Tiger Woods won the U.S. Open, dispelling Nicklaus's racist assumption forever.) Nicklaus's and Snyder's views of black athleticism both see athletic aptitude as inborn, physical, and even genetic; such traits as intelligence, skill, perseverance, and dedication do not come into play.

Black male models present a problem for the fashion industry, argues Hilton Als, where they "still tend to generate lurid fantasies of subway 'gangstas,' and many American designers aren't sure that black men can *sell.*" Lauren has found a way out of this problem: transformed into a metaphorical satyr—half man, half horse—Beckford is freed from the specificity of contemporary black masculinity, thus making him more accessible to the white reader. This effect is also achieved, as John Hoberman points out in *Darwin's Athletes: How Sport Has Damaged Black America and Preserved the Myth of Race*, by dissolving ethnic blackness into a genteel and nonviolent "sporting world that is exclusively and impeccably white: golfing, fishing, tennis, rowing, sailing, and polo—the sports of dynamic imperial males unwinding from the rigors of colonial administration."

Yet Lauren's "Polo man" is only allowed to join this world as the counterpart to one of its beautiful, imperial animals. A handsome model, black or white, can help lure the consumer into the fantasy that buying a particular garment will grant him access to the garment's aura of beauty. The risk, however, is that the consumer may also feel competitive with or even threatened by another man's attractiveness. The very presence of black models, then, challenges the often unconscious desires of white men to see themselves as superior to black men. To some extent, Lauren neutralizes these competitive feelings by inviting us to see mirrored in the face of his mahogany "Polo man" the features of an animal prized for its physical endowments.

Too often, white people acknowledge a particular strength in a black colleague, sports figure, politician, or entertainer but dilute their recognition with the same kind of ambivalence implicit in the Lauren ad. In a study of the racial attitudes of sports reporters, for example, *Boston Globe* writer Derek Jackson analyzed the coverage of five National Collegiate Athletic Association basketball games and seven National Football League play-off games during a single season. More than three-quarters of the adjectives used to describe white football players referred to their brains, while just under two-thirds of the adjectives used for black players referred to their brawn. In basketball, the ratio was 63 percent brains for white players, 77 percent brawn for black players.

Cultural and social institutions controlled by white people have been slow to reward black accomplishment not because African Americans don't excel but because such rewards declare that a black person may, in fact, be more talented, more intelligent, or more beautiful than his white peers. One need look no further than the film industry to see white people's indifference to black people's excellence. Although African Americans buy movie tickets in the disproportionate numbers (they make up 12 percent of the population but 25 percent of movie patrons), black people in Hollywood rarely achieve crossover superstar status, or are thought capable of carrying a movie, or receive such markers of success as Academy Award nominations. The 1997 Oscars were a case in point: all twenty acting nominees were white and a number of their performances were less than outstanding; overlooked were the extraordinary and critically acclaimed work of black actors Djimon Hounsou in *Amistad*; Samuel L. Jackson, Debbi Morgan, and Lynn Whitfield in *Eve's Bayou*; and Pam Grier in *Jackie Brown*. The argument, advanced by several white critics, that these films were weak and thus placed their actors at a disadvantage for Oscar nominations is specious: *Eve's Bayou* was widely praised by critics (though the film apparently did not reach white audiences) and Grier's and Hounsou's white co-stars, Robert Forster and Anthony Hopkins, were nominated. In the end, most black men in Hollywood—from Denzel Washington to James Earl Jones—remain character actors: "In other words, they are *safe*," observes actress Ellen Holly in an op-ed piece in *The New York Times* on the obstacles faced by black actors in the film industry. "They may be doing some of the most riveting work in film . . . but none is breaking the sexual taboos that keep a black man from becoming a high-wattage star."

Mainstream American culture's avoidance of black talent and excellence suggests one of the greatest deficiencies of whiteness: its inability to celebrate and learn from the strengths and accomplishments of black people. Too often, white people live by the rules of self-protection, competitiveness, and self-aggrandizement—rules which tell us that black men may be no more handsome or intelligent than the polo ponies on which their rich white brothers ride.

4

Am I Thin Enough Yet?

Sharlene Hesse-Biber

"Ever since I was ten years old, I was just a very vain person. I always wanted to be the thinnest, the prettiest. 'Cause I thought, if I look like this, then I'm going to have so many boyfriends, and guys are going to be so in love with me, and I'll be taken care of for the rest of my life. I'll never have to work, you know?"—Delia, college senior

What's Wrong with This Picture?

Pretty, vivacious, and petite, Delia was a picture of fashionable perfection when she first walked into my office. Her tight blue jeans and fringed Western shirt showed off her thin, 5-ft frame; her black cowboy boots and silver earrings completed a presentation that said, "Look at me!"

The perfect picture had a serious price. Delia had come to talk about her "problem." She is bulimic. In secret, she regularly binges on large amounts of food, then forces herself to vomit. It has become a powerful habit, one that she is afraid to break because it so efficiently maintains her thin body. For Delia, as for so many others, being thin is everything.

"I mean, how many bumper stickers have you seen that say 'No Fat Chicks,' you know? Guys don't like fat girls. Guys like little girls. I guess because it makes them feel bigger and, you know, they want somebody who looks pretty. Pretty to me is you have to be thin and you have to have like good facial features. It's both. My final affirmation of myself is how many guys look at me when I go into a bar. How many guys pick up on me. What my boyfriend thinks about me."

Delia's Story

Delia is the eldest child, and only girl, in a wealthy Southern family. Her father is a successful dentist and her mother has never worked outside the home. They fought a lot when she was young—her father was an alcoholic—and they eventually divorced. According to Delia, both parents doted on her.

"I've never been deprived of anything in my entire life. I was spoiled, I guess, because I've never felt any pressure from my parents to do anything. My Dad would say, 'Whatever you want to do, if you want to go to Europe, if you want to go to law school, if you don't want to do anything . . . whatever you want to do, just be happy.' No pressure."

He was unconcerned about her weight, she said, but emphasized how important it was to be pretty. Delia quickly noticed this message everywhere, especially in the media.

"I am so affected by *Glamour* magazine and *Vogue* and all that, because that's a line of work I want to get into. I'm looking at all these beautiful women. They're thin. I want to be just as beautiful. I want to be just as thin. Because that is what guys like."

When I asked what her mother wanted for her, she recited, "To be nice and pretty and sweet and thin and popular and smart and successful and have everything that I could ever want and just to be happy." "Sweet and pretty and thin" meant that from the age of ten she was enrolled in a health club, and learned to count calories. Her mom, who at 45 is "beautiful, gorgeous, thin," gave her instructions on how to eat.

"'Only eat small amounts. Eat a thousand calories a day; don't overeat.' My mom was never critical like, 'You're fat.' But one time, I went on a camping trip and I gained four pounds and she said, 'You've got to lose weight.' I mean, she watched what I ate. Like if I was going to get a piece of cake she would be, 'Don't eat that.'"

At age 13 she started her secret bingeing and vomiting. "When I first threw up I thought, well, it's so easy," she told me. "I can eat and not get the calories and not gain weight. And I was modeling at the time, and I wanted to look like the girls in the magazines."

Delia's preoccupation with thinness intensified when she entered high school. She wanted to be a cheerleader, and she was tiny enough to make it. "When I was sixteen I just got into this image thing, like tiny, thin . . . I started working out more. I was Joe Healthy Thin Exercise Queen and I'd just fight eating because I was working out all the time, you know? And so I'm going to aerobics two or three times a day sometimes, eating only salad and a bagel, and like, no fat. I just got caught up in this circle."

College in New England brought a new set of social pressures. She couldn't go running every day because of the cold. She hated the school gym, stopped working out, and gained four pounds her freshman year. Her greatest stress at college had nothing to do with academics. "The most stressful thing for me is whether I'm going to eat that day, and what am I going to eat," she told me, "more than getting good grades."

After freshman year Delia became a cheerleader again. "Going in, I know I weighed like 93 or 94 pounds, which to me was this enormous hang-up, because I'd never weighed more than 90 pounds in my entire life. And I was really freaked out. I knew people were going to be looking at me in the crowd and I'm like, I've got to lose this weight. So I would just not eat, work out all the time. I loved being on the squad, but my partner was a real jerk. He would never work out, and when we would do lifts he'd always be, 'Delia, go run. Go run, you're too heavy.' I hadn't been eating that day. I had already run seven or eight miles and he told me to run again. And I was surrounded by girls who were all so concerned about their weight, and it was just really this horrible situation."

College life also confirmed another issue for Delia, a cultural message from her earliest childhood. She did *not* want to be a breadwinner. She put it this way, "When I was eight I wanted to be President of the United States. As I grew older and got to college I was like, wow, it's hard for women. I mean, I don't care what people say. If they say the society's liberated, they're wrong. It's still really hard for women. It's like they look through a glass window [*sic*]. They're vice presidents, but they aren't the president. And I just figured, God, how much easier would it be for me to get married to somebody I know is going to make a lot of money and just be taken care of . . . I want somebody else to be the millionaire." . . .

Economic and career achievement is a primary definition of success for men. (Of course, men can also exhibit some self-destructive behaviors in pursuit of this success, such as workaholism or substance abuse.) Delia's upbringing and environment defined success for her in a different way. She was not interested in having a job that earned $150,000 a year, but in marrying the guy who did. She learned to use any tool she could to stay thin, to look good, and to have a shot at her goal.

No wonder she was reluctant to give up her behavior. She was terrified of losing the important benefits of her membership in the Cult of Thinness. She knew she was hurting psychologically and physically, but, in the final analysis, being counted among "the chosen" justified the pain.

"God forbid anybody else gets stuck in this trap. But I'm already there, and I don't really see myself getting out, because I'm just so obsessed with how I look. I get personal satisfaction from looking thin, and receiving attention from guys."

I told Delia about women who have suggested other ways of coping with weight issues. There are even those who advocate fat liberation, or who suggest that fat is beautiful. She was emphatic about these solutions.

"Bullshit. They live in la-la land . . . I can hold onto my boyfriend because he doesn't need to look anywhere else. The bottom line is that appearance counts. And you can sit here and go, 'I feel good about myself twenty pounds heavier,' but who is the guy going to date?"

A Woman's Sense of Worth

Delia's devotion to the rituals of beauty work involved a great deal of time and energy. She weighed herself three times a day. She paid attention to what she put in her mouth; when she had too much, she knew she must get rid of it. She had to act and look a certain way, buy the right clothes, the right makeup. She also watched out for other women who might jeopardize her chances as they vied for the rewards of the system.

A woman's sense of worth in our culture is still greatly determined by her ability to attract a man. Social status is largely a function of income and occupation. Women's access to these resources is generally indirect, through marriage.[1] Even a woman with a successful and lucrative career may fear that her success comes at the expense of her femininity. . . .

Cultural messages on the rewards of thinness and the punishments of obesity are everywhere. Most women accept society's standards of beauty as "the way things are," even though these standards may undermine self-image, self-esteem, or physical well-being. Weight concerns or even obsessions are so common among women and girls that they escape notice. Dieting is not considered abnormal behavior, even among women who are not overweight. But only a thin line separates "normal" dieting from an eating disorder.[2] . . .

Profiting from Women's Bodies

Because women feel their bodies fail the beauty test, American industry benefits enormously, continually nurturing feminine insecurities. Ruling patriarchal interests, like corporate culture, the traditional family, the government, and the media also benefit. If women are so busy trying to control their bodies through dieting, excessive exercise, and self-improvement activities, they lose control over other important aspects of selfhood that might challenge the status quo.[3] In the words of one critic, "A secretary who bench-presses 150 pounds is still stuck in a dead-end job; a housewife who runs the marathon is still financially dependent on her husband."[4]

In creating women's concept of the ideal body image, the cultural mirror is more influential than the mirror reflecting peer group attitudes. Research has shown that women overestimate how thin a body their male and female peers desire. In a recent study using body silhouettes, college students of both sexes were asked to indicate an ideal female figure, the one that they believed most attractive to the same-sex peer and other-sex peer. Not only did the women select a thinner silhouette than the men,[5] but when asked to choose a *personal* ideal, rather than a peer ideal, the women selected an even skinnier model.

Advertisements and Beauty Advice: Buy, Try, Comply

Capitalism and patriarchy most often use the media to project the culturally desirable body to women. These images are everywhere—on TV, in the movies, on billboards, in print. Women's magazines, with their glossy pages of advertising, advertorials, and beauty advice, hold up an especially devious mirror. They offer "help" to women, while presenting a standard nearly impossible to attain. As one college student named Nancy noted in our interviews,

The advertisement showed me exactly what I should be, not what I was. I wasn't tall, I wasn't blonde, I wasn't skinny. I didn't have thin thighs, I didn't have a flat stomach. I am short, have brown curly hair, short legs. They did offer me solutions like dying my hair or a workout or the use of this cream to take away cellulite. . . .

Not everyone is taken in, of course. One student I interviewed dismissed the images she saw in the advertising pages of magazines as "constructed people."

I just stopped buying women's magazines. They are all telling you how to dress, how to look, what to wear, the type of clothes. And I think they are just ridiculous. . . . You can take the most gorgeous model and make her look terrible. Just like you can take a person who is not that way and make them look beautiful. You can use airbrushing and many other techniques. These are not really people. They are constructed people.

Computer-enhanced photography has advanced far beyond the techniques that merely airbrushed blemishes, added highlights to hair, and lengthened the legs with a camera angle. The September 1994 issue of *Mirabella* featured as a cover model "an extraordinary image of great American beauty." According to the magazine, the photographer "hints that she's something of a split personality . . . it wasn't easy getting her together. Maybe her identity has something to do with the microchip floating through space, next to that gorgeous face . . . true American beauty is a combination of elements from all over the world." In other words, the photo is a computerized composite. It is interesting that *Mirabella's* "melting pot" American beauty has white skin and predominantly Caucasian features, with just a hint of other ethnicities.

There are a number of industries that help to promote image, weight, and body obsession, especially among women. If we examine the American food and weight loss industries, we'll understand how their corporate practices and advertising campaigns perpetuate the American woman's dissatisfaction with her looks.

The American Food Industry: Fatten Up and Slim Down

. . . It is not uncommon for the average American to have a diet cola in one hand and high-fat fries and a burger in the other. Food and weight loss are inescapably a key part of the culture of the 1990's. The media bombard us with images of every imaginable type of food — snack foods, fast foods, gourmet foods, health foods, and junk foods. Most of these messages target children, who are very impressionable, and women, who make the purchasing decisions for themselves and their families. At the same time women are subjected to an onslaught of articles, books, videos, tapes, and TV talk shows devoted to dieting and the maintenance of sleek and supple figures. The conflicting images of pleasurable consumption and an ever leaner body type give us a food consciousness loaded with tension and ambivalence.

Social psychologist Brett Silverstein explains that the food industry, like all industries under capitalism, is always striving to maximize profit, growth, concentration, and control. It does so at the expense of the food consumer. "[It] promotes snacking so that consumers will have more than three opportunities a day to consume food, replaces free water with purchased soft drinks, presents desserts as the ultimate reward, and bombards women and children with artificially glamorized images of highly processed foods."[6]

Diet foods are an especially profitable segment of the business. . . .

In 1983, the food industry came up with a brilliant marketing concept, and introduced 91 new "lite" fat-reduced or calorie-reduced foods.[7] The success of lite products has been phenomenal. The consumer equated "lightness" with health. The food industry seemed to equate it with their own expenses—lite foods have lower production costs than "regular" lines, but they are often priced higher. . . .

The Diet and Weight-Loss Industry: We'll Show You the Way

. . . Increasingly, American women are told that they can have the right body if only they consume more and more products. They can change the color of their eyes with tinted contacts, they can have a tanned skin by using self-tanning lotion. They can buy cellulite control cream, spot firming cream, even contouring shower and bath firming gel to get rid of the "dimpled" look. One diet capsule on the market is supposed to be the "fat cure." It is called Anorex-eck, evoking the sometimes fatal eating disorder known as anorexia. It promises to "eliminate the cause of fat formation . . . so quickly and so effectively you will know from the very start why it has taken more than 15 years of research . . . to finally bring you . . . an ultimate cure for fat!"[8] . . .

There are currently more than 17,000 different diet plans, products, and programs from which to choose.[9] Typically, these plans are geared to the female market. They are loaded with promises of quick weight loss and delicious low-calorie meals. . . .

Many of these programs produce food products that they encourage the dieter to buy. The Jenny Craig member receives a set of pre-packaged meals that cost about $10 per day. (It allows for some outside food as well.) Some diet companies are concerned with the problem of gaining weight back and have developed "maintenance" products. Maintenance programs are often expensive and their long-term outcomes are unproven. What *can* be proven are bigger profits and longer dependence on their programs.

The Dis-eased Body: Medicalizing Women's Body Issues

The therapeutic and medical communities tend to categorize women's eating and weight problems as a disease.[10] In this view, behavior like self-starvation or compulsive eating is often called an addiction. An addiction model of behavior assumes that the cause and the cure of the problem lies within the individual. Such an emphasis fails to examine the larger mirrors that society holds up to the individual.[11]

. . . While a disease model lessens the burden of guilt and shame and may free people to work on change, it also has political significance. According to feminist theorist Bette S. Tallen, "The reality of oppression is replaced with the metaphor of addiction." It places the problem's cause within a biological realm, away from outside social forces.[12] Issues such as poverty, lack of education and opportunity, racial and gender inequality remain unexamined. More important, a disease-oriented model of addiction, involving treatment by the health care system, results in profits for the medical-industrial complex. Addiction, Tallen notes, suggests a solution that is personal—"Get treatment!"—rather than political—"Smash patriarchy!" It replaces the feminist view, that the personal is political, with the attitude of "therapism," that the "political is personal."[13] One of Bette Tallen's students told her that she had learned a lot from reading *Women Who Love Too Much* after her divorce from a man who had beaten her. Tallen suggested that "perhaps the best book to read would not be about women who love too much but about men who hit too much."[14]

The idea that overweight is a disease, and overeating represents an addiction, reinforces the dis-ease that American women feel about their bodies. The capitalist and patriarchal mirror held before them supports and maintains their obsession and insecurity. . . .

Women continue to follow the standards of the ideal thin body because of how they are rewarded by being in the right body. Thinness gives women access to a number of important resources: feelings of power, self-confidence, even femininity; male attention or protection; and the social and economic benefits that can follow. . . .

NOTES

1. Pauline B. Bart, "Emotional and Social Status of the Older Woman," in *No Longer Young: The Older Woman in America. Proceedings of the 26th Annual Conference on Aging*, ed. Pauline Bart et al. (Ann Arbor: University of Michigan Institute of Gerontology, 1975), pp. 3–21; Daniel Bar-Tal and Leonard Saxe, "Physical Attractiveness and Its Relationship to Sex-Role Stereotyping," *Sex Roles* 2 (1976): 123–133; Peter Blumstein and Pepper W. Schwartz, *American Couples: Money, Work and Sex* (New York: Willian Morrow, 1983); Glen H. Elder, "Appearance and Education in Marriage Mobility," *American Sociological Review* 34 (1969): 519–533; Susan Sontag, "The Double Standard of Aging," *Saturday Review* (September, 1972), pp. 29–38.

2. J. Polivy and C. P. Herman, "Dieting and Binging: A Causal Analysis," *American Psychologist* 40 (1985):193–201.

3. Ilana Attie and J. Brooks-Gunn, "Weight Concerns as Chronic Stressors in Women," in *Gender and Stress*, eds. Rosalind K. Barnett, Lois Biener, and Grace Baruch (New York: Free Press, 1987), pp. 218–252.

4. Katha Pollitt, "The Politically Correct Body," *Mother Jones* (May 1982): 67. I don't want to disparage the positive benefits of exercising and the positive self-image that can

come from feeling good about one's body. This positive image can spill over into other areas of one's life, enhancing, for example, one's self-esteem, or job prospects.

5. See Lawrence D. Cohn and Nancy E. Adler, "Female and Male Perceptions of Ideal Body Shapes: Distorted Views Among Caucasian College Students," *Psychology of Women Quarterly* 16 (1992): 69–79; A. Fallon and P. Rozin, "Sex Differences in Perceptions of Desirable Body Shape," *Journal of Abnormal Psychology* 94 (1985): 102–105.

6. Brett Silverstein, *Fed Up!* (Boston: South End Press, 1984), pp. 4, 47, 110. Individuals may be affected in many different ways, from paying too much (in 1978, concentration within the industry led to the overcharging of consumers by $12 to $14 billion [p. 47]) to the ingestion of unhealthy substances.

7. Warren J. Belasco, "'Lite' Economics: Less Food, More Profit," *Radical History Review* 28–30 (1984): 254–278; Hillel Schwartz, *Never Satisfied* (New York: Free Press, 1986), p. 241.

8. Advertised in *Parade* magazine (December 30, 1984).

9. Deralee Scanlon, *Diets That Work* (Chicago: Contemporary Books, 1991), p. 1.

10. See Stanton Peele, *Diseasing of America: Addiction Treatment Out of Control* (Lexington, MA: D.C. Heath and Co., 1989).

11. There are a few recovery books that point to the larger issues of the addiction model. Anne Wilson Schaef's book, *When Society Becomes an Addict,* looks at the wider institutions of society that perpetuate addiction. She notes that society operates on a scarcity model. This is the "Addictive System." This model assumes that there is never enough of anything to go around and we need to get what we can. Schaef sees society as made up of three systems: A White Male System (the Addictive System), A Reactive Female System (one where women respond passively to men by being subject to their will), and the Emerging Female System (a system where women lead with caring and sensitivity). Society needs to move in the direction of the Emerging Female System in order to end addiction. Another important book is Stanton Peele's *Love and Addiction.* Another book by Stanton Peele, *The Diseasing of America: How the Addiction Industry Captured Our Soul* (Lexington, MA: Lexington Books, 1989), stresses the importance of social change in societal institutions and advocates changing the given distribution of resources and power within the society as a way to overcome the problem of addiction. See Anne Wilson Schaef, *When Society Becomes an Addict* (New York: Harper & Row, 1987), and Stanton Peele, *Love and Addiction* (New York: New American Library, 1975).

12. Bette S. Tallen, "Twelve Step Programs: A Lesbian Feminist Critique," *NWSA Journal* 2 (1990): 396.

13. Tallen, "Twelve Step Programs: A Lesbian Feminist Critique," 404–405.

14. Tallen, "Twelve Step Programs: A Lesbian Feminist Critique," 405.

5

Sex and Race:
The Analogy of Social Control

William Chafe

. . . Analogies should not be limited to issues of substance alone, nor is their purpose to prove that two categories or objects are exactly identical. According to the dictionary, an analogy is "a relation of likeness . . . consisting in the resemblance not of the things themselves but of two or more attributes, circumstances or effects." Within this context, the purpose of an analogy is to illuminate a process or relationship which might be less discernible if only one or the other side of the comparison were viewed in isolation. What, then, if we look at sex and race as examples of how social control is exercised in America, with the primary emphasis on what the analogy tells us about the modes of control emanating from the dominant culture? . . . What if the nature of the analogy is not in the *substance* of the material existence which women and blacks have experienced but in the *forms* by which others have kept them in "their place" and prevented them from challenging the status quo?

The virtues of such an approach are many. First, it provides greater flexibility in exploring how the experience of one group can inform the study of another. Second, it has the potential of developing insights into the larger processes by which the status quo is perpetuated from generation to generation. In this sense, it can teach us about the operation of society as a whole and the way in which variables like sex and race have been made central to the division of responsibilities and power within the society. If the forms of social control used with blacks and women resemble each other in "two or more attributes, circumstances, or effects," then it may be possible to learn something both about the two groups and how the status quo has been maintained over time. The best way to pursue this, in turn, is through looking closely at the process of social control as it has operated on one group, and then comparing it with the process and experience of the second group.

In his brilliant autobiographical novel *Black Boy*, Richard Wright describes what it was like to grow up black in the Jim Crow South. Using his family, the church, his classmates, his jobs, and his fantasies as stage-pieces for his story,

Wright plays out the themes of hunger, fear, and determination which permeated his young life. Above all, he provides a searing account of how white Southerners successfully controlled the lives and aspirations of blacks. A series of concentric circles of social control operated in devastating fashion to limit young blacks to two life options—conformity to the white system, or exile.*

The outermost circle of control, of course, consisted of physical intimidation. When Richard asked his mother why black men did not fight white men, she responded, "The white men have guns and the black men don't." Physical force, and ultimately the threat of death, served as a constant reminder that whites held complete power over black lives. Richard saw that power manifested repeatedly. When his Uncle Hoskins dared to start his own saloon and act independently of the white power structure, he was lynched. The brother of one of Richard's schoolmates suffered a similar fate, allegedly for fooling with a white prostitute. When Richard worked for a clothing store, he frequently saw the white manager browbeat or physically attack black customers who had not paid their bills on time. When one woman came out of the store in a torn dress and bleeding, the manager said, "That's what we do to niggers when they don't pay their bills."[1]

The result was pervasive fear, anchored in the knowledge that whites could unleash vicious and irrational attacks without warning. Race consciousness could be traced, at least in part, to the tension which existed between anger at whites for attacking blacks without reason, and fear that wanton violence could strike again at any time, unannounced and unrestrained. "The things that influenced my conduct as a Negro," Richard wrote, "did not have to happen to me directly; I needed but to hear of them to feel their full effects in the deepest layers of my consciousness. Indeed the white brutality that I had not seen was a more effective control of my behavior than that which I knew . . . as long as it remained something terrible and yet remote, something whose horror and blood might descend upon me at any moment, I was compelled to give my entire imagination over to it, an act which blocked the springs of thought and feelings in me."[2]

The second circle of control rested in white domination of the economic status of black people. If a young black did not act the part of "happy nigger" convincingly, the employer would fire him. Repeatedly, Richard was threatened with the loss of work because he did not keep his anger and independence from being communicated to his white superiors. "Why don't you laugh and talk like the other niggers?" one employer asked. "Well, sir, there is nothing much to say or smile about," Richard said. "I don't like your looks nigger. Now git!" the boss ordered.

---

*Despite the problems created by using a novel for purposes of historical analysis, the interior perspective that is offered outweighs the limitation of "subjectiveness." Wright has been criticized for being overly harsh and elitist in his judgment of his black peers. His depiction of the conditions blacks had to cope with, on the other hand, corresponds well with the historical record. In the cases of both women and blacks, novels provide a vividness of detail and personal experience necessary to understand the larger processes at work in the society, but for the most part unavailable in conventional historical sources. (For amplification of Wright's experience with Jim Crow, see Selection 2 in Part I of this book.)

Only a limited number of economic roles were open to blacks, and if they were not played according to the rules, the job would be lost. A scarce supply of work, together with the demand that it be carried out in a deferential manner, provided a powerful guarantee that blacks would not get out of line.[3]

Significantly, the highest status jobs in the black community—teachers, ministers, civil servants—all depended ultimately upon acting in ways that pleased the white power structure.[*] One did not get the position at the post office or in the school system without being "safe"—the kind of person who would not make trouble. The fundamental precondition for success in the black community, therefore, was acting in ways that would not upset the status quo. When Richard tried to improve his own occupational chances and learn the optical trade, the white men who were supposed to teach him asked: "What are you trying to do, get smart, nigger?"[4]

The third circle of control consisted of the psychological power of whites to define and limit the reach of black aspirations. The sense people have of who they are and what they might become is tied intimately to the expectations communicated to them by others. The verbal cues, the discouragement or encouragement of authority figures, the picture of reality transmitted by friends or teachers—all of these help to shape how people think of themselves and their life chances. Stated in another way, human beings can envision careers as doctors and lawyers or a life of equality with others only to the extent that someone holds forth these ideals as viable possibilities.

Within this realm of social psychology, white Southerners exerted a pervasive and insidious control upon blacks. When Richard took his first job in a white household, he was given a bowl of molasses with mold on it for breakfast, even as his employers ate bacon and eggs. The woman he worked for asked what grade he was in, and when he replied the seventh, she asked, "Then why are you going to school?" When he further answered, "Well, I want to be a writer," she responded: "You'll never be a writer . . . who on earth put such ideas into your nigger head?" By her response, the woman attempted to undercut whatever sense of possibility Richard or other young blacks might have entertained for such a career. In effect, the woman had defined from a white perspective the outer boundaries of a black person's reality. As Richard noted, "She had assumed that she knew my place in life, what I felt, what I ought to be, and I resented it with all my heart . . . perhaps I would never be a writer; but I did not want her to say so." In his own time Richard Wright was able to defy the limits set upon his life by white people. But for the overwhelming majority of his fellow blacks, the ability of whites to intimidate them

---

[*]There is an important distinction, of course, between jobs which were tied to white support and those with an indigenous base in the black community. Black doctors, morticians, and barbers, for example, looked to the black community itself for their financial survival; hence they could be relatively free of white domination. On the other hand, the number of such independent positions was small. Although many people would include ministers in such a category, the visibility of the ministerial role created pressure from blacks concerned with the stability and safety of their churches for ministers to avoid a radical protest position. That started to change during the civil rights movement.

psychologically diminished the chance that they would be able to aspire realistically to a life other than that assigned them within a white racist social structure.[5]

The most devastating control of all, however, was that exercised by the black community itself out of self-defense. In the face of a world managed at every level by white power, it became an urgent necessity that black people train each other to adapt in order to survive. Thus the most profound and effective socialization toward accepting the racial status quo came from Richard's own family and peer group. It was Richard's mother who slapped him into silence "out of her own fear" when he asked why they had not fought back after Uncle Hoskins's lynching. To even ask the question posed a threat to safety. Similarly, it was Richard's Uncle Tom who insisted that Richard learn, almost by instinct, how to be accommodating. If Richard did not learn, the uncle said, he would never amount to anything and would end up on the gallows. Indeed, Richard would survive only if somebody broke his spirit and set the "proper" example.[6]

The instances of social control from within the black community abound in Wright's *Black Boy*. It was not only the white employer, but almost every black he knew, who opposed Richard's writing aspirations. "From no quarter," he recalled, "with the exception of the Negro newspaper editor, had there come a single encouraging word . . . I felt that I had committed a crime. Had I been aware of the full extent to which I was pushing against the current of my environment, I would have been frightened altogether out of my attempts at writing." The principal of his school urged vehemently that Richard give a graduation speech written by the principal rather than by Richard himself so that the proper tone of accommodation could be struck; the reward for going along was a possible teaching job. Griggs, Richard's best friend, was perhaps the most articulate in demanding that Richard control his instincts. "You're black and you don't act a damn bit like it." When Richard replied, "Oh Christ, I can't be a slave," Griggs responded with the ultimate lesson of reality: "But you've got to eat . . . when you are in front of white people, think before you act, think before you speak . . . you may think I'm an Uncle Tom, but I'm not. I hate these white people, hate them with all my heart. But I can't show it; if I did, they'd kill me." No matter where he went or whom he talked to in his own community, Richard found, not support for his protest, but the warning that he must behave externally in the manner white people expected. Whatever the hope of ultimate freedom, survival was the immediate necessity. One could not fight another day if one was not alive.[7]

Paradoxically, even the outlets for resistance within the system provided a means of reinforcing it. There were many ways of expressing unhappiness with one's lot, and all were essential to let off steam. The gang on the corner constantly verbalized resentment and anger against the white oppressor. Yet the very fact that the anger had to be limited to words and out of the earshot of whites meant that in practical terms it was ineffectual. Humor was another form of resistance. Richard and his friends joked that, if they ate enough black-eyed peas and buttermilk, they would defeat their white enemies in a race riot with "poison gas." But the end of the joke was an acknowledgment that the only way in reality to cope with the "mean" white folks was to leave.[8]

Indeed, the most practical form of resistance—petty theft—almost seemed a ploy by white people to perpetuate the system. Just as modern-day department store owners tolerate a certain degree of employee theft as a means of making the workers think they are getting away with something so they will not demand higher wages, so white employers of black people appear to have intentionally closed their eyes to a great deal of minor stealing. By giving blacks a small sense of triumph, white employers were able to tie them even more closely into the system, and prevent them from contemplating outright defiance. As Wright observed:[9]

> No Negroes in my environment had ever thought of organizing . . . and petitioning their white employers for higher wages. . . . They knew that the whites would have retaliated with swift brutality. So, pretending to conform to the laws of the whites, grinning, bowing, they let their fingers stick to what they could touch. And the whites seemed to like it.
>
> But I, who stole nothing, who wanted to look them straight in the face, who wanted to talk and act like a man, inspired fear in them. The southern whites would rather have had Negroes who stole work for them than Negroes who knew, however dimly, the worth of their own humanity. Hence, whites placed a premium upon black deceit; they encouraged irresponsibility, and their rewards were bestowed upon us blacks in the degree that we could make them feel safe and superior.

From a white point of view, a minor exercise of indirect and devious power by blacks was a small price to pay for maintaining control over the entire system. Thus, whites held the power to define black people's options, even to the point of controlling their modes of resistance.*

The result of all this was a system that functioned smoothly, with barely a trace of overt protest or dissension. Everyone seemed outwardly content with their place. At a very early age, Wright observed, "the white boys and the black boys began to play our traditional racial roles as though we had been born to them, as though it was in our blood, as though we were guided by instinct." For most people, the impact of a pervasive system of social control was total: resignation, a lowering of aspirations, a recognition of the bleakness of the future and the hopelessness of trying to achieve major change. In Wright's images life was like a train on a track; once headed in a given direction, there was little possibility of changing one's course.[10]

Wright himself, of course, was the exception. "Somewhere in the dead of the southern night," he observed, "my life had switched onto the wrong track, and without my knowing it, the locomotive of my heart was rushing down a dangerously

---

*It is important to remember that there existed a life in the black community less susceptible to white interference on a daily basis. Black churches, lodges, and family networks provided room for individual self-expression and supplied emotional reinforcement and sustenance. In this connection it is no accident that black institutions are strongest in the South where, until recently, the vast majority of blacks resided. On the other hand, the freedom which did exist came to a quick end wherever blacks attempted to enter activities, occupations, or areas of aspiration involving whites; or defined as white-controlled. Thus even the realm where freedom existed was partially a reflection of white control.

steep slope, heading for a collision, heedless of the warning red lights that blinked all about me, the sirens and the bells and the screams that filled the air." Wright had chosen the road of exile, of acute self-consciousness and alienation. For most blacks of his era, though, the warning red lights, the sirens, the bells, and the screams produced at least outward conformity to the status quo. In the face of forms of social control which effectively circumscribed one's entire life, there seemed no other choice.[11]

Obviously, women have not experienced overtly and directly the same kind of consistent physical intimidation that served so effectively to deter the black people of Richard Wright's childhood from resisting their condition. On the other hand, it seems clear that the physical strength and alleged dominance of men have been an important instrument of controlling women's freedom of action. The traditional image of the male as "protector" owes a great deal to the notion that women cannot defend themselves and that men must therefore take charge of their lives physically. The same notion of male strength has historically been responsible for restricting jobs involving heavy labor to men. Nor is the fear with which women view the potential of being struck or raped by a male lover, husband, or attacker an insignificant reality in determining the extent to which women historically have accepted the dominance of the men in their lives. Richard Wright observed that "the things that influenced my conduct . . . did not have to happen to me directly; I needed but to hear of them to feel their full effects. . . ." Similarly, women who have grown up with the image of powerful and potentially violent men need not have experienced a direct attack to share a sense of fear and intimidation. "Strength," the psychologist Jerome Kagan has observed, "is a metaphor for power." Thus, despite the substantive difference in the way women and blacks have been treated, the form of social control represented by physical strength has operated similarly for both groups.[12]

An even stronger case can be made for the way in which economic controls have succeeded in keeping blacks and women in their place. In 1898 Charlotte Perkins Gilman argued in *Women and Economics* that the root of women's subjection was their economic dependency on men. As long as women were denied the opportunity to earn their own living, she argued, there could never be equality between the sexes. The fact that women had to please their mates, both sexually and through other services, to ensure their survival made honest communication and mutual respect impossible. The prospect of a "present" from a generous husband, or a new car or clothes, frequently served to smooth over conflict, while the implicit threat of withholding such favors could be used to discourage carrying conflict too far.[13]

In fact, the issue of women not controlling their own money has long been one of the most painful and humiliating indexes of inequality between the sexes, especially in the middle class. Since money symbolizes power, having to ask others for it signifies subservience and an inferior status. Carol Kennicott, the heroine of Sinclair Lewis's *Main Street*, recognized the problem. After begging prettily for her household expenses early in her marriage, she started to demand her own separate funds. "What was a magnificent spectacle of generosity to you," she told her husband, "was a humiliation to me. You *gave* me money—gave it to your mistress if she was complaisant." Beth Phail, a character in Marge Piercy's novel *Small Changes*, experienced the same conflict with her husband, who was immediately threatened by the idea of her economic autonomy. Indeed, few examples of psychological control seem more pointed than those represented in husbands' treating their wives as not mature enough to handle their own money.[14]

Even the women who held jobs reflected the pattern by which economic power was used to control women's freedom of action. Almost all women workers were concentrated in a few occupations delineated as "woman's" work. As secretaries, waitresses, cooks, and domestic workers, women on the job conformed to the "service" image of their sex. Significantly, the highest status jobs available— nurses and teachers—tended to reinforce a traditional image of women and the status quo between the sexes, just as the highest jobs available within the black community—teachers and civil servants—reinforced a pattern of accommodation with the existing white power structure. Any woman who chose a "man's job" automatically risked a loss of approval, if not total hostility. For most, the option simply did not exist.

Even those in the most prestigious positions illustrated how money could be used as an instrument of social control. If they were to succeed in raising funds, college administrators in black and women's schools frequently found that they had to shape their programs in conformity to social values that buttressed the status quo. Booker T. Washington represented the most outstanding example of this phenomenon. Repeatedly he was forced to appease white racist presumptions in order to get another donation for Tuskegee. As the funnel through which all white philanthropic aid to blacks was channeled, Washington had to ensure that no money would be spent in a way which might challenge the political values of his contributors, even though privately he fought those political values. But Washington was not alone. During the 1830's Mary Lyons, head of Mt. Holyoke Seminary, agreed not to attend trustee meetings lest she offend male sensibilities, and Mary Alice Baldwin, the very effective leader of the Women's College of Duke University, felt it necessary to pay homage to the conservative tradition of "the Southern lady" as the price for sustaining support of women's education at Duke.[15]

In all of these instances, economic controls functioned in parallel ways to limit the freedom of women and blacks. If a group is assigned a "place," there are few more effective ways of keeping it there than economic dependency. Not only must the group in question conform to the expectations of the dominant class in order to get money to live; those who would do otherwise are discouraged by the fact that no economic incentives exist to reward those who challenge the status quo. The absence of financial support for those who dare to deviate from prescribed norms has served well to perpetuate the status quo in the condition of both women and blacks. "I don't want to be a slave," Richard Wright observed. "But you have to eat," Griggs replied.

The strongest parallel, however, consists of the way in which blacks and women have been given the psychological message that they should be happy with their "place." In both instances, this form of control has effectively limited aspiration to non-conventional roles. Although Beth Phail of *Small Changes* wanted to go to college and law school, her family insisted that her highest aspiration should be marriage and homemaking. A woman should not expect a career. Similarly, when Carol Kennicott told her college boyfriend, "I want to do something with my life," he responded eagerly: "What's better than making a comfy home and bringing up some cute kids . . . ?" The small town atmosphere of Gopher Prairie simply reinforced the pressure to conform. Carol was expected to be a charming hostess, a dutiful wife, and a good homemaker, but not a career woman. Thus, as Sinclair Lewis observed, she was a "woman with a working brain and no work." The messages Carol received from her surroundings were not designed to give her high self-esteem. Her husband called her "an extravagant little rabbit," and his poker partners, she noted, simply expected her "to wait on them like a servant."[16]

Although Carol's personality was atypical, her social experience was not. When high school girls entertained the possibility of a career, they were encouraged to be nurses, not doctors. The qualities that received the most praise were those traditionally associated with being a "lady," not an assertive individual ready to face the world. Significantly, both women and blacks were the victims of two devices designed to discourage non-conformity. Those who sought to protest their status, for example, were subjected to ridicule and caricature. The black protestor was almost certain to be identified with subversive activity, just as the women's rights advocate was viewed as unsexed and a saboteur of the family. (Ordinary blacks and females were subject to a gentler form of humor, no less insidious, as in the characters of Amos 'n Andy's "King Fish" or Lucille Ball's "Lucy.") In addition, it was not uncommon for blacks to be set against blacks and women against women in a competition which served primarily the interests of the dominant group. According to Judith Bardwick and Elizabeth Donavan, girls are socialized to use oblique forms of aggression largely directed at other females, while men's aggression is overt. The stereotype of women doing devious battle over an attractive man is an ingrained part of our folk tradition. Nor is the "divide and conquer" strategy a stranger to the history of black people, as when white workers sowed seeds of suspicion between Richard Wright and another black worker in order to make them fight each other for the entertainment of whites.[17]

In both cases the psychological form of social control has operated in a similar fashion. The aspirations, horizons, and self-images of blacks and women have been defined by others in a limiting and constrictive way. More often than not, the result historically has been an acceptance of society's perception of one's role. The prospect of becoming an architect, an engineer, or a carpenter is not easy to sustain in an environment where the very idea is dismissed as foolish or unnatural. Instead of encouragement to aspire to new horizons of achievement, the message transmitted to blacks and women has been the importance of finding satisfaction with the status quo.

But in the case of women, as with blacks, the most effective instrument of continued control has been internal pressure from the group itself. From generation to generation, mothers teach daughters to please men, providing the instruction that prepares the new generation to assume the roles of mothers and housewives. Just as blacks teach each other how to cope with "whitey" and survive within the system, women school each other in how to win a man, how to appear charming, where to "play a role" in order to avoid alienating a potential husband. When Beth in *Small Changes* rebelled against her husband and fought the idea of tying herself down with a child, it was the other women in her family who urged her to submit and at least give the *appearance* of accepting the role expected of her.[18]

In fact, dissembling in order to conform to social preconceptions has been a frequent theme of women's socialization. As Mirra Komarovsky has demonstrated, college women in the 1940's were taught to hide their real ability in order to make their male friends feel superior. "My mother thinks that it is very nice to be smart in college," one of Komarovsky's students noted, "but only if it doesn't take too much effort. She always tells me not to be too intellectual on dates, to be clever in a light sort of way." It is not difficult to imagine one woman saying to another as Griggs said to Richard Wright, "When you are around white people [men] you have to act the part that they expect you to act." Even if deception was the goal, however, the underlying fact was that members of the "oppressed" group acted as accomplices in perpetuating the status quo.[19]

The most effective device for maintaining internal group discipline was to ostracize those who did not conform. Richard Wright found himself singled out for negative treatment because he refused to accept authority and to smile and shuffle before either his teachers or white people. Beth Phail was roundly condemned by her sisters and mother for not pleasing her husband, and above all for not agreeing to have a child. And Carol Kennicott received hostile glances when she violated her "place" by talking politics with men or seeking to assume a position of independent leadership in the community of Gopher Prairie. The disapproval of her female peers was the most effective weapon used to keep her in line, and, when it appeared that she finally was going to have a child, her women friends applauded the fact that in becoming a mother she would finally get over all her strange ideas and settle down. As Sinclair Lewis observed, "She felt that willy-nilly she was being initiated into the assembly of housekeepers; with the baby for hostage, she would never escape."[20]

The pressure of one's own group represented a double burden. In an environment where success was defined as marriage, and fulfillment as being a happy homemaker, it was hard enough to fight the tide in the first place. If one did, however, there was the additional problem of being seen as a threat to all the other members of the group who had conformed. The resistance of blacks toward Richard Wright and of women toward Carol Kennicott becomes more understandable in light of the fact that in both cases the individual protestors, through their refusal to play the game according to the rules, were also passing judgment on those who accepted the status quo. Thus, historically, women and blacks have kept each other in line not only as a means of group self-defense—protecting the new generation from harm and humiliation—but also as a means of maintaining self-respect by defending the course they themselves have chosen.

Indeed, for women as well as for blacks, even the vehicles for expressing resentment became reinforcements of the status quo. For both groups, the church provided a central emotional outlet—a place where solidarity with one's own kind could be found, and where some protest was possible. Women's church groups provided not only a means of seeking reform in the larger society but also for talking in confidence to other women about the frustrations of being a woman in a male-dominated society. What social humorists have called "hen-sessions" were in fact group therapy encounters where women had a chance to voice their gripes. Humor was frequently a vehicle for expressing a bittersweet response to one's situation, bemoaning, even as one laughed, the pain of being powerless. But as in the case with blacks, venting one's emotions about a life situation—although necessary for survival—was most often an instrument for coping with the situation, rather than for changing it.

Perhaps the most subversive and destructive consequence of a pervasive system of social control is how it permeates every action, so that even those who are seeking to take advantage of the "enemy" end up supporting the system. When Shorty, the elevator man in *Black Boy* known for his wit and hostility to whites, needed some money for lunch one day, he told a white man he would not move the elevator until he got a quarter. "I'm hungry, Mr. White Man. I'm dying for a quarter," Shorty said. The white man responded by asking what Shorty would do for a quarter. "You can kick me for a quarter," Shorty said, bending over. At the end of the elevator ride, Shorty had his quarter. "This monkey's got the peanuts," he said. Shorty was right. He had successfully used racial stereotypes and his own role as a buffoon to get himself some lunch money. But in the process, the entire system of racial imbalance had been strengthened.[21]

Similar patterns run through the history of women's relationships to men. The coquette role is only the most extreme example of a type of manipulative behavior by women that seems to confirm invidious stereotypes. In the classic case of a wife trying to persuade her husband to go along with a desired course of action, the woman may play up to a man's vanity and reinforce his stereotyped notions about being a tower of strength and in control. Similarly, a female employee wishing advancement may adopt a flirtatious attitude toward a male superior. By playing a semi-seductive role and implying a form of sexual payoff for services rendered, she may achieve her immediate goal. But in each of these cases, the price is to become more entrapped in a set of distorted and unequal sex role stereotypes. The fact that overt power is not available and that the ability to express oneself honestly and openly has been denied leads to the use of covert and manipulative power. Thus, a woman may play dumb or a black may act deferential—conforming in each case to a stereotype—as a means of getting his or her way. But the result is pathological power that simply perpetuates the disease. The irony is that, even in trying to outwit the system of social control, the system prevails.

Basic to the entire system, of course, has been the extent to which a clearly defined role was "woven into the texture of things." For blacks the crucial moment might come as soon as they developed an awareness of whites. In the case of women, it more likely took place at puberty when the need to begin pleasing potential husbands was emphasized. In either case, what Richard Wright said about the process of socialization could be said of both groups. "I marveled," he wrote:[22]

> at how smoothly the black boys [women] acted out the role . . . mapped out for them. Most of them were not conscious of living a special, separate, stunted way of life. Yet I knew that in some period of their growing up—a period that they had no doubt forgotten—there had been developed in them a delicate, sensitive controlling mechanism that shut off their minds and emotions from all that the white race [society] had said was taboo. Although they lived in America where in theory there existed equality of opportunity, they knew unerringly what to aspire to and what not to aspire to.

The corollary for both women and blacks, at least metaphorically, has been that those unable or unwilling to accept the role prescribed for them have been forced into a form of physical or spiritual exile. Richard Wright understood that continued accommodation with the white Southern system of racial oppression would mean the destruction of his integrity and individuality. "Ought one to surrender to authority even if one believed that the authority was wrong?" Wright asked. "If the answer was yes, then I knew that I would always be wrong, because I could never do it. . . . How could one live in a world in which one's mind and perceptions meant nothing and authority and tradition meant everything?" The only alternative to psychological death was exile, and Wright pursued that course, initially in Chicago, later in Paris. In her own way Carol Kennicott attempted the same journey. "I've got to find out what my work is," she told her husband. "I've been ruled too long by fear of being called things. I'm going away to be quiet and think. I'm—I'm going. I have a right to my own life." And Beth Phail finally fled her home and family because it was the only way to grow up, to find out what "she wanted," to learn how to be a person in her own right in the world.[23]

Although in reality only a few blacks and women took the exact course adopted by Richard Wright, Carol Kennicott, and Beth Phail, all those who chose to resist the status quo shared to some extent in the metaphor of exile. Whether the person was a feminist like Charlotte Perkins Gilman, a pioneer career woman such as Elizabeth Blackwell, a runaway slave like Frederick Douglass, or a bold race leader like W. E. B. Du Bois, the act of challenging prevailing norms meant living on the edge of alienation and apart from the security of those who accepted the status quo. Until and unless protest generated its own community of support which could provide a substitute form of security and reinforcement, the act of deviance promised to be painful and solitary.

This condition, in turn, reflected an experience of marginality which many blacks and women shared. In sociological terms, the "marginal" personality is someone who moves in and out of different groups and is faced with the difficulty of adjusting behavior to the norms of the different groups. By definition, most blacks and most women have participated in that experience, especially as they have been required to accommodate the expectations of the dominant group of white males. The very fact of having to adopt different modes of behavior for different audiences introduces an element of complexity and potential conflict to the lives of those who are most caught up in a marginal existence. House slaves, for example, faced the inordinately difficult dilemma of being part of an oppressed group of slaves even as they lived in intimacy with and under the constant surveillance of the white master-class, thereby experiencing in its most extreme form the conflict of living in two worlds.[24]

Ordinarily, the tension implicit in such a situation is deflected, or as Richard Wright observed, "contained and controlled by reflex." Most house slaves seemed to learn how to live with the conflict by repressing their anger and uneasiness. Coping with the situation became a matter of instinct. But it is not surprising that many slave revolts were led by those house slaves who could not resolve the conflict by reflex, and instead were driven to alienation and protest. For the minority of people who misinterpreted the cues given them or learned too late how to cope, consciousness of the conflict made instinctive conformity impossible. As Richard Wright observed, "I could not make subservience an automatic part of my behavior. . . . while standing before a white man . . . I had to figure out how to say each word . . . I could not grin . . . I could not react as the world in which I lived expected me to." The pain of self-consciousness made the burden almost unbearable. As Maya Angelou has written, awareness of displacement "is the rust on the razor that threatens the throat." In an endless string of injuries, it was the final insult.[25]

Dissenting blacks and women have shared this experience of being "the outsider." Unable to accept the stereotyped behavior prescribed for their group, they have, in Vivian Gornick's words, "stood beyond the embrace of their fellows." With acute vision, Gornick writes, the outsider is able to "see deeply into the circle, penetrating to its very center, his vision a needle piercing the heart of life. Invariably, what he sees is intolerable." On the basis of such a vision, exile is the only alternative available. Yet, ironically, it too serves to reinforce the status quo by removing from the situation those most likely to fight it. Until the members willing to resist become great enough, the system of social control remains unaltered.[26]

It seems fair to conclude, therefore, that a significant resemblance has existed in the forms of social control used to keep women and blacks in their "place." Despite profound substantive differences between women and blacks, and white women and black women, all have been victims of a process, the end product of which has been to take away the power to define one's own aspirations, destiny, and sense of self. In each case a relationship of subservience to the dominant group has been perpetuated by physical, economic, psychological, and internal controls that have functioned in a remarkably similar way to discourage deviancy and place a premium on conformity. "It was brutal to be Negro and have no control over my life," Maya Angelou observes in her autobiography. "It was brutal to be young and already trained to sit quietly." From a feminist perspective, the same words describe the process of control experienced by most women.[27]

The core of this process has been the use of a visible, physical characteristic as the basis for assigning to each group a network of duties, responsibilities, and attributes. It is the physical foundation for discriminatory treatment which makes the process of social control on sex and race distinctive from that which has applied to other oppressed groups. Class, for example, comes closest to sex and race as a source of massive social inequity and injustice. Yet in an American context, class has been difficult to isolate as an organizing principle. Because class is not associated with a visible physical characteristic and many working class people persist in identifying with a middle-class life-style, class is not a category easy to identify in terms of physical or psychological control. (The very tendency to abjure class consciousness in favor of a social mobility ethic, of course, is its own form of psychological control.) Ethnicity too has frequently served as a basis for oppression, but the ease with which members of most ethnic minorities have been able to "pass" into the dominant culture has made the structure of social control in those cases both porous and complicated. Thus although in almost every instance invidious treatment has involved the use of some form of physical, economic, psychological, or internal controls, the combinations have been different and the exceptions frequent.

The analogy of sex and race is distinctive, therefore, precisely to the extent that it highlights in pure form the process of social control which has operated to maintain the existing structure of American society. While many have been victimized by the same types of control, only in the case of sex and race—where physical attributes are ineradicable—have these controls functioned systematically and clearly to define from birth the possibilities to which members of a group might aspire. Perhaps for that reason sex and race have been cornerstones of the social system, and the source of values and attitudes which have both reinforced the power of the dominant class and provided a weapon for dividing potential opposition.

Finally, the analogy provides a potential insight into the strategies and possibilities of social change. If women and blacks have been kept in their "place" by similar forms of social control, the prerequisites for liberation may consist of overcoming those forms of social control through a similar process. In the case of both women and blacks, the fundamental problem has been that others have controlled the power to define one's existence. Thus, to whatever extent women and blacks act or think in a given way solely because of the expectation of the dominant group rather than from their own choice, they remain captive to the prevailing system of social control. The prototypical American woman, writes Vivian Gornick, is perceived as "never taking, always being taken, never absorbed by her own desire, preoccupied only with whether or not she is desired." Within such a context, the "other" is always more important than the "self" in determining one's sense of individual identity. It is for this reason that efforts by blacks and women toward group solidarity, control over one's own institutions, and development of an autonomous and positive self-image may be crucial in breaking the bonds of external dominance.[28]

Yet such a change itself depends on development of a collective consciousness of oppression and a collective commitment to protest. As long as social and political conditions, or the reluctance of group members to participate, preclude the emergence of group action, the individual rebel has little chance of effecting change. Thus the issue of social control leads inevitably to the question of how the existing cycle is broken. What are the preconditions for the evolution of group protest? How do external influences stimulate, or forestall, the will to resist? And through what modes of organization and action does the struggle for autonomy proceed? For these questions too, the analogy of sex and race may provide a useful frame of reference.

Whatever the case, it seems more productive to focus on forms of control or processes of change than to dwell on the substantive question of whether blacks and women have suffered comparable physical and material injury. Clearly, they have not. On the other hand when two groups exist in a situation of inequality, it may be self-defeating to become embroiled in a quarrel over which is more unequal or the victim of greater oppression. The more salient question is how a condition of inequality for both is maintained and perpetuated—through what modes is it reinforced? By that criterion, continued exploration of the analogy of sex and race promises to bring added insight to the study of how American society operates.

NOTES

1. Richard Wright, *Black Boy* (New York, 1937), pp. 48, 52, 150, 157. Quotations used by permission of the publishers Harper and Row, New York.

2. Wright, pp. 65, 150–51.

3. Wright, p. 159.

4. Wright, p. 164.

5. Wright, pp. 127–29.

6. Wright, pp. 139–40.

7. Wright, pp. 147, 153–55, 160–61.

8. Wright, pp. 68–71, 200.

9. Wright, p. 175.

10. Wright, p. 72.

11. Wright, p. 148.

12. Wright, pp. 150–51; Susan Brownmiller, *Against Our Will* (New York, 1975); Jerome Kagan and H. A. Moss, *Birth to Maturity* (New York, 1962).

13. Carl Degler, "Introduction," *The History of Women* (Oxford, 1975).

14. Sinclair Lewis, *Main Street* (New York, 1920), pp. 74, 167; Marge Piercy, *Small Changes* (Greenwich, Conn., 1972), p. 33.

15. Louis P. Harlan, *Booker T. Washington 1856–1901* (New York, 1972); Ralph Ellison, *Invisible Man* (New York, 1952); Eleanor Flexner, *Century of Struggle* (Cambridge, Mass., 1959), p. 33; and Dara DeHaven, "On Educating Women—The Co-ordinate Ideal at Trinity and Duke University," Master's thesis, Duke University, 1974.

16. Piercy, *Small Changes*, pp. 19–20, 29, 40–41; Lewis, *Main Street*, pp. 14–15, 86, 283.

17. Judith Bardwick and Elizabeth Donovan, "Ambivalence: The Socialization of Women" in *Women in Sexist Society: Studies in Power and Powerlessness*, eds. Barbara Moran and Vivian Gornick (New York, 1971); Wright, *Black Boy*, pp. 207–13.

18. Piercy, *Small Changes*, pp. 31, 34, 316–17.

19. Piercy, pp. 30–31, 34, 39; Mirra Komarovsky, "Cultural Contradictions and Sex Roles," *American Journal of Sociology* 52 (November 1946).

20. Lewis, *Main Street*, p. 234.

21. Wright, *Black Boy*, p. 199.

22. Wright, p. 172.

23. Wright, p. 144; Lewis, *Main Street*, pp. 404–5; Piercy, *Small Changes*, p. 41.

24. See Everett Hughes, "Social Change and Status Protest: An Essay on the Marginal Man," *Phylon* 10 (December 1949); and Robert K. Merton, *Social Theory and Social Structure* (New York, 1965), pp. 225–50.

25. Wright, *Black Boy*, p. 130; Maya Angelou, *I Know Why the Caged Bird Sings* (New York, 1970), p. 3.

26. Vivian Gornick, "Woman as Outsider," in Moran and Gornick, pp. 126–44.

27. Angelou, p. 153.

28. Gornick, p. 140.

6

Pulling Train

Peggy R. Sanday

This article discusses certain group rituals of male bonding on a college campus, in particular, a phenomenon called "pulling train." According to a report issued by the Association of American Colleges in 1985, "pulling train," or "gang banging" as it is also called, refers to a group of men lining up like train cars to take turns having sex with the same woman (Ehrhart and Sandler 1985, 2). This report labels "pulling train" as gang rape. Bernice Sandler, one of its authors, recently reported that she had found more than seventy-five documented cases of gang rape on college campuses in recent years (*Atlanta Constitution*, 7 June 1988). Sandler labeled these incidents gang rape because of the coercive nature of the sexual behavior. The incidents she and Julie K. Ehrhart described in their 1985 report display a common pattern. A vulnerable young woman, one who is seeking acceptance or who is high on drugs or alcohol, is taken to a room. She may or may not agree to have sex with one man. She then passes out, or is too weak or scared to protest, and

From Peggy R. Sanday, *Fraternity Gang Rape: Sex, Brotherhood, and Privilege on Campus*. Copyright © 1990. Reprinted by permission of New York University Press.

a train of men have sex with her. Sometimes the young woman's drinks are spiked without her knowledge, and when she is approached by several men in a locked room, she reacts with confusion and panic. Whether too weak to protest, frightened, or unconscious, as has been the case in quite a number of instances, anywhere from two to eleven or more men have sex with her. In some party invitations the possibility of such an occurrence is mentioned with playful allusions to "gang bang" or "pulling train" (Ehrhart and Sandler 1985, 1–2).

The reported incidents occurred at all kinds of institutions: "public, private, religiously affiliated, Ivy League, large and small" (ibid.). Most of the incidents occurred at fraternity parties, but some occurred in residence halls or in connection with college athletics. Incidents have also been reported in high schools. . . .

Just a few examples taken from the Ehrhart and Sandler report (1985, 1–2) are sufficient to demonstrate the coercive nature of the sexual behavior.

> The 17-year-old freshman woman went to the fraternity "little sister" rush party with two of her roommates. The roommates left early without her. She was trying to get a ride home when a fraternity brother told her he would take her home after the party ended. While she waited, two other fraternity members took her into a bedroom to "discuss little sister matters." The door was closed and one of the brothers stood blocking the exit. They told her that in order to become a little sister (honorary member) she would have to have sex with a fraternity member. She was frightened, fearing they would physically harm her if she refused. She could see no escape. Each of the brothers had sex with her, as did a third who had been hiding in the room. During the next two hours a succession of men went into the room. There were never less than three men with her, sometimes more. After they let her go, a fraternity brother drove her home. He told her not to feel bad about the incident because another woman had also been "upstairs" earlier that night. (Large southern university)

> It was her first fraternity party. The beer flowed freely and she had much more to drink than she had planned. It was hot and crowded and the party spread out all over the house, so that when three men asked her to go upstairs, she went with them. They took her into a bedroom, locked the door and began to undress her. Groggy with alcohol, her feeble protests were ignored as the three men raped her. When they finished, they put her in the hallway, naked, locking her clothes in the bedroom. (Small eastern liberal arts college)

> A 19-year-old woman student was out on a date with her boyfriend and another couple. They were all drinking beer and after going back to the boyfriend's dorm room, they smoked two marijuana cigarettes. The other couple left and the woman and her boyfriend had sex. The woman fell asleep and the next thing she knew she awoke with a man she didn't know on top of her trying to force her into having sex. A witness said the man was in the hall with two other men when the woman's boyfriend came out of his room and invited them to have sex with his unconscious girlfriend. (Small midwestern college)

Although Ehrhart and Sandler boldly labeled the incidents they described as rape, few of the perpetrators were prosecuted. Generally speaking, the male participants are protected and the victim is blamed for having placed herself in a compromising social situation where male adolescent hormones are known, as the saying goes, "to get out of hand." For a number of reasons, people say, "She asked for it." As the above examples from the Ehrhart and Sandler report suggest, the victim may be a vulnerable young woman who is seeking acceptance or who is weakened by the ingestion of drugs or alcohol. She may or may not agree to having sex with one man. If she has agreed to some sexual activity, the men assume that she has agreed to all sexual activity regardless of whether she is conscious or not. In the minds of the boys involved the sexual behavior is not rape. On many campuses this opinion is shared by a significant portion of the campus community. . . .

The XYZ Express

I first learned about "pulling train" in 1983 from a student who was then enrolled in one of my classes. Laurel had been out of class for about two weeks. I noticed her absence and worried that she was getting behind on her work. When she came back to class she told me that she had been raped by five or six male students at a fraternity house after one of the fraternity's weekly Thursday night parties. Later, I learned from others that Laurel was drunk on beer and had taken four hits of LSD before going to the party. According to the story Laurel told to a campus administrator, after the party she fell asleep in a first-floor room and when she awoke was undressed. One of the brothers dressed her and carried her upstairs, where she was raped by "guys" she did not know but said she could identify if photographs were available. She asked a few times for the men to get off her, but to no avail. According to her account, she was barely conscious and lacked the strength to push them off her.

There is no dispute that Laurel had a serious drinking and drug problem at the time of the party. People at the party told me that during the course of the evening she acted like someone who was "high," and her behavior attracted quite a bit of attention. They described her as dancing provocatively to the beat of music only she could hear. She appeared disoriented and out of touch with what was happening. Various fraternity brothers occasionally danced with her, but she seemed oblivious to the person she was dancing with. Some of the brothers teased her by spinning her around in a room until she was so dizzy she couldn't find her way out. At one point during the evening she fell down a flight of stairs. Later she was pulled by the brothers out of a circle dance, a customary fraternity ritual in which only brothers usually took part.

After the other partyers had gone home, the accounts of what happened next vary according to who tells the story. The differences of opinion do not betray a Rashomon effect as much as they reflect different definitions of a common sexual event. No one disputes that Laurel had sex with at least five or six male students, maybe more. When Anna, a friend of the XYZ brothers, saw Laurel the next day and heard the story from the brothers, her immediate conclusion was that they had raped Laurel. Anna based her conclusion on seeing Laurel's behavior at the party and observing her the following day. It seemed to Anna that Laurel was incapable of consenting to sex, which is key for determining a charge of rape. Anna's opinion was later confirmed by the Assistant District Attorney for Sex Crimes, who investigated but did not prosecute the case.

The brothers claimed that Laurel had lured them into a "gang bang" or "train," which they preferred to call an "express." Their statements and actions during the days after the event seemed to indicate that they considered the event a routine part of their "little sisters program," something to be proud of. Reporting the party activities on a sheet posed on their bulletin board in the spot where the house minutes are usually posted, Anna found the following statement, which she later showed me:

> Things are looking up for the [XYZ] sisters program. A prospective leader for the group spent some time interviewing several [brothers] this past thursday and friday. Possible names for the little sisters include [XYZ] "little wenches" and "The [XYZ] express."

. . . The ideology that promotes "pulling train" is seen in the discourse and practices associated with some parties on campus. Party invitations expressing this ideology depict a woman lying on a pool table, or in some other position suggestive of sexual submission. The hosts of the party promote behavior aimed at seduction. *Seduction* means plying women with alcohol or giving them drugs in order to "break down resistance." A drunken woman is not defined as being in need of protection and help, but as "asking for it." If the situation escalates into sexual activity, the brothers watch each other perform sexual acts and then brag about "getting laid." The event is referred to as "drunken stupidity, women chasing, and all around silliness." The drama enacted parodies the image of the gentleman. Its male participants brag about their masculinity and its female participants are degraded to the status of what the boys call "red meat" or "fish." The whole scenario joins men in a no-holds-barred orgy of togetherness. The woman whose body facilitates all of this is sloughed off at the end like a used condom. She may be called a "nympho" or the men may believe that they seduced her—a practice known as "working a yes out"—through promises of becoming a little sister, by getting her drunk, by promising her love, or by some other means. Those men who object to this kind of behavior run the risk of being labeled "wimps" or, even worse in their eyes, "gays" or "faggots."

The rationalization for this behavior illustrates a broader social ideology of male dominance. Both the brothers and many members of the broader community excuse the behavior by saying that "boys will be boys" and that if a woman gets into trouble it is because "she asked for it," "she wanted it," or "she deserved it." The ideology inscribed in this discourse represents male sexuality as more natural and more explosive than female sexuality. This active, "naturally" explosive nature of male sexuality is expected to find an outlet either in the company of male friends or in the arms of prostitutes. In these contexts men are supposed to use women to satisfy explosive urges. The women who satisfy these urges are included as passive actors in the enactment of a sexual discourse where the male, but not the female, sexual instinct is characterized as an insatiable biological instinct and psychological need.

Men entice one another into the act of "pulling train" by implying that those who do not participate are unmanly or homosexual. This behavior is full of contradictions because the homoeroticism of "pulling train" seems obvious. A group of men watch each other having sex with a woman who may be unconscious. One might well ask why the woman is even necessary for the sexual acts these men stage for one another. As fraternity practices described in this book suggest, the answer seems to lie in homophobia. One can suggest that in the act of "pulling train" the polymorphous sexuality of homophobic men is given a strictly heterosexual form.

Polymorphous sexuality, a term used by Freud to refer to diffuse sexual interests with multiple objects, means that men will experience desire for one another. However, homophobia creates a tension between polymorphous sexual desire and compulsory heterosexuality. This tension is resolved by "pulling train": the brothers vent their interest in one another through the body of a woman. In the sociodrama that is enacted, the idea that heterosexual males are superior to women and to homosexuals is publicly expressed and probably subjectively absorbed. Thus, both homophobia and compulsory heterosexuality can be understood as strategies of knowledge and power centering on sex that support the social stratification of men according to sexual preference.

In group sex, homoerotic desire is simultaneously indulged, degraded, and extruded from the group. The fact that the woman involved is often unconscious highlights her status as a surrogate victim in a drama where the main agents are males interacting with one another. The victim embodies the sexual urges of the brothers; she is defined as "wanting it"—even though she may be unconscious during the event—so that the men can satisfy their urges for one another at her expense. By defining the victim as "wanting it," the men convince themselves of their heterosexual prowess and delude themselves as to the real object of their lust. If they were to admit to the real object, they would give up their position in the male status hierarchy as superior, heterosexual males. The expulsion and degradation of the victim both brings a momentary end to urges that would divide the men and presents a social statement of phallic heterosexual dominance.

By blaming the victim for provoking their own sexual aggression, men control and define acceptable and unacceptable female sexual behavior through the agency of fear. The fear is that a woman who does not guard her behavior runs the risk of becoming the target of uncontrollable male sexual aggression. Thus, although women are ostensibly the controlling agent, it is fear of the imagined explosive nature of male sexuality that ultimately reigns for both sexes. This fear instills in some men and women consciousness of their sexual and social identities.

In sum, the phenomenon of "pulling train" has many meanings. In addition to those meanings that have been mentioned, it is a bonding device that can permanently change a young man's understanding of masculinity. The bonding is accomplished by virtue of coparticipation in a "forbidden" act. As Ward Goodenough (1963) points out, sharing in the forbidden as part of initiation to a group is a powerful bonding device. For example, criminal gangs may require the initiate to perform a criminal act in order to be accepted as a member, an act that once performed is irrevocable. Participation in a "train" performs the same function of bonding the individual to the group and changing his subjectivity. Such bridge-burning acts of one kind or another are standard parts of ritualized identity-change procedures.

The Conditions Promoting "Pulling Train"

We cannot assume that all entering college students have well-established sexual and social identities or ethical positions regarding sexual harassment and abuse. Recent research by psychologists on human subjectivity argues that subjectivity is dynamic and changes as individuals move through the life cycle. The evidence presented here suggests that the masculine subjectivity of insecure males may be shaped, or at least reinforced, by experiences associated with male bonding at college.

[One] example is fraternity initiation rituals in which young men who admit to feelings of low self-esteem upon entering the college setting are forced to cleanse and purify themselves of the despised and dirty feminine, "nerdy," "faggot" self bonded to their mothers. The ritual process in these cases humiliates the pledges in order to break social and psychological bonds to parental authority and to establish new bonds to the brotherhood. The traumatic means employed to achieve these goals induces a state of consciousness that makes abuse of women a means to renew fraternal bonds and assert power as a brotherhood. . . .

. . . Cross-cultural research demonstrates that whenever men build and give allegiance to a mystical, enduring, all-male social group, the disparagement of women is, invariably, an important ingredient of the mystical bond, and sexual aggression the means by which the bond is renewed (Sanday 1981, 1986). As long as exclusive male clubs exist in a society that privileges men as a social category, we must recognize that collective sexual aggression provides a ready stage on which some men represent their social privilege and introduce adolescent boys to their future place in the status hierarchy.

Why has the sexual abuse of women and the humiliation of generations of pledges been tolerated for so long? The answer lies in a historical tendency to privilege male college students by failing to hold them accountable. Administrators protect young men by dissociating asocial behavior from the perpetrator and attributing it to something else. For example, one hears adult officials complaining about violence committed by fraternity brothers at the same time they condone the violence by saying that "things got out of hand" because of alcohol, adolescence, or some other version of "boys will be boys." Refusing to take serious action against young offenders promotes the male privilege that led to the behavior in the first place. At some level, perhaps, administrators believe that by taking effective action to end all forms of abuse they deny young men a forum for training for masculinity. Where this is the case women students cannot possibly experience the same social opportunities or sense of belonging at college as their male peers, even though they spend the same amount of money for the privilege of attending. As colleges and universities face an increasing number of legal suits deriving from rape, murder, and the other forms of abuse reported in fraternities, athletic settings, and dorms, change is clearly imminent. . . .

REFERENCES

Ehrhart, Julie K., and Bernice R. Sandler. 1985. "Campus Gang Rape: Party Games?" Washington, D.C.: Project on the Status of Women, Association of American Colleges.

Goodenough, Ward Hunt. 1963. *Cooperation in Change.* New York: Russell Sage Foundation.

Sanday, Peggy Reeves. 1981. "The Socio-Cultural Context of Rape." *Journal of Social Issues* 37: 5–27.

_____. 1986. "Rape and the Silencing of the Feminine." In *Rape: A Collection of Essays,* edited by Roy Porter and Sylvana Tomaselli. London: Basil Blackwell.

7

Failing at Fairness:
How America's Schools Cheat Girls

Myra and David Sadker

Sitting in the same classroom, reading the same textbook, listening to the same teacher, boys and girls receive very different educations. From grade school through graduate school, female students are more likely to be invisible members of classrooms. Teachers interact with males more frequently, ask them better questions, and give them more precise and helpful feedback. Over the course of years, the uneven distribution of teacher time, energy, attention, and talent, with boys getting the lion's share, takes its toll on girls. Since gender bias is not a noisy problem, most people are unaware of secret sexist lessons and the quiet losses they engender.

Girls are the majority of our nation's schoolchildren, yet they are second-class educational citizens. The problems they face—loss of self-esteem, decline in achievement, and closing of career options—are at the heart of the educational process. Until educational sexism is eradicated, more than half our children will be shortchanged and their gifts lost to society.

Award-winning author Susan Faludi discovered that backlash "is most powerful when it goes private, when it lodges inside a woman's mind and turns her vision inward, until she imagines the pressure is all in her head, until she begins to enforce the backlash too—on herself." Psychological backlash internalized by adult women is a frightening concept. But it is even more terrifying when a curriculum of sexist school lessons becomes a secret mind game played against children, our daughters, tomorrow's women.

After almost two decades of research grants and thousands of hours of classroom observation, we remain amazed at the stubborn persistence of hidden sexist lessons at school.

Like a thief in school, sexist lessons subvert education, twist it into a system of socialization that robs potential. Consider this record of silent, devastating losses.

- In the early grades girls are ahead of or equal to boys on almost every standardized measure of achievement and psychological well-being. By the time they graduate from high school or college they have fallen back. Girls are the only students in America who start out ahead and leave behind.
- In high school, girls score behind on the SAT and ACT, tests critical for college admission. The greatest gender gap is in the crucial areas of science and math.
- Girls are far behind on College Board Achievement tests required by most of the highly selective colleges.
- Boys are much more likely to be awarded national, state, and college scholarships.
- The gap does not close in college. Women are still behind, scoring lower on all sections of the Graduate Record Exam, necessary for entrance to most graduate programs.
- Women also trail on most tests needed to enter professional schools: lower on the GMAT for business school, lower on the LSAT for law school, and lower on the MCAT for medicine.
- From elementary school through higher education, female students receive less active instruction—both in quantity and quality of teacher time and attention.
- As girls go through school, their self-esteem plummets, and the danger of depression increases.
- Economic penalties follow women after graduation. "Women's careers" such as teaching and nursing are poorly paid. Even when women work in the same jobs as men, they earn less money. Most of America's poor live in households headed by women.

If the cure for cancer is stirring in the mind of one of our daughters, we are less likely to unlock the miracle than if it is forming in the mind of one of our sons. Until this changes, everybody loses.

Candid Camera would have a field day in elementary school. No need to create embarrassing situations. Just set the camera to take a photograph every 60 seconds. Since classroom action moves so swiftly, snapshots slow down the pace and reveal subliminal gender lessons.

Snapshot 1   Tim answers a question.
Snapshot 2   The teacher reprimands Alex.
Snapshot 3   Judy and Alice sits with hands raised while Brad answers a question.
Snapshot 4   Sally answers a question.
Snapshot 5   The teacher praises Marcus for skill in spelling.
Snapshot 6   The teacher helps Sam with a spelling mistake.
Snapshot 7   The teacher compliments Alice on her neat paper.
Snapshot 8   Students are in lines for a spelling bee. Boys are on one side of the room and girls are on the other.

As the snapshots continue, the underlying gender messages become clear. The classroom consists of two worlds: one of boys in action, the other of girls' inaction. Male students control classroom conversation. They ask and answer more questions. They receive more praise for the intellectual quality of their ideas. They get criticized. They get help when they are confused. They are the heart and center of interaction. Watch how boys dominate the discussion in this upper elementary class about presidents.

The fifth-grade class is almost out-of-control. "Just a minute," the teacher admonishes. "There are too many of us here to all shout out at once. I want you to raise your hands, and then I'll call on you. If you shout out, I'll pick somebody else."

Order is restored. Then Stephen, enthusiastic to make his point, calls out:

Stephen:	I think Lincoln was the best president.He held the country together during the war.
Teacher:	A lot of historians would agree with you.
Mike:	(seeing that nothing happened to Stephen, calls out) I don't. Lincoln was O.K. But my Dad liked Reagan. He always said Reagan was a great president.
David:	(calling out) Reagan? Are you kidding?
Teacher:	Who do you think our best President was, Dave?
David:	FDR. He saved us from the depression.
Max:	(calling out) I don't think it is right to pick one best president. There were a lot of good ones.
Teacher:	That's interesting.
Kimberly:	(calling out)I don't think the presidents today are as good as the ones we used to have.
Teacher:	O.K. Kimberly. But you forgot the rule. You're supposed to raise your hand.

The classroom is the only place in society where so many different, young, and restless individuals are crowded into close quarters for an extended period of time day after day. Teachers sense the undertow of raw energy and restlessness that threatens to engulf the classroom. To preserve order from impending chaos, most teachers use established conventions of the classroom, such as "Raise your hand if you want to talk."

Intellectually, teachers know they should apply this rule consistently. But when the discussion gets going, fast-paced and furious, good intentions are often swept aside. When this rule falls by the wayside and the shouting out begins, it is an open invitation for male dominance. Our research shows that boys call out eight times more often than girls. Sometimes what they say has little or nothing to do with the teacher's questions. Whether male comments are insightful or irrelevant, teachers respond to them. However, a fascinating pattern occurs when girls call out. Suddenly the teacher remembers the rule: "Don't forget you're supposed to raise your hand before you talk." So the girl, not as assertive as her brother to begin with, is deftly and swiftly put back in her place. . . .

This micro-iniquity has a powerful cumulative impact. And most insidious of all, it happens subliminally.

At surface glance, girls appear to be doing well. They get better grades and less punishment than boys. Quieter and more conforming, they are the elementary school's ideal students. "If it ain't broke, don't fix it," is the school's operating principle as girls' good behavior frees the teacher to work with the more hard-to-manage boys. The result: girls get less time, less challenge, and less help. Reinforced for passivity, their independence and self-esteem suffer. Victims of benign neglect, penalized for doing what they should, girls lose ground as they go through school. In contrast, boys get reinforced for breaking the rules; they are rewarded for grabbing more than their fair share of the teacher's time and attention.

Even when teachers remember to apply the rules consistently, boys are still the ones who get noticed. When girls raise their hands, it is often at a right angle, arm bent at the elbow, a cautious, tentative, almost insecure gesture. At other times they do raise their arms straight and high, but they signal silently. In contrast, when boys raise their hands, they fling them wildly in the air, up and down, up and down, again and again. . . .

In the social studies class about presidents, we saw boys as a group grabbing attention while girls as a group were left out of the action. Another way to observe in the classroom is to focus on individual children and record and describe their behavior for an extended period of time. Here is what we found when we watched two children for a 45-minute class. . . .

The fifth-grade boy sits in the 4th seat, second row. Since there are more than 30 other children in the class, getting the teacher's attention is a very competitive game. Watch how he plays.

First the boy waves his hand straight in the air so the teacher will select him from the surrounding forest of mainly male arms. He waves and pumps for almost three minutes without success. Evidently tiring, he puts his right arm down only to replace it with the left. Wave and pump. Wave and pump. Another two minutes go by. Still no recognition. Down with the left hand, up with the right. He moves to strategy two—the sounds: "Ooh me. C'mon. C'mon. Pleeze. OOOOh!" Another minute without notice. Strategy three: he gets out of his seat, stands in front of his desk, and waves with sound effects for another 30 seconds. He slumps back into his seat, momentarily discouraged. Five seconds later the right arm is up again in the strategy-four effort. He holds his right arm up in the air by resting it on his left as he leans on his elbow. Three more minutes go by.

"Tom." His name. Recognition. For a brief shining moment he has the floor. The eyes of the teacher and his classmates are on him, the center of attention. He has spent more than nine minutes of ceaseless effort to get his half-minute in the sun. Post response he sits for four quiet minutes. Then up shoots the arm again.

There is another student in the same class on the other side of the room, a little more toward the front. She begins the class with her arm held high, her face is animated, her body leans forward. Clearly she has something she wants to say. She keeps her right hand raised for more than a minute, switches to the left for another 45 seconds. She is not called on. She doesn't make noises or jump out of her seat. But it looks as though her arm is getting tired. She reverts to propping the right arm up with the left, a diagonal signal she maintains for two more minutes. Still no recognition. The hand comes down.

She sits quietly, stares out the window, plays with the hair of the girl in front of her. Her face is no longer animated. She crosses her arms on the desk and rests her head on the pillow she has created. She spends the final twelve minutes of class time with her head on the desk. Her eyes are open, but it is impossible to tell if she is listening. The period ends. The girl has not said a word.

When we videotape classrooms and play back tapes, most teachers are stunned to see themselves teaching subtle gender lessons along with math and spelling. The teacher in the social studies class about presidents was completely unaware she gave male students more attention. Only after several viewings of her videotape did she notice how she let boys call out answers but reprimanded girls for similar behavior. The teacher who taught Tom and the silent girl did not realize what effort it took to get attention. Surprised and saddened, he watched his initially eager female student, caught on videotape, wilt before his eyes, symbolically fading from the classroom.

In our workshops for educators we call boys like Tom "star students" or "green-arms." Teachers smile with weary recognition as we describe students whose hands are up in the air so high and so long that the blood drains out and gangrene sets in. Our research shows that in a typical class of 25 students, two or three green-arm students capture approximately 25 percent of the teacher's attention.

Most students are not so salient. Rather, nominally involved, they get one or two questions from the teacher each class period. Even though nominal students don't wave arms and make birdlike noises, they do exhibit their own distinguishable patterns. If you were a nominal student, you can probably remember the following from your own school days. As the teacher approaches, you tense. Your question comes, adrenaline pumps, shoulders rise, your heart pounds so loud the teacher's voice is barely audible. You answer. Correct! Exhale, relief. The teacher's shadow and cologne move on. You've paid your dues. . . .

In the typical classroom we found that approximately 10 percent of students are green-arms and 70 percent are nominal. Who's left? Those four or five students, in most classrooms about 20 percent, who do not say anything at all. Of course some boys are shy, and some girls assertive. But in our research we found that male students are more often stars and female students are more often stifled. Other researchers have found that for every eight star-boys there is only one star-girl. . . .

Girls in general receive less attention than boys in general, but here's where the shocker kicks in. Unlike the smart boy who flourishes in the classroom, the gifted girl is the student least likely to be recognized.

When we analyzed the computer printouts from our research for intersection between gender and race, an intriguing trend emerged. The students most likely to receive teacher attention were white males; second, minority males; third, white females; and at the bottom of the ladder, minority females. In elementary school, being paid attention to by the teacher is enormously important for achievement and self-esteem. Later in life, being paid money is important, and the salary pecking order parallels the classroom: white males on the top rung and minority females at the bottom. In her classroom interaction studies, Jacqueline Jordan Irvine found that black girls were active, assertive, and salient in the primary grades; but as they moved up through elementary school, they became the most invisible members of classrooms.

Recent research clarifies the connection between self-esteem and academic achievement, especially in math and science. Girls and boys who enjoy science and math consider themselves more important, like themselves more, and feel better about their school work and family relationships. They are also more likely to hold professional career goals. Thirty-one percent of girls say they are good in math in elementary school. By middle school, only 18 percent think they are mathematically capable. When girls lose confidence in their ability to do math and science, they avoid these subjects. When they believe they can't succeed, they become less willing to attempt new science and math problems and tasks. As they have fewer and fewer experiences with math and science, they become less capable. As their competence withers, so does their self-esteem. And so the vicious, connected cycle—attenuation of self-confidence, leading to loss of mental ability, resulting in diminishment of self-confidence—continues. The order of this downward spiral is crucial. First comes the plunge in confidence. The drop in achievement follows. It is during middle school that the fabled gender gap in math emerges and in science it gets greater. The brightest girls suffer most. In Terman's famous studies of gifted men and women, boys' I.Q.s fell three points during adolescence. Girls' dropped an eye-opening thirteen points.

By the end of middle school, smart girls report they feel more worried and afraid, less encouraged and appreciated than they were in elementary school.

Poised on the edge of adolescence, girls struggle to keep their balance, retain their authenticity and vitality, move on, and emerge as secure and capable adults. But now so many pitfalls surround them: physical vulnerability, the closing of options, the emphasis on thin, pretty and popular, the ascendancy of social success over academic achievement, the silencing of their honest feelings, the message that math and science are male domains, the short-circuiting of ability that renders them helpless, the subtle insinuations that boys are really the smart ones (they just don't try). Girls who succumb to these messages are at emotional and academic risk, in danger of losing not only their confidence, not only their achievement, but the very essence of themselves.

8

Tracking

Mary Kennedy Carter

A recent *New York Teacher* article reminded us of the experiences we had with our son's education. My observations and experiences tend to indicate that "tracking" starts at an early age through a variety of means.

Our son, Keith, started school knowing how to read. In first grade, however, he was put into the bottom reading group until it was learned that I was a teacher and was volunteering in the school's learning center. At that point, Keith was moved into the middle reading group. This placement continued until third grade when I requested that he be given the opportunity to work with the top group. Fortunately, the teacher agreed and Keith did excellent work in that group.

In sixth grade, when it was time for junior high school and honors classes, Keith was recommended for math and social studies, but not for science, although his grades justified honors placement. When I questioned this, I was told by the principal that they did not think that Keith could handle three honors. Most of his white friends were going into four honors. Through our intervention, Keith was placed in science—three honors. How many African-American children were kept out of honors through such an attitude and then considered lazy or troublemakers when the regular classes left them unchallenged and unmotivated?

Throughout junior and senior high school, Keith was one of a very small number of African-American boys or girls in the honors classes. He graduated in the top 10 percent of his class, made National Honor Society and was accepted by leading universities, including Princeton and Cornell. Incidentally, he worked for three years during high school in a computer store after school. Presently, Keith is a junior at Rensselaer Polytechnic Institute in Troy where he has made dean's list each year while following a rigorous schedule and participating in various campus activities.

As an educator, it has been of great concern to me that we had to play such an active role in assuring that our son receive the opportunities that an "excellent school system" had to offer. What about the many children whose parents are intimidated by the system or who trust it to provide the best for their youngsters?

From *New York Teacher*, April 18, 1994, p. 23. © Mary Kennedy Carter. Reprinted with permission of *New York Teacher*.

I would contend that it is the role of education to expect and encourage the best in each of our students.

Unfortunately many in education, consciously and unconsciously, expect more from some and less from others, and in many instances, race still is the deciding factor. Statistics support the philosophy that students rise to their highest level if expected to do so and given the opportunity to do so. By the same token, they will fail or be in the bottom classes if that is expected of them.

I do not think that the "Arlenes and Keiths" in the *New York Teacher* article are the exception. They were fortunate to have parents and some teachers who trusted in their potential and encouraged them to work to their highest abilities against whatever odds and regardless of their color. Only when educators and parents join together in the endeavor will we see a rise in academic standards, classes that accurately represent race and gender, and development of an educated populace prepared to take on the role of leadership and service that our nation needs and deserves.

9

Media Magic:
Making Class Invisible

Gregory Mantsios

Of the various social and cultural forces in our society, the mass media is arguably the most influential in molding public consciousness. Americans spend an average twenty-eight hours per week watching television. They also spend an undetermined number of hours reading periodicals, listening to the radio, and going to the movies. Unlike other cultural and socializing institutions, ownership and control of the mass media is highly concentrated. Twenty-three corporations own more than one-half of all the daily newspapers, magazines, movie studios, and radio and television outlets in the United States.[1] The number of media companies is shrinking and their control of the industry is expanding. And a relatively small number of media outlets is producing and packaging the majority of news and entertainment programs. For the most part, our media is national in nature and single-minded (profit-oriented) in purpose. This media plays a key role in defining our cultural tastes, helping us locate ourselves in history, establishing our national identity, and ascertaining the range of national and social possibilities. In this essay, we will examine the way the mass media shapes how people think about each other and about the nature of our society.

The United States is the most highly stratified society in the industrialized world. Class distinctions operate in virtually every aspect of our lives, determining the nature of our work, the quality of our schooling, and the health and safety of our loved ones. Yet remarkably, we, as a nation, retain illusions about living in an egalitarian society. We maintain these illusions, in large part, because the media hides gross inequities from public view. In those instances when inequities are revealed, we are provided with messages that obscure the nature of class realities and blame the victims of class-dominated society for their own plight. Let's briefly examine what the news media, in particular, tells us about class.

About the Poor

The news media provides meager coverage of poor people and poverty. The coverage it does provide is often distorted and misleading.

The Poor Do Not Exist

For the most part, the news media ignores the poor. Unnoticed are forty million poor people in the nation—a number that equals the entire population of Maine, Vermont, New Hampshire, Connecticut, Rhode Island, New Jersey, and New York combined. Perhaps even more alarming is that the rate of poverty is increasing twice as fast as the population growth in the United States. Ordinarily, even a calamity of much smaller proportion (e.g., flooding in the Midwest) would garner a great deal of coverage and hype from a media usually eager to declare a crisis, yet less than one in five hundred articles in the *New York Times* and one in one thousand articles listed in the *Readers Guide to Periodic Literature* are on poverty. With remarkably little attention to them, the poor and their problems are hidden from most Americans.

When the media does turn its attention to the poor, it offers a series of contradictory messages and portrayals.

The Poor Are Faceless

Each year the Census Bureau releases a new report on poverty in our society and its results are duly reported in the media. At best, however, this coverage emphasizes annual fluctuations (showing how the numbers differ from previous years) and ongoing debates over the validity of the numbers (some argue the number should be lower, most that the number should be higher). Coverage like this desensitizes us to the poor by reducing poverty to a number. It ignores the human tragedy of poverty—the suffering, indignities, and misery endured by millions of children and adults. Instead, the poor become statistics rather than people.

The Poor Are Undeserving

When the media does put a face on the poor, it is not likely to be a pretty one. The media will provide us with sensational stories about welfare cheats, drug addicts, and greedy panhandlers (almost always urban and Black). Compare these images and the emotions evoked by them with the media's treatment of middle-class (usually white) "tax evaders," celebrities who have a "chemical dependency," or wealthy businesspeople who use unscrupulous means to "make a profit." While the behavior of the more affluent offenders is considered an "impropriety" and a deviation from the norm, the behavior of the poor is considered repugnant, indicative of the poor in general, and worthy of our indignation and resentment.

The Poor Are an Eyesore

When the media does cover the poor, they are often presented through the eyes of the middle class. For example, sometimes the media includes a story about community resistance to a homeless shelter or storekeeper annoyance with panhandlers. Rather than focusing on the plight of the poor, these stories are about middle-class opposition to the poor. Such stories tell us that the poor are an inconvenience and an irritation.

The Poor Have Only Themselves to Blame

In another example of media coverage, we are told that the poor live in a personal and cultural cycle of poverty that hopelessly imprisons them. They routinely center on the Black urban population and focus on perceived personality or cultural traits that doom the poor. While the women in these stories typically exhibit an "attitude" that leads to trouble or a promiscuity that leads to single motherhood, the men possess a need for immediate gratification that leads to drug abuse or an unquenchable greed that leads to the pursuit of fast money. The images that are seared into our mind are sexist, racist, and classist. Census figures reveal that most of the poor are white, not Black or Hispanic, that they live in rural or suburban areas, not urban centers, and hold jobs at least part of the year.[2] Yet, in a fashion that is often framed in an understanding and sympathetic tone, we are told that the poor have inflicted poverty on themselves.

The Poor Are Down on Their Luck

During the Christmas season, the news media sometimes provides us with accounts of poor individuals or families (usually white) who are down on their luck. These stories are often linked to stories about soup kitchens or other charitable activities and sometimes call for charitable contributions. These "Yule time" stories are as much about the affluent as they are about the poor: they tell us that the affluent in our society are a kind, understanding, giving people—which we are not.* The series of unfortunate circumstances that have led to impoverishment are presumed to be a temporary condition that will improve with time and a change in luck.

Despite appearances, the messages provided by the media are not entirely disparate. With each variation, the media informs us what poverty is not (i.e., systemic and indicative of American society) by informing us what it is. The media tells us that poverty is either an aberration of the American way of life (it doesn't exist, it's just another number, it's unfortunate but temporary) or an end product of the poor themselves (they are a nuisance, do not deserve better, and have brought their predicament upon themselves).

By suggesting that the poor have brought poverty upon themselves, the media is engaging in what William Ryan has called "blaming the victim."[3] The media identifies in what ways the poor are different as a consequence of deprivation, then defines those differences as the cause of poverty itself. Whether blatantly hostile or cloaked in sympathy, the message is that there is something fundamentally wrong with the victims—their hormones, psychological makeup, family environment, community, race, or some combination of these—that accounts for their plight and their failure to lift themselves out of poverty.

But poverty in the United States is systemic. It is a direct result of economic and political policies that deprive people of jobs, adequate wages, or legitimate support. It is neither natural nor inevitable: there is enough wealth in our nation to eliminate poverty if we chose to redistribute existing wealth or income. The plight of the poor is reason enough to make the elimination of poverty the nation's first priority. But poverty also impacts dramatically on the nonpoor. It has a dampening effect on wages in general (by maintaining a reserve army of unemployed and underemployed anxious for any job at any wage) and breeds crime and violence (by maintaining conditions that invite private gain by illegal means and rebellion-like behavior, not entirely unlike the urban riots of the 1960s). Given the extent of poverty in the nation and the impact it has on us all, the media must spin considerable magic to keep the poor and the issue of poverty and its root causes out of the public consciousness.

---

*American households with incomes of less than $10,000 give an average of 5.5 percent of their earning to charity or to a religious organization, while those making more than $100,000 a year give only 2.9 percent. After changes in the 1986 tax code reduced the benefits of charitable giving, taxpayers earning $500,000 or more slashed their average donation by nearly one-third. Furthermore, many of these acts of benevolence do not help the needy. Rather than provide funding to social service agencies that aid the poor, the voluntary contributions of the wealthy go to places and institutions that entertain, inspire, cure, or educate wealthy Americans—art museums, opera houses, theaters, orchestras, ballet companies, private hospitals, and elite universities. (Robert Reich, "Secession of the Successful," *New York Times Magazine*, February 17, 1991, p. 43.)

About Everyone Else

Both the broadcast and the print news media strive to develop a strong sense of "we-ness" in their audience. They seek to speak to and for an audience that is both affluent and like-minded. The media's solidarity with affluence, that is, with the middle and upper class, varies little from one medium to another. Benjamin DeMott points out, for example, that the *New York Times* understands affluence to be intelligence, taste, public spirit, responsibility, and a readiness to rule and "conceives itself as spokesperson for a readership awash in these qualities."[4] Of course, the flip side to creating a sense of "we," or "us," is establishing a perception of the "other." The other relates back to the faceless, amoral, undeserving, and inferior "underclass." Thus, the world according to the news media is divided between the "underclass" and everyone else. Again the messages are often contradictory.

The Wealthy Are Us

Much of the information provided to us by the news media focuses attention on the concerns of a very wealthy and privileged class of people. Although the concerns of a small fraction of the populace, they are presented as though they were the concerns of everyone. For example, while relatively few people actually own stock, the news media devotes an inordinate amount of broadcast time and print space to business news and stock market quotations. Not only do business reports cater to a particular narrow clientele, so do the fashion pages (with $2,000 dresses), wedding announcements, and the obituaries. Even weather and sports news often have a class bias. An all news radio station in New York City, for example, provides regular national ski reports. International news, trade agreements, and domestic policies issues are also reported in terms of their impact on business climate and the business community. Besides being of practical value to the wealthy, such coverage has considerable ideological value. Its message: the concerns of the wealthy are the concerns of us all.

The Wealthy (as a Class) Do Not Exist

While preoccupied with the concerns of the wealthy, the media fails to notice the way in which the rich as a class of people create and shape domestic and foreign policy. Presented as an aggregate of individuals, the wealthy appear without special interests, interconnections, or unity in purpose. Out of public view are the class interests of the wealthy, the interlocking business links, the concerted actions to preserve their class privileges and business interests (by running for public office, supporting political candidates, lobbying, etc.). Corporate lobbying is ignored, taken for granted, or assumed to be in the public interest. (Compare this with the media's portrayal of the "strong arm of labor" in attempting to defeat trade legislation that is harmful to the interests of working people.) It is estimated that two-thirds of the U.S. Senate is composed of millionaires.[5] Having such a preponderance of millionaires in the Senate, however, is perceived to be neither unusual nor antidemocratic; these millionaire senators are assumed to be serving "our" collective interests in governing.

The Wealthy Are Fascinating and Benevolent

The broadcast and print media regularly provide hype for individuals who have achieved "super" success. These stories are usually about celebrities and superstars from the sports and entertainment world. Society pages and gossip columns serve to keep the social elite informed of each others' doings, allow the rest of us to gawk at their excesses, and help to keep the American dream alive. The print media is also fond of feature stories on corporate empire builders. These stories provide an occasional "insider's" view of the private and corporate life of industrialists by suggesting a rags to riches account of corporate success. These stories tell us that corporate success is a series of smart moves, shrewd acquisitions, timely mergers, and well thought out executive suite shuffles. By painting the upper class in a positive light, innocent of any wrongdoing (labor leaders and union organizations usually get the opposite treatment), the media assures us that wealth and power are benevolent. One person's capital accumulation is presumed to be good for all. The elite, then, are portrayed as investment wizards, people of special talent and skill, whom even their victims (workers and consumers) can admire.

The Wealthy Include a Few Bad Apples

On rare occasions, the media will mock selected individuals for their personality flaws. Real estate investor Donald Trump and New York Yankees owner George Steinbrenner, for example, are admonished by the media for deliberately seeking publicity (a very un-upper class thing to do); hotel owner Leona Helmsley was caricatured for her personal cruelties; and junk bond broker Michael Milkin was condemned because he had the audacity to rob the rich. Michael Parenti points out that by treating business wrongdoings as isolated deviations from the socially beneficial system of "responsible capitalism," the media overlooks the features of the system that produce such abuses and the regularity with which they occur. Rather than portraying them as predictable and frequent outcomes of corporate power and the business system, the media treats abuses as if they were isolated and atypical. Presented as an occasional aberration, these incidents serve not to challenge, but to legitimate, the system.[6]

The Middle Class Is Us

By ignoring the poor and blurring the lines between the working people and the upper class, the news media creates a universal middle class. From this perspective, the size of one's income becomes largely irrelevant: what matters is that most of "us" share an intellectual and moral superiority over the disadvantaged. As *Time* magazine once concluded, "Middle America is a state of mind."[7] "We are all middle class," we are told, "and we all share the same concerns": job security, inflation, tax burdens, world peace, the cost of food and housing, health care, clean air and water, and the safety of our streets. While the concerns of the wealthy are quite distinct from those of the middle class (e.g., the wealthy worry about investments, not jobs), the media convinces us that "we [the affluent] are all in this together."

The Middle Class Is a Victim

For the media, "we" the affluent not only stand apart from the "other"—the poor, the working class, the minorities, and their problems—"we" are also victimized by the poor (who drive up the costs of maintaining the welfare roles), minorities (who commit crimes against us), and workers (who are greedy and drive companies out and prices up). Ignored are the subsidies to the rich, the crimes of corporate America, and the policies that wreak havoc on the economic well-being of middle America. Media magic convinces us to fear, more than anything else, being victimized by those less affluent than ourselves.

The Middle Class Is Not a Working Class

The news media clearly distinguishes the middle class (employees) from the working class (i.e., blue collar workers) who are portrayed, at best, as irrelevant, outmoded, and a dying breed. Furthermore, the media will tell us that the hardships faced by blue collar workers are inevitable (due to progress), a result of bad luck (chance circumstances in a particular industry), or a product of their own doing (they priced themselves out of a job). Given the media's presentation of reality, it is hard to believe that manual, supervised, unskilled, and semiskilled workers actually represent more than 50 percent of the adult working population.[8] The working class, instead, is relegated by the media to "the other."

In short, the news media either lionizes the wealthy or treats their interests and those of the middle class as one in the same. But the upper class and the middle class do not share the same interests or worries. Members of the upper class worry about stock dividends (not employment), they profit from inflation and global militarism, their children attend exclusive private schools, they eat and live in a royal fashion, they call on (or are called upon by) personal physicians, they have few consumer problems, they can escape whenever they want from environmental pollution, and they live on streets and travel to other areas under the protection of private police forces.*[9]

---

*The number of private security guards in the United States now exceeds the number of public police officers. (Robert Reich, "Secession of the Successful," *New York Times Magazine*, February 17, 1991, p. 42.)

The wealthy are not only a class with distinct life-styles and interests, they are a ruling class. They receive a disproportionate share of the country's yearly income, own a disproportionate amount of the country's wealth, and contribute a disproportionate number of their members to governmental bodies and decision-making groups—all traits that William Domhoff, in his classic work *Who Rules America,* defined as characteristic of a governing class.[10]

This governing class maintains and manages our political and economic structures in such a way that these structures continue to yield an amazing proportion of our wealth to a minuscule upper class. While the media is not above referring to ruling classes in other countries (we hear, for example, references to Japan's ruling elite),[11] its treatment of the news proceeds as though there were no such ruling class in the United States.

Furthermore, the news media inverts reality so that those who are working class and middle class learn to fear, resent, and blame those below, rather than those above, them in the class structure. We learn to resent welfare, which accounts for only two cents out of every dollar in the federal budget (approximately $10 billion) and provides financial relief for the needy,[*] but learn little about the $11 billion the federal government spends on individuals with incomes in excess of $100,000 (not needy),[12] or the $17 billion in farm subsidies, or the $214 billion (twenty times the cost of welfare) in interest payments to financial institutions.

Middle-class whites learn to fear African Americans and Latinos, but most violent crime occurs within poor and minority communities and is neither interracial[†] nor interclass. As horrid as such crime is, it should not mask the destruction and violence perpetrated by corporate America. In spite of the fact that 14,000 innocent people are killed on the job each year, 100,000 die prematurely, 400,000 become seriously ill, and 6 million are injured from work-related accidents and diseases, most Americans fear government regulation more than they do unsafe working conditions.

Through the media, middle-class—and even working-class—Americans learn to blame blue collar workers and their unions for declining purchasing power and economic security. But while workers who managed to keep their jobs and their unions struggled to keep up with inflation, the top 1 percent of American families saw their average incomes soar 80 percent in the last decade.[13] Much of the wealth at the top was accumulated as stockholders and corporate executives moved their companies abroad to employ cheaper labor (56 cents per hour in El Salvador) and avoid paying taxes in the United States. Corporate America is a world made up of

---

[*] A total of $20 billion is spent on welfare when you include all state funding. But the average state funding also comes to only two cents per state dollar.

[†] In 92 percent of the murders nationwide the assailant and the victim are of the same race (46 percent are white/white, 46 percent are black/black), 5.6 percent are black on white, and 2.4 percent are white on black. (FBI and Bureau of Justic Statistics, 1985–1986, quoted in Raymond S. Franklin, *Shadows of Race and Class,* University of Minnesota Press, Minneapolis, 1991, p. 108.)

ruthless bosses, massive layoffs, favoritism and nepotism, health and safety violations, pension plan losses, union busting, tax evasions, unfair competition, and
price gouging, as well as fast buck deals, financial speculation, and corporate
wheeling and dealing that serve the interests of the corporate elite, but are generally wasteful and destructive to workers and the economy in general.

It is no wonder Americans cannot think straight about class. The mass media
are neither objective, balanced, independent, nor neutral. Those who own and direct the mass media are themselves part of the upper class, and neither they nor
the ruling class in general have to conspire to manipulate public opinion. Their
interest is in preserving the status quo, and their view of society as fair and equitable comes naturally to them. But their ideology dominates our society and justifies what is in reality a perverse social order—one that perpetuates unprecedented
elite privilege and power on the one hand and widespread deprivation on the
other. A mass media that did not have its own class interests in preserving the status quo would acknowledge that inordinate wealth and power undermines democracy and that a "free market" economy can ravage a people and their
communities.

NOTES

1. Martin Lee and Norman Solomon, *Unreliable Sources*, Lyle Stuart (New York,
1990), p. 71. See also Ben Bagdikian, *The Media Monopoly*, Beacon Press (Boston, 1990).

2. Department of Commerce, Bureau of the Census, "Poverty in the United States:
1992," *Current Population Reports, Consumer Income*, Series P60–185, pp. xi, xv, 1.

3. William Ryan, *Blaming the Victim*, Vintage (New York, 1971).

4. Benjamin Demott, *The Imperial Middle*, William Morrow (New York, 1990),
p. 123.

5. Fred Barnes, "The Zillionaires Club," *The New Republic*, January 29, 1990, p. 24.

6. Michael Parenti, *Inventing Reality*, St. Martin's Press (New York, 1986), p. 109.

7. *Time*, January 5, 1979, p. 10.

8. Vincent Navarro, "The Middle Class—A Useful Myth," *The Nation*, March 23,
1992, p. 1.

9. Charles Anderson, *The Political Economy of Social Class*, Prentice Hall
(Englewood Cliffs, N.J., 1974), p. 137.

10. William Domhoff, *Who Rules America*, Prentice Hall (Englewood Cliffs, N.J.,
1967), p. 5.

11. Lee and Solomon, *Unreliable Sources*, p. 179.

12. *Newsweek*, August 10, 1992, p. 57.

13. *Business Week*, June 8, 1992, p. 86.

Blaming the Victim

William Ryan

Twenty years ago, Zero Mostel used to do a sketch in which he impersonated a Dixiecrat Senator conducting an investigation of the origins of World War II. At the climax of the sketch, the Senator boomed out, in an excruciating mixture of triumph and suspicion, "What was Pearl Harbor *doing* in the Pacific?" This is an extreme example of Blaming the Victim.

Twenty years ago, we could laugh at Zero Mostel's caricature. In recent years, however, the same process has been going on every day in the arena of social problems, public health, anti-poverty programs, and social welfare. A philosopher might analyze this process and prove that, technically, it is comic. But it is hardly ever funny.

Consider some victims. One is the miseducated child in the slum school. He is blamed for his own miseducation. He is said to contain within himself the causes of his inability to read and write well. The shorthand phrase is "cultural deprivation," which, to those in the know, conveys what they allege to be inside information: that the poor child carries a scanty pack of cultural baggage as he enters school. He doesn't know about books and magazines and newspapers, they say. (No books in the home; the mother fails to subscribe to *Readers' Digest*.) They say that if he talks at all—an unlikely event since slum parents don't talk to their children—he certainly doesn't talk correctly. (Lower-class dialect spoken here, or even—God forbid!—Southern Negro.) (*Ici on parle nigra.*) If you can manage to get him to sit in a chair, they say, he squirms and looks out the window. (Impulse-ridden, these kids, motoric rather than verbal.) In a word he is "disadvantaged" and "socially deprived," they say, and this, of course, accounts for his failure (*his* failure, they say) to learn much in school.

Note the similarity to the logic of Zero Mostel's Dixiecrat Senator. What is the culturally deprived child *doing* in the school? What is wrong with the victim? In pursuing this logic, no one remembers to ask questions about the collapsing buildings and torn textbooks, the frightened, insensitive teachers, the six additional desks in the room, the blustering, frightened principals, the relentless segregation, the callous administrator, the irrelevant curriculum, the bigoted or cowardly members of the school board, the insulting history book, the stingy taxpayers, the fairy-tale readers, or the self-serving faculty of the local teachers' college. We are encouraged to confine our attention to the child and to dwell on all his alleged defects. Cultural deprivation becomes an omnibus explanation for the educational disaster area known as the inner-city school. This is Blaming the Victim.

Pointing to the supposedly deviant Negro family as the "fundamental weakness of the Negro community" is another way to blame the victim. Like "cultural deprivation," "Negro family" has become a shorthand phrase with stereotyped connotations of matriarchy, fatherlessness, and pervasive illegitimacy. Growing up in the "crumbling" Negro family is supposed to account for most of the racial evils in America. Insiders have the word, of course, and know that this phrase is supposed to evoke images of growing up with a long-absent or never-present father (replaced from time to time perhaps by a series of transient lovers) and with bossy women ruling the roost, so that the children are irreparably damaged. This refers particularly to the poor, bewildered male children, whose psyches are fatally wounded and who are never, alas, to learn the trick of becoming upright, downright, forthright all-American boys. Is it any wonder the Negroes cannot achieve equality? From such families! And, again, by focusing our attention on the Negro family as the apparent *cause* of racial inequality, our eye is diverted. Racism, discrimination, segregation, and the powerlessness of the ghetto are subtly, but thoroughly, downgraded in importance.

The generic process of Blaming the Victim is applied to almost every American problem. The miserable health care of the poor is explained away on the grounds that the victim has poor motivation and lacks health information. The problems of slum housing are traced to the characteristics of tenants who are labeled as "Southern rural migrants" not yet "acculturated" to life in the big city. The "multiproblem" poor, it is claimed, suffer the psychological effects of impoverishment, the "culture of poverty," and the deviant value system of the lower classes; consequently, though unwittingly, they cause their own troubles. From such a viewpoint, the obvious fact that poverty is primarily an absence of money is easily overlooked or set aside.

The growing number of families receiving welfare are fallaciously linked together with the increased number of illegitimate children as twin results of promiscuity and sexual abandon among members of the lower orders. Every important social problem—crime, mental illness, civil disorder, unemployment—has been analyzed within the framework of the victim-blaming ideology. . . .

I have been listening to the victim-blamers and pondering their thought processes for a number of years. That process is often very subtle. Victim-blaming is cloaked in kindness and concern, and bears all the trappings and statistical furbelows of scientism; it is obscured by a perfumed haze of humanitarianism. In observing the process of Blaming the Victim, one tends to be confused and disoriented because those who practice this art display a deep concern for the victims that is quite genuine. In this way, the new ideology is very different from the open prejudice and reactionary tactics of the old days. Its adherents include sympathetic social scientists with social consciences in good working order, and liberal politicians with a genuine commitment to reform. They are very careful to dissociate themselves from vulgar Calvinism or crude racism; they indignantly condemn any notions of innate wickedness or genetic defect. "The Negro is *not born* inferior," they shout apoplectically. "Force of circumstance," they explain in reasonable tones, "has *made* him inferior." And they dismiss with self-righteous contempt any claims that the poor man in America is plainly unworthy or shiftless or enamored of idleness. No, they say, he is "caught in the cycle of poverty." He is trained to be poor by his culture and his family life, endowed by his environment (perhaps by his ignorant mother's outdated style of toilet training) with those unfortunately unpleasant characteristics that make him ineligible for a passport into the affluent society.

Blaming the Victim is, of course, quite different from old-fashioned conservative ideologies. The latter simply dismissed victims as inferior, genetically defective, or morally unfit; the emphasis is on the intrinsic, even hereditary, defect. The former shifts its emphasis to the environmental causation. The old-fashioned conservative could hold firmly to the belief that the oppressed and the victimized were born that way—"that way" being defective or inadequate in character or ability. The new ideology attributes defect and inadequacy to the malignant nature of poverty, injustice, slum life, and racial difficulties. The stigma that marks the victim and accounts for his victimization is an acquired stigma, a stigma of social, rather than genetic, origin. But the stigma, the defect, the fatal difference—though derived in the past from environmental forces—is still located *within* the victim, inside his skin. With such an elegant formulation, the humanitarian can have it both ways. He can, all at the same time, concentrate his charitable interest on the defects of the victim, condemn the vague social and environmental stresses that produced the defect (some time ago), and ignore the continuing effect of victimizing social forces (right now). It is a brilliant ideology for justifying a perverse form of social action designed to change, not society, as one might expect, but rather society's victim.

As a result, there is a terrifying sameness in the programs that arise from this kind of analysis. In education, we have programs of "compensatory education" to build up the skills and attitudes of the ghetto child, rather than structural changes in the schools. In race relations, we have social engineers who think up ways of "strengthening" the Negro family, rather than methods of eradicating racism. In health care, we develop new programs to provide health information (to correct the supposed ignorance of the poor) and to reach out and discover cases of untreated illness and disability (to compensate for their supposed unwillingness to seek treatment). Meanwhile, the gross inequities of our medical care delivery systems are left completely unchanged. As we might expect, the logical outcome of analyzing social problems in terms of the deficiencies of the victim is the development of programs aimed at correcting those deficiencies. The formula for action becomes extraordinarily simple: change the victim.

All of this happens so smoothly that it seems downright rational. First, identify a social problem. Second, study those affected by the problem and discover in what ways they are different from the rest of us as a consequence of deprivation and injustice. Third, define the differences as the cause of the social problem itself. Finally, of course, assign a government bureaucrat to invent a humanitarian action program to correct the differences.

Now no one in his right mind would quarrel with the assertion that social problems are present in abundance and are readily identifiable. God knows it is true that when hundreds of thousands of poor children drop out of school—or even graduate from school—they are barely literate. After spending some ten thousand hours in the company of professional educators, these children appear to have learned very little. The fact of failure in their education is undisputed. And the racial situation in America is usually acknowledged to be a number one item on the nation's agenda. Despite years of marches, commissions, judicial decisions, and endless legislative remedies, we are confronted with unchanging or even widening racial differences in achievement. In addition, despite our assertions that Americans get the best health care in the world, the poor stubbornly remain unhealthy. They lose more work because of illness, have more carious teeth, lose more babies as a result of both miscarriage and infant death, and die considerably younger than the well-to-do.

The problems are there, and there in great quantities. They make us uneasy. Added together, these disturbing signs reflect inequality and a puzzlingly high level of unalleviated distress in America totally inconsistent with our proclaimed ideals and our enormous wealth. This thread—this rope—of inconsistency stands out so visibly in the fabric of American life, that it is jarring to the eye. And this must be explained, to the satisfaction of our conscience as well as our patriotism. Blaming the Victim is an ideal, almost painless, evasion.

The second step in applying this explanation is to look sympathetically at those who "have" the problem in question, to separate them out and define them in some way as a special group, a group that is *different* from the population in general. This is a crucial and essential step in the process, for that difference is in itself hampering and maladaptive. The Different Ones are seen as less competent, less skilled, less knowing—in short, less human. The ancient Greeks deduced from a single characteristic, a difference in language, that the barbarians—that is, the "babblers" who spoke a strange tongue—were wild, uncivilized, dangerous, rapacious, uneducated, lawless, and, indeed, scarcely more than animals. Automatically labeling strangers as savages, weird and inhuman creatures (thus explaining difference by exaggerating difference) not infrequently justifies mistreatment, enslavement, or even extermination of the Different Ones.

Blaming the Victim depends on a very similar process of identification (carried out, to be sure, in the most kindly, philanthropic, and intellectual manner) whereby the victim of social problems is identified as strange, different—in other words, as a barbarian, a savage. Discovering savages, then, is an essential component of, and prerequisite to, Blaming the Victim, and the art of Savage Discovery is a core skill that must be acquired by all aspiring Victim Blamers. They must learn how to demonstrate that the poor, the black, the ill, the jobless, the slum tenants, are different and strange. They must learn to conduct or interpret the research that shows how "these people" think in different forms, act in different patterns, cling to different values, seek different goals, and learn different truths. Which is to say that they are strangers, barbarians, savages. This is how the distressed and disinherited are redefined in order to make it possible for us to look at society's problems and to attribute their causation to the individuals affected. . . .

Blaming the Victim can take its place in a long series of American ideologies that have rationalized cruelty and injustice.

Slavery, for example, was justified—even praised—on the basis of a complex ideology that showed quite conclusively how useful slavery was to society and how uplifting it was for the slaves.[1] Eminent physicians could be relied upon to provide the biological justification for slavery since after all, they said, the slaves were a separate species—as, for example, cattle are a separate species. No one in his right mind would dream of freeing the cows and fighting to abolish the ownership of cattle. In the view of the average American of 1825, it was important to preserve slavery, not simply because it was in accord with his own group interests (he was not fully aware of that), but because reason and logic showed clearly to the reasonable and intelligent man that slavery was good. In order to persuade a good and moral man to *do* evil, then, it is not necessary first to persuade him to *become* evil. It is only necessary to teach him that he is doing good. No one, in the words of a legendary newspaperman, thinks of himself as a son of a bitch.

In late-nineteenth-century America there flowered another ideology of injustice that seemed rational and just to the decent, progressive person. But Richard Hofstadter's analysis of the phenomenon of Social Darwinism[2] shows clearly its functional role in the preservation of the *status quo*. One can scarcely imagine a better fit than the one between this ideology and the purposes and actions of the robber barons, who descended like piranha fish on the America of this era and picked its bones clean. Their extraordinarily unethical operations netted them not only hundreds of millions of dollars but also, perversely, the adoration of the nation. Behavior that would be, in any more rational land (including today's America), more than enough to have landed them all in jail, was praised as the very model of a captain of modern industry. And the philosophy that justified their thievery was such that John D. Rockefeller could actually stand up and preach it in church. Listen as he speaks in, of all places, Sunday school: "The growth of a large business is merely a survival of the fittest. . . . The American Beauty rose can be produced in the splendor and fragrance which bring cheer to its beholder only by sacrificing the early buds which grow up around it. This is not an evil tendency in business. It is merely the working-out of a law of nature and a law of God."[3]

This was the core of the gospel, adapted analogically from Darwin's writings on evolution. Herbert Spencer and, later, William Graham Sumner and other beginners in the social sciences considered Darwin's work to be directly applicable to social processes: ultimately as a guarantee that life was progressing toward perfection but, in the short run, as a justification for an absolutely uncontrolled laissez-faire economic system. The central concepts of "survival of the fittest," "natural selection," and "gradualism" were exalted in Rockefeller's preaching to the status of laws of God and Nature. Not only did this ideology justify the criminal rapacity of those who rose to the top of the industrial heap, defining them automatically as naturally superior (this was bad enough), but at the same time it also required that those at the bottom of the heap be labeled as patently *unfit*—a label based solely on their position in society. According to the law of natural selection, they should be, in Spencer's judgment, eliminated. "The whole effort of nature is to get rid of such, to clear the world of them and make room for better."

For a generation, Social Darwinism was the orthodox doctrine in the social sciences, such as they were at that time. Opponents of this ideology were shut out of respectable intellectual life. The philosophy that enabled John D. Rockefeller to justify himself self-righteously in front of a class of Sunday school children was not the product of an academic quack or a marginal crackpot philosopher. It came directly from the lectures and books of leading intellectual figures of the time, occupants of professorial chairs at Harvard and Yale. Such is the power of an ideology that so neatly fits the needs of the dominant interests of society.

If one is to think about ideologies in America in 1970, one must be prepared to consider the possibility that a body of ideas that might seem almost self-evident is, in fact, highly distorted and highly selective; one must allow that the inclusion of a specific formulation in every freshman sociology text does not guarantee that the particular formulation represents abstract Truth rather than group interest. It is important not to delude ourselves into thinking that ideological monstrosities were constructed by monsters. They were not; they are not. They are developed through a process that shows every sign of being valid scholarship, complete with tables of numbers, copious footnotes, and scientific terminology. Ideologies are quite often academically and socially respectable and in many instances hold positions of exclusive validity, so that disagreement is considered unrespectable or radical and risks being labeled as irresponsible, unenlightened, or trashy.

Blaming the Victim holds such a position. It is central in the mainstream of contemporary American social thought, and its ideas pervade our most crucial assumptions so thoroughly that they are hardly noticed. Moreover, the fruits of this ideology appear to be fraught with altruism and humanitarianism, so it is hard to believe that it has principally functioned to block social change.

A major pharmaceutical manufacturer, as an act of humanitarian concern, has distributed copies of a large poster warning, "LEAD PAINT CAN KILL!" The poster, featuring a photograph of the face of a charming little girl, goes on to explain that if children *eat* lead paint, it can poison them, they can develop serious symptoms, suffer permanent brain damage, even die. The health department of a major American city has put out a coloring book that provides the same information. While the poster urges parents to prevent their children from eating paint, the coloring book is more vivid. It labels as neglectful and thoughtless the mother who does not keep her infant under constant surveillance to keep it from eating paint chips.

Now, no one would argue against the idea that it is important to spread knowledge about the danger of eating paint in order that parents might act to forestall their children from doing so. But to campaign against lead paint *only* in these terms is destructive and misleading and, in a sense, an effective way to support and agree with slum landlords—who define the problem of lead poisoning in precisely these terms.

This is an example of applying an exceptionalistic solution to a universalistic problem. It is not accurate to say that lead poisoning results from the actions of individual neglectful mothers. Rather, lead poisoning is a social phenomenon supported by a number of social mechanisms, one of the most tragic by-products of the systematic toleration of slum housing. In New Haven, which has the highest reported rate of lead poisoning in the country, several small children have died and many others have incurred irreparable brain damage as a result of eating peeling paint. In several cases, when the landlord failed to make repairs, poisonings have occurred time and again through a succession of tenancies. And the major reason for the landlord's neglect of this problem was that the city agency responsible for enforcing the housing code did nothing to make him correct this dangerous condition.

The cause of the poisoning is the lead in the paint on the walls of the apartment in which the children live. The presence of the lead is illegal. To use lead paint in a residence is illegal; to permit lead paint to be exposed in a residence is illegal. It is not only illegal, it is potentially criminal since the housing code does provide for criminal penalties. The general problem of lead poisoning, then, is more accurately analyzed as the result of a systematic program of lawbreaking by one interest group in the community, with the toleration and encouragement of the public authority charged with enforcing that law. To ignore these continued and repeated law violations, to ignore the fact that the supposed law enforcer actually cooperates in lawbreaking, and then to load a burden of guilt on the mother of a dead or dangerously ill child is an egregious distortion of reality. And to do so *under the guise* of public-spirited and humanitarian service to the community is intolerable.

But this is how Blaming the Victim works. The righteous humanitarian concern displayed by the drug company, with its poster, and the health department, with its coloring book, is a genuine concern, and this is a typical feature of Blaming the Victim. Also typical is the swerving away from the central target that requires systematic change and, instead, focusing in on the individual affected. The ultimate effect is always to distract attention from the basic causes and to leave the primary social injustice untouched. And, most telling, the proposed remedy for the problem is, of course, to work on the victim himself. Prescriptions for cure, as written by the Savage Discovery set, are invariably conceived to revamp and revise the victim, never to change the surrounding circumstances. They want to change his attitudes, alter his values, fill up his cultural deficits, energize his apathetic soul, cure his character defects, train him and polish him and woo him from his savage ways.

Isn't all of this more subtle and sophisticated than such old-fashioned ideologies as Social Darwinism? Doesn't the change from brutal ideas about survival of the fit (and the expiration of the unfit) to kindly concern about characterological defects (brought about by stigmas of social origin) seem like a substantial step forward? Hardly. It is only a substitution of terms. The old, reactionary exceptionalistic formulations are replaced by new progressive, humanitarian exceptionalistic formulations. In education, the outmoded and unacceptable concept of racial or class differences in basic inherited intellectual ability simply gives way to the new notion of cultural deprivation: there is very little functional difference between these two ideas. In taking a look at the phenomenon of poverty, the old concept of unfitness or idleness or laziness is replaced by the newfangled theory of the culture of poverty. In race relations, plain Negro inferiority—which was good enough for old-fashioned conservatives—is pushed aside by fancy conceits about the crumbling Negro family. With regard to illegitimacy, we are not so crass as to concern ourselves with immorality and vice, as in the old days; we settle benignly on the explanation of the "lower-class pattern of sexual behavior," which no one condemns as evil, but which is, in fact, simply a variation of the old explanatory idea. Mental illness is no longer defined as the result of hereditary taint or congenital character flaw; now we have new causal hypotheses regarding the ego-damaging emotional experiences that are supposed to be the inevitable consequence of the deplorable child-rearing practices of the poor.

In each case, of course, we are persuaded to ignore the obvious: the continued blatant discrimination against the Negro, the gross deprivation of contraceptive and adoption services to the poor, the heavy stresses endemic in the life of the poor. And almost all our make-believe liberal programs aimed at correcting our urban problems are off target; they are designed either to change the poor man or to cool him out.

We come finally to the question, Why? It is much easier to understand the process of Blaming the Victim as a way of thinking than it is to understand the motivation for it. Why do Victim Blamers, who are usually good people, blame the victim? The development and application of this ideology, and of all the mythologies associated with Savage Discovery, are readily exposed by careful analysis as hostile acts—one is almost tempted to say acts of war—directed against the disadvantaged, the distressed, the disinherited. It is class warfare in reverse. Yet those who are most fascinated and enchanted by this ideology tend to be progressive, humanitarian, and, in the best sense of the word, charitable persons. They would usually define themselves as moderates or liberals. Why do they pursue this dreadful war against the poor and the oppressed?

Put briefly, the answer can be formulated best in psychological terms—or, at least, I, as a psychologist, am more comfortable with such a formulation. The highly charged psychological problem confronting this hypothetical progressive, charitable person I am talking about is that of reconciling his own self-interest with the promptings of his humanitarian impulses. This psychological process of reconciliation is not worked out in a logical, rational, conscious way; it is a process that takes place far below the level of sharp consciousness, and the solution—Blaming the Victim—is arrived at subconsciously as a compromise that apparently satisfies both his self-interest and his charitable concerns. Let me elaborate.

First, the question of self-interest or, more accurately, class interest. The typical Victim Blamer is a middle-class person who is doing reasonably well in a material way; he has a good job, a good income, a good house, a good car. Basically, he likes the social system pretty much the way it is, at least in broad outline. He likes the two-party political system, though he may be highly skilled in finding a thousand minor flaws in its functioning. He heartily approves of the profit motive as the propelling engine of the economic system despite his awareness that there are abuses of that system, negative side effects, and substantial residual inequalities.

On the other hand, he is acutely aware of poverty, racial discrimination, exploitation, and deprivation, and, moreover, he wants to do something concrete to ameliorate the condition of the poor, the black, and the disadvantaged. This is not an extraneous concern; it is central to his value system to insist on the worth of the individual, the equality of men, and the importance of justice.

What is to be done, then? What intellectual position can he take, and what line of action can he follow that will satisfy both of these important motivations? He quickly and self-consciously rejects two obvious alternatives, which he defines as "extremes." He cannot side with an openly reactionary, repressive position that accepts continued oppression and exploitation as the price of a privileged position for his own class. This is incompatible with his own morality and his basic political principles. He finds the extreme conservative position repugnant.

He is, if anything, more allergic to radicals, however, than he is to reactionaries. He rejects the "extreme" solution of radical social change, and this makes sense since such radical social change threatens his own well-being. A more equitable distribution of income might mean that he would have less—a smaller or older house, with fewer yews or no rhododendrons in the yard, a less enjoyable job, or, at the least, a somewhat smaller salary. If black children and poor children were, in fact, reasonably educated and began to get high S.A.T. scores, they would be competing with *his* children for the scarce places in the entering classes of Harvard, Columbia, Bennington, and Antioch.

So our potential Victim Blamers are in a dilemma. In the words of an old Yiddish proverb, they are trying to dance at two weddings. They are old friends of both brides and fond of both kinds of dancing, and they want to accept both invitations. They cannot bring themselves to attack the system that has been so good to them, but they want so badly to be helpful to the victims of racism and economic injustice.

Their solution is a brilliant compromise. They turn their attention to the victim in his post-victimized state. They want to bind up wounds, inject penicillin, administer morphine, and evacuate the wounded for rehabilitation. They explain what's wrong with the victim in terms of social experiences *in the past*, experiences that have left wounds, defects, paralysis, and disability. And they take the cure of these wounds and the reduction of these disabilities as the first order of business. They want to make the victims less vulnerable, send them back into battle with better weapons, thicker armor, a higher level of morale.

In order to do so effectively, of course, they must analyze the victims carefully, dispassionately, objectively, scientifically, empathetically, mathematically, and hardheadedly, to see what made them so vulnerable in the first place.

What weapons, now, might they have lacked when they went into battle? Job skills? Education?

What armor was lacking that might have warded off their wounds? Better values? Habits of thrift and foresight?

And what might have ravaged their morale? Apathy? Ignorance? Deviant lower-class cultural patterns?

This is the solution of the dilemma, the solution of Blaming the Victim. And those who buy this solution with a sigh of relief are inevitably blinding themselves to the basic causes of the problems being addressed. They are, most crucially, rejecting the possibility of blaming, not the victims, but themselves. They are all unconsciously passing judgments on themselves and bringing in a unanimous verdict of Not Guilty.

If one comes to believe that the culture of poverty produces persons *fated* to be poor, who can find any fault with our corporation-dominated economy? And if the Negro family produces young men *incapable* of achieving equality, let's deal with that first before we go on to the task of changing the pervasive racism that informs and shapes and distorts our every social institution. And if unsatisfactory resolution of one's Oedipus complex accounts for all emotional distress and mental disorder, then by all means let us attend to that and postpone worrying about the pounding day-to-day stresses of life on the bottom rungs that drive so many to drink, dope, and madness.

That is the ideology of Blaming the Victim, the cunning Art of Savage Discovery. The tragic, frightening truth is that it is a mythology that is winning over the best people of our time, the very people who must resist this ideological temptation if we are to achieve nonviolent change in America.

NOTES

1. For a good review of this general ideology, see I. A. Newby, *Jim Crow's Defense* (Baton Rouge: Louisiana State University Press, 1965).

2. Richard Hofstadter, *Social Darwinism in American Thought* (revised ed.; Boston: Beacon Press, 1955).

3. William J. Ghent, *Our Benevolent Feudalism* (New York: The Macmillan Co., 1902), p. 29.

Suggestions for Further Reading

Basow, Susan. *Gender: Stereotypes and Roles.* Pacific Grove, CA: Brooks/Cole Publishing, 1992.

Goings, Kenneth W. *Mammy and Uncle Mose: Black Collectibles and American Stereotyping.* Bloomington: Indiana University Press, 1994.

Harding, S., and M. B. Hintikka. *Discovering Reality: Feminist Perspectives on Epistemology, Metaphysics, Methodology, and Philosophy of Science.* Boston: D. Reidel Publishing, 1983.

Holtzman, Linda. *Media Messages: What Film, Television, and Popular Music Teach Us about Race, Class, Gender, and Sexual Orientation.* Armonk, NY: M.E. Sharp, 2000.

hooks, bell. *Teaching to Transgress: Education as the Practice of Freedom.* New York: Routledge, 1994.

Kramarae, C., M. Schultz, and W.M. O'Barr, eds. *Language and Power.* Beverly Hills, CA: Sage Press, 1984.

Loewen, James. *Lies My Teacher Told Me.* New York: Touchstone Books, 1996.

Lee, Martin A., and Norman Solomon. *Unreliable Sources.* New York: Lyle Stuart, 1990.

Mazzocco, Dennis W. *Networks of Power: Corporate TV's Threat to Democracy.* Boston: South End Press, 1994.

Oakes, J. *Keeping Track: How Schools Structure Inequality.* New Haven: Yale University Press, 1985.

Orenstein, Peggy. *School Girls.* New York: Doubleday, 1994.

Parenti, Michael. *Inventing Reality.* New York: St. Martin's Press, 1986.

Sadker, Myra, and David Sadker. *Failing at Fairness: How America's Schools Cheat Girls.* New York: Scribner's, 1994.

Spender, D. *Man Made Language,* 2d ed. Boston: Routledge & Kegan Paul. 1985.

Thompson, Becky W. *A Hunger So Wide and So Deep.* Minneapolis: University of Minnesota Press, 1994.

Wolf, Naomi. *The Beauty Myth.* New York: Doubleday/Anchor, 1992.

PART VIII

Making a Difference

AN ADEQUATE UNDERSTANDING OF THE NATURE and causes of race, class, and gender oppression is a critical first step toward moving beyond them. Solutions to problems are generated, at least in part, by the way we pose them. That is why so much of this book is devoted to defining and analyzing the nature of these systems of oppression. Only when we appreciate the subtle and complex factors that operate together to create a society in which wealth, privilege, and opportunity are unequally divided will we be able to formulate viable proposals for changing these conditions.

What, then, have the selections in this book told us about racism, sexism, heterosexism, and class divisions? First, that there is no single cause. Eliminating these forms of oppression will involve changes at the personal, social, political, and economic levels. It will require us to think differently about ourselves and others and think about the world using new categories. We will have to learn to pay close attention to our attitudes and behavior and ask what values and what kinds of relationships they are creating and maintaining, both consciously and unconsciously. We will have to reevaluate virtually every institution in society and critically appraise the ways in which they intentionally or unintentionally perpetuate the forms of discrimination we have been studying, and we will have to act to change them. In short, we must scrutinize every aspect of economic, political, and social life with a view to asking whose interests are served and whose are denied when the world is organized in this way.

In Selections 1 and 2, Audre Lorde and Gloria Anzaldúa suggest that we will need to begin by redefining and rethinking the idea of difference. While acknowledging that real differences of race, age, and sexuality exist, Lorde argues that it is not these differences that separate us as much as it is our refusal to acknowledge them and the role they play in shaping our relationships and social institutions. Denying or distorting those differences keeps us apart, but embracing these differences can provide a new starting point from which to work together to reconstruct our world. Gloria Anzaldúa is concerned with the way women of color deal with differences among themselves; she argues that many women of color have learned to see each other through the categories of inferiority/superiority that white people have constructed and urges women of color to reject these categories and stand "on the ground of our own ethnic being."

In Selection 3, bell hooks continues one of the projects of this book—understanding the way in which sex, race, and class function as interlocking, mutually supportive systems of domination. Like Lorde and Anzaldúa, she urges us to rethink difference. While acknowledging past failures of much feminist theory to adequately address issues of race, racism, and class, hooks maintains that a revisioned feminism can provide the most comprehensive perspective from which to challenge all forms of oppression and domination. This is true, she maintains, because sexism is the form of oppression we confront daily: "sexism directly shapes and determines relations of power in our private lives, in familiar social spaces, in that most intimate context—home—and in that most intimate sphere of relations—family." hooks envisions a process of education and consciousness raising whereby women from diverse backgrounds come together in small groups to talk about feminism and to learn from each other, but she calls on men as well to commit themselves to overthrowing patriarchal domination.

As many of the readings in this book make clear, significant and lasting changes in our society will come about only when each of us assumes responsibility for making a difference. Racism, sexism, class inequities, and heterosexism and homophobia are everybody's problem. They undermine the quality of life for all of us—ironically, even for those people who seem, at least in the short run, to profit from them. While the enormity of the work to be done can seem overwhelming, in Selection 4 Andrea Ayvazian suggests that one way to overcome a sense of immobilization is to adopt the role of an ally. According to Ayvazian "an ally is a member of a dominant group in our society who works to dismantle any form of oppression from which she or he receives the benefit." By acting consciously and deliberately to challenge oppression and to make privilege visible, allies provide role models for us all and demonstrate ways in which each of us can act as a powerful agent of change. Several of the articles that follow provide concrete examples of what this might mean.

In Selection 5, Harlon L. Dalton argues that white people in the United States need to own the race problem as a first step toward working to solve it. To this end, he enumerates some of the ways in which many of us who are white routinely distance ourselves from issues of race and racism. According to Dalton, white people have in common a tendency to blame people of color for the conditions that are really the result of years of institutional racism and to hold people of color responsible for changing these conditions—as if this could happen by a sheer effort of will. Another avoidance strategy involves "turning the tables" by focusing on "the victimization of the white male," suggesting that it is white men, not people of color, who are the real targets of unfair treatment. Finally, Dalton takes issue with those academics who argue that class privilege, not racism, is the real cause of the race problem in the United States. While agreeing that economic issues are significant, Dalton sees the new emphasis on class as yet another way to deflect attention from what he terms "the enduring problem of race."

A very concrete way that those of us who are white can own the race problem and take steps toward solving it is suggested by Fletcher A. Blanchard in Selection 6. Blanchard reports on a study he did that showed the importance and value of condemning racist harassment whenever we come upon it. In his study, college students who overheard someone else speak out against racism were much more likely to express strong anti-racist views themselves. He concludes that "each of us can affect others' concern for eliminating racism by taking strong public stands condemning bigotry on campuses." Selection 7 by Michael Bronski expresses a similar concern for the need to stand up to and speak out against anti-gay violence. Bronski maintains that since anti-gay hatred, like all hatred, is learned, violence against lesbian women and gay men will continue until all of us own the problem and act to end it. Some of the strategies Bronski advocates are not turning a deaf ear when people use the term "fag" or tell homophobic jokes, supporting education that includes positive information about lesbians and gays, and providing lesbian and gay friends and relatives with support.

A new vision of society will require new choices and options for men as well as women. In Selection 8, Cooper Thompson is profoundly critical of the way in which boys are socialized to believe that violence is an acceptable—even desirable—way to establish their manhood and to negotiate differences. He believes that this socialization leads to both misogyny and homophobia and makes it difficult for men to form warm and loving friendships with members of both sexes. Because the social costs of prevailing conceptions of masculinity are so high, Thompson urges us to develop a new vision of manhood, one that allows boys to claim many of the qualities previously defined as "feminine." Thompson concludes with a warning: "The survival of our society may rest on the degree to which we are able to teach men to cherish life."

Selections 9 and 10 provide us with two examples of how life experience can change people and make them more aware of the systems of oppression that operate in our society. The first takes a look at changes in corporate culture brought about by Lewis E. Platt, currently Chair at Hewlett-Packard. Hewlett-Packard came into the news in July of 1999 when Carly Fiorina was appointed chief executive of the firm, becoming only the third woman to head a Fortune 500 company. Platt had major responsibility for transforming what he described as formerly "a white male haven" into a corporate culture that is more welcoming to women. When his wife, Susan, died of cancer, Platt found himself a single parent with two daughters, 9 and 11, to raise. Platt reports that his sudden vulnerability shattered his old assumption that any difficulties women had in the workplace were of their own making. When he became chief executive officer some years later, he played a leadership role in designing women-friendly/family-friendly policies and then actively campaigned for their use. Interestingly, Platt himself admits that the company has been less successful in recruiting and promoting Blacks. And ironically, instead of using her new position to serve as an ally to others, in one of her early public statements Fiorina seemed to bend over backward to deny that there was gender discrimination, or any other kind of unequal treatment, in corporate America. Nonetheless, the role played by Lewis Platt at Hewlett-Packard provides an encouraging example of what can happen when we learn to see the world through each other's eyes and then use our own privilege to redress existing inequities.

Selection 10 introduces C. P . Ellis, business manager of the International Union of Operating Engineers and former president of the Durham, North Carolina, chapter of the Ku Klux Klan. In this interview, conducted by Studs Terkel, we hear firsthand of Ellis's evolution into someone who clearly functions as an ally and agent of social change. In Ellis's case, an awareness of the role that racism plays in perpetuating class privilege seems to have been key to his personal transformation. Working closely on community issues in conjunction with African Americans, and returning to school to study for his high school diploma through a program in which he was one of the only whites, helped to shatter some of the racist stereotypes that Ellis had spent a lifetime learning. Working within the union movement brought him a first-hand awareness of how racism is used to divide poor and working people of all colors and to maintain the privilege of those at the top. Ellis would undoubtably agree with Michael Hout and Samuel Lucas, authors of Selection 11, who believe that narrowing the gap between rich and poor is essential to achieving both social justice and economic health in the United States.

While race in America is a white problem, grievances among communities of color, as we have seen, are a continuing fact of life in contemporary U.S. society. In Selection 12, Eric Yamamoto examines the two colliding impulses within communities of color: on the one hand, the impulse to form interracial alliances in order to respond to the attack on affirmative action and other progressive social policies and, on the other, the impulse to distrust other people of color who are members of a different racial/ethnic group or who are suspected of having different class interests. In this essay, Yamamoto addresses the key question: "How do communities of color heal our racial wounds—not only those inflicted by white America, but also those apparently opened, or rubbed raw, by other racial groups?"

This Part and our study ends with a poem by Aurora Levins Morales, "Child of the Americas," which encourages us to look to the future and helps us envision a new paradigm, one that embraces difference and sees in it the basis for creating a new sense of community.

1

Age, Race, Class, and Sex:
*Women Redefining Difference**

Audre Lorde

Much of Western European history conditions us to see human differences in simplistic opposition to each other: dominant/subordinate, good/bad, up/down, superior/inferior. In a society where the good is defined in terms of profit rather than in terms of human need, there must always be some group of people who, through systematized oppression, can be made to feel surplus, to occupy the place of the dehumanized inferior. Within this society, that group is made up of Black and Third World people, working-class people, older people, and women.

As a forty-nine-year-old Black lesbian feminist socialist mother of two, including one boy, and a member of an interracial couple, I usually find myself a part of some group defined as other, deviant, inferior, or just plain wrong. Traditionally, in american society, it is the members of oppressed, objectified groups who are expected to stretch out and bridge the gap between the actualities of our lives and the consciousness of our oppressor. For in order to survive, those of us for whom oppression is as american as apple pie have always had to be watchers, to become familiar with the language and manners of the oppressor, even sometimes adopting them for some illusion of protection. Whenever the need for some pretense of communication arises, those who profit from our oppression call upon us to share our knowledge with them. In other words, it is the responsibility of the oppressed to teach the oppressors their mistakes. I am responsible for educating teachers who dismiss my children's culture in school. Black and Third World people are expected to educate white people as to our humanity. Women are expected to educate men. Lesbians and gay men are expected to educate the heterosexual world. The oppressors maintain their position and evade responsibility for their own actions. There is a constant drain of energy which might be better used in redefining ourselves and devising realistic scenarios for altering the present and constructing the future.

*Paper delivered at the Copeland Colloquium, Amherst College, April 1980.

Institutionalized rejection of difference is an absolute necessity in a profit economy which needs outsiders as surplus people. As members of such an economy, we have *all* been programmed to respond to the human differences between us with fear and loathing and to handle that difference in one of three ways: ignore it, and if that is not possible, copy it if we think it is dominant, or destroy it if we think it is subordinate. But we have no patterns for relating across our human differences as equals. As a result, those differences have been misnamed and misused in the service of separation and confusion.

Certainly there are very real differences between us of race, age, and sex. But it is not those differences between us that are separating us. It is rather our refusal to recognize those differences, and to examine the distortions which result from our misnaming them and their effects upon human behavior and expectation.

Racism, the belief in the inherent superiority of one race over all others and thereby the right to dominance. Sexism, the belief in the inherent superiority of one sex over the other and thereby the right to dominance. Ageism. Heterosexism. Elitism. Classism.

It is a lifetime pursuit for each one of us to extract these distortions from our living at the same time as we recognize, reclaim, and define those differences upon which they are imposed. For we have all been raised in a society where those distortions were endemic within our living. Too often, we pour the energy needed for recognizing and exploring difference into pretending those differences are insurmountable barriers, or that they do not exist at all. This results in a voluntary isolation, or false and treacherous connections. Either way, we do not develop tools for using human difference as a springboard for creative change within our lives. We speak not of human difference, but of human deviance.

Somewhere, on the edge of consciousness, there is what I call a *mythical norm,* which each one of us within our hearts knows "that is not me." In america, this norm is usually defined as white, thin, male, young, heterosexual, christian, and financially secure. It is with this mythical norm that the trappings of power reside within society. Those of us who stand outside that power often identify one way in which we are different, and we assume that to be the primary cause of all oppression, forgetting other distortions around difference, some of which we ourselves may be practicing. By and large within the women's movement today, white women focus upon their oppression as women and ignore differences of race, sexual preference, class, and age. There is a pretense to a homogeneity of experience covered by the word *sisterhood* that does not in fact exist.

Unacknowledged class differences rob women of each others' energy and creative insight. Recently a women's magazine collective made the decision for one issue to print only prose, saying poetry was a less "rigorous" or "serious" art form. Yet even the form our creativity takes is often a class issue. Of all the art forms, poetry is the most economical. It is the one which is the most secret, which requires the least physical labor, the least material, and the one which can be done between shifts, in the hospital pantry, on the subway, and on scraps of surplus paper. Over the last few years, writing a novel on tight finances, I came to appreciate the enormous differences in the material demands between poetry and prose. As we reclaim our literature, poetry has been the major voice of poor, working class, and Colored women. A room of one's own may be a necessity for writing prose, but so are reams of paper, a typewriter, and plenty of time. The actual requirements to produce the visual arts also help determine, along class lines, whose art is whose. In this day of inflated prices for material, who are our sculptors, our painters, our photographers? When we speak of broadly based women's culture, we need to be aware of the effect of class and economic differences on the supplies available for producing art.

As we move toward creating a society within which we can each flourish, ageism is another distortion of relationship which interferes with our vision. By ignoring the past, we are encouraged to repeat its mistakes. The "generation gap" is an important social tool for any repressive society. If the younger members of a community view the older members as contemptible or suspect or excess, they will never be able to join hands and examine the living memories of the community, nor ask the all important question, "Why?" This gives rise to a historical amnesia that keeps us working to invent the wheel every time we have to go to the store for bread.

We find ourselves having to repeat and relearn the same old lessons over and over that our mothers did because we do not pass on what we have learned, or because we are unable to listen. For instance, how many times has this all been said before? For another, who would have believed that once again our daughters are allowing their bodies to be hampered and purgatoried by girdles and high heels and hobble skirts?

Ignoring the differences of race between women and the implications of those differences presents the most serious threat to the mobilization of women's joint power.

As white women ignore their built-in privilege of whiteness and define woman in terms of their own experience alone, then women of Color become "other," the outsider whose experience and tradition is too "alien" to comprehend. An example of this is the signal absence of the experience of women of Color as a resource for women's studies courses. The literature of women of Color is seldom included in women's literature courses and almost never in other literature courses, nor in women's studies as a whole. All too often, the excuse given is that the literatures of women of Color can only be taught by Colored women, or that they are too difficult to understand, or that classes cannot "get into" them because they come out of experiences that are "too different." I have heard this argument presented by white women of otherwise quite clear intelligence, women who seem to have no trouble at all teaching and reviewing work that comes out of the vastly different experiences of Shakespeare, Molière, Dostoyefsky, and Aristophanes. Surely there must be some other explanation.

This is a very complex question, but I believe one of the reasons white women have such difficulty reading Black women's work is because of their reluctance to see Black women as women and different from themselves. To examine Black women's literature effectively requires that we be seen as whole people in our actual complexities—as individuals, as women, as human—rather than as one of those problematic but familiar stereotypes provided in this society in place of genuine images of Black women. And I believe this holds true for the literatures of other women of Color who are not Black.

The literatures of all women of Color recreate the textures of our lives, and many white women are heavily invested in ignoring the real differences. For as long as any difference between us means one of us must be inferior, then the recognition of any difference must be fraught with guilt. To allow women of Color to step out of stereotypes is too guilt provoking, for it threatens the complacency of those women who view oppression only in terms of sex.

Refusing to recognize difference makes it impossible to see the different problems and pitfalls facing us as women.

Thus, in a patriarchal power system where whiteskin privilege is a major prop, the entrapments used to neutralize Black women and white women are not the same. For example, it is easy for Black women to be used by the power structure against Black men, not because they are men, but because they are Black. Therefore, for Black women, it is necessary at all times to separate the needs of the oppressor from our own legitimate conflicts within our communities. This same problem does not exist for white women. Black women and men have shared racist oppression and still share it, although in different ways. Out of that shared oppression we have developed joint defenses and joint vulnerabilities to each other that are not duplicated in the white community, with the exception of the relationship between Jewish women and Jewish men.

On the other hand, white women face the pitfall of being seduced into joining the oppressor under the pretense of sharing power. This possibility does not exist in the same way for women of Color. The tokenism that is sometimes extended to us is not an invitation to join power; our racial "otherness" is a visible reality that makes that quite clear. For white women there is a wider range of pretended choices and rewards for identifying with patriarchal power and its tools.

Today, with the defeat of ERA, the tightening economy, and increased conservatism, it is easier once again for white women to believe the dangerous fantasy that if you are good enough, pretty enough, sweet enough, quiet enough, teach the children to behave, hate the right people, and marry the right men, then you will be allowed to co-exist with patriarchy in relative peace, at least until a man needs your job or the neighborhood rapist happens along. And true, unless one lives and loves in the trenches it is difficult to remember that the war against dehumanization is ceaseless.

But Black women and our children know the fabric of our lives is stitched with violence and with hatred, that there is no rest. We do not deal with it only on the picket lines, or in dark midnight alleys, or in the places where we dare to verbalize our resistance. For us, increasingly, violence weaves through the daily tissues of our living—in the supermarket, in the classroom, in the elevator, in the clinic and the schoolyard, from the plumber, the baker, the saleswoman, the bus driver, the bank teller, the waitress who does not serve us.

Some problems we share as women, some we do not. You fear your children will grow up to join the patriarchy and testify against you, we fear our children will be dragged from a car and shot down in the street, and you will turn your backs upon the reasons they are dying.

The threat of difference has been no less blinding to people of Color. Those of us who are Black must see that the reality of our lives and our struggle does not make us immune to the errors of ignoring and misnaming difference. Within Black communities where racism is a living reality, differences among us often seem dangerous and suspect. The need for unity is often misnamed as a need for homogeneity, and a Black feminist vision mistaken for betrayal of our common interests as a people. Because of the continuous battle against racial erasure that Black women and Black men share, some Black women still refuse to recognize that we are also oppressed as women, and that sexual hostility against Black women is practiced not only by the white racist society, but implemented within our Black communities as well. It is a disease striking the heart of Black nationhood, and silence will not make it disappear. Exacerbated by racism and the pressures of powerlessness, violence against Black women and children often becomes a standard within our communities, one by which manliness can be measured. But these woman-hating acts are rarely discussed as crimes against Black women.

As a group, women of Color are the lowest paid wage earners in america. We are the primary targets of abortion and sterilization abuse, here and abroad. In certain parts of Africa, small girls are still being sewed shut between their legs to keep them docile and for men's pleasure. This is known as female circumcision, and it is not a cultural affair as the late Jomo Kenyatta insisted, it is a crime against Black women.

Black women's literature is full of the pain of frequent assault, not only by a racist patriarchy, but also by Black men. Yet the necessity for and history of shared battle have made us, Black women, particularly vulnerable to the false accusation that anti-sexist is anti-Black. Meanwhile, womanhating as a recourse of the powerless is sapping strength from Black communities, and our very lives. Rape is on the increase, reported and unreported, and rape is not aggressive sexuality, it is sexualized aggression. As Kalamu ya Salaam, a Black male writer, points out, "As long as male domination exists, rape will exist. Only women revolting and men made conscious of their responsibility to fight sexism can collectively stop rape."[1]

Differences between ourselves as Black women are also being misnamed and used to separate us from one another. As a Black lesbian feminist comfortable with the many different ingredients of my identity, and a woman committed to racial and sexual freedom from oppression, I find I am constantly being encouraged to pluck out some one aspect of myself and present this as the meaningful whole, eclipsing or denying the other parts of self. But this is a destructive and fragmenting way to live. My fullest concentration of energy is available to me only when I integrate all the parts of who I am, openly, allowing power from particular sources of my living to flow back and forth freely through all my different selves, without the restrictions of externally imposed definition. Only then can I bring myself and my energies as a whole to the service of those struggles which I embrace as part of my living.

A fear of lesbians, or of being accused of being a lesbian, has led many Black women into testifying against themselves. It has led some of us into destructive alliances, and others into despair and isolation. In the white women's communities, heterosexism is sometimes a result of identifying with the white patriarchy, a rejection of that interdependence between women-identified women which allows the self to be, rather than to be used in the service of men. Sometimes it reflects a diehard belief in the protective coloration of heterosexual relationships, sometimes a self-hate which all women have to fight against, taught us from birth.

Although elements of these attitudes exist for all women, there are particular resonances of heterosexism and homophobia among Black women. Despite the fact that woman-bonding has a long and honorable history in the African and African-american communities, and despite the knowledge and accomplishments of many strong and creative women-identified Black women in the political, social and cultural fields, heterosexual Black women often tend to ignore or discount the existence and work of Black lesbians. Part of this attitude has come from an understandable terror of Black male attack within the close confines of Black society, where the punishment for any female self-assertion is still to be accused of being a lesbian and therefore unworthy of the attention or support of the scarce Black male. But part of this need to misname and ignore Black lesbians comes from a very real fear that openly women-identified Black women who are no longer dependent upon men for their self-definition may well reorder our whole concept of social relationships.

Black women who once insisted that lesbianism was a white woman's problem now insist that Black lesbians are a threat to Black nationhood, are consorting with the enemy, are basically un-Black. These accusations, coming from the very women to whom we look for deep and real understanding, have served to keep many Black lesbians in hiding, caught between the racism of white women and the homophobia of their sisters. Often, their work has been ignored, trivialized, or misnamed, as with the work of Angelina Grimke, Alice Dunbar-Nelson, Lorraine Hansberry. Yet women-bonded women have always been some part of the power of Black communities, from our unmarried aunts to the amazons of Dahomey.

And it is certainly not Black lesbians who are assaulting women and raping children and grandmothers on the streets of our communities.

Across this country, as in Boston during the spring of 1979 following the unsolved murders of twelve Black women, Black lesbians are spearheading movements against violence against Black women.

What are the particular details within each of our lives that can be scrutinized and altered to help bring about change? How do we redefine difference for all women? It is not our differences which separate women, but our reluctance to recognize those differences and to deal effectively with the distortions which have resulted from the ignoring and misnaming of those differences.

As a tool of social control, women have been encouraged to recognize only one area of human difference as legitimate, those differences which exist between women and men. And we have learned to deal across those differences with the urgency of all oppressed subordinates. All of us have had to learn to live or work or coexist with men, from our fathers on. We have recognized and negotiated these differences, even when this recognition only continued the old dominant/subordinate mode of human relationship, where the oppressed must recognize the masters' difference in order to survive.

But our future survival is predicated upon our ability to relate within equality. As women, we must root our internalized patterns of oppression within ourselves if we are to move beyond the most superficial aspects of social change. Now we must recognize differences among women who are our equals, neither inferior nor superior, and devise ways to use each others' difference to enrich our visions and our joint struggles.

The future of our earth may depend upon the ability of all women to identify and develop new definitions of power and new patterns of relating across difference. The old definitions have not served us, nor the earth that supports us. The old patterns, no matter how cleverly rearranged to imitate progress, still condemn us to cosmetically altered repetitions of the same old exchanges, the same old guilt, hatred, recrimination, lamentation, and suspicion.

For we have, built into all of us, old blueprints of expectation and response, old structures of oppression, and these must be altered at the same time as we alter the living conditions which are a result of those structures. For the master's tools will never dismantle the master's house.

As Paulo Freire shows so well in *The Pedagogy of the Oppressed*,[2] the true focus of revolutionary change is never merely the oppressive situations which we seek to escape, but that piece of the oppressor which is planted deep within each of us, and which knows only the oppressors' tactics, the oppressors' relationships.

Change means growth, and growth can be painful. But we sharpen self-definition by exposing the self in work and struggle together with those whom we define as different from ourselves, although sharing the same goals. For Black and white, old and young, lesbian and heterosexual women alike, this can mean new paths to our survival.

> We have chosen each other
> and the edge of each others battles
> the war is the same
> if we lose
> someday women's blood will congeal
> upon a dead planet
> if we win
> there is no telling
> we seek beyond history
> for a new and more possible meaning.[3]

NOTES

1. From "Rape: A Radical Analysis, An African-American Perspective" by Kalamu ya Salaam in *Black Books Bulletin*, vol. 6, no. 4 (1980).

2. Seabury Press, New York, 1970.

3. From "Outlines," unpublished poem.

2

En rapport, In Opposition:
Cobrando cuentas a las nuestras

Gloria Anzaldúa

Watch for Falling Rocks

The first time I drove from El Paso to San Diego, I saw a sign that read *Watch for Falling Rocks*. And though I watched and waited for rocks to roll down the steep cliff walls and attack my car and me, I never saw any falling rocks. Today, one of the things I'm most afraid of are the rocks we throw at each other. And the resultant guilt we carry like a corpse strapped to our backs for having thrown rocks. We colored women have memories like elephants. The slightest hurt is recorded deep within. We do not forget the injury done to us and we do not forget the injury we have done another. For unfortunately we do not have hides like elephants. Our vulnerability is measured by our capacity for openness, intimacy. And we all know that our own kind is driven through shame or self-hatred to poke at all our open wounds. And we know they know exactly where the hidden wounds are.

> I keep track of all distinctions. Between past and present. Pain and pleasure. Living and surviving. Resistance and capitulation. Will and circumstances. Between life and death. Yes. I am scrupulously accurate. I have become a keeper of accounts.
> —Irena Klepfisz[1]

One of the changes that I've seen since *This Bridge Called My Back* was published[2] is that we no longer allow white women to efface us or suppress us. Now we do it to each other. We have taken over the missionary's "let's civilize the savage role," fixating on the "wrongness" and moral or political inferiority of some of our sisters, insisting on a profound difference between oneself and the *Other*. We have been indoctrinated into adopting the old imperialist ways of conquering and dominating, adopting a way of confrontation based on differences while standing on the ground of ethnic superiority.

In the "dominant" phase of colonialism, European colonizers exercise direct control of the colonized, destroy the native legal and cultural systems, and negate non-European civilizations in order to ruthlessly exploit the resources of the subjugated with the excuse of attempting to "civilize" them. Before the end of this phase, the natives internalize Western culture. By the time we reach the "neocolonialist" phase, we've accepted the white colonizers' system of values, attitudes, morality, and modes of production.[3] It is not by chance that in the more rural towns of Texas Chicano neighborhoods are called *colonias* rather than *barrios*.

There have always been those of us who have "cooperated" with the colonizers. It's not that we have been "won" over by the dominant culture, but that it has exploited pre-existing power relations of subordination and subjugation within our native societies.[4] The great White ripoff and they are still cashing in. Like our exploiters who fixate on the inferiority of the natives, we fixate on the fucked-upness of our sisters. Like them we try to impose our version of "the ways things should be"; we try to impose one's self on the *Other* by making her the recipient of one's negative elements, usually the same elements that the Anglo projected on us. Like them, we project our self-hatred on her; we stereotype her, we make her generic.

Just How Ethnic Are You?

One of the reasons for this hostility among us is the forced cultural penetration, the rape of the colored by the white, with the colonizers depositing their perspective, their language, their values in our bodies. External oppression is paralleled with our internalization of that oppression. And our acting out from that oppression. They have us doing to those within our own ranks what they have done and continue to do to us—*Othering* people. That is, isolating them, pushing them out of the herd, ostracizing them. The internalization of negative images of ourselves, our self-hatred, poor self-esteem, makes our own people the *Other*. We shun the white-looking Indian, the "high yellow" Black woman, the Asian with the white lover, the Native woman who brings her white girl friend to the Pow Wow, the Chicana who doesn't speak Spanish, the academic, the uneducated. Her difference makes her a person we can't trust. *Para que sea "legal,"* she must pass the ethnic legitimacy test we have devised. And it is exactly our internalized whiteness that desperately wants boundary lines (this part of me is Mexican, this Indian) marked out and woe to any sister or any part of us that steps out of our assigned places, woe to anyone who doesn't measure up to our standards of ethnicity. *Si no cualifica,* if she fails to pass the test, *le aventamos mierda en la cara, le aventamos piedras, la aventamos.* We throw shit in her face, we throw rocks, we kick her out. *Como gallos de pelea nos atacamos unas a las otras—mexicanas de nacimiento contra* the born-again *mexicanas.* Like fighting cocks, razor blades strapped to our fingers, we slash out at each other. We have turned our anger against ourselves. And our anger is immense. *Es un acido que corroe.*

Internal Affairs *o las que niegan a su gente*

> *Tu traición yo la llevo aquá muy dentro,*
> *la llevo dentro de mi alma*
> *dentro de mi corazón.*
> *Tu traición.*
> > —Cornelio Reyna[5]

I get so tired of constantly struggling with my sisters. The more we have in common, including love, the greater the heartache between us, the more we hurt each other. It's excruciatingly painful, this constant snarling at our own shadows. Anything can set the conflict in motion: the lover getting more recognition by the community, the friend getting a job with higher status, a break-up. As one of my friends said, "We can't fucking get along."

So we find ourselves *entreguerras,*[6] a kind of civil war among intimates, an in-class, in-race, in-house fighting, a war with strategies, tactics that are our coping mechanisms, that once were our survival skills and which we now use upon one another,[7] producing intimate terrorism—a modern form of *las guerras floridas,* the war of flowers that the Aztecs practiced in order to gain captives for the sacrifices. Only now we are each other's victims, we offer the *Other* to our politically correct altar.

El deniego. The hate we once cast at our oppressors we now fling at women of our own race. Reactionary—we have gone to the other extreme—denial of our own. We struggle for power, compete, vie for control. Like kin, we are there for each other, but like kin we come to blows. And the differences between us and this new *Other* are not racial but ideological, not metaphysical but psychological. *Nos negamos a si mismas y el deniego nos causa daño.*

Breaking Out of the Frame

> I'm standing at the sea end of the truncated Berkeley pier. A boat had plowed into the black posts gouging out a few hundred feet of structure, cutting the pier in two. I stare at the sea, surging silver-plated, between me and the loped-off corrugated arm, the wind whipping my hair. I look down, my head and shoulders, a shadow on the sea. Yemaya pours strings of light over my dull jade, flickering body, bubbles

pop out of my ears. I feel the tension easing and, for the first time in months, the litany of work yet to do, of deadlines, that sings incessantly in my head, blows away with the wind.

Oh, Yemaya, I shall speak the words
     you lap against the pier.

But as I turn away I see in the distance a ship's fin fast approaching. I see fish heads lying listless in the sun, smell the stench of pollution in the waters.

From where I stand, *queridas carnalas*—in a feminist position—I see, through a critical lens with variable focus, that we must not drain our energy breaking down the male/white frame (the whole of Western culture) but turn to our own kind and change our terms of reference. As long as we see the world and our experiences through white eyes—in a dominant/subordinate way—we're trapped in the tar and pitch of the old manipulative and strive-for-power ways.

Even those of us who don't want to buy in get sucked into the vortex of the dominant culture's fixed oppositions, the duality of superiority and inferiority, of subject and object. Some of us, to get out of the internalized neocolonial phase, make for the fringes, the Borderlands. And though we have not broken out of the white frame, we at least see it for what it is. Questioning the values of the dominant culture which imposes fundamental difference on those of the "wrong" side of the good/bad dichotomy is the first step. Responding to the *Other* not as irrevocably different is the second step. By highlighting similarities, downplaying divergences, that is, by *rapprochement* between self and *Other* it is possible to build a syncretic relationship. At the basis of such a relationship lies an understanding of the effects of colonization and its resultant pathologies.

We have our work cut out for us. Nothing is more difficult than identifying emotionally with a cultural alterity, with the *Other*. *Alter*: to make different; to castrate. *Altercate*: to dispute angrily. *Alter ego*: another self or another aspect of oneself. *Alter idem*: another of the same kind. Nothing is harder than identifying with an interracial identity, with a mestizo identity. One has to leave the permanent boundaries of a fixed self, literally "leave" oneself and see oneself through the eyes of the *Other*. Cultural identity is "nothing more nor less than the mean between selfhood and otherness. . . ."[8] Nothing scares the Chicana more than a quasi Chicana; nothing disturbs a Mexican more than an acculturated Chicana; nothing agitates a Chicana more than a Latina who lumps her with the *norteamericanas*. It is easier to retreat to the safety of difference behind racial, cultural and class borders. Because our awareness of the *Other* as object often swamps our awareness of ourselves as subject, it is hard to maintain a fine balance between cultural ethnicity and the continuing survival of that culture, between traditional culture and an evolving hybrid culture. How much must remain the same, how much must change.

For most of us our ethnicity is still the issue. Ours continues to be a struggle of identity—not against a white background so much as against a colored background. *Ya no estamos afuera o atras del marco de la pintura*—we no longer stand outside nor behind the frame of the painting. We are both the foreground, the background and the figures predominating. Whites are not the central figure, they are not even in the frame, though the frame of reference is still white, male and heterosexual. But the white is still there, invisible, under our skin—we have subsumed the white.

El desengaño/Disillusionment

And yes I have some criticism, some self-criticism. And no I will not make everything nice. There is shit among us we need to sift through. Who knows, there may be some fertilizer in it. I've seen collaborative efforts between us end in verbal abuse, cruelty and trauma. I've seen collectives fall apart, dumping their ideals by the wayside and treating each other worse than they'd treat a rabid dog. My momma said, "Never tell other people our business, never divulge family secrets." Chicano dirt you do not air out in front of white folks, nor lesbian dirty laundry in front of heterosexuals. The cultural things stay with la Raza. Colored feminists must present a united front in front of whites and other groups. But the fact is we are not united. (I've come to suspect that unity is another Anglo invention like their one sole god and the myth of the monopole.⁹) We are not going to cut through *la mierda* by sweeping the dirt under the rug.

We have a responsibility to each other, certain commitments. The leap into self-affirmation goes hand in hand with being critical of self. Many of us walk around with reactionary, self-righteous attitudes. We preach certain political behaviors and theories and we do fine with writing about them. Though we want others to live their lives by them, we do not live them. When we are called on it, we go into a self-defensive mode and denial just like whites did when we started asking them to be accountable for their race and class biases.

Las opuestas/Those in Opposition

In us, intra- and cross-cultural hostilities surface in not so subtle put-downs. *Las no comprometidas, las que negan a sus gente. Fruncemos las caras y negamos toda responsabilidad.* Where some of us racially mixed people are stuck in now is denial and its damaging effects. Denial of the white aspects that we've been forced to acquire, denial of our sisters who for one reason or another cannot "pass" as 100% ethnic—as if such a thing exists. Racial purity, like language purity, is a fallacy. Denying the reality of who we are destroys the basis needed from which to talk honestly and deeply about the issues between us. We cannot make any real connections because we are not touching each other. So we sit facing each other and before the words escape our mouths the real issues are blanked in our consciousness, erased before they register because it hurts too much to talk about them, because it makes us vulnerable to the hurt the *carnala* may dish out, because we've been wounded too deeply and too often in the past. So we sit, a paper face before another paper face—two people who suddenly cease to be real. *La no compasiva con la complaciente, lo incomunicado atorado en sus gargantas.*

We, the new Inquisitors, swept along with the "swing to the right" of the growing religious and political intolerance, crusade against racial heretics, mow down with the sickle of righteous anger our dissenting sisters. The issue (in all aspects of life) has always been when to resist changes and when to be open to them. Right now, this rigidity will break us.

Recobrando/Recovering

Una luz fria y cenicienta bañada en la plata palida del amanecer entra a mi escritorio and I think about the critical stages we feminists of color are going through, chiefly that of learning to live with each other as *carnalas, parientes, amantes,* as kin, as friends, as lovers. Looking back on the road that we've walked on during the last decade, I see many emotional, psychological, spiritual, political gains—primarily developing an understanding and acceptance of the spirituality of our root ethnic cultures. This has given us the ground from which to see that our spiritual lives are not split from our daily acts. *En recobrando* our affinity with nature and her forces (deities), we have "recovered" our ancient identity, digging it out like dark clay, pressing it to our current identity, molding past and present, inner and outer. Our clay-streaked faces acquiring again images of our ethnic self and self-respect taken from us by the *colonizadores.* And if we've suffered losses, if often in the process we have momentarily "misplaced" our *carnala*hood, our sisterhood, there beside us always are the women, *las mujeres.* And that is enough to keep us going.

By grounding in the earth of our native spiritual identity, we can build up our personal and tribal identity. We can reach out for the clarity we need. Burning sage and sweetgrass by itself won't cut it, but it can be a basis from which we act.

And yes, we are elephants with long memories, but scrutinizing the past with binocular vision and training it on the juncture of past with present, and identifying the options on hand and mapping out future roads, will ensure us survival.

So if we won't forget past grievances, let us forgive. Carrying the ghosts of past grievances *no vale la pena.* It is not worth the grief. It keeps us from ourselves and each other; it keeps us from new relationships. We need to cultivate other ways of coping. I'd like to think that the in-fighting that we presently find ourselves doing is only a stage in the continuum of our growth, an offshoot of the conflict that the process of biculturation spawns, a phase of the internal colonization process, one that will soon cease to hold sway over our lives. I'd like to see it as a skin we will shed as we are born into the 21st century.

And now in these times of the turning of the century, of harmonic conversion, of the end of *El Quinto Sol* (as the ancient Aztecs named our present age), it is time we began to get out of the state of opposition and into *rapprochement,* time to get our heads, words, ways out of white territory. It is time that we broke out of the invisible white frame and stood on the ground of our own ethnic being.

NOTES

1. Irena Klepfisz, *Keeper of Accounts* (Montpelier, VT: Sinister Wisdom, 1982), 85.

2. According to Chela Sandoval, the publication of *Bridge* marked the end of the second wave of the women's movement in its previous form. *U.S. Third World Feminist Criticism: The Theory and Method of Oppositional Consciousness*, a dissertation in process.

3. Abdul R. JanMohamed, "The Economy of Manichean Allegory: The Function of Racial Difference in Colonialist Literature," *"Race," Writing, and Difference*, ed. Henry Louis Gates, Jr. (Chicago: University of Chicago Press, 1985), 80–81.

4. JanMohamed, 81.

5. A Chicano from Texas who sings and plays *bajo-sexto* in his *música norteña/conjunto*. *"Tu Traición"* is from the album *15 Exitasos*, Reyna Records, 1981.

6. *Entreguerras, entremundos/Inner Wars Among the Worlds* is the title of a forthcoming book of narratives/novel.

7. Sarah Hoaglund, "Lesbian Ethics: Intimacy & Self-Understanding," *Bay Area Women's News*, May/June 1987, vol. 1, no. 2, 7.

8. Nadine Gordimer is quoted in JanMohamed's essay, 88.

9. Physicists are searching for a single law of physics under which all other laws will fall.

3

Feminism:
A Transformational Politic

bell hooks

We live in a world in crisis—a world governed by politics of domination, one in which the belief in a notion of superior and inferior, and its concomitant ideology—that the superior should rule over the inferior—affects the lives of all people everywhere, whether poor or privileged, literate or illiterate. Systematic dehumanization, worldwide famine, ecological devastation, industrial contamination, and the possibility of nuclear destruction are realities which remind us daily that we are in crisis. Contemporary feminist thinkers often cite sexual politics as the origin of this crisis. They point to the insistence on difference as that factor which becomes the occasion for separation and domination and suggest that differentiation of status between females and males globally is an indication that patriarchal domination of the planet is the root of the problem. Such an assumption has fostered the notion that elimination of sexist oppression would necessarily lead to the eradication of all forms of domination. It is an argument that has led influential Western white women to feel that feminist movement should be *the* central political agenda for females globally. Ideologically, thinking in this direction enables Western women, especially privileged white women, to suggest that racism and class exploitation are merely the offspring of the parent system: patriarchy. Within feminist movement in the West, this has led to the assumption that resisting patriarchal domination is a more legitimate feminist action than resisting racism and other forms of domination. Such thinking prevails despite radical critiques made by black women and other women of color who question this proposition. To speculate that an oppositional division between men and women existed in early human communities is to impose on the past, on these non-white groups, a world view that fits all too neatly within contemporary feminist paradigms that name man as the enemy and woman as the victim.

Clearly, differentiation between strong and weak, powerful and powerless, has been a central defining aspect of gender globally, carrying with it the assumption that men should have greater authority than women, and should rule over them. As significant and important as this fact is, it should not obscure the reality that women can and do participate in politics of domination, as perpetrators as well as victims—that we dominate, that we are dominated. If focus on patriarchal domination masks this reality or becomes the means by which women deflect attention from the real conditions and circumstances of our lives, then women cooperate in suppressing and promoting false consciousness, inhibiting our capacity to assume responsibility for transforming ourselves and society.

Thinking speculatively about early human social arrangement, about women and men struggling to survive in small communities, it is likely that the parent-child relationship with its very real imposed survival structure of dependency, of strong and weak, of powerful and powerless, was a site for the construction of a paradigm of domination. While this circumstance of dependency is not necessarily one that leads to domination, it lends itself to the enactment of a social drama wherein domination could easily occur as a means of exercising and maintaining control. This speculation does not place women outside the practice of domination, in the exclusive role of victim. It centrally names women as agents of domination, as potential theoreticians, and creators of a paradigm for social relationships wherein those groups of individuals designated as "strong" exercise power both benevolently and coercively over those designated as "weak."

Emphasizing paradigms of domination that call attention to woman's capacity to dominate is one way to deconstruct and challenge the simplistic notion that man is the enemy, woman the victim; the notion that men have always been the oppressors. Such thinking enables us to examine our role as women in the perpetuation and maintenance of systems of domination. To understand domination, we must understand that our capacity as women and men to be either dominated or dominating is a point of connection, of commonality. Even though I speak from the particular experience of living as a black woman in the United States, a white-supremacist, capitalist, patriarchal society, where small numbers of white men (and honorary "white men") constitute ruling groups, I understand that in many places in the world oppressed and oppressor share the same color. I understand that right here in this room, oppressed and oppressor share the same gender. Right now as I speak, a man who is himself victimized, wounded, hurt by racism and class exploitation is actively dominating a woman in his life—that even as I speak, women who are ourselves exploited, victimized, are dominating children. It is necessary for us to remember, as we think critically about domination, that we all have the capacity to act in ways that oppress, dominate, wound (whether or not that power is institutionalized). It is necessary to remember that it is first the potential oppressor within that we must resist—the potential victim within that we must rescue—otherwise we cannot hope for an end to domination, for liberation.

This knowledge seems especially important at this historical moment when black women and other women of color have worked to create awareness of the ways in which racism empowers white women to act as exploiters and oppressors. Increasingly this fact is considered a reason we should not support feminist struggle even though sexism and sexist oppression is a real issue in our lives as black women (see, for example, Vivian Gordon's *Black Women, Feminism, Black Liberation: Which Way?*). It becomes necessary for us to speak continually about the convictions that inform our continued advocacy of feminist struggle. By calling attention to interlocking systems of domination—sex, race, and class—black women and many other groups of women acknowledge the diversity and complexity of female experience, of our relationship to power and domination. The intent is not to dissuade people of color from becoming engaged in feminist movement. Feminist struggle to end patriarchal domination should be of primary importance to women and men globally not because it is the foundation of all other oppressive structures but because it is that form of domination we are most likely to encounter in an ongoing way in everyday life.

Unlike other forms of domination, sexism directly shapes and determines relations of power in our private lives, in familiar social spaces, in that most intimate context—home—and in that most intimate sphere of relations—family. Usually, it is within the family that we witness coercive domination and learn to accept it, whether it be domination of parent over child, or male over female. Even though family relations may be, and most often are, informed by acceptance of a politic of domination, they are simultaneously relations of care and connection. It is this convergence of two contradictory impulses—the urge to promote growth and the urge to inhibit growth—that provides a practical setting for feminist critique, resistance, and transformation.

Growing up in a black, working-class, father-dominated household, I experienced coercive adult male authority as more immediately threatening, as more likely to cause immediate pain than racist oppression or class exploitation. It was equally clear that experiencing exploitation and oppression in the home made one feel all the more powerless when encountering dominating forces outside the home. This is true for many people. If we are unable to resist and end domination in relations where there is care, it seems totally unimaginable that we can resist and end it in other institutionalized relations of power. If we cannot convince the mothers and/or fathers who care not to humiliate and degrade us, how can we imagine convincing or resisting an employer, a lover, a stranger who systematically humiliates and degrades?

Feminist effort to end patriarchal domination should be of primary concern precisely because it insists on the eradication of exploitation and oppression in the family context and in all other intimate relationships. It is that political movement which most radically addresses the person—the personal—citing the need for transformation of self, of relationships, so that we might be better able to act in a revolutionary manner, challenging and resisting domination, transforming the world outside the self. Strategically, feminist movement should be a central component of all other liberation struggles because it challenges each of us to alter our person, our personal engagement (either as victims or perpetrators or both) in a system of domination.

Feminism, as liberation struggle, must exist apart from and as a part of the larger struggle to eradicate domination in all its forms. We must understand that patriarchal domination shares an ideological foundation with racism and other forms of group oppression, that there is no hope that it can be eradicated while these systems remain intact. This knowledge should consistently inform the direction of feminist theory and practice. Unfortunately, racism and class elitism among women has frequently led to the suppression and distortion of this connection so that it is now necessary for feminist thinkers to critique and revise much feminist theory and the direction of feminist movement. This effort at revision is perhaps most evident in the current widespread acknowledgement that sexism, racism, and class exploitation constitute interlocking systems of domination—that sex, race, and class, and not sex alone, determine the nature of any female's identity, status, and circumstance, the degree to which she will or will not be dominated, the extent to which she will have the power to dominate.

While acknowledgement of the complex nature of woman's status (which has been most impressed upon everyone's consciousness by radical women of color) is a significant corrective, it is only a starting point. It provides a frame of reference which must serve as the basis for thoroughly altering and revising feminist theory and practice. It challenges and calls us to re-think popular assumptions about the nature of feminism that have had the deepest impact on a large majority of women, on mass consciousness. It radically calls into question the notion of a fundamentally common female experience which has been seen as the prerequisite for our coming together, for political unity. Recognition of the inter-connectedness of sex, race, and class highlights the diversity of experience, compelling redefinition of the terms for unity. If women do not share "common oppression," what then can serve as a basis for our coming together?

Unlike many feminist comrades, I believe women and men must share a common understanding—a basic knowledge of what feminism is—if it is ever to be a powerful mass-based political movement. In *Feminist Theory: from margin to cen-*

ter, I suggest that defining feminism broadly as "a movement to end sexism and sexist oppression" would enable us to have a common political goal. We would then have a basis on which to build solidarity. Multiple and contradictory definitions of feminism create confusion and undermine the effort to construct feminist movement so that it addresses everyone. Sharing a common goal does not imply that women and men will not have radically divergent perspectives on how that goal might be reached. Because each individual starts the process of engagement in feminist struggle at a unique level of awareness, very real differences in experience, perspective, and knowledge make developing varied strategies for participation and transformation a necessary agenda.

Feminist thinkers engaged in radically revisioning central tenets of feminist thought must continually emphasize the importance of sex, race, and class as factors which *together* determine the social construction of femaleness, as it has been so deeply ingrained in the consciousness of many women active in feminist movement that gender is the sole factor determining destiny. However, the work of education for critical consciousness (usually called consciousness-raising) cannot end there. Much feminist consciousness-raising has in the past focussed on identifying the particular ways men oppress and exploit women. Using the paradigm of sex, race, and class means that the focus does not begin with men and what they do to women, but rather with women working to identify both individually and collectively the specific character of our social identity.

Imagine a group of women from diverse backgrounds coming together to talk about feminism. First they concentrate on working out their status in terms of sex, race, and class using this as the standpoint from which they begin discussing patriarchy or their particular relations with individual men. Within the old frame of reference, a discussion might consist solely of talk about their experiences as victims in relationship to male oppressors. Two women—one poor, the other quite wealthy—might describe the process by which they have suffered physical abuse by male partners and find certain commonalities which might serve as a basis for bonding. Yet if these same two women engaged in a discussion of class, not only would the social construction and expression of femaleness differ, so too would their ideas about how to confront and change their circumstances. Broadening the discussion to include an analysis of race and class would expose many additional differences even as commonalities emerged.

Clearly the process of bonding would be more complex, yet this broader discussion might enable the sharing of perspectives and strategies for change that would enrich rather than diminish our understanding of gender. While feminists have increasingly given "lip service" to the idea of diversity, we have not developed strategies of communication and inclusion that allow for the successful enactment of this feminist vision.

Small groups are no longer the central place for feminist consciousness-raising. Much feminist education for critical consciousness takes place in Women's Studies classes or at conferences which focus on gender. Books are a primary source of education, which means that already masses of people who do not read have no access. The separation of grassroots ways of sharing feminist thinking across kitchen tables from the spheres where much of that thinking is generated, the academy, undermines feminist movement. It would further feminist movement if new feminist thinking could be once again shared in small group contexts, integrating critical analysis with discussion of personal experience. It would be useful to promote anew the small group setting as an arena for education for critical consciousness, so that women and men might come together in neighborhoods and communities to discuss feminist concerns.

Small groups remain an important place for education for critical consciousness for several reasons. An especially important aspect of the small group setting is the emphasis on communicating feminist thinking, feminist theory, in a manner that can be easily understood. In small groups, individuals do not need to be equally literate or literate at all because the information is primarily shared through conversation, in dialogue which is necessarily a liberatory expression. (Literacy should be a goal for feminists even as we ensure that it not become a requirement for participation in feminist education.) Reforming small groups would subvert the appropriation of feminist thinking by a select group of academic women and men, usually white, usually from privileged class backgrounds.

Small groups of people coming together to engage in feminist discussion, in dialectical struggle make a space where the "personal is political" as a starting point for education for critical consciousness can be extended to include politicization of the self that focusses on creating understanding of the ways sex, race, and class together determine our individual lot and our collective experience. It would further feminist movement if many well known feminist thinkers would participate in small groups, critically re-examining ways their works might be changed by incorporating broader perspectives. All efforts at self-transformation challenge us to engage in ongoing, critical self-examination and reflection about feminist practice, about how we live in the world. This individual commitment, when coupled with engagement in collective discussion, provides a space for critical feedback which strengthens our efforts to change and make ourselves new. It is in this commitment to feminist principles in our words and deeds that the hope of feminist revolution lies.

Working collectively to confront difference, to expand our awareness of sex, race, and class as interlocking systems of domination, of the ways we reinforce and perpetuate these structures, is the context in which we learn the true meaning of solidarity. It is this work that must be the foundation of feminist movement. Without it, we cannot effectively resist patriarchal domination; without it, we remain estranged and alienated from one another. Fear of painful confrontation often leads women and men active in feminist movement to avoid rigorous critical encounter, yet if we cannot engage dialectically in a committed, rigorous, humanizing manner, we cannot hope to change the world. True politicization—coming to critical consciousness—is a difficult, "trying" process, one that demands that we give up set ways of thinking and being, that we shift our paradigms, that we open ourselves to the unknown, the unfamiliar. Undergoing this process, we learn what it means to struggle and in this effort we experience the dignity and integrity of being that comes with revolutionary change. If we do not change our consciousness, we cannot change our actions or demand change from others.

Our renewed commitment to a rigorous process of education for critical consciousness will determine the shape and direction of future feminist movement. Until new perspectives are created, we cannot be living symbols of the power of feminist thinking. Given the privileged lot of many leading feminist thinkers, both in terms of status, class, and race, it is harder these days to convince women of the primacy of this process of politicization. More and more, we seem to form select interest groups composed of individuals who share similar perspectives. This limits our capacity to engage in critical discussion. It is difficult to involve women in new processes of feminist politicization because so many of us think that identifying men as the enemy, resisting male domination, gaining equal access to power and privilege is the end of feminist movement. Not only is it not the end, it is not even the place we want revitalized feminist movement to begin. We want to begin as women seriously addressing ourselves, not solely in relation to men, but in relation to an entire structure of domination of which patriarchy is one part. While the struggle to eradicate sexism and sexist oppression is and should be the primary thrust of feminist movement, to prepare ourselves politically for this effort we must first learn how to be in solidarity, how to struggle with one another.

Only when we confront the realities of sex, race, and class, the ways they divide us, make us different, stand us in opposition, and work to reconcile and resolve these issues will we be able to participate in the making of feminist revolution, in the transformation of the world. Feminism, as Charlotte Bunch emphasizes again and again in *Passionate Politics*, is a transformational politics, a struggle against domination wherein the effort is to change ourselves as well as structures. Speaking about the struggle to confront difference, Bunch asserts:

> A crucial point of the process is understanding that reality does not look the same from different people's perspective. It is not surprising that one way feminists have come to understand about differences has been through the love of a person from another culture or race. It takes persistence and motivation—which love often engenders—to get beyond one's ethnocentric assumptions and really learn about other perspectives. In this process and while seeking to eliminate oppression, we also discover new possibilities and insights that come from the experience and survival of other peoples.

Embedded in the commitment to feminist revolution is the challenge to love. Love can be and is an important source of empowerment when we struggle to confront issues of sex, race, and class. Working together to identify and face our differences—to face the ways we dominate and are dominated—to change our actions, we need a mediating force that can sustain us so that we are not broken in this process, so that we do not despair.

Not enough feminist work has focussed on documenting and sharing ways individuals confront differences constructively and successfully. Women and men need to know what is on the other side of the pain experienced in politicization.

We need detailed accounts of the ways our lives are fuller and richer as we change and grow politically, as we learn to live each moment as committed feminists, as comrades working to end domination. In reconceptualizing and reformulating strategies for future feminist movement, we need to concentrate on the politicization of love, not just in the context of talking about victimization in intimate relationships, but in a critical discussion where love can be understood as a powerful force that challenges and resists domination. As we work to be loving, to create a culture that celebrates life, that makes love possible, we move against dehumanization, against domination. In *Pedagogy of the Oppressed*, Paulo Freire evokes this power of love, declaring:

> I am more and more convinced that true revolutionaries must perceive the revolution, because of its creative and liberating nature, as an act of love. For me, the revolution, which is not possible without a theory of revolution—and therefore science—is not irreconcilable with love . . . The distortion imposed on the word "love" by the capitalist world cannot prevent the revolution from being essentially loving in character, nor can it prevent the revolutionaries from affirming their love of life.

That aspect of feminist revolution that calls women to love womanness, that calls men to resist dehumanizing concepts of masculinity, is an essential part of our struggle. It is the process by which we move from seeing ourselves as objects to acting as subjects. When women and men understand that working to eradicate patriarchal domination is a struggle rooted in the longing to make a world where everyone can live fully and freely, then we know our work to be a gesture of love. Let us draw upon that love to heighten our awareness, deepen our compassion, intensify our courage, and strengthen our commitment.

4

Interrupting the Cycle of Oppression:

The Role of Allies as Agents of Change

Andrea Ayvazian

Many of us feel overwhelmed when we consider the many forms of systemic oppression that are so pervasive in American society today. We become immobilized, uncertain about what actions we can take to interrupt the cycles of oppression and violence that intrude on our everyday lives. One way to overcome this sense of immobilization is to assume the role of an ally. Learning about this role—one that each and every one of us is capable of assuming—can offer us new ways of behaving and a new source of hope.

Through the years, experience has taught us that isolated and episodic actions—even dramatic, media-grabbing events—rarely produce more than a temporary blip on the screen. What does seem to create real and lasting change is highly-motivated individuals—usually only a handful at first—who are so clear and consistent on an issue that they serve as a heartbeat in a community, steadily sending out waves that touch and change those in their path. These change agents or allies have such a powerful impact because their actions embody the values they profess: their behavior and beliefs are congruent.

What Is an Ally?

An ally is a member of a dominant group in our society who works to dismantle any form of oppression from which she or he receives the benefit. Allied behavior means taking personal responsibility for the changes we know are needed in our society, and so often ignore or leave to others to deal with. Allied behavior is intentional, overt, consistent activity that challenges prevailing patterns of oppression, makes privileges that are so often invisible visible, and facilitates the empowerment of persons targeted by oppression.

From *Fellowship* (January–February 1995), pp. 7–10.

I use the term"oppresion" to describe the combination of prejudice plus access to social, political, and economic power on the part of a dominant group. Racism, a core component of oppression, has been defined by David Wellman as a system of advantage based on race. Wellman's definition can be altered slightly to describe every other form of oppression. Hence we can say that sexism is a system of advantage based on gender, that heterosexism is a system of advantge based on sexual orientation, and so on. In each form of oppression there is a dominant group—the one that receives the unearned advantage, benefit, or privilege—and a targeted group—the one that is denied that advantage, benefit, or privilege. We know the litany of dominants: white people, males, Christians, heterosexuals, able-bodied people, those in their middle years, and those who are middle or upper class.

We also know that everyone has multiple social identities. We are all dominant and targeted simultaneously. I, for instance, am simultaneously dominant as a white person and targeted as a woman. A white able-bodied man may be dominant in those categories, but targeted as a Jew or Muslim or as a gay person. Some people are, at some point in their lives, entirely dominant; but if they are, they won't be forever. Even a white, able-bodied, heterosexual, Christian male will literally grow out of his total dominance if he reaches old age.

When we consider the different manifestations of systematic oppression and find ourselves in any of the categories where we are dominant—and therefore receive the unearned advantages that accrue to that position of advantage—we have the potential to be remarkably powerful agents of change as allies. Allies are whites who identify as anti-racists, men who work to dismantle sexism, able-bodied people who are active in the disability rights movement, Christians who combat anti-Semitism and other forms of religious prejudice. Allied behavior usually involves talking to other dominants about their behavior: whites confronting other whites on issues of racism, men organizing with other men to combat sexism, and so on. Allied behavior is clear action aimed at dismantling the oppression of others in areas where you yourself benefit—it is proactive, intentional, and often involves taking a risk.

To tether these principles to everyday reality, just think of the group Parents, Families and Friends of Lesbians and Gays (PFLAG) as the perfect example of allied behavior. PFLAG is an organization of (mainly) heterosexuals who organize support groups and engage in advocacy and education among other heterosexuals around issues of gay and lesbian liberation. PFLAG speakers can be heard in houses of worship, schools, and civic organizations discussing their own commitment to securing gay and lesbian civil rights. Because they are heterosexuals speaking (usually) to other heterosexuals, they often have a significant impact.

The anti-racism trainer Kenneth Jones, an African-American, refers to allied behavior as "being at my back." He has said to me, "Andrea, I know you are at my back on the issue of race equity—you're talking to white people who cannot hear me on this topic, you're out there raising these issues repeatedly, you're organizing with other whites to stand up to racism. And I'm at your back. I'm raising issues of gender equity with men, I am talking to men who cannot hear you, I've made a commitment to combat sexism."

Available to each one of us in the categories where we are dominant is the proud and honorable role of ally: the opportunity to raise hell with others like us and to interrupt the cycle of oppression. Because of our very privilege, we have the potential to stir up good trouble, to challenge the status quo, and to inspire real and lasting change. William Stickland, an aide to Jesse Jackson, once said: "When a critical mass of white people join together, rise up, and shout a thunderous 'No' to racism, we will actually alter the course of history."

Reducing Violence

When I ponder the tremendous change a national network of allies can make in this country, I think not only of issues of equity and empowerment, but also of how our work could lead to diminishing levels of violence in our society. Let us consider for a moment the critical connection between oppression and violence on one hand, and the potential role of allied behavior in combating violence on the other.

A major source of violence in our society is the persistent inequity between dominant and targeted groups. Recall that oppression is kept in place by two factors:

1. Ideology, or the propagation of doctrines that purport to legitimize inequality; and
2. Violence (or the threat of violence) by the dominant group against the targeted group.

The violence associated with each form of systemic oppression noticeably decreases when allies (or dominants) rise up and shout a thunderous "No" to the perpetuation of these inequities. Because members of the dominant group are conferred with considerable social power and privilege, they carry significant authority when confronting perpetrators of violence in their own group—when whites deter other whites from using violence against people of color, when heterosexuals act to prevent gay bashing, and so on.

Research studies have confirmed what observers and allies have been saying for years: that when a woman is the victim of ongoing, violent domestic abuse, it makes no difference to her chances of survival if she has counseling, takes out a restraining order, or learns to fight back. According to the studies, the only factor that statistically increases a woman's chances of survival is if the victimizer himself is exposed to direct and ongoing anti-battering intervention.

These studies have inspired the creation of model mentoring programs in places like Quincy, Massachusetts, Duluth, Minnesota, and New York City—programs in which men prone to violence against women work with other men through a series of organized interventions. The success of these programs has demonstrated that it is actually possible to interrupt and stop the cycle of violence among batterers. In 1992, for instance, the model program in Quincy helped cut the incidence of domestic homicide to zero. The Batterers Anonymous groups, in which men who are former perpetrators work with men who are current batterers, have also had remarkable success in breaking the habit of violence. These groups are allied behavior made manifest; their success in reducing the incidence of violence against women is now statistically proven.

In our society, oppression and violence are woven together: one leads to the other, one justifies the other. Furthermore, members of the dominant group who are not perpetrators of violence often collude, through their silence and inactivity, with those who are. Allied behavior is an effective way of interrupting the cycle of violence by breaking the silence that reinforces the cycle, and by promoting a new set of behavior through modeling and mentoring.

Providing Positive Role Models

Not only does allied behavior contribute to an increase in equity and a decrease in violence, but allies provide positive role models that are sorely needed by today's young people. The role of ally offers young people who are white, male, and in other dominant categories a positive, proactive, and proud identity. Rather than feeling guilty, shameful, and immobilized as the "oppressor," whites and other dominants can assume the important and useful role of social change agent. There have been proud allies and change agents throughout the history of this nation, and there are many alive today who can inspire us with their important work.

I often speak in high school classes and assemblies, and in recent years I have taken to doing a little informal survey from the podium. I ask the students if they can name a famous living white racist. Can they? Yes. They often name David Duke—he ran for President in their lifetime—or they sometimes name Senator Jesse Helms; and when I was in the midwest, they named Marge Schott, the owner of the Cincinnati Reds. It does not take long before a hand shoots up, or someone just calls out one of those names.

Following that little exercise, I ask the students, "Can you name a famous living white anti-racist (or civil rights worker, or someone who fights racism)?" Can they? Not very often. Sometimes there is a whisper or two, but generally the room is very quiet. So, recently, I have been saying: forget the famous part. Just name for me any white person you know in your community, or someone you have heard of, who has taken a stand against racism. Can they? Sometimes. Occasionally someone says "my mom," or "my dad." I have also heard "my rabbi, my teacher, my minister." But not often enough.

I believe that it is difficult for young people to grow up and become something they have never heard of. It is hard for a girl to grow up and become a commercial airline pilot if it has never occurred to her that woman can and do fly jet planes.

Similarly, it is hard for young people to grow up and fight racism if they have never met anyone who does.

And there *are* many remarkable role models whom we can claim with pride, and model ourselves after. People like Laura Haviland, who was a conductor on the Underground Railroad and performed unbelievably brave acts while the slave-catchers were right on her trail; Virginia Foster Durr, a southern belle raised with great wealth and privilege who, as an adult, tirelessly drove black workers to and from their jobs during the Montgomery bus boycott; the Rev. James Reeb, who went south during the Mississippi Freedom Summer of 1964 to organize and march; Hodding Carter, Jr., editor and publisher of a newspaper in the Mississippi Delta who used his paper to battle for racial equity and who took considerable heat for his actions. And more: the Grimke sisters, Lucretia Mott, William Lloyd Garrison, John Brown, Viola Liuzzo.

There are also many contemporary anti-racists like Morris Dees, who gave up a lucrative law practice to start the Southern Poverty Law Center and Klan Watch in Alabama and bring white supremacists to trial; Anne Braden, active for decades in the civil rights struggle in Kentucky; Rev. Joseph Barndt, working within the religious community to make individual churches and entire denominations proclaim themselves as anti-racist institutions. And Peggy McIntosh, Judith Katz, and Myles Horton. And so many others. Why don't our young people know these names? If young people knew more about these dedicated allies, perhaps they would be inspired to engage in more anti-racist activities themselves.

Choosing Our Own Roles

We also need to consider our role as allies. In our own communities, would young people, if asked the same questions, call out our names as anti-racists? In areas where we are dominant, is our struggle for equity and justice evident? When we think about our potential role as allies, we need to recall a Quaker expression: "Let your life be your teaching." The Quakers understand that our words carry only so much weight, that it is our actions, our daily behaviors, that tell the true story.

In my own life I struggle with what actions to take, how to make my beliefs and my behaviors congruent. One small step that has had interesting repercussions over the last decade is the fact that my partner (who is male) and I have chosen not to be legally married until gay and lesbian couples can be married and receive the same benefits and legal protection that married heterosexual couples enjoy. A small step, but it has allowed us to talk with folks at the YMCA about their definition of "family" when deciding who qualifies for their "family plan"; to challenge people at Amtrak about why some "family units" receive discounts when traveling together and others do not; and to raise questions in the religious community about who can receive formal sanction for their loving unions and who cannot. These are not earth-shattering steps in the larger picture, but we believe that small steps taken by thousands of people will eventually change the character of our communities.

When we stop colluding and speak out about the unearned privileges we enjoy as members of a dominant group—privileges we have been taught for so long to deny or ignore—we have the potential to undergo and inspire stunning transformation. Consider the words of Gandhi: "As human beings, our greatness lies not so much in being able to remake the world, as in being able to remake ourselves."

In my own community, I have been impressed by the efforts of three middle-aged males who have remade themselves into staunch allies for women. Steven Botkin established the Men's Resource Center in Amherst, Massachusetts twelve years ago and put a commitment to eliminating sexism in its very first mission statement. Another Amherst resident, Michael Burkart, travels nationwide and works with top executives in Fortune 500 companies on the issue of gender equity in their corporations. And Geoff Lobenstine, a social worker who identifies as an anti-sexist male, brings these issues to his work in Holyoke, Massachusetts.

Charlie Parker once said this about music: "Music is your own experience, your thoughts, your wisdom. If you don't live it, it won't come out of your horn." I think the same is true about us in our role as allies—it is our own experience, our thoughts, our wisdon. If we don't live it, it won't come out of our horn.

Preparing for the Long Haul

Now I would be the first to admit that personally and professionally the role of ally is often exhausting. I know that it involves challenges—being an ally is difficult work, and it can often be lonely. We must remember to take care of ourselves along this journey, to sustain our energy and our zest for those ongoing challenges.

We must also remember that it is hard to go it alone: allies need allies. As with any other struggle in our lives, we need supportive people around us to help us to persevere. Other allies will help us take the small, daily steps that will, in time, alter the character of our communities. We know that allied behavior usually consists of small steps and unglamorous work. As Mother Teresa once said: "I don't do any great things. I do small things with great love."

Finally two additional points about us in our role as allies: First, we don't always see the results of our efforts. Sometimes we do, but often we touch and even change lives without ever knowing it. Consequently, we cannot measure our success in quantitative terms. Like waves upon the shore, we are altering the landscape—but exactly how, may be hard to discern.

Doubts inevitably creep up about our effectiveness, about our approach, about the positions we assume or the actions we take. But we move forward, along with the doubts, the uncertainly, and often the lack of visible results. In our office, we have a famous William James quote on the wall to sustain us: "I will act as though what I do makes a difference." And, speaking personally, although my faith gets rattled, I try to act as though what I do does make a difference.

Second, there is no such thing as a perfect ally. Perfection is not our goal. When I asked my colleague Kenneth Jones what stood out for him as the most important characteristic of a strong ally, he said simply: "being consistently conscious." He didn't say "never stumbling," or "never making mistakes." He said: "being consistently conscious." And so we do our best: taking risks, being smart, making errors, feeling foolish, doing what we believe is right, based on our best judgment at the time. We are imperfect, but we are steady. We are courageous but not faultless. As Lani Guinier said: "It is better to be vaguely right than precisely wrong." If we obsess about looking good instead of doing good, we will get caught in a spiral of ineffective action. Let's not get side-tracked or defeated because we are trying to be perfect.

And so we move ahead, pushing ourselves forward on our growing edge. We know that although none of us are beginners in dealing with issues of oppression and empowerment, none of us are experts either. These issues are too complex, too painful, and too pervasive for us to achieve a state of clarity and closure once and for all. The best we can hope for is to strive each day to be our strongest and clearest selves, transforming the world one individual at a time, one family at a time, one community at a time. May we summon the wisdom to be devoted allies today. May we walk the walk, living as though equity, justice and freedom for all have already arrived.

Like most activists, I carry a dream inside me. As I travel nationwide for my work, I can actually see signs of it becoming true. The dream is that we will create in this country a nonviolent army of allies that will challenge and break the cycle of oppression and usher in a new era of liberation, empowerment, and equity for persons historically targeted by systemic oppression. Within each individual is the potential to effect enormous change. May we move foward, claiming with pride our identities as allies, interrupting the cycle of oppression, and modeling a new way of behaving and believing.

5

What White Folks Must Do

Harlon L. Dalton

"America has a race problem." Those five words seem innocuous enough, perhaps even a bit bland. But I can still recall how they surged through me the first time I encountered them. I was in my early teens, I think, and was hanging around the house waiting for dinner. While thumbing through the latest issue of *Ebony* magazine, I happened upon a serious-looking essay by historian Lerone Bennett, Jr. Instead of skipping over it in favor of something a bit lighter, I decided to check it out. I'm not sure I ever got to the essay's main point, for I was mesmerized by something Bennett said early on. He said, in essence, that we Negroes should stop thinking that *we* have a race problem and start recognizing that *America* has a race problem.

The effect on me was electric. Until that moment, I did not realize how thoroughly I had bought into the notion that racial injustice was "the Black man's burden." Sure, we could implore White America to set things straight, but weren't we the ones who were suffering? It was a short step from thinking that we had a problem to believing that we *were* the problem, and I was already in mid-stride. Lerone Bennett understood how psychologically debilitating such beliefs can be, and he reached across the printed page to save me.

Thinking of race as "the Black man's burden" is also debilitating to Whites. It leaves them powerless to effect change. It deprives them of the opportunity to be moral agents and to participate in the cleansing of this nation's great stain. It reinscribes a vertical relationship, even for people who are philosophically committed to equality. Moreover, sitting on the sidelines virtually guarantees that America's future will be bleak. We don't have a person to waste. We cannot build a healthy modern economy while disempowering and undervaluing a large segment of the workforce. We owe our children more; not just a thriving economy and a clean environment, but also a nation free of permanent divisions and human decay. As a practical matter, people of color cannot do it alone. We are busy enough just getting by. Besides, the scale of the problem is such that we need all hands on deck. In order to redistribute advantage and rethink how we relate to one another, everyone's participation is needed.

From *Racial Healing: Confronting the Fear between Blacks and Whites* (New York: Anchor Books, 1995), pp. 117–126.

So it is imperative that White folk accept joint ownership of America's race problem. But first they must *un*learn the many ways in which they commonly *dis*own race. For example, Whites often excuse themselves from taking an active role by engaging in a heightened rhetoric of Black responsibility. Sometimes it seems as if every race conversation gets turned into a discussion of what Black people need to do to get their own house in order. "They" need to become more ambitious, to take education more seriously, to be willing to meet Whites halfway, to stop victimizing each other.[1]

An especially galling version of table turning is "let's talk about Black-on-Black crime." I do not mean to suggest that Black-on-Black crime is not a serious issue. On the contrary. The Black community has viewed it as critical for years. Part of the reason that Louis Farrakhan is held in such high esteem in the Black community in spite of his many failings is that he has steadfastly taken the community to task for preying on its own. Similarly, Jesse Jackson has preached for years that there is nothing manly or honorable about victimizing one another. The same message has echoed from pulpits, podiums, and street corners in Black neighborhoods across America for at least a decade. Since 1993, Black-on-Black crime has topped *Ebony's* annual readers' poll as "the most pressing issue facing Black America."

Given all that, there is something deeply insulting about the implication that Black people have not focused on the issue, or worse, that we aren't concerned about it, or worse still, that we wouldn't be concerned about it if White folk did not wave it in our faces. Moreover, there is something passing strange about the sudden interest in Black-on-Black crime to the seeming exclusion of Black-on-*White* crime. In any event, the dominance of this and other issues of Black responsibility serve to deflect attention away from our joint obligation to transform America's relation to race.

A second way in which White folk sometimes disown the race problem is by treating Black people as if they were fully in control of their own fate. "Why don't they just . . . ?" Why don't they just go get a job? Why don't they just move out of the inner city? Why don't they just stop having babies? Why don't they just exercise more control over their children? Why don't they just take the bull by the horns? (Does anyone ever say what you are supposed to do with the bull once you've grabbed hold of it?)

The problem is that such questions are often posed rhetorically. Moreover, even when serious answers are sought, some answers seem to fall outside the pale. Thus, it just wouldn't do to respond, "Because you wouldn't hire them," or "Because you wouldn't be interested in having them as next-door neighbors." Yet there is much truth in these answers. Black people do not, in and of themselves, control the real estate market, the job market, the economy, the welfare system, the school system, or the streets. The problem with the questions and the anticipated answers is that they assume a false world in which Black people are both the problem and the solution. The net effect is that the posing of such questions tends to deflect attention away from the possibility of joint ownership of both.

A third way in which White people sometimes avoid dealing with the impact of racism on Black America is by turning the tables. In particular, the notion that White men have suffered greatly at the hands of people of color (and White women) has been responsible for the death of many trees of late. "White, Male and Worried," proclaimed *Business Week*.[2] "White Male Fear" graced the pages of *The Economist*.[3] Perhaps less surprisingly, *Playboy* ran a two-part series entitled "The Myth of Male Power."[4] And *Newsweek* hit the nail on the head with "White Male Paranoia."[5] Actor/director Michael Douglas has even managed to create a virtual cottage industry with his portrayals of victimized White males.[6]

Assuming for the moment that *Business Week*, *Newsweek*, and the rest are onto something terribly important, we make a mistake in allowing it to drown out or eclipse our concern for the plight of people of color. Justice is not a limited resource. We do not have to choose between doing right by one group and doing right by another. Nor are the aspirations of White men (or women) necessarily in conflict with those of people of color. If we were to take joint responsibility for cleaning up the racial mess, we could search for creative solutions that expand opportunities for everyone. Moreover, upon reflection thoughtful Whites might discover that sometimes less is more. That has certainly been my experience as a male. Ceding the right to, as Humphrey Bogart put it in *Casablanca*, "make the decisions for both of us" has been enormously liberating. Similarly, in a very real sense Black liberation holds the promise of White liberation as well.

The attention given to the "victimization of the White male" is troubling in a second respect. It is insensitive to power and position and ignores issues of quality and scale. Several years ago, lesbian and gay male students at a small private law school in the Northeast which shall remain nameless were the victims of a series of belligerent acts. Someone had ascertained their sexual orientation (by, I suspect, taking note of who received a rather distinctive party invitation) and placed hateful messages in their student mail slots. Vulgar graffiti directed at lesbians were scratched into an elevator wall. Threatening messages were slipped under at least one student's dorm-room door.

Eventually, the law school's dean called a town meeting at which students, faculty, and staff could come together as a community to share information and express solidarity with those who had been attacked. As it happens, the president of the university was in the building that afternoon, and was invited to join the rest of us in the courtyard. After listening to several gay students speak of how frightened, vulnerable, and angry they felt, he approached the microphone. "I know how you feel," he told the students, or words to that effect (I am paraphrasing from memory). "I know what it is like to be under attack." He then proceeded to describe the ongoing labor strife between the university administration and the clerical and technical workers' union and to emphasize how personally stung he had been when workers in the heat of passion had called him names.

The students stared at him dumbstruck. Although he claimed to be empathizing with them, it was obvious that the president had been unnerved by their emotionalism and was indirectly urging them to respond with more dispassion. But beyond that, how could he dare equate his experience with theirs? He was the president of an exceedingly wealthy university that historically had treated its clerical and technical workers as if they were vassals. He should be able to handle a little negative feedback. The gay students, on the other hand, were being stalked by an anonymous assailant simply for being who they were. They had no ready way to defend themselves, no sense of when the belligerence would end, and no idea how far things might go.

Equating the current plight of the angry White male with that of historically oppressed people of color is a little like that. Although the contrasts are not as sharp and the parallel is less than perfect, the error is the same. The comparison only makes sense if you sweep aside issues of hierarchy and control. Somehow, despite his vaunted victimization, the angry White male seems to have done rather well for himself in effecting a political sea change in 1994. Meanwhile, America's hidden wound continues to fester.

A fourth way in which the race problem is disowned is by simply removing race from the picture. "Wouldn't you agree," I am often asked, "that these days the problems of Black people have much more to do with class than race?" Before I can even object to the leading question, a follow-up is posed: "Wouldn't it make more sense to formulate social policies that target class concerns rather than racial ones?"

These statements (dressed up as questions) suffer from at least two fundamental defects. First, they assume that race and class are independent of one another and can be readily teased apart. Sociologists have long known, however, that race and class are sometimes interrelated in complex ways.[7] It's often difficult to determine whether what one is observing is a race effect, a class effect, a combination of the two, or an interaction between the two. (Not to mention the effect of mass culture. When it comes to watching the Super Bowl or purchasing Nike shoes, we are probably all more American than anything else.) Second, the sentiment that we should really be focusing on class either assumes that a forced choice is required or is a disguised way of saying that race is irrelevant. After all, if we aren't artificially limited to one choice, and if racism is indeed alive and well, then the simple answer is that we should focus on both.

As is too often the case, my fellow pointy-heads in the academy bear a measure of responsibility for stirring the pot. For some time, social scientists have been asking, in one form or another, the following queston: to what extent can differences between the races (in attitudes, in behavior, in social location) be explained by class? The answer usually comes back that when you control for class, many or even most (depending on the study) racial disparities disappear. I do not quarrel with these results. I simply question what they mean.

Which disparities remain, and are they significant in the life of the Black community? Does statistically controlling for class tell us anything at all about what would happen in the real world if we sought to make the Black class structure mirror that which presently exists for Whites? How would we go about doing that? Would we, for example, employ economic (as distinct from racial) affirmative action? What would be the impact of this class shifting on Whites? If we could

simply wave a magic wand and equalize the class structures, why not use it to eliminate racism as well? More fundamentally, why does the difference in class structure exist in the first place? Might not racism have something to do with it? And if
so, what reason is there for believing that we can just focus on class without also focusing on race?

In fairness, I should note that some who suggest that we worry less about race
and more about class are making a rather different point. They might well concede the case that is powerfully made in Ellis Cose's *The Rage of a Privileged
Class*[8]—namely, that racism remains a problem for Blacks who break through the
class barrier. They question, however, whether racism is an important concern of
the so-called Black "underclass." Surely for the folk who can't afford to buy Cose's
book, runs the argument, class is much more important than race. Therefore, by
continuing to focus on race, we favor the relatively well-off Black middle class over
the much more numerous and needy underclass.

Despite its surface appeal, this position is seriously flawed. Of course the problems of the underclass are largely economic. But that doesn't mean that the poor
don't also suffer from racism. It may well take a different form than is true for the
middle class. An underemployed single mother in the inner city is a hell of a lot
less likely to be concerned about bumping against a glass ceiling than about being
left behind. But the cause of her predicament is not solely her class position, for
the racial pecking order is largely responsible for the fact that Blacks are massed at
the bottom of the economic pile. And race-related indifference is largely responsible for our unwillingness to do what is necessary to improve the lot of the poor.
Furthermore, while the material position of inner-city Blacks may not be apprecia-
bly different from that of, say, many rural Whites, the color line serves to divide
economic like from like, thus increasing the likelihood that nothing will be done
to improve their lives.

I honestly believe that many who push the "it's all class" line have the best of
intentions. I also happen to believe that many others are simply looking for a way
to get off the race hook. But either way, the practical effect is the same: to deflect
attention from the enduring problem of race, with only the most theoretical of payoffs in return.

Finally, rather than disown the race problem altogether, many Whites simply
make their participation in bringing about change conditional. I can't tell you how
many times I have heard, "I'd be willing to help, if you would only . . ." Be less
shrill. Get your own house in order first. Meet me halfway. (Guess who gets to determine where that point is.) Inevitably, I experience these preconditions as a kind
of muscle flexing or throwing down of the gauntlet. In case I forgot, I am being
shown who is still in charge.

That White folk would resist owning the race problem is perfectly understandable. Dealing with race takes a considerable psychic toll, especially on those who
are most attuned to the felt grievances of people of color. To recognize other people's pain and to contemplate that one might have contributed to or benefited

from it is not easy. It is no wonder that genuinely decent White people sometimes try to make race disappear. How do you make peace with the fact that people like you have subordinated others in your name?

Then there is the small matter of coping with change. For most of us change is anxiety-producing even when it promises to serve us well. I suspect that most White folk would be in favor of marked progress for people of color if they could be guaranteed that their own lives would not be significantly affected.[9] But that is not in the cards. We all must change if we are to promote racial healing and aspire to racial justice. All of our lives will be altered in some respects—for example, our neighborhoods may change complexion and our employment prospects may differ—but the biggest changes will be in how we think. And abandoning old attitudes and familiar patterns of belief is never easy.

NOTES

1. See generally Wellman, *White Racism,* for a discussion of White peoples' thinking in this regard.

2. Michele Galen and Ann Therese Palmer, "White, Male, and Worried," *Business Week,* 31 January 1994, 50-55.

3. "White Male Fear," *Economist,* 29 January 1994, 34.

4. Warren Farrel, "The Myth of Male Power," parts 1 and 2, *Playboy,* July 1993, August 1993.

5. David Gates, "White Male Paranoia," *Newsweek,* 29 March 1993, 48-53.

6. J. Hoberman, "Victim Victorious: Well-Fed Yuppie Michael Douglas Leads the Charge for Resentful White Men," *Village Voice,* 7 March 1995, 31-33; "Tapping Male Fears: Michael Douglas Finds Success as 'Victim,'" *Cleveland Plain Dealer,* 31 December 1994; Ellen Goodman, "'Disclosure' Uncovers Hollywood Distortion," *Chicago Tribune,* 20 December 1994.

7. See generally Robert C. Smith and Richard Seltzer, *Race, Class, and Culture: A Study in Afro-American Mass Opinion* (Albany: State University of New York Press, 1992), chapter one.

8. Ellis Cose, *The Rage of a Privileged Class* (New York: HarperCollins, 1993).

9. Wellman, *White Racism,* 112.

6

Combatting Intentional Bigotry and Inadvertently Racist Acts

Fletcher A. Blanchard

What you say about racial discrimination matters: Your vocal opinions affect what others think and say. A series of experiments that I and my students and colleagues conducted demonstrate that racial prejudice is much more malleable than many researchers, policy makers, and educational leaders believe. In the wake of the verdict in the case of four Los Angeles policemen accused of beating Rodney King and the violence that followed it, the search for ways to lessen the devastating consequences of racism in America has intensified. If we understand that simply overhearing others condemn or condone racial harassment dramatically affects people's reactions to racism, we may be able to help find solutions to tensions and bigotry—both on campuses and in the larger society.

In the experiments we conducted, the first two of which are described in an article in *Psychological Science* (March, 1991), we briefly interviewed students as they walked between classes. In some portions of the experiment, the interviewer also stopped a second person, ostensibly another student but in reality a member of the research team, who offered her programmed opinions first. After hearing someone else condemn racism, college students expressed anti-racist sentiments much more strongly than those who heard someone express equivocal views. However, students who first heard someone condone racism then voiced views that reflected strong acceptance of racism.

The large differences that we observed appeared both when research participants spoke their views publicly and when we measured their opinions more anonymously by asking them to complete a questionaire and return it to the researcher in a sealed envelope. The elasticity of privately held views regarding racism appears to reveal a lack of knowledge about the nature of racism and uncertainty about how institutions and individuals might appropriately respond to expressions of racism.

Originally published in *The Chronicle of Higher Education*, May 13, 1992, section 2, pp. B1–B2.

I suspect that one of the reasons that opinions about racism are so easily influenced derives from the high level of racial segregation that still characterizes contemporary American society. Indeed, one wonders just how much people's ignorance about racism and lack of contact with other races contributed to the verdict in the King case. Although a recent survey by People for the American Way indicated that many young Americans say they have a friend of another race, most still know little about other racial and ethnic groups.

Public-opinion polls over the last several decades portray largely favorable trends regarding whites' attitudes toward African Americans, but those attitudes and opinions derive from little direct experience. Few white college students have grown up in integrated neighborhoods, attended schools with integrated classrooms, or observed their parents interact in a friendly manner with people of color.

Even fewer of the white students entering college today have had the chance to learn from black teachers, work for black employers, or participate in voluntary activities and organizations where the adult leaders, coaches, or advisers were black. America's campuses constitute the first multiracial social setting encountered by many young people.

As a result, few of the many whites who have reached an honest commitment to egalitarian values have had the opportunity to acquire the full range of interpersonal skills, sensibilities, and knowledge that might allow them to fulfill that commitment. Few, for example, have vicariously experienced the pain felt by a friend who has suffered racial harassment. Few have discovered the ways that everyday language may communicate disrespect for a particular group. Thus the elasticity of reactions to racism appears to reflect the uncertainty that the inexperienced, but well intentioned, bring to their first interracial setting.

Although there has been an alarming increase in racial harassment on campuses and in society at large, the results of opinion polls showing a trend toward more egalitarian racial attitudes among Americans make it difficult to attribute the racist attacks to any increase in racial prejudice among the many. Instead, much of the harassment should be understood to represent open hostility expressed by the strongly prejudiced few. Efforts to reduce racial harassment and enhance tolerance must acknowledge the many who are naive, inexperienced, and often well intentioned, on the one hand, and the few who are genuinely mean spirited, on the other. Strategies that are effective for one group may be less so for the other.

Many colleges and universities are responding to the current wave of racist attacks by creating policies that attempt to define and regulate racial harassment. However, none of the new codes of conduct acknowledges the important differences between the intentional behavior of the committed bigot and the inadvertent behavior of the profoundly inexperienced.

The least controversial variety of code, aimed squarely at the committed bigot, borrows language from federal and state civil-rights statutes and anti-harassment regulations. By narrowly framing the boundaries of unacceptable behavior, this approach provides a basis for punishing some behavior of the mean-spirited few.

Unfortunately, the federal and state regulations that define and bar racial harassment are neither as articulate nor as encompassing as those governing sexual harassment. Until state and federal rules barring racial harassment recognize how seemingly less-odious behaviors can accumulate to produce an atmosphere of intimidation, codes of conduct that rely on them will restrain only the most flagrant forms of attack.

A second approach to regulating racial harassment, aimed squarely at the well-intentioned many, consists of urging civility. Instead of defining the limits of impropriety and barring behavior that oversteps those bounds, civility codes encourage general tolerance and acceptance, leaving it to administrators and adjudicating bodies to apply the rules to particular instances of unacceptable behavior.

These policies rarely offer the specific guidance required by those inexperienced with racism. Little controversy follows the promulgation of such codes. Rather, it more often attends their application to particular instances of objectionable behavior—behavior that falls somewhere between civility and clearly illegal harassment.

A third variety of code attempts to define and forbid a much broader range of impropriety than currently is addressed by federal and most state regulations. The prohibitions often embrace both the intentional behavior of the committed bigot and the careless behavior of those inexperienced with interracial contacts. Although both classes of behavior cause harm, the new policies fail to acknowledge the different motivations of the actors, and thus the need for different remedies.

Most important, it is difficult to write such codes so that they enhance freedom from discrimination but also preserve the broader freedom of speech. These are the policies that have generated the most interesting debate and the most belligerent contention. Some of the opposition has been raised by those who would safeguard the use of racial epithets under the guise of defending First Amendment freedoms. Other opponents have resorted to ridicule and name calling, perhaps to avoid acknowledging the prevalence of racial harassment and bias in our society. The principled portions of the discussion undoubtedly have enhanced both our understanding of the boundaries of free speech and of the causes of contemporary racism.

The principal virtue of all of the codes I have outlined is that each encourages consensus regarding proper conduct. It is this consensus—the shared sense of what is right and what is wrong—that steers social behavior much more effectively than mere rules and regulations. Articulate codes that are widely distributed and discussed can contribute to a consensus that rejects bigotry.

No one of these three strategies for regulating racism is complete, however. The most effective policies must combine elements of all three approaches. The best policies must proscribe illegal racial harassment, thereby providing punishment for the mean-spirited few, as well as prescribe expectations for tolerance and respect, thereby providing guidance for the inexperienced many. The best policies also will step beyond the boundaries of current statutes, recognizing, for example, that racial epithets directed at individuals are intolerable in humane society.

By linking codes of conduct with statements of academic mission, effective policies signal a strong institutional commitment to the protection of civil rights. Yet no code of conduct, no matter how comprehensively it is framed, can create by itself the sort of accepting and respectful communities that we need.

Other forms of attention to the discriminatory consequences of behavior are required if colleges and universities are to become the sort of educational settings where everyone can thrive. The fact that people of color often find themselves numerically underrepresented in academic institutions exaggerates the discomfort and pain that arise out of insensitive acts.

Consider an organization in which 10 percent of the people are black and 90 percent are white. Imagine a department of that organization in which 10 people work, nine of whom are white and one of whom is black. Imagine further that all nine of the whites perceive themselves to be unprejudiced and have adopted a genuine commitment to egalitarian values. If each of those well-intentioned whites makes only one insensitive "mistake" a month, the one black target of the nine naive whites would experience, on average, some hurtful and isolating behavior every third day.

The well-intentioned white is aware of only one insensitive event over the last month—if, in fact, he or she has been informed of that lapse. But the personal experience of the person of color reflects a high rate of discriminatory behavior. Reduce the proportion of African Americans or add an intentional racist and the resulting setting becomes even more intolerable. This imbalance in perceptions of the rate of discrimination and insensitivity exacerbates the potential for misunderstanding.

Until college students bring with them from high school more extensive experience with interracial interaction, massive commitments to remedial education and training will be required to reduce the rate of unintentional harm caused by these "interracially incompetent" people. I suspect that the best educational techniques will take advantage of the positive motivation to "do the right thing" that characterizes most entering students—by emphasizing vivid and concrete examples of the hurtful and harmful behavior of the naive. One-shot "workshops" presented during first-year orientation probably will not be sufficient. Rather, activities or programs that foster the early formation of strong interracial friendships will contribute most to intergroup understanding.

Until inexperienced students master the behaviors that reflect their egalitarian commitments, we must maintain havens for minority students that protect them from intentional harassment and naive disrespect, including cultural centers and organizations for particular minority groups. By also introducing programs and activities that foster formation of strong interracial friendships, it may be possible, over time, to reduce the need for safe havens.

It is solid interracial friendships that help insulate targets of harassment from the most devastating consequences of anonymous racist attacks and exaggerated feelings of isolation. Such friendships also will provide the basis for the sort of interracial learning that has been absent from the experience of many who enter college today.

The research that I described at the outset suggests that each of us can affect others' concern for eliminating racism by taking strong public stands condemning bigotry on campuses. Just as anti-smoking attitudes among non-smokers eventually led to regulations banning smoking in public places, a broad consensus that eschews bigotry surely can reduce the display of intentional bias and inadvertent discriminatory behavior on campuses.

Our research suggests that no one need wait for administrators to take the lead. Each of us can influence each other by criticizing the willful bigotry of the mean-spirited few and gently guiding the well-intentioned efforts of the inexperienced many.

7

Confronting Anti-Gay Violence

Michael Bronski

Several weeks ago I was walking with my lover in a quiet neighborhood in Cambridge, Massachusetts, on our way to a late afternoon movie. We were holding hands in an offhanded sort of way, chatting together, when a group of young teens sitting on a front stoop across the street (the oldest was probably 14, the youngest maybe 12) yelled "faggot"; then they laughed and threw some plastic soda bottles at us before they ran off. We thought for a moment of chasing and confronting them—this didn't seem particularly dangerous and I have always felt that confronting this sort of harassment, if not immediately dangerous, is always better than ignoring it—but they were already a block away and it did not seem worth the time or energy. We went off to the movies, but the incident was deeply disquieting. Gay men and lesbians have always been aware of anti-gay violence. It becomes a way of life, just as it is for many people of color in America and for women making their way through the world everyday. In the past months we have heard—in the mainstream media—that there is a new focus on gay bashing. And the message here is that this new focus will bring about a new understanding and the end to it. Aside from the Matthew Shepard murder in Laramie, Wyoming, by Russell Henderson and Aaron McKinney, both 21, last October other murders of gay people have been deemed newsworthy:

On January 17 Kevin Tryals and Laaron Morris of Galveston, Texas, were found in a burning car on a dead-end road outside of city limits. Both bodies were severely burned. The medical examiner's office ruled that both men were dead before the car was ignited and that both men died from multiple gunshot wounds. Police have ruled out robbery and are treating the murders as anti-gay violence.

On February 20 the burned remains of Billy Jack Gaither, 39, a factory worker were discovered in Sylacauga, a small town in Alabama. He had been beaten to death (or near death) with an ax handle and thrown onto a stack of tires and set afire. His attackers, 21-year-old Charles Butler and 25-year-old Steven Mullins, claim he made a pass at them.

On March 1, the severed head of Henry Edward Northington, 39, was found on a pathway to a park known as a gay men's cruising spot outside of Alexandria, Virginia. Northington was homeless and gay. No one has been arrested.

ZNet Commentary, April 9, 1999.

On March 12, in Los Angeles, Juan Chavez, 34, pleaded guilty of murdering five gay men by luring them to their homes supposedly for sex and then robbing and strangling them. He also was accused of taking the victims' cars after killing them. He claimed he commited the murders to stop the spread of AIDS.

On March 15 the body of Michael Barber, 56, was discovered in his apartment in Fort Lauderdale, Florida, encased in a zippered plastic bag. He had died of multiple stab wounds. Barber, an ex-Marine, had worked as a gardener in the area. Six months ago Charles Squires, 64, of nearby Wilton Manors, Florida, was found stabbed to death and wrapped in plastic inside his home. Police are treating both as anti-gay crimes.

On March 19, Bradley Davis, 24, of San Francisco, was found bleeding and semiconscious between two parked cars at 12:15 A.M. near 18th and Castro Streets by police officers who were called to the scene. Officers arrested three suspects— Ban Doc Im, 21; Henry Sai Kwong, 19; Thang Cao Truong, 18—who were seen by witnesses attacking Davis after standing on Castro shouting anti-gay and anti–African American epithets. There is no doubt that since the Shepard murder anti-gay violence has been deemed more newsworthy, while some analysts are claiming that violence against gay, lesbian, and transgendered people is rising. The Triangle Foundation, a gay rights advocacy group in Detroit, documented two Michigan anti-gay murders in 1997 and six in 1998; by March of 1999, they were investigating five. But the reality is that there have always been an enormous num- ber of murders, beatings, attacks, and harassments; what has changed are both the rate of reporting and the attention of the media. Generally speaking, queer com- mentators and activists see this as a positive trend; it seems to me that increased visi- bility for homophobic violence is only a first, albeit important, but rather small step. The enormous coverage given to the Shepard murder—and we will see much more once the trial starts—is, in itself, a study of what can go wrong. It is clear that Matthew Shepard's place as a media star was predicated on several factors: his mur- der was brutal and shocking, and his age, race, good looks, and class status made him the perfect victim for a national media looking for a good story. But will this coverage have any lasting effect on how both the media and public policy deal with anti-gay violence? If Matthew Shepard had been an African American teenage hus- tler, the story would have been different: there would not have been a story. Are the media simply going to go for the most sensational stories of anti-gay violence: be- headings, public burnings, dead bodies in zippered bags? The only reason the press reported on the Castro Street beating was that it took place in the dead-center of the most famous public gay neighborhood in the world.

Anywhere else it would not be news. In the past three decades U.S. culture has made some significant changes in how some issues about violence and discrimina- tion are perceived and acted upon. Rape (although it still occurs all the time) is now treated more seriously by the police and the courts. The same is true of do- mestic violence. As recent events in New York have shown, the uphill, and fero- ciously waged, battle to have police violence against people of color is alive, well, and even making some progress. These changes all came about because of com- mitted, sustained grass-roots organizing, an insistence that the issues be taken seriously—as a moral imperative—and a demand that the popular media both pay attention and act more responsibly. But will this coverage of anti-gay violence engender substantive change? If it has any chance to, it must move beyond simple sentimentalization and pity for "nice" victims: the bulk of reported anti-gay assaults in Manhattan, for instance, are faced by African American and Latino transgendered sex workers. The other thing that has to change is that anti-gay violence cannot continue to be viewed outside of a broader political and social context of the personal lives of heterosexuals. This may be beginning to happen. An editorial in the *St. Louis Dispatch* on March 10 noted "the ideas allowed to fester into the kind of murderous hatred that killed Gaither and Shepard . . . sprouted long before any blows were struck, any triggers were pulled, any fires were set. Like all hatred, anti-gay hatred is learned. Don't turn a deaf ear when your kid calls another child a 'fag' on the playground. Don't laugh at homophobic jokes in the office. Support education that includes positive information on gays and lesbians. Let gay and lesbian acquaintances or friends or relatives know they have your support. To condemn the brutal slayings of these men without examining the routine homophobia in our daily lives would by hypocrisy." I have deep suspicions of the ability of the mainstream media to effect any positive social change. I think of the young men—boys, really—who shouted and threw a bottle at me in the emblematically liberal city of Cambridge. I am old enough to be their grandfather, my lover is old enough to be their father. The men—boys?—accused of killing the "innocent" Matthew Shepard were his age. How do we work on building a common consensus that hating gay people enough to attack them is wrong in a culture that supports, or doesn't care about, the most murderous aspects of U.S. foreign policy? How do we discuss "accepting"—never mind valuing—homosexuality in a country in which the complexity of race is still, for the most part, undiscussable? Gay and lesbian activists have been organizing around violence issues for decades, and to a large degree they have not been taken seriously by many other political, religious, or social institutions. It is one thing to advise that men and women not laugh at fag jokes in the office, but we have to realize that not laughing at—or rebuking the teller of—fag jokes often labels someone a fag himself. One of the main problems in fighting anti-gay prejudice is that the specter of homosexuality is everywhere, implicating anyone who counters the sentiment. The mainstream press's coverage of anti-gay violence may be a beginning of a more complex, fruitful public discourse, but it is only one facet of how the problem is confronted. Gay activists have to begin, or continue, building coalitions with other anti-violence and social action groups. Individuals doing political work on the left also have to take more time and energy in examining the myriad ways sexuality—in all its manifestations—impacts on social, national, and international policies and politics. In the meantime I am still going to hold my lover's hand wherever and whenever I want to. But I am also going to watch my back and be more purposeful in challenging people when faced with harassment or violence. If we had chased and confronted those boys, they might have thought twice before doing this again.

8

A New Vision of Masculinity

Cooper Thompson

I was once asked by a teacher in a suburban high school to give a guest presentation on male roles. She hoped that I might help her deal with four boys who exercised extraordinary control over the other boys in the class. Using ridicule and their status as physically imposing athletes, these four wrestlers had succeeded in stifling the participation of the other boys, who were reluctant to make comments in class discussions.

As a class we talked about the ways in which boys got status in that school and how they got put down by others. I was told that the most humiliating put-down was being called a "fag." The list of behaviors which could elicit ridicule filled two large chalkboards, and it was detailed and comprehensive; I got the sense that a boy in this school had to conform to rigid, narrow standards of masculinity to avoid being called a fag. I, too, felt this pressure and became very conscious of my mannerisms in front of the group. Partly from exasperation, I decided to test the seriousness of these assertions. Since one of the four boys had some streaks of pink in his shirt, and since he had told me that wearing pink was grounds for being called a fag, I told him that I thought he was a fag. Instead of laughing, he said, "I'm going to kill you."

Such is the stereotypic definition of strength that is associated with masculinity. But it is a very limited definition of strength, one based on dominance and control and acquired through the humiliation and degradation of others.

Contrast this with a view of strength offered by Pam McAllister in her introduction to *Reweaving the Web of Life:*

> The "Strength" card in my Tarot deck depicts, not a warrior going off to battle with his armor and his mighty sword, but a woman stroking a lion. The woman has not slain the lion nor maced it, not netted it, nor has she put on it a muzzle or a leash. And though the lion clearly has teeth and long sharp claws, the woman is not hiding, nor has she sought a protector, nor has she grown muscles. She doesn't appear to be talking to the lion nor flattering it, nor tossing it fresh meat to distract its hungry jaws.

The woman on the "Strength" card wears a flowing white dress and a garland of flowers. With one hand she cups the lion's jaws, with the other she caresses its nose. The lion on the card has big yellow eyes and a long red tongue curling out of its mouth. One paw is lifted and the mane falls in thick red curls across its broad torso. The woman. The lion. Together they depict strength.

This image of strength stands in direct contrast to the strength embodied in the actions of the four wrestlers. The collective strength of the woman and the lion is a strength unknown in a system of traditional male values. Other human qualities are equally foreign to a traditional conception of masculinity. In workshops I've offered on the male role stereotype, teachers and other school personnel easily generate lists of attitudes and behaviors which boys typically seem to not learn. Included in this list are being supportive and nurturant, accepting one's vulnerability and being able to ask for help, valuing women and "women's work," understanding and expressing emotions (except for anger), the ability to empathize with and empower other people, and learning to resolve conflict in nonaggressive, noncompetitive ways.

Learning Violence

All of this should come as no surprise. Traditional definitions of masculinity include attributes such as independence, pride, resiliency, self-control, and physical strength. This is precisely the image of the Marlboro man, and to some extent, these are desirable attributes for boys and girls. But masculinity goes beyond these qualities to stress competitiveness, toughness, aggressiveness, and power. In this context, threats to one's status, however small, cannot be avoided or taken lightly. If a boy is called a fag, it means that he is perceived as weak or timid—and therefore not masculine enough for his peers. There is enormous pressure for him to fight back. Not being tough at these moments only proves the allegation.

Violence is learned not just as a way for boys to defend allegations that they are feminized, but as an effective, appropriate way for them to normally behave. In "The Civic Advocacy of Violence" [M., Spring 1982] Wayne Ewing clearly states:

> I used to think that we simply tolerated and permitted male abusiveness in our society. I have now come to understand rather, that we advocate physical violence. Violence is presented as effective. Violence is taught as the normal, appropriate and necessary behavior of power and control. Analyses which interweave advocacy of male violence with "SuperBowl Culture" have never been refuted. Civic expectations—translated into professionalism, financial commitments, city planning for recreational space, the raising of male children for competitive sport, the corporate ethics of business ownership of athletic teams, profiteering on entertainment—all result in the monument of the National Football League, symbol and reality at once of the advocacy of violence.

Ultimately, violence is the tool which maintains what I believe are the two most critical socializing forces in a boy's life: *homophobia*, the hatred of gay men (who are stereotyped as feminine) or those men believed to be gay, as well as the fear of being perceived as gay; and *misogyny*, the hatred of women. The two forces are targeted at different classes of victims, but they are really just the flip sides of the same coin. Homophobia is the hatred of feminine qualities in men while misogyny is the hatred of feminine qualities in women. The boy who is called a fag is the target of other boys' homophobia as well as the victim of his own homophobia. While the overt message is the absolute need to avoid being feminized, the implication is that females—and all that they traditionally represent—are contemptible. The United States Marines have a philosophy which conveniently combines homophobia and misogyny in the belief that "When you want to create a group of male killers, you kill 'the woman' in them."

The pressures of homophobia and misogyny in boys' lives have been poignantly demonstrated to me each time that I have repeated a simple yet provocative activity with students. I ask them to answer the question, "If you woke up tomorrow and discovered that you were the opposite sex from the one you are now, how would you and your life be different?" Girls consistently indicate that there are clear advantages to being a boy—from increased independence and career opportunities to decreased risks of physical and sexual assault—and eagerly answer the question. But boys often express disgust at this possibility and even refuse sometimes to answer the question. In her reports of a broad-based survey using this question, Alice Baumgartner reports the following responses as typical of boys: "If I were a girl, I'd be stupid and weak as a string"; "I would have to wear makeup, cook, be a mother, and yuckky stuff like that"; "I would have to hate snakes. Everything would be miserable"; "If I were a girl, I'd kill myself."

The Costs of Masculinity

The costs associated with a traditional view of masculinity are enormous, and the damage occurs at both personal and societal levels. The belief that a boy should be tough (aggressive, competitive, and daring) can create emotional pain for him. While a few boys experience short-term success for their toughness, there is little security in the long run. Instead, it leads to a series of challenges which few, if any, boys ultimately win. There is no security in being at the top when so many other boys are competing for the same status. Toughness also leads to increased chances of stress, physical injury, and even early death. It is considered manly to take extreme physical risks and voluntarily engage in combative, hostile activities.

The flip side of toughness—nurturance—is not a quality perceived as masculine and thus not valued. Because of this boys and men experience a greater emotional distance from other people and few opportunities to participate in meaningful interpersonal relationships. Studies consistently show that fathers spend very small amounts of time interacting with their children. In addition, men report that they seldom have intimate relationships with other men, reflecting their homophobia. They are afraid of getting too close and don't know how to take down the walls that they have built between themselves.

As boys grow older and accept adult roles, the larger social costs of masculinity clearly emerge. Most women experience male resistance to an expansion of women's roles; one of the assumptions of traditional masculinity is the belief that women should be subordinate to men. The consequence is that men are often not willing to accept females as equal, competent partners in personal and professional settings. Whether the setting is a sexual relationship, the family, the streets, or the battlefield, men are continuously engaged in efforts to dominate. Statistics on child abuse consistently indicate that the vast majority of abusers are men, and that there is no "typical" abuser. Rape may be the fastest growing crime in the United States. And it is men, regardless of nationality, who provoke and sustain war. In short, traditional masculinity is life threatening.

New Socialization for Boys

Masculinity, like many other human traits, is determined by both biological and environmental factors. While some believe that biological factors are significant in shaping some masculine behavior, there is undeniable evidence that cultural and environmental factors are strong enough to override biological impulses. What is it, then, that we should be teaching boys about being a man in a modern world?

- Boys must learn to accept their vulnerability, learn to express a range of emotions such as fear and sadness, and learn to ask for help and support in appropriate situations.
- Boys must learn to be gentle, nurturant, cooperative and communicative, and in particular, learn nonviolent means of resolving conflicts.
- Boys must learn to accept those attitudes and behaviors which have traditionally been labeled feminine as necessary for full human development—thereby reducing homophobia and misogyny. This is tantamount to teaching boys to love other boys and girls.

Certain qualities like courage, physical strength, and independence, which are traditionally associated with masculinity, are indeed positive qualities for males, provided that they are not manifested in obsessive ways nor used to exploit or dominate others. It is not necessary to completely disregard or unlearn what is traditionally called masculine. I believe, however, that the three areas above are crucial for developing a broader view of masculinity, one which is healthier for all life.

These three areas are equally crucial for reducing aggressive, violent behavior among boys and men. Males must learn to cherish life for the sake of their *own* wholeness as human beings, not just *for* their children, friends, and lovers. If males were more nurturant, they would be less likely to hurt those they love.

Leonard Eron, writing in the *American Psychologist,* puts the issue of unlearning aggression and learning nurturance in clear-cut terms:

> Socialization is crucial in determining levels of aggression. No matter how aggression is measured or observed, as a group males always score higher than females. But this is not true for all girls. There are some girls who seem to have been socialized like boys who are just as aggressive as boys. Just as some females can learn to be aggressive, so males can learn *not* to be aggressive. If we want to reduce the level of aggression in society, we should also discourage boys from aggression very early on in life and reward them too for others' behaviors; in other words, we should socialize boys more like girls, and they should be encouraged to develop socially positive qualities such as tenderness, cooperation, and aesthetic appreciation. The level of individual aggression in society will be reduced only when male adolescents and young adults, as a result of socialization, subscribe to the same standards of behavior as have been traditionally encouraged for women.

Where will this change in socialization occur? In his first few years, most of a boy's learning about masculinity comes from the influences of parents, siblings and images of masculinity such as those found on television. Massive efforts will be needed to make changes here. But at older ages, school curriculum and the school environment provide powerful reinforcing images of traditional masculinity. This reinforcement occurs through a variety of channels, including curriculum content, role modeling, and extracurricular activities, especially competitive sports.

School athletics are a microcosm of the socialization of male values. While participation in competitive activities can be enjoyable and healthy, it too easily becomes a lesson in the need for toughness, invulnerability, and dominance. Athletes learn to ignore their own injuries and pain and instead try to injure and inflict pain on others in their attempts to win, regardless of the cost to themselves or their opponents. Yet the lessons learned in athletics are believed to be vital for full and complete masculine development, and as a model for problem-solving in other areas of life.

In addition to encouraging traditional male values, schools provide too few experiences in nurturance, cooperation, negotiation, nonviolent conflict resolution, and strategies for empathizing with and empowering others. Schools should become places where boys have the opportunity to learn these skills; clearly, they won't learn them on the street, from peers, or on television.

Setting New Examples

Despite the pressures on men to display their masculinity in traditional ways, there are examples of men and boys who are changing. "Fathering" is one example of a positive change. In recent years, there has been a popular emphasis on child-care activities, with men becoming more involved in providing care to children, both professionally and as fathers. This is a clear shift from the more traditional view that child rearing should be delegated to women and is not an appropriate activity for men.

For all of the male resistance it has generated, the Women's Liberation Movement has at least provided a stimulus for some men to accept women as equal partners in most areas of life. These are the men who have chosen to learn and grow from women's experiences and together with women are creating new norms for relationships. Popular literature and research on male sex roles is expanding, reflecting a wider interest in masculinity. Weekly news magazines such as *Time* and *Newsweek* have run major stories on the "new masculinity," suggesting that positive changes are taking place in the home and in the workplace. Small groups of men scattered around the country have organized against pornography, battering, and sexual assault. Finally there is the National Organization for Changing Men which has a pro-feminist, pro-gay, pro–"new man" agenda, and its ranks are slowly growing.

In schools where I have worked with teachers, they report that years of efforts to enhance educational opportunities for girls have also had some positive effects on boys. The boys seem more tolerant of girls' participation in coed sports activities and in traditionally male shops and courses. They seem to have a greater respect for the accomplishments of women through women's contributions to literature and history. Among elementary school aged males, the expression of vulnerable feelings is gaining acceptance. In general, however, there has been far too little attention paid to redirecting male role development.

Boys Will Be Boys

I think back to the four wrestlers and the stifling culture of masculinity in which they live. If schools were to radically alter this culture and substitute for it a new vision of masculinity, what would that look like? In this environment, boys would express a full range of behaviors and emotions without fear of being chastised. They would be permitted and encouraged to cry, to be afraid, to show joy, and to express love in a gentle fashion. Extreme concern for career goals would be replaced by a consideration of one's need for recreation, health, and meaningful work. Older boys would be encouraged to tutor and play with younger students. Moreover, boys would receive as much recognition for artistic talents as they do for athletics, and, in general, they would value leisure-time, recreational activities as highly as competitive sports.

In a system where maleness and femaleness were equally valued, boys might no longer feel that they have to "prove" themselves to other boys; they would simply accept the worth of each person and value those differences. Boys would realize that it is permissible to admit failure. In addition, they would seek out opportunities to learn from girls and women. Emotional support would be commonplace, and it would no longer be seen as just the role of the female to provide the support. Relationships between boys and girls would no longer be based on limited roles, but instead would become expressions of two individuals learning from and supporting one another. Relationships between boys would reflect their care for one another rather then their mutual fear and distrust.

Aggressive styles of resolving conflicts would be the exception rather than the norm. Girls would feel welcome in activities dominated by boys, knowing that they were safe from the threat of being sexually harassed. Boys would no longer boast of beating up another boy or of how much they "got off" of a girl the night before. In fact, the boys would be as outraged as the girls at rape or other violent crimes in the community. Finally, boys would become active in efforts to stop nuclear proliferation and all other forms of military violence, following the examples set by activist women.

The development of a new conception of masculinity based on this vision is an ambitious task, but one which is essential for the health and safety of both men and women. The survival of our society may rest on the degree to which we are able to teach men to cherish life.

9

A Push from the Top Shatters a Glass Ceiling

Reed Abelson

PALO, ALTO, Calif.   Hewlett-Packard's elevation of Carly Fiorina to the post of chief executive last month solidified the company's reputation as a bastion of egalitarianism in a male-dominated corporate world. With more than a quarter of Hewlett-Packard's managers women—including one who was a main rival of Ms. Fiorina for the top job—it seemed incontestable that the glass ceiling that stops the rise of female executives at so many other companies had been shattered.

But who hurled the rock?

The surprising answer: a middle-aged white guy who never thought much about women in the workplace—until he was thrust suddenly into the challenging role of single parent.

The struggle of Lewis E. Platt, now the company's 58-year-old chairman, to juggle the competing duties of father and breadwinner when he was a rising senior executive nearly two decades ago had a happy ending for Hewlett-Packard. And his success in turning company policy around from the traditional "man rules the roost" culture to a gender-blind ethos holds an important lesson for the rest of corporate America: A litte direction at the top can go a long way.

It all began in 1981. Back then, Mr. Platt was a general manager, and Hewlett-Packard was what he describes as a "white male haven," populated by graduates of engineering schools in dark suits with starched white shirts. He was, he says, quite comfortable working in that male-dominated environment and leaving the child-rearing and housekeeping chores to his wife of 16 years, Susan.

Then, his world fell apart: Susan died of cancer, and suddenly, he was the one who had to make dinner for his two daughters, Laura and Caryn, then 9 and 11, get them to school, make sure they did their homework in the evenings and even find the time to go grocery shopping.

"My mother had really been the one running the show on the home front," said Caryn, now 29, who runs her own social services business. She has memories of standing with her father and her sister in a supermarket aisle wondering whether there were enough varieties of Hamburger Helper, one of the few dishes Mr. Platt could prepare, to dine on that week.

His sudden vulnerability, Mr. Platt says, shattered his old assumption that any difficulties women had in the workplace were of their own making. "Here I was a white male, doing really well at H.P.," Mr. Platt recalled in an interview at the company's headquarters in Palo Alto, Calif. "I was suddenly thrust into a different role." In the position of having double duty at home and at work. "I couldn't cope any better than they did," he said.

For six months after his wife's death, he said, his co-workers allowed him to grieve and concentrate on getting his personal life in order instead of putting his full energy into his career. "I was probably a pretty marginal performer," he admitted, but he came to understand the ebb and flow of careers. "One day I would be back and give the time and energy to be a senior manager," he said.

As the months rolled by, his life remained frantic, he says, a never-ending grind of traveling, working late in the office, getting up early to be with his children and turning to grandparents or nannies to care for them when he was not around. At one point, he debated leaving Hewlett-Packard; but as a lifelong employee, who had joined right out of business school in 1966 and worked his way up the ladder, he soldiered on.

When he married again in 1983, his second wife, Joan, took over the household responsibilities, freeing him to indulge his workaholic tendencies. But rather than retreating to his old way of thinking, he found he sympathized with the plight of the average working woman more than ever. The new Mrs. Platt had two daughters of her own, Amanda and Hillary, then 9 and 7, and surrounded as he was as the sole male, he had little choice but to look at their side of things, noted his daughter, Caryn. "We would gang up on him pretty mercilessly," she recalled. All four daughters are now working.

Named a vice president in 1983, Mr. Platt continued his ascent at Hewlett-Packard, managing various parts of the company's computer business before becoming an executive vice president in 1987. During that time, more women were rising to the level of manager, but few were making it to the highest ranks.

By the time he became chief executive in 1992, he says, droves of those women managers were leaving. "The pipeline didn't look very good," he said. After an outside consultant conducted interviews with many of these women, he came to realize that despite his own open-mindedness on the subject, the company's policies were not flexible enough to accommodate their lives outside the workplace.

What concerned him in particular were the women in their late 30's who left the company to devote more time to their children, never to be seen again. "They were gone," Mr. Platt said. "We were no longer connected to them."

So he decided to take action. Working with other top executives, Mr. Platt developed what for Hewlett-Packard was a new workplace strategy. Over the next several years, the company began to encourage employees to adjust their workweeks, arrange flexible work schedules, work at home if necessary and even share jobs — all so that they could meet their personal responsibilities. They could even take sabbaticals — yearlong unpaid leaves from the company — no questions asked.

While many companies offer these options, few corporations actually encourage their use. Hewlett-Packard did. Mr. Platt made speeches, reminding managers that they needed to consider seriously any of their employees' requests to take advantage of this new flexibility, and he put his name on memos sent to managers across the world. "Work/life issues are a business priority," one statement said. "Attention to work/life issues strengthens H.P.'s competitive edge and improves teamwork within H.P."

Even high-level employees take advantage of the new flexibility. Janice Chaffin, an 18-year Hewlett-Packard employee and general manager in charge of providing large computer systems to companies, for example, shared that position, just one rank below division president at the company, for a year.

Ms. Chaffin says she has never come under any pressure to put in time in the office for the sake of appearance — her bosses' boss even encouraged her to make clear to her own manager, who was known for spending nearly every waking hour at the office, that she would not do the same. "It was never an issue," she said.

Nearly all employees determine their own hours to some extent, according to the company, and large numbers opt to work at home at least some of the time. About 12 percent have formal telecommuting arrangements, and employees are routinely asked about how receptive their managers are to their needs in balancing work with the rest of their lives.

Perhaps most important, Mr. Platt has been vocal on the issue, according to Jerry Cashman, the company's director of programs that encourage work-life balance and diversity. He also likes to remind male colleagues of some of the built-in disadvantages women operate under; he never tires of noting that while the vast majority of them are married to men who work, two-thirds of male managers have stay-at-home wives.

Mr. Platt says the new policy is not just the right thing to do—it is the smart thing. "Anything you can do to attract and retain the best talent is really critical," he said.

The results, in fact, have been dramatic. In the early 90's, the turnover for women was twice that of men, according to the company; now, the gap has been eliminated and the rates are almost identical. Moreover, the company says it loses fewer than 5 percent of its employees each year, compared with an industry average that the consulting firm William M. Mercer puts at 17 percent.

Brenda Vathauer, a high-powered marketing manager, says the freedom to set her own agenda persuaded her to return to Hewlett-Packard after her maternity leave. But she found herself in an odd position: She did not want a part-time job, which she noted is too often considered a "subjob" at most companies, but she did not want to work the 60 hours of a typical full-time job, either.

The solution: She teamed up with another working mother to share a full-time management position in customer service. Each woman now puts in three 10-hour days a week, each receives three-quarters pay and benefits—and each gets to spend four days a week at home, counting weekends. "You can keep your career more on track," explained Karen Walker, her partner in the enterprise and a mother of three.

Men make use of the company's programs, too. Bill Hornung, also a customer-service manager, describes himself as "a telecommuter poster child" for other men because he works at home so can he care for his two children, 5 and 9, when his wife, a flight attendant, is in the air.

To be sure, Hewlett-Packard is not an equal-opportunity utopia. Mr. Platt readily admits that the company has had difficulty recruiting and promoting blacks. The company said it does not disclose the percentage of managers within certain ethnic groups.

Even so, to the outside world, the promotion of Ms. Fiorina to chief executive—she is only the third woman now heading a Fortune 500 company—was seen as a groundbreaking event. And though it was greeted as policy as usual inside the company, some Hewlett-Packard employees reveled in the symbolism. Just as the victory of the American women's soccer team provided important role models for young women, so did the selection of Ms. Fiorina, they say.

Bart Coddington, who works with analysts studying the computer industry for the company, says his 3-year-old granddaughter, Sydney, "will grow up with all that."

"I'm just so excited for her," he said.

Now that the white, middle-aged guy responsible for ushering in this era of equality will step down as chairman at the end of the year, what about the woman who replaced him as chief executive? When she was appointed, Ms. Fiorina made a widely reported, controversial assertion that there was no glass ceiling. She has since told colleagues that her remark may not apply throughout corporate America, and she has emphasized the need to look for talent wherever it can be found, regardless of sex, race or age. She is not giving interviews.

As for Mr. Platt, he is leaving it up to the company's employees to make sure Hewlett-Packard does not revert to its old self. Specific programs are not important, he says. "It's the core values."

10

C. P. Ellis

Studs Terkel

We're in his office in Durham, North Carolina. He is the business manager of the International Union of Operating Engineers. On the wall is a plaque: "Certificate of Service, in recognition to C. P. Ellis, for your faithful service to the city in having served as a member of the Durham Human Relations Council. February 1977."

At one time, he had been president (exalted cyclops) of the Durham chapter of the Ku Klux Klan . . .

He is fifty-three years old.

My father worked in a textile mill in Durham. He died at forty-eight years old. It was probably from cotton dust. Back then, we never heard of brown lung. I was about seventeen years old and had a mother and sister depending on somebody to make a livin'. It was just barely enough insurance to cover his burial. I had to quit school and go to work. I was about eighth grade when I quit.

My father worked hard but never had enough money to buy decent clothes. When I went to school, I never seemed to have adequate clothes to wear. I always left school late afternoon with a sense of inferiority. The other kids had nice clothes, and I just had what Daddy could buy. I still got some of those inferiority feelin's now that I have to overcome once in a while.

I loved my father. He would go with me to ball games. We'd go fishin' together. I was really ashamed of the way he'd dress. He would take this money and give it to me instead of putting it on himself. I always had the feeling about somebody looking at him and makin' fun of him and makin' fun of me. I think it had to do somethin' with my life.

My father and I were very close, but we didn't talk about too many intimate things. He did have a drinking problem. During the week, he would work every day, but weekend he was ready to get plastered. I can understand when a guy looks at his paycheck and looks at his bills, and he's worried hard all the week, and his bills are larger than his paycheck. He'd done the best he could the entire week, and there seemed to be no hope. It's an illness thing. Finally you just say: "The heck with it. I'll just get drunk and forget it."

My father was out of work during the depression, and I remember going with him to the finance company uptown, and he was turned down. That's something that's always stuck.

My father never seemed to be happy. It was a constant struggle with him just like it was for me. It's very seldom I'd see him laugh. He was just tryin' to figure out what he could do from one day to the next.

After several years pumping gas at a service station, I got married. We had to have children. Four. One child was born blind and retarded, which was a real additional expense to us. He's never spoken a word. He doesn't know me when I go to see him. But I see him, I hug his neck. I talk to him, tell him I love him. I don't know whether he knows me or not, but I know he's well taken care of. All my life, I had work, never a day without work, worked all the overtime I could get and still could not survive financially. I began to say there's somethin' wrong with this country. I worked my butt off and just never seemed to break even.

I had some real great ideas about this great nation. (Laughs.) They say to abide by the law, go to church, do right and live for the Lord, and everything'll work out. But it didn't work out. It just kept gettin' worse and worse.

I was workin' a bread route. The highest I made one week was seventy-five dollars. The rent on our house was about twelve dollars a week. I will never forget: outside of this house was a 265-gallon oil drum, and I never did get enough money to fill up that oil drum. What I would do every night, I would run up to the store and buy five gallons of oil and climb up the ladder and pour it in that 265-gallon drum. I could hear that five gallons when it hits the bottom of that oil drum, splatters, and it sounds like it's nothin' in there. But it would keep the house warm for the night. Next day you'd have to do the same thing.

I left the bread route with fifty dollars in my pocket. I went to the bank and I borrowed four thousand dollars to buy the service station. I worked seven days a week, open and close, and finally had a heart attack. Just about two months before the last payments of that loan. My wife had done the best she could to keep it runnin'. Tryin' to come out of that hole, I just couldn't do it.

I really began to get bitter. I didn't know who to blame. I tried to find somebody. I began to blame it on black people. I had to hate somebody. Hatin' America is hard to do because you can't see it to hate it. You gotta have somethin' to look at to hate. (Laughs.) The natural person for me to hate would be black people, because my father before me was a member of the Klan. As far as he was concerned, it was the savior of the white people. It was the only organization in the world that would take care of the white people. So I began to admire the Klan.

I got active in the Klan while I was at the service station. Every Monday night, a group of men would come by and buy a Coca-Cola, go back to the car, take a few drinks, and come back and stand around talkin'. I couldn't help but wonder: Why are these dudes comin' out every Monday? They said they were with the Klan and have meetings close-by. Would I be interested? Boy, that was an opportunity I really looked forward to! To be part of somethin'. I joined the Klan, went from member to chaplain, from chaplain to vice-president, from vice-president to president. The title is exalted cyclops.

The first night I went with the fellas, they knocked on the door and gave the signal. They sent some robed Klansmen to talk to me and give me some instructions. I was led into a large meeting room, and this was the time of my life! It was thrilling. Here's a guy who's worked all his life and struggled all his life to be something, and here's the moment to be something. I will never forget it. Four robed Klansmen led me into the hall. The lights were dim, and the only thing you could see was an illuminated cross. I knelt before the cross. I had to make certain vows and promises. We promised to uphold the purity of the white race, fight communism, and protect white womanhood.

After I had taken my oath, there was loud applause goin' throughout the buildin', musta been at least four hundred people. For this one little ol' person. It was a thrilling moment for C. P. Ellis.

It disturbs me when people who do not really know what it's all about are so very critical of individual Klansmen. The majority of 'em are low-income whites, people who really don't have a part in something. They have been shut out as well as the blacks. Some are not very well educated either. Just like myself. We had a lot of support from doctors and lawyers and police officers.

Maybe they've had bitter experiences in this life and they had to hate somebody. So the natural person to hate would be the black person. He's beginnin' to come up, he's beginnin' to learn to read and start votin' and run for political office. Here are white people who are supposed to be superior to them, and we're shut out.

I can understand why people join extreme right-wing or left-wing groups. They're in the same boat I was. Shut out. Deep down inside, we want to be part of this great society. Nobody listens, so we join these groups.

At one time, I was state organizer of the National Rights party. I organized a youth group for the Klan. I felt we were getting old and our generation's gonna die. So I contacted certain kids in schools. They were havin' racial problems. On the first night, we had a hundred high school students. When they came in the door, we had "Dixie" playin'. These kids were just thrilled to death. I begin to hold weekly meetin's with 'em, teachin' the principles of the Klan. At that time, I believed Martin Luther King had Communist connections. I began to teach that Andy Young was affiliated with the Communist party.

I had a call one night from one of our kids. He was about twelve. He said: "I just been robbed downtown by two niggers." I'd had a couple of drinks and that really teed me off. I go downtown and couldn't find the kid. I got worried. I saw two young black people. I had the .32 revolver with me. I said: "Nigger, you seen a little young white boy up here? I just got a call from him and was told that some niggers robbed him of fifteen cents." I pulled my pistol out and put it right at his head. I said: "I've always wanted to kill a nigger and I think I'll make you the first one." I nearly scared the kid to death, and he struck off.

This was the time when the civil rights movement was really beginnin' to peak. The blacks were beginnin' to demonstrate and picket downtown stores. I never will forget some black lady I hated with a purple passion. Ann Atwater. Every time I'd go downtown, she'd be leadin' a boycott. How I hated—pardon the expression, I don't use it much now—how I just hated that black nigger. (Laughs.) Big, fat, heavy woman. She'd pull about eight demonstrations, and first thing you know they had two, three blacks at the checkout counter. Her and I have had some pretty close confrontations.

I felt very big, yeah. (Laughs.) We're more or less a secret organization. We didn't want anybody to know who we were, and I began to do some thinkin'. What am I hidin' for? I've never been convicted of anything in my life. I don't have any court record. What am I, C. P. Ellis, as a citizen and a member of the United Klansmen of America? Why can't I go the city council meeting and say: "This is the way we feel about the matter? We don't want you to purchase mobile units to set in our schoolyards. We don't want niggers in our schools."

We began to come out in the open. We would go to the meetings, and the blacks would be there and we'd be there. It was a confrontation every time. I didn't hold back anything. We began to make some inroads with the city councilmen and county commissioners. They began to call us friend. Call us at night on the telephone: "C. P., glad you came to that meeting last night." They didn't want integration either, but they did it secretively, in order to get elected. They couldn't stand up openly and say it, but they were glad somebody was sayin' it. We visited some of the city leaders in their home and talk to 'em privately. It wasn't long before councilmen would call me up: "The blacks are comin' up tonight and makin' outrageous demands. How about some of you people showin' up and have a little balance?" I'd get on the telephone: "The niggers is comin' to the council meeting tonight. Persons in the city's called me and asked us to be there."

We'd load up our cars and we'd fill up half the council chambers, and the blacks the other half. During these times, I carried weapons to the meetings, outside my belt. We'd go there armed. We would wind up just hollerin' and fussin' at each other. What happened? As a result of our fightin' one another, the city council still had their way. They didn't want to give up control to the blacks nor the Klan. They were usin' us.

I began to realize this later down the road. One day I was walkin' downtown and a certain city council member saw me comin'. I expected him to shake my hand because he was talkin' to me at night on the telephone. I had been in his home and visited with him. He crossed the street. Oh shit, I began to think, somethin's wrong here. Most of 'em are merchants or maybe an attorney, an insurance agent, people like that. As long as they kept low-income whites and low-income blacks fightin', they're gonna maintain control.

I began to get that feeling after I was ignored in public. I thought: Bullshit, you're not gonna use me anymore. That's when I began to do some real serious thinkin'.

The same thing is happening in this country today. People are being used by those in control, those who have all the wealth. I'm not espousing communism. We got the greatest system of government in the world. But those who have it simply don't want those who don't have it to have any part of it. Black and white. When it comes to money, the green, the other colors make no difference. (Laughs.)

I spent a lot of sleepless nights. I still didn't like blacks. I didn't want to associate with 'em. Blacks, Jews, or Catholics. My father said: "Don't have anything to do with 'em." I didn't until I met a black person and talked with him, eyeball to eyeball, and met a Jewish person and talked to him, eyeball to eyeball. I found out they're people just like me. They cried, they cussed, they prayed, they had desires. Just like myself. Thank God, I got to the point where I can look past labels. But at that time, my mind was closed.

I remember one Monday night Klan meeting. I said something was wrong. Our city fathers were using us. And I didn't like to be used. The reactions of the others was not too pleasant: "Let's just keep fightin' them niggers."

I'd go home at night and I'd have to wrestle with myself. I'd look at a black person walkin' down the street, and the guy'd have ragged shoes or his clothes would be worn. That began to do somethin' to me inside. I went through this for about six months. I felt I just had to get out of the Klan. But I wouldn't get out.

Then something happened. The state AFL-CIO received a grant from the Department of HEW, a $78,000 grant: how to solve racial problems in the school system. I got a telephone call from the president of the state AFL-CIO. "We'd like to get some people together from all walks of life." I said: "All walks of life? Who you talkin' about?" He said: "Blacks, whites, liberals, conservatives, Klansmen, NAACP people."

I said: "No way am I comin' with all those niggers. I'm not gonna be associated with those type of people." A White Citizens Council guy said: "Let's go up there and see what's goin' on. It's tax money bein' spent." I walk in the door, and there was a large number of blacks and white liberals. I knew most of 'em by face 'cause I seen 'em demonstratin' around town. Ann Atwater was there. (Laughs.) I just forced myself to go in and sit down.

The meeting was moderated by a great big black guy who was bushy-headed. (Laughs.) That turned me off. He acted very nice. He said: "I want you all to feel free to say anything you want to say." Some of the blacks stand up and say it's white racism. I took all I could take. I asked for the floor and I cut loose. I said: "No, sir, it's black racism. If we didn't have niggers in the schools, we wouldn't have the problems we got today."

I will never forget. Howard Clements, a black guy, stood up. He said: "I'm certainly glad C. P. Ellis come because he's the most honest man here tonight." I said: "What's that nigger tryin' to do?" (Laughs.) At the end of that meeting, some blacks tried to come up shake my hand, but I wouldn't do it. I walked off.

Second night, same group was there. I felt a little more easy because I got some things off my chest. The third night, after they elected all the committees, they want to elect a chairman. Howard Clements stood up and said: "I suggest we elect two co-chairpersons." Joe Beckton, executive director of the Human Relations Commission, just as black as he can be, he nominated me. There was a reaction from some blacks. Nooo. And, of all things, they nominated Ann Atwater, that big old fat black gal that I had just hated with a purple passion, as co-chairman. I thought to myself: Hey, ain't no way I can work with that gal. Finally, I agreed to accept it, 'cause at this point, I was tired of fightin', either for survival or against black people or against Jews or against Catholics.

A Klansman and a militant black woman, co-chairmen of the school committee. It was impossible. How could I work with her? But after about two or three days, it was in our hands. We had to make it a success. This gave me another sense of belongin', a sense of pride. This helped this inferiority feelin' I had. A man who has stood up publicly and said he despised black people, all of a sudden he was willin' to work with 'em. Here's a chance for a low-income white man to be somethin'. In spite of all my hatred for blacks and Jews and liberals, I accepted the job. Her and I began to reluctantly work together. (Laughs.) She had as many problems workin' with me as I had workin' with her.

One night, I called her: "Ann, you and I should have a lot of differences and we got 'em now. But there's somethin' laid out here before us, and if it's gonna be a success, you and I are gonna have to make it one. Can we lay aside some of these feelin's?" She said: "I'm willing if you are." I said: "Let's do it."

My old friends would call me at night: "C. P., what the hell is wrong with you? You're sellin' out the white race." This begin to make me have guilt feelin's. Am I doin' right? Am I doin' wrong? Here I am all of a sudden makin' an about-face and tryin' to deal with my feelin's, my heart. My mind was beginnin' to open up. I was beginnin' to see what was right and what was wrong. I don't want the kids to fight forever.

We were gonna go ten nights. By this time, I had went to work at Duke University, in maintenance. Makin' very little money. Terry Sanford give me this ten days off with pay. He was president of Duke at the time. He knew I was a Klansman and realized the importance of blacks and whites getting along.

I said: "If we're gonna make this thing a success, I've got to get to my kind of people." The low-income whites. We walked the streets of Durham, and we knocked on doors and invited people. Ann was goin' into the black community. They just wasn't respondin' to us when we made these house calls. Some of 'em were cussin' us out. "You're sellin' us out, Ellis, get out of my door. I don't want to talk to you." Ann was gettin' the same response from blacks: "What are you doin' messin' with that Klansman?"

One day, Ann and I went back to the school and we sat down. We began to talk and just reflect. Ann said: "My daughter came home cryin' every day. She said her teacher was makin' fun of me in front of the other kids." I said: "Boy, the same thing happened to my kid. White liberal teacher was makin' fun of Tim Ellis's father, the Klansman. In front of other peoples. He came home cryin'." At this point—(he pauses, swallows hard, stifles a sob)—I begin to see, here we are, two people from the far ends of the fence, havin' identical problems, except hers bein' black and me bein' white. From that moment on, I tell ya, that gal and I worked together good. I begin to love the girl, really. (He weeps.)

The amazing thing about it, her and I, up to that point, had cussed each other, bawled each other, we hated each other. Up to that point, we didn't know each other. We didn't know we had things in common.

We worked at it, with the people who came to these meetings. They talked about racism, sex education, about teachers not bein' qualified. After seven, eight nights of real intense discussion, these people, who'd never talked to each other before, all of a sudden came up with resolutions. It was really somethin', you had to be there to get the tone and feelin' of it.

At that point, I didn't like integration, but the law says you do this and I've got to do what the law says, okay? We said: "Let's take these resolutions to the school board." The most disheartening thing I've ever faced was the school system refused to implement any one of these resolutions. These were recommendations from the people who pay taxes and pay their salaries. (Laughs.)

I thought they were good answers. Some of 'em I didn't agree with, but I been in this thing from the beginning, and whatever comes of it, I'm gonna support it. Okay, since the school board refused, I decided I'd just run for the school board.

I spent eighty-five dollars on the campaign. The guy runnin' against me spent several thousand. I really had nobody on my side. The Klan turned against me. The low-income whites turned against me. The liberals didn't particularly like me. The blacks were suspicious of me. The blacks wanted to support me, but they couldn't muster up enough to support a Klansman on the school board. (Laughs.) But I made up my mind that what I was doin' was right, and I was gonna do it regardless what anybody said.

It bothered me when people would call and worry my wife. She's always supported me in anything I wanted to do. She was changing, and my boys were too. I got some of my youth corps kids involved. They still followed me.

I was invited to the Democratic women's social hour as a candidate. Didn't have but one suit to my name. Had it six, seven, eight years. I had it cleaned, put on the best shirt I had and a tie. Here were all this high-class wealthy candidates shakin' hands. I walked up to the mayor and stuck out my hand. He give me that handshake with that rag type of hand. He said: "C. P., I'm glad to see you." But I could tell by his handshake he was lyin' to me. This was botherin' me. I know I'm a low-income person. I know I'm not wealthy. I know they were sayin': "What's this little ol' dude runnin' for school board?" Yet they had to smile and make like they're glad to see me. I begin to spot some black people in that room. I automatically went to 'em and that was a firm handshake. They said: "I'm glad to see you, C. P." I knew they meant it—you can tell about a handshake.

Every place I appeared, I said I will listen to the voice of the people. I will not make a major decision until I first contacted all the organizations in the city. I got 4,640 votes. The guy beat me by two thousand. Not bad for eighty-five bucks and no constituency.

The whole world was openin' up, and I was learnin' new truths that I had never learned before. I was beginnin' to look at a black person, shake hands with him, and see him as a human bein'. I hadn't got rid of all this stuff. I've still got a little bit of it. But somethin' was happenin' to me.

It was almost like bein' born again. It was a new life. I didn't have these sleepless nights I used to have when I was active in the Klan and slippin' around at night. I could sleep at night and feel good about it. I'd rather live now than at any other time in history. It's a challenge.

Back at Duke, doin' maintenance, I'd pick up my tools, fix the commode, unstop the drains. But this got in my blood. Things weren't right in this country, and what we done in Durham needs to be told. I was so miserable at Duke, I could hardly stand it. I'd go to work every morning just hatin' to go.

My whole life had changed. I got an eighth-grade education, and I wanted to complete high school. Went to high school in the afternoons on a program called PEP—Past Employment Progress. I was about the only white in class, and the oldest. I begin to read about biology. I'd take my books home at night, 'cause I was determined to get through. Sure enough, I graduated. I got the diploma at home.

I come to work one mornin' and some guy says: "We need a union." At this time I wasn't pro-union. My daddy was anti-labor, too. We're not gettin' paid much, we're havin' to work seven days in a row. We're all starvin' to death. The next day, I meet the international representative of the Operating Engineers. He give me authorization cards. "Get these cards out and we'll have an election." There was eighty-eight for the union and seventeen no's. I was elected chief steward for the union.

Shortly after, a union man come down from Charlotte and says we need a full-time rep. We've got only two hundred people at the two plants here. It's just barely enough money comin' in to pay your salary. You'll have to get out and organize more people. I didn't know nothin' about organizin' unions, but I knew how to organize people, stir people up. (Laughs.) That's how I got to be business agent for the union.

When I began to organize, I began to see far deeper. I began to see people again bein' used. Blacks against whites. I say this without any hesitancy: management is vicious. There's two things they want to keep: all the money and all the say-so. They don't want these poor workin' folks to have none of that. I begin to see management fightin' me with everything they had. Hire anti-union law firms, badmouth unions. The people were makin' a dollar ninety-five an hour, barely able to get through weekends. I worked as a business rep for five years and was seein' all this.

Last year, I ran for business manager of the union. He's elected by the workers. The guy that ran against me was black, and our membership is seventy-five percent black. I thought: Claiborne, there's no way you can beat that black guy. People know your background. Even though you've made tremendous strides, those black people are not gonna vote for you. You know how much I beat him? Four to one. (Laughs.)

The company used my past against me. They put out letters with a picture of a robe and a cap: Would you vote for a Klansman? They wouldn't deal with the issues. I immediately called for a mass meeting. I met with the ladies at an electric component plant. I said: "Okay, this is Claiborne Ellis. This is where I come from. I want you to know right now, you black ladies here, I was at one time a member of the Klan. I want you to know, because they'll tell you about it."

I invited some of my old black friends. I said: "Brother Joe, Brother Howard, be honest now and tell these people how you feel about me." They done it. (Laughs.) Howard Clements kidded me a little bit. He said: "I don't know what I'm doin' here, supportin' an ex-Klansman." (Laughs.) He said: "I know what C. P. Ellis come from. I knew him when he was. I knew him as he grew, and growed with him. I'm tellin' you now: follow, follow this Klansman." (He pauses, swallows hard.) "Any questions?" "No," the black ladies said. "Let's get on with the meeting, we need Ellis." (He laughs and weeps.) Boy, black people sayin' that about me. I won one thirty-four to forty-one. Four to one.

It makes you feel good to go into a plant and butt heads with professional union busters. You see black people and white people join hands to defeat the racist issues they use against people. They're tryin' the same things with the Klan. It's still happenin' today. Can you imagine a guy who's got an adult high school diploma runnin' into professional college graduates who are union busters? I gotta compete with 'em. I work seven days a week, nights, and on Saturday and Sunday. The salary's not that great, and if I didn't care, I'd quit. But I care and I can't quit. I got a taste of it. (Laughs.)

I tell people there's a tremendous possibility in this country to stop wars, the battles, the struggles, the fights between people. People say: "That's an impossible dream. You sound like Martin Luther King." An ex-Klansman who sounds like Martin Luther King. (Laughs.) I don't think it's an impossible dream. It's happened in my life. It's happened in other people's lives in America.

I don't know what's ahead of me. I have no desire to be a big union official. I want to be right out here in the field with the workers. I want to walk through their factory and shake hands with that man whose hands are dirty. I'm gonna do all that one little ol' man can do. I'm fifty-two years old, and I ain't got many years left, but I want to make the best of 'em.

When the news came over the radio that Martin Luther King was assassinated, I got on the telephone and begin to call other Klansmen. We just had a real party at the service station. Really rejoicin' 'cause that son of a bitch was dead. Our troubles are over with. They say the older you get, the harder it is for you to change. That's not necessarily true. Since I changed, I've set down and listened to tapes of Martin Luther King. I listen to it and tears come to my eyes 'cause I know what he's sayin' now. I know what's happenin'.

POSTSCRIPT: *The phone rings. A conversation. . . .*

"This was a black guy who's director of Operation Breakthrough in Durham. I had called his office. I'm interested in employin' some young black person who's interested in learnin' the labor movement. I want somebody who's never had an opportunity, just like myself. Just so he can read and write, that's all."

11

Narrowing the Income Gap between Rich and Poor

Michael Hout and Samuel R. Lucas

The growing income gap between rich and poor Americans has become a key issue in this political season. The gap is larger now than at any point in the last 75 years. But a heated political and academic debate is under way about what the numbers mean. Some politicians and commentators try to dismiss income inequality with a variety of false assertions. They claim that inequality is inevitable because every society has its rich and poor; that it is a reflection of Americans' unequal talents; that it is necessary for economic growth; or that it may be unfortunate but must be tolerated because of the prohibitive expense of initiating government programs to redistribute wealth.

The results of a year-long research project that we and four colleagues in the sociology department at the University of California at Berkeley conducted contradict all of these propositions, as we document in *Inequality by Design: Cracking the Bell Curve Myth*, Princeton University Press (1996). Social inequality is not a force beyond our control.

Recent American history and the experience of several European nations show that economic inequality depends on the choices we make—how we regulate corporations and unions, how we distribute the tax burden, how we finance or do not finance education, and how we set wages. Nor is "taxing and spending" our only option.

Perhaps the most telling argument against the inevitability of our current situation is that not only is the inequality in income between the richest and the poorest in the United States greater now than in the past, but it is also greater than that of any other populous, industrialized country. Workers in such countries also have had to deal with the globalization of trade and the disruptions caused by new technology; yet only workers in the United States have lost so much ground. For exam-

From *The Chronicle of Higher Education*, August 8, 1995, pp. 81–82. Michael Hout is professor of sociology and Director, Survey Research Center, University of California, Berkeley. Samuel R. Lucas is assistant professor of sociology, University of California, Berkeley. This article draws on their forthcoming book, *Inequality by Design: Cracking the Bell Curve Myth* (co-authored with Claude S. Fischer, Martin Sanchez Jankowski, Ann Swidler, and Kim Voss; Princeton University Press). Reprinted by permission of the authors.

ple, in 1974 the chief executive officers of American corporations made about $35 for every worker's dollar; in 1995, they made $224 for every worker's dollar. By contrast, the chief executive officers of German corporations make about 21 deutsche marks (about $14) for every one earned by workers. Clearly, different economic choices produce different outcomes.

While every society has its rich and poor, inequality is mainly a matter of degree. In 1974, when the gap between the incomes of the richest and poorest Americans was at a historic low, the top 10 percent of U.S. households had incomes 31 times those of the poorest 10 percent and four times those of median-income households. By 1994, those numbers were 55 times the poorest and six times the median. Not only is inequality growing; its growth is accelerating. Inequality surged between 1991 and 1993 as the most recent recession lowered incomes for all but the richest Americans. Executives killed jobs in ways that would be illegal in Germany and France—for example, shutting down plants in some regions and relocating them in jurisdictions with right-to-work laws. Wall Street rewarded the executives with a mid-recession rally that boosted the value of their stock options.

Viewing inequality as inevitable absolves us of responsibility for reducing it. The current differences among nations mean that Americans need to be activist, not fatalistic, in the face of growing inequality. They also suggest that inequality is not produced by the genetic or other immutable personal characteristics that doom many workers to low wages. In their controversial book *The Bell Curve: The Reshaping of American Life by Differences in Intelligence* (Free Press, 1994), the political scientist Charles Murray and the late psychologist Richard J. Herrnstein tried to explain the rising inequality of incomes in the United States by claiming that the economy now rewards intelligence more than in the past.

Our reanalysis of their data shows conclusively that the test scores that they relied on to gauge intelligence reflect home environments—particularly parents' socio-economic levels—as well as the quality of the schools people attended. For example, if I.Q. tests measure innate ability, people's scores on them ought to correlate equally well with their educational achievements both before and after the test. But the data used by Mr. Murray and Mr. Herrnstein show that people's scores correlate much more closely with their educational achievements at the time of the test than they do with their subsequent educational achievements. Schools create intelligence; they do not merely certify it. Thus the "intelligence" measured by tests is affected by a person's environment and is not solely the result of inborn characteristics.

Certainly, cognitive skills—though not innate—are important to one's earnings. However, errors and omissions in *The Bell Curve* also exaggerate the role of I.Q. in American inequality. Our reanalysis of the book's data shows that refining and enriching people's social environment makes I.Q. just one variable among many affecting inequality. Would that talent alone decided where a person ended up in society. Being born rich is still at least as much of an advantage as performing well on tests. . . .

Nor are the growing disparities in income an unavoidable negative effect of economic growth. Our review of the latest economic research concludes that such disparities may actually hinder growth. Since 1945, societies that have had greater inequality in incomes between the richest and poorest families have tended to have lower, not higher, subsequent economic growth.

The German and Italian economies grew faster between 1975 and 1989 than did that of the United States, but the gap between the incomes of the richest and the poorest citizens in those countries did not increase. In the United States, the period from 1955 through 1974 was the era of the greatest economic growth in this century, and also the era of the greatest equality of incomes in this century. The richest 5 percent of U.S. households saw their incomes go up rapidly during that period, but their share of total household income fell from 22 percent to 16 percent as the incomes of poor and middle-income households rose even faster.

Greater equality of income between the richest and poorest does not harm productivity, either. In a comparative analysis of Western nations spanning the 1970s and 1980s, the Northwestern University economist Rebecca Blank found that factors including job-security laws (such as tenure laws for workers in some European countries), homeowner subsidies (such as tax deductions for mortgage interest in the United States), health insurance, and public child care did not inhibit the flexibility of businesses to shift resources, for example from one set of priorities or products to another.

Growing inequality of incomes may actually be hurting our economic performance. In a study of more than 100 U.S. businesses, Douglass Cowherd of the Brookings Institution and our Berkeley colleague David Levine found that the smaller the wage gap between managers and workers, the higher the quality of the business's products. Considering how the gap between management compensation and workers' wages has grown in recent years, this analysis suggests that the quality of some companies' products may be suffering.

Do we have to raise taxes and spend on welfare programs to have less inequality of income? Research shows that many social programs can reduce inequality, but it also shows that many countries have low inequality without high spending on social programs. Rates of poverty among children are sensitive indicators of overall inequality. At 22 percent, the proportion of poor children in the United States is higher than that in any other populous, industrial country. Australia and Canada are next, with 14 percent of their children living in poverty—a rate more than 30 percent below that of the United States. The rate of childhood poverty is 10 percent in Britain and Italy, and in the single digits in Germany (7 percent), France (6 percent), and the Netherlands (6 percent).

Some countries achieve their lower rates with expensive social programs, but others don't. Childhood poverty would be substantially higher in France (25 percent) and in Britain (30 percent) if there were no taxes and no welfare programs to redistribute income in those two countries. Their welfare states bring their rates of childhood poverty below that of the United States. But the percentage of children living in poverty already is low before the government transfers any money to poor people in Germany (where the rate is 9 percent before counting the taxes and welfare spending that lower it to 7 percent) and in Italy (12 percent as opposed to the 10 percent after social spending). The rate of childhood poverty is moderate in the Netherlands (14 percent before social programs lower it to 6 percent). Those nations do not need extensive welfare spending to keep children out of poverty, because the economy itself does not generate as much inequality as we see in France, Britain, or the United States.

Germany, Italy, and the Netherlands have less poverty because they have no working poor. They boost the bottom of the income distribution with a minimum wage guaranteeing that full-time workers' children will not be poor. With the current minimum wage of $4.25 per hour, however, an American parent of two can work full time and still fall below the poverty line. Even though Congress has approved a bill raising the minimum wage to $5.25 in September 1997, that will still be true. Indeed, it would be true even if we raised the minimum wage to $6.50 per hour. The continuing debates about the minimum wage in this country have not contradicted this essential point: Young workers and their children are not as poor in countries with higher minimum wages.

Many European countries also use national wage agreements to control inequality. The details differ, but these countries all use some form of collective bargaining that makes management accountable to workers. In Austria and Norway, national associations of employers in different industries bargain with representatives of national unions to determine wages for workers in each sector of the economy. In Germany and Italy, bargaining goes on between unions and employers' associations in each industry or region. The government then routinely extends the terms of these agreements to non-union workers and companies.

In the United States, workers' wages are negotiated with a specific employer, either by individual employees or by a local union. In many jobs, the employer simply offers the job at a preset wage with little or no negotiation. This extremely decentralized system weakens the bargaining power of workers. Research by the Harvard University economist Richard Freeman, reported in *Working Under Different Rules* (Russell Sage Foundation, 1994), shows that the distribution of wages for workers of the same age, education, gender, and occupation is much wider in the United States than in countries with more centralized methods of setting wages.

Unions are the key to more uniform policies for setting wages. They help lower the inequality of income because they typically make management more accountable to workers, particularly when managers try to raise their own pay. The decline of unions in the United States in recent decades has meant that workers have lost the power to claim their share of economic growth. Between 1970 and 1990, the proportion of workers in the private sector belonging to unions dropped from 30 percent to just 11 percent, the lowest rate of union membership in the industrialized world except, possibly, for Japan.

Even as unions were declining, American workers set records in productivity (output per working hour). Between 1949 and 1974, increases in productivity were rewarded by increases in wages. Since 1974, productivity increased 68 percent in manufacturing and 50 percent in the service sector of the economy, but real wages grew less than 10 percent. The gains in productivity fueled both executive compensation—up 600 percent since 1974, according to research by the economic writer Graeff Crystal—and the stock market, where the Dow Jones Industrial Average has risen from 1,500 to more than 5,500 since 1974. Workers have set the table for an American economic feast for over two decades, but they have not received their slice of the growing pie.

The reports about economic inequality keep appearing. Political leaders, with the exception of the Republican Presidential candidate Patrick Buchanan, have been surprisingly passive. The action gap is almost as big as the income gap.

Our review of recent American history and of the actions of our competitors makes it clear that the country need not accept ever-more-extreme income disparities. Nor is the unpopular combination of high taxes and social spending our only remedy. In the past, investments in our schools and colleges helped to equalize opportunity for many citizens. Institutions such as labor unions empowered workers who wanted to claim a share of their own productivity. Today, the economies of countries that have national-incomes policies that include a voice for workers are growing faster than is the economy of the United States, and they are doing a better job of sharing the wealth.

That suggests that the solutions to America's problems of inequality of income are in the classrooms, boardrooms, and workplaces around the country. Washington's role should be to foster opportunity through education and to find ways to bring employers and workers together on an equal footing, so they can solve economic problems directly. For example, we need changes in the policies of the National Labor Relations Board to make it easier to form unions and easier for unions to force employers to engage in binding arbitration over contracts and other disputes.

12

Interracial Justice:
Healing Our Own

Eric K. Yamamoto

For this keynote address I will talk about something that links us, divides us, and has the potential for binding us closely—something, however, that we often find difficult to discuss and write about. That something is, first, grievances among our communites of color that sometimes prevent us from building deep alliances; and second, ways to heal the wounds resulting from those grievances.[1]

Our time together today will be largely what we call in Hawai`i: "Talk Story." Its meaning lies in the messy stories of interracial grievance and healing I will tell, and in the greater clarity those stories bring to your own similar experiences.

Let us start by acknowledging that for many of us these are Alice-in-Wonderland times. Times in which "Civil Rights Initiative" means the dismantling of affirmative action,[2] in which "civil rights victory" can mean an agreement to *end* a school desegregation consent decree in San Francisco backed by the NAACP,[3] in which a progressive civil rights group pays a large sum to a white teacher to forestall a Supreme Court ruling.[4]

In this milieu we observe two colliding impulses in our racial communities. One impulse is the desire of nonwhite racial groups to build interracial alliances. The broad multiracial coalition opposing California's anti-affirmative action, Proposition 209, in one of many examples.

The other impulse, amid shifting racial and class demographics, is to distrust "others," to doubt their motivations and question their actions. Consider the rapid dissolution of multiracial coalitions following the South Central Los Angeles rebellion-riot in 1992 fueled by accusations and countercharges. This latter impulse militates against building deep alliances.

How, then, are we to deal with this complex, dissonant reality—a movement toward interracial alliances characterized partially by anger and distrust?

As framed, this question is one that many in our racial communities prefer to avoid. By focusing attention on interracial tensions, the question can be twisted to obscure what David Roediger calls the "wages of whiteness"—continuing white domi-

Keynote address, First National Law Teachers of Color Conference, Chicago, 1999. Reprinted by permission of the author.

nance in most aspects of American life.[5] By acknowledging interracial grievances, the question also airs dirty laundry, with no easy affirming answers. Indeed, as Elizabeth Martinez says, the answers "require a knowledge and wisdom we have yet to attain."[6]

Nevertheless the question is worth our time and commitment. By avoiding it, racial communities risk having someone else frame the concepts and language of interracial grievance and the methods of reconciliation. A recent new article headline, for instance, coarsely framed interracial relations as "Asians, Blacks and Intolerance." "Given Asian prejudice against blacks," the article said, "it's not surprising many blacks resent Asians."[7] Inflammatory more than informative.

Dealing forthrightly with the dissonant impulses just described requires that we develop sharper ways for handling deep group-on-group grievances that underlie many surface face-to-face conflicts. This means grappling with what we see and hear but do not often discuss: amid changing racial conditions, groups can be simultaneously harmed in one relationship and complicitious in the harm of others in another.

The question then for communities of color is not so much "can we all get along?" but rather, "how" do we get along? To ground this question, let us turn to Seattle and New Orleans: vastly different stories, but with common threads. I ask you to listen with an open ear—some of it is hard to hear, and my brief accounts are at best incomplete.

Seattle

In July of 1999, 6,000 journalists of color congregated in Seattle. Four journalists' associations—African American, Hispanic, Native American, and Asian American—met, as they did five years ago, to deal with the media's role in shaping race issues, to build coalitions around specific tasks (for example, challenging stereotyping in newscasts), and to forge larger reportorial alliances.

Despite general agreement about continuing white dominance in the media, and despite many cooperative efforts, simmering grievances among the associations threatened to turn disagreements about specifics (where to hold a Native American ceremony; how to respond to Washington's version of Proposition 209) into intergroup fires. The escalation sense of mistrust ("are they just out for themselves?") and grievance ("in here is no different from out there") threatened their larger effort to collectively shape the tenor of race understanding in America—all before the conference begins.[8]

New Orleans

In the hot New Orleans summer of 1996, neighborhood tension erupted in a street brawl between Tho Nguyen's son and Ulysses Narcisse.[9] African American residents and the Committee for Justice boycotted Nguyen's PNT grocery store. They accused the owners of assult and discrimination as well as "refusing to accept pennies, taxing food stamps and allowing neighborhood drunkards to loiter." The

Nguyens brought charges of their own about African Americans' untrustworthiness and years of obscene language and repeated taunts of "go back to your own country."

A rally at the Greater Antioch Full Gospel Church demanded that African American proprietors take over the store. "It's time to reclaim the community from a stream of foreigners who invade our neighborhood and bleed it for money." A state politician encouraged the protesters to "fight on," and a minister hoped that the "campaign against outside shop owners in African American neighborhoods [would] spread all over the city."

The city's Human Relations Commission and the United States Department of Justice offered to mediate the escalating dispute. The Committe for Justice declined to participate, however, stating that the Human Relations director was siding with the "mean-spirited grocer" who "operated a reign of terror" and should be "rendered penniless."

How did the Nguyens respond? They closed the store permanently and took to the courts. "The defendants [Committee and Church] are not merely exercising their First Amendment right to peacefully assemble and protest," their federal court compaint said. "Rather, they are engaged in a pattern or practice of economic terrorism" against Vietnamese immigrants. African American spokespersons, on the other hand, describe the storeowners as foreign shopkeepers. "It is clear that some groups just arriving in America see us as the bottom of the pecking order and intend to use us as a stepping stone to their own prosperity." For both sides, these kinds of stock stories caried the day.

And the legal process and media reporting failed to unravel those stories. They failed to engage the community in a probing analysis of what it was that transformed a street brawl into a widespread interracial controversy. The entire dispute resolution process (including mediation) failed to offer, and the Nguyens and the neighborhood residents failed to develop, a thoughtful account of each other's histories and present-day struggles in the area. The process also did not generate a complex understanding of African American, white American, and Vietnamese American relations in New Orleans: the harsh unique effects on African American of southern slavery, Jim Crow apartheid, and contemporary white racism; the existence of stark poverty in both the black and Vietnamese communities; the recent southern violence against Vietnamese immigrants; the publicized inner-city conflicts between Asian American merchants and African American customers. It did not generate deep understanding of New Orleans' history of racial hierarchy, including its middle positioning of Creoles (and potentially Asian Americans) below whites and above blacks.

Three separate attemps at formal dispute resolution failed. Mediation and negotiation sessions focused narrowly on the sale of the store and looked past the healing of deep, personally felt wounds and the repairing of broken group relationships.

Seven months after the altercation, the Nguyens sold the store to a Palestinian. The residents welcomed the new owner, they said, because Palestinian owners treated blacks well. The picketing stopped, but the lawsuit's damage claim and the interracial distrust remained.

For this reason, 350 Vietnamese Americans and African Americans from five community churches gathered to promote "understanding of our cultural and ethnic heritages." "Let us celebrate what we can become," said Reverend Thomas Glasgo. Monsignor Dominic Luong hoped the prayer service in English and Vietnamese would help unify multiracial eastern New Orleans. Fourteen-year-old Hoang Tran "liked how they all come together as a community. There was no fighting or anything like that. It was without racsim."

The warm sense of harmony, however, was largely ephemeral. The prayer service glossed over difficult racial issues. It provided few tools for critically examining and acting on the PNT grocers controversy and others like it. Yet the service was a start. People were talking and hoping. Was this healing? False grace? Or something else?

In the fall of 1997 the new Palestinian owner of the store was shot and killed during a store robbery.

✻   ✻   ✻

How do we think about Seattle and New Orleans? We can start with this: How do communities of color heal our racial wounds—not only those inflicted directly by white America, but also those apparently opened, or rubbed raw, by other racial groups? How can communities of color build relationships, reconciling where appropriate, so that we can live together peaceably and work together politically? And what is the role of legal scholars and activists?

Think again about New Orleans. Why is it there that a civil rights lawsuit and the rhetoric of discrimination (generated initially to meet white-against-black discrimination) appeared to be a stark misfit? Why did three narrowly focused alternative dispute resolution efforts fails? Think about the Lowell High School suit brought by Chinese American plaintiffs to invalidate a San Francisco school desegregation order obtained by the NAACP. Why is it there that plaintiffs deployed civil rights law and the rhetoric of equality so uncritically and so destructively?[10]

How do we develop the concepts, language, and methods our communities need to deal with intergroup grievances in ways that build, rather than destroy, relationships, so that 6,000 journalists or color, attempting to coalesce and powerfully shape public understandings of race in American, do not themselves fracture along the subsurface fault lines of racial grievance?

One suggestion I make is that we focus, in instances, on interracial justice. As developed in another work,[11] within a larger setting of continuing white racism, interracial justice entails hard acknowledgment of the historical and contemporary ways in which racial groups harm one another, along with affirmative efforts to address deeper group grievances and to rearticulate and restructure present-day relations. It means grappling with the challenge of dismantling "a system in which one group (usually but not always white) dominates others and of providing for a new order without producing oppressive structures and attitudes".[12] So conceived and practically implemented, I believe interracial justice opens a path toward building relationships among communities of color.

I will not describe here how this conception of interracial justice draws from disciplines of law, theology, social psychology, ethics, political science, and indigenous group healing practices. Now will I explain the practical framework for inquiry and action in concrete situations—a framework marked by four Rs: Recognition, Responsibility, Reconstruction, and Reparation.[13]

What I will do in closing is highlight the significance, and difficulty, of interracial efforts to heal, reconcile, and build relationships through the legal process and beyond. And in doing so, highlight what we, as legal scholars and teachers drawing on our individual experiences, might turn our collective powers to. Taunya Banks has done just that with her insightful new article in the *Asian Law Journal*, "Both Edges of the Margin: Blacks and Asians in Mississippi Masala, Barriers to Coalition Building."[14]

So think broadly about the recent international and domestic phenomenon of groups participating, sometimes meaningfully, sometimes fatuously, in processes of truth-telling, joint analysis of history and the current political economy, and apology and reparation: Japanese American internment; Rosewood; Tuskegee experiment; Tulsa riots; Texaco; Rutgers University's President; South Africa; Swiss Banks; Australia's aborigines; the Baptists and slavery; the Lutherans and anti-Semitism; Queen Elizabeth and imperialism; French President Chirac and Nazi complicity; Pope John Paul II and . . . lots of things; Bill Clinton and American slavery; and others.[15]

As I said, "some meaningful efforts, and some fatuous." But how can we tell the difference? And how can we help guide the differenc in future actions?

More specifically, concerning interracial grievances, recall Seattle—how the four journalists of color associations search hard for a way to deal with interracial mistrust—for a way to creatively struggle through lingering group grievances that transcend individuals. Prior to their convention, they dealt with cross-culture mediators, and no lawyers or academics involved. What does that say about how our work is perceived?

Also recall eastern New Orleans: 350 community residents, five churches, and government officials—all trying not only to bridge a cultural divide, but also to heal the African American/Asian American wounds inflamed by racial tiering, the media, and a limited court system's notion of "dispute resolution."

Think about Hawaii—certain Asian Americans and indigenous Hawaiians struggling with a chill in their relations characterized by, in their words, a "mutual demeaning stereotyping and mistrust",[16] coming to grips (through historical-cultural analysis and apologies and reparations) with partial Asian American complicity in keeping Hawaiians down during the 100 years following the overthrow of the Hawaiian government by U.S. businessmen and military—even while Asian Americans there were the objects of white racism.[17]

And even though these kinds of self-critical affirmative efforts by community groups and by frontline civil rights workers, teachers, lawyers, clergy, organizers and scholars bear the risk of mischaracterization by those on the Right, think of the rich, complex possibilities. For healing. For building alliances.

NOTES

1. For a fully developed discussion on interracial grievances and healings, see Eric K. Yamamota, *Interracial Justice: Conflict and Reconciliation in Post-Civil Rights America* (1999). See generally, Nicholas Tavuchis, *Mea Culpa: A Sociology of Apology and Reconciliation* (1991); Martha Minow, *Between Vengeance and Forgiveness* (1998).

2. 1996 Cal. Legis. Serv. Prop. 209 (West), enacted as Cal. Const. art. I §31 in 1996, "The State shall not discriminate against or grant preferential treatment to any individual or group on the basis of race, sex, color, ethnicity, or national origin in the operation of public employment, public education, or public contracting".

3. See Eric K. Yamamoto, "Critical Race Praxis: Race Theory and Political Lawyering Practice in Post-Civil Rights America," (1997) *Michigan Law Review* 95:821 describing settlement of Chinese American claims of discrimination in *Ho v. San Francisco United Sch. Dist.*, (N.D. Cal. Mar. 8, 1986) (No. C-94-2418-WHO).

4. See *Taxman v. Board of Education of the Township of Piscataway*, 91 F.3d 1547 (3d Cir. 1996), *cert dismissed*, 118 S. Ct. 595 (1997). Sharon Taxman, a white schoolteacher, was laid off while an equally qualified black teacher was retained. Her appeal, pending before the Supreme Court, was withdrawn as part of a settlement of $433,500, paid partially by a civil rights organization which sought to preclude the conservative Court from ruling on the case. See also "Black & White Case," *American Bar Association Journal* 84:33 (January 1998).

5. David Roediger, *Towards the Abolition of Whiteness: Essays on Race, Politics, and Working Class History* 1 (1994).

6. Elizabeth Martinez, "Beyond Black/White: The Racisms of Our Time," *Social Justice* 20:22 (1991).

7. See Yamamoto, *Interracial Justice*, describing media attempts to fill the void by narrowly portraying conflicts between African American and Asian American communities.

8. Interview with Diane Wong, Executive Director of Unity 99, in San Francisco, California (March 23, 1999).

9. See Yamamoto, *Interracial Justice*, The following account and quotes arising from the incident between Nguyen's son and Narcisse are drawn from this section of the book.

10. See Yamamoto, "Critical Race Praxis," note 3.

11. See Yamamoto, *Interracial Justice*, note 1.

12. Lisa Lowe, "Heterogeneity, Hybridity, Multiplicity: Marking Asian American Differences," *Diaspora*, 1:24, 28 (1991) (presenting Franz Fanon's argument).

13. "The first dimension is *recognition*. It asks racial group members to recognize and empathize with the anger and hope of those wounded; to acknowledge the disabling social constraints imposed by one group on another and the resulting group wounds; to identify related justice grievances often underlying current group conflict; and to critically examine stock stories of racial group attributes and interracial relations ostensibly legitimating those constraints and grievances. The second dimension is *responsibility*. It suggests that amid struggles over identity and power, racial groups can be simultaneously subordinated in some

relationships and subordinating in others. In some situations, a group's power is both enlivened and constrained by specific social and economic conditions and political alignments. Responsibility therefore asks racial groups to assess carefully the dynamics of group agency for imposing disabling constraints on others and, when appropriate, to accept group responsibility for healing the resulting wounds.

The third dimension is *reconstruction*. It entails active steps (performance) toward healing the social and psychological wounds resulting from disabling group constraints. Those steps might include apologies by the aggressors and, when appropriate, forgiveness by those injured and a joint reframing of stories of group identities and intergroup relations. The fourth dimension, closely related to the third, is *reparation*. It seeks to repair the damage to the material conditions of racial group life in order to attenuate one group's power over another. This means material changes in the structure of the relationship (social, economic, political) to guard against 'cheap reconciliation,' in which healing efforts are 'just talk.'" See Yamamoto, *Interracial Justice*.

14. Taunya Lovell Banks, "Both Edges of the Margin: Blacks and Asians in Mississippi Masala, Barriers to Coalition Building," *Asian Law Journal*; 5:7(1998).

15. See Eric K. Yamamoto, *Race Apologies, Iowa Journal of Gender, Race & Justice* 47 (1997) (cataloging national and international trends of race apologies).

16. Eric K. Yamamoto, "Rethinking Alliances: Agency, Responsibility and Interracial Justice," UCLA *Asian Pacific American Law Journal* 3:33 (1995).

17. For a more in-depth discussion on Asian American and Native Hawaiian apology and redress, see Yamamoto, "Rethinking Alliances."

13

Child of the Americas

Aurora Levins Morales

I am a child of the Americas,
a light-skinned mestiza of the Caribbean,
a child of many diaspora, born into this continent at a crossroads.

I am a U. S. Puerto Rican Jew,
a product of the ghettos of New York I have never known.
An immigrant and the daughter and granddaughter of immigrants.
I speak English with passion: it's the tongue of my consciousness,
a flashing knife blade of crystal, my tool, my craft.

From Aurora Levins Morales and Rosario Morales, *Getting Home Alive* (Ithaca, NY: Firebrand Books, 1986).

I am Caribeña, island grown. Spanish is in my flesh,
ripples from my tongue, lodges in my hips:
the langauge of garlic and mangoes,
the singing in my poetry, the flying gestures of my hands.
I am of Latinoamerica, rooted in the history of my continent:
I speak from that body.

I am not african. Africa is in me, but I cannot return.
I am not taína. Taîno is in me, but there is no way back.
I am not european. Europe lives in me, but I have no home there.

I am new. History made me. My first language was spanglish.
I was born at the crossroads
and I am whole.

Suggestions for Further Reading

Colby, A., and W. Damon. *Some Do Care: Contemporary Lives of Moral Commitment.* New York: Free Press, 1992.

Dees, Morris. *A Season of Justice: A Lawyer's Own Story of Victory over America's Hate Groups.* New York: Touchstone Books, 1991.

Economists Policy Group on Women's Issues. *Women's Policy Agenda.* Washington, DC: Institute for Women's Policy Research, 1992.

Eisenstein, Zillah R. *The Color of Gender: Reimagining Democracy.* Berkeley: Univeristy of California Press, 1994.

Kaufman, Michael, ed. *Beyond Patriarchy.* Toronto: Oxford University Press, 1987.

Kiang, Peter N. *We Could Shape It: Organizing for Asian Pacific American Student Empowerment.* Boston: Univeristy of Massachusetts Press, 1996.

Kivel, Paul. *Uprooting Racism: How White People Can Work for Racial Justice.* New York: New Society Publishers, 1996.

Lynch, James. *Prejudice Reduction in the Schools.* New York: Nichols Publishing, 1987.

Marable, Manning. *Beyond Black and White.* London and New York: Verso Books, 1995.

Pogrebin, L. C. *Growing Up Free.* New York: Bantam Books, 1981.

Reddy, Maureen T. *Everyday Acts against Racism.* Seattle: Seal Press, 1996.

Shalom, Steve. *Socialist Visions.* Boston: South End Press, 1980.

Spring, J. *Deculturalization and the Struggle for Equality: A Brief History of the Education of Dominated Cultures in the U. S.* New York: McGraw-Hill, 1997.

Stoltenberg, Jon. *The End of Manhood: A Book for Men of Conscience.* New York: Dutton, 1993.

West, Cornel. *Race Matters.* Boston: Beacon Press, 1993.

Index